The O'Leary Series

Microsoft® Office PowerPoint® 2003

Introductory Edition

Timothy J. O'Leary
Arizona State University

Linda I. O'Leary

Boston Burr Ridge, IL Dubuque, IA Madison, WI New York San Francisco St. Louis
Bangkok Bogotá Caracas Kuala Lumpur Lisbon London Madrid Mexico City
Milan Montreal New Delhi Santiago Seoul Singapore Sydney Taipei Toronto

Mc Graw Hill Technology Education

MICROSOFT® OFFICE POWERPOINT® 2003, INTRODUCTORY EDITION
Published by McGraw-Hill Technology Education, an imprint of the McGraw-Hill Companies, Inc. 1221 Avenue of the Americas, New York, NY, 10020.

This book is printed on acid-free paper.

2 3 4 5 6 7 8 9 0 QPD/QPD 0 9 8 7 6 5

ISBN 0-07-283606-7

Editor-in-Chief: *Bob Woodbury*
Sponsoring editor: *Don Hull*
Developmental editor: *Jennie Yates*
Marketing manager: *Andy Bernier*
Media producer: *Mark Christianson*
Project manager: *Jim Labeots*
Manager, new book production: *Heather D. Burbridge*
Coordinator freelance design: *Artemio Ortiz Jr.*
Photo research coordinator: *Ira C. Roberts*
Supplement producer: *Matthew Perry*
Senior digital content specialist: *Brian Nacik*
Cover design: *Asylum Studios*
Interior design: *Artemio Ortiz Jr.*
Typeface: *10.5/13 New Aster*
Compositor: *Rogondino & Associates/Cecelia G. Morales*
Printer: *Quebecor World Dubuque Inc.*

Library of Congress Control Number 2003113384

www.mhhe.com

McGraw-Hill Technology Education

At McGraw-Hill Technology Education, we publish instructional materials for the technology education market—in particular, for computer instruction in post secondary education that ranges from introductory courses in traditional four-year universities to continuing education and proprietary schools. McGraw-Hill Technology Education presents a broad range of innovative products—texts, lab manuals, study guides, testing materials, and technology-based training and assessment tools.

We realize that technology has created and will continue to create new mediums for professors and students to use in managing resources and communicating information to one another. McGraw-Hill Technology Education provides the most flexible and complete teaching and learning tools available and offers solutions to the changing needs of the classroom. McGraw-Hill Technology Education is dedicated to providing the tools for today's instructors and students, which will enable them to successfully navigate the world of Information Technology.

- McGraw-Hill/Osborne—This division of The McGraw-Hill Companies is known for its best-selling Internet titles, Harley Hahn's *Internet & Web Yellow Pages* and the *Internet Complete Reference.* For more information, visit Osborne at www.osborne.com.
- Digital Solutions—Whether you want to teach a class online or just post your "bricks-n-mortar" class syllabus, McGraw-Hill Technology Education is committed to publishing digital solutions. Taking your course online doesn't have to be a solitary adventure, nor does it have to be a difficult one. We offer several solutions that will allow you to enjoy all the benefits of having your course material online.
- Packaging Options—For more information about our discount options, contact your McGraw-Hill Sales representative at 1-800-338-3987 or visit our website at **www.mhhe.com/it**.

McGraw-Hill Technology Education is dedicated to providing
the tools for today's instructors and students.

What does this logo mean?

It means this courseware has been approved by the Microsoft® Office Specialist Program to be among the finest available for learning *Microsoft Office Word 2003, Microsoft Office Excel 2003, Microsoft Office Access 2003*, and *Microsoft Office PowerPoint 2003*. It also means that upon completion of this courseware, you may be prepared to take an exam for Microsoft Office Specialist qualification.

What is a Microsoft Office Specialist?

A Microsoft Office Specialist is an individual who has passed exams for certifying his or her skills in one or more of the Microsoft Office desktop applications such as Microsoft Word, Microsoft Excel, Microsoft PowerPoint, Microsoft Outlook, Microsoft Access, or Microsoft Project. The Microsoft Office Specialist Program typically offers certification exams at the "Specialist" and "Expert" skill levels.* The Microsoft Office Specialist Program is the only program in the world approved by Microsoft for testing proficiency in Microsoft Office desktop applications and Microsoft Project. This testing program can be a valuable asset in any job search or career advancement.

More Information:

To learn more about becoming a Microsoft Office Specialist, visit www.microsoft.com/officespecialist

To learn about other Microsoft Office Specialist approved courseware from McGraw-Hill Technology Education, visit http://www.mhhe.com/catalogs/irwin/it/mous/index.mhtml

---

* The availability of Microsoft Office Specialist certification exams varies by application, application version and language. Visit www.microsoft.com/officespecialist for exam availability.

Who benefits from Microsoft Office Specialist certification?

Employers
Microsoft Office Specialist certification helps satisfy employers' needs for qualitative assessments of employees' skills. Training, coupled with Microsoft Office Specialist certification, offers organizations of every size the ability to enhance productivity and efficiency by enabling their employees to unlock many advanced and laborsaving features in Microsoft Office applications. Microsoft Office Specialist certification can ultimately improve the bottom line.

Employees
Microsoft Office Specialist certification demonstrates employees' productivity and competence in Microsoft Office applications, the most popular business applications in the world. Achieving Microsoft Office Specialist certification verifies that employees have the confidence and ability to use Microsoft Office applications in meeting and exceeding their work challenges.

Instructors
Microsoft Office Specialist certification validates instructors' knowledge and skill in using Microsoft Office applications. It serves as a valuable credential, demonstrating their potential to teach students these essential applications. The Microsoft Office Specialist Authorized Instructor program is also available to those who wish to further demonstrate their instructional capabilities.

Students
Microsoft Office Specialist certification distinguishes students from their peers. It demonstrates their efficiency in completing assignments and projects, leaving more time for other studies. Improved confidence toward meeting new challenges and obstacles is yet another benefit. Achieving Microsoft Office Specialist certification gives students the marketable skills necessary to set them apart in the competitive job market.

To learn more about becoming a Microsoft Office Specialist, visit www.microsoft.com/officespecialist

To purchase a Microsoft Office Specialist certification exam, visit www.DesktopIQ.com

---

Brief Contents

Labs

Detailed Contents

Acknowledgments

The new edition of The O'Leary Series has been made possible only through the enthusiasm and dedication of a great team of people. Because the team spans the country, literally from coast to coast, we have utilized every means of working together including conference calls, FAX, e-mail, and document collaboration. We have truly tested the team approach and it works!

Leading the team from McGraw-Hill are Don Hull, Sponsoring Editor, and Jennie Yates, Developmental Editor. Their renewed commitment, direction, and support have infused the team with the excitement of a new project.

The production staff is headed by James Labeots, Project Manager, whose planning and attention to detail has made it possible for us to successfully meet a very challenging schedule. Members of the production team include: Artemio Ortiz, Designer; Pat Rogondino and Cecelia Morales, Compositors; Susan Defosset, Copy Editor; Heather Burbridge, Production Supervisor; Matthew Perry, Supplement Coordinator; and Elizabeth Mavetz, Media Producer. We would particularly like to thank Pat, Cecelia, and Susan—team members for many past editions whom we can always depend on to do a great job.

Finally, we are particularly grateful to a small but very dedicated group of people who helped us develop the manuscript. Colleen Hayes, Susan Demar, and Kathy Duggan have helped on the last several editions and continue to provide excellent developmental support. To Steve Willis, Carol Cooper, and Sarah Martin who provide technical expertise, youthful perspective, and enthusiasm, our thanks for helping get the manuscripts out the door and meeting the deadlines.

Preface

Introduction

The 20th century not only brought the dawn of the Information Age, but also rapid changes in information technology. There is no indication that this rapid rate of change will be slowing—it may even be increasing. As we begin the 21st century, computer literacy will undoubtedly become prerequisite for whatever career a student chooses. The goal of the O'Leary Series is to assist students in attaining the necessary skills to efficiently use these applications. Equally important is the goal to provide a foundation for students to readily and easily learn to use future versions of this software. This series does this by providing detailed step-by-step instructions combined with careful selection and presentation of essential concepts.

About the Authors

Tim and Linda O'Leary live in the American Southwest and spend much of their time engaging instructors and students in conversation about learning. In fact, they have been talking about learning for more than 25 years. Something in those early conversations convinced them to write a book, to bring their interest in the learning process to the printed page. Today, they are as concerned as ever about learning, about technology, and about the challenges of presenting material in new ways, both in terms of content and the method of delivery.

A powerful and creative team, Tim combines his years of classroom teaching experience with Linda's background as a consultant and corporate trainer. Tim has taught courses at Stark Technical College in Canton, Ohio, Rochester Institute of Technology in upper New York state, and is currently a professor at Arizona State University in Tempe, Arizona. Tim and Linda have talked to and taught students from ages 8 to 80, all of them with a desire to learn something about computers and the applications that make their lives easier, more interesting, and more productive.

About the Book

Times are changing, technology is changing, and this text is changing, too. Do you think the students of today are different from yesterday? There is no doubt about it—they are. On the positive side, it is amazing how much effort students will put toward things they are convinced are relevant to them. Their effort directed at learning application programs and exploring the Web seems at times limitless. On the other hand, students can often be shortsighted, thinking that learning the skills to use the application is the only objective. The mission of the series is to build upon and extend this interest by not only teaching the specific application skills but by introducing the concepts that are common to all applications, providing students with the confidence, knowledge, and ability to easily learn the next generation of applications.

Same Great Features as the Office XP Edition with some new additions!

- **Introduction to Computer Essentials**—A brief introduction to the basics of computer hardware and software (appears in Office Volume I only).

- **Introduction to Outlook**—A lab devoted to Microsoft Office Outlook 2003 basics (appears in Office Volume I only).
- **Introduction to Microsoft Office 2003**—Presents an overview to the Microsoft Office 2003 components: Office Word, Excel, Access, PowerPoint, and Outlook. Includes a hands-on section that introduces the features that are common to all Office 2003 applications, including using menus, task panes, and the Office Help system.
- **Lab Organization**—The lab text is organized to include main and subtopic heads by grouping related tasks. For example, tasks such as changing fonts and applying character effects appear under the "Formatting" topic head. This results in a slightly more reference-like approach, making it easier for students to refer back to the text to review. This has been done without losing the logical and realistic development of the case.
- **Relevant Cases**—Four separate running cases demonstrate the features in each application. Topics are of interest to students—At Arizona State University, over 600 students were surveyed to find out what topics are of interest to them.
- **Focus on Concepts**—Each lab focuses on the concepts behind the application. Students learn the concepts, so they can succeed regardless of the software package they might be using. The concepts are previewed at the beginning of each lab and summarized at the end of each lab.
- All **Numbered Steps** and bullets appear in left margin space making it easy not to miss a step.
- **Clarified Marginal Notes**—Marginal notes have been enhanced by more clearly identifying the note content with box heads and the use of different colors.

  Additional Information—Brief asides with expanded discussion of features.

  Having Trouble?—Procedural tips advising students of possible problems and how to overcome them.

  Another Method—Alternative methods of performing a procedure.

- **Focus on Careers**—A new feature, appearing at the end of each lab, which provides an example of how the material covered may be applied in the "real world."
- A **Microsoft Office Specialist Skills** table, appearing at the end of each lab, contains page references to Microsoft Office Specialist skills learned in the lab.
- **End-of-Chapter Material**
    - Screen Identification (appears in the first lab of each application)
    - Matching
    - Multiple Choice
    - Fill-In
    - True/False

  Hands-On Practice Exercises—Students apply the skills and concepts they learned to solve case-based exercises. Many cases in the practice exercises tie to a running case used in another application lab. This helps to demonstrate the use of the four applications across a common case setting. For example, the Adventure Travel Tours case used in the Word labs is continued in practice exercises in Excel, Access, and PowerPoint.

    - Step-by-Step
    - On Your Own

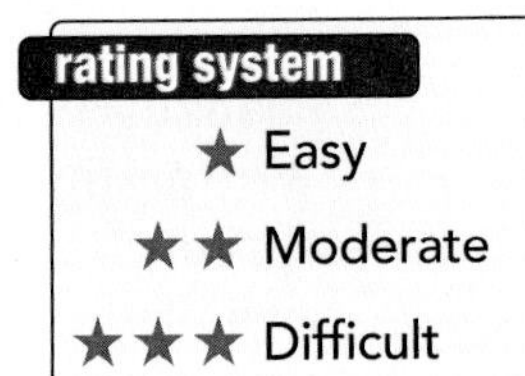

- **Rating System**—The 3-star rating system identifies the difficulty level of each practice exercise in the end-of-lab materials.

- **Continuing Exercises**—A continuing exercise icon identifies exercises that build off of exercises completed in earlier labs.

- **Working Together Labs**—At the completion of the brief and introductory texts, a final lab demonstrates the integration of the MS Office applications.
- **References**

  Command Summary—Provides a table of all commands used in the labs.

  Glossary of Key Terms—Includes definitions for all bolded terms used in the labs and included in the Key Terms list at the end of each lab.

  Data File List—Helps organize all data and solution files.

  Microsoft Office Specialist Certification Guide—Links all Microsoft Office Specialist objectives to text content and end-of-chapter exercises.

Instructor's Guide

We understand that, in today's teaching environment, offering a textbook alone is not sufficient to meet the needs of the many instructors who use our books. To teach effectively, instructors must have a full complement of supplemental resources to assist them in every facet of teaching from preparing for class, to conducting a lecture, to assessing students' comprehension. ***The O'Leary Series*** offers a fully-integrated supplements package and Web site, as described below.

Instructor's Resource Kit

The **Instructor's Resource Kit** contains a computerized Test Bank, an Instructor's Manual, and PowerPoint Presentation Slides. Features of the Instructor's Resource Kit are described below.

- **Instructor's Manual** The Instructor's Manual contains lab objectives, concepts, outlines, lecture notes, and command summaries. Also included are answers to all end-of-chapter material, tips for covering difficult materials, additional exercises, and a schedule showing how much time is required to cover text material.
- **Computerized Test Bank** The test bank contains over 1,300 multiple choice, true/false, and discussion questions. Each question will be accompanied by the correct answer, the level of learning difficulty, and corresponding page references. Our flexible Diploma software allows you to easily generate custom exams.
- **PowerPoint Presentation Slides** The presentation slides will include lab objectives, concepts, outlines, text figures, and speaker's notes. Also included are bullets to illustrate key terms and FAQs.

Online Learning Center/Web Site

Found at **www.mhhe.com/oleary**, this site provides additional learning and instructional tools to enhance the comprehension of the text. The OLC/Web Site is divided into these three areas:

- **Information Center** Contains core information about the text, supplements, and the authors.
- **Instructor Center** Offers instructional materials, downloads, and other relevant links for professors.
- **Student Center** Contains data files, chapter competencies, chapter concepts, self-quizzes, flashcards, additional Web links, and more.

Skills Assessment

SimNet (Simulated Network Assessment Product) provides a way for you to test students' software skills in a simulated environment.

- Pre-testing options
- Post-testing options
- Course placement testing
- Diagnostic capabilities to reinforce skills
- Proficiency testing to measure skills
- Web or LAN delivery of tests.
- Computer-based training tutorials

For more information on skills assessment software, please contact your local sales representative, or visit us at **www.mhhe.com/it**.

Digital Solutions to Help You Manage Your Course

PageOut is our Course Web Site Development Center that offers a syllabus page, URL, McGraw-Hill Online Learning Center content, online exercises and quizzes, gradebook, discussion board, and an area for student Web pages.

Available free with any McGraw-Hill Technology Education product, PageOut requires no prior knowledge of HTML, no long hours of coding, and a way for course coordinators and professors to provide a full-course Web site. PageOut offers a series of templates—simply fill them with your course information and click on one of 16 designs. The process takes under an hour and leaves you with a professionally designed Web site. We'll even get you started with sample Web sites, or enter your syllabus for you! PageOut is so straightforward and intuitive, it's little wonder why over 12,000 college professors are using it. For more information, visit the PageOut Web site at www.pageout.net.

Online courses are also available. Online Learning Centers (OLCs) are your perfect solutions for Internet-based content. Simply put, these Centers are "digital cartridges" that contain a book's pedagogy and supplements. As students read the book, they can go online and take self-grading quizzes or work through interactive exercises. These also provide students appropriate access to lecture materials and other key supplements.

Online Learning Centers can be delivered through any of these platforms:

- Blackboard.com
- WebCT (a product of Universal Learning Technology)

McGraw-Hill has partnerships with WebCT and Blackboard to make it even easier to take your course online. Now you can have McGraw-Hill content delivered through the leading Internet-based learning tool for higher education.

Computing Concepts

Computing Essentials 2004 and ***Computing Today*** offer a unique, visual orientation that gives students a basic understanding of computing concepts. *Computing Essentials* and *Computing Today* are some of the few books on the market that are written by a professor who still teaches the courses every semester and loves it. The books encourage "active" learning with their exercises, explorations, visual illustrations, and inclusion of screen shots and numbered steps. While combining the "active" learning style with current topics and technology, these texts provide an accurate snapshot of computing trends. When bundled with software application lab manuals, students are given a complete representation of the fundamental issues surrounding the personal computing environment.

Select features of these texts include:

- **Using Technology**—Engaging coverage of hot, high-interest topics, such as phone calls via the Internet, using the Internet remotely with a Personal Digital Assistant (PDA), and Client and Server operating systems. These Web-related projects direct the student to explore current popular uses of technology.
- **Expanding Your Knowledge**—Geared for those who want to go into greater depth on a specific topic introduced within the chapter. These projects meet the needs of instructors wanting more technical depth of coverage.
- **Building Your Portfolio**—Develops critical thinking and writing skills while students examine security, privacy, and ethical issues in technology. By completing these exercises, students will be able to walk away from the class with something to show prospective employers.
- **Making IT Work for You**—Based on student surveys, *Computing Essentials* identified several special interest topics and devoted a two-page section on each in the corresponding chapter. Making IT Work for You sections engage students by presenting high interest topics that directly relate to the concepts presented in the chapter. Topics include downloading music from the Internet, creating personal Web sites, and using the Internet to make long-distance phone calls. Many of these are supported by short video presentations that will be available via CD and the Web.
- **On the Web Explorations**—Appear throughout the margins of the text and encourage students to go to the Web to visit several informative and established sites in order to learn more about the chapter's featured topic.
- **A Look to the Future Sections**—Provide insightful information about the future impact of technology and forecasts of how upcoming enhancements in the world of computing will play an important and powerful role in society.
- **End-of-Chapter Material**—A variety of material including objective questions (key terms, matching, multiple choice, and short answer completion) and critical thinking activities. This will help to reinforce the information just learned.

STUDENT'S GUIDE

As you begin each lab, take a few moments to read the **Case Study** and the Concept Preview. The case study introduces a real-life setting that is interwoven throughout the entire lab, providing the basis for understanding the use of the application. Also, notice the Additional Information, Having Trouble?, and Another Method boxes scattered throughout the book. These tips provide more information about related topics, help get you out of trouble if you are having problems, and offer suggestions on other ways to perform the same task. Finally, read the text between the steps. You will find the few minutes more it takes you is well worth the time when you are completing the practice exercises.

Many learning aids are built into the text to ensure your success with the material and to make the process of learning rewarding. The pages that follow call your attention to the key features in the text.

Objectives

Appear at the beginning of the lab and identify the main features you will be learning.

Case Study

Introduces a real-life setting that is interwoven throughout the lab, providing the basis for understanding the use of the application.

Creating and Editing a Document LAB 1

Objectives

After you have read this chapter, you should be able to:

1. Develop a document as well as enter and edit text.
2. Insert and delete text and blank lines.
3. Reveal formatting marks.
4. Use AutoCorrect, AutoText, and AutoComplete.
5. Use automatic spelling and grammar checking.
6. Save, close, and open files.
7. Select text.
8. Undo and redo changes.
9. Change fonts and type sizes.
10. Bold and color text.
11. Change alignment.
12. Insert, size, and move pictures.
13. Preview and print a document.
14. Set file properties.

WD1.1

Case Study

Adventure Travel Tours

As a recent college graduate, you have accepted a job as advertising coordinator for Adventure Travel Tours, a specialty travel company that organizes active adventure vacations. The company is headquartered in Los Angeles and has locations in other major cities throughout the country. You are responsible for coordination of the advertising program for all locations. This includes the creation of many kinds of promotional materials: brochures, flyers, form letters, news releases, advertisements, and a monthly newsletter. You are also responsible for creating Web pages for the company Web site.

Adventure Travel is very excited about four new tours planned for the upcoming year. They want to promote them through informative presentations held throughout the country. Your first job as advertising coordinator will be to create a flyer advertising the four new tours and the presentations about them. The flyer will be modified according to the location of the presentation.

The software tool you will use to create the flyer is the word processing application Microsoft Word Office 2003. It helps you create documents such as letters, reports, and research papers. In this lab, you will learn how to enter, edit, and print a document while you create the flyer (shown right) to be distributed in a mailing to Adventure Travel Tours clients.

© PhotoDisc

WD1.2

• Objectives, Case Study
• Concept Preview, Another Method, Having Trouble?

Concept Preview

Provides an overview to the concepts that will be presented throughout the lab.

Another Method

Offers additional ways to perform a procedure.

Having Trouble?

Helps resolve potential problems as you work through each lab.

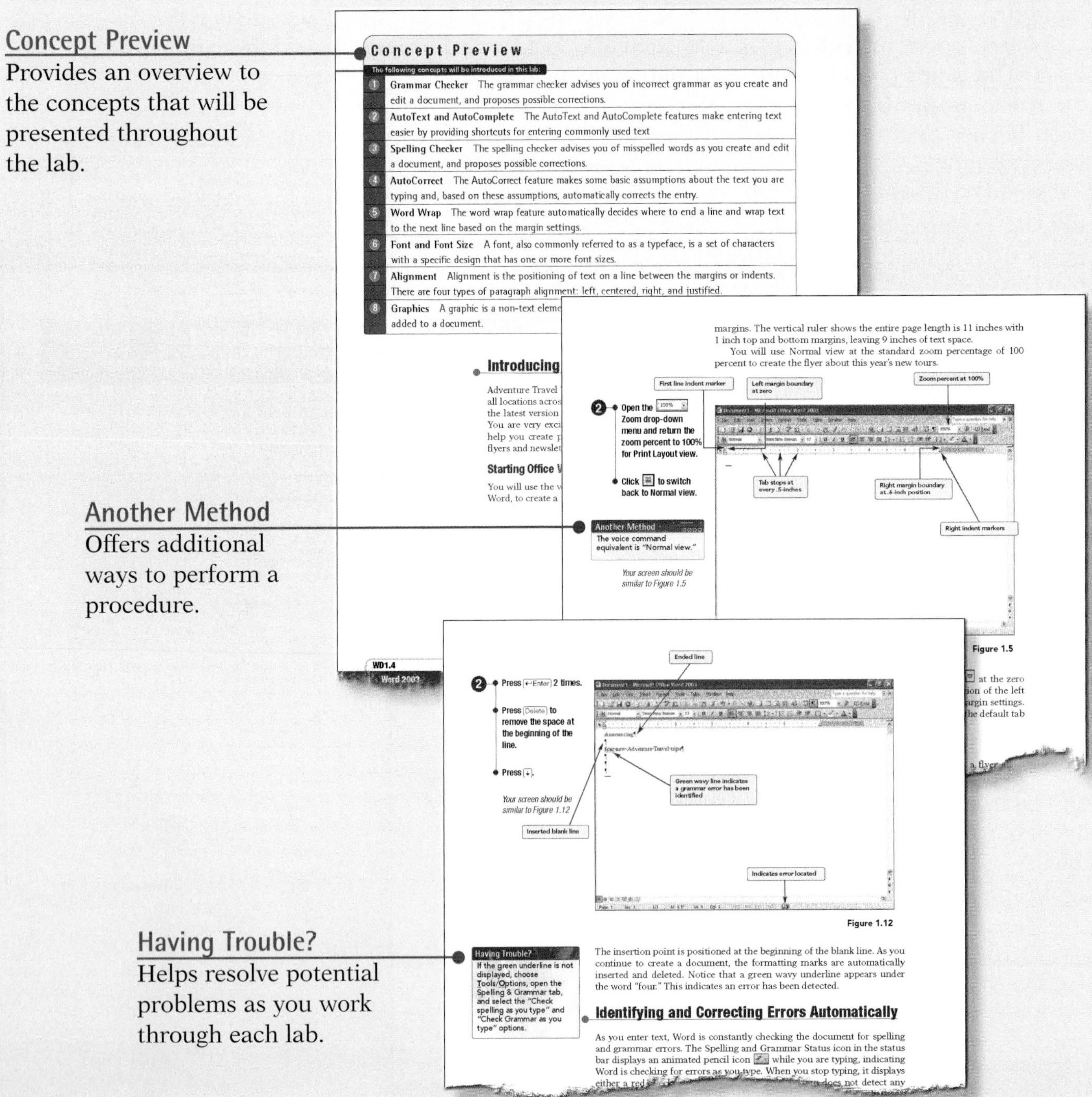

• Numbered and Bulleted Steps, Additional Information

Numbered and Bulleted Steps

Provide clear Step-by-Step Instructions on how to complete a task, or series of tasks.

Additional Information

Offers brief asides with expanded coverage of content.

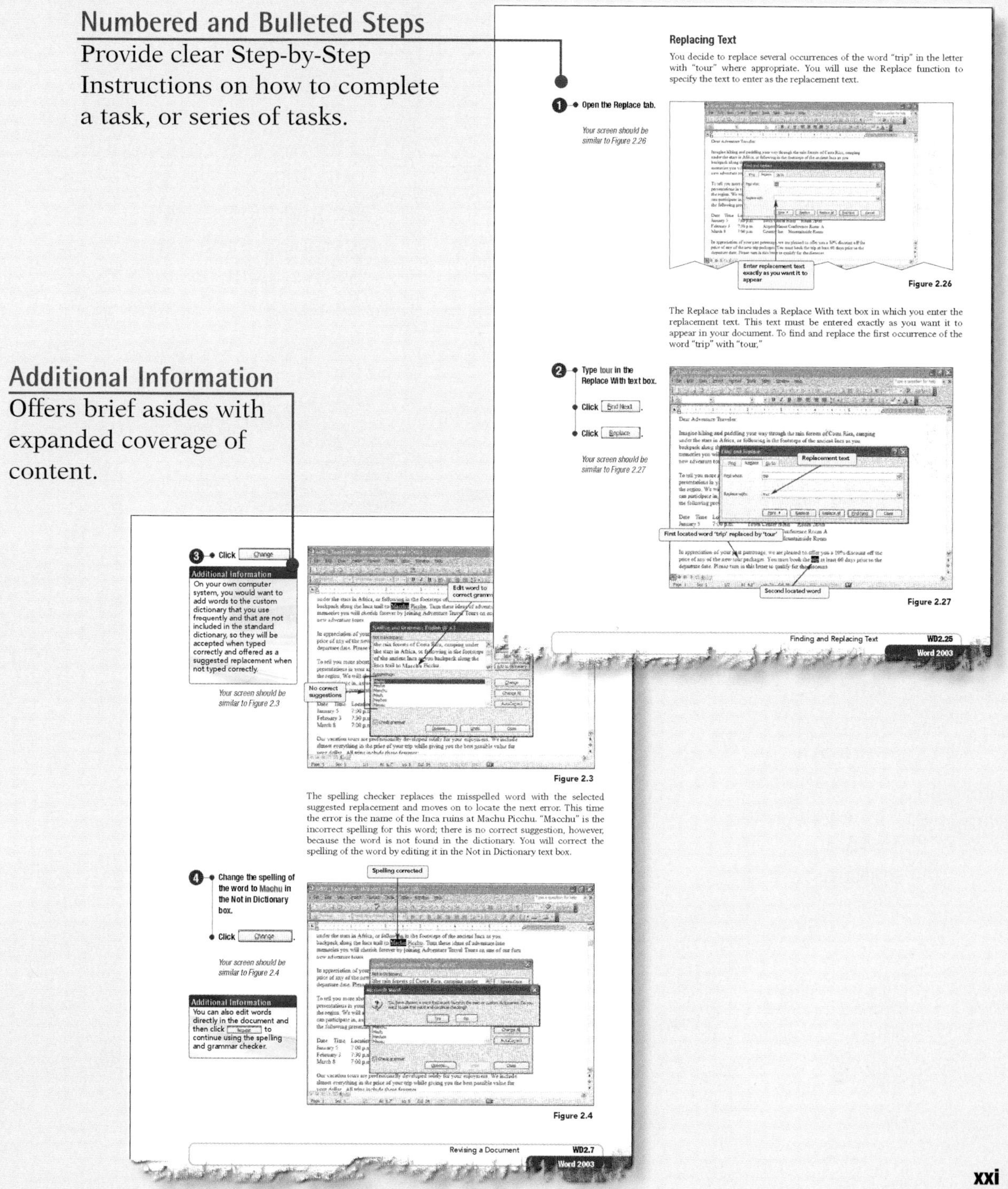

• Figures and Callouts, Tables

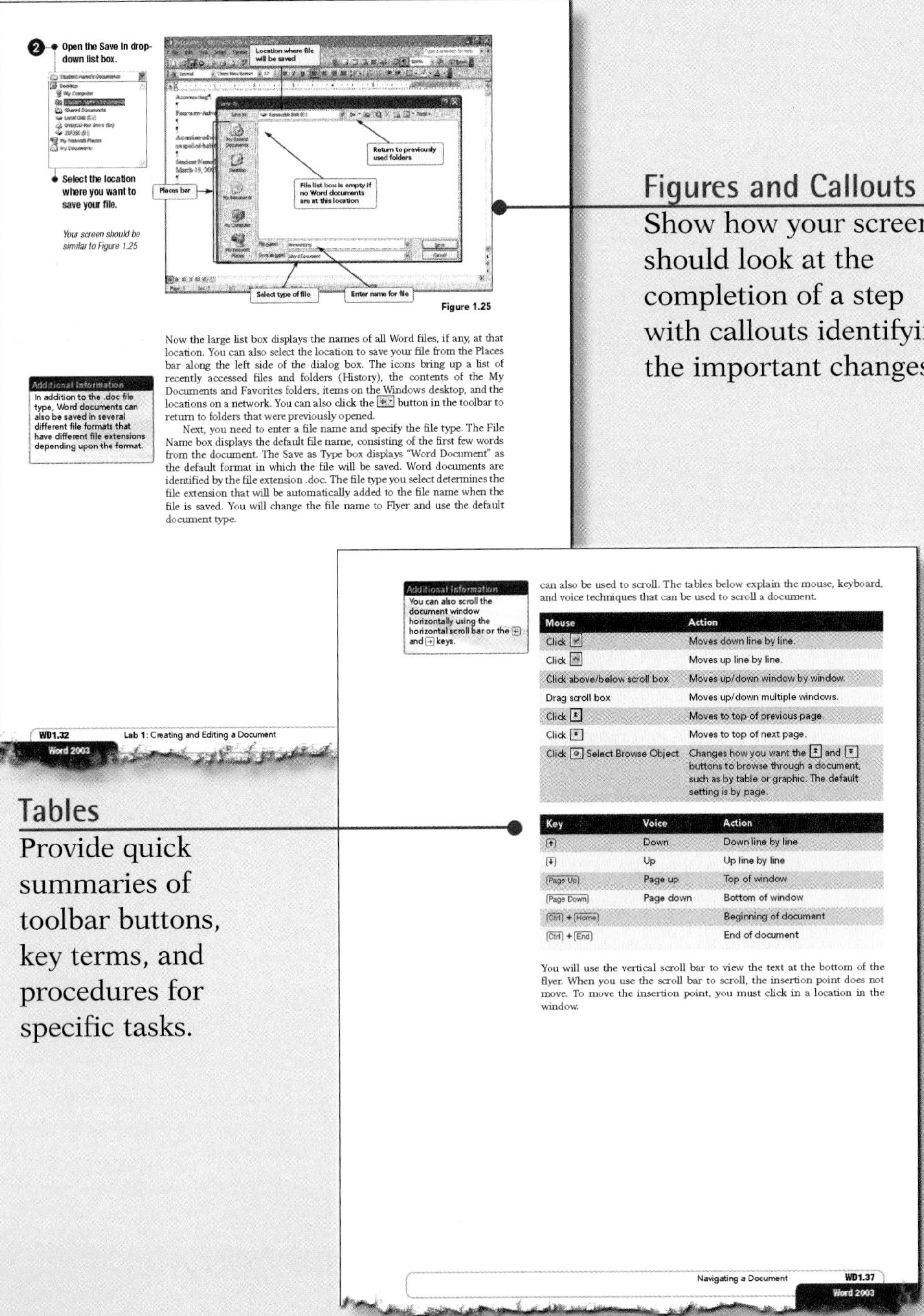

Figures and Callouts

Show how your screen should look at the completion of a step with callouts identifying the important changes.

Tables

Provide quick summaries of toolbar buttons, key terms, and procedures for specific tasks.

• Focus on Careers, Concept Summary

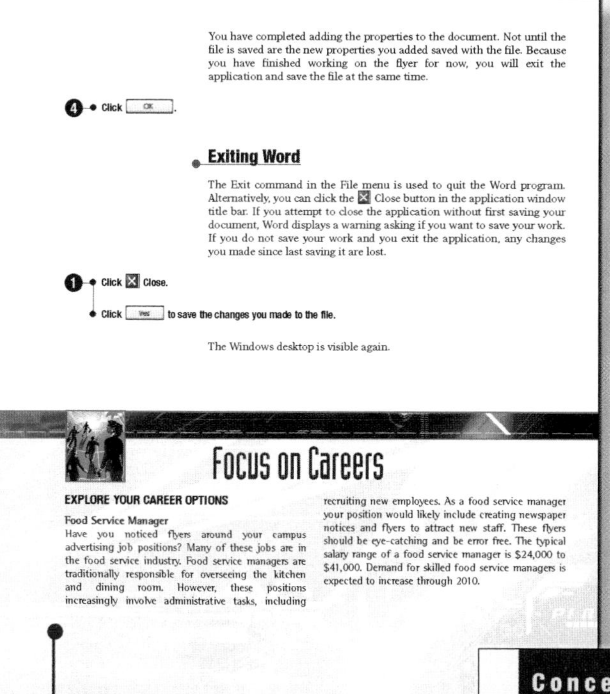

You have completed adding the properties to the document. Not until the file is saved are the new properties you added saved with the file. Because you have finished working on the flyer for now, you will exit the application and save the file at the same time.

4 Click OK.

Exiting Word

The Exit command in the File menu is used to quit the Word program. Alternatively, you can click the ☒ Close button in the application window title bar. If you attempt to close the application without first saving your document, Word displays a warning asking if you want to save your work. If you do not save your work and you exit the application, any changes you made since last saving it are lost.

1 Click ☒ Close.

Click Yes to save the changes you made to the file.

The Windows desktop is visible again.

Focus on Careers

EXPLORE YOUR CAREER OPTIONS

Food Service Manager

Have you noticed flyers around your campus advertising job positions? Many of these jobs are in the food service industry. Food service managers are traditionally responsible for overseeing the kitchen and dining room. However, these positions increasingly involve administrative tasks, including recruiting new employees. As a food service manager your position would likely include creating newspaper notices and flyers to attract new staff. These flyers should be eye-catching and be error free. The typical salary range of a food service manager is $24,000 to $41,000. Demand for skilled food service managers is expected to increase through 2010.

Exiting Word

Concept Summary

Offers a visual summary of the concepts presented throughout the lab.

Focus on Careers

Provides an example of how the material covered may be applied in the "real world."

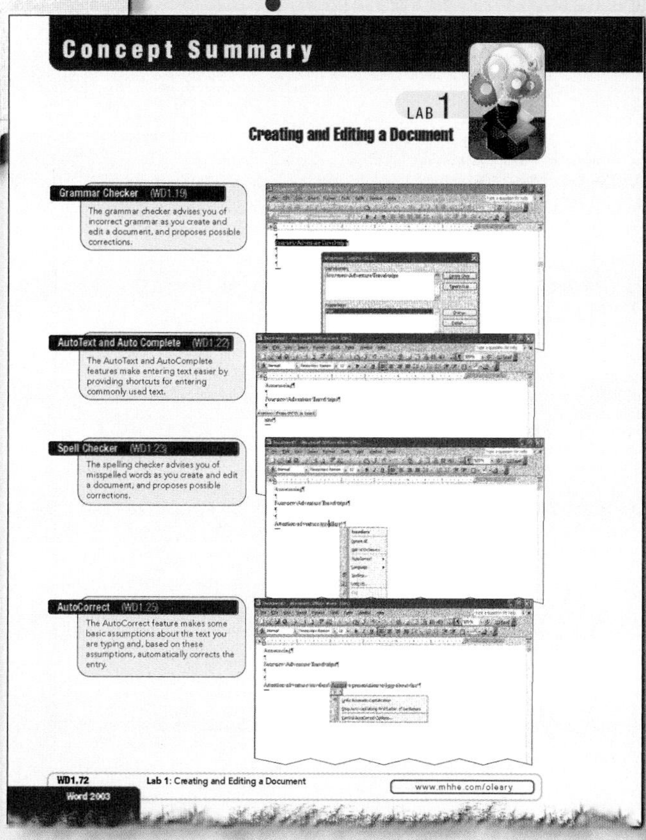

Concept Summary

LAB 1

Creating and Editing a Document

Grammar Checker (WD1.19)

The grammar checker advises you of incorrect grammar as you create and edit a document, and proposes possible corrections.

AutoText and Auto Complete (WD1.22)

The AutoText and AutoComplete features make entering text easier by providing shortcuts for entering commonly used text.

Spell Checker (WD1.23)

The spelling checker advises you of misspelled words as you create and edit a document, and proposes possible corrections.

AutoCorrect (WD1.25)

The AutoCorrect feature makes some basic assumptions about the text you are typing and, based on these assumptions, automatically corrects the entry.

WD1.72 Lab 1: Creating and Editing a Document www.mhhe.com/oleary

Word 2003

• Key Terms and Microsoft Office Specialist Skills, Command Summary

Key Terms and Microsoft Office Specialist Skills

Includes a list of all bolded terms with page references and a table showing the Microsoft Office Specialist certification skills that were covered in the lab.

Command Summary

Provides a table of commands and keyboard and toolbar shortcuts for all commands used in the lab.

lab review

LAB 3

Creating Reports and Tables

key terms

alignment WD1.58
AutoComplete WD1.22
AutoCorrect WD1.25
AutoText WD1.22
character formatting WD1.50
cursor WD1.5
custom dictionary WD1.23
default WD1.68
document window WD1.5
drawing object WD1.60
edit WD1.11
embedded object WD1.60
end-of-file marker WD1.5
file property WD1.69
font WD1.51
font size WD1.51
format WD1.11
formatting mark WD1.14
Formatting toolbar WD1.5
grammar checker WD1.16
graphic WD1.60
Insert mode WD1.40
insertion point WD1.5
main dictionary WD1.23
object WD1.60
Overtype mode WD1.41
pane WD1.6
paragraph formatting WD1.50
picture WD1.60
ruler WD1.5
sans serif font WD1.51
select WD1.6
selection rectangle WD1.65
serif font WD1.51
sizing handles WD1.65
Smart Tag WD1.29
soft space WD1.58
source program WD1.60
spelling checker WD1.23
Standard toolbar WD1.5
thumbnail WD1.62
TrueType WD1.52
typeface WD1.51
word wrap WD1.28

microsoft office specialist skills

The Microsoft Office Specialist (MOS) certification program is designed to measure your proficiency in performing basic tasks using the Office 2003 applications. Getting certified demonstrates that you have the skills and provides a valuable industry credential for employment. After completing this lab, you have learned the following Microsoft Office Specialist skills:

Skill	Description	Page
Creating Content	Insert and edit text, symbols, and special characters	WD1.XX
	Insert frequently used and predefined text	WD1.XX,
	Insert, position, and size graphics	WD1.XX
Formatting Content	Format text	WD1.XX
	Format paragraphs	WD1.XX
Formatting and Managing Documents	Preview and print documents	WD1.XX
	Review and modify document properties	WD1.XX
	Save documents in appropriate formats for different uses	WD1.XX
	Print documents, envelopes, and labels	WD1.XX
	Preview documents and Web pages	WD1.XX
	Change and organize document views and windows	WD1.XX

WD1.74 Lab 1: Creating and Editing a Document www.mhhe.com/oleary

Word 2003

command summary

Command	Shortrtcut Key	Button	Voice	Action
File/Page Setup				Changes layout of page including margins, paper size, and paper source
File/Versions				Saves, opens, and deletes document versions
Edit/Cut	Ctrl + X		Cut	Cuts selection to Clipboard
Edit/Copy	Ctrl + C		Copy	Copies selection to Clipboard
Edit/Paste	Ctrl + V		Paste	Pastes item from Clipboard
Edit/Find	Ctrl + F			Locates specified text
Edit/Replace	Ctrl + H			Locates and replaces specified text
Insert/Break/Page break	Ctrl + ←Enter			Inserts hard page break
Insert/Date and Time				Inserts current date or time, maintained by computer system, in selected format
Insert/AutoText				Enters predefined text
Insert/AutoText/AutoText				Create new AutoText entries
Insert/Picture/AutoShapes		AutoShapes ▾		Inserts selected AutoShape
Format/Font/Font/ Underline style/Single	Ctrl + U	U		Underlines selected text with a single line
Format/Paragraph/Indents and Spacing/Special/First Line				Indents first line of paragraph from left margin
Format/Paragraph/Indents and Spacing/Line Spacing	Ctrl + #			Changes amount of white space between lines
Format/Bullets and Numbering				Creates a bulleted or numbered list
Format /Tabs				Specifies types and position of tab stops
Format/Styles and Formatting				Displays the Styles and Formatting Task pane

Lab Review WD2.71

Word 2003

• Lab Exercises: Screen Identification, Matching, Multiple Choice, True/False, Fill-in

Lab Exercises

Reinforce the terminology and concepts presented in the lab through Screen Identification, Matching, Multiple Choice, True/False, and Fill-in questions.

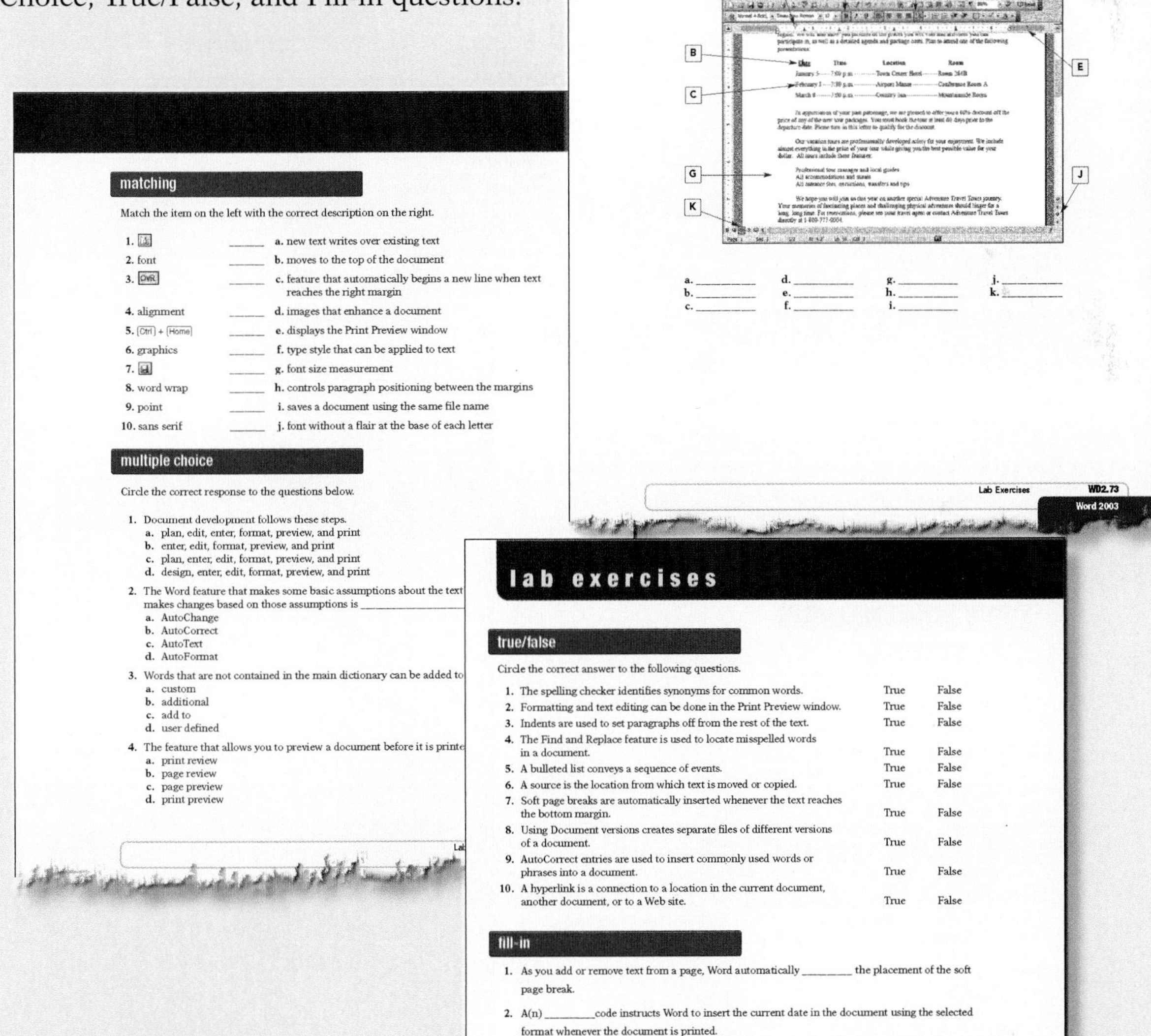

• Lab Exercises: Step-by-Step, On Your Own

Lab Exercises

Provide hands-on practice and develop critical thinking skills through step-by-step and on-your-own practice exercises. These exercises have a rating system from easy to difficult and test your ability to apply the knowledge you have gained in each lab. Exercises that build off of previous exercises are noted with a Continuing Exercise icon.

On Your Own

lab exercises

rating system
★ Easy
★★ Moderate
★★★ Difficult

step-by-step

Writing a Memo ★

1. Adventure Travel Tours is planning to update its World Wide Web site in the near future. You have been asked to solicit suggestions from the travel agents about changes they would like to see made to the current Web site. You decide to send all the travel agents a memo asking them for their input. Your completed memo is shown here.
   a. Open a blank Word document and create the following memo in Normal view. Press Tab twice after you type colons (:) in the To, From, and Date lines. This will make the information following the colons line up evenly. Enter a blank line between paragraphs.

   To: Travel Agents
   From: Student Name
   Date: [Current date]
   Next month we plan to begin work on updating the current Adventure Travel Tours Web site. In preparation for this project, I would like your input about the current Web site. In the next few days as you use the Web site, pay attention to such things as the layout, colors, and content. Then send your comments back to me about both the positive and negative features of the current Web site and suggestions for changes you would like to see made in the new Web site.

   Thank you in advance for your input.

   b. Turn on the display of formatting marks.
   c. Correct any spelling and grammar errors that are identified.
   d. Delete the word "current" from the first and second sentences. Delete the phrase "such things ... hird sentence. Insert the text "ease of use," after the word "colors," in the third

   ...aragraph beginning with the third sentence. Include a blank line between

   ...t size for the entire memo to 14 pt and the alignment of the body of the memo to

   ...line insert the AutoText reference line "RE:".

...1: Creating and Editing a Document   www.mhhe.com/oleary

---

p. Increase the font size of the line above "Roast Coffee" to 18 pt. Reset its line spacing to single. Insert a blank line below it.
q. Copy the remaining paragraph from the wd02_Coffee Flyer document, and insert it at the bottom of the new document. Include two blank lines between the table and the paragraph.
r. Bold and center the final paragraph. Remove the hyperlink format from the URL. Format the URL as italic, bold, and red.
s. Increase the top, left, and right margins to 1.5 inches.
t. Create the Explosion 1 AutoShape from Stars and Banners. Enter and center the word Sale! in red within it, and choose the gold fill color. Size the shape appropriately. Move the shape to the top left corner of the document. Delete the drawing canvas.
u. Add your name and a field with the current date several lines below the final paragraph.
v. Save the document as Coffee Flyer2. Preview and print it.

on your own

Requesting a Reference ★

1. Your first year as a biology major is going well and you are looking for a summer internship with a local research lab. You have an upcoming interview and want to come prepared with a letter of reference from your last position. Write a business letter directed to your old supervisor, Rachel McVey, at your former lab, AMT Research. Use the modified block letter style shown in the lab. Be sure to include the date, a salutation, two paragraphs, a closing, and your name as a signature. Spell-check the document, save the document as Reference Letter, and print it.

Long Distance Rates Survey ★

2. American Consumer Advocates conducted a survey in October, 2002 comparing the costs of long distance rates. Create a tabbed table using the information shown below. Bold and underline the column heads. Add style 2 tab leaders to the table entries. Above the table, write a paragraph explaining the table contents.

Company	Per Minute	Monthly Fee	Customer Service Wait
Zone LD	3.5¢	$2.00	Less than 1 minute
Pioneer Telephone	3.9¢	none	1 minute
Capsule	3.9¢	none	17 minutes
ECG	4.5¢	$1.99	5 minutes
IsTerra	4.9¢	none	10 minutes

Include your name and the date below the table. Save the document as Phone Rates and print the document.

Lab Exercises   WD2.85
Word 2003

The O'Leary Series

Microsoft® Office PowerPoint® 2003

Introductory Edition

Introduction to Microsoft Office 2003

Objectives

After completing the Introduction to Microsoft Office 2003, you should be able to:

1. Describe Office System 2003.
2. Describe the Office 2003 applications.
3. Start an Office 2003 application.
4. Recognize the basic application window features.
5. Use menus, shortcut menus, and shortcut keys.
6. Use toolbars and task panes.
7. Use Office Help.
8. Exit an Office 2003 application.

What Is Microsoft Office System 2003?

Microsoft Office System 2003 is a comprehensive, integrated system of programs, servers and services designed to solve a wide array of business needs. Although the programs can be used individually, they are designed to work together seamlessly making it easy to connect people and organizations to information, business processes and each other. The applications include tools used to create, discuss, communicate, and manage projects. If you share a lot of documents with other people, these features facilitate access to common documents. This version has expanded and refined the communication and collaboration features and integration with the World Wide Web. In addition, several new interface features are designed to make it easier to perform tasks and help users take advantage of all the features in the applications.

The Microsoft Office System 2003 is packaged in different combinations of components. The major components and a brief description are provided in the following table.

Component	Description
Microsoft Office 2003	
Office Word 2003	Word Processor
Office Excel 2003	Spreadsheet
Office Access 2003	Database manager
Office PowerPoint 2003	Presentation graphics
Office Outlook 2003	Desktop information manager
Office FrontPage 2003	Web site creation and management
Office InfoPath 2003	Creates XML forms and documents
Office OneNote 2003	Note-taking
Office Publisher 2003	Desktop publishing
Office Visio 2003	Drawing and diagramming
Office SharePoint Portal Server v2.0 and Services	

The five components of Microsoft Office 2003—Word, Excel, Access, PowerPoint, and Outlook—are the applications you will learn about in this series of labs. They are described in more detail in the following sections.

Office Word 2003

Office Word 2003 is a word processing software application whose purpose is to help you create text-based documents. Word processors are one of the most flexible and widely used application software programs. A word processor can be used to manipulate text data to produce a letter, a report, a memo, an e-mail message, or any other type of correspondence.

Two documents you will produce in the first two Word labs, a letter and flyer, are shown here.

A letter containing a tabbed table, indented paragraphs, and text enhancements is quickly created using basic Word features.

March 25, 2005

Dear Adventure Traveler:

Imagine hiking and paddling your way through the rain forests of Costa Rica, camping under the stars in Africa, or following in the footsteps of the ancient Inca as you backpack along the Inca trail to Machu Picchu. Turn these dreams of adventure into memories you will cherish forever by joining Adventure Travel Tours on one of our four new adventure tours.

To tell you more about these exciting new adventures, we are offering several presentations in your area. These presentations will focus on the features and cultures of the region. We will also show you pictures of the places you will visit and activities you can participate in, as well as a detailed agenda and package costs. Plan to attend one of the following presentations:

Date	Time
January 5 -----	7:00 p.m. --------
February 3 ----	7:30 p.m. --------
March 8 -------	7:00 p.m. --------

In appreciation of your past patr
price of any of the new tour packages. Y
departure date. Please turn in this letter t

Our vacation tours are professio
almost everything in the price of your to
dollar. All tours include these features:

- **Professional tour manager and**
- **All accommodations and meals**
- **All entrance fees, excursions, t**

We hope you will join us this ye
Your memories of fascinating places an
long, long time. For reservations, please
directly at 1-800-777-0004.

Announcing

New Adventure Travel Tours

Attention adventure travelers! Attend an Adventure Travel presentation to learn about some of the earth's greatest unspoiled habitats and find out how you can experience the adventure of a lifetime. This year we are introducing four new tours and offering you a unique opportunity to combine many different outdoor activities while exploring the world.

India Wildlife Adventure
Inca Trail to Machu Picchu
Safari in Tanzania
Costa Rica Rivers and Rain Forests

Presentation dates and times are January 5 at 7:00 p.m., February 3 at 7:30 p.m., and March 8 at 7:00 p.m. All presentations are held at convenient hotel locations. The hotels are located in downtown Los Angeles, in Santa Clara, and at the airport.

Call 1-800-777-0004 for presentation locations, a full color brochure, and itinerary information, costs, and trip dates.

Visit our Web site at www.AdventureTravelTours.com

A flyer incorporating many visual enhancements such as colored text, varied text styles, and graphic elements is both eye-catching and informative.

The beauty of a word processor is that you can make changes or corrections as you are typing. Want to change a report from single spacing to double spacing? Alter the width of the margins? Delete some paragraphs and add others from yet another document? A word processor allows you to do all these things with ease.

Word 2003 includes many group collaboration features to help streamline how documents are developed and changed by group members. You can also create and send e-mail messages directly from within Word using all its features to create and edit the message. In addition, you can send an entire document as your e-mail message, allowing the recipient to edit the document directly without having to open or save an attachment.

Word 2003 is closely integrated with the World Wide Web, detecting when you type a Web address and automatically converting it to a hyperlink. You can also create your own hyperlinks to locations within documents, or to other documents, including those at external locations such as a Web site or file server. Its many Web-editing features, including a Web Page Wizard that guides you step by step, help you quickly create a Web page.

Office Excel 2003

Office Excel 2003 is an electronic worksheet that is used to organize, manipulate, and graph numeric data. Once used almost exclusively by accountants, worksheets are now widely used by nearly every profession. Marketing professionals record and evaluate sales trends. Teachers record grades and calculate final grades. Personal trainers record the progress of their clients.

Excel includes many features that not only help you create a well-designed worksheet, but one that produces accurate results. Formatting features include visual enhancements such as varied text styles, colors, and graphics. Other features help you enter complex formulas and identify and correct formula errors. You can also produce a visual display of data in the form of graphs or charts. As the values in the worksheet change, charts referencing those values automatically adjust to reflect the changes.

Excel also includes many advanced features and tools that help you perform what-if analysis and create different scenarios. And like all Office 2003 applications, it is easy to incorporate data created in one application into another. Two worksheets you will produce in Labs 2 and 3 of Excel are shown on the next page.

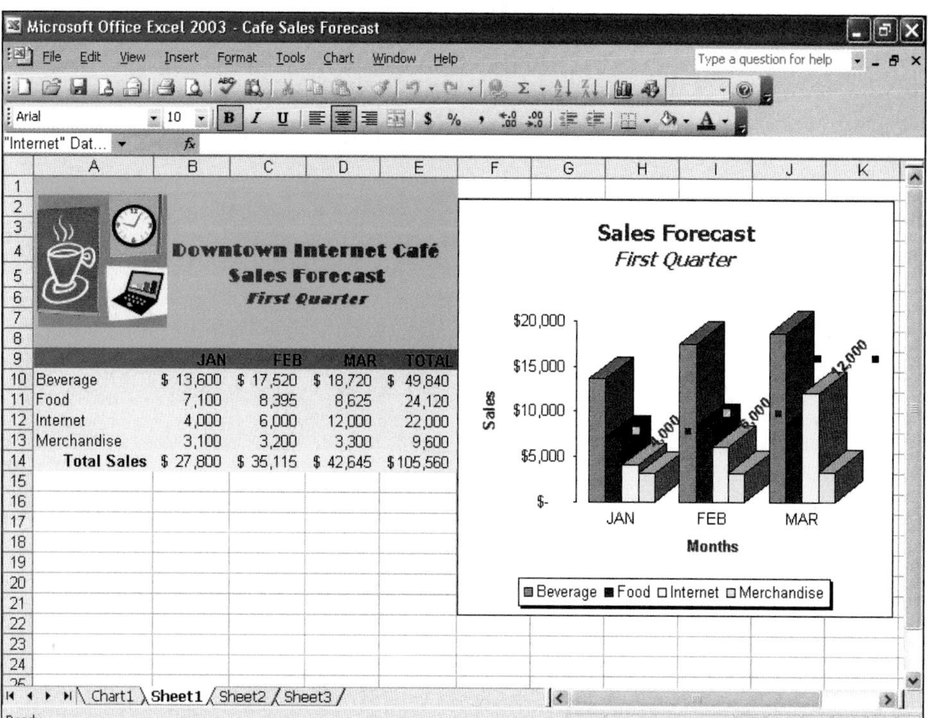

A worksheet showing the quarterly sales forecast containing a graphic, text enhancements, and a chart of the data is quickly created using basic Excel features.

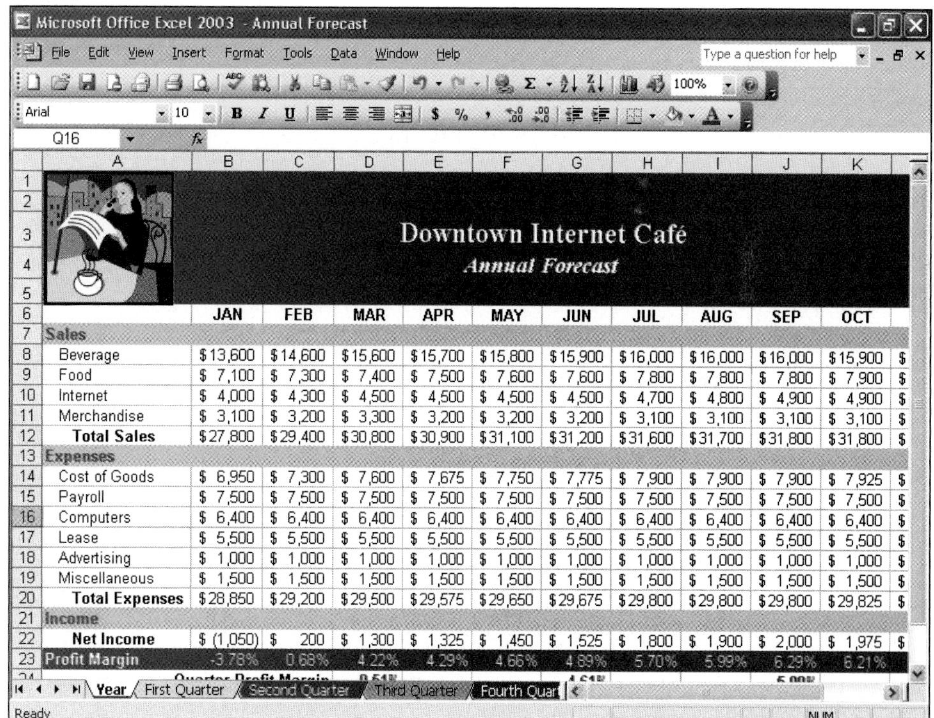

A large worksheet incorporating more complex formulas, visual enhancements such as colored text, varied text styles, and graphic elements is both informative and attractive.

You will see how easy it is to analyze data and make projections using what-if analysis and what-if graphing in Lab 3 and to incorporate Excel data in a Word document as shown in the following figures.

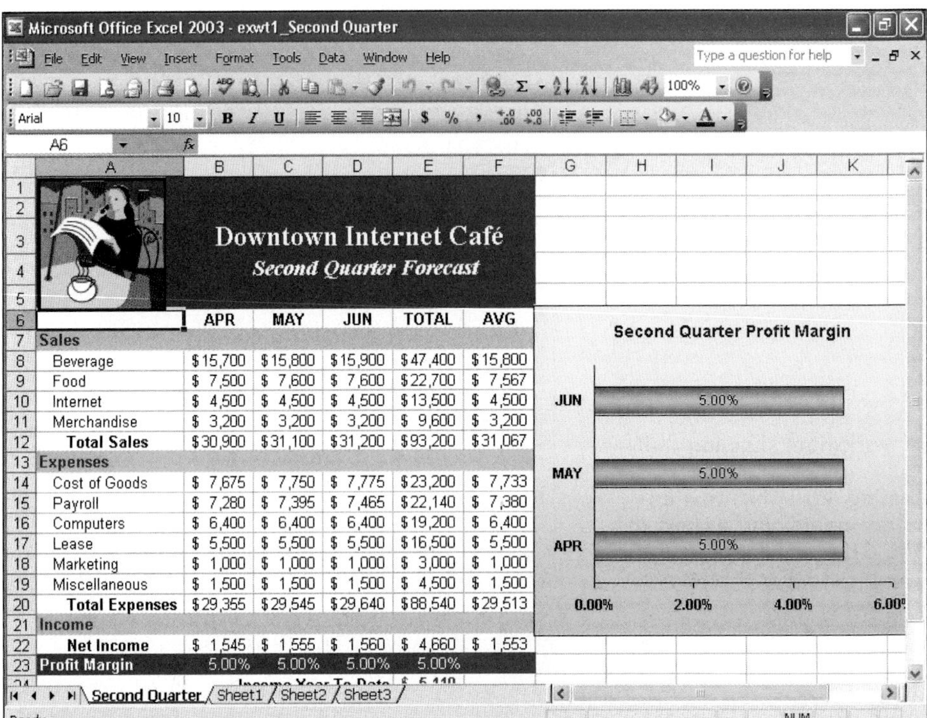

Changes you make in worksheet data while performing what-if analysis are automatically reflected in charts that reference that data.

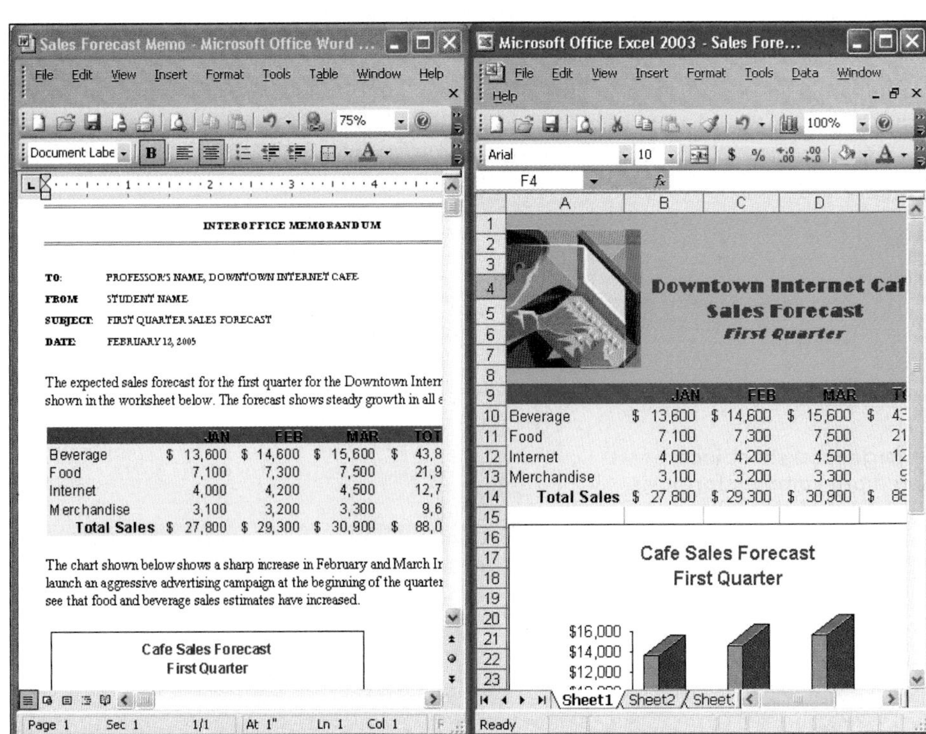

Worksheet data and charts can be copied and linked to other Office documents such as a Word document.

Office Access 2003

Office Access 2003 is a relational database management application that is used to create and analyze a database. A database is a collection of related data. In a relational database, the most widely used database structure, data is organized in linked tables. Tables consist of columns (called fields) and rows (called records). The tables are related or linked to one another by a common field. Relational databases allow you to create smaller and more manageable database tables, since you can combine and extract data between tables.

The program provides tools to enter, edit, and retrieve data from the database as well as to analyze the database and produce reports of the output. One of the main advantages of a computerized database is the ability to quickly add, delete, and locate specific records. Records can also be easily rearranged or sorted according to different fields of data, resulting in multiple table arrangements that provide more meaningful information for different purposes. Creation of forms makes it easier to enter and edit data as well. In the Access labs you will create and organize the database table shown below.

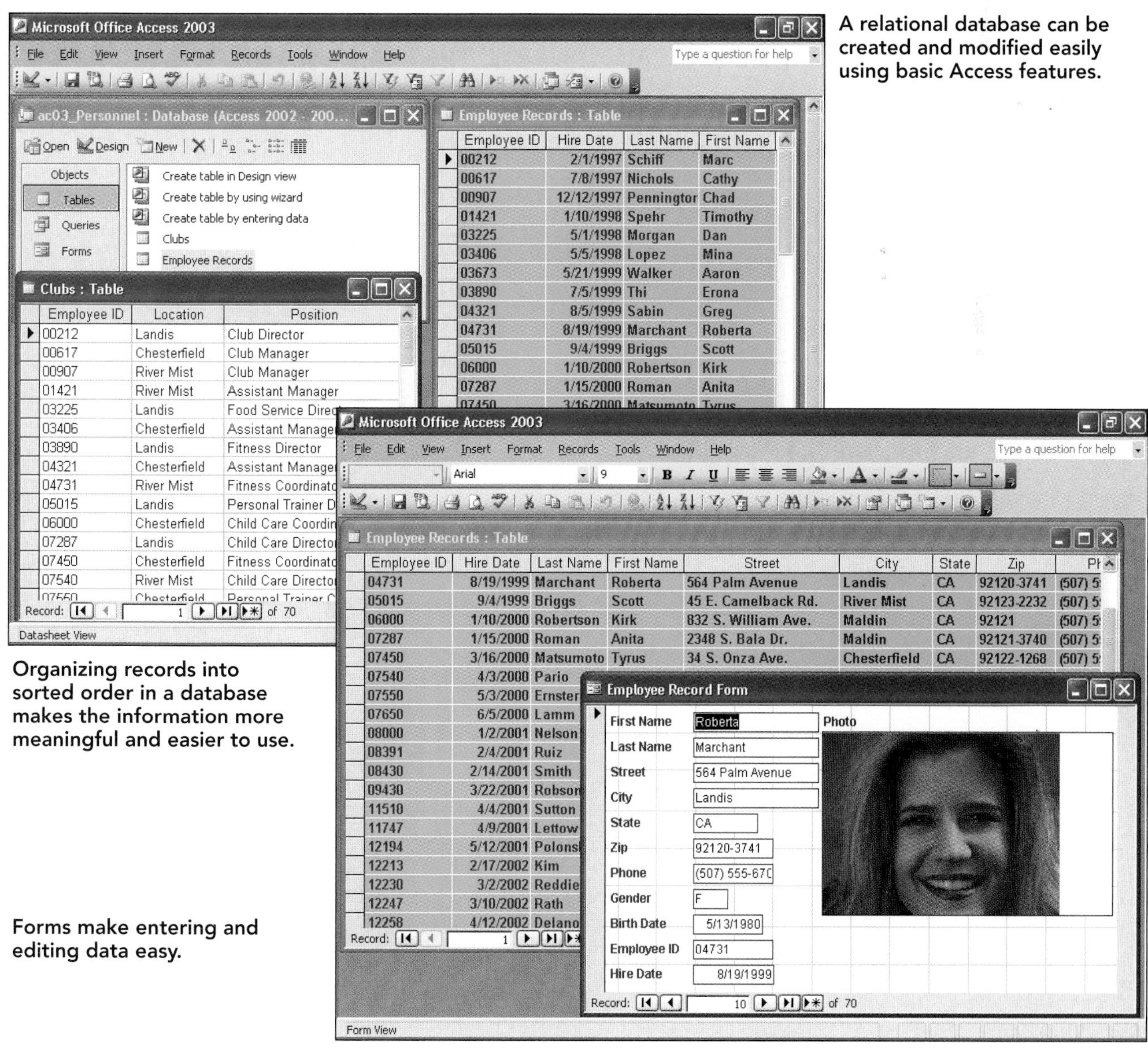

A relational database can be created and modified easily using basic Access features.

Organizing records into sorted order in a database makes the information more meaningful and easier to use.

Forms make entering and editing data easy.

Another feature is the ability to analyze the data in a table and perform calculations on different fields of data. Additionally, you can ask questions or query the table to find only certain records that meet specific conditions to be used in the analysis. Information that was once costly and time-consuming to get is now quickly and readily available. This information can then be quickly printed out in the form of reports ranging from simple listings to complex, professional-looking reports in different layout styles, or with titles, headings, subtotals, or totals.

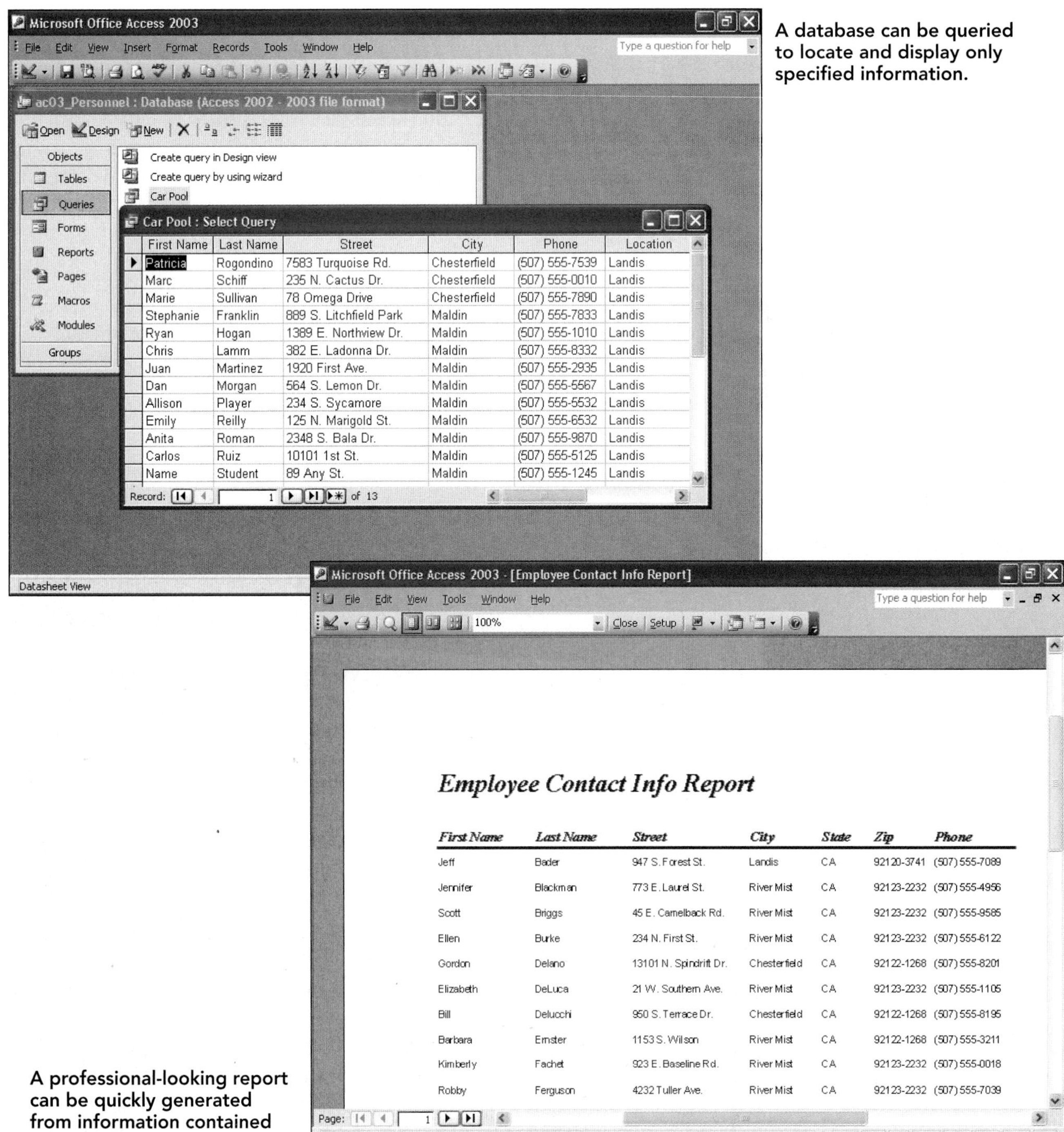

A database can be queried to locate and display only specified information.

A professional-looking report can be quickly generated from information contained in a database.

Office PowerPoint 2003

Office PowerPoint 2003 is a graphics presentation program designed to help you produce a high-quality presentation that is both interesting to the audience and effective in its ability to convey your message. A presentation can be as simple as overhead transparencies or as sophisticated as an on-screen electronic display. In the first two PowerPoint labs you will create and organize the presentation shown on the next page.

A presentation consists of a series of pages or "slides" presenting the information you want to convey in an organized and attractive manner.

When running an onscreen presentation, each slide of the presentation is displayed full-screen on your computer monitor or projected onto a screen.

Office Outlook 2003

Office Outlook 2003 is a personal information manager (PIM) program that is designed to get you organized and keep you organized. PIMs, also known as desktop managers, are designed to maximize your personal productivity by making it efficient and easy to perform everyday tasks such as scheduling meetings, recording contact information, and communicating with others, to name a few. Outlook 2003 includes an integrated e-mail program, a calendar, and contact and task management features.

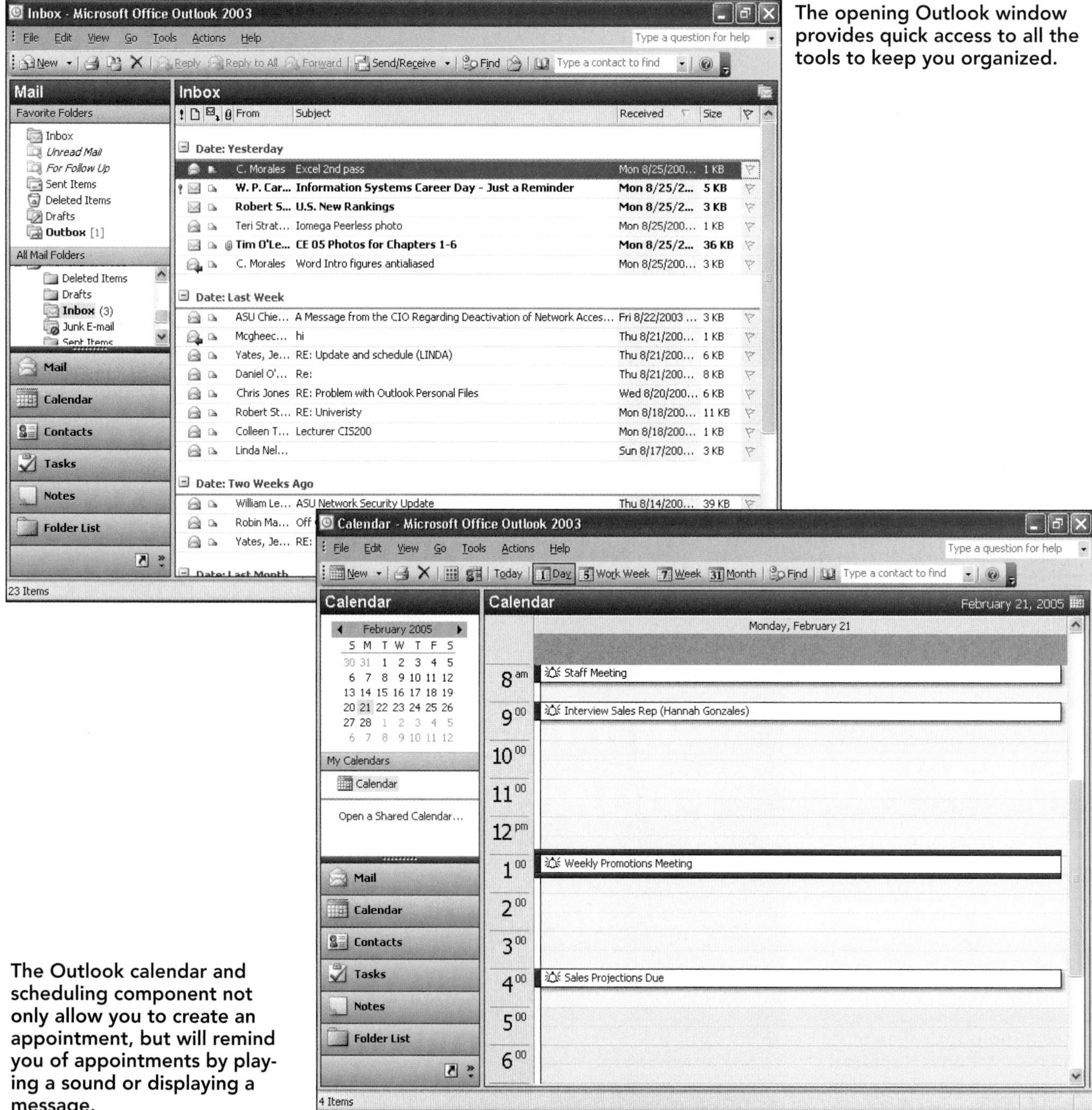

The opening Outlook window provides quick access to all the tools to keep you organized.

The Outlook calendar and scheduling component not only allow you to create an appointment, but will remind you of appointments by playing a sound or displaying a message.

Common Office 2003 Features

Additional Information

Please read the Before You Begin and Instructional Conventions sections in the Overview to Office PowerPoint 2003 (PPO.3) before starting this section.

Additional Information

It is assumed that you are already familiar with basic Windows operating system features. To review these features, refer to your Windows text or if available, the O'Leary Series *Introduction to Windows* text.

Now that you know a little about each of the applications in Microsoft Office 2003, we will take a look at some of the features that are common to all Office 2003 applications. This is a hands-on section that will introduce you to the features and allow you to get a feel for how Office 2003 works. Although Word 2003 will be used to demonstrate how the features work, only common features will be addressed. These features include using menus, Office Help, task panes, toolbars, and starting and exiting an application. The features that are specific to each application will be introduced individually in each application text.

Starting an Office 2003 Application

There are several ways to start an Office 2003 application. The two most common methods are by using the Start menu or by clicking a desktop shortcut for the program if it is available. If you use the Start menu, the steps will vary slightly depending on the version of Windows you are using.

1. **Click start to display the Start menu.**

   Select All Programs.

Having Trouble?

If you are using Windows 2002 or earlier, select Programs.

   Select Microsoft Office.

   Choose Microsoft Office Word 2003.

OR

1. **Double-click the** Microsoft Office Word 2003 **shortcut on the desktop.**

2. **If necessary, click Maximize in the title bar to maximize the window.**

Additional Information

Your window may appear with olive green or silver colors, depending upon the Windows settings on your computer.

Your screen should be similar to Figure 1

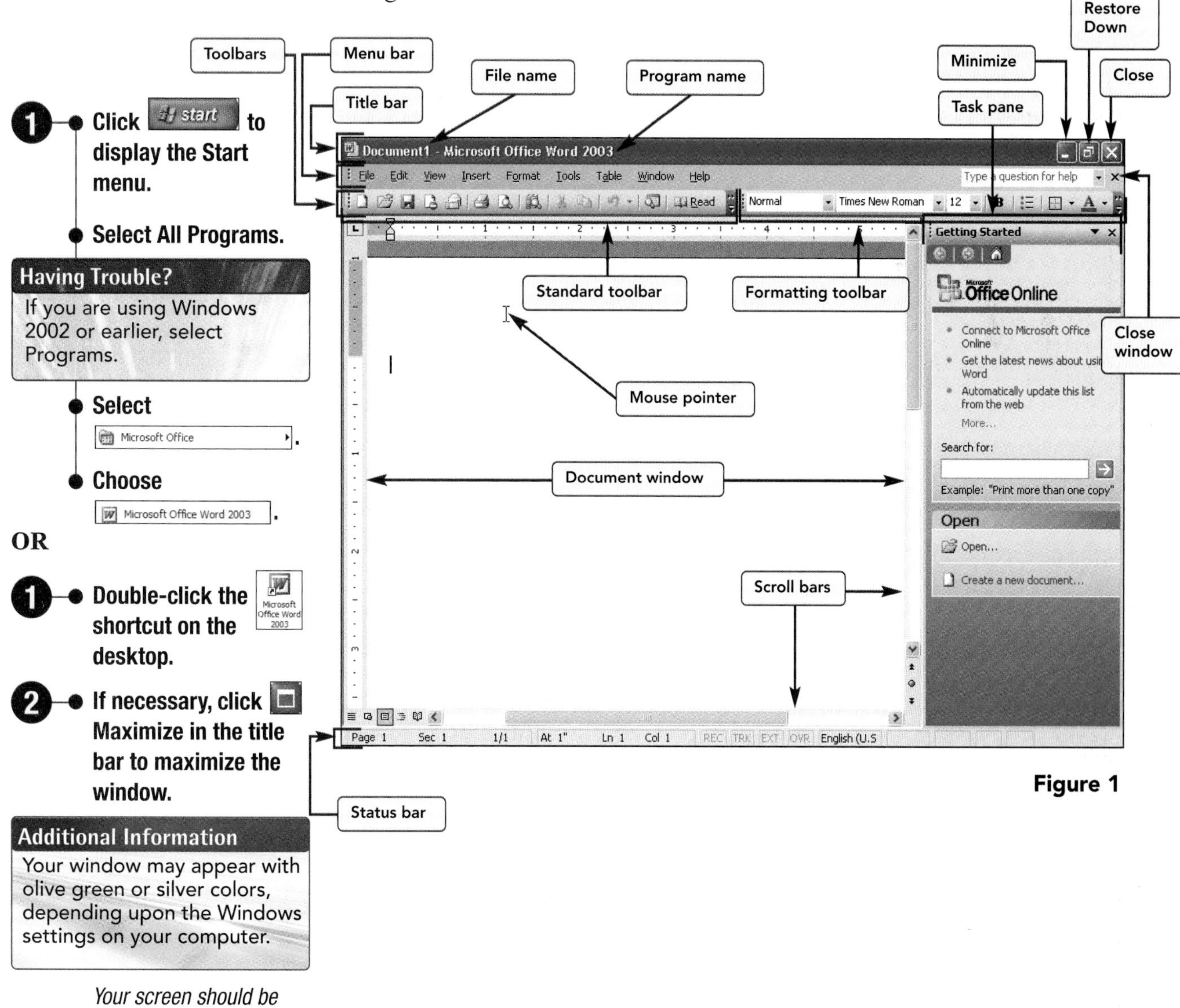

Figure 1

Additional Information

Application windows can be sized, moved, and otherwise manipulated like any other windows on the desktop.

The Word program is started and displayed in a window on the desktop. The left end of the application window title bar displays the file name followed by the program name, Microsoft Office Word 2003. The right end of the title bar displays the Minimize, Restore Down, and Close buttons. They perform the same functions and operate in the same way as all Windows versions.

The **menu bar** below the title bar displays the application's program menu. The right end displays the document window's Close Window button. As you use the Office applications, you will see that the menu bar contains many of the same menus, such as File, Edit, and Help. You will also see several menus that are specific to each application.

The **toolbars** located below the menu bar contain buttons that are mouse shortcuts for many of the menu items. Commonly, the Office applications will display two toolbars when the application is first opened: Standard and Formatting. They may appear together on one row (as in Figure 1), or on separate rows.

The large center area of the program window is the **document window** where open application files are displayed. Currently, there is a blank Word document open. In Word, the mouse pointer appears as I when positioned in the document window and as a when it can be used to select items. The **task pane** is displayed on the right side of the document window. Task panes provide quick access to features as you are using the application. As you perform certain actions, different task panes automatically open. In this case, since you just started an application, the Getting Started task pane is automatically displayed, providing different ways to create a new document or open an existing document.

Additional Information

Use Tools/Options and select Startup task pane to display the Getting Started task pane when starting the application.

The **status bar** at the bottom of the window displays location information and the status of different settings as they are used. Different information is displayed in the status bar for different applications.

On the right and bottom of the document window, are vertical and horizontal scroll bars. A **scroll bar** is used with a mouse to bring additional lines of information into view in a window. The vertical scroll bar is used to move up or down, and the horizontal scroll bar moves side to side in the window.

As you can see, many of the features in the Word window are the same as in other Windows applications. The common user interface makes learning and using new applications much easier.

Using Menus

Additional Information

Use Tools/Customize/Options and check or clear the "Always show full menus" option to change how your menus operate.

A menu is one of many methods you can use to accomplish a task in a program. When opened, a menu displays a list of commands. When an Office program menu is first opened, it may display a short version of commands. The short menu is a personalized version of the menu that displays basic and frequently used commands and hides those used less often. An expanded version will display automatically after the menu is open for a few seconds.

1 Click **F**ile to open the File menu.

Point to each menu in the menu bar to see the full menu for each.

Additional Information

Once one menu is expanded, others expand automatically until you choose a command or perform another action.

Point to the **V**iew menu.

Your screen should be similar to Figure 2

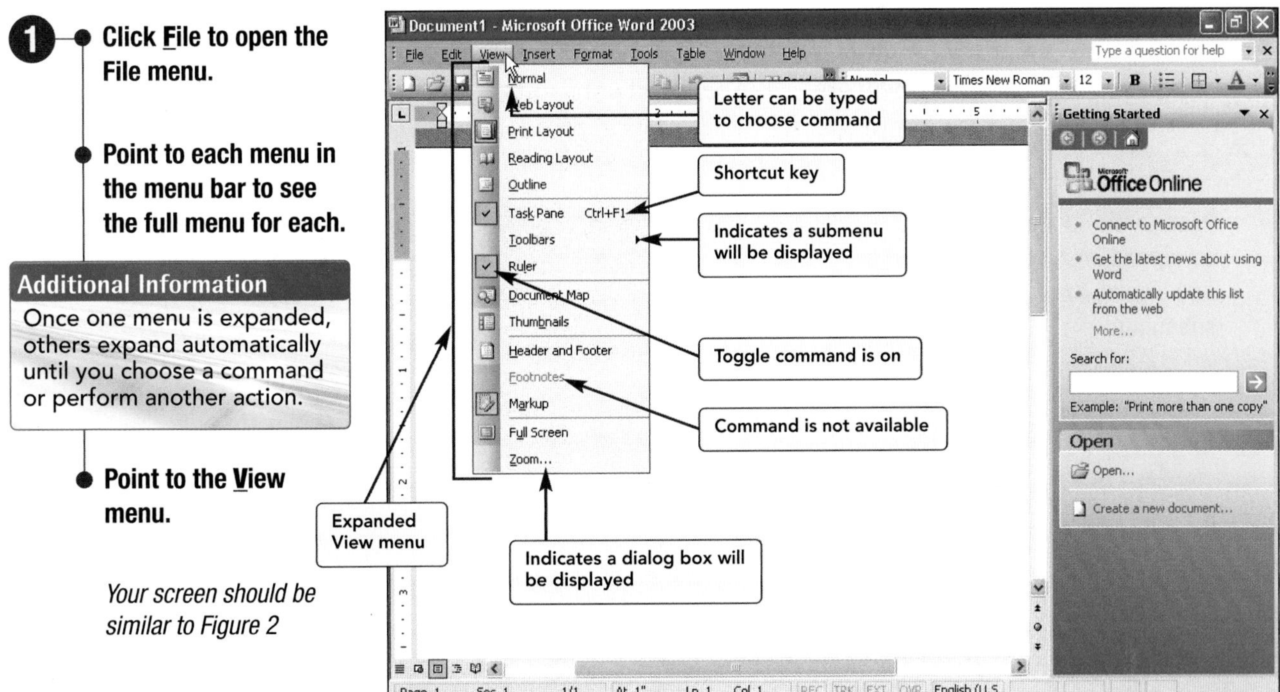

Figure 2

Additional Information

If you do not want to wait for the expanded menu to appear, you can click [expand button] at the bottom of the menu or double-click the menu name to display the full menu immediately.

Many commands have images next to them so you can quickly associate the command with the image. The same image appears on the toolbar button for that feature. Menus may include the following features (not all menus include all features):

Feature	Meaning
Ellipsis (...)	Indicates a dialog box will be displayed.
▸	Indicates a submenu will be displayed.
Dimmed	Indicates the command is not available for selection until certain other conditions are met.
Shortcut key	A key or key combination that can be used to execute a command without using the menu.
Checkmark	Indicates a toggle type of command. Selecting it turns the feature on or off. A checkmark indicates the feature is on.
Underlined letter	Indicates the letter you can type to choose the command.

Additional Information

If underlined command letters are not displayed, this feature is not active on your system.

On the View menu, two options, Task Pane and Ruler, are checked, indicating these features are on. The Task Pane option also displays the shortcut key combination, Ctrl + F1, after the option. This indicates the command can be chosen by pressing the keys instead of using the menu. The Footnotes option is dimmed because it is not currently available. The Toolbars option will display a submenu when selected, and the Zoom command a dialog box of additional options.

Once a menu is open, you can select a command from the menu by pointing to it. A colored highlight bar, called the **selection cursor**, appears over the selected command.

2 **Point to the Toolbars command to select it and display the submenu.**

Your screen should be similar to Figure 3

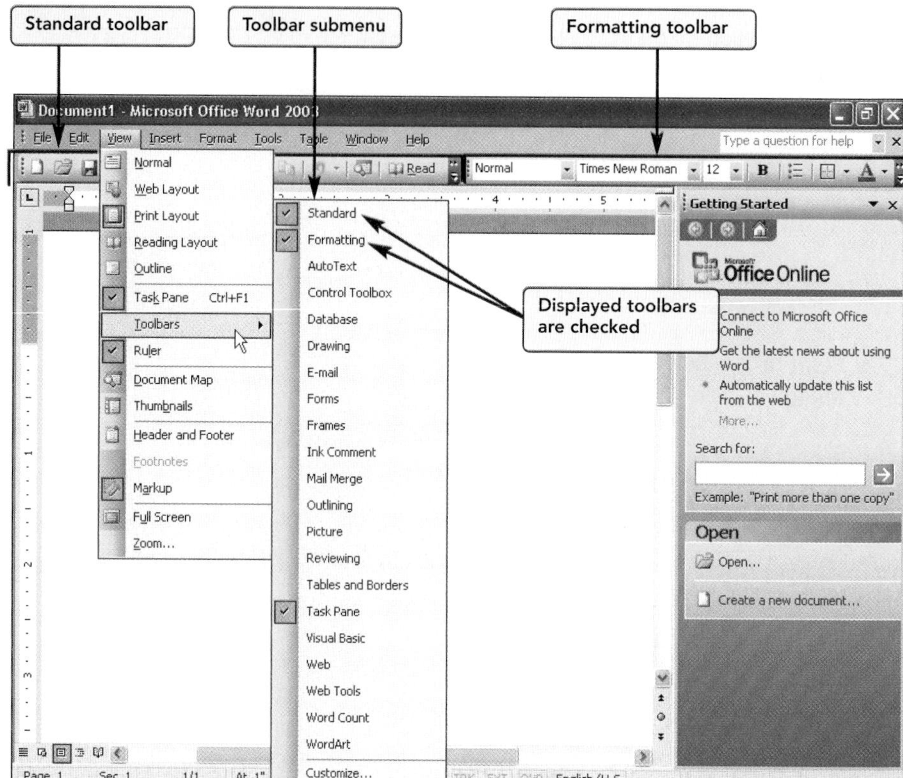

Figure 3

Currently there are three selected (checked) Toolbar options: Standard, Formatting, and although not technically a toolbar, the Task Pane. If other toolbars are selected in your menu, this is because once a toolbar has been turned on, it remains on until turned off.

To choose a command, you click on it. When the command is chosen, the associated action is performed. You will close the task pane and any other open toolbars and display the Drawing toolbar.

3

- **Click on Task Pane to turn off this feature.**
- **Open the View menu again, select Toolbars, and if it is not already selected, click on the Drawing toolbar option to turn it on.**
- **If necessary, choose View/Toolbars again and deselect any other toolbar options (there should be 3 selected toolbar options).**

Your screen should be similar to Figure 4

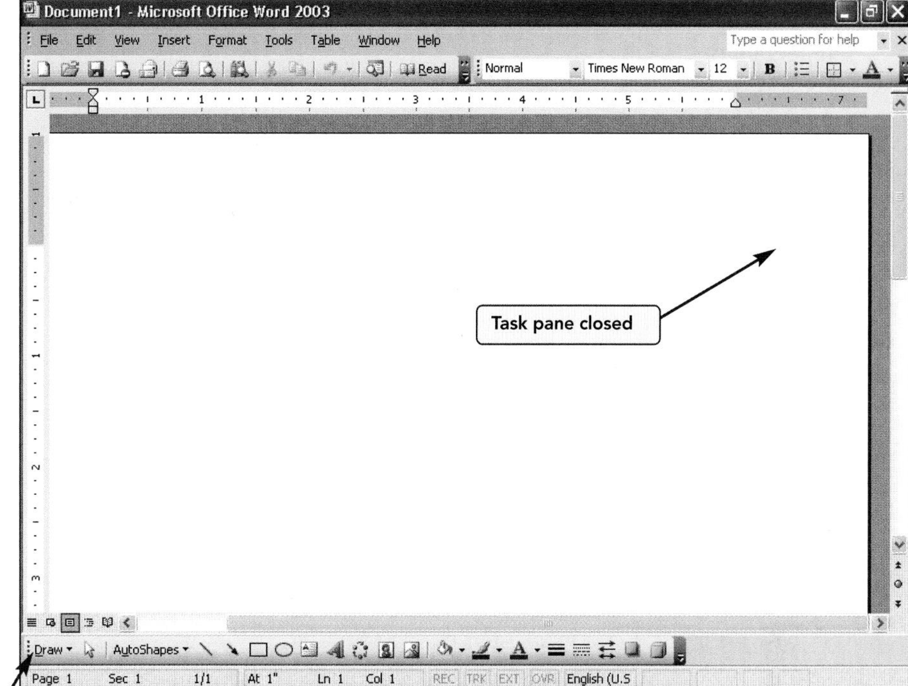

Figure 4

> **Additional Information**
> If you have a microphone and have installed and trained the Speech Recognition feature, you can speak the command sequences to open menus and choose commands. For example, to open a toolbar, you would say "View Toolbars."

> **Additional Information**
> Using voice commands, saying "Right click" will open the shortcut menu for the selected item.

The task pane is closed and the Drawing toolbar is displayed above the status bar. Any other toolbars that were open which you deselected are closed.

Using Shortcut Menus

Another way to access menu options is to use the **shortcut menu**. The shortcut menu is opened by right-clicking on an item on the screen. This menu displays only those options associated with the item. For example, right-clicking on any toolbar will display the toolbar menu options only. You will use this method to hide the Drawing toolbar again.

Point to the Drawing toolbar and right-click.

Your screen should be similar to Figure 5

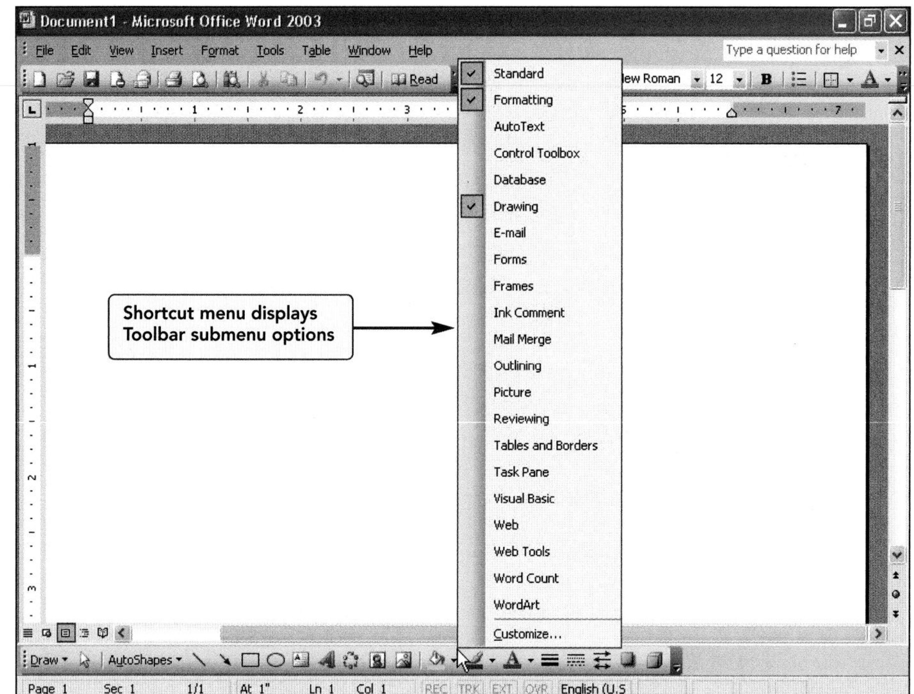

Figure 5

Additional Information

The Customize option can be used to change features of toolbars and menus.

The shortcut menu displays only the Toolbar submenu options on the View menu. Using a shortcut menu saves time over selecting the main menu command sequence.

Choose Drawing to turn off this feature.

Your screen should be similar to Figure 6

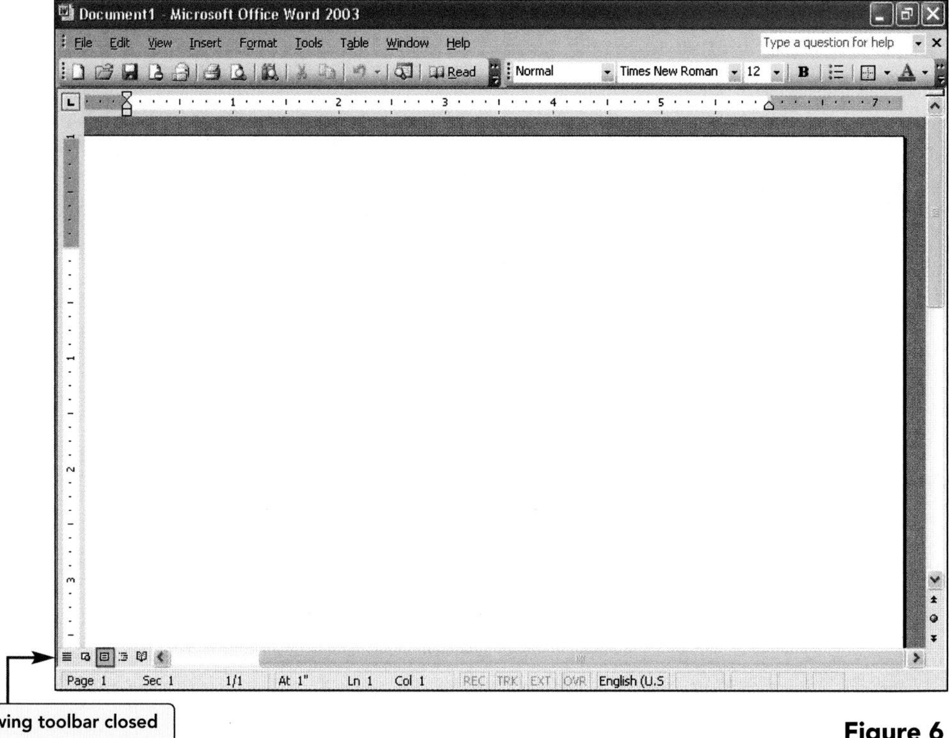

Figure 6

The Drawing toolbar is no longer displayed.

Using Shortcut Keys

A third way to perform a command is to use the shortcut key or key combination associated with a particular command. If you will recall, the shortcut key associated with the View/Task Pane command is Ctrl + F1. To use the key combination, you hold down the first key while pressing the second.

Additional Information
Not all commands have shortcut keys.

1 **Hold down Ctrl and press the F1 function key.**

Having Trouble?
Function keys are located above the numeric keys on the keyboard.

Your screen should be similar to Figure 7

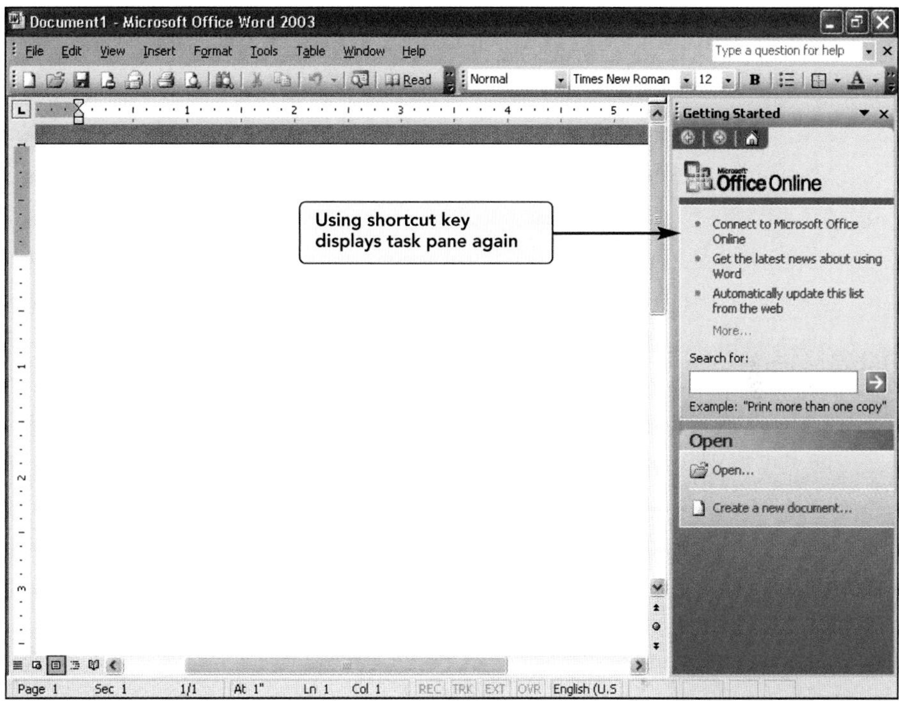

Figure 7

The task pane is displayed again. Using shortcut keys is the quickest way to perform many actions; however, you need to remember the key combination in order to use it.

Additional Information
Using the Speech Recognition feature, you can also use voice shortcuts for many commands. For example, to show the task pane, you would say "show task pane." Many voice commands also have several different words you can say to initiate the command. You could also say "task pane" or "view task pane."

Using Toolbars

Initially, Word displays two toolbars, Standard and Formatting, below the menu bar (see Figure 3). The **Standard toolbar** contains buttons that are used to complete the most frequently used menu commands. The **Formatting toolbar** contains buttons that are used to change the appearance or format of the document. There are many features that can be used to make working with toolbars easier.

Displaying Toolbars on Separate Rows

The default toolbar arrangement is to display both toolbars on one row. Because there is not enough space to display all the buttons on both toolbars on a single row, many buttons are hidden. The Toolbar Options button located at the end of a toolbar displays a drop-down button list of those buttons that are not displayed. Toolbars initially display the basic buttons. Like menus, they are personalized automatically, displaying those buttons you use frequently and hiding others. When you use a button from this list, it then is moved to the toolbar, and a button that has not been used recently is moved to the Toolbar Options list. It also contains an option to display the toolbars on separate rows. You will use this option to quickly see all the toolbar buttons.

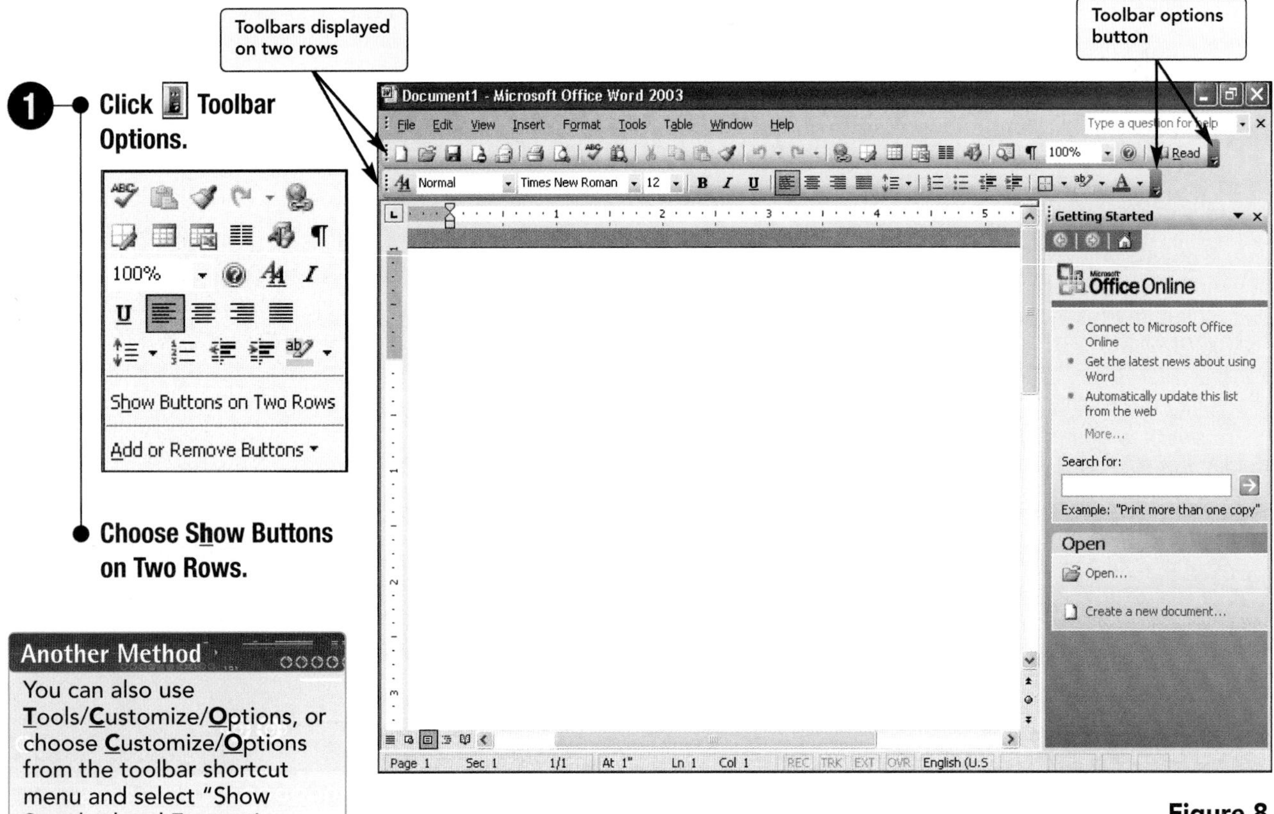

Figure 8

Another Method

You can also use Tools/Customize/Options, or choose Customize/Options from the toolbar shortcut menu and select "Show Standard and Formatting toolbars on two rows."

Your screen should be similar to Figure 8

Additional Information

The Add or Remove Buttons option allows you to customize existing toolbars by selecting those buttons you want to display and by creating your own customized toolbars.

The two toolbars now occupy separate rows, providing enough space for all the buttons to be displayed. Now using Toolbar Options is no longer necessary, and when selected only displays the options to return the toolbars display to one row and the Add or Remove Buttons option.

When a toolbar is open, it may appear docked or floating. A **docked toolbar** is fixed to an edge of the window and displays a vertical bar, called the move handle, on the left edge of the toolbar. Dragging this bar up or down allows you to move the toolbar. If multiple toolbars share the same row, dragging the bar left or right adjusts the size of the toolbar. If docked, a toolbar can occupy a row by itself, or several can be on a row together. A **floating toolbar** appears in a separate window and can be moved anywhere on the desktop.

Docked toolbar

2 **Point to the move handle of the Standard toolbar and, when the mouse pointer appears as ✥, drag the toolbar into the document window.**

Your screen should be similar to Figure 9

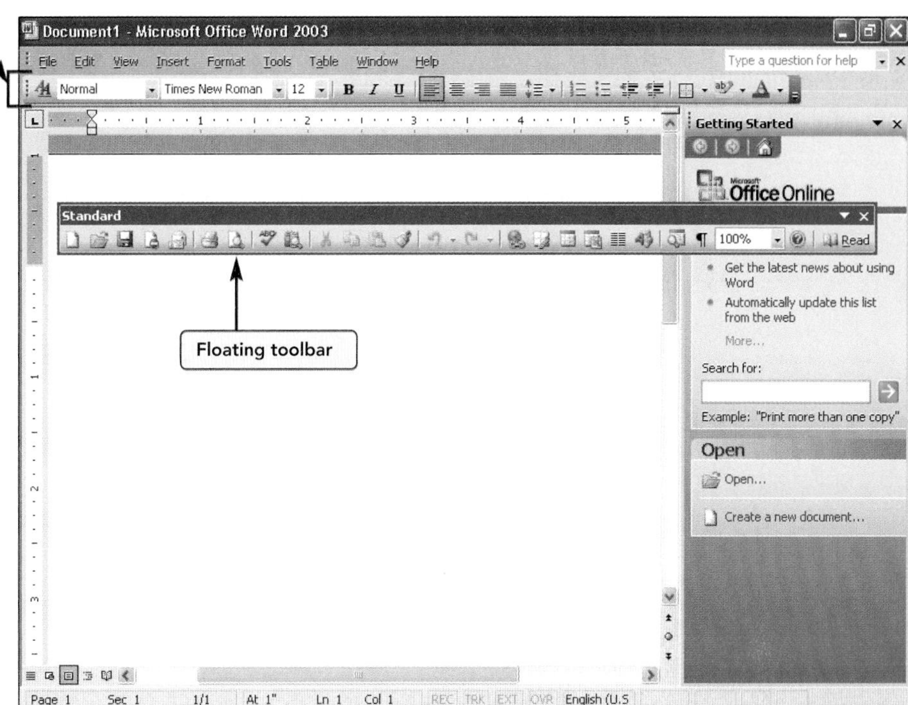

Figure 9

The Standard toolbar is now a floating toolbar and can be moved to any location in the window by dragging the title bar. If you move a floating toolbar to the edge of the window, it will attach to that location and become a docked toolbar. A floating toolbar can also be sized by dragging the edge of the toolbar.

Toolbars docked and displayed on two rows again

3 **Drag the title bar of the floating toolbar (the mouse pointer appears as ✥) to move the toolbar to the row below the Formatting toolbar.**

Move the Formatting toolbar below the Standard toolbar.

Align both toolbars with the left edge of the window by dragging the move handle horizontally.

Your screen should be similar to Figure 10

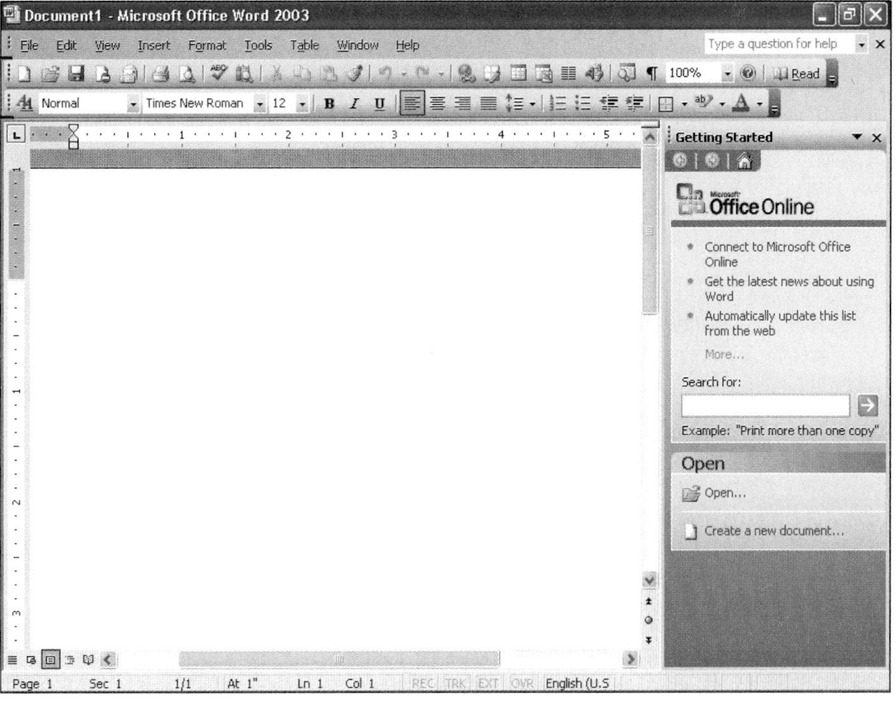

Figure 10

The two toolbars again occupy two rows. To quickly identify the toolbar buttons, you can display the button name by pointing to the button.

4 Point to any button on the Standard toolbar.

Your screen should be similar to Figure 11

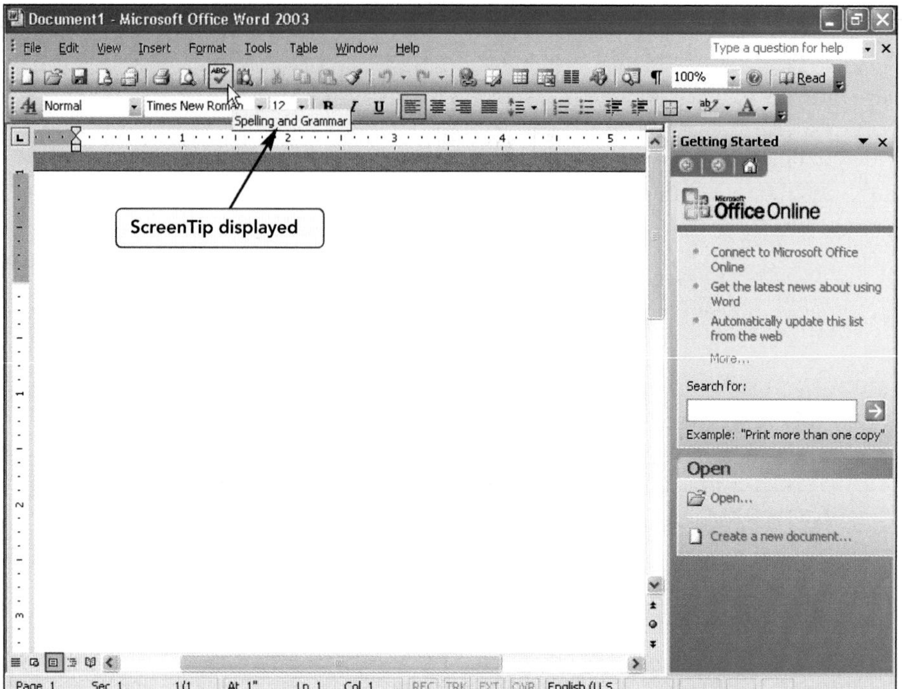

Figure 11

A ScreenTip containing the button name appears next to the mouse pointer. Clicking on a button will perform the associated action. You will use the Help button to access Microsoft Word Help.

5 Click Microsoft Office Word Help.

Another Method

You can also choose Help/Microsoft Office Word Help, or press F1 to access Help.

Your screen should be similar to Figure 12

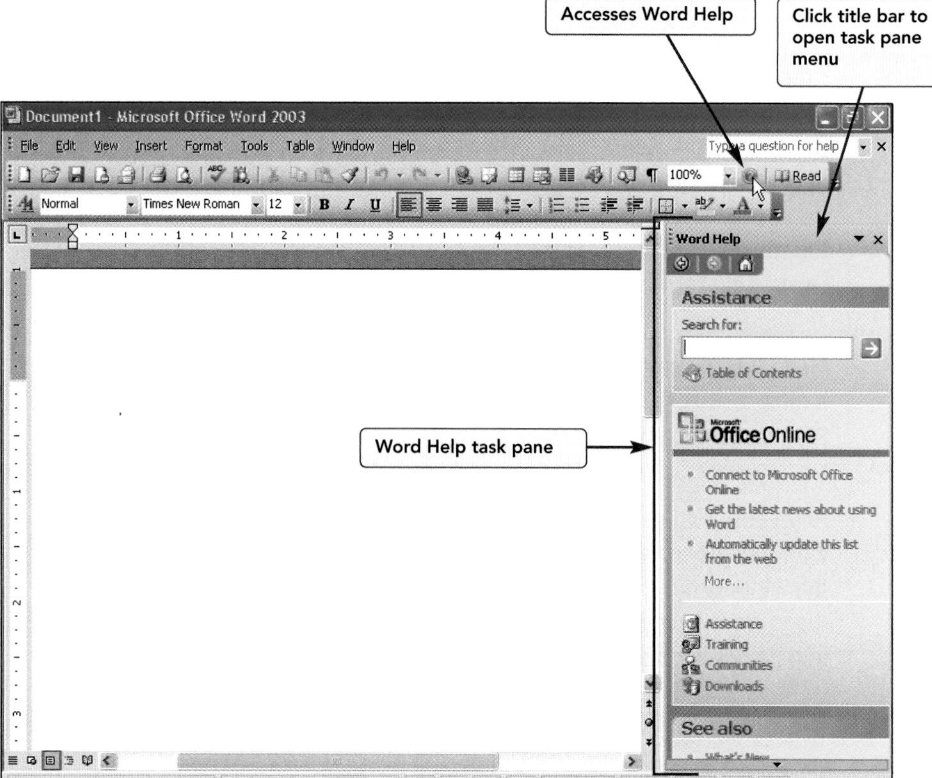

Figure 12

The Getting Started task pane is replaced by the Microsoft Word Help task pane. The name of the task pane appears in the task pane title bar.

Using Task Panes

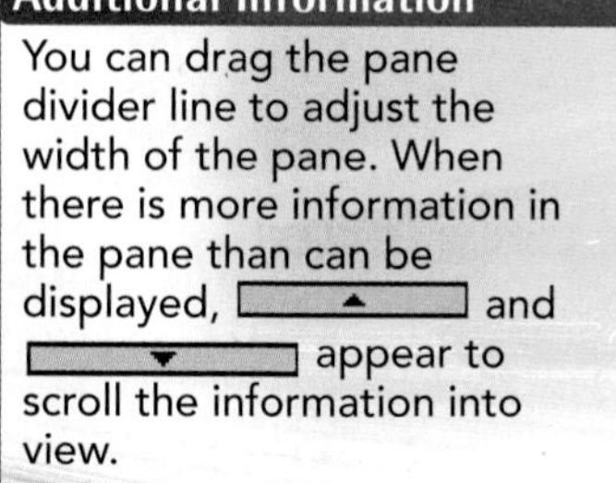

Additional Information

You can drag the pane divider line to adjust the width of the pane. When there is more information in the pane than can be displayed, [up scroll button] and [down scroll button] appear to scroll the information into view.

Task panes appear automatically when certain features are used. They can also be opened manually from the task pane menu. Clicking the task pane title bar displays a drop-down menu of other task panes you can select. In Word there are 14 different task panes. You will redisplay the Getting Started task pane. Then you will quickly return to the previously displayed task pane using the Back toolbar button in the task pane.

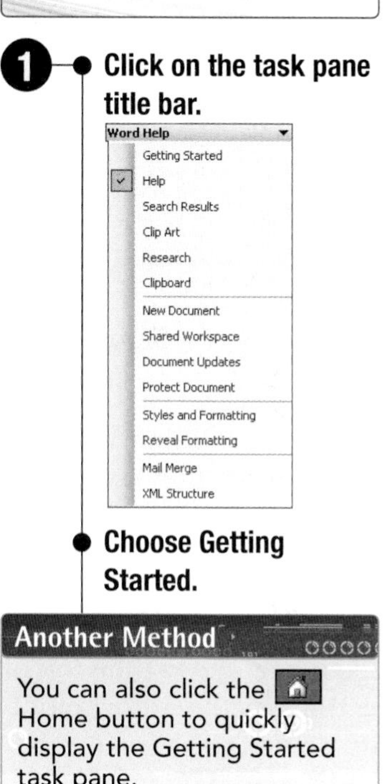

1 **Click on the task pane title bar.**

- **Choose Getting Started.**

Another Method

You can also click the Home button to quickly display the Getting Started task pane.

- **Click Back.**

Your screen should be similar to Figure 13

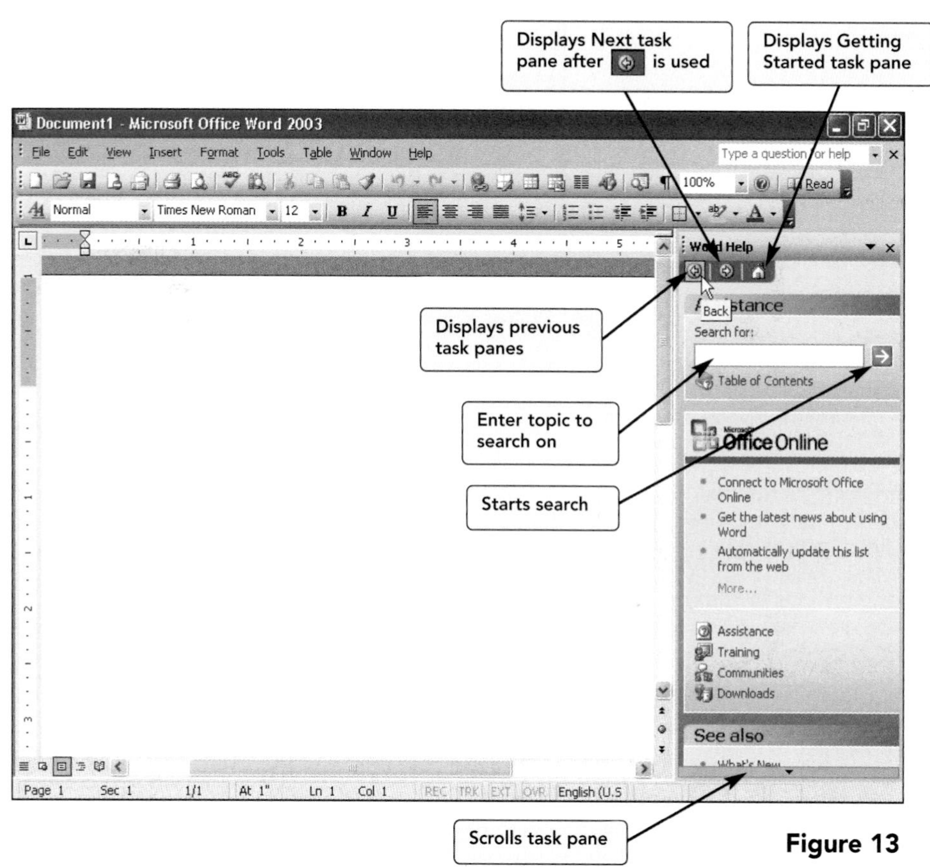

Figure 13

The Help task pane is displayed again. Likewise, clicking the Forward button will display the task pane that was viewed before using Back.

Using Office Help

There are several ways you can get help. One method is to conduct a search of the available help information by entering a sentence or question you want help on in the Search text box of the Help task pane. Notice the insertion point is positioned in the Search text box. This indicates it is ready for you to type an entry. You will use this method to learn about getting Help while you work.

Additional Information

Although you can also simply enter a word or phrase in the Search box, the best results occur when you type a complete sentence or question.

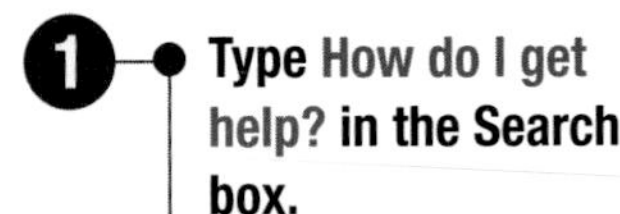

Type How do I get help? in the Search box.

Having Trouble?

If the insertion point is not displayed in the Search box, simply click in the box to activate it.

Click Start Searching.

Your screen should be similar to Figure 14

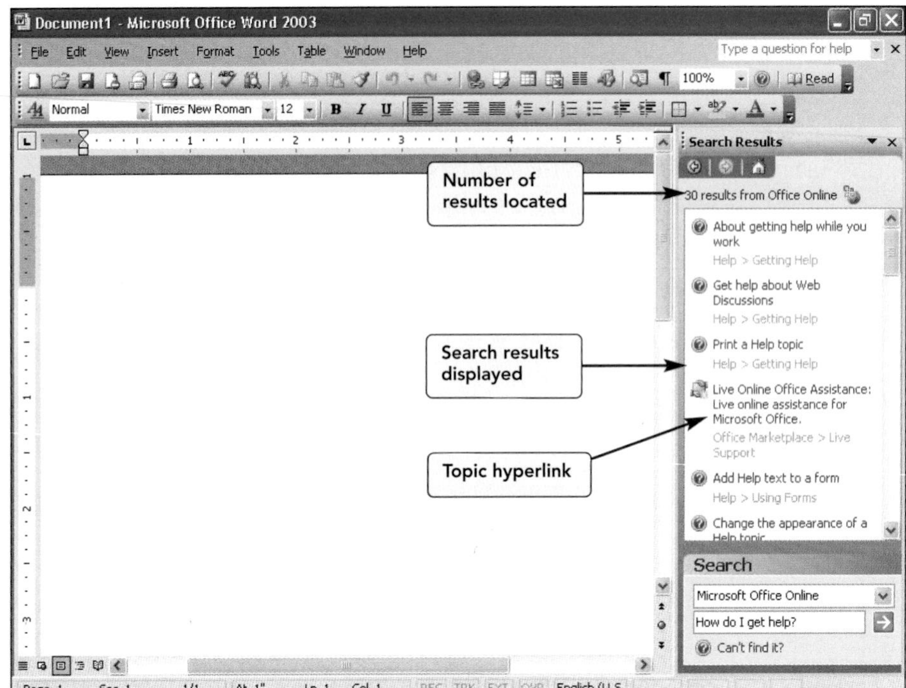

Figure 14

Additional Information

In addition to being connected to the Internet, the Online Content settings must be selected. Click Online Content Settings in the Help task pane and select all the options to turn on these features.

Additional Information

The number of results located and where they were found is displayed at the top of the list.

If you are connected to the Internet, the Microsoft Office Online Web site is searched and the results are displayed in the Search Results task pane. If you are not connected, the offline help information that is provided with the application and stored on your computer is searched. Generally the search results are similar, but fewer in number.

The Search Results pane displays a list of located results. The results are shown in order of relevance, with the most likely matches at the top of the list. Each result is a **hyperlink** or connection to the information located on the Online site or in Help on your computer. Clicking the hyperlink accesses and displays the information associated with the hyperlink.

You want to read the information in the topic "About getting help while you work."

2 **From the Search Results list click the "About getting help while you work" hyperlink.**

Additional Information

When you point to the hyperlink, it appears underlined and the mouse pointer appears as 👆.

Your screen should be similar to Figure 15

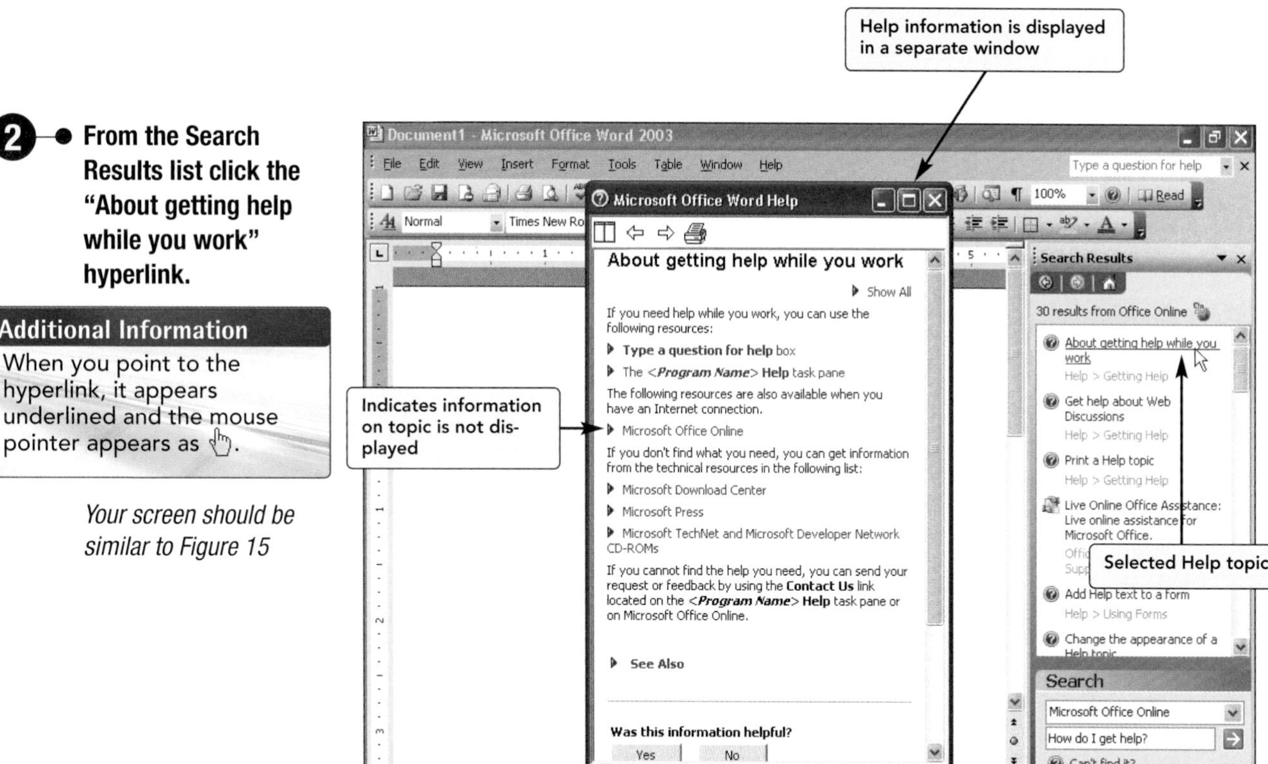

Figure 15

The information on the selected topic is displayed in a separate Help window. The Help window on your screen will probably be a different size and arrangement than in Figure 15. Depending on the size of your Help window, you may need to scroll the window to see all the Help information provided. As you are reading the help topic, you will see many subtopics preceded with ▸. This indicates the information in the subtopic is not displayed. Clicking on the subtopic heading displays the information about the topic.

3

- If necessary, use the scroll bar to scroll the Help window to see the information on this topic.
- Scroll back up to the top of the window.

Additional Information

Clicking the scroll arrows scrolls the text in the window line by line, and dragging the scroll bar up or down moves to a general location within the window area.

- Click the "Type a question for help box" subtopic.
- Click the "The <Program name> Help task pane" subtopic.
- Read the information on both subtopics.

Your screen should be similar to Figure 16

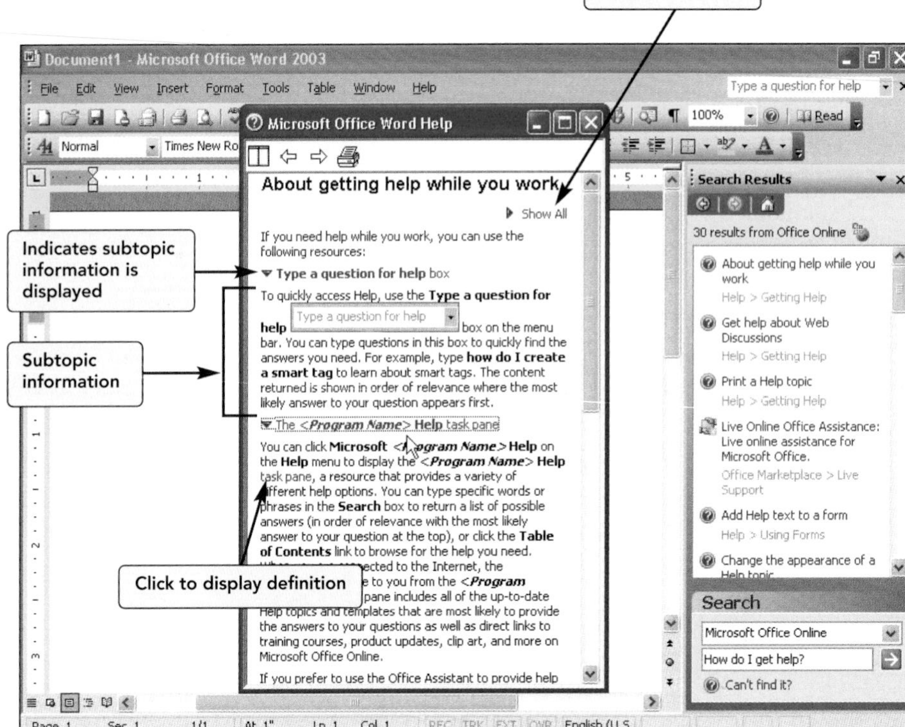

Figure 16

The [▸] preceding the subtopic has changed to [▾] indicating the subtopic content is displayed. The selected subtopics provide information about accessing Help using the "Type a question for help" box and the Help task pane. Notice the blue words "task pane" within the subtopic content. This indicates that clicking on the text will display a definition of the term. You can continue to click on the subtopic headings to display the information about each topic individually, or you can click Show All to display all the available topic information.

4

- Click "task pane" to see the definition.
- Click Show All at the top of the Help window.
- Scroll the window to see the Microsoft Office Online subtopic.
- Read the information on this subtopic.

Your screen should be similar to Figure 17

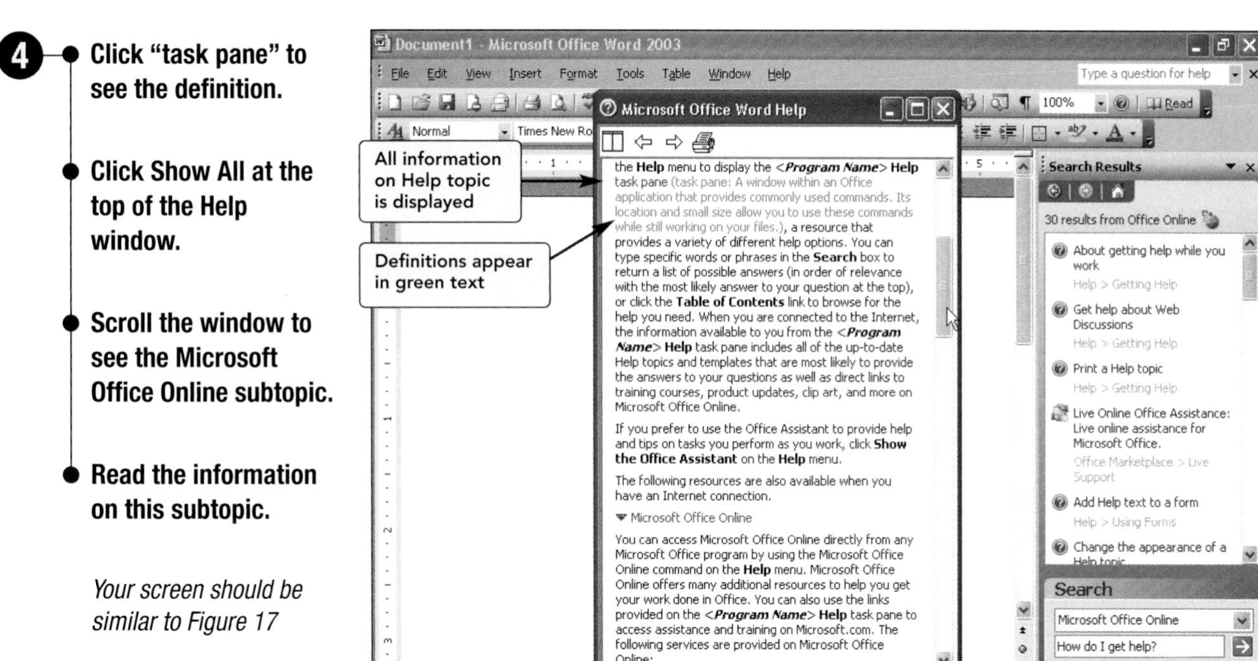

Figure 17

The information under all the subtopics is fully displayed, including definitions.

Using the Help Table of Contents

Another source of help is to use the Help table of contents. Using this method allows you to browse the Help topics to locate topics of interest to you.

1

- Click Close in the Help window title bar to close the Help window.
- Click Back in the task pane.
- Click Table of Contents (below the Search box).

Your screen should be similar to Figure 18

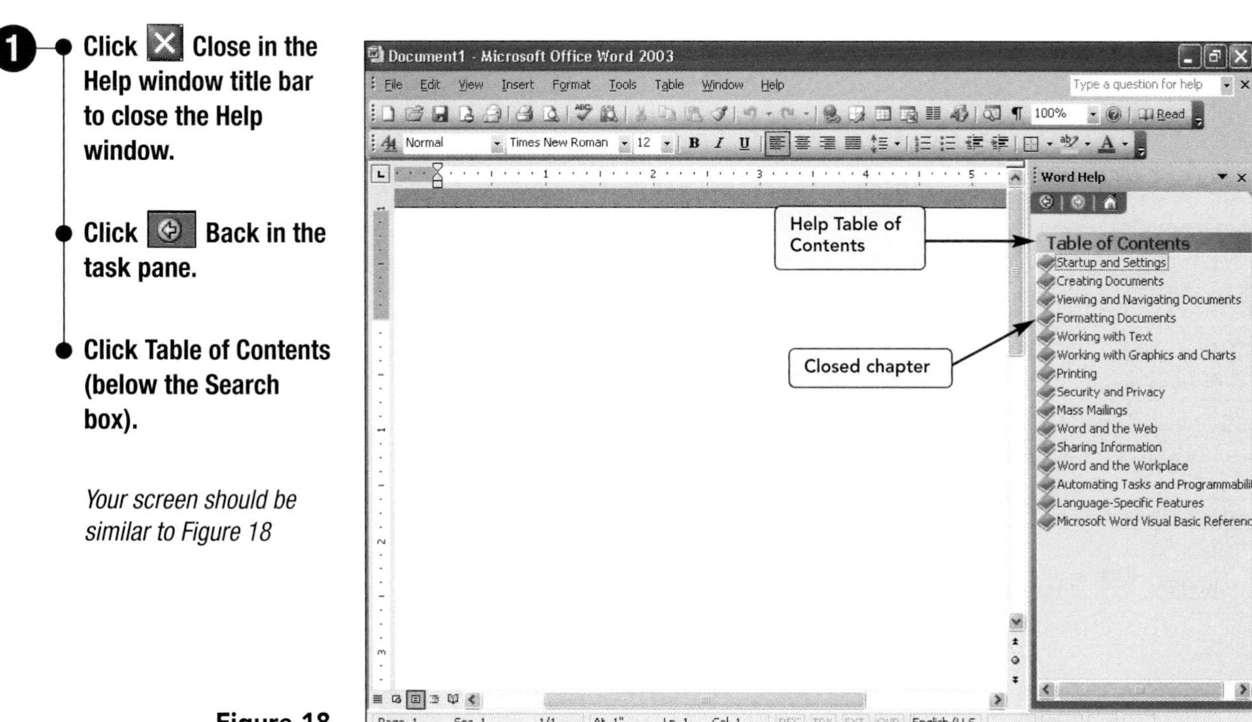

Figure 18

The entire Word Help Table of Contents is displayed in the Help task pane. Clicking on an item preceded with a Closed Book icon opens a chapter, which expands to display additional chapters or topics. The Open Book icon identifies those chapters that are open. Clicking on an item preceded with displays the specific Help information.

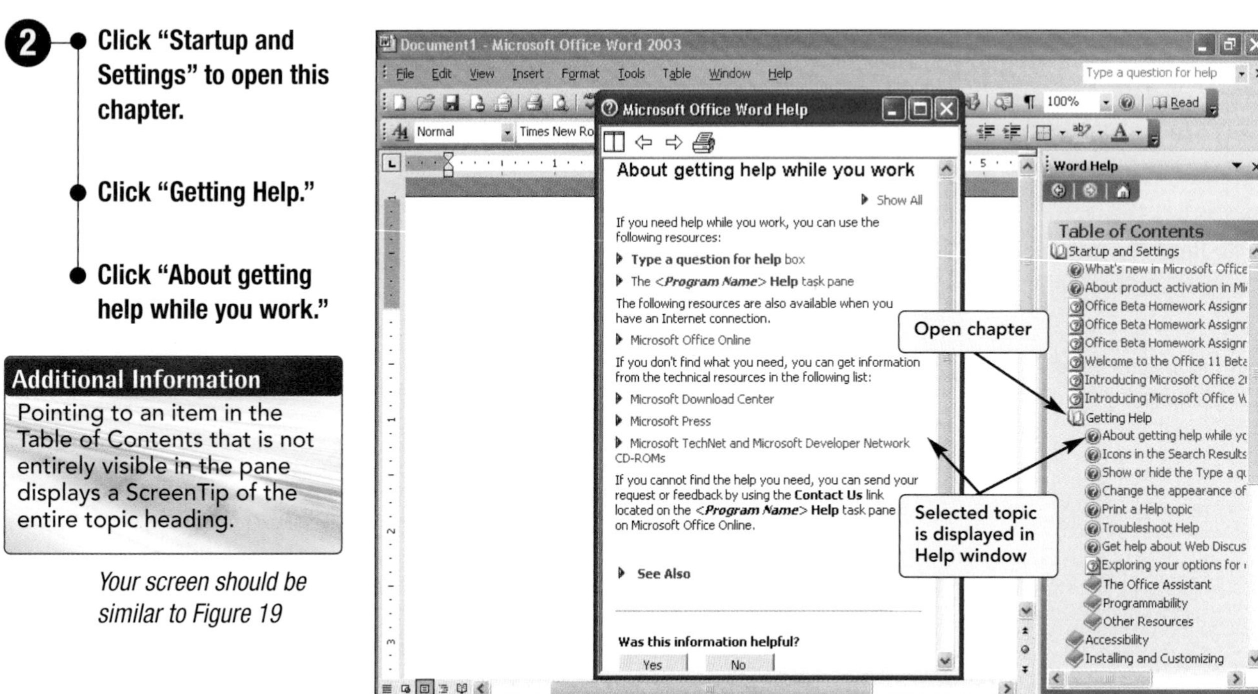

2

- **Click "Startup and Settings" to open this chapter.**
- **Click "Getting Help."**
- **Click "About getting help while you work."**

Additional Information

Pointing to an item in the Table of Contents that is not entirely visible in the pane displays a ScreenTip of the entire topic heading.

Your screen should be similar to Figure 19

Figure 19

The Help window opens again and displays the information on the selected topic. To close a chapter, click the icon.

Exiting an Office 2003 Application

Now you are ready to close the Help window and exit the Word program. The Exit command on the File menu can be used to quit most Windows programs. Alternatively, you can click the Close button in the program window title bar.

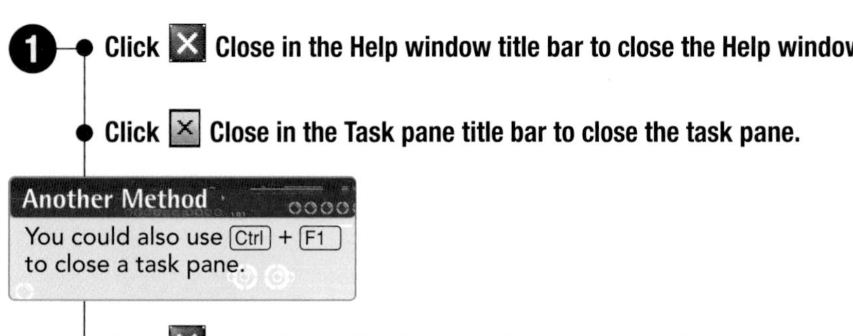

1

- **Click Close in the Help window title bar to close the Help window.**
- **Click Close in the Task pane title bar to close the task pane.**

Another Method

You could also use Ctrl + F1 to close a task pane.

- **Click Close in the Word window title bar to exit Word.**

The program window is closed and the desktop is visible again.

Introduction to Microsoft Office 2003

key terms

docked toolbar I.18
document window I.12
floating toolbar I.18
Formatting toolbar I.17
hyperlink I.22
menu bar I.12
scroll bar I.12
selection cursor I.14
shortcut menu I.15
Standard toolbar I.17
status bar I.12
task pane I.12
toolbar I.12

command summary

Command	Shortcut Key	Button	Voice	Action
start/All Programs				Opens program menu
File/E**x**it	Alt + F4	✕		Exits Office program
View/**T**oolbars			View toolbars	Hides or displays toolbars
View/Tas**k** Pane	Ctrl + F1		Task pane Show task pane View task pane Hide task pane	Hides or displays task pane
Tools/**C**ustomize/**O**ptions				Changes settings associated with toolbars and menus
Help/Microsoft Word **H**elp	F1	?		Opens Help window

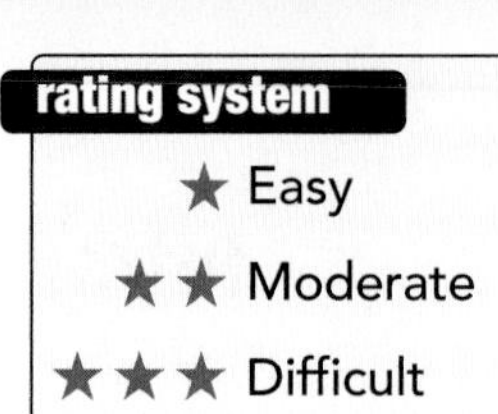

step-by-step

Using an Office Application ★

1. All Office 2003 applications have a common user interface. You will explore the Excel 2003 application and use many of the same features you learned about while using Word 2003 in this lab.

   a. Use the Start menu or a shortcut icon on your desktop to start Office Excel 2003. Close the Getting Started Task Pane.
   b. What shape is the mouse pointer when positioned in the document window area? ________
   c. Excel also has nine menus. Which menu is not the same as in Word? ________ Open the Tools Menu. How many commands in the Tools menu will display a submenu when selected? ______ How many commands are listed in the Formula Auditing submenu? __________
   d. Click on a blank space near the Formatting toolbar to open the toolbar shortcut menu. How many toolbars are available in Excel? ________
   e. Display the Chart toolbar. Dock the Chart toolbar above the Status bar. Change it to a floating toolbar. Close the Chart toolbar.
   f. Use the shortcut key combination to display the Task Pane. How many Task Panes are available? __________
   g. Display the Help Task Pane and search for help information on "worksheet." How many search results were returned? ______ Read the "About viewing workbooks and worksheets" topic. What is the definition of a worksheet? ____
   ____
   h. Close the Help window. Close the Excel window to exit the program.

on your own

Exploring Microsoft Help ★

1. In addition to the Help information you used in this lab, Office 2003 Online Help also includes many interactive tutorials. Selecting a Help topic that starts a tutorial will open the browser program on your computer. Both audio and written instructions are provided. You will use one of these tutorials to learn more about using Office 2003. Start Word 2003 and search for Help on "shortcut keys." Then select the "Work with the Keyboard in Office" topic. Follow the directions in the tutorial to learn about this feature. When you are done, close the browser window and the Word window.

Overview of Microsoft Office PowerPoint 2003

What Is a Presentation Program?

You are in a panic! Tomorrow you are to make a presentation to an audience and you want it to be good. To the rescue comes a powerful tool: graphics presentation programs. These programs are designed to help you create an effective presentation, whether to the board of directors of your company or to your fellow classmates. An effective presentation gets your point across clearly and in an interesting manner.

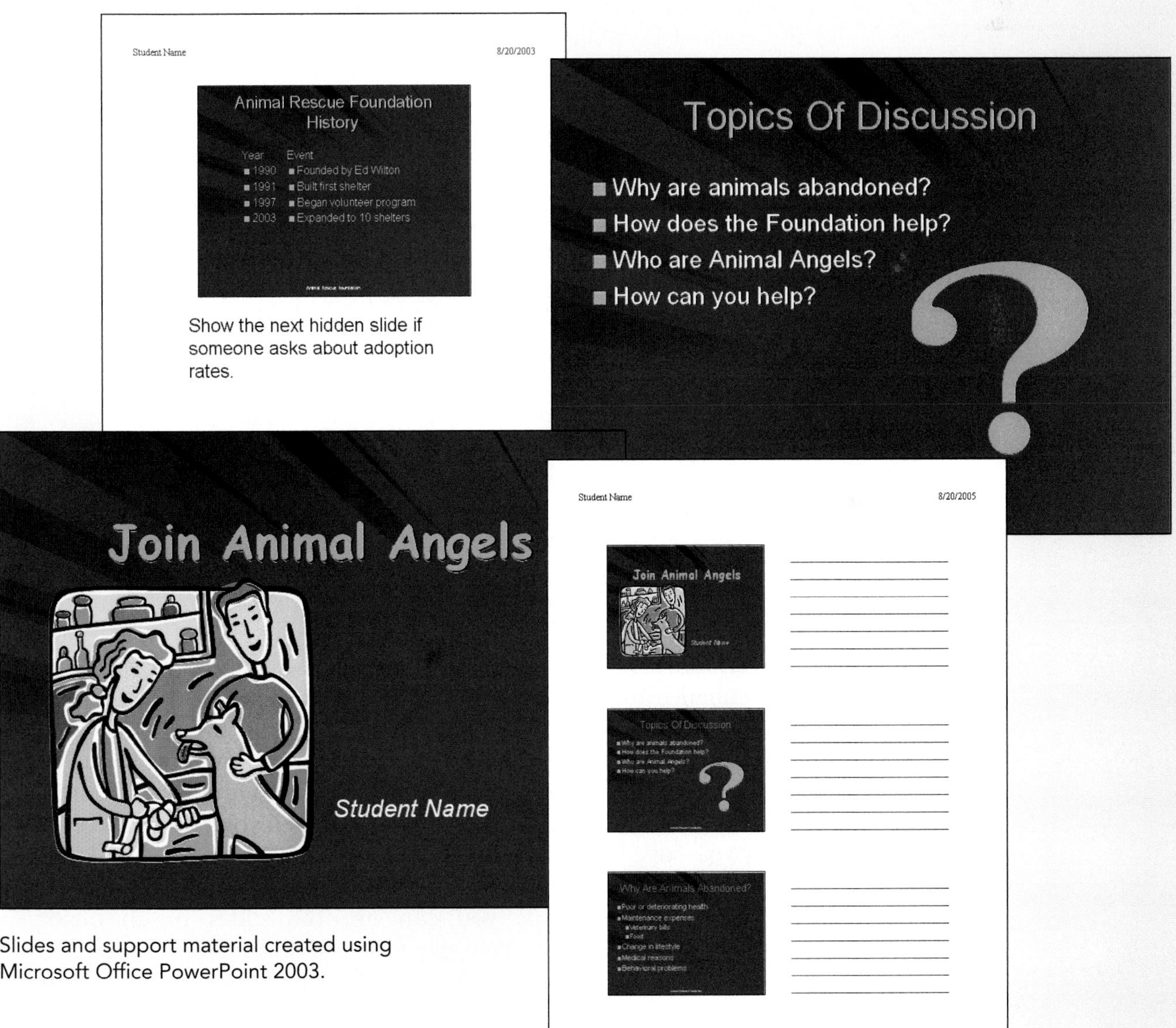

Slides and support material created using Microsoft Office PowerPoint 2003.

Graphics presentation programs are designed to help you produce a high-quality presentation that is both interesting to the audience and effective in its ability to convey your message. A presentation can be as simple as overhead transparencies or as sophisticated as an onscreen electronic display. Graphics presentation programs can produce black-and-white or color overhead transparencies, 35mm slides, onscreen electronic presentations called screen shows, Web pages for Web use, and support materials for both the speaker and the audience.

The graphics presentation program includes features such as text handling, outlining, graphing, drawing, animations, clip art, and multimedia support. With a few keystrokes, the user can quickly change, correct, and update the presentation. In addition, graphics presentation programs suggest layouts for different types of presentations and offer professionally designed templates to help you produce a presentation that is sure to keep your audience's attention.

Office PowerPoint 2003 Features

Creating an effective presentation is a complicated process. Graphics presentation programs help simplify this process by providing assistance in the content development phase, as well as in the layout and design phase. In addition, these programs produce the support materials you can use when making a presentation to an audience.

The content development phase includes deciding on the topic of your presentation, the organization of the content, and the ultimate message you want to convey to the audience. As an aid in this phase, PowerPoint 2003 helps you organize your thoughts based on the type of presentation you are making. Several common types of presentations sell a product or idea, suggest a strategy, or report on the progress of a program. Based on the type of presentation, the program suggests ideas and organization tips. For example, if you are making a presentation on the progress of a sales campaign, the program would suggest that you enter text on the background of the sales campaign as the first page, called a slide; the current status of the campaign as the next slide; and accomplishments, schedule, issues and problems, and where you are heading on subsequent slides.

The layout for each slide is the next important decision. Again, PowerPoint 2003 helps you by suggesting text layout features such as title placement, bullets, and columns. You can also incorporate graphs of data, tables, organizational charts, clip art, and other special text effects in the slides.

PowerPoint 2003 also includes professionally designed templates to further enhance the appearance of your slides. These templates include features that standardize the appearance of all the slides in your presentation. Professionally selected combinations of text and background colors, common typefaces and sizes, borders, and other art designs take the worry out of much of the design layout.

After you have written and designed the slides, you can then have the slides made into black-and-white or color overhead transparencies or 35mm slides. Alternatively, you can use the slides in an onscreen electronic presentation or a Web page for use on the Web. An electronic presentation uses the computer to display the slides on an overhead projection screen. When you use this type of presentation, many programs also include a rehearsal feature, allowing you to practice and time your presentation. The length of time to display each slide can be set and your entire presentation can be completed within the allotted time. A presentation can be modified to display on a Web site and to run using a Web browser.

Finally, with PowerPoint 2003 you can also print out the materials you have created. You can print an outline of the text showing the titles of the slides and main text but not the art. The outline allows you to check the organizational logic of your presentation. You can also print speaker notes to which you can refer to while making your presentation. These notes generally consist of a small printout of each slide with any notes on topics you want to discuss while the slides are displayed. Finally, you can create printed handouts of the slides for the audience. The audience can refer to the slide and make notes on the handout page as you speak.

Case Study for Office PowerPoint 2003 Labs

You have volunteered at the Animal Rescue Foundation, a nonprofit organization that rescues unwanted animals from local animal shelters and finds foster homes for them until a suitable adoptive family can be found. With your computer skills, you have been asked to create a powerful and persuasive presentation to entice the community to volunteer.

The organization has recently purchased the graphics presentation program Microsoft Office PowerPoint 2003. You will use this application to create the presentation.

Lab 1: You use PowerPoint to enter and edit the text for your presentation. You also learn how to reorganize the presentation and enhance it with different text attributes and by adding a picture. Finally, you learn how to run a slide show and print handouts.

Lab 2: You learn about many more features to enhance the appearance of your slides. These include changing the slide design and color scheme and adding clip art, animation, and sound. You also learn how to add transition effects to make the presentation more interesting. Finally, you create speaker notes to help you keep your cool during the presentation.

Working Together: Demonstrates the sharing of information between applications. First you learn how to copy and embed a table created in Word into a slide. Then you learn how to link a chart created in Excel to another slide.

Before You Begin

To the Student

The following assumptions have been made:

- The Microsoft Office PowerPoint 2003 program has been installed on your computer system.

- You have the data files needed to complete the series of PowerPoint 2003 Labs and practice exercises. These may be supplied by your instructor and are also available at the online learning center Web site found at www.mhhe.com/oleary.
- You have completed the McGraw-Hill Windows Labs or you are already familiar with how to use Windows and a mouse.

To the Instructor

It is assumed that the complete version of the program has been installed prior to students using the labs. In addition, please be aware that the following settings are assumed to be in effect for the PowerPoint 2003 program. These assumptions are necessary so that the screens and directions in the text are accurate.

- The Getting Started task pane is displayed on startup (use Tools/Options/View).
- The status bar is displayed (use Tools/Options/View).
- The vertical ruler is displayed (use Tools/Options/View).
- The Paste Options buttons are displayed (use Tools/Options/Edit).
- The Standard, Formatting, Drawing, and Outlining toolbars are on (use Tools/Customize/Toolbars).
- The Standard and Formatting toolbars are displayed on separate rows (use Tools/Customize/Options).
- Full menus are always displayed (use Tools/Customize/Options).
- The Office Assistant feature is enabled but not on (right-click on the Assistant, choose Options, and clear the Use the Office Assistant option).
- Normal view is on (use View/Normal).
- The Clip Organizer is installed on the local disk or network.
- The automatic spelling check feature is on (use Tools/Options/Spelling and Style/Check spelling as you type).
- The style check feature is off (use Tools/Options/Spelling and Style and clear the Check Style option).
- All the options in the View tab are selected (use Tools/Options/View).
- All slide design templates have been installed.
- The feature to access Online Help is on (choose Online Content Settings from the Help task pane and select the Show content and links from Microsoft Office Online option).

In addition, all figures in the manual reflect the use of a standard VGA display monitor set at 800 by 600. If another monitor setting is used, it may display more or fewer lines of text displayed in the windows than in the figures. This setting can be changed using Windows setup.

Microsoft Office Language Bar

The Microsoft Office Language bar may be displayed when you start the application. Commonly, it will appear in the title bar, however, it may appear in other locations depending upon your setup. The Language bar provides buttons to access and use the Speech Recognition and Handwriting recognition features of Office. To display the Language bar, choose Toolbars/Language bar from the Taskbar Shortcut menu.

Instructional Conventions

Hands-on instructions that you are to perform appear as a sequence of numbered steps. Within each step, a series of bullets identifies the specific actions that must be performed. Step numbering begins over within each topic heading throughout the lab.

Command sequences that you are to issue appear following the word "Choose." Each menu command selection is separated by a /. If the menu command can be selected by typing a letter of the command, the letter will appear underlined and bold. Items that need to be selected will follow the word "Select" and will appear in black text. You can select items with the mouse or directional keys. (See Example A.)

Example A

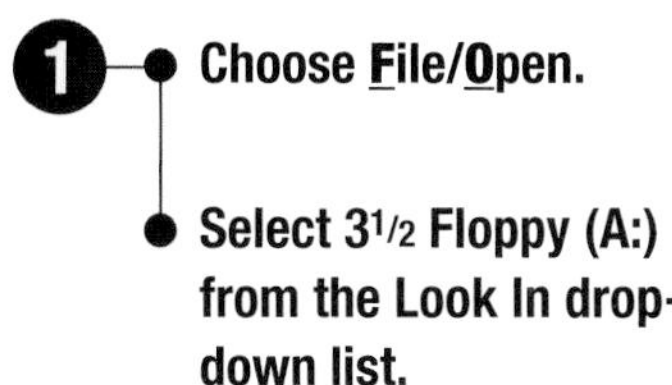

Commands that can be initiated using a button and the mouse appear following the word "Click." The icon (and the icon name if the icon does not include text) is displayed following "Click." The menu equivalent, keyboard shortcut and/or voice command appear in an Another Method margin note when the action is first introduced. (See Example B.)

Example B

Another Method

The menu equivalent is **F**ile/**O**pen, the keyboard shortcut is Ctrl + O, and the voice command is "Open."

Plain blue text identifies file names. Information you are asked to type appears in blue and bold. (See Example C.)

Example C

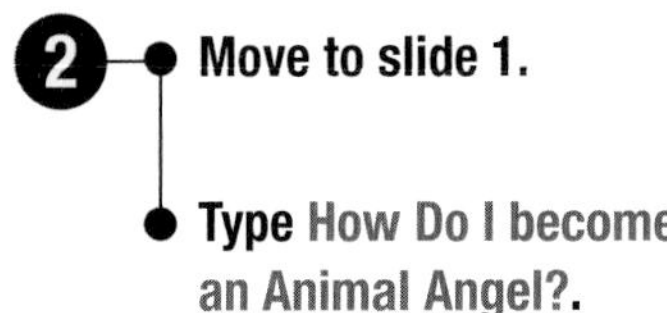

Creating a Presentation

LAB 1

Objectives

After completing this lab, you will know how to:

1. Use the AutoContent wizard to create a presentation.
2. View and edit a presentation.
3. Save, close, and open a presentation.
4. Check spelling.
5. Delete, move, and insert slides.
6. Size and move placeholders.
7. Run a slide show.
8. Change fonts and formatting.
9. Insert pictures and clip art.
10. Preview and print a presentation.

Case Study

Animal Rescue Foundation

You are the Volunteer Coordinator at the local Animal Rescue Foundation. This nonprofit organization rescues unwanted pets from local animal shelters and finds foster homes for them until a suitable adoptive family can be found. The agency has a large volunteer group called the Animal Angels that provides much-needed support for the foundation.

The agency director has decided to launch a campaign to increase community awareness about the Foundation. As part of the promotion, you have been asked to create a powerful and persuasive presentation to entice more members of the community to join Animal Angels.

The agency director has asked you to preview the presentation at the weekly staff meeting tomorrow and has asked you to present a draft of the presentation by noon today.

Although we would all like to think that our message is the core of the presentation, the presentation materials we use can determine whether the message reaches the audience. To help you create the presentation, you will use Microsoft Office PowerPoint 2003, a graphics presentation application that is designed to create presentation materials such as slides, overheads, and handouts. Using Office PowerPoint 2003, you can create a high-quality and interesting onscreen presentation with pizzazz that will dazzle your audience.

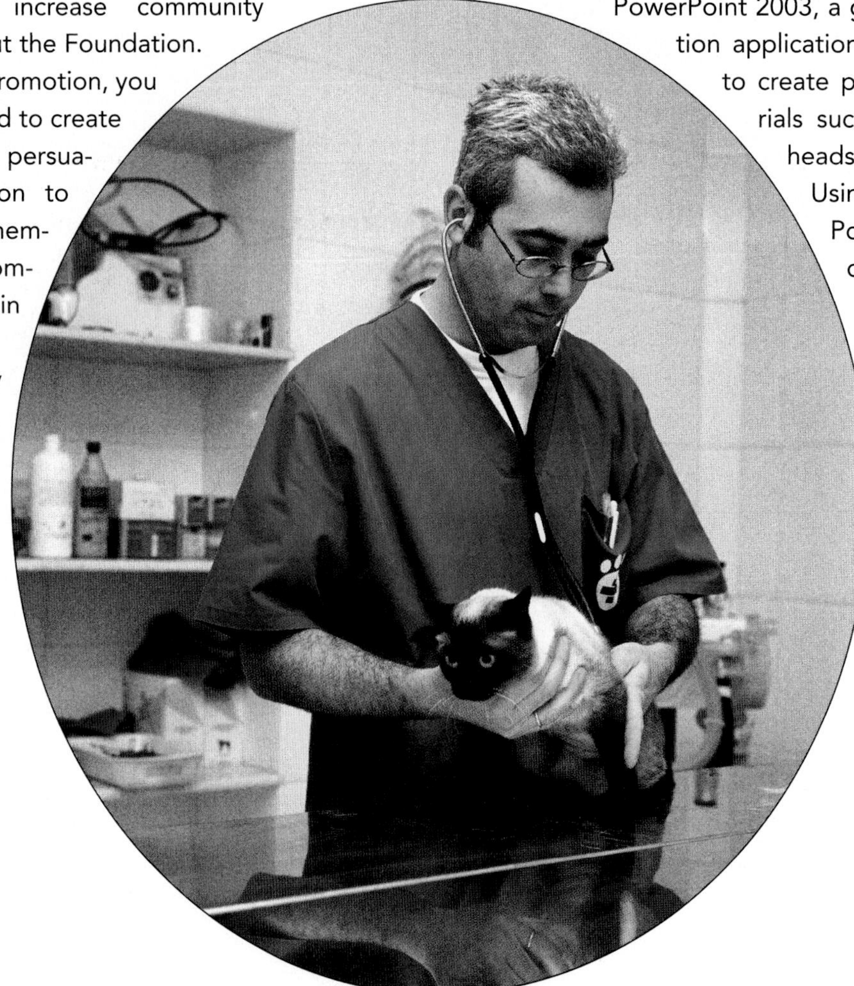

© Andy Sotiriou/Getty Images

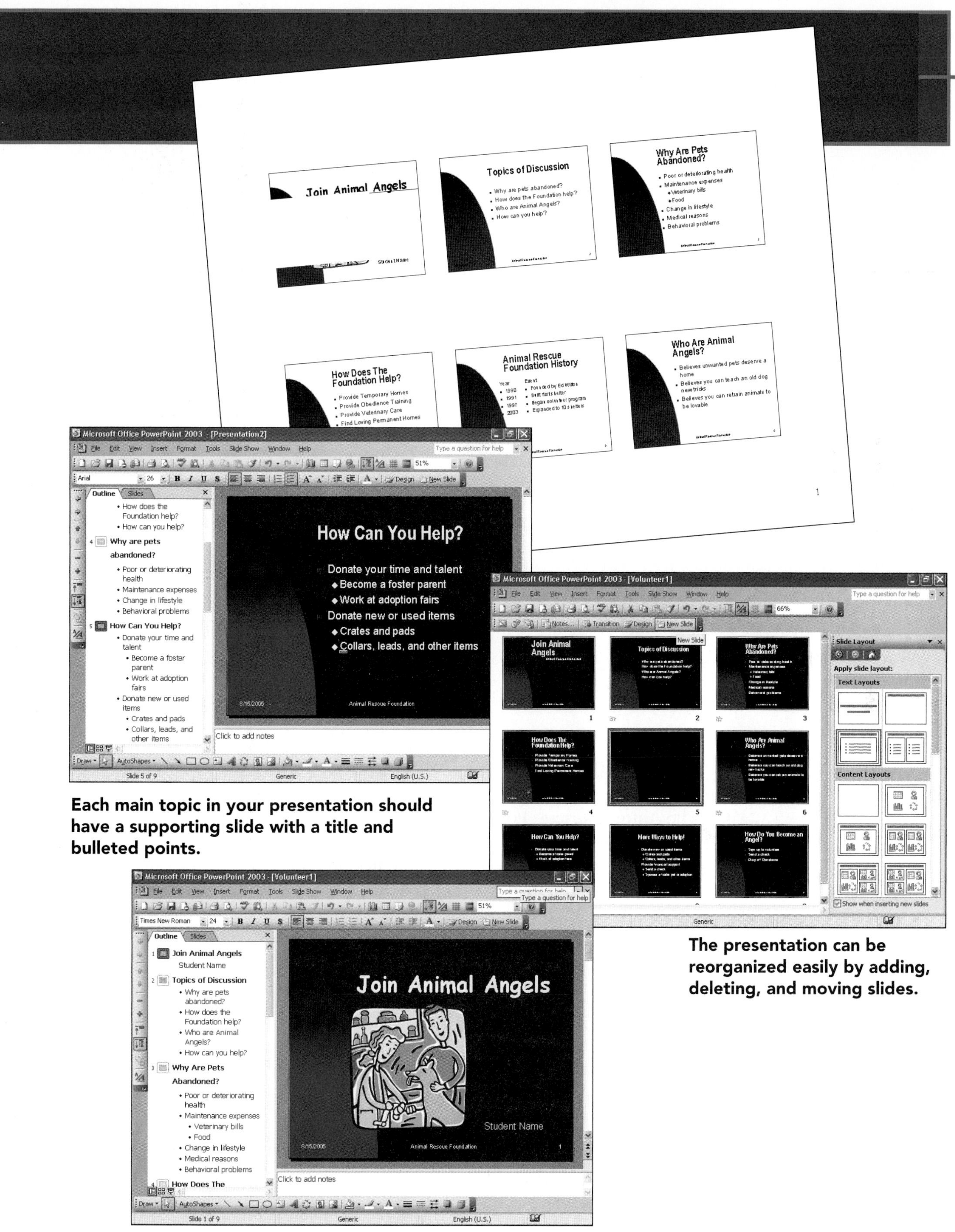

Each main topic in your presentation should have a supporting slide with a title and bulleted points.

The presentation can be reorganized easily by adding, deleting, and moving slides.

Enhance the presentation with the addition of graphics and text colors.

Concept Preview

The following concepts will be introduced in this lab:

1. **Template** A template is a file containing predefined settings that can be used as a pattern to create many common types of presentations.
2. **Presentation Style** A PowerPoint presentation can be made using five different styles: onscreen presentations, Web presentations, black-and-white or color overheads, and 35mm slides.
3. **Slide** A slide is an individual "page" of your presentation.
4. **AutoCorrect** The AutoCorrect feature makes some basic assumptions about the text you are typing and, based on these assumptions, automatically corrects the entry.
5. **Spelling Checker** The spelling checker locates all misspelled words, duplicate words, and capitalization irregularities as you create and edit a presentation, and proposes possible corrections.
6. **Layout** The layout controls the way items are arranged on a slide.
7. **Font and Font Size** A font, also commonly referred to as a typeface, is a set of characters with a specific design. Each font has one or more sizes.
8. **Graphics** A graphic is a non-text element or object, such as a drawing or picture, that can be added to a slide.
9. **Stacking Order** Stacking order is the order in which objects are inserted into different layers of the slide.

Introducing Office PowerPoint 2003

The Animal Rescue Foundation has just installed the latest version of the Microsoft Office Suite of applications, Office 2003, on their computers. You will use the graphics presentation program, Microsoft Office PowerPoint 2003, included in the office suite to create your presentation. Using this program, you should have no problem creating the presentation in time for tomorrow's staff meeting.

Starting Office PowerPoint 2003

1 **Start the Office PowerPoint 2003 application.**

Having Trouble?

See "Introduction to Office System 2003" for information on starting the application and for a discussion of features that are common to all Office 2003 applications.

Your screen should be similar to Figure 1.1

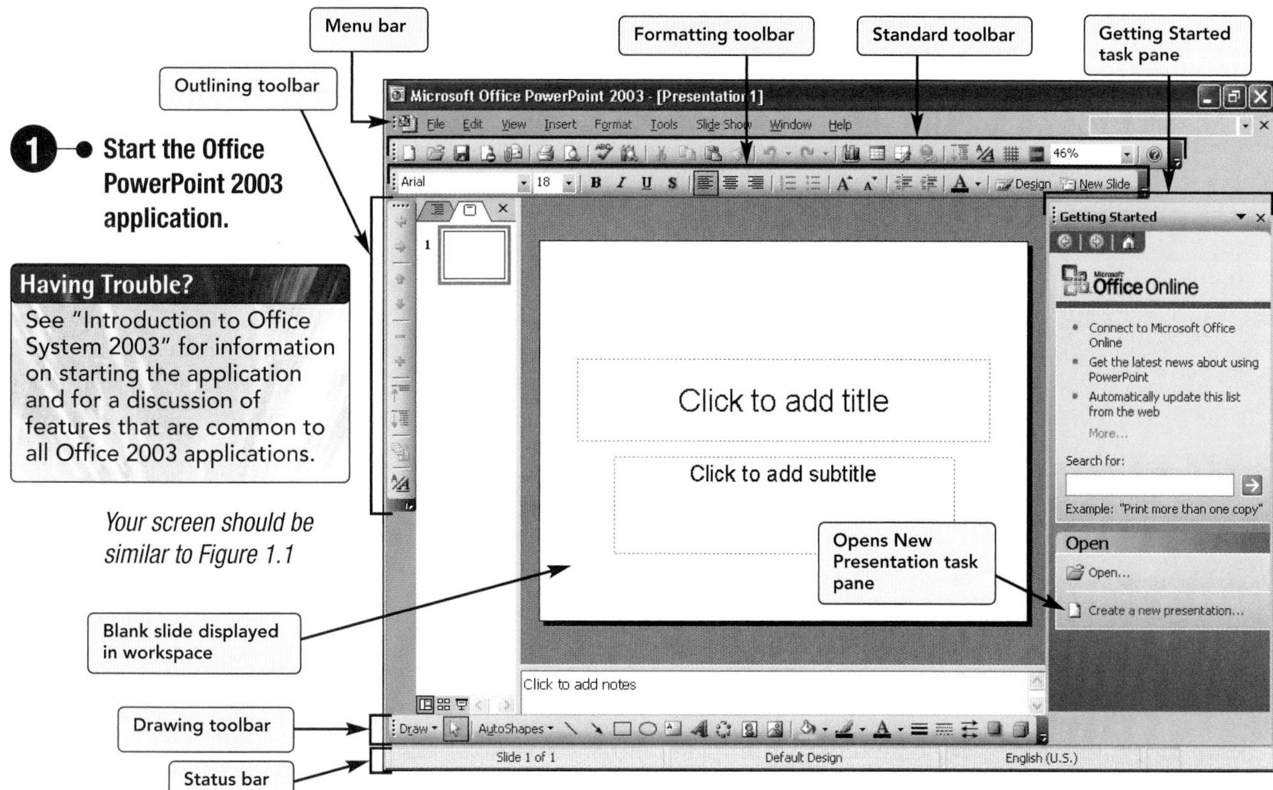

Figure 1.1

Additional Information

Because the Office 2003 applications remember settings that were on when the program was last exited, you screen may look slightly different.

Additional Information

If you have installed the Speech Recognition feature the voice command to display toolbars is "View Toolbars" and to display the task pane is "Task pane."

The PowerPoint application window is displayed. The menu bar below the title bar displays the PowerPoint program menu. It consists of nine menus that provide access to the commands and features you will use to create and modify a presentation.

Located below the menu bar are the Standard and Formatting toolbars. The Standard toolbar contains buttons that are used to complete the most frequently used menu commands. The Formatting toolbar contains buttons that are used to change the appearance or format of the document. The **Drawing toolbar** is displayed along the bottom edge of the window. It contains buttons that are used to enhance text and create shapes. In addition, the **Outlining toolbar** may be displayed along the left edge of the window. It is used to enter and modify the content of the presentation. PowerPoint 2003 has 13 different toolbars. Many of the toolbars appear automatically as you use different features. Other toolbars may be displayed if they were on when the program was last exited.

2 **If necessary, make the following changes to your screen to make it look like Figure 1.1:**

- **Use View/Toolbars and select or deselect the appropriate toolbar to display or hide it. There should be four toolbars displayed.**
- **The Standard, Formatting, Drawing and Outlining toolbars should be displayed.**
- **If your task pane is not displayed, choose View/Task Pane.**

Additional Information

Sixteen different task panes can be displayed depending on the task being performed.

The large area containing the blank slide is the **workspace** where your presentations are displayed as you create and edit them. Because you just started the program, the Getting Started task pane is automatically displayed on the right side of the window. It is used to open an existing presentation or create new presentations. The status bar at the bottom of the PowerPoint window displays messages and information about various PowerPoint settings.

Developing New Presentations

During your presentation you will present information about the Animal Rescue Foundation and why someone should want to join the Animal Angels volunteer group. As you prepare to create a new presentation, you should follow several basic steps: plan, create, edit, enhance, and rehearse.

Step	Description
Plan	The first step in planning a presentation is to understand its purpose. You also need to find out the length of time you have to speak, who the audience is, what type of room you will be in, and what kind of audiovisual equipment is available. These factors help to determine the type of presentation you will create.
Create	To begin creating your presentation, develop the content by typing your thoughts or notes into an outline. Each main idea in your presentation should have a supporting slide with a title and bulleted points.
Edit	While typing, you are will probably make typing and spelling errors that need to be corrected. This is one type of editing. Another type is to revise the content of what you have entered to make it clearer, or to add or delete information. To do this, you might insert a slide, add or delete bulleted items, or move text to another location.
Enhance	You want to develop a presentation that grabs and holds the audience's attention. Choose a design that gives your presentation some dazzle. Wherever possible add graphics to replace or enhance text. Add effects that control how a slide appears and disappears, and that reveal text in a bulleted list one bullet at a time.
Rehearse	Finally, you should rehearse the delivery of your presentation. For a professional presentation, your delivery should be as polished as your materials. Use the same equipment that you will use when you give the presentation. Practice advancing from slide to slide and then back in case someone asks a question. If you have a mouse available, practice pointing or drawing on the slide to call attention to key points.

After rehearsing your presentation, you may find that you want to go back to the editing phase. You may change text, move bullets, or insert a new slide. Periodically, as you make changes, rehearse the presentation again to see how the changes affect your presentation. By the day of the presentation, you will be confident about your message and at ease with the materials.

During the planning phase, you have spoken with the Foundation director regarding the purpose of the presentation and the content in general. The purpose of your presentation is to educate members of the community about the organization and to persuade many to volunteer. In addition, you want to impress the director by creating a professional presentation.

Creating a Presentation

When you first start PowerPoint, a new blank presentation is opened. It is like a blank piece of paper that already has many predefined settings. These settings, called **default** settings, are generally the most commonly used settings and are stored as a presentation template.

Concept 1

Template

1 A **template** is a file containing predefined settings that can be used as a pattern to create many common types of presentations. Every PowerPoint presentation is based on a template. The default settings for a basic blank presentation are stored in the default design template file. Whenever you create a new presentation using this template, the same default settings are used.

Many other templates that are designed to help you create professional-looking presentations are also available within PowerPoint and in the Microsoft Office Template Gallery on the Microsoft Office Web site. They include design templates, which provide a design concept, fonts, and color scheme; and content templates, which suggest content for your presentation based on the type of presentation you are making. You can also design and save your own presentation templates.

The Getting Started task pane is used to specify how you want to start using the PowerPoint program. It provides a variety of ways to start a new presentation or to open an existing presentation. More options for starting a new presentation are available in the New Presentation task pane.

1 Click Create a new presentation in the Getting Started task pane.

Another Method

You could also select the task pane to open from the Other Task Panes drop-down menu.

Your screen should be similar to Figure 1.2

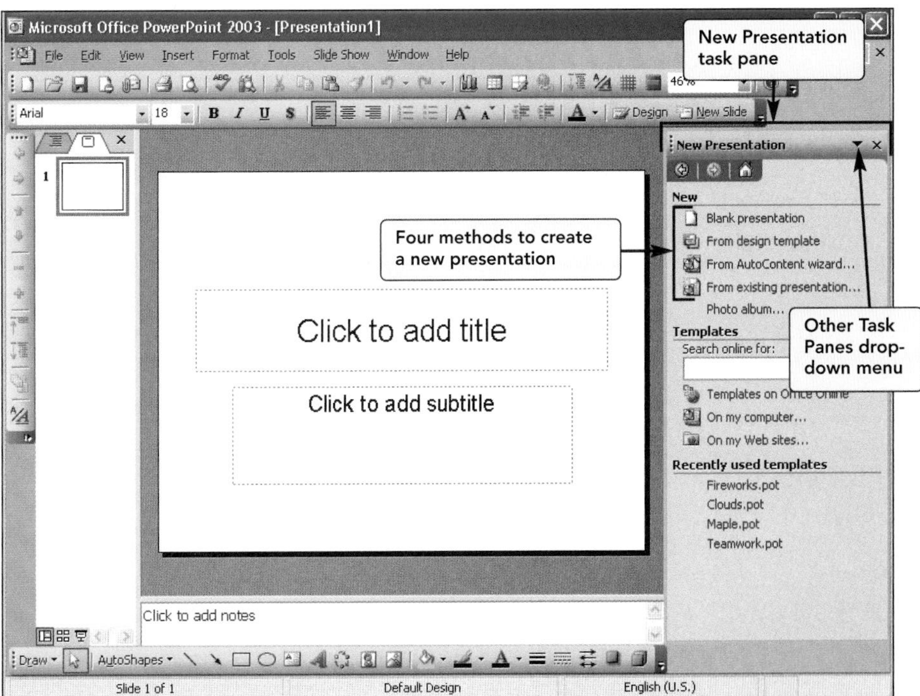

Figure 1.2

Additional Information

The Photo Album option allows you to create a specialized type of presentation consisting of pictures only.

Four methods can be used to create a presentation. The first method is to start with a blank presentation that has minimal design elements and add your own content and design changes. Another is to use one of the many design templates as the basis for your new presentation. The third method is to use the AutoContent wizard. A **wizard** is an interactive approach that guides you through the process of performing many complicated tasks. The AutoContent wizard creates a presentation that contains suggested content and design based on the answers you provide. Finally, you can use an existing presentation as the base for your new presentation by making the design or content changes you want for the new presentation.

Using the AutoContent Wizard

Because this is your first presentation created using PowerPoint, you decide to use the AutoContent wizard.

2 **From the New Presentation task pane, select From AutoContent wizard.**

Your screen should be similar to Figure 1.3

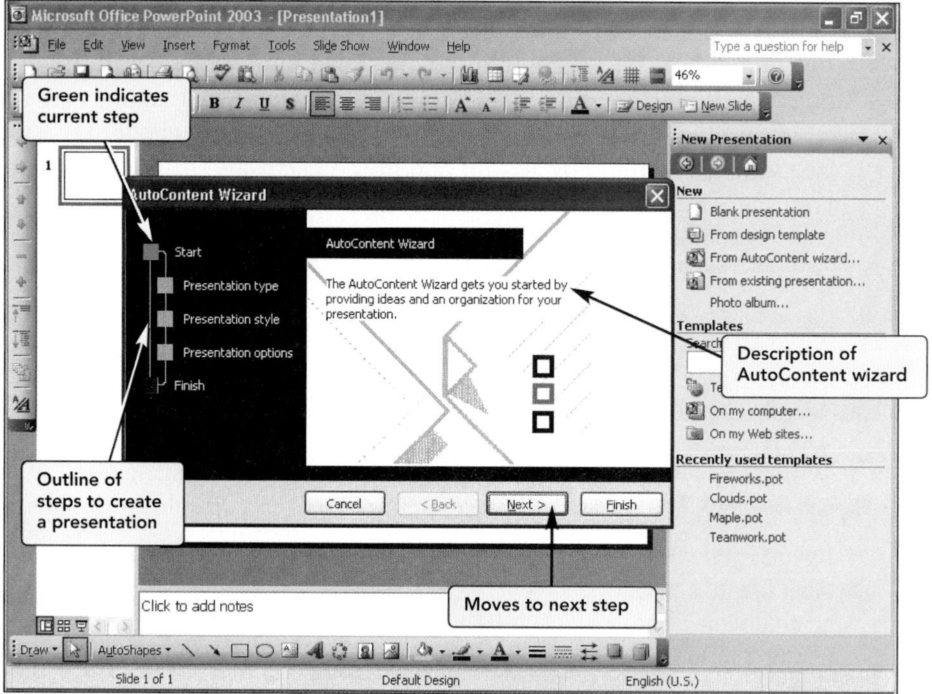

Figure 1.3

The opening dialog box of the AutoContent wizard briefly describes how the feature works. As the AutoContent wizard guides you through creating the presentation, it shows your progress through the steps in the outline on the left side of the dialog box. The green box identifies the current step.

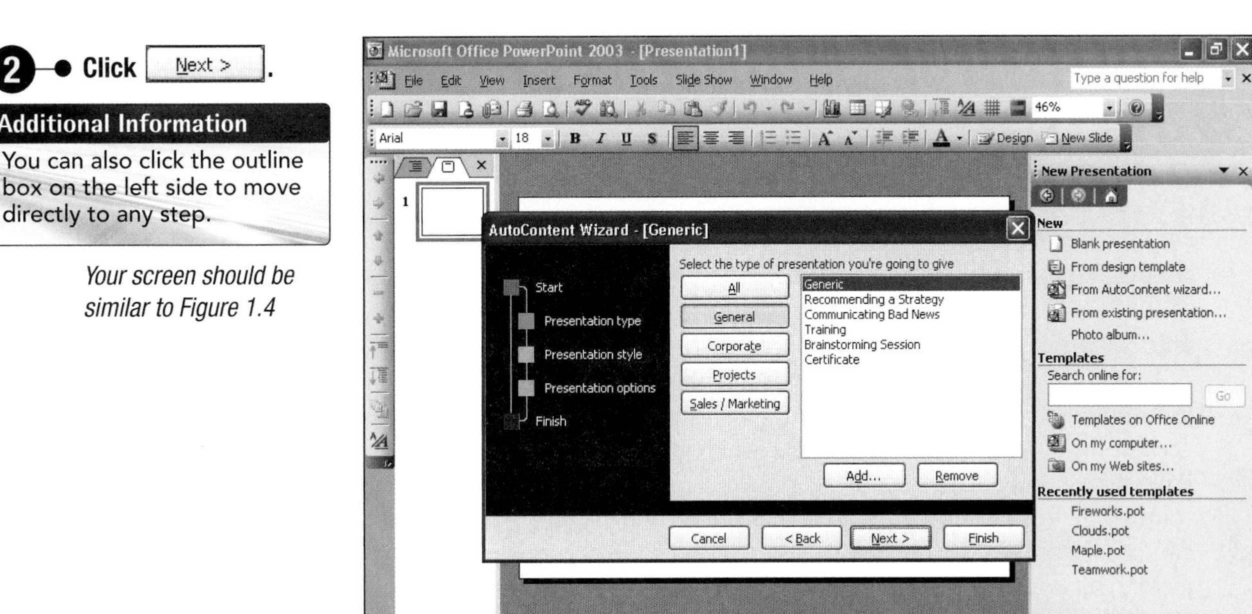

2 Click Next >.

Additional Information

You can also click the outline box on the left side to move directly to any step.

Your screen should be similar to Figure 1.4

Figure 1.4

In the Presentation Type step, you are asked to select the type of presentation you are creating. PowerPoint offers 24 different types of presentations, each with a different recommended content and design. Each type is indexed under a category. Currently, only the names of the six presentation types in the General category appear in the list box. You will use the Generic presentation option.

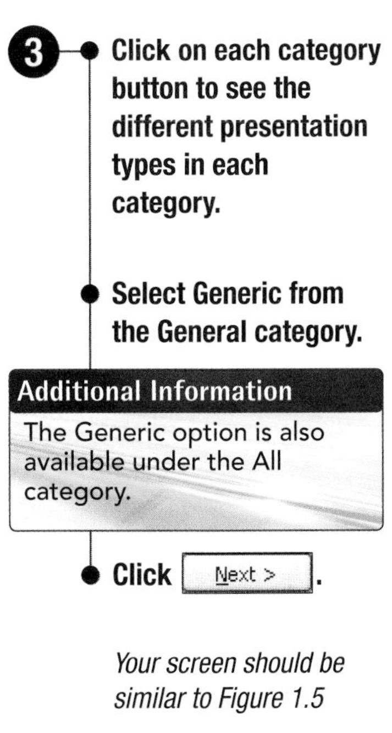

3

- **Click on each category button to see the different presentation types in each category.**
- **Select Generic from the General category.**

Additional Information

The Generic option is also available under the All category.

- **Click** Next >.

Your screen should be similar to Figure 1.5

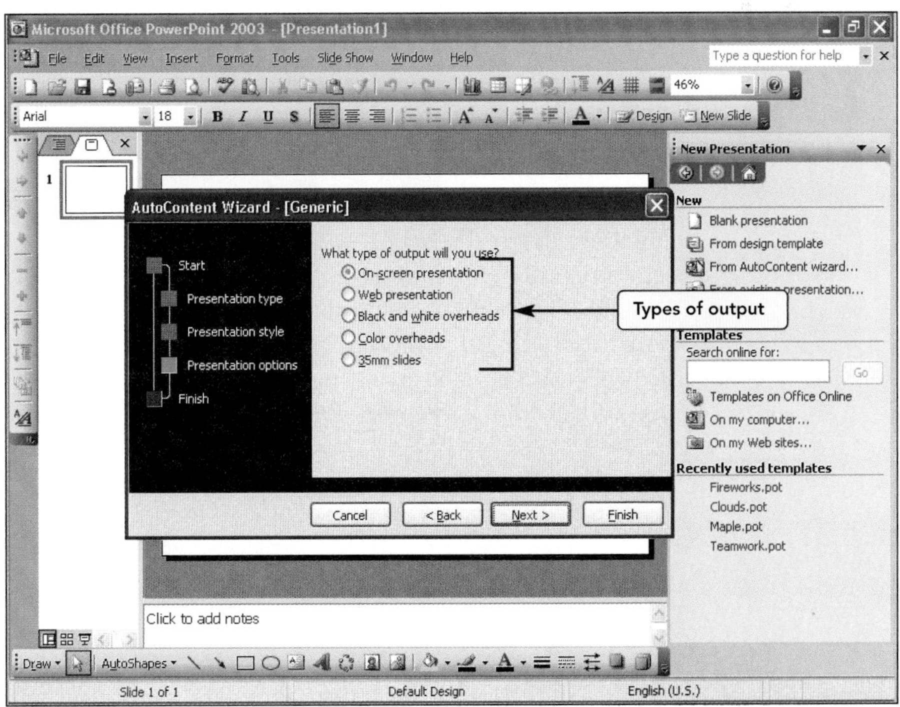

Figure 1.5

In the Presentation Style step, you select the type of output your presentation will use.

Concept 2

Presentation Style

2 A PowerPoint presentation can be made using five different styles: onscreen presentations, Web presentations, black-and-white or color overheads, and 35mm slides. The type of equipment that is available to you will affect the style of presentation that you create.

If you have computer projection equipment that displays the current monitor image on a screen, you should create a full-color onscreen presentation. You can also design your onscreen presentation specifically for the World Wide Web, where a browser serves as the presentation tool. Often you will have access only to an overhead projector, in which case you can create color or black-and-white transparencies. Most laser printers will print your overheads directly on plastic transparencies, or you can print your slides and have transparencies made at a copy center. If you have access to a slide projector, you may want to use 35mm slides. You can send your presentation to a service bureau that will create the slides for you.

The room in which you will be using to make your presentation is equipped with computer projection equipment, so you will create an onscreen presentation. The Wizard selects the color scheme best suited to the type of output you select. Because On-screen Presentation is the default selection, you will accept it and move to the next step.

Your screen should be similar to Figure 1.6

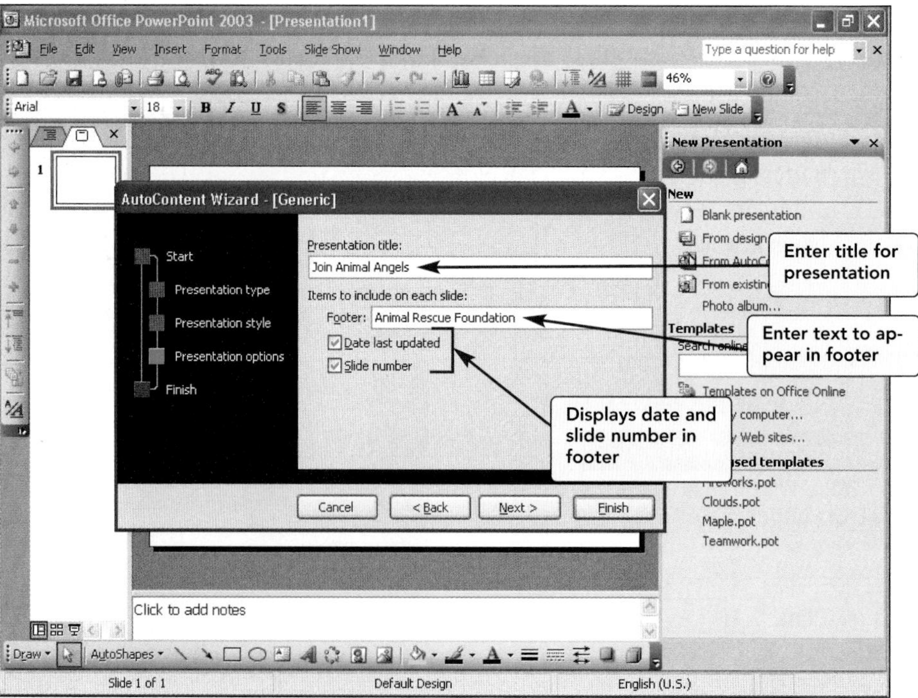

Figure 1.6

In the Presentation Options step, you are asked to enter some basic information that will appear on the title slide and in the footer of each slide in the presentation.

Concept 3

Slide

3 A **slide** is an individual "page" of your presentation. The first slide of a presentation is the title slide which is used to introduce your presentation. Additional slides are used to support each main point in your presentation. The slides give the audience a visual summary of the words you speak, which helps them understand the content and keeps them entertained. The slides also help you, the speaker, organize your thoughts, and prompt you during the presentation.

You would like to have the name of the presentation appear as the title on the first slide, and to have the name of the organization, date of the presentation, and the slide number appear on the footer of each slide. A **footer** consists of text or graphics that appear at the bottom of each slide. Because the options to display the date that the presentation was last updated and slide number are already selected, you only need to enter the title text and footer text.

5

- **Click in the Presentation title text box to display the insertion point.**
- **Type Join Animal Angels.**

Having Trouble?

If you make a typing error, use the Backspace key to delete the characters to the left of the insertion point and then retype the current text.

- **Press Tab.**
- **Type Animal Rescue Foundation in the Footer text box.**

Your screen should be similar to Figure 1.7

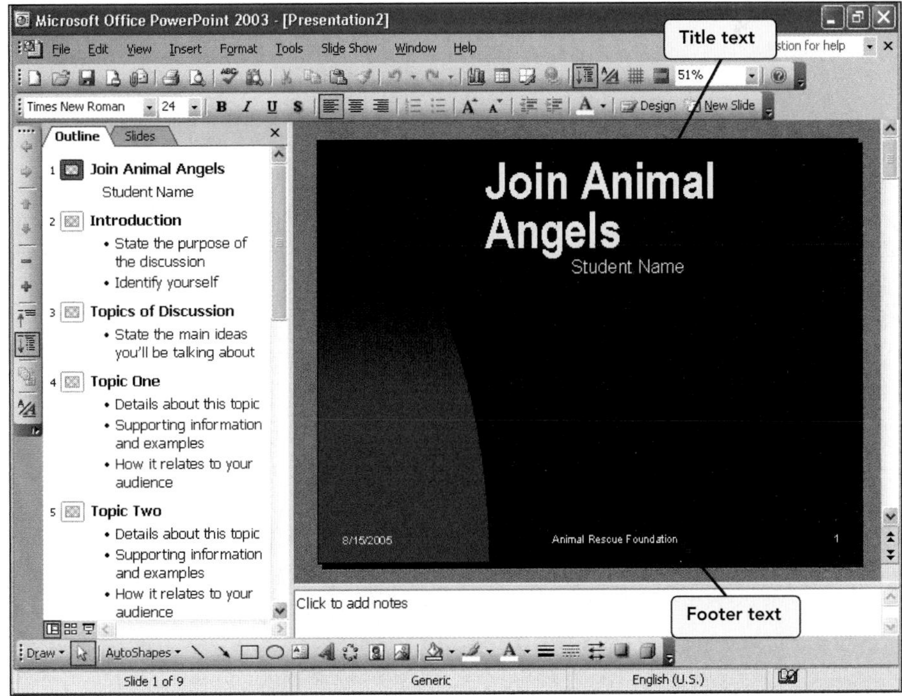

Figure 1.7

You have entered all the information PowerPoint needs to create your presentation.

6 Click Next >.

Click Finish.

If necessary, maximize the document window.

Your screen should be similar to Figure 1.8

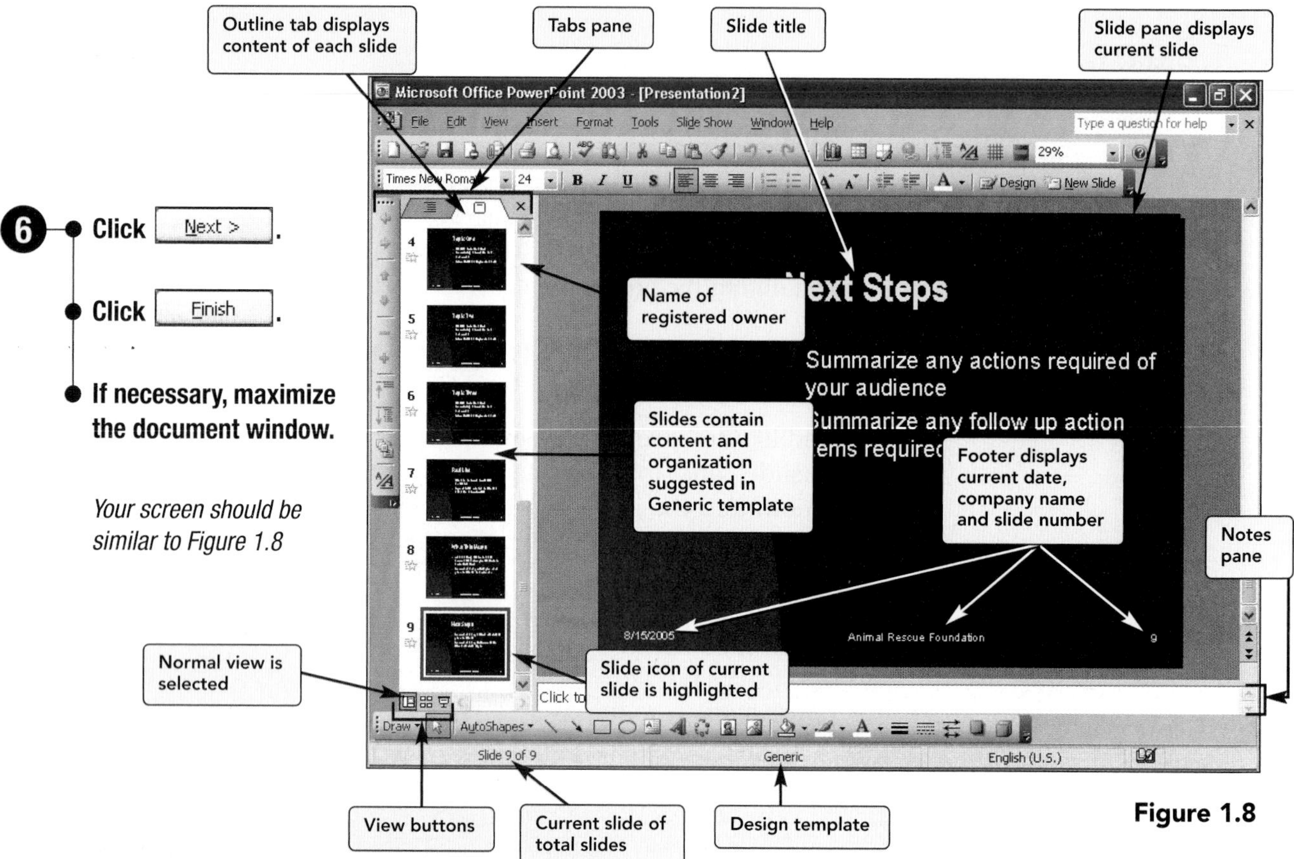

Figure 1.8

Viewing the Presentation

Additional Information

You will learn how to change the color and design in Lab 2.

Based on your selections and entries, the AutoContent wizard creates a presentation and displays it in the workspace. The colors and design were selected by the wizard when you selected the Generic presentation type.

The presentation is initially displayed in Normal view showing the Outline tab. A **view** is a way of looking at a presentation. PowerPoint provides several views you can use to look at and modify your presentation. Depending on what you are doing, one view may be preferable to another. The commands to change views are located on the View menu. In addition, the three view buttons to the left of the horizontal scroll bar can be used to switch quickly from one view to another. The menu commands, buttons, and voice commands for the three main views are described in the table on the next page.

Additional Information

Many voice commands have several different words you can say to initiate the command.

View	Command	Button	Voice	Description
Normal	View/Normal		Normal or Normal view	Provides three working areas of the window that allow you to work on all aspects of your presentation in one place.
Slide Sorter	View/Slide Sorter		Slide sorter	Displays a miniature of each slide to make it easy to reorder slides, add special effects such as transitions, and set timing between slides.
Slide Show	View/Slide Show		View show, Begin slide show, Start slide show, or Slide show view	Displays each slide in final form using the full screen space so you can practice or present the presentation.

Using Normal View

Additional Information
Normal view is often referred to as a tri-pane view because it displays three panes simultaneously.

Normal view is displayed by default because it is the main view you use while creating a presentation. In Normal view, three working areas, called **panes**, are displayed. These panes allow you to work on all components of your presentation in one convenient location. The pane on the left side includes tabs that alternate between viewing the presentation in outline format and as slide miniatures. The pane on the right displays the selected slide. The notes pane below the slide pane includes space for you to enter speaker notes.

Additional Information
You will learn about speaker notes in Lab 2.

Currently, the Outline tab is open and displays the title and text for each slide in the presentation. It is used to organize and develop the content of your presentation. To the left of each slide title in the Outline tab is a slide icon and a number that identifies each slide (see Figure 1.8). The icon of the current slide is highlighted, and the current slide is displayed in the main working area, called the slide pane. The text for the first slide consists of the title and the footer text you specified when using the AutoContent wizard. Below the title, the name of the registered owner of the application program is displayed automatically. The other slides shown in the Outline tab contain sample text that is included by the Wizard based upon the type of presentation you selected. The sample text suggests the content for each slide to help you organize your presentation's content. Because the current view is Normal, the button is highlighted. The status bar displays the number of the current slide and total number of slides, and the name of the design template used.

Additional Information
You can adjust the size of each pane by dragging the splitter bar that borders each pane.

The Slides tab is used to display each slide in the presentation as a thumbnail. A **thumbnail** is a miniature representation of a picture, in this case of a slide. Clicking on the thumbnail selects the slide, making it the current slide, and displays it in the slide pane.

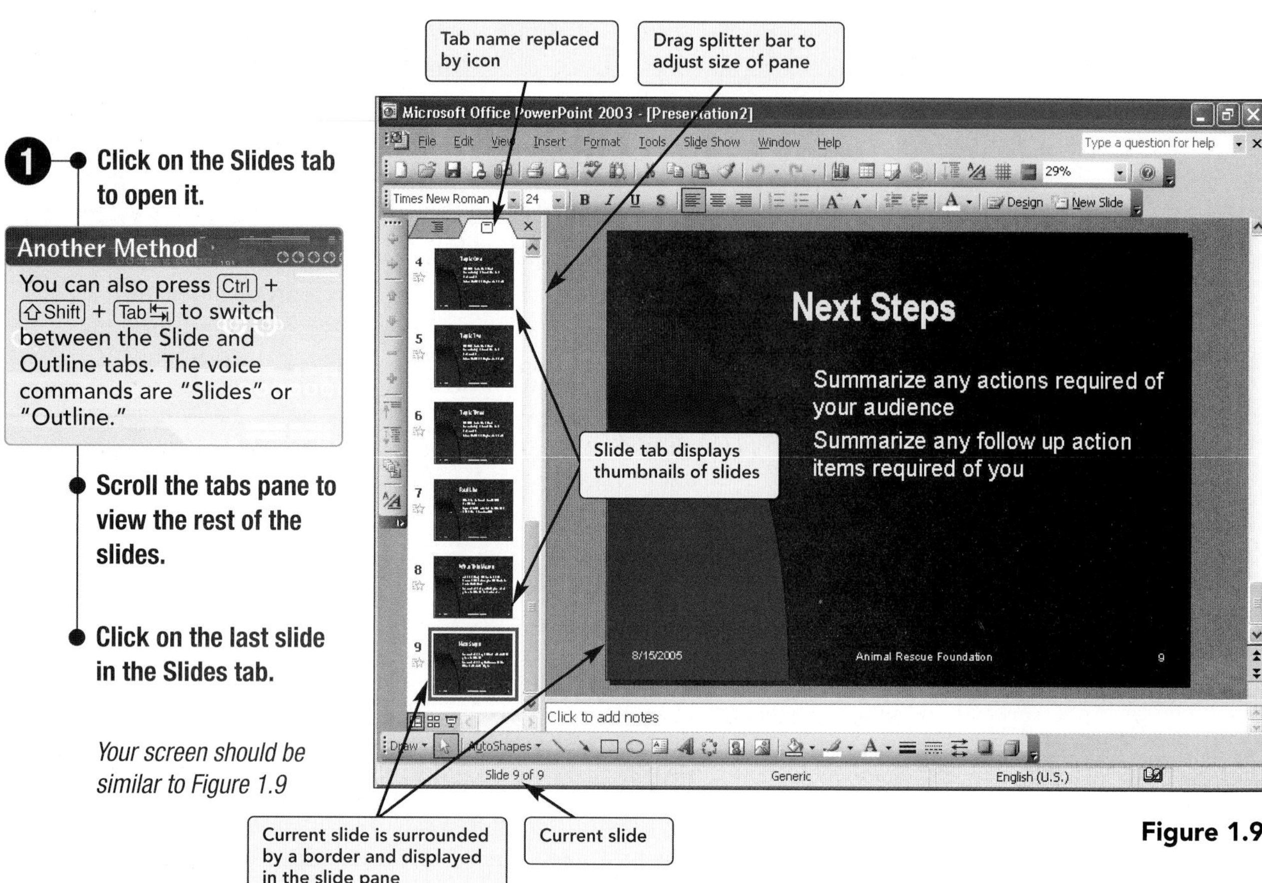

Figure 1.9

Additional Information

You can make the thumbnails larger by increasing the width of the tabs pane.

The size of the tabs pane adjusted to be just large enough to display the thumbnails. In addition, because the pane is narrower, the tab names are replaced by icons. The presentation has a total of nine slides. The status bar displays the number of the current slide.

Using Slide Sorter View

The second main view that is used while creating a presentation is Slide Sorter view. This view also displays thumbnails of the slides.

1 Click Slide Sorter View.

Having Trouble?

Pointing to a view button displays its name in a ScreenTip.

Your screen should be similar to Figure 1.10

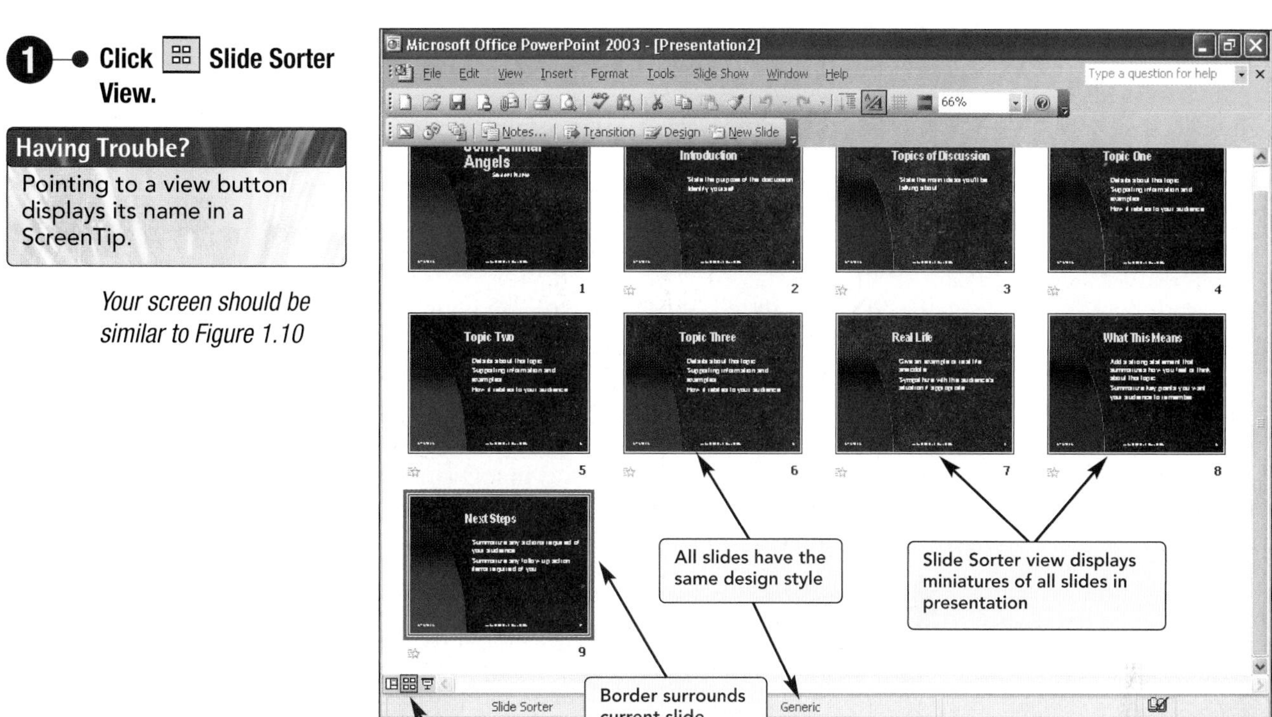

Figure 1.10

This view displays a miniature of each slide in the window. All the slides use the same design style, associated with a generic presentation. The design style sets the background design and color, as well as the text style, color, and layout. The currently selected slide, slide 9, appears with a blue border around it. Clicking on a thumbnail selects the slide and makes it the **current slide**, or the slide that will be affected by any changes you make.

Click on slide 1.

Your screen should be similar to Figure 1.11

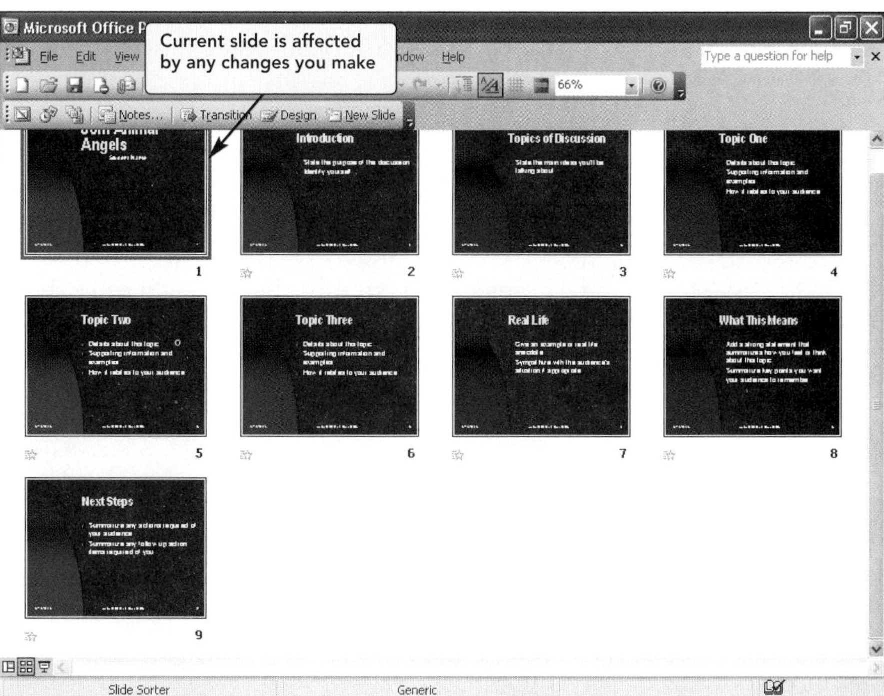

Figure 1.11

Editing a Presentation

After creating a presentation using the AutoContent wizard, you need to replace the sample content with the appropriate information for your presentation. Editing involves making text changes and additions to the content of your presentation. It also includes making changes to the organization of content. This can be accomplished quickly by rearranging the order of bulleted items on slides as well as the order of slides.

While editing, you will need to move to specific locations in the text. You can use the mouse to move to selected locations simply by clicking on the location. An insertion point appears to show your location in the text. You can also use the arrow keys located on the numeric keypad or the directional keypad to move the insertion point. The keyboard directional keys and voice commands used to move within text are described in the following table.

Key	Voice	Movement
→	Right	One character to right
←	Left	One character to left
↑	Up	One line up
↓	Down	One line down
Ctrl + →	Next word	One word to right
Ctrl + ←	Back word	One word to left
Home	Home	Left end of line
End	Go end	Right end of line

Additional Information

You can use the directional keys on the numeric keypad or the dedicated directional keypad area. If you use the numeric keypad, make sure the Num Lock feature is off, otherwise numbers will be entered in the document. The Num Lock indicator light above the keypad is lit when on. Press Num Lock to turn it off.

Holding down a directional key or key combination moves the insertion point quickly in the direction indicated, saving multiple presses of the key. Many of the insertion point movement keys can be held down to execute multiple moves.

While editing you will also need to select text. To select text using the mouse, first move the insertion point to the beginning or end of the text to be selected, and then drag when the mouse pointer is an I-beam to highlight the text you want selected. You can select as little as a single letter or as much as the entire document. To remove highlighting and deselect text, simply click anywhere in the document.

You can also quickly select a block of text, such as a word or line. The following table summarizes the mouse techniques used to select standard blocks.

To Select	Procedure
Word	Double-click in the word.
Sentence	Press Ctrl and click within the sentence.
All text in a bullet	Triple-click in the bulleted text.
Multiple lines and bullets	Drag up or down across the lines

You can also select text with the keyboard or using voice commands shown in the following table.

Keyboard	Voice	Action
⇧Shift + →		Selects the next space or character.
⇧Shift + ←		Selects the previous space or character.
Ctrl + ⇧Shift + →	Select next word	Selects the next word.
Ctrl + ⇧Shift + ←	Select last word	Selects the last word.
Ctrl + ⇧Shift + ↑	Select last line	Selects text going backward.
Ctrl + ⇧Shift + ↓	Select next line	Selects text going forward.
Ctrl + A	Select all	Selects the entire document.

Using the Outline Tab

The easiest way to make text-editing changes is to use the Outline tab in Normal view. When working in the Outline tab, the Outlining toolbar is displayed. It is used to modify the presentation outline.

1 • **Click Normal View to switch to Normal view again.**

• **Click the Outline tab.**

Your screen should be similar to Figure 1.12

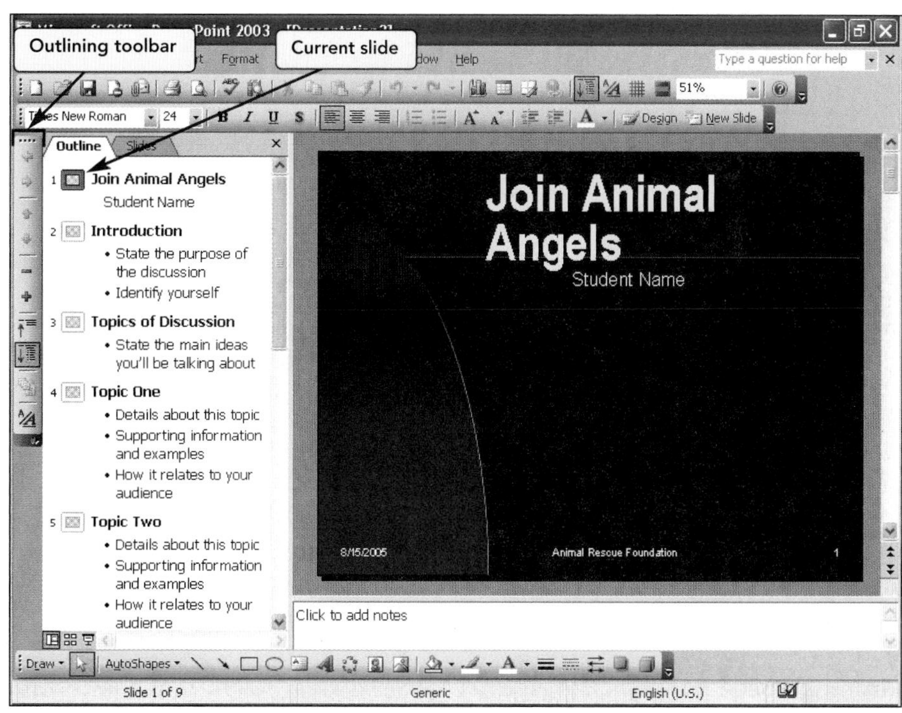

Figure 1.12

Slide 1 is still the current slide. The first change you want to make is to select the owner name on the first slide and delete it.

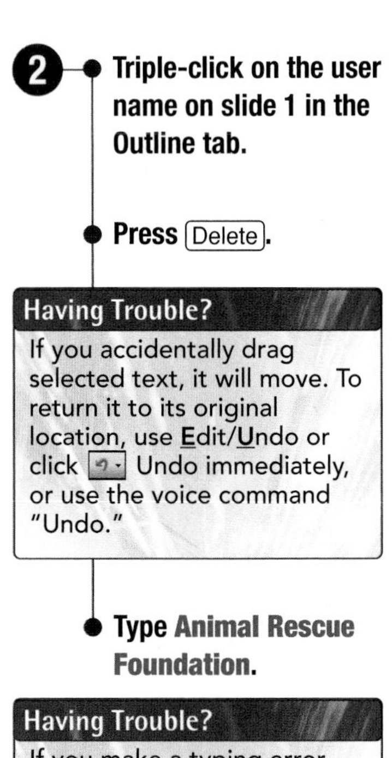

2

- **Triple-click on the user name on slide 1 in the Outline tab.**
- **Press Delete.**

Having Trouble?

If you accidentally drag selected text, it will move. To return it to its original location, use Edit/Undo or click Undo immediately, or use the voice command "Undo."

- **Type Animal Rescue Foundation.**

Having Trouble?

If you make a typing error, press Backspace to delete the characters to the error and retype the entry.

Your screen should be similar to Figure 1.13

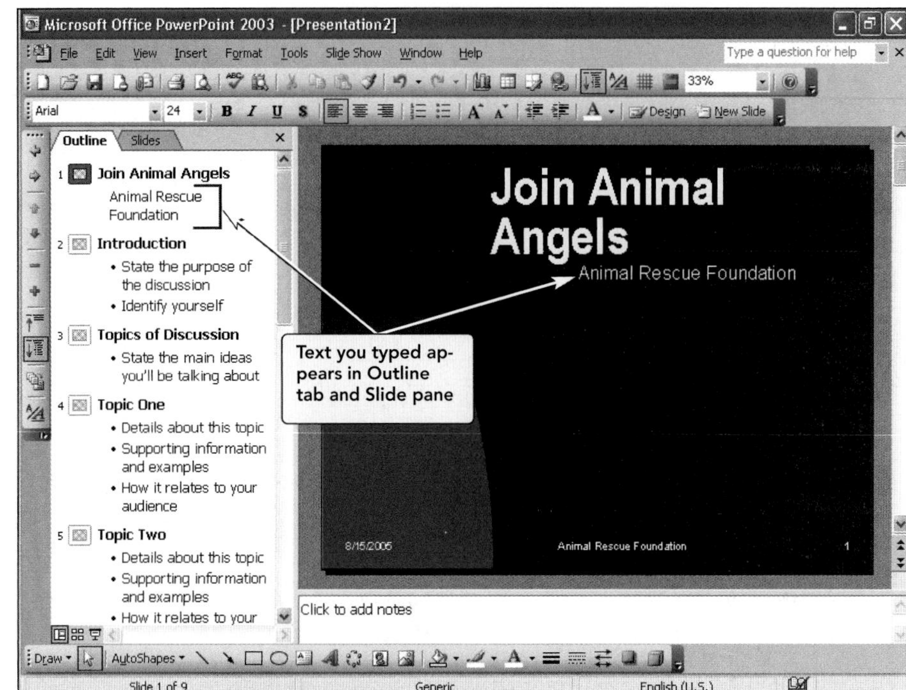

Figure 1.13

Additional Information

If you click the slide icon to the right of the slide number, all text on the slide is selected.

The selected text is removed and the new text is entered in the Outline tab as well as in the slide displayed in the slide pane. As you make changes in the Outline tab, the slide pane updates immediately.

The next change you want to make is in the Introduction slide. The sample text in this slide recommends that you enter an opening statement to explain the purpose of the discussion and to introduce yourself. You must replace the sample text next to the first bullet with the text for your slide. In the Outline tab, you can also select an entire paragraph and all subparagraphs by pointing to the left of the line and clicking when the mouse pointer is a ✥.

3

- Click on the slide 2 icon.
- Click to the left of the sample text "State the purpose of the discussion" in the Outline tab when the mouse pointer is a ✥.
- Type **volunter** (this word is intentionally misspelled).
- Press Spacebar.

Your screen should be similar to Figure 1.14

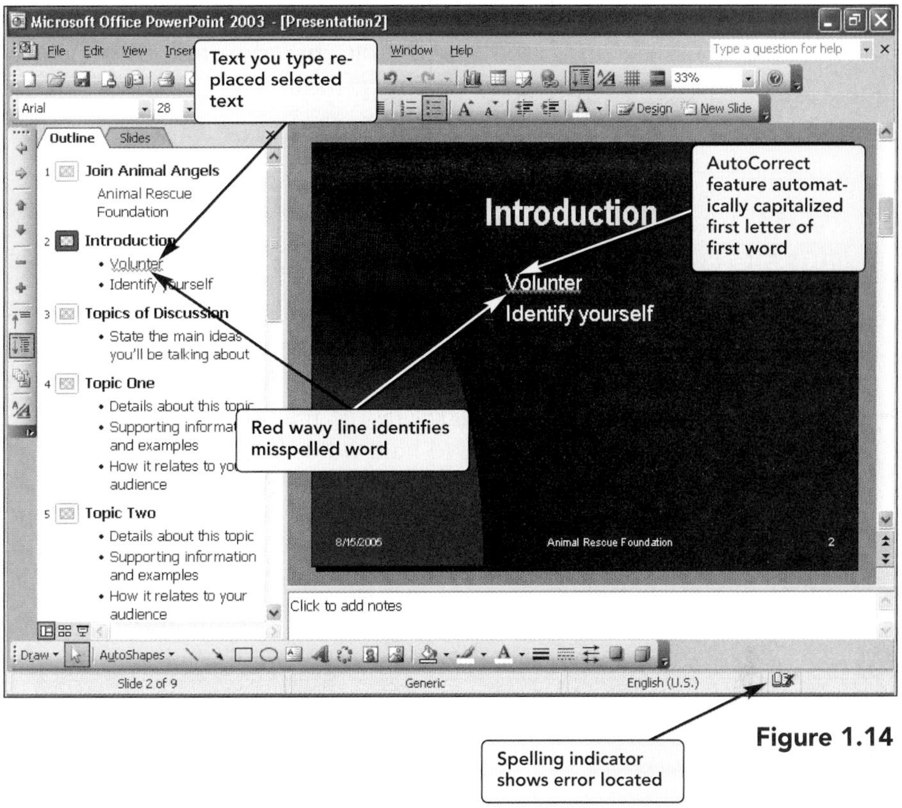

Figure 1.14

Additional Information

Bulleted items in a presentation are capitalized in sentence case format. Ending periods, however, are not included.

As soon as you pressed a key, the selected text was deleted and replaced by the new text you typed. Also, as you enter text, the program checks words for accuracy. First, PowerPoint capitalized the first letter of the word. This is part of the AutoCorrect feature of PowerPoint.

Concept 4

AutoCorrect

4 The AutoCorrect feature makes some basic assumptions about the text you are typing and, based on these assumptions, automatically corrects the entry. The AutoCorrect feature automatically inserts proper capitalization at the beginning of sentences and in the names of days of the week. It will also change to lowercase letters any words that were incorrectly capitalized due to the accidental use of the Caps Lock key. In addition, it also corrects many common typing and spelling errors automatically.

One way the program makes corrections automatically is by looking for certain types of errors. For example, if two capital letters appear at the beginning of a word, the second capital letter is changed to a lowercase letter. If a lowercase letter appears at the beginning of a sentence, the first letter of the first word is capitalized. If the name of a day begins with a lowercase letter, the first letter is capitalized.

Another way the program makes corrections is by checking all entries against a built-in list of words that are commonly spelled incorrectly or typed incorrectly. If it finds the entry on the list, the program automatically replaces the error with the correction. For example, the typing error "aboutthe" is automatically changed to "about the" because the error is on the AutoCorrect list. You can also add words to the AutoCorrect list that you want to be corrected automatically. Any such words are added to the list on the computer you are using and will be available to anyone who uses the machine after you.

Next, PowerPoint identified the word as misspelled by underlining it with a wavy red line. In addition, the spelling indicator in the status bar appears as [icon], indicating that the automatic spelling check feature has found a spelling error.

Concept 5

Spelling Checker

5 The **spelling checker** locates all misspelled words, duplicate words, and capitalization irregularities as you create and edit a presentation, and proposes possible corrections. This feature works by comparing each word to a dictionary of words. If the word does not appear in the main dictionary or in a custom dictionary, it is identified as misspelled. The **main dictionary** is supplied with the program; a **custom dictionary** is one you can create to hold words you commonly use, such as proper names and technical terms, but that are not included in the main dictionary.

If the word does not appear in either dictionary, the program identifies it as misspelled by displaying a red wavy line below the word. You can then correct the misspelled word by editing it. Alternatively, you can display a list of suggested spelling corrections for that word and select the correct spelling from the list to replace the misspelled word in the presentation.

Additional Information

The spelling checker works just as it does in the other Microsoft Office 2003 applications.

Because you have discovered this error very soon after typing it, and you know that the correct spelling of this word is "volunteer," you can quickly correct it by using the Backspace key. The Backspace key removes the character or space to the left of the insertion point; therefore, it is particularly useful when you are moving from right to left (backward) along a line of text. You will correct this word and continue entering the text for this slide.

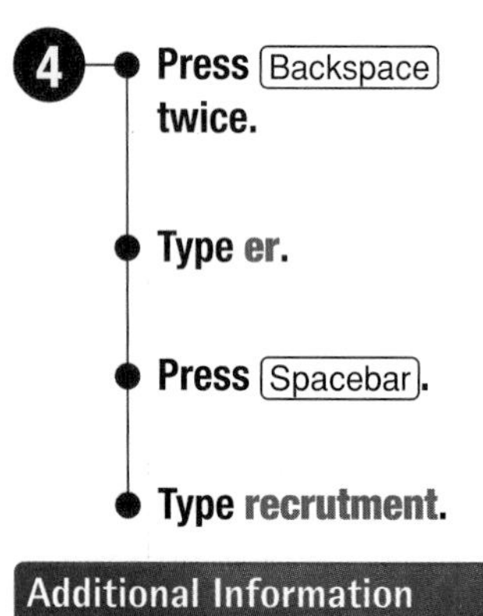

4

- **Press** Backspace **twice.**
- **Type er.**
- **Press** Spacebar.
- **Type recrutment.**

Additional Information

As you type, an animated pen appears over the spelling indicator while the spelling checker is in the process of checking for errors. When no spelling errors are located, the indicator appears as [icon].

Your screen should be similar to Figure 1.15

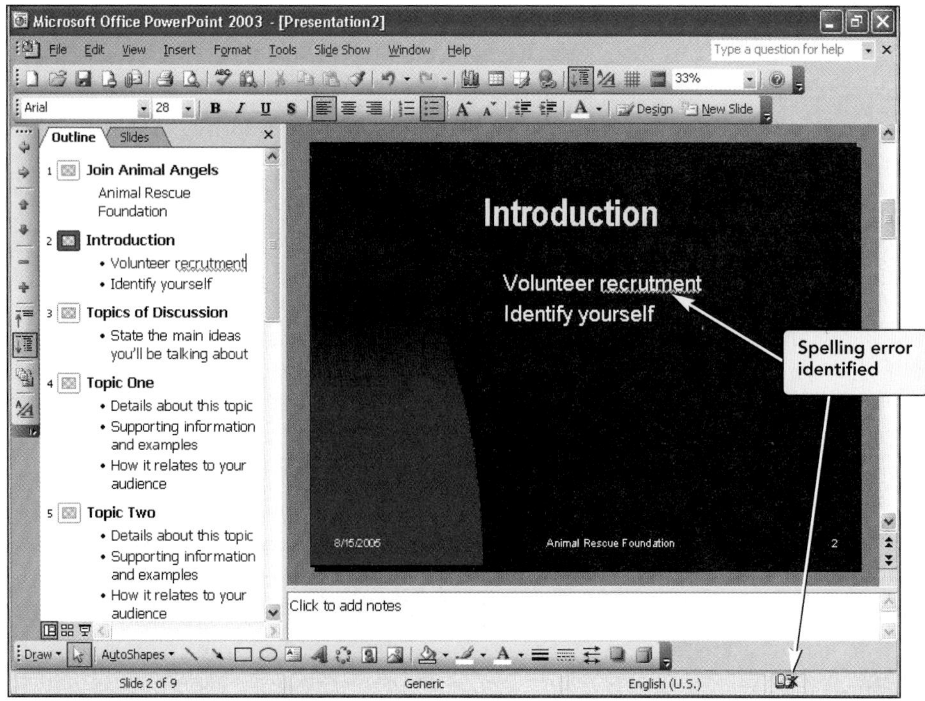

Figure 1.15

Again, the program has identified a word as misspelled. Another way to quickly correct a misspelled word is to select the correct spelling from a list of suggested spelling corrections displayed on the shortcut menu.

5 **Right-click on the misspelled word in the Outline tab to display the shortcut menu.**

Your screen should be similar to Figure 1.16

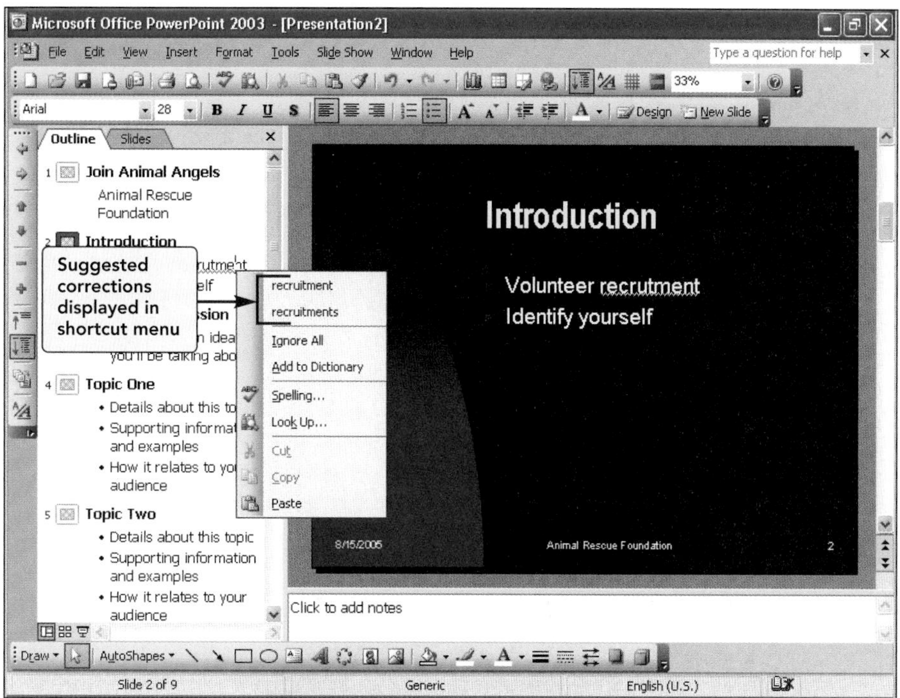

Figure 1.16

The shortcut menu displays two suggested correct spellings. The menu also includes several related menu options described below.

Option	Effect
Ignore All	Instructs PowerPoint to ignore the misspelling of this word throughout the rest of this session.
Add to Dictionary	Adds the word to the custom dictionary list. When a word is added to the custom dictionary, PowerPoint will always accept that spelling as correct.
Spelling	Starts the spelling checker to check the entire presentation.
Look Up	Checks the spelling of text in another language.

Additional Information

If only one suggested spelling correction is offered, the correction is automatically inserted.

Sometimes no suggested replacements are offered because PowerPoint cannot locate any words in its dictionary that are similar in spelling, or the suggestions offered are not correct. If either situation happens, you must edit the word manually. In this case, you will replace the word with the correct spelling and enter your name on this slide.

6 Choose "recruitment."

- Select "Identify yourself" in the Outline tab.
- Type **your name.**

Your screen should be similar to Figure 1.17

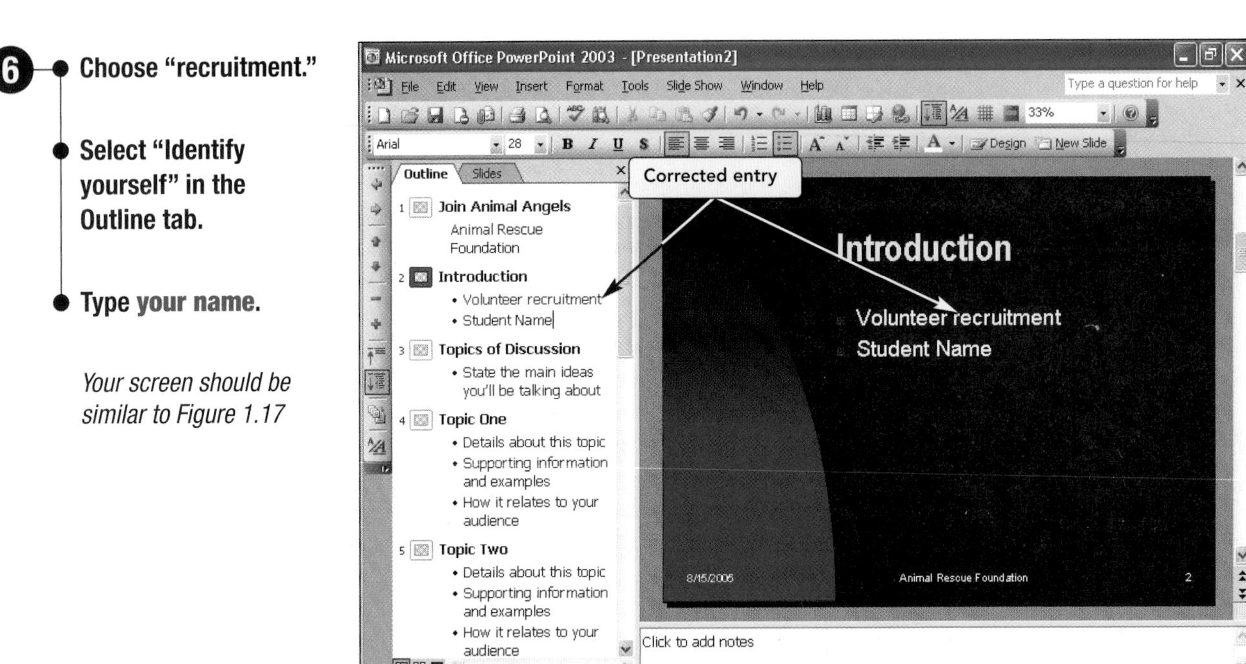

Figure 1.17

You are now ready to update the third slide in your presentation by entering the three main topics you will be discussing. You want to enter each topic on a separate bulleted line. The first bullet is already displayed and contains sample text that you will replace. To add additional lines and bullets, you simply press ←Enter.

7 In slide 3 of the Outline tab, select "State the main ideas you'll be talking about."

- Type **Why are pets abandoned?.**
- Press ←Enter.
- Type **How can you help?.**
- Press ←Enter.
- Type **How does the Foundation help?** (do not press ←Enter).

Having Trouble?

If you accidentally insert an extra bullet and blank line, press Backspace twice to remove them.

Your screen should be similar to Figure 1.18

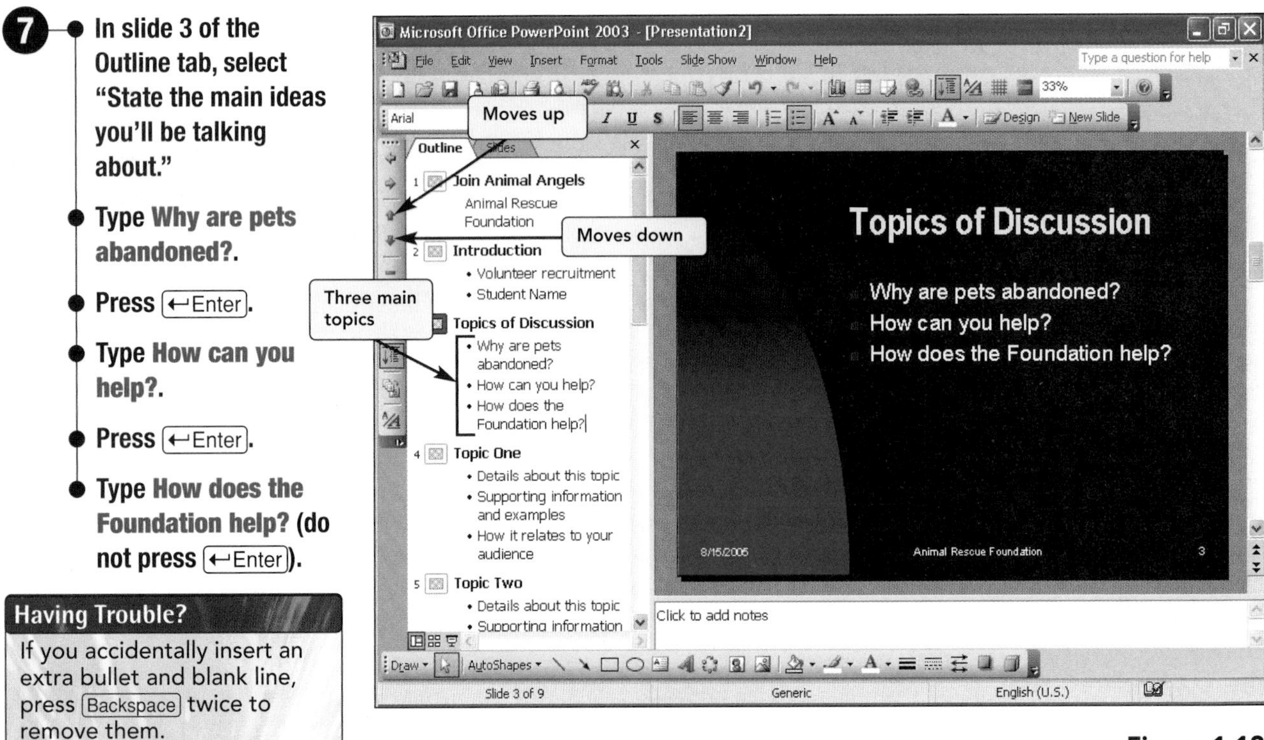

Figure 1.18

You realize that you entered the topics in the wrong order. You want the last item to be the second item in the list. A bulleted point can be moved easily by selecting it and dragging it to a new location, or by using the Move Up or Move Down buttons in the Outlining toolbar. When using the buttons, the insertion point must be on the bulleted item you want to move. You will move the bulleted item on the current line up one line.

8 Click Move Up.

Your screen should be similar to Figure 1.19

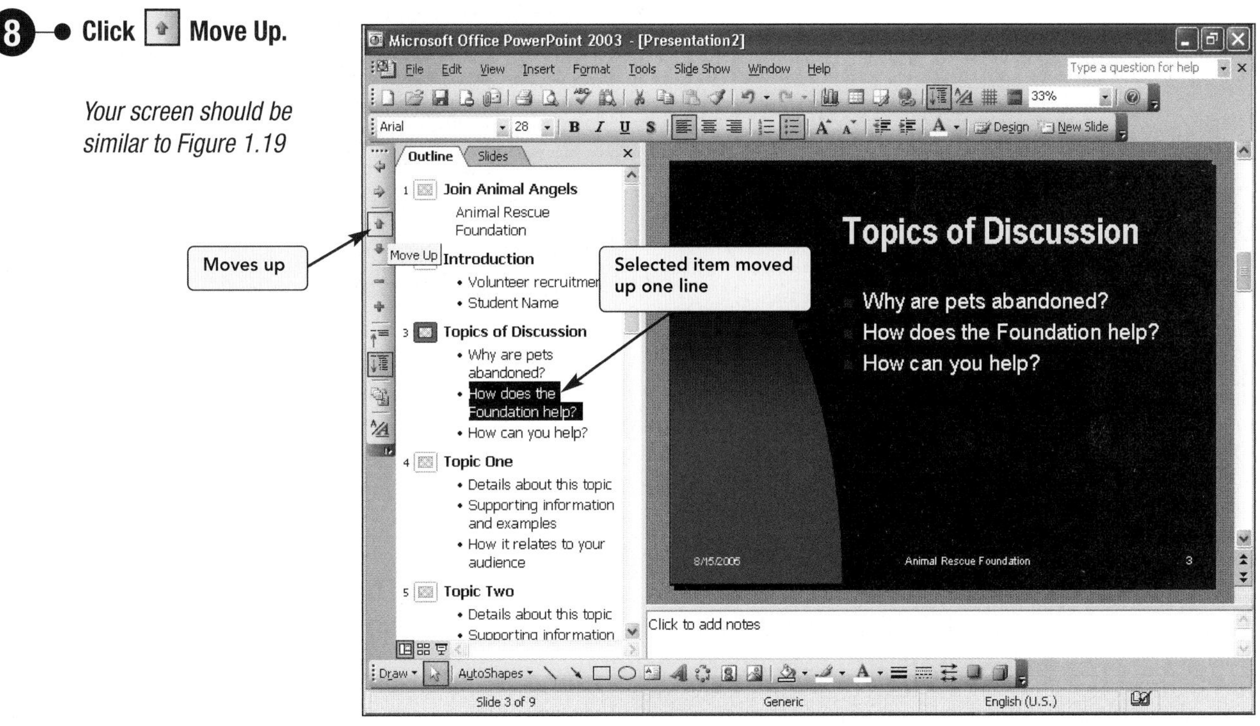

Figure 1.19

Editing in the Slide Pane

Next, you want to update the content of the fourth slide. The fourth slide contains the title "Topic One" and a list of three bulleted items. The title and the bulleted list are two separate elements or placeholders on the slide. **Placeholders** are boxes that are designed to contain specific types of items or **objects** such as the slide title text, bulleted item text, charts, tables, and pictures. Each slide can have several different types of placeholders. To indicate which placeholder to work with, you must first select it. You will change the sample text in the title placeholder first in the slide pane.

1 Click on slide 4 in the Outline tab to display it in the slide pane.

Click anywhere on the slide title text in the slide pane.

Your screen should be similar to Figure 1.20

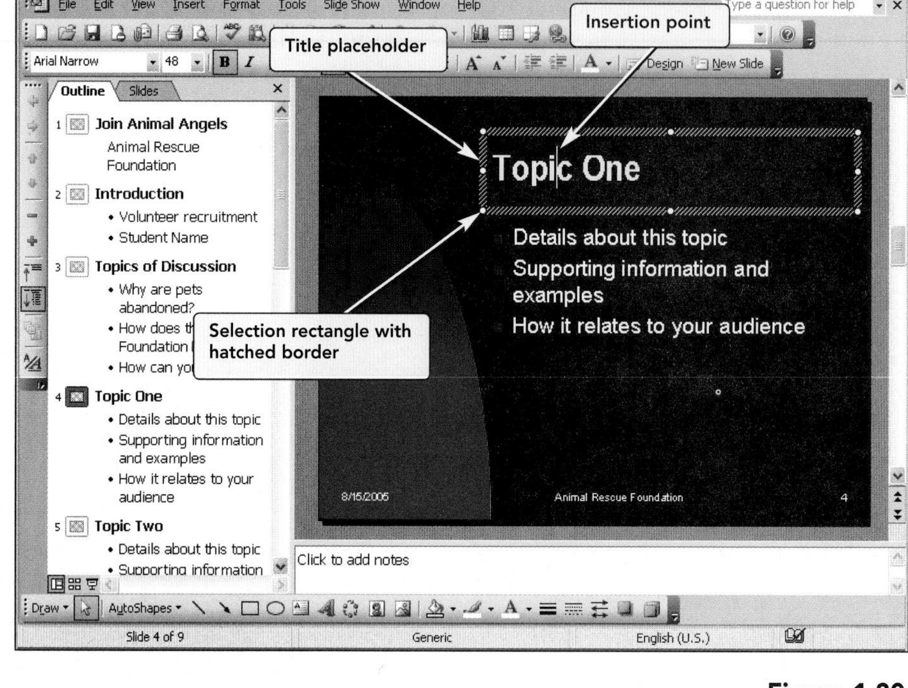

Figure 1.20

Additional Information

You can also enter and edit text in Dictation mode using the Speech Recognition feature.

Additional Information

A dotted border around a selected object indicates that you can format the box itself. Clicking the hatch-marked border changes it to a dotted border.

The title placeholder is now a selected object and is surrounded by a **selection rectangle**. The hatch-marked border of the selection rectangle indicates that you can enter, delete, select, and format the text inside the placeholder. An insertion point is displayed to show your location in the text and to allow you to select and edit the text. The mouse pointer appears as an I-beam to be used to position the insertion point. You will enter the new title for this slide.

2 Select the title text.

Having Trouble?

Drag to select a portion of the text, double-click to select a word, or triple-click to select a line.

Type **Why Are Pets Abandoned?**.

Your screen should be similar to Figure 1.21

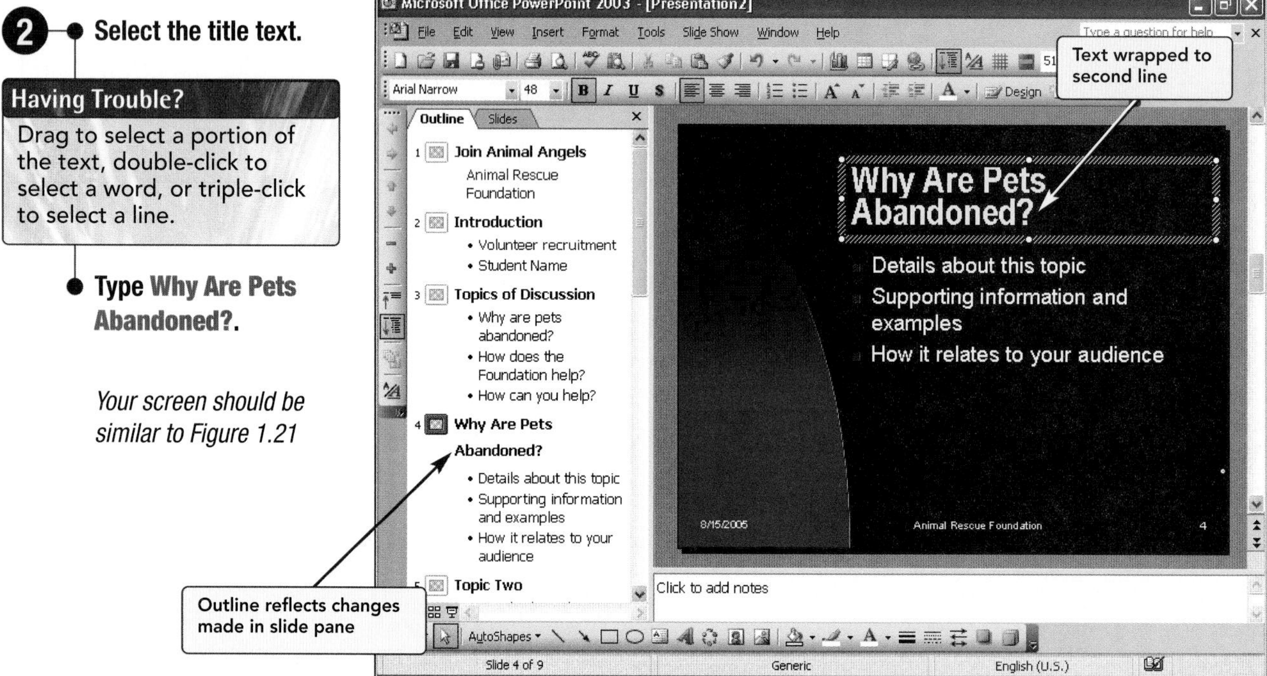

Figure 1.21

Notice that the text automatically wrapped to a second line when the length exceeded the width of the box. The Outline tab reflects the changes as they are made in the slide pane. Next, you need to replace the sample text in the bulleted list.

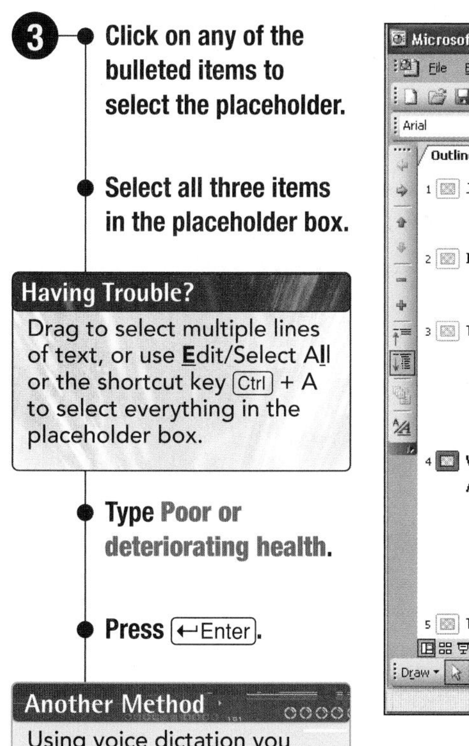

3

- **Click on any of the bulleted items to select the placeholder.**
- **Select all three items in the placeholder box.**

Having Trouble?

Drag to select multiple lines of text, or use Edit/Select All or the shortcut key Ctrl + A to select everything in the placeholder box.

- **Type Poor or deteriorating health.**
- **Press ←Enter.**

Another Method

Using voice dictation you would say "Enter" to start a new line.

- **Enter the following text for the next three bullets:**

  Maintenance expenses

  Change in lifestyle

  Behavioral problems

Your screen should be similar to Figure 1.22

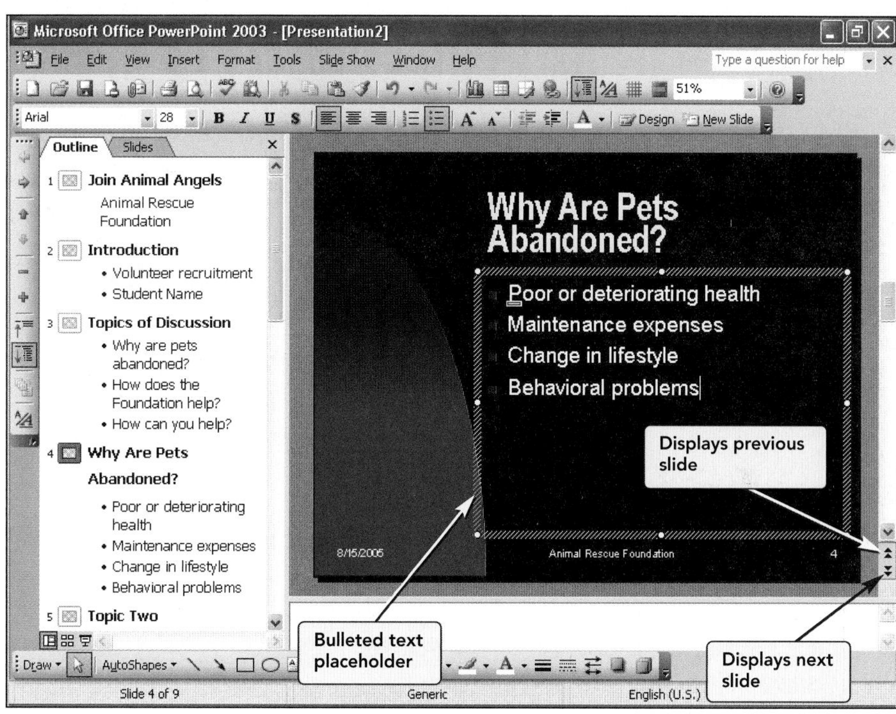

Figure 1.22

In the next slide you will enter information about how people can help the Animal Rescue Foundation. In addition to clicking on the slide in the Outline tab, the following features can be used to move to other slides in Normal view.

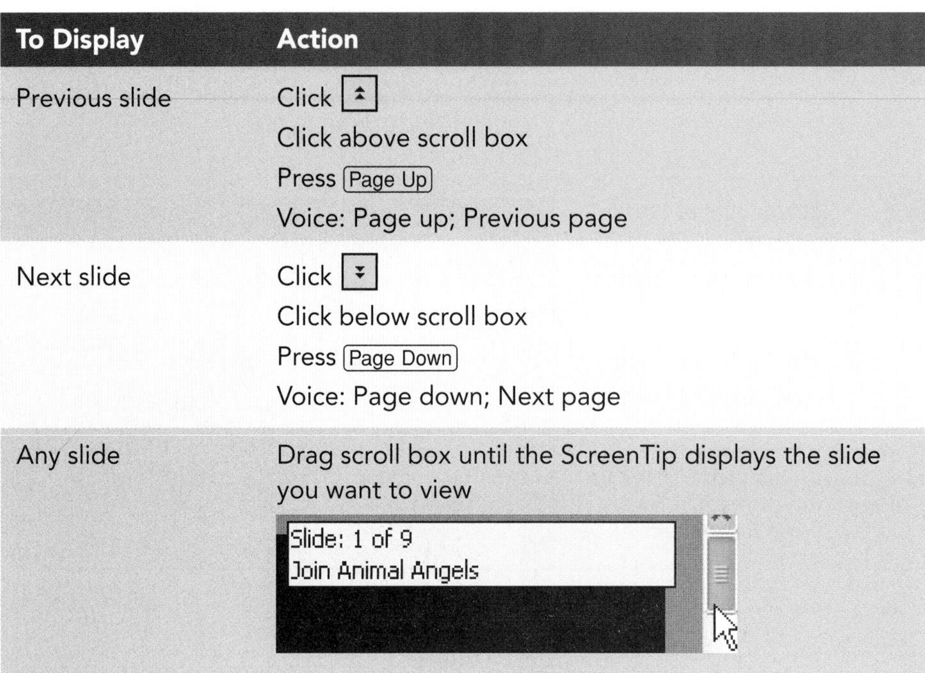

To Display	Action
Previous slide	Click [▲] Click above scroll box Press Page Up Voice: Page up; Previous page
Next slide	Click [▼] Click below scroll box Press Page Down Voice: Page down; Next page
Any slide	Drag scroll box until the ScreenTip displays the slide you want to view Slide: 1 of 9 Join Animal Angels

You will enter a new slide title and text for the bulleted items.

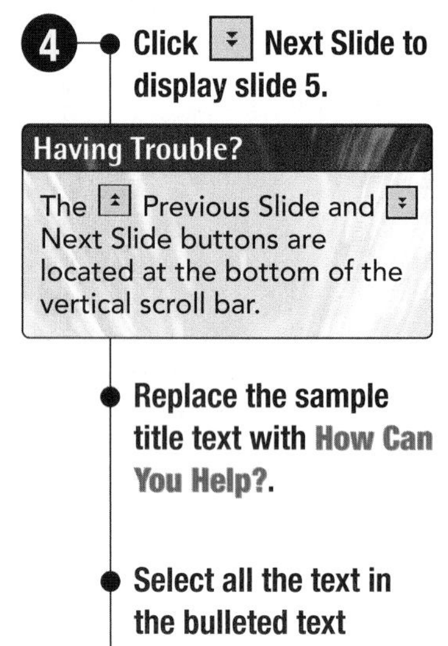

4 **Click [▼] Next Slide to display slide 5.**

Having Trouble?

The [▲] Previous Slide and [▼] Next Slide buttons are located at the bottom of the vertical scroll bar.

- **Replace the sample title text with How Can You Help?.**
- **Select all the text in the bulleted text placeholder.**
- **Type Donate your time and talent.**
- **Press ←Enter.**

Your screen should be similar to Figure 1.23

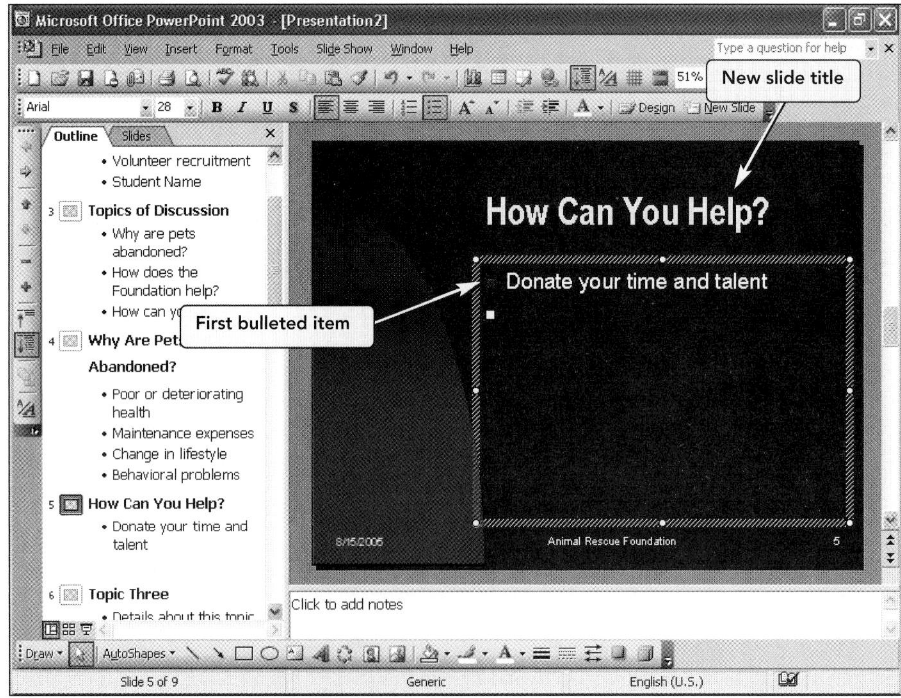

Figure 1.23

Demoting and Promoting Bulleted Items

You want the next bulleted item to be indented below the first bulleted item. Indenting a bulleted point to the right **demotes** it, or makes it a lower or subordinate topic in the outline hierarchy.

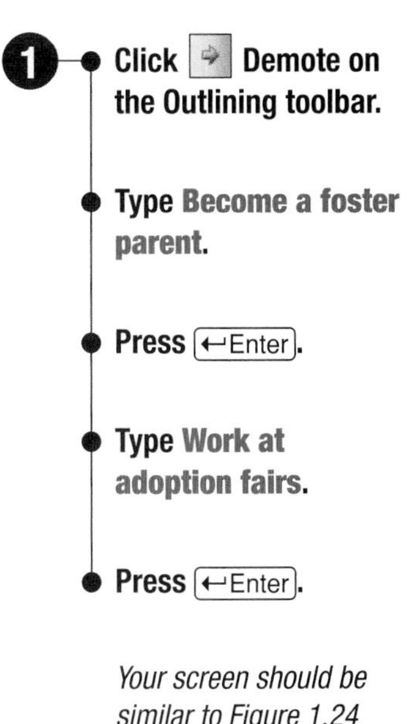

Additional Information

You can also demote and promote bulleted items in the Outline tab using the same procedure. In addition, in the Outline tab you can drag a selected item to the left or right to promote or demote it.

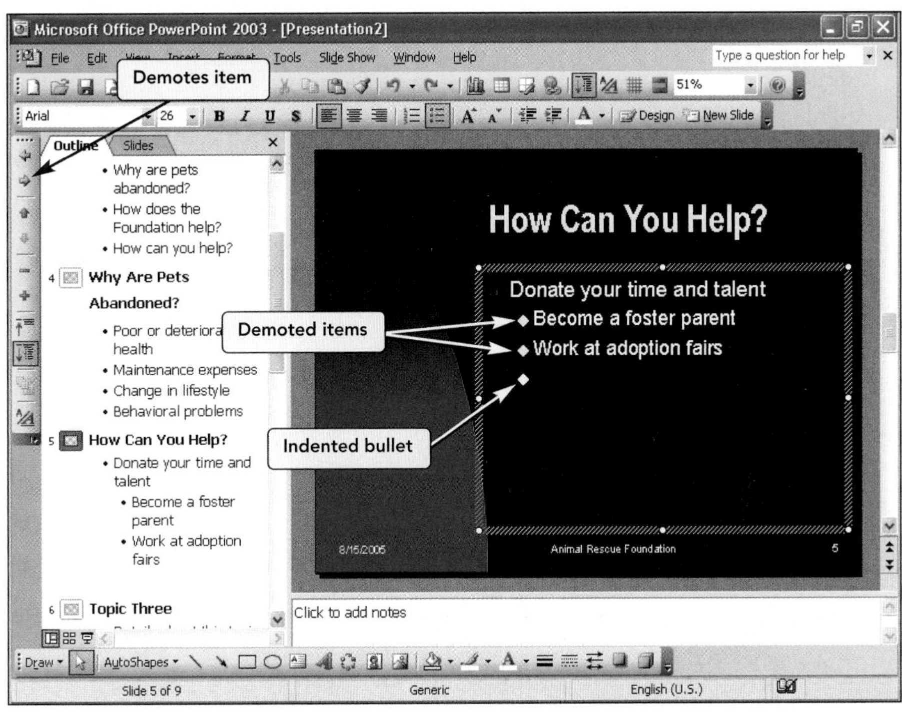

Figure 1.24

The bullet style of the demoted lines is ◆. When you demote a bulleted point, PowerPoint continues to indent to the same level until you cancel the indent. Before entering the next item, you want to remove the indentation, or **promote** the line. Promoting a line moves it to the left, or up a level in the outline hierarchy.

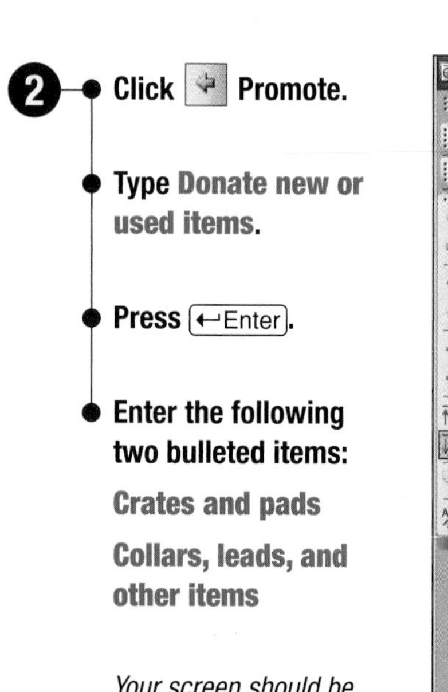

2 Click Promote.

- Type **Donate new or used items.**
- Press Enter.
- Enter the following two bulleted items:

  Crates and pads

  Collars, leads, and other items

Your screen should be similar to Figure 1.25

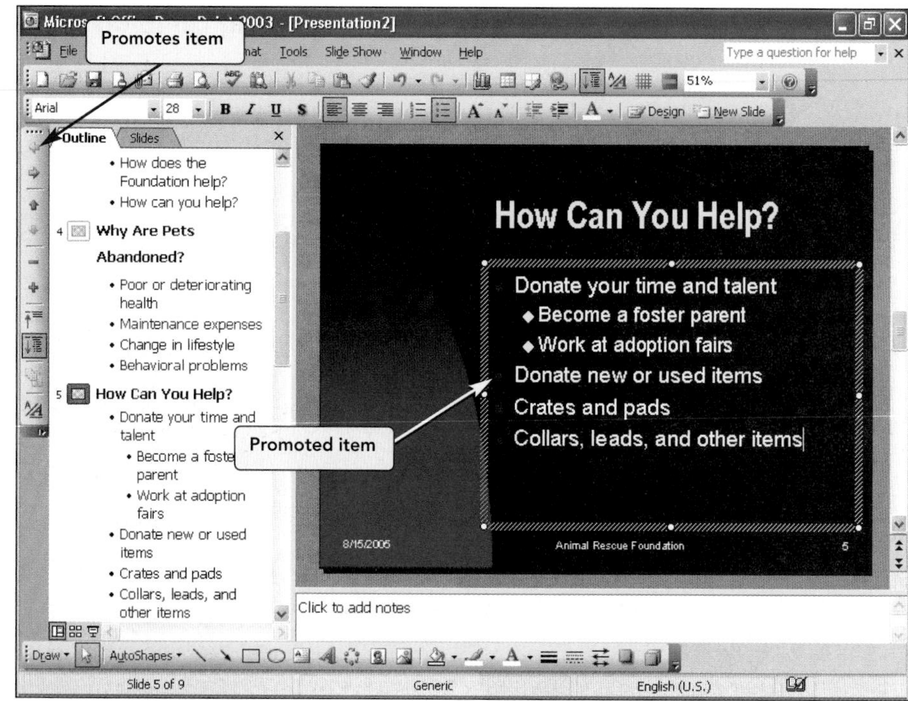

Figure 1.25

You can also promote or demote bulleted items after the text has been entered. The insertion point can be anywhere on the line to be promoted or demoted.

3 Demote the items "Crates and pads" and "Collars, leads, and other items."

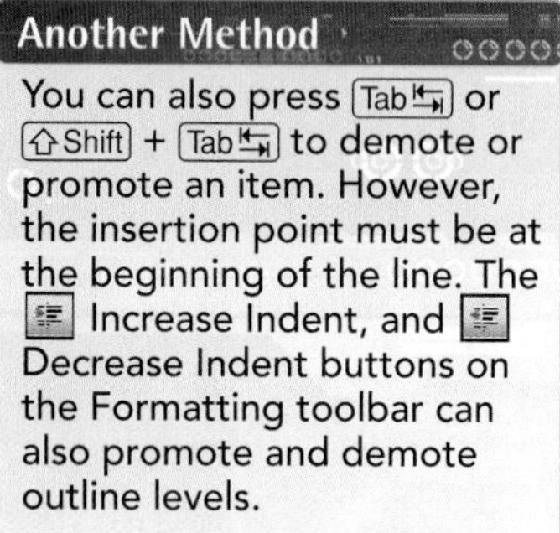

Another Method

You can also press Tab or Shift + Tab to demote or promote an item. However, the insertion point must be at the beginning of the line. The Increase Indent, and Decrease Indent buttons on the Formatting toolbar can also promote and demote outline levels.

Your screen should be similar to Figure 1.26

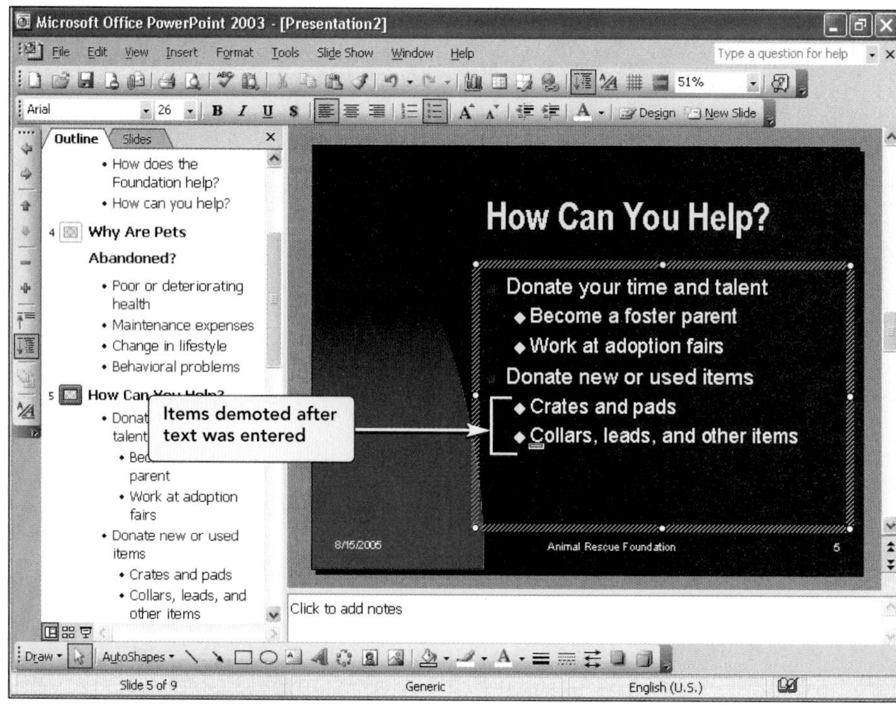

Figure 1.26

You still have three more bulleted items to add to this text placeholder. Notice, however, that the last item is near the bottom of the placeholder box. As you type the text the AutoFit feature will automatically reduce the line spacing and if needed the size of the text until the spillover text fits inside the placeholder.

4

- **Move to the end of "Collars, leads, and other items"**
- **Press ←Enter.**
- **Type Provide financial support**
- **Press ←Enter.**
- **Enter the following three bulleted items:**

  Send a donation

  Sponsor a foster pet

  Sponsor an adoption
- **Promote the "Provide Financial Support" bullet.**

Your screen should be similar to Figure 1.27

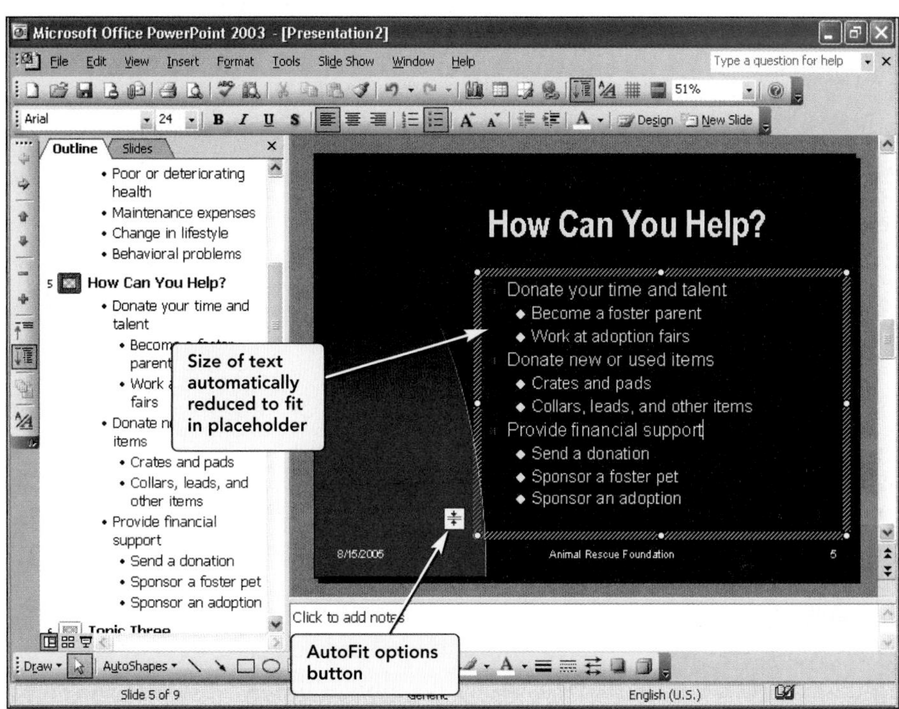

Figure 1.27

Additional Information

As you increase or decrease the size of the placeholder, the AutoFit feature will adjust the line spacing and text size appropriately.

As you continued entering more bulleted items, the text size reduced even more. Also notice that the AutoFit Options button appears next to the placeholder. It contains options that allow you to control the AutoFit feature and to handle the over-spilling text.

Splitting Text Between Slides

Generally when creating slides, it is a good idea to limit the number of bulleted items on a slide to six. It is also recommended that the number of words on a line should not exceed five. In this case, because there are ten bulleted items on this slide, you want to split the slide content between two slides.

1 Click the AutoFit Options button.

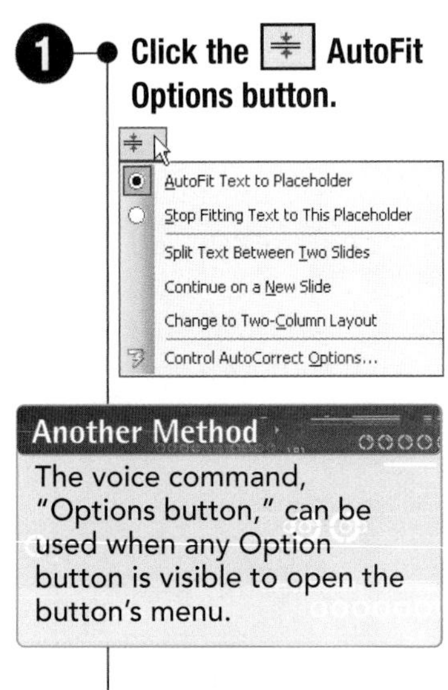

> **Another Method**
> The voice command, "Options button," can be used when any Option button is visible to open the button's menu.

- Choose Split Text Between Two Slides.

Your screen should be similar to Figure 1.28

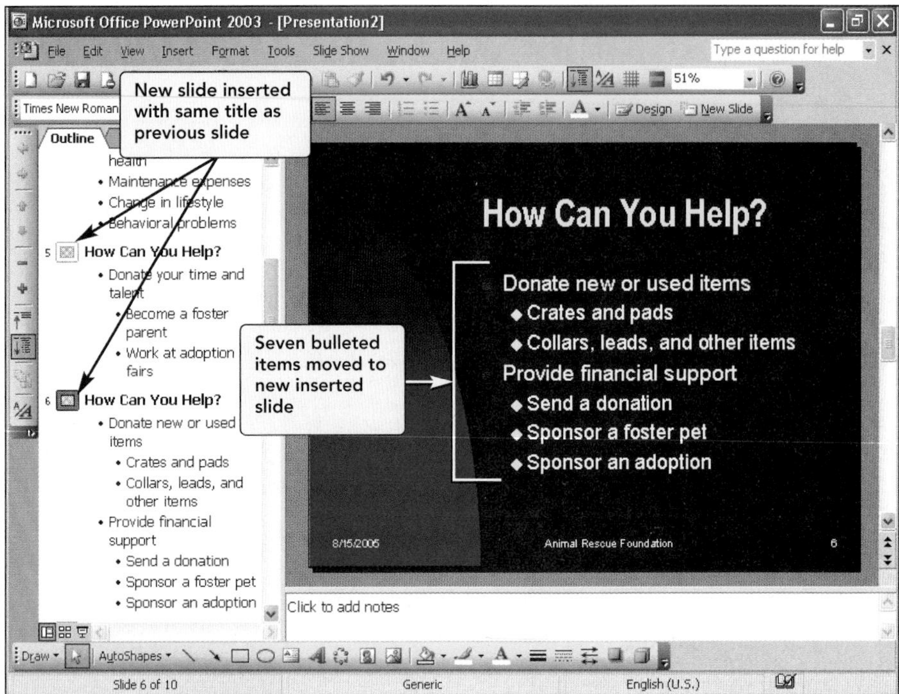

Figure 1.28

> **Another Method**
> You can split text into two slides in the Outline tab by positioning the insertion point at the end of a bulleted item and pressing ←Enter. Then promote it until a new slide icon and number appear. All text after the insertion point will become bulleted items on the new slide.

A new slide is inserted into the presentation containing the same title as the previous slide and the last two bulleted topic groups. Because the split occurs at a main topic, there are still seven bulleted items on the new slide. You will combine two items into one to reduce the number to six and change the title of the slide.

2 Click the title placeholder.

- Replace the title text with **More Ways to Help!**.
- Move to the end of the sixth bulleted item and press Delete.
- Edit the item to be "Sponsor a foster pet or adoption."

Your screen should be similar to Figure 1.29

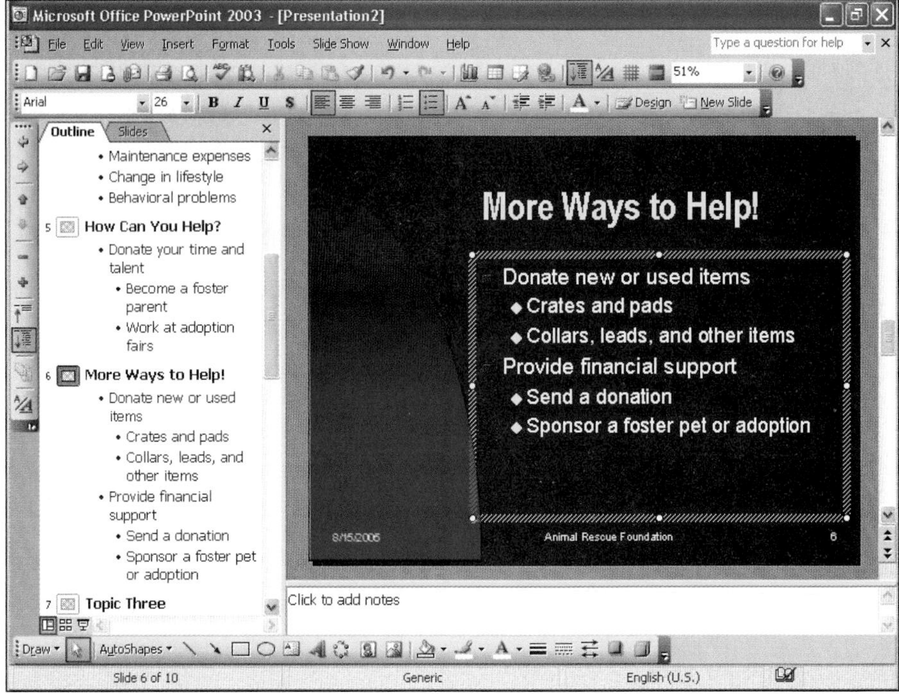

Figure 1.29

Saving, Closing, and Opening a Presentation

You have just been notified about an important meeting that is to begin in a few minutes. Before leaving for the meeting, you want to save the presentation. As you enter and edit text to create a new presentation, the changes you make are immediately displayed onscreen and are stored in your computer's memory. However, they are not permanently stored until you save your work to a file on a disk. After a presentation is saved as a file, it can be closed and opened again at a later time to be edited further.

As a backup against the accidental loss of work caused by a power failure or other mishap, Office 2003 includes an AutoRecover feature. When this feature is on, as you work you may see a pulsing disk icon briefly appear in the status bar. This icon indicates that the program is saving your work to a temporary recovery file. The time interval between automatic saving can be set to any period you specify; the default is every 10 minutes. When you start up again, the recovery file containing all changes you made up to the last time it was saved by AutoRecover is opened automatically. You then need to save the recovery file. If you do not save it, it is deleted when closed. While AutoRecover is a great feature for recovering lost work, it should not be used in place of regularly saving your work.

Saving the Presentation

You will save the work you have done so far on the presentation. The Save or Save As commands on the File menu are used to save files. The Save command or the Save button will save the active file using the same file name by replacing the contents of the existing file with the document as it appears on your screen. The Save As command allows you to save a file with a new file name and/or to a new location. This action leaves the original file unchanged. When a presentation is saved for the first time, either command can be used. It is especially important to save a new presentation very soon after you create it because the AutoRecover feature does not work until a file name has been specified.

1 Click Save.

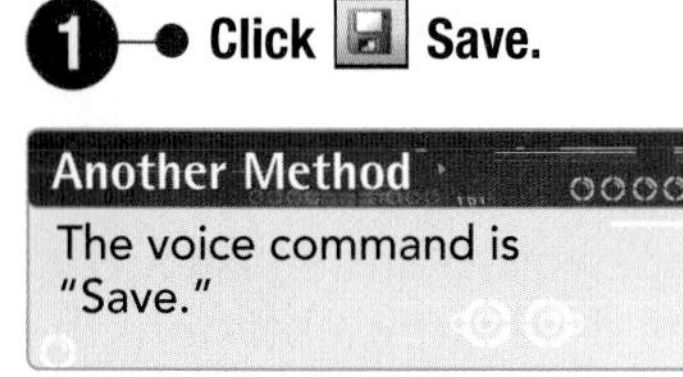

Another Method

The voice command is "Save."

Your screen should be similar to Figure 1.30

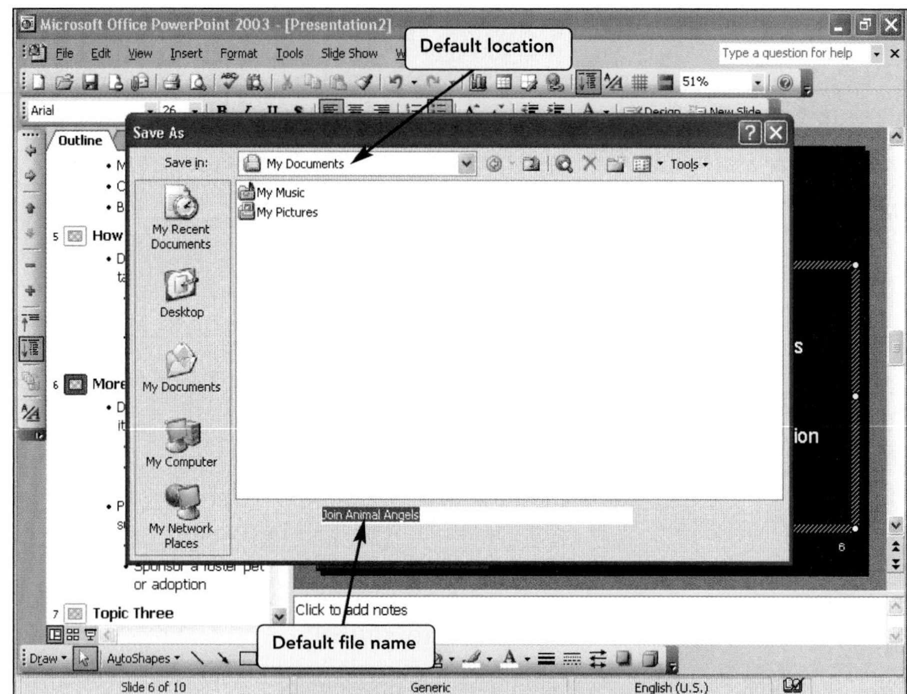

Figure 1.30

Additional Information

Windows documents can have up to 256 characters in the file name. Names can contain letters, numbers, and spaces; the symbols /,\,?,:,*,", <, > cannot be used.

The Save As dialog box is displayed in which you specify the location to save the file and the file name. The Save In list box displays the default location where files are stored. The File Name text box displays the title from the first slide as the default file name. You will change the location to the location where you save your files and the file name. Notice that the default name is highlighted, indicating that it is selected and will be replaced as you type the new name.

2 **Type Volunteer.**

Additional Information

The file name can be entered in either uppercase or lowercase letters and will appear exactly as you type it.

- **Open the Save In list box.**

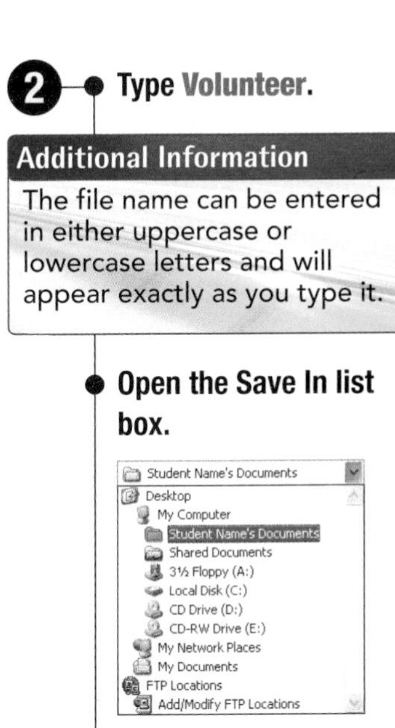

Having Trouble?

Click the text box arrow to open the drop-down list.

- **Select the location where you will save your files from the Save In drop-down list.**

Having Trouble?

If you are saving to a floppy disk and an error message is displayed, check that your disk is properly inserted in the drive and click OK.

Your screen should be similar to Figure 1.31

Having Trouble?

If your dialog box does not display file extensions, your Windows program has this option deactivated.

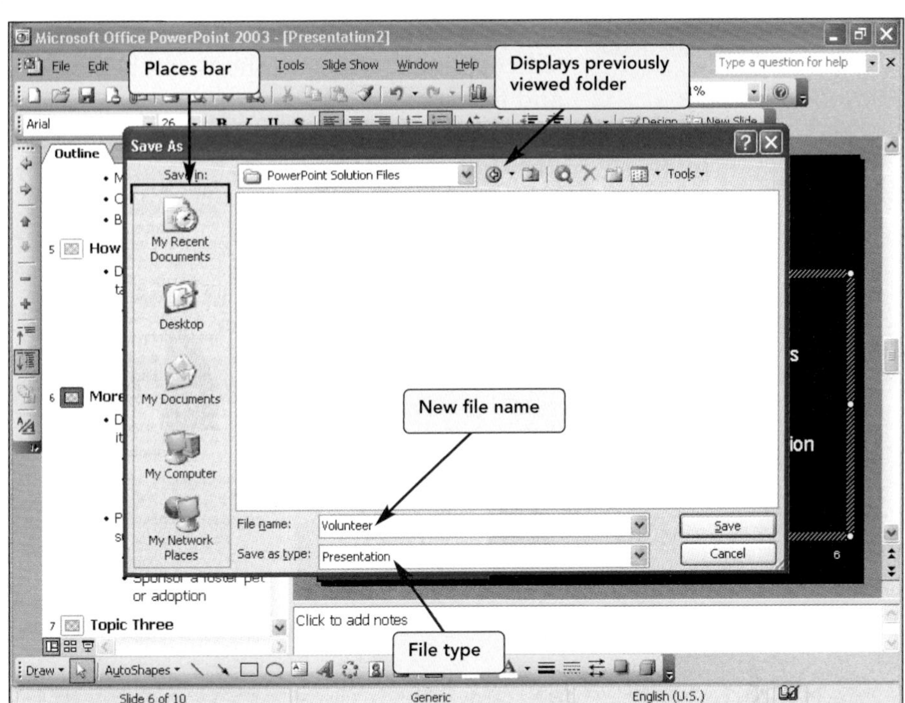

Figure 1.31

The large list box displays the names of any PowerPoint files (if any) stored in that location. Only PowerPoint presentation files are listed, because the selected file type in the Save As Type list box is Presentation. Presentation files have a default file extension of .ppt.

Additional Information

If your system uses Windows NT, My Network Places is Network Neighborhood.

You can also select the save location from the Places bar along the left side of the dialog box. The icons bring up a list of recently accessed files and folders, the contents of the My Documents and Favorites folders, the Windows desktop, and folders that reside on a network or Web through the My Network Places. Selecting a folder from one of these lists changes to that location. You can also click the button in the toolbar to return to folders that were previously opened during the current session.

3 Click .

Your screen should be similar to Figure 1.32

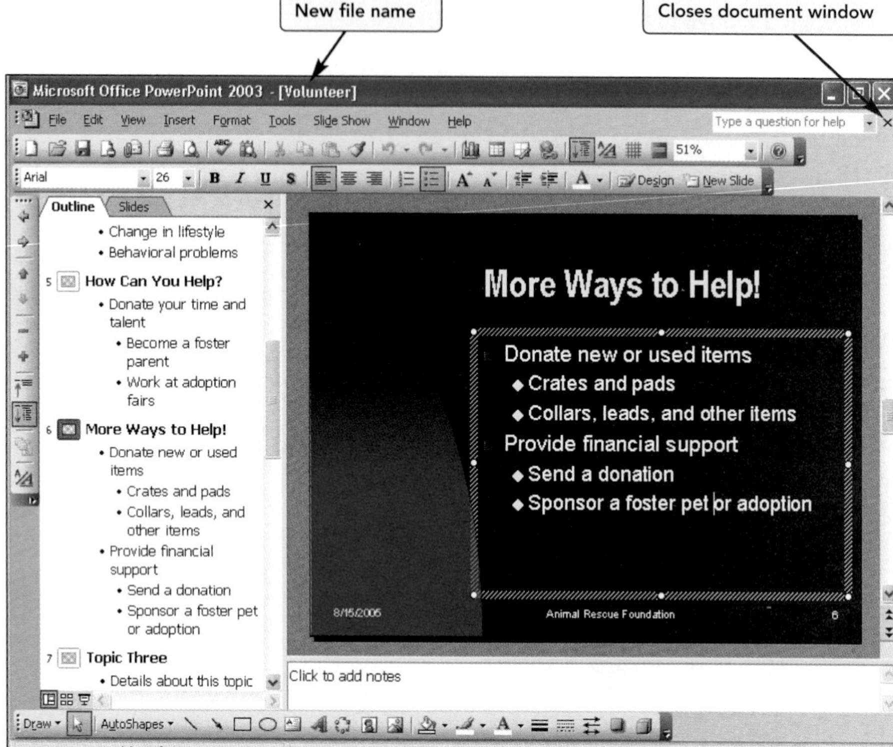

Figure 1.32

The new file name is displayed in the window title bar. The presentation is now saved in a new file named Volunteer. The view in use at the time the file is saved is also saved with the file.

Closing a Presentation

You are now ready to close the file.

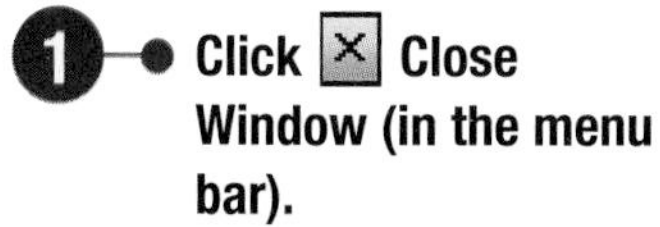

Click Close Window (in the menu bar).

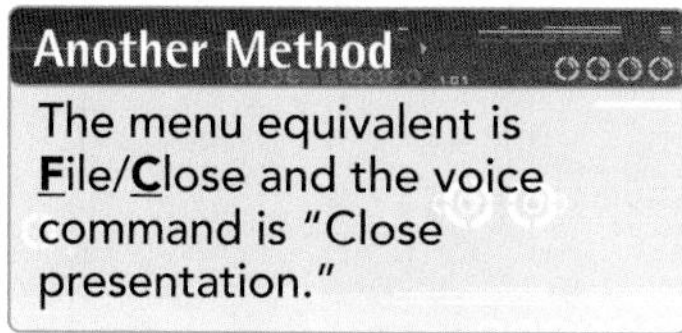

Another Method

The menu equivalent is File/Close and the voice command is "Close presentation."

Your screen should be similar to Figure 1.33

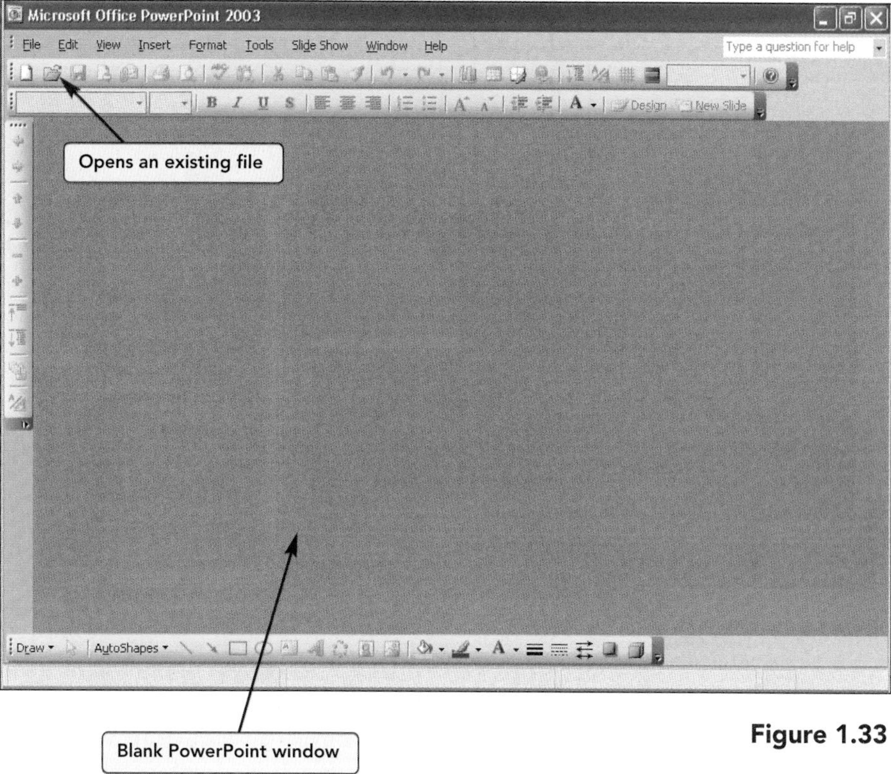

Figure 1.33

The presentation is closed, and a blank PowerPoint window is displayed. Always save your slide presentation before closing a file or leaving the PowerPoint program. As a safeguard against losing your work if you forget to save the presentation, PowerPoint will remind you to save any unsaved presentation before closing the file or exiting the program.

Note: If you are ending your lab session now, choose File/Exit to exit the program.

Opening an Existing Presentation

After returning from your meeting, you hastily continued to enter the information for several more slides and saved the presentation using a new file name. You will open this file to see the information in the new slides and will continue working on the presentation.

Click Open.

Another Method

The menu equivalent is File/Open, the keyboard shortcut is Ctrl + O, and the voice command is "Open."

- **If necessary, select the location containing your data files from the Look In drop-down list box.**
- **Select** pp01_Volunteer1.

Your screen should be similar to Figure 1.34

Having Trouble?

The files in your file list and the previewed file may be different than shown in Figure 1.34. If a preview is not displayed, click Views and select Preview.

Additional Information

The File/New command or the button opens a blank new presentation. You can also quickly open a recently used file by selecting it from the list of file names displayed at the bottom of the File menu and at the bottom of the Getting Started task pane.

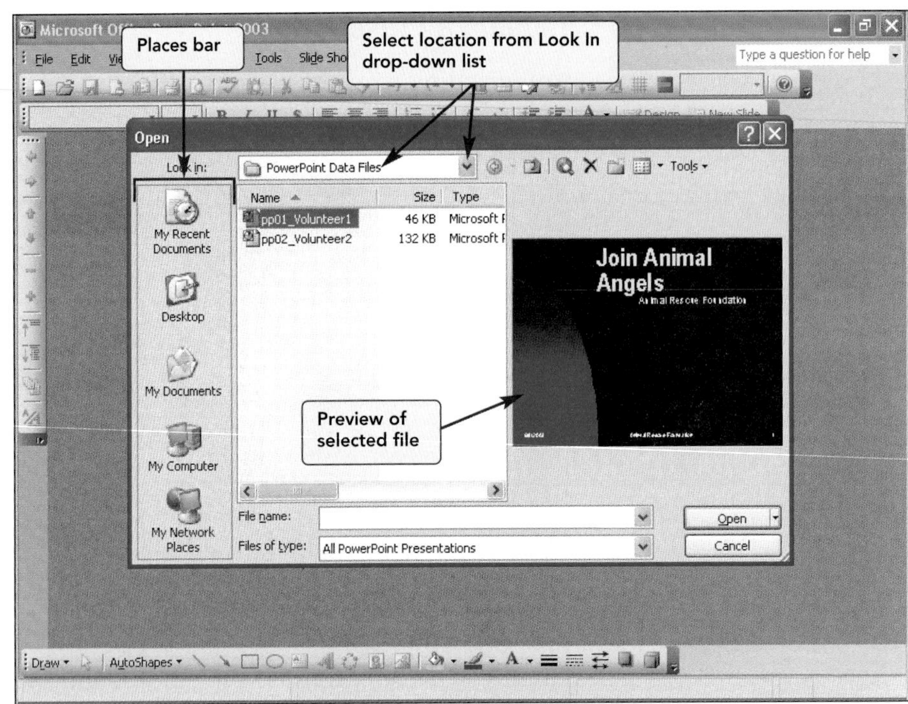

Figure 1.34

In the Open dialog box you specify the location and name of the file you want to open. The Look In drop-down list box displays the last specified location, in this case the location where you saved the Volunteer presentation. The large list box displays the names of PowerPoint presentation files only, as specified by the setting in the Files of Type box. As in the Save As dialog box, the Places bar can be used to quickly access recently used files. A preview of the selected file is displayed in the right side of the dialog box.

You will open the selected file next.

2 Click Open.

Another Method
You could also double-click the file name to both select it and choose Open.

- If necessary, open the Outline tab.
- Edit slide 2 in the slide pane to display your name.
- Scroll the Outline pane to see the additional content that has been added to the presentation.

Your screen should be similar to Figure 1.35

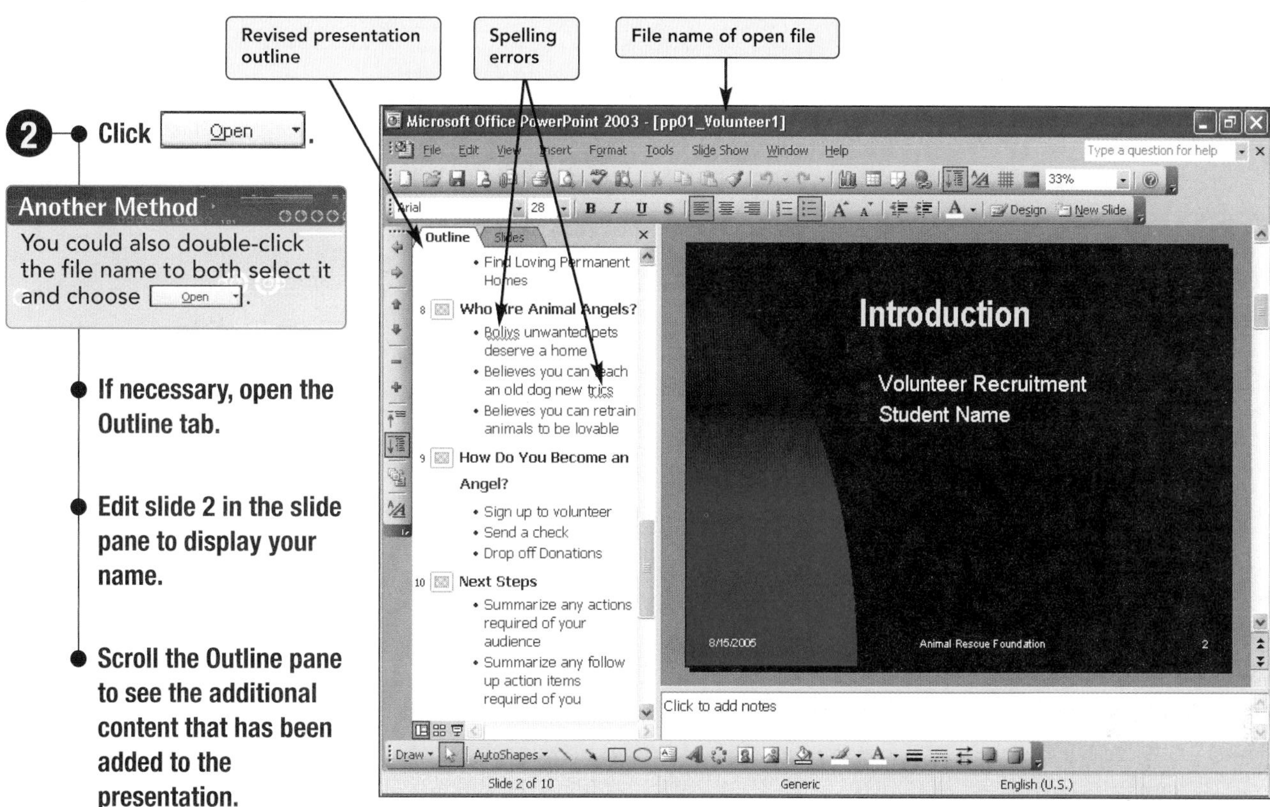

Figure 1.35

The presentation still contains ten slides, and all the sample text has been replaced with text for the volunteer recruitment presentation except for slide 10.

Checking Spelling

As you entered the information on the additional slides, you left several typing errors uncorrected. To correct the misspelled words and grammatical errors, you can use the shortcut menu to correct each individual word or error, as you learned earlier. However, in many cases you may find it more efficient to wait until you are finished writing before you correct any spelling or grammatical errors. Rather than continually breaking your train of thought to correct errors as you type, you can check the spelling on all slides of the presentation at once.

1 Click Speling.

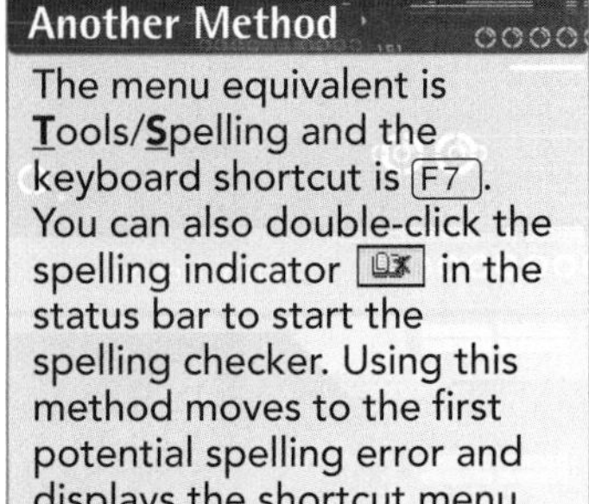

Another Method

The menu equivalent is Tools/Spelling and the keyboard shortcut is F7. You can also double-click the spelling indicator in the status bar to start the spelling checker. Using this method moves to the first potential spelling error and displays the shortcut menu.

Your screen should be similar to Figure 1.36

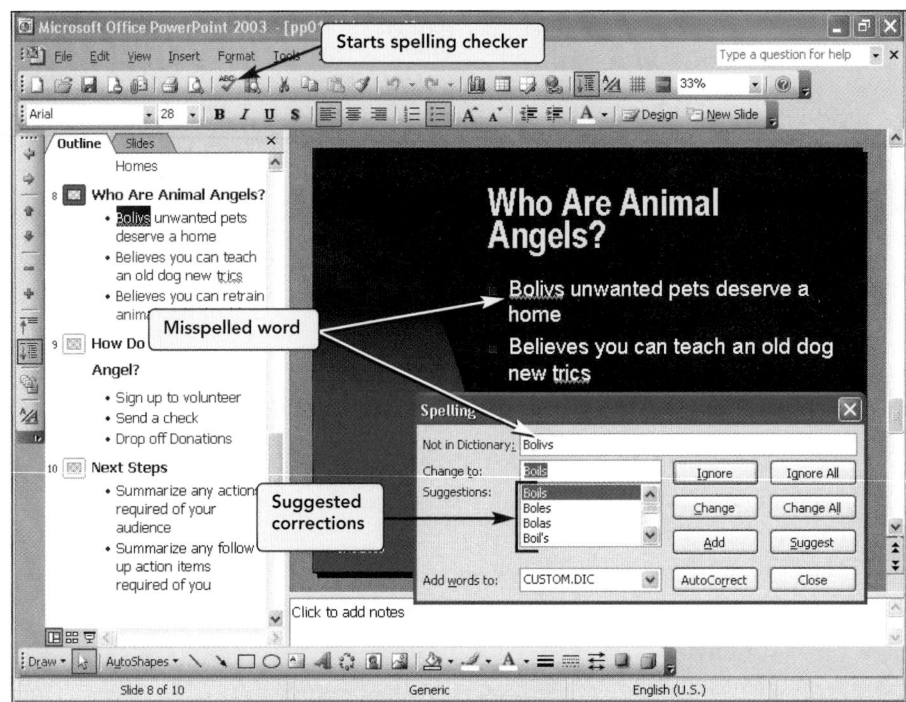

Figure 1.36

Additional Information

The spelling checker identifies many proper names and technical terms as misspelled. To stop this from occurring, use the Add Words To option to add those names to the custom dictionary.

The program jumps to slide 8, highlights the first located misspelled word, "Bolivs," in the Outline pane, and opens the Spelling dialog box. The Spelling dialog box displays the misspelled word in the Not in Dictionary text box. The Suggestions list box displays the words the spelling checker has located in the dictionary that most closely match the misspelled word. The first word is highlighted.

Although the list displays several additional suggestions, none of them is correct. Sometimes the spelling checker does not display any suggested replacements because it cannot locate any words in the dictionaries that are similar in spelling. If there are no suggestions, the Not in Dictionary text box simply displays the word that is highlighted in the text. When none of the suggestions is correct, you must edit the word yourself by typing the correction in the Change To text box.

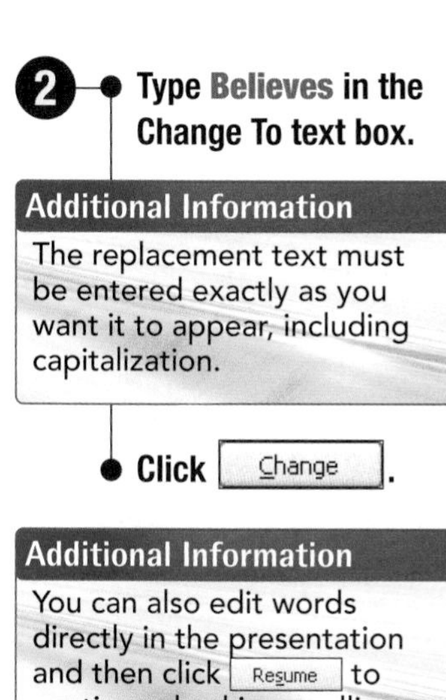

2 **Type Believes in the Change To text box.**

Additional Information

The replacement text must be entered exactly as you want it to appear, including capitalization.

Click Change**.**

Additional Information

You can also edit words directly in the presentation and then click Resume to continue checking spelling.

Your screen should be similar to Figure 1.37

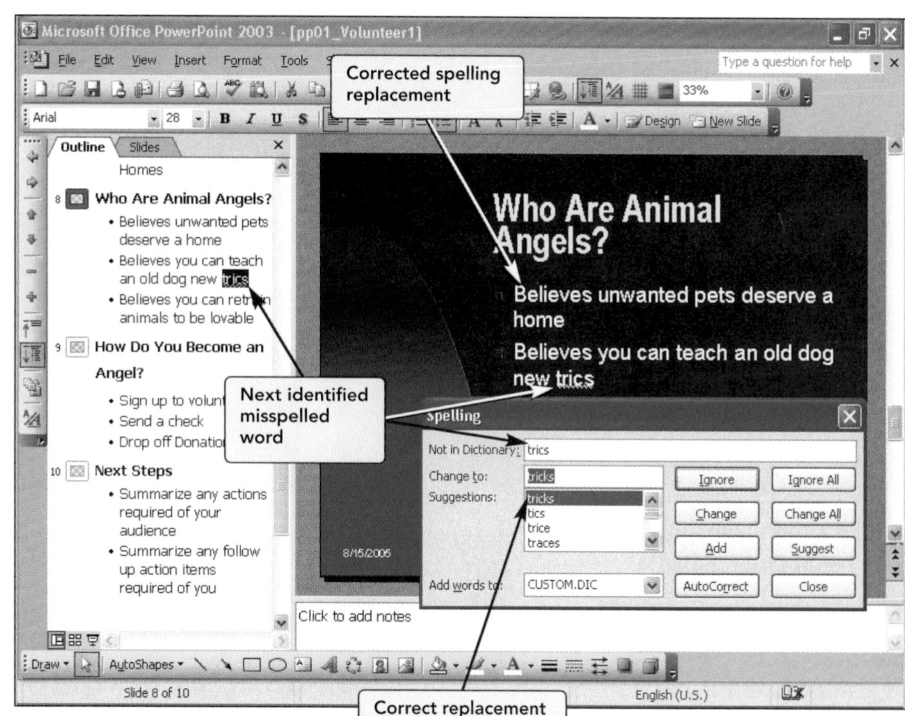

Figure 1.37

The corrected replacement is made in the slide. After the Spelling dialog box is open, the spelling checker continues to check the entire presentation for spelling errors. The next misspelled word, "trics," is identified. In this case, the suggested replacement is correct.

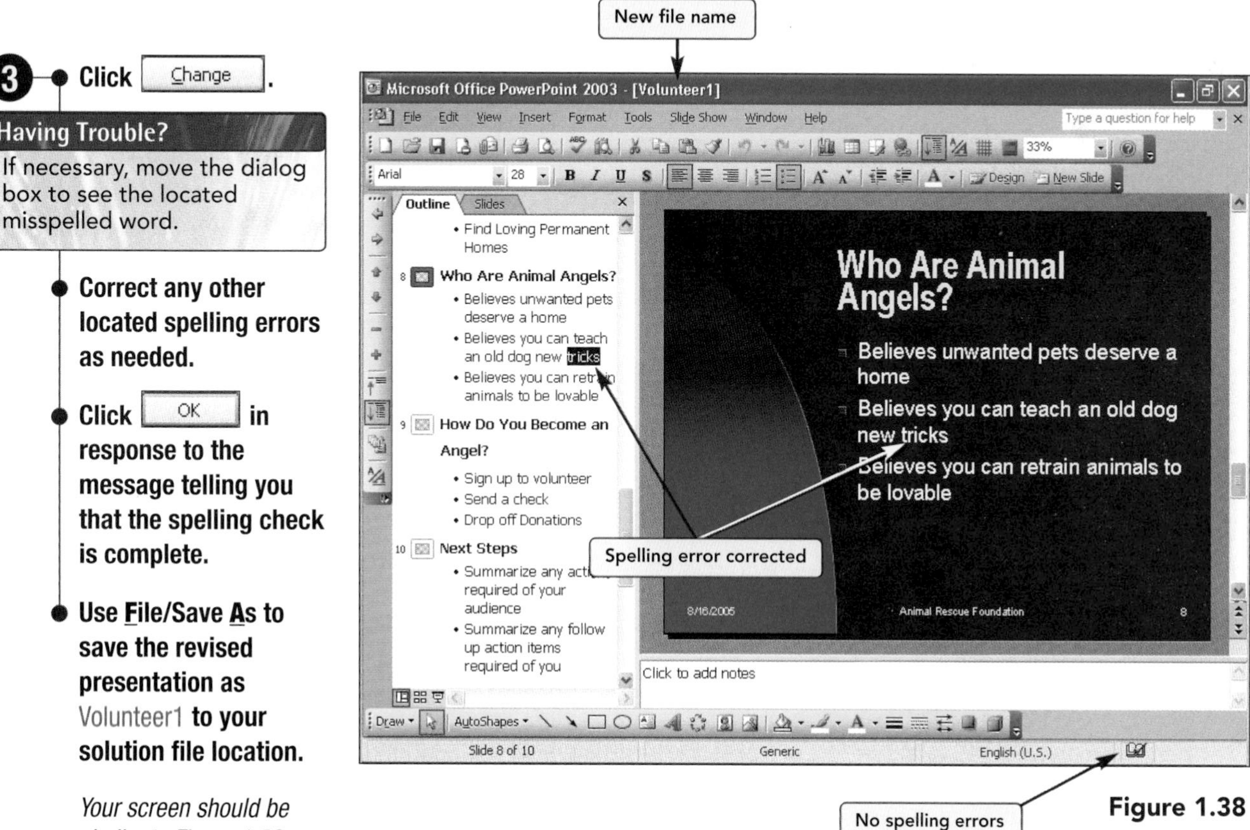

3 **Click** Change**.**

Having Trouble?

If necessary, move the dialog box to see the located misspelled word.

Correct any other located spelling errors as needed.

Click OK **in response to the message telling you that the spelling check is complete.**

Use File/Save As to save the revised presentation as Volunteer1 **to your solution file location.**

Your screen should be similar to Figure 1.38

Figure 1.38

Working with Slides

To get a better overall picture of all slides in the presentation, you will switch to Slide Sorter view.

1 • **Click [icon] Slide Sorter view.**

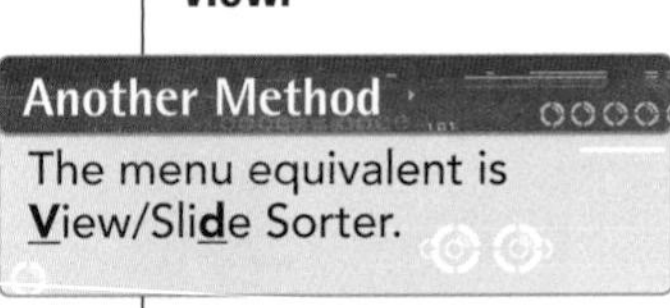

Another Method

The menu equivalent is View/Slide Sorter.

• **If necessary, move the Slide Sorter toolbar below the Standard toolbar.**

Having Trouble?

If the Slide Sorter toolbar is not displayed, select it from the toolbar shortcut menu and display it below the Standard toolbar.

Your screen should be similar to Figure 1.39

Having Trouble?

Do not be concerned if your screen displays a different number of slides per row. This is a function of your monitor settings.

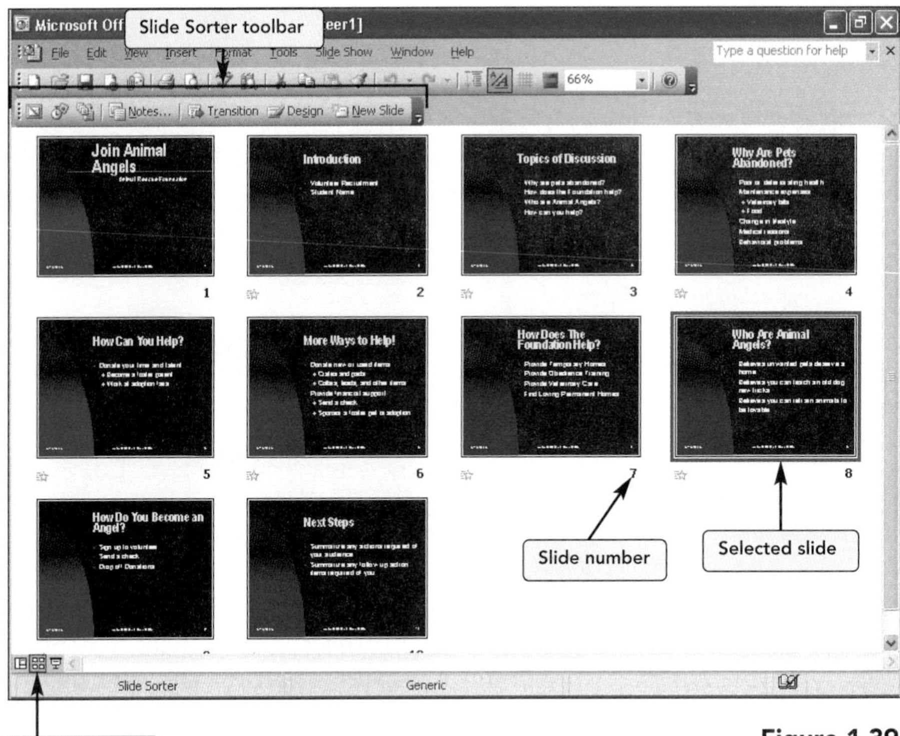

Figure 1.39

Viewing the slides side by side helps you see how your presentation flows. You can now see that slides 7 and 8 are out of order and do not follow the sequence of topics in the Topics for Discussion slide. You also see that you need to delete slide 10. As you continue to look at the slides, you also decide the second slide does not really add much to the presentation and you want to delete it.

This view also displays the Slide Sorter toolbar that is used to add enhancements to your presentation. The Formatting toolbar is not displayed because you cannot format slides in this view.

Deleting Slides

First you will delete slide 10 and then slide 2.

1 **Select slide 10.**

Having Trouble?

Clicking on a slide selects it.

- **Press Delete.**
- **In the same manner, select and delete slide 2.**

Another Method

The menu equivalent is Edit/Delete Slide.

Your screen should be similar to Figure 1.40

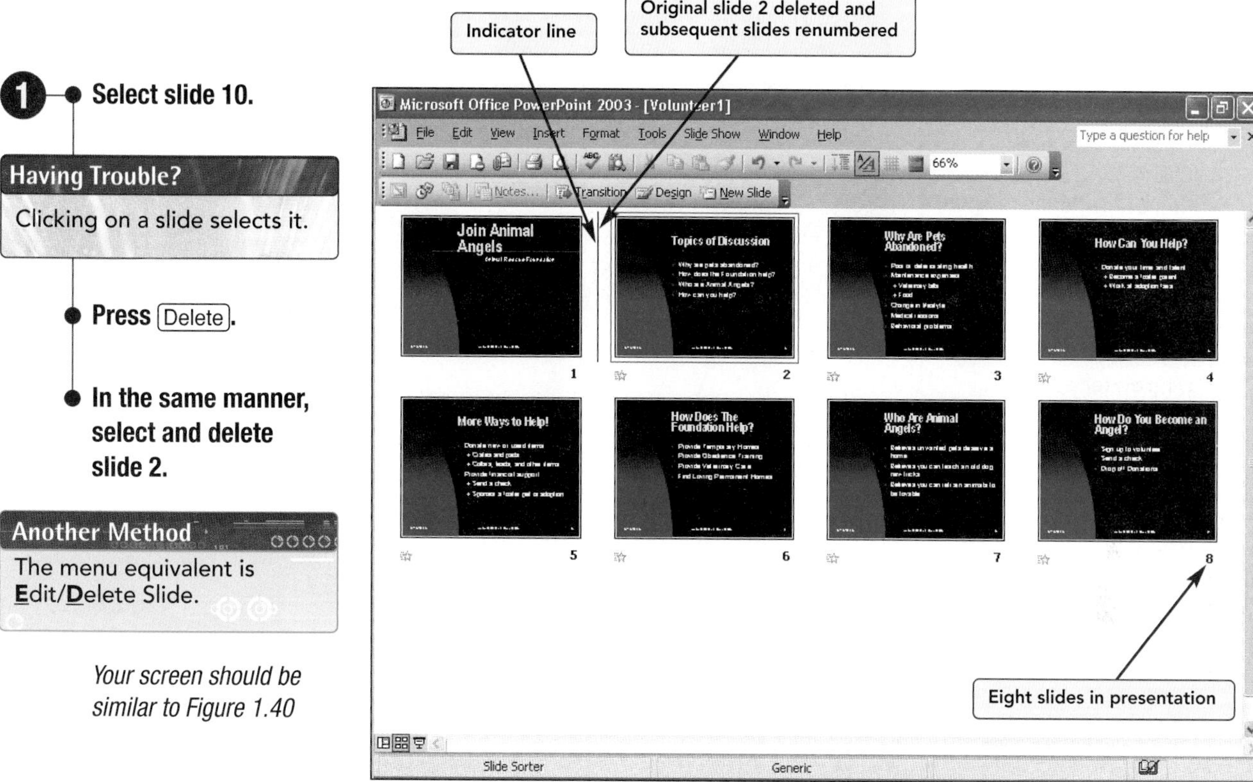

Figure 1.40

The slides have been deleted, and all remaining slides have been appropriately renumbered. An indicator line appears between slides 1 and 2 where the deleted slide once existed.

Moving Slides

Now you want to correct the organization of the slides by moving slide 6, How Does the Foundation Help?, and slide 7, Who Are Animal Angels?, before slide 4, How Can You Help?. To reorder a slide in Slide Sorter view, you drag it to its new location using drag and drop. As you drag the mouse, an indicator line appears to show you where the slide will appear in the presentation. When the indicator line is located where you want the slide to be placed, release the mouse button. You will select both slides and move them at the same time.

1 Select slide 6.

- Hold down Ctrl and click on slide 7.
- Point to either selected slide and drag the mouse until the indicator line is displayed before slide 4.

Additional Information

The mouse pointer appears as [pointer icon] when you drag to move a slide.

- Release the mouse button.

Another Method

You can also use the Edit/Cut and Edit/Paste commands to move slides in Slide Sorter view or the voice commands "Cut" and "Paste."

Your screen should be similar to Figure 1.41

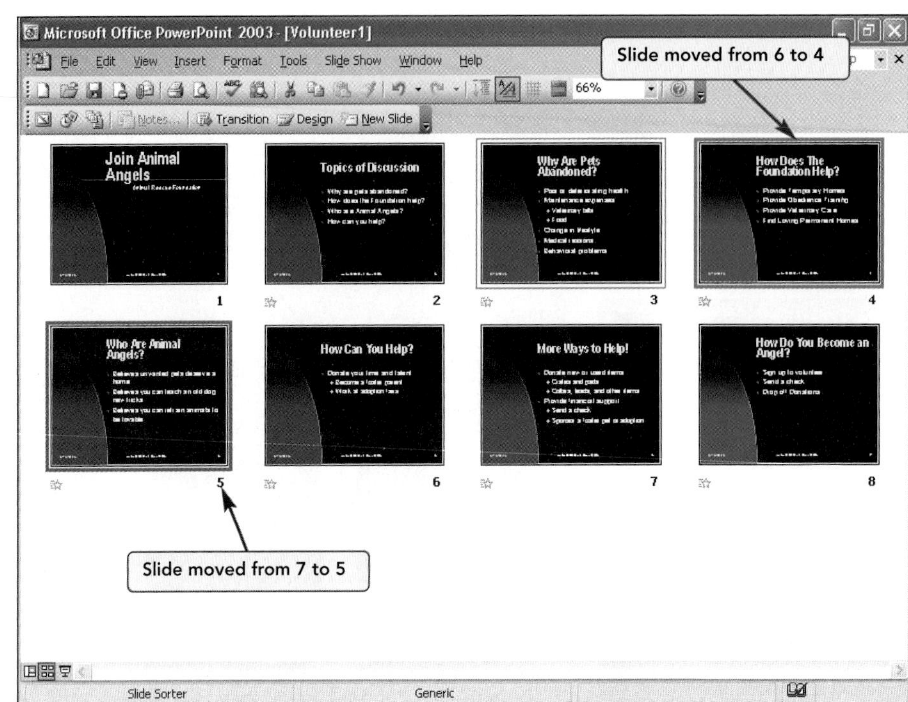

Figure 1.41

The slides now appear in the order you want them.

Inserting Slides

During your discussion with the Foundation director, it was suggested that you add a slide showing the history of the organization. To include this information in the presentation, you will insert a new slide after slide 4.

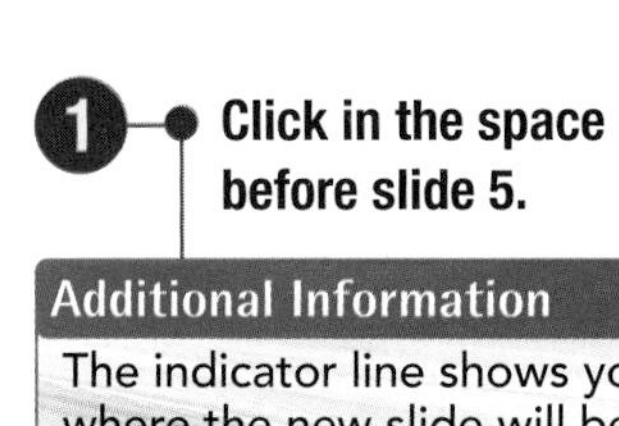

Click in the space before slide 5.

Additional Information

The indicator line shows you where the new slide will be added.

Click New Slide.

Another Method

The menu equivalent is **I**nsert/**N**ew Slide, the keyboard shortcut is Ctrl + M and the voice command is "New slide."

Your screen should be similar to Figure 1.42

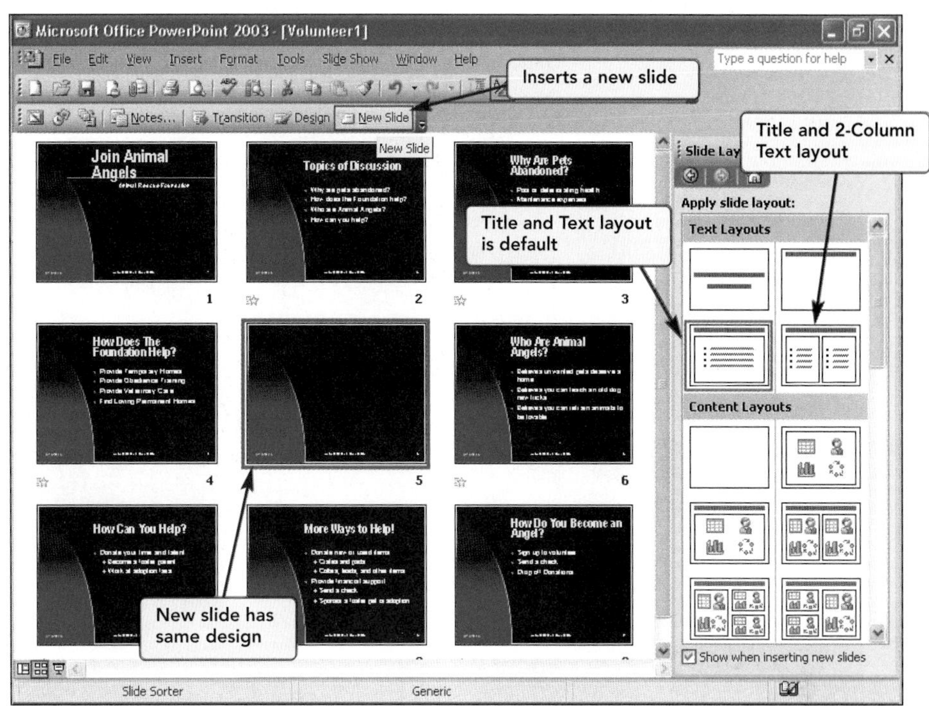

Figure 1.42

A blank new slide is inserted. It has the same design elements as the other slides in the presentation.

Selecting the Slide Layout

The Slide Layout task pane is automatically displayed so that you can select a slide layout for the new slide.

Concept 6

Layout

6 The **layout** controls the way items are arranged on a slide. A layout contains placeholders for the different items such as bulleted text, titles, charts, and so on. PowerPoint includes 27 predefined layouts that can be selected and applied to slides. For example, there are text layouts that include placeholders for a title and bulleted text, and content layouts that include placeholders for a table, diagram, chart, or clip art.

You can change the layout of an existing slide by selecting a new layout. If the new layout does not include placeholders for objects that are already on your slide (for example, if you created a chart and the new layout does not include a chart placeholder), you do not lose the information. All objects remain on the slide and the selected layout is automatically adjusted by adding the appropriate type of placeholder for the object. Alternatively, as you add new objects to a slide, the layout automatically adjusts by adding the appropriate type of placeholder. You can also rearrange, size, and format placeholders on a slide any way you like to customize the slide's appearance.

To make creating slides easy, use the predefined layouts. The layouts help you keep your presentation format consistent and, therefore, more professional.

The Slide Layout task pane displays examples of the 27 layout designs organized into four categories. Pointing to a layout displays the layout name in a ScreenTip. The default layout, Title and Text, is selected.

Because this slide will contain two columns of text about the history of the organization, you will use the two-column text layout.

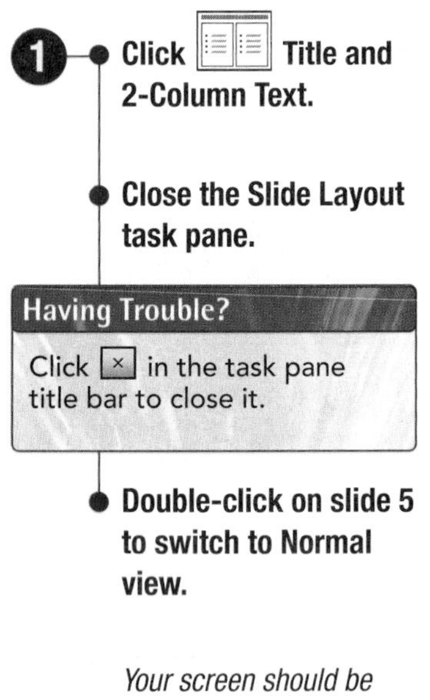

1 **Click Title and 2-Column Text.**

Close the Slide Layout task pane.

Having Trouble?

Click ☒ in the task pane title bar to close it.

Double-click on slide 5 to switch to Normal view.

Your screen should be similar to Figure 1.43

Additional Information

The layout of an existing slide can be changed using Format/Slide Layout.

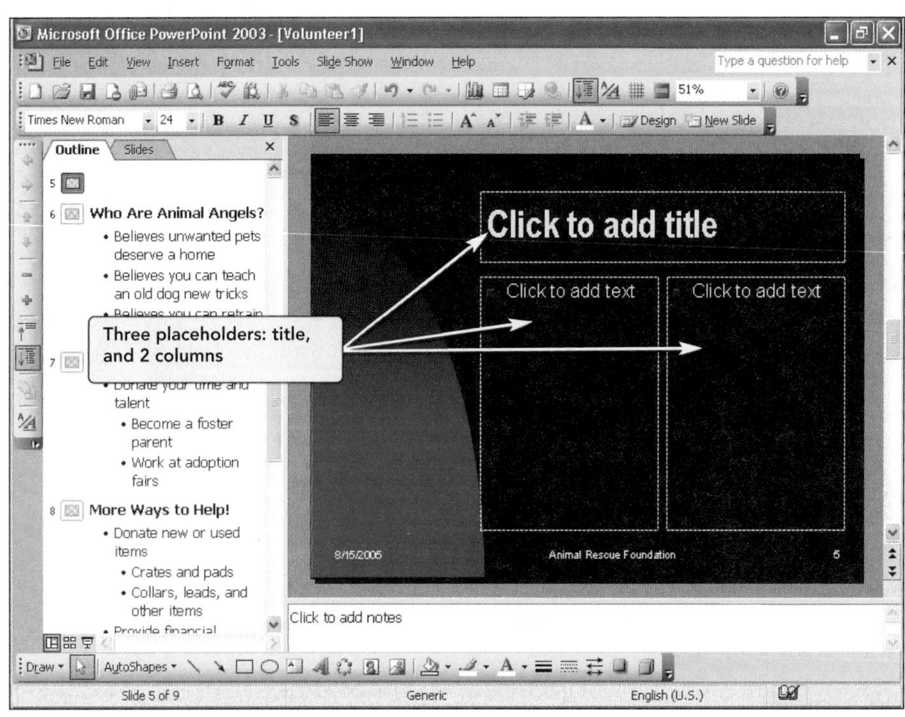

Figure 1.43

The slide displays the three placeholders created by the two-column text layout. Next, you will add text to the slide presenting a brief history of the Animal Rescue Foundation. First, you will enter the slide title and then the list of dates and events.

2

- Click in the title placeholder.
- Type **Animal Rescue Foundation History.**
- Click in the left text placeholder.
- Type **Year.**
- Press ←Enter.
- Continue entering the information shown below. Remember to press ←Enter to create a new line.

  1990

  1991

  1997

  2003
- In the same manner, enter the following text in the right text placeholder:

  Event

  Founded by Ed Wilton

  Built first shelter

  Began volunteer program

  Expanded to 10 shelters

Your screen should be similar to Figure 1.44

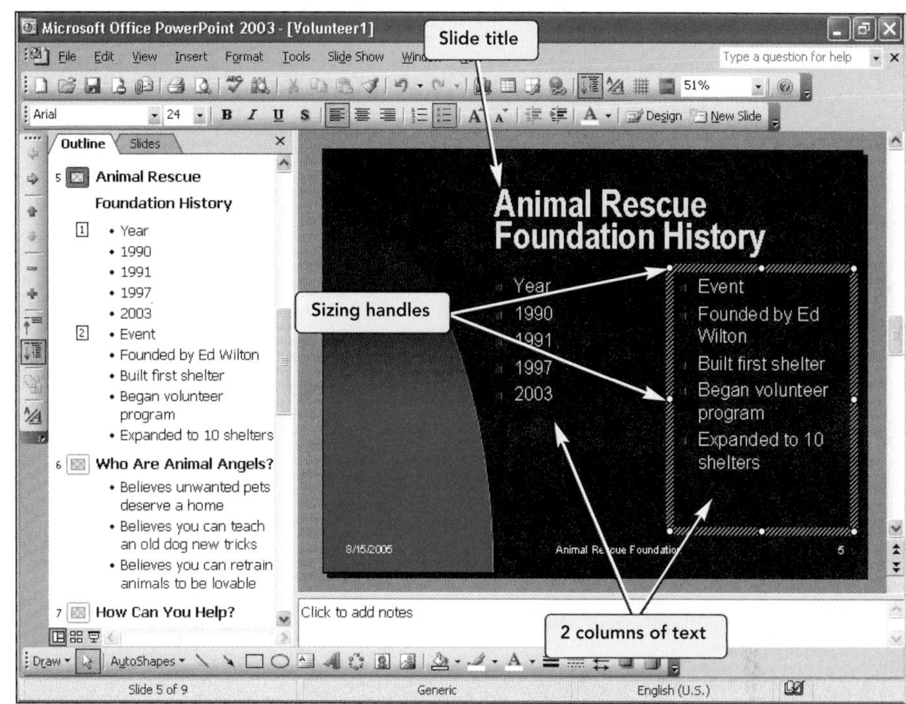

Figure 1.44

The left placeholder is too big for its contents, and the right placeholder is too small. To correct the size, you can adjust the size of the placeholders.

Sizing a Placeholder

The eight boxes in the selection rectangle are **sizing handles** that can be used to adjust the size of the placeholder. Dragging the corner sizing handles will adjust both the height and width at the same time, whereas the center handles adjust the side borders to which they are associated. When you point to the sizing handle, the mouse pointer appears as ↔ indicating the direction in which you can drag the border to adjust the size.

1 On the right text placeholder, drag the left-center sizing handle to the left until each item appears on a single line (see Figure 1.45).

Select the left text placeholder and drag the right-center sizing handle to the left (see Figure 1.45).

Your screen should be similar to Figure 1.45

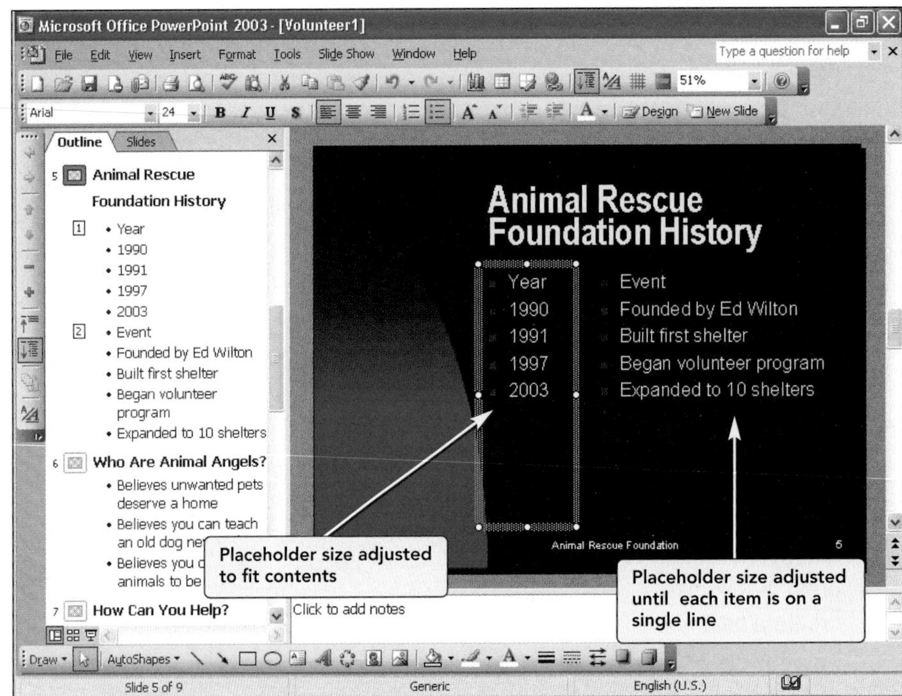

Figure 1.45

Moving a Placeholder

Next, you want to move the Year column placeholder closer to the Event column. Then you want to move both placeholders so they appear more centered in the space. An object can be moved anywhere on a slide by dragging the selection rectangle. The mouse pointer appears as ✥ when you can move a placeholder. You will select both placeholders and move them at the same time. As you drag the placeholder a dotted outline is displayed to show your new location.

1

- Point to the Year column selection rectangle (not a handle) and drag the selected placeholder to the right, closer to the Event column.
- With the left placeholder still selected, hold down Ctrl while clicking on the right placeholder to select both.
- Drag the selected placeholders to the left to their new location (see Figure 1.46).
- Save your changes to the presentation using the same file name.

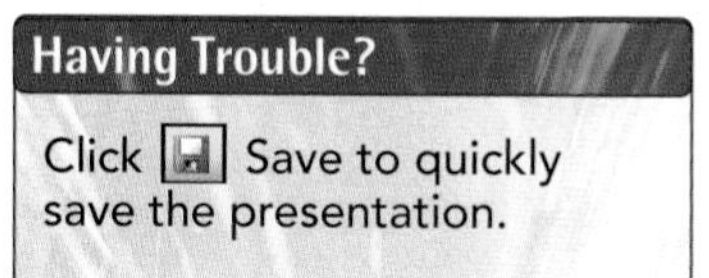

Having Trouble?

Click Save to quickly save the presentation.

Your screen should be similar to Figure 1.46

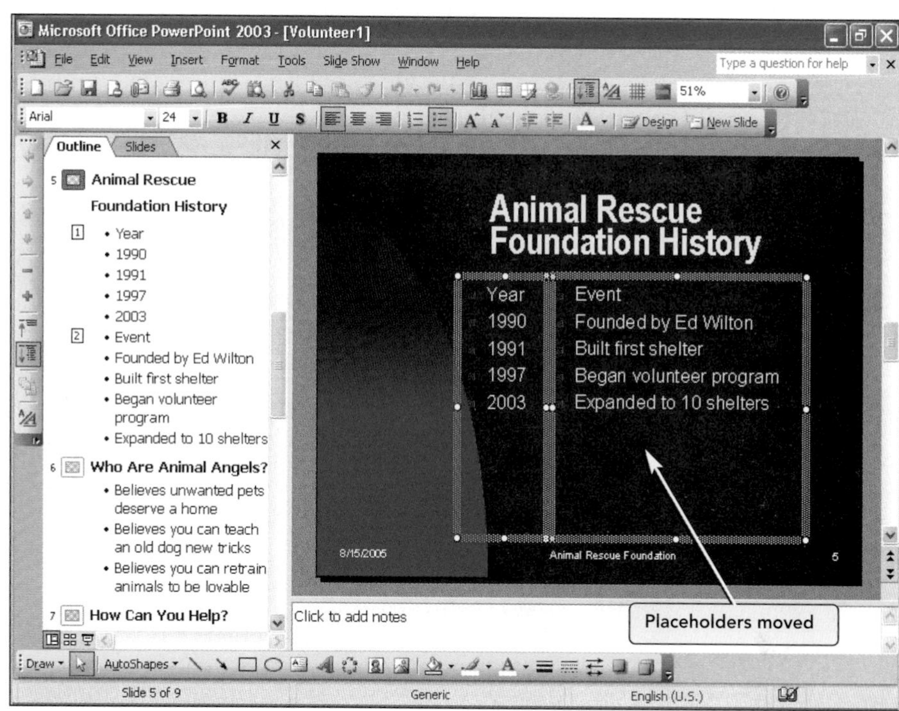

Figure 1.46

Rehearsing a Presentation

Now that the slides are in the order you want, you would like to see how the presentation would look when viewed by an audience. Rather than set up the presentation as you would to present it for an audience, a simple way to rehearse a presentation is to view it electronically on your screen as a slide show. A **slide show** displays each slide full screen and in order. While the slide show is running, you can plan what you want to say to supplement the information provided on the slides.

Using Slide Show View

When you view a slide show, each slide fills the screen, hiding the PowerPoint application window, so you can view the slides as your audience would. You will begin the slide show starting with the first slide.

Additional Information

Using [Slide Show button] starts the slide show beginning with the currently selected slide.

Another Method

The menu equivalent is View/Slide Show and the voice command is "View show." Using these methods starts the slide show beginning with the first slide in the presentation.

Your screen should be similar to Figure 1.47

Figure 1.47

The presentation title slide is displayed full screen, as it will appear when projected on a screen using computer projection equipment. The easiest way to see the next slide is to click the mouse button. You can also use the keys shown below to move to the next or previous slide.

Additional Information

Pressing F1 while in Slide Show opens a Help window describing the actions you can use during the slide show.

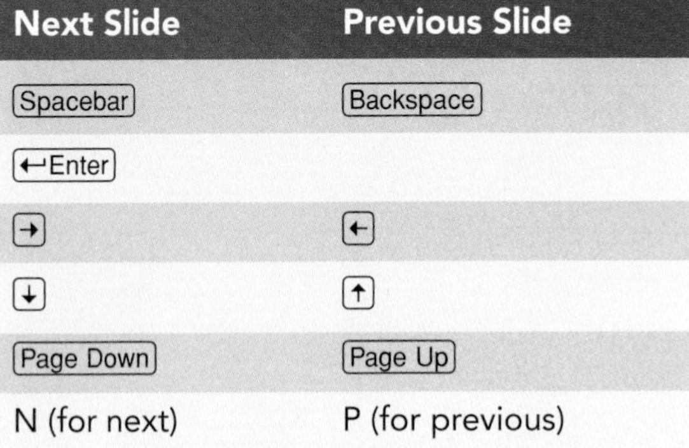

Next Slide	Previous Slide
Spacebar	Backspace
←Enter	
→	←
↓	↑
Page Down	Page Up
N (for next)	P (for previous)

You can also select **N**ext, **P**revious, or Last **V**iewed from the shortcut menu. Additionally, moving the mouse pointer in Slide Show displays the Slide Show toolbar in the lower left corner of the window. Clicking [previous button] or [next button] moves to the previous or next slide and [menu button] opens the shortcut menu.

Slide Show toolbar

2

- Click to display the next slide.
- Using each of the methods described, slowly display the entire presentation.
- When the last slide displays a black window, click again to end the slide show.

Additional Information

You can press Esc or use End Show on the shortcut menu at any time to end the slide show.

Your screen should be similar to Figure 1.48

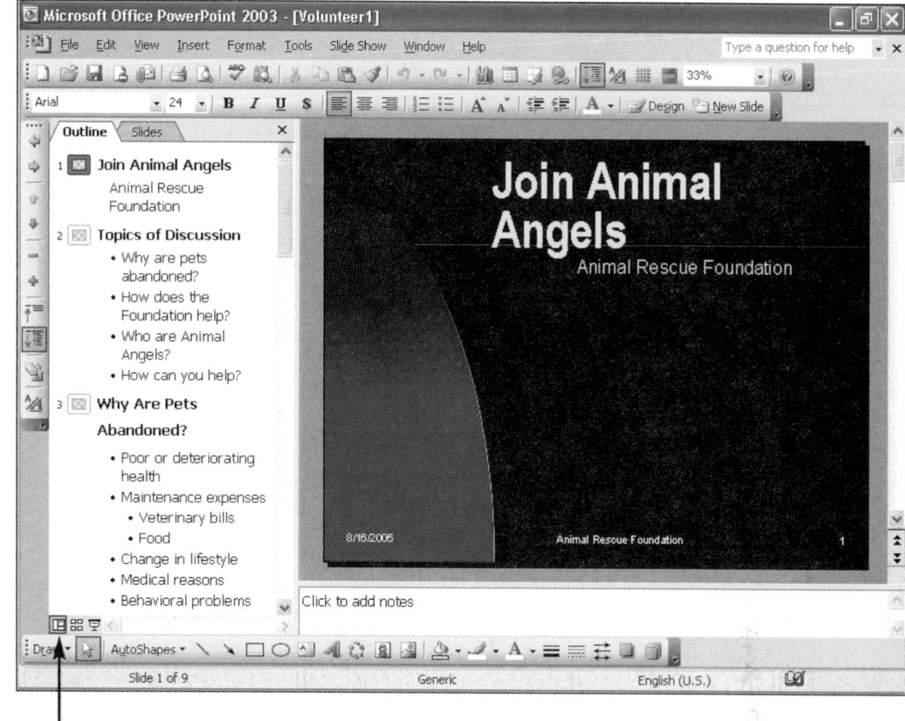

Figure 1.48

After the last slide is displayed, the program returns to the view you were last using, in this case Normal view.

Formatting Slide Text

While looking at the slide show, you decide that the title slide needs to have more impact. You also want to remove the bullets from the items on the history slide. Enhancing the appearance of the slide to make it more readable or attractive is called **formatting**. The default design template already includes many basic formatting features.

Applying different formatting to characters and paragraphs can greatly enhance the appearance of the slide. **Character formatting** features affect the selected characters only. They include changing the character style and size, applying effects such as bold and italics, changing the character spacing, and adding animated text effects. **Paragraph formatting** features affect an entire paragraph. A paragraph is text that has a carriage return from pressing ←Enter at the end of it. Each item in a bulleted list, title, and subtitle is a paragraph. Paragraph formatting features include the position of the paragraph or its alignment between the margins, paragraph indentation, spacing above and below a paragraph, and line spacing within a paragraph.

Changing Fonts

First, you will improve the appearance of the presentation title by changing the font of the title text.

Concept 7

Font and Font Size

7 A **font**, also commonly referred to as a **typeface**, is a set of characters with a specific design. The designs have names such as Times New Roman and Courier. Using fonts as a design element can add interest to your presentation and give your audience visual cues to help them find information quickly.

There are two basic types of fonts: serif and sans serif. **Serif** fonts have a flair at the base of each letter that visually leads the reader to the next letter. Two common serif fonts are Roman and Times New Roman. Serif fonts generally are used for text in paragraphs. **Sans serif** fonts do not have a flair at the base of each letter. Arial and Helvetica are two common sans serif fonts. Because sans serif fonts have a clean look, they are often used for headings in documents. It is good practice to use only two or three different fonts in a presentation because too many can distract from your presentation content and can look unprofessional.

Each font has one or more sizes. Font size is the height and width of the character and is commonly measured in **points**, abbreviated pt. One point equals about 1/72 inch, and text in most documents is 10 pt or 12 pt.

Several common fonts in different sizes are shown in the following table.

Font Name	Font Type	Font Size
Arial	Sans serif	This is 10 pt. This is 16 pt.
Courier New	Serif	This is 10 pt. This is 16 pt.
Times New Roman	Serif	This is 10 pt. This is 16 pt.

To change the font before typing the text, use the command and then type. All text will appear in the specified setting until another font setting is selected. To change a font setting for existing text, select the text you want to change and then use the command. If you want to apply font formatting to a word, simply move the insertion point to the word and the formatting is automatically applied to the entire word.

1 **Select the text "Join Animal Angels" in the slide pane.**

Additional Information

The font used in the title is Arial Narrow, as displayed in the Arial Narrow button.

- **Open the Arial Narrow Font drop-down list.**

- **Scroll the list and choose Comic Sans MS.**

Another Method

The menu equivalent is Format/Font/Font.

Your screen should be similar to Figure 1.49

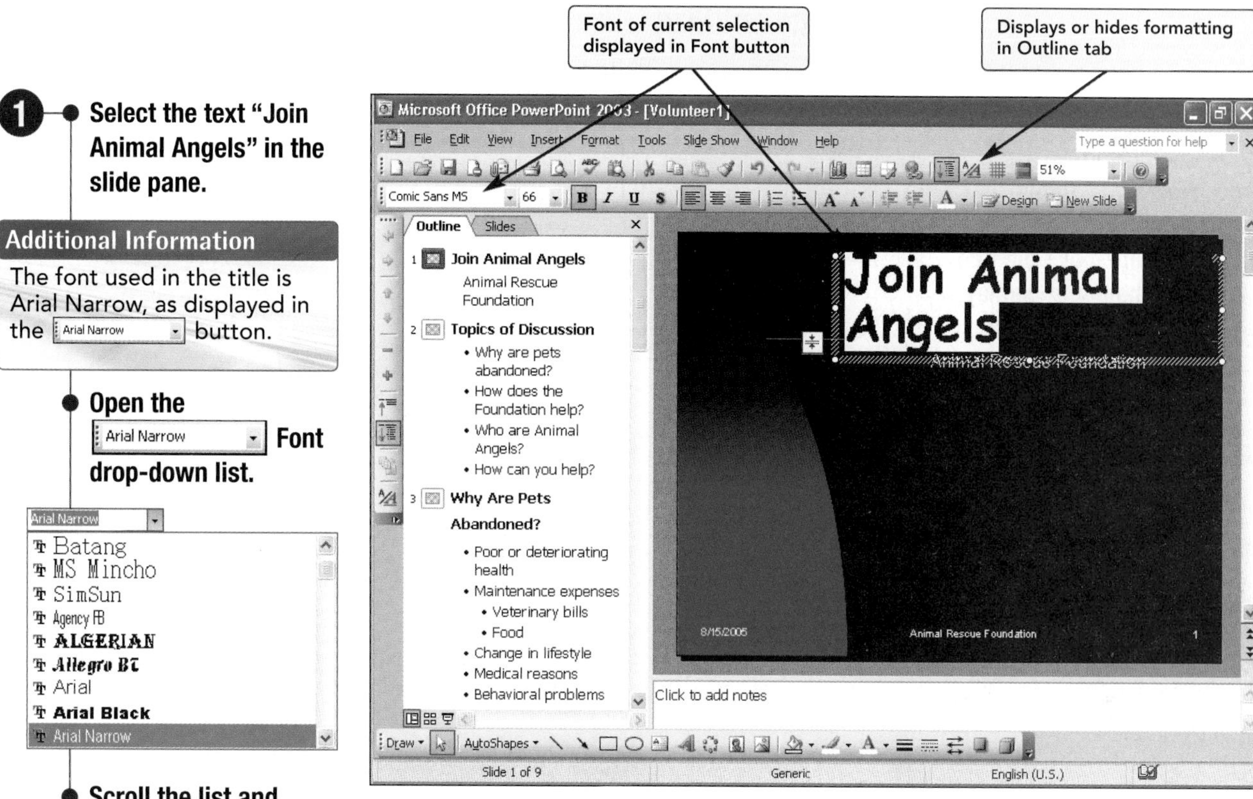

Figure 1.49

Additional Information

You can show or hide the text formatting in the Outline tab using Show Formatting.

The text has changed to the new font style, and the Font button displays the font name used in the current selection. The formatting effects appear in the slide pane but are not displayed in the Outline tab.

Changing Font Size

The title text is also a little larger than you want it to be.

1 **Click Decrease Font Size 2 times.**

- **Size and move the title placeholder to display the title on one line above the red graphic line.**

Additional Information

Use Increase Font Size to incrementally increase the point size of selected text.

Another Method

You could also specify the point size from the 18 Font Size drop-down list or use Format/Font/Size.

Your screen should be similar to Figure 1.50

Additional Information

If a selection includes text in several different sizes, the smallest size appears in the Font Size button followed by a + sign.

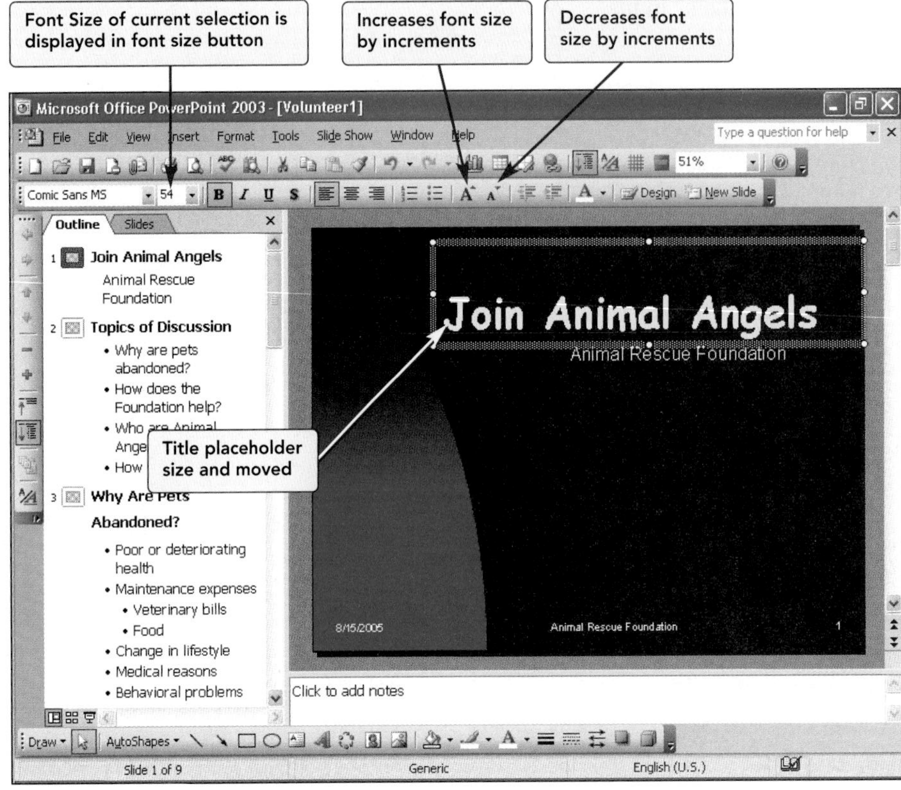

Figure 1.50

The Font Size button displays the point size of the current selection.

2 **Replace the subtitle text with your name.**

- **Reduce the size of the subtitle placeholder to fit the contents.**

Having Trouble?

Drag the sizing handles to size the placeholder.

- **Move the placeholder to the location shown in Figure 1.51.**

Your screen should be similar to Figure 1.51

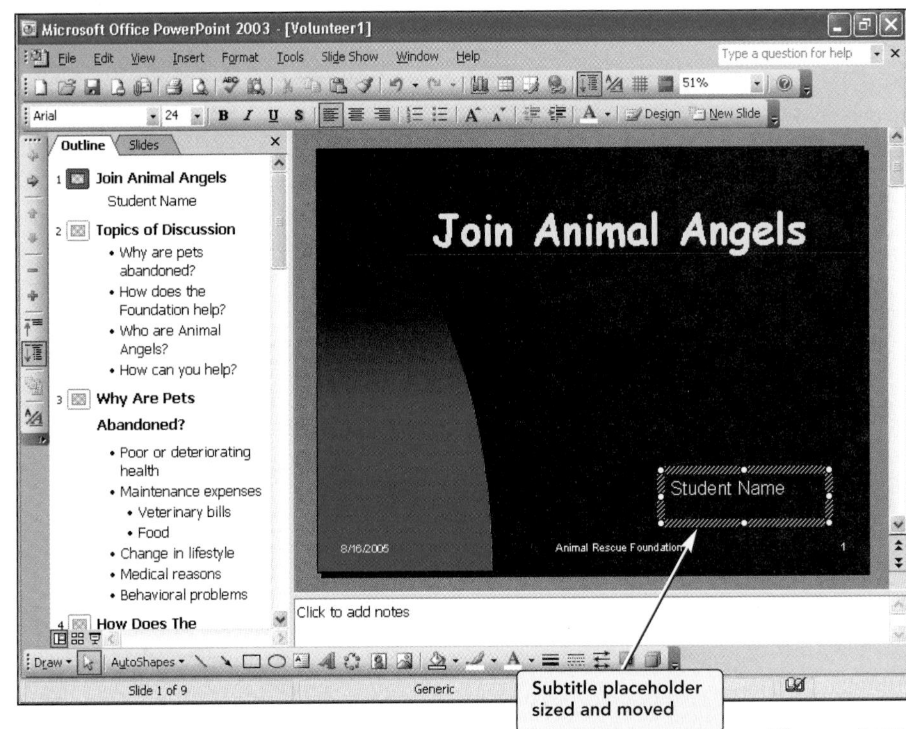

Figure 1.51

Adding and Removing Bullets

Next, you want to remove the bullets from the items on the history slide. You can quickly apply and remove bullets using Bullets on the Formatting toolbar. This button applies the bullet style associated with the design template you are using. Because the placeholder items already include bullets, using this button will remove them.

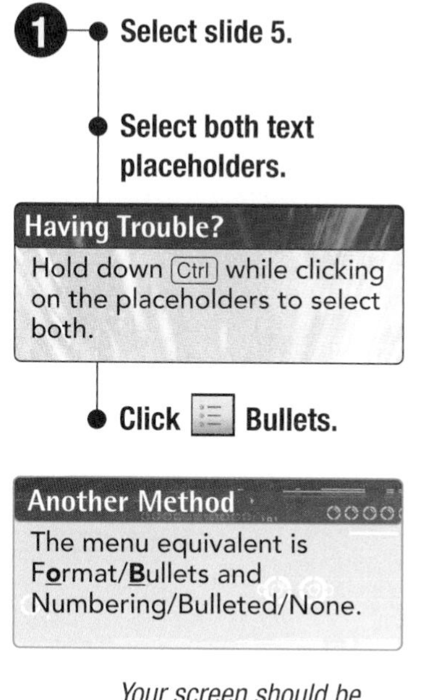

1 **Select slide 5.**

Select both text placeholders.

Having Trouble?

Hold down Ctrl while clicking on the placeholders to select both.

Click Bullets.

Another Method

The menu equivalent is Format/Bullets and Numbering/Bulleted/None.

Your screen should be similar to Figure 1.52

Applies or removes bullets

Bullets removed from items in both placeholders

Figure 1.52

The bullets are removed from all the items in both placeholders. Now, however, you think it would look better to add bullets back to the four items under each column heading.

2

- **Select the four years in the left column.**
- **Click Bullets.**
- **Apply bullets to the four events in the right column.**
- **Click outside the selected object to deselect it.**
- **Save the presentation again.**

Your screen should be similar to Figure 1.53

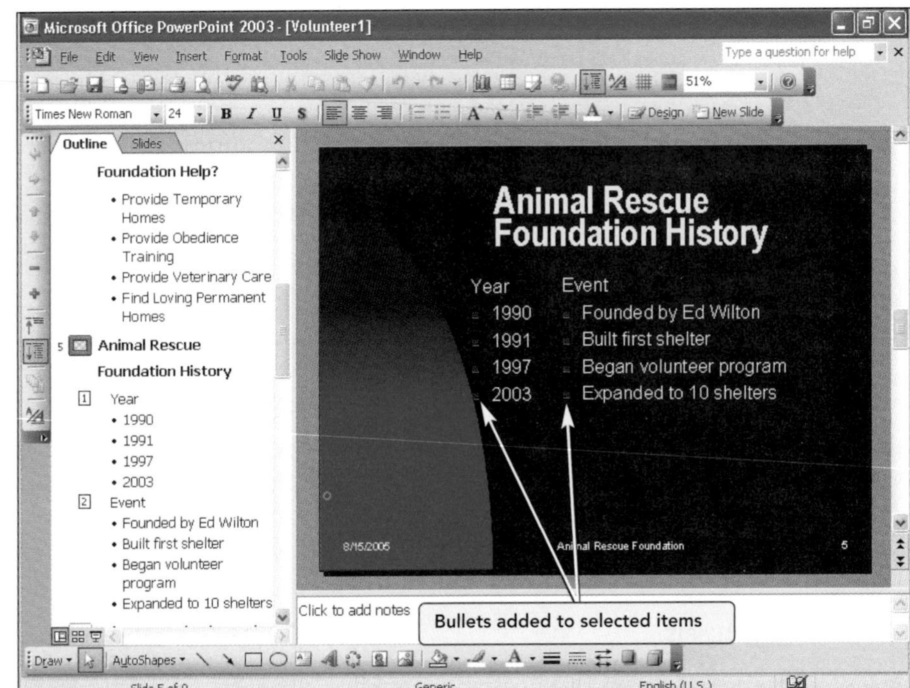

Figure 1.53

Bullets appear before the selected text items only.

Working with Graphics

Finally, you want to add a picture to the title slide. A picture is one of several different graphic objects that can be added to a slide.

Concept 8

Graphics

8 A **graphic** is a non-text element or object, such as a drawing or picture, that can be added to a slide. A graphic can be a simple **drawing object** consisting of shapes such as lines and boxes that can be created using features on the Drawing toolbar. A drawing object is part of your presentation document. A **picture** is an image such as a graphic illustration or a scanned photograph. Pictures are graphics that were created from another program and are inserted in a slide as embedded objects. An **embedded object** becomes part of the presentation file and can be opened and edited using the **source program**, the program in which it was created. Several examples of drawing objects and pictures are shown below.

Add graphics to your presentation to help the audience understand concepts, to add interest, and to make your presentation stand out from others.

Photograph

Clip Art

Drawing Object

Inserting a Graphic from the Clip Organizer

Additional Information

You can also scan a picture and insert it directly into a slide without saving it as a file first.

You want to add a graphic to the slide below the title line. Graphic files can be obtained from a variety of sources. Many simple drawings called **clip art** are available in the Clip Organizer that comes with Office 2003. The Clip Organizer's files, or clips, include art, sound, animation, and movies you can add to a presentation.

You can also create graphic files using a scanner to convert any printed document, including photographs, to an electronic format. Most images that are scanned and inserted into documents are stored as Windows bitmap files (.bmp). All types of graphics, including clip art, photographs, and other types of images, can be found on the Internet. These files are commonly stored as .jpg or .pcx files. Keep in mind that any images you locate on the Internet may be protected by copyright and should only be used with permission. You can also purchase CDs containing graphics for your use.

You decide to check the Clip Organizer to find a suitable graphic.

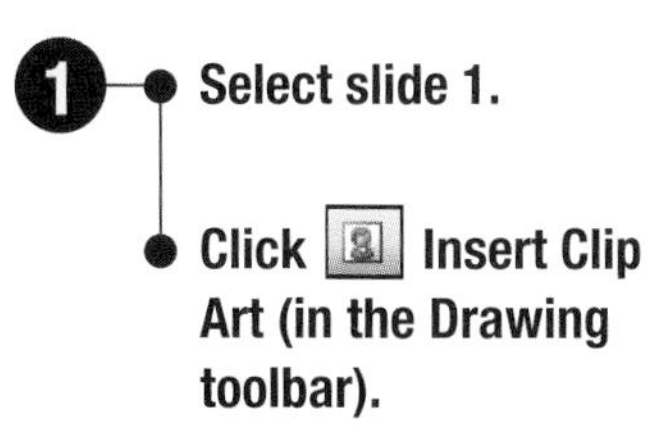

1 **Select slide 1.**

Click Insert Clip Art (in the Drawing toolbar).

Another Method

The menu equivalent is Insert/Picture/Clip Art. You could also display the Getting Started task pane and select Clip Art from the task pane menu.

Your screen should be similar to Figure 1.54

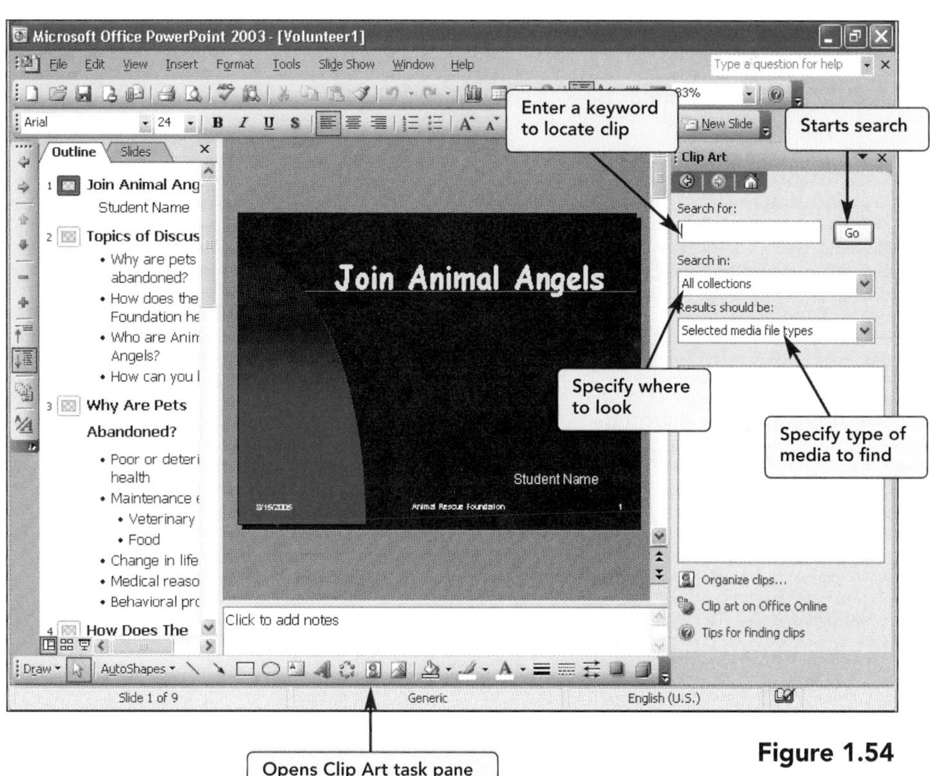

Figure 1.54

Additional Information

You can also insert graphics directly from files on your computer using Insert/Picture/From File.

The Clip Art task pane appears in which you can enter a keyword, a word or phrase that is descriptive of the type of graphic you want to locate. The graphics in the Clip Organizer are organized by topic and are identified with several keywords that describe the graphic. You can also specify the locations to search and the type of media files, such as clip art, movies, photographs or sound, to display in the search results. You want to find clip art and photographs of animals.

2

- **If necessary, select any existing text in the Search For text box.**
- **In the Search for text box, type animal.**
- **If All Collections is not displayed in the Search In text box, select Everywhere from the drop-down list.**
- **Open the Results Should Be drop-down list.**
- **Select Photographs and Clip Art and deselect Movies and Sounds.**

Having Trouble?

Click the box next to an option to select or deselect (clear the checkmark).

- **Click outside the drop-down list to close it.**
- **Click Go.**
- **Point to a thumbnail in the Results area.**

Your screen should be similar to Figure 1.55

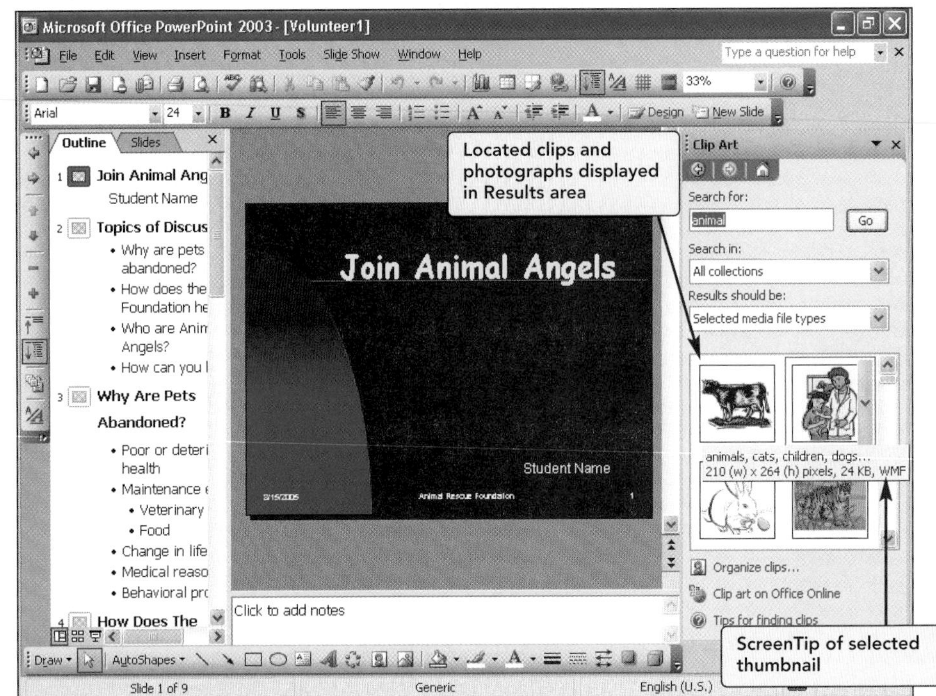

Figure 1.55

The program searches all locations on your computer and, if you have an Internet connection established, searches Microsoft's Clip Art and Media Web site for clip art and graphics that match your search term. The Results area displays thumbnails of all located graphics. Pointing to a thumbnail displays a ScreenTip containing the **keywords** associated with the picture and information about the picture properties. It also displays a drop-down list bar that accesses the item's shortcut menu.

3 **Scroll the results list to the bottom to view all of the located clips and photographs.**

Your screen should be similar to Figure 1.56

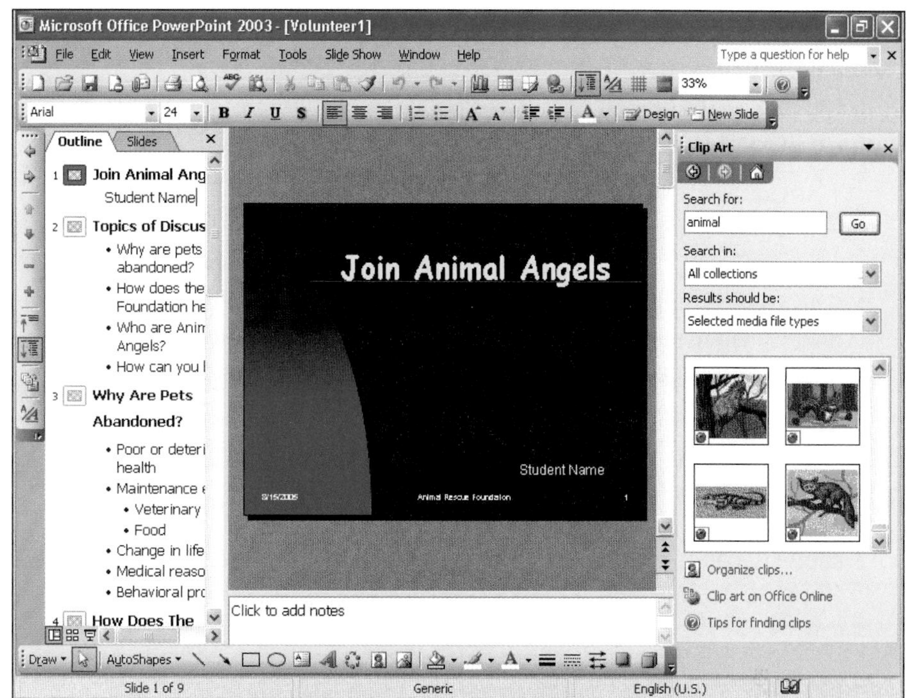

Figure 1.56

Additional Information

Entering keywords separated with a comma requires that either keyword be associated with the graphic and therefore expands the search.

Because so many pictures were located, you decide to narrow your search to display pictures of animals and healthcare only. Adding a second word to your search will narrow the number of graphics located. This is because it requires that both words must be associated with the graphic in order for it to appear in the results. Additionally, because the graphic is sometimes difficult to see, you can preview it in a larger size.

4 Add the word **healthcare** following the word "animal" in the Search For text box.

- Click **Go**.
- If necessary, scroll the results area to see the graphic of two people and a dog.
- Point to the graphic and click ▾ to open the shortcut menu.

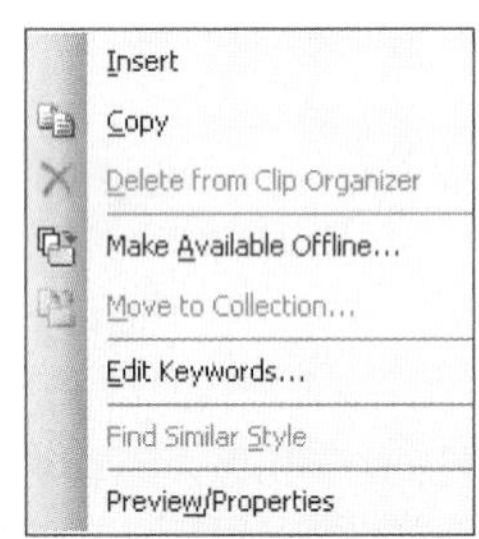

Additional Information

The shortcut menu commands are used to work with and manage the items in the Clip Organizer.

- Choose **Preview/Properties.**

Your screen should be similar to Figure 1.57

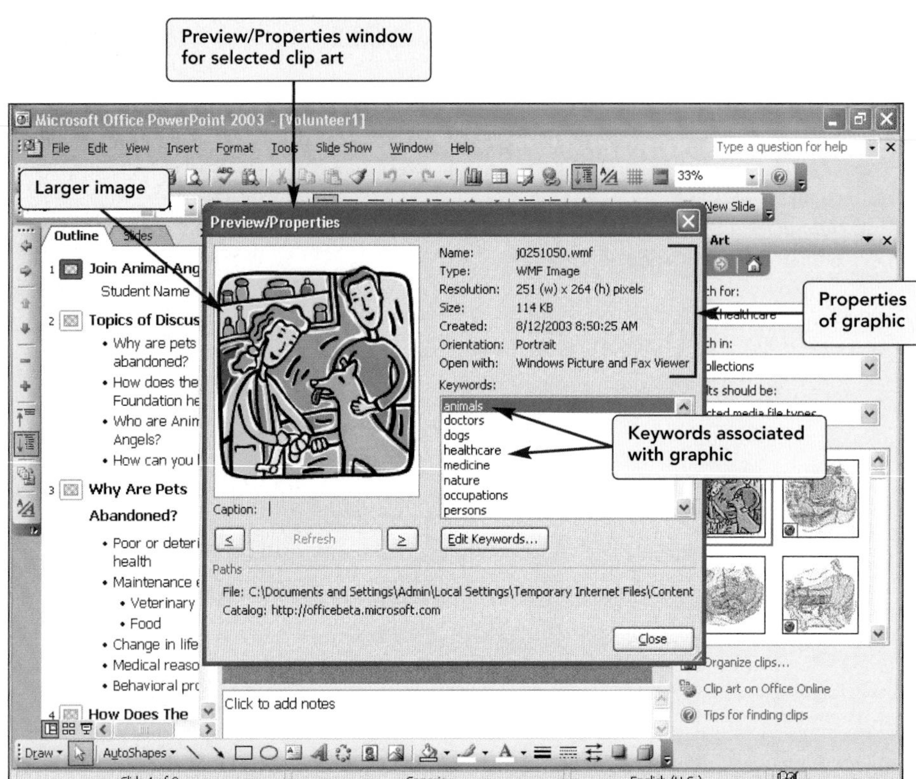

Figure 1.57

Having Trouble?

If this graphic is not available in the Clip Organizer, close the Clip Art task pane and choose Insert/Picture/From File and insert pp01_Animalcare.bmp from your data file location. Skip to below Figure 1.58.

Because the search term is more specific, fewer results are displayed. The Preview/Properties dialog box displays the selected graphic larger so it is easier to see. It also displays more information about the properties associated with the graphic. You can now see that animals and healthcare are both keywords associated with this graphic. You think this looks like a good choice and will insert it into the document.

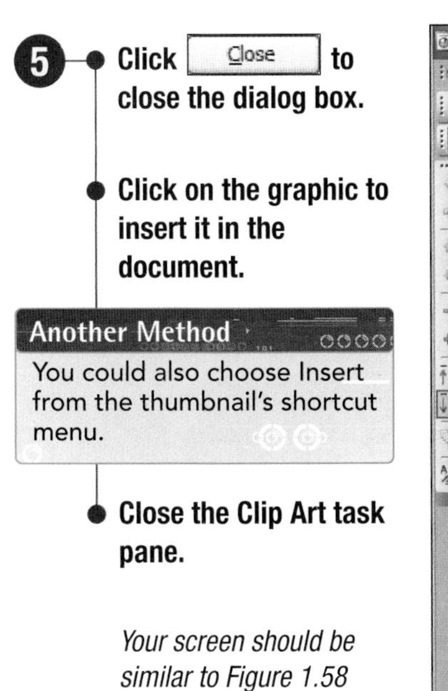

5 Click Close to close the dialog box.

- Click on the graphic to insert it in the document.

Another Method

You could also choose Insert from the thumbnail's shortcut menu.

- Close the Clip Art task pane.

Your screen should be similar to Figure 1.58

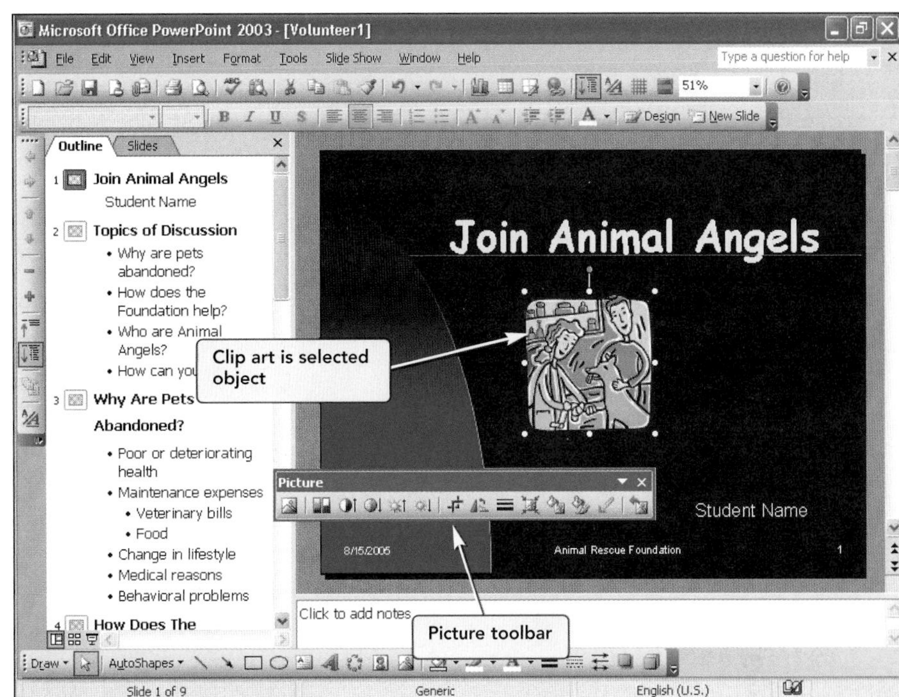

Figure 1.58

The clip art graphic is inserted in the center of the slide. It is a selected object and can be sized and moved like any other selected object. The **Picture toolbar** is also automatically displayed and is used to modify the graphic.

Inserting a Graphic from a File

Although you think this graphic looks good, you want to see how a photograph you recently scanned of a puppy would look instead. The photograph has been saved as pp01_Puppy.jpg.

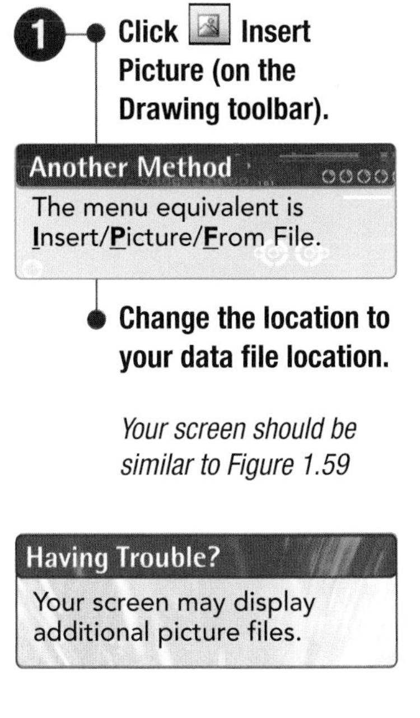

1 Click Insert Picture (on the Drawing toolbar).

Another Method

The menu equivalent is Insert/Picture/From File.

- Change the location to your data file location.

Your screen should be similar to Figure 1.59

Having Trouble?

Your screen may display additional picture files.

Figure 1.59

Having Trouble?

If the thumbnail preview is not displayed, click Views and choose Thumbnails.

The Insert Picture dialog box is similar to the Open and Save dialog boxes, except that the only types of files listed are files with picture file extensions. A thumbnail preview of each picture is displayed above the file name.

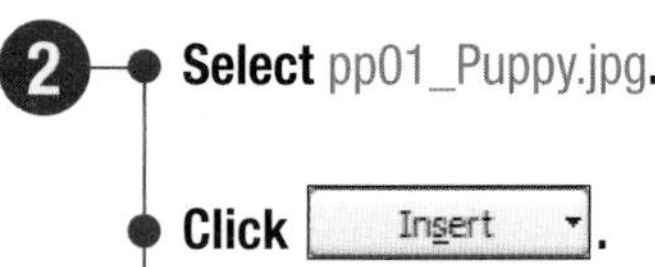

2 **Select** pp01_Puppy.jpg.

Click Insert.

Move the picture to the right to see the underlying clip art.

Your screen should be similar to Figure 1.60

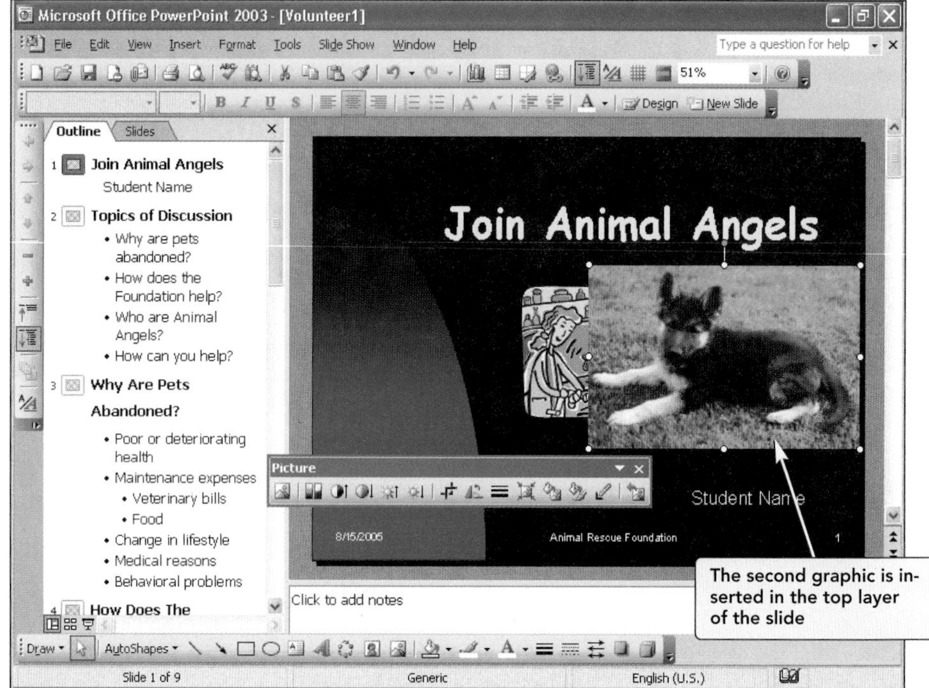

Figure 1.60

The second graphic is inserted on the slide on top of the clip art object. As objects are added to a slide, they automatically stack in individual layers.

Concept 9

Stacking Order

9 **Stacking order** is the order in which objects are inserted into different layers of the slide. As each object is added to the slide, it is added to the top layer. Adding objects to separate layers allows each object to be positioned precisely on the page, including in front of and behind other objects. As objects are stacked in layers, they may overlap. To change the stacking order, open the Draw menu on the Drawing toolbar and select Order.

Additional Information

Sometimes it is easy to lose an object behind another. If this happens, you can press Tab to cycle forward or Shift + Tab to cycle backward through the stacked objects until the one you want is selected.

Because the photograph was the last object added to the slide, it is on the top layer of the stack. Although the photograph looks good, you think the clip art introduces the topic of volunteering better.

3 Click Undo (2 times).

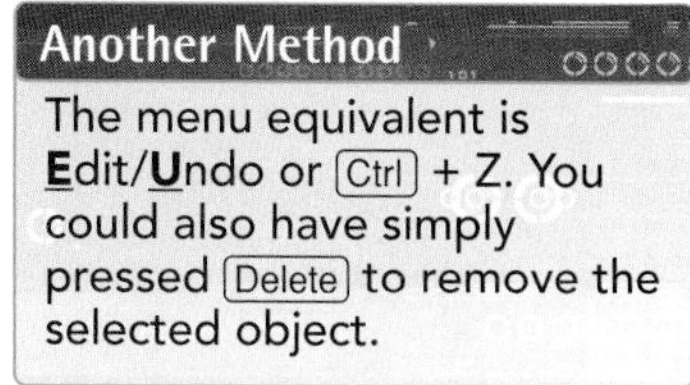

Another Method

The menu equivalent is **E**dit/**U**ndo or Ctrl + Z. You could also have simply pressed Delete to remove the selected object.

Your screen should be similar to Figure 1.61

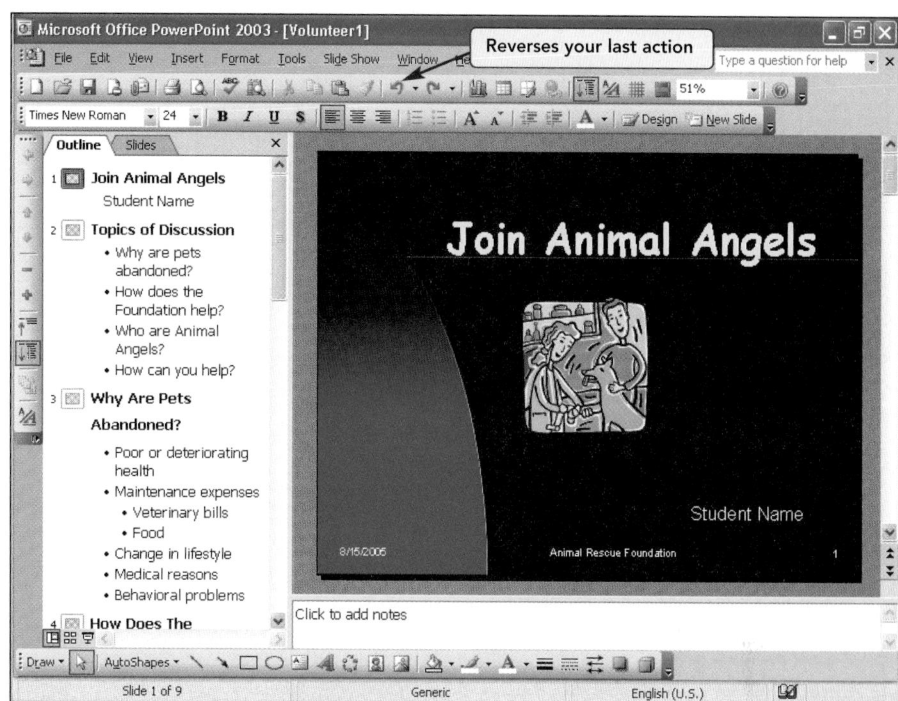

Figure 1.61

Using Undo reverses your last action. Notice that the Undo button includes a drop-down list button. Clicking this button displays a list of the most recent actions that can be reversed, with the most recent action at the top of the list. When you select an action from the drop-down list, you also undo all actions above it in the list.

Sizing and Moving a Graphic

Frequently, when a graphic is inserted, its size or placement will need to be adjusted. A graphic object is sized and moved just like a placeholder. You want to increase the graphic size slightly and position it in the space below the title.

1 Click on the graphic to select it.

Drag the bottom left corner sizing handle to increase its size to that shown in Figure 1.62.

Drag the graphic to position it as shown in Figure 1.62.

Click outside the graphic to deselect it.

Your screen should be similar to Figure 1.62

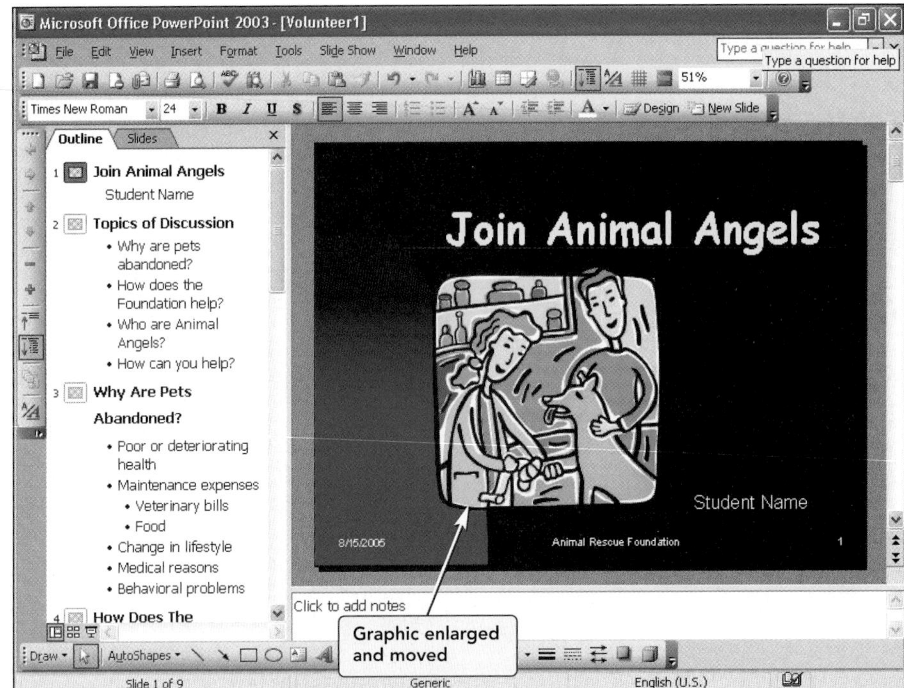

Figure 1.62

Now you think the title slide will make a much better impression. To see how the changes and enhancements you have made to the presentation will look full screen, you will run the slide show again.

2 Save the presentation again.

Run the slide show from the first slide.

Previewing and Printing the Presentation

Although you still plan to make many changes to the presentation, you want to give a copy of the slides to the Foundation director to get feedback regarding the content and layout. Although your presentation looks good on your screen it may not look good when printed. Previewing the presentation allows you to see how it will look before you waste time and paper printing it out. Many times, you will want to change the print and layout settings to improve the appearance of the output.

Previewing the Presentation

Shading, patterns, and backgrounds that look good on the screen can make printed handouts unreadable, so you want to preview how the printout will look before making a copy for the director.

1 • **Click [Print Preview icon] Print Preview.**

Another Method

The menu equivalent is File/Print Preview and the voice command is "Print preview."

Your screen should be similar to Figure 1.63

Having Trouble?

Your Print Preview may appear in color if you have a color printer.

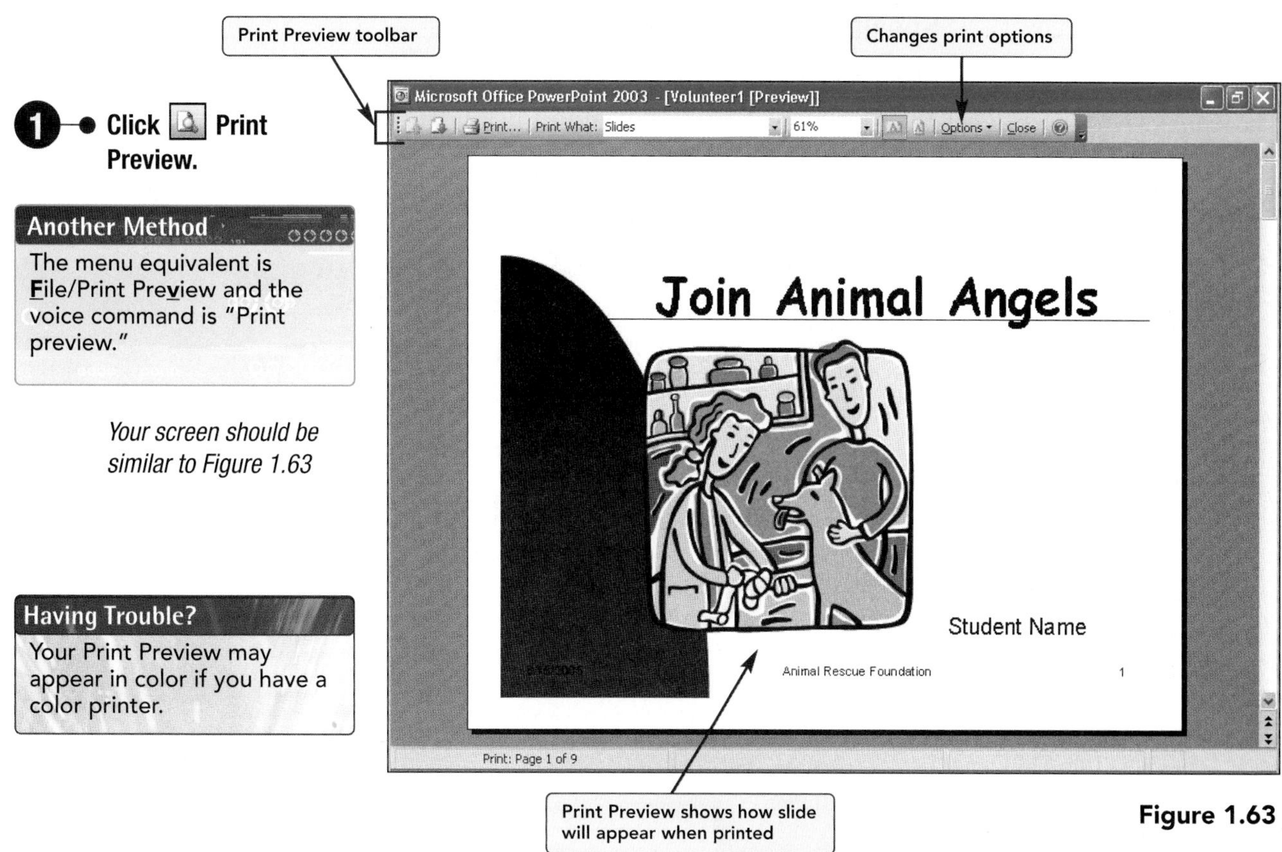

Figure 1.63

The Print Preview window displays the first slide in the presentation as it will appear when printed using the selected printer. It is displayed in color if your selected printer is a color printer; otherwise, it appears in grayscale (shades of gray) as in Figure 1.63. Even if you have a color printer, you want to print the slides in grayscale. The Print Preview window also includes its own toolbar that lets you modify the default print settings.

2 • **If you need to change to grayscale, click [Options].**

• **Choose Color/Grayscale/Grayscale.**

The default grayscale setting (shown in Figure 1.63) shows you how the slide would look with some of the background in white, with black text, and with patterns in grayscale.

Specifying Printed Output

The Preview window displays a single slide on the page as it will appear when printed. This is the default print setting. You can change the type of printed output using the Print What option. The output types are described in the table below. Only one type of output can be printed at a time.

Output Type	Description
Slides	Prints one slide per page.
Handouts	Prints multiple slides per page.
Outline View	Prints the slide content as it appears in Outline view.
Notes Pages	Prints the slide and the associated notes on a page.

Additional Information

You will learn about notes in Lab 2.

You want to change the print setting to Handouts to print several slides on a page.

1 **Open the Print What drop-down menu.**

Choose Handouts (6 slides per page).

Your screen should be similar to Figure 1.64

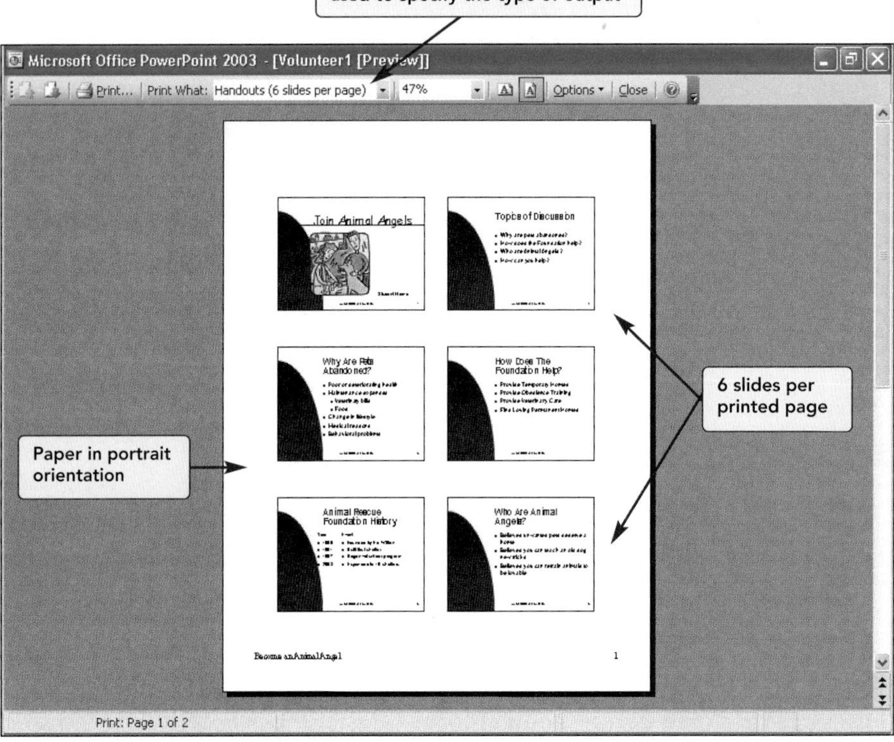

Figure 1.64

Changing Page Orientation

You also want to change the orientation or the direction the output is printed on a page. The default orientation for handouts is **portrait**. This setting prints across the width of the page. You will change the orientation to **landscape** so that the slides print across the length of the paper. Then you will preview the other pages.

❶ • Click [Landscape icon] Landscape.

• Click [Next Page icon] Next Page to view page 2 of the handout.

Your screen should be similar to Figure 1.65

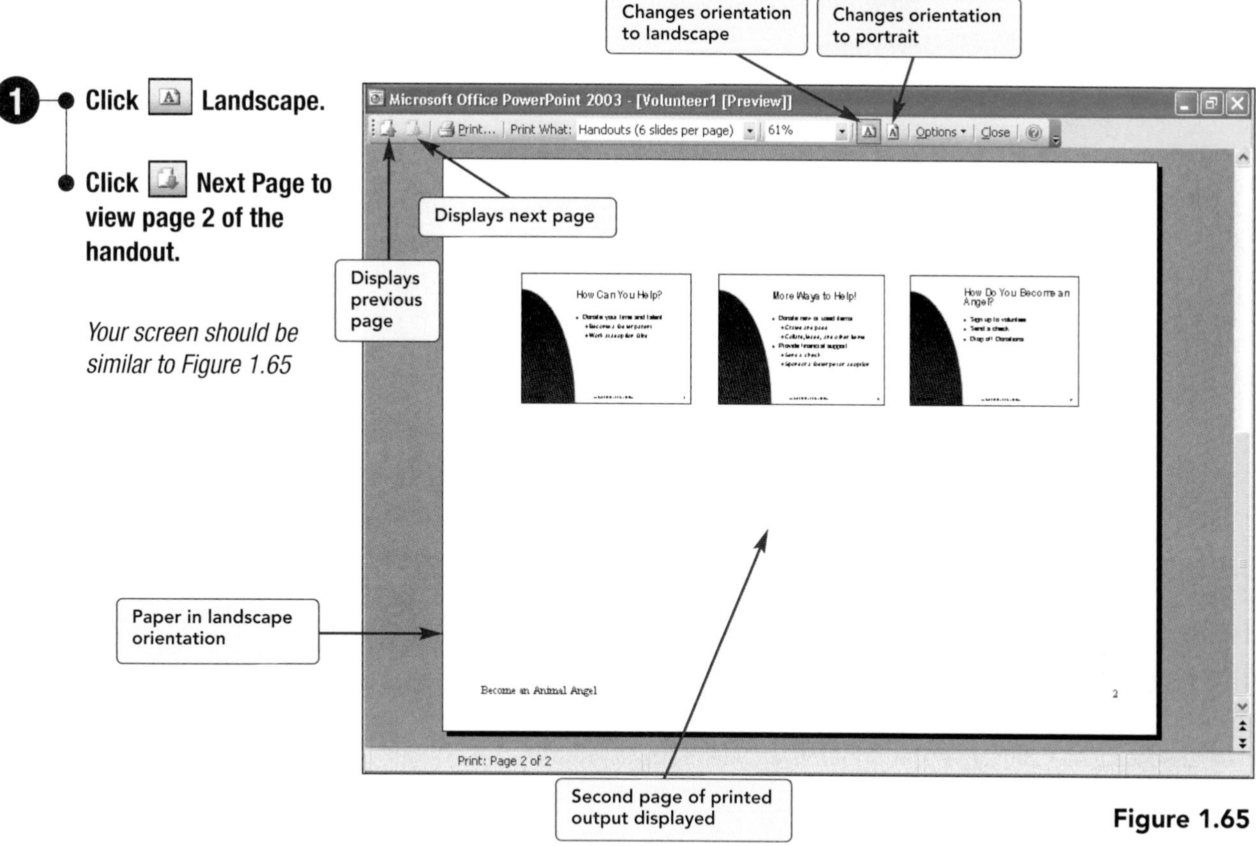

Figure 1.65

The last three slides in the presentation are displayed on the second page in landscape orientation.

Printing the Presentation

Now, you are ready to print the handouts.

❶ • Click [Print...].

Another Method

The menu equivalent is File/Print and the keyboard shortcut is Ctrl + P. You can use [Print icon] Print on the Standard toolbar if you do not need to make any changes to the default print settings.

Your screen should be similar to Figure 1.66

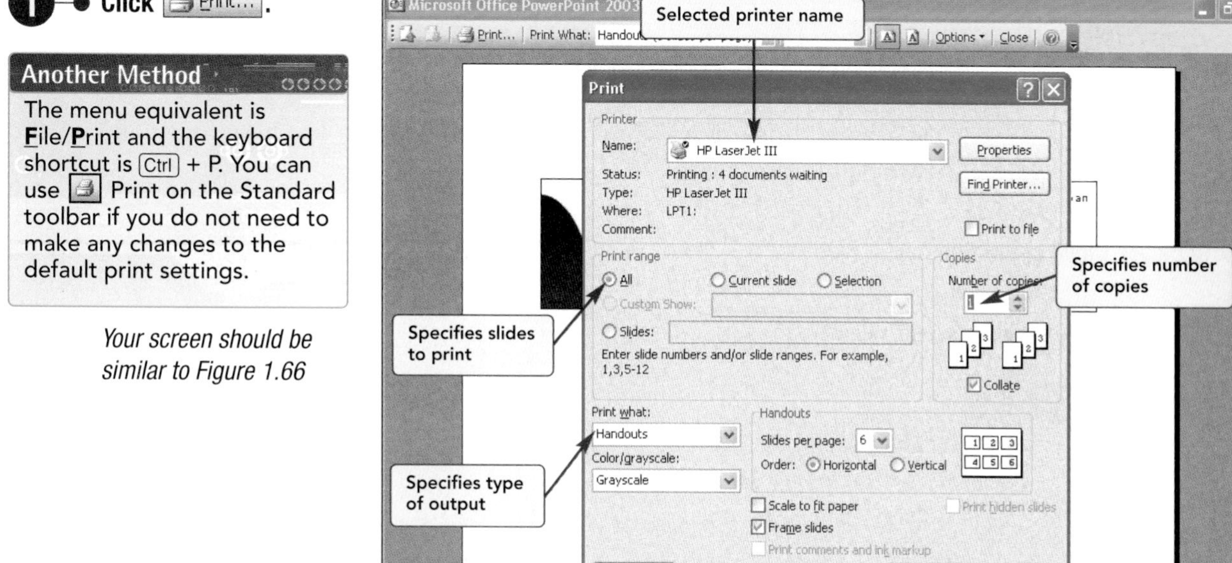

Figure 1.66

Note: Please consult your instructor for printing procedures that may differ from the following directions.

The Name text box in the Printer section displays the name of the selected printer. You may need to specify the printer you will be using. (Your instructor will provide the printer to select.) The Print Range settings specify the slides to print. The default setting, All, prints all the slides, while Current Slide prints only the slide you are viewing. The Slides option is used to specify individual slides or a range of slides to print by entering the slide numbers in the text box. The Copies section is used to specify the number of copies of the specified print range. The default is to print one copy.

At the bottom of the dialog box, PowerPoint displays options that allow you to print color slides as black-and-white slides, to make the slide images fill the paper, and to add a frame around the slide. The grayscale and handout options you specified in the Print Preview window are already selected. The Frame Slides option is selected by default and displays a border around each slide.

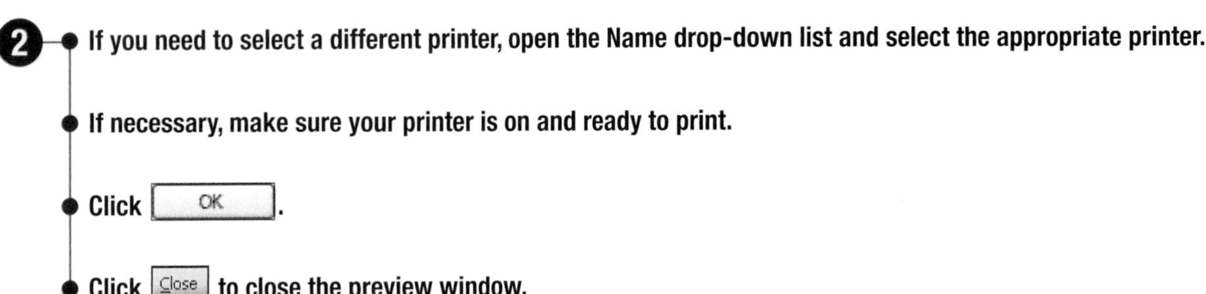

The Printer icon appears in the status bar, indicating that the program is sending data to the Print Manager, and your handouts should be printing. Your printed output should be similar to that shown in the Case Study at the beginning of the lab.

Exiting PowerPoint

You have finished working on the presentation for now and will exit the PowerPoint program.

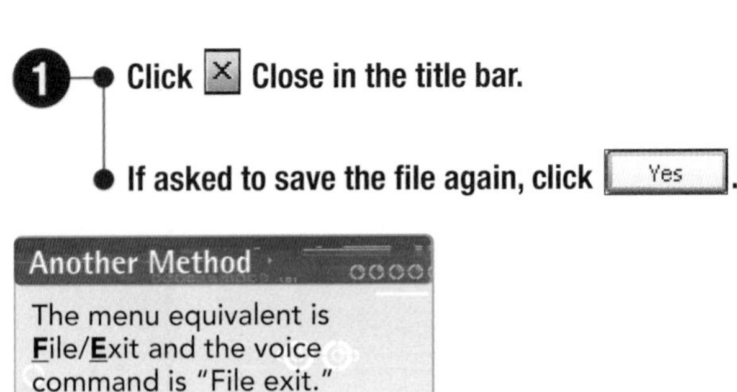

Another Method

The menu equivalent is File/Exit and the voice command is "File exit."

Focus on Careers

EXPLORE YOUR CAREER OPTIONS

Account Executive

Sales is an excellent entry point for a solid career in any company. Account Executive is just one of many titles that a sales professional may have; Field Sales and Sales Representative are two other titles. Account executives take care of customers by educating them on the company's latest products, designing solutions using the company's product line, and closing the deal to make the sale and earn their commission. These tasks require the use of effective PowerPoint presentations that educate and motivate potential customers. The salary range of account executives is limited only by his/her ambition; salaries range from $27,450 to more than $102,000. To learn more about this career visit http://www.bls.gov/oco/ocos119.htm, the Web site for the Bureau of Labor Statistics of the U.S. Department of Labor.

LAB 1 Creating a Presentation

Template (PP1.7)

A template is a file containing predefined settings that can be used as a pattern to create many common types of presentations.

Presentation Style (PP1.10)

A PowerPoint presentation can be made using five different styles: onscreen presentations, Web presentations, black-and-white or color overheads, and 35mm slides.

Slide (PP1.11)

A slide is an individual "page" of your presentation.

AutoCorrect (PP1.19)

The AutoCorrect feature makes some basic assumptions about the text you are typing and, based on these assumptions, automatically identifies and/or corrects the entry.

Spelling Checker (PP1.20)

The spelling checker locates all misspelled words, duplicate words, and capitalization irregularities as you create and edit a presentation, and proposes possible corrections.

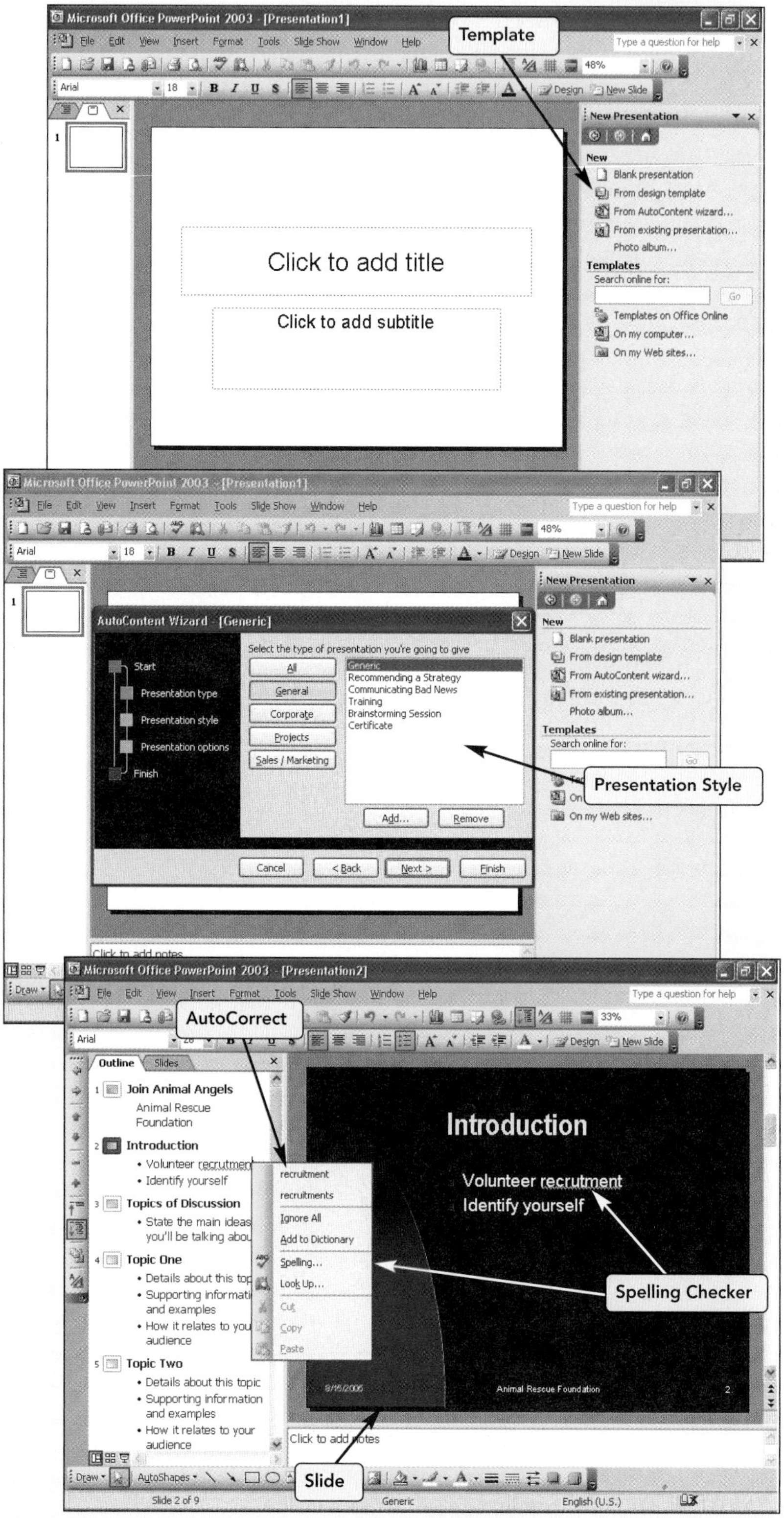

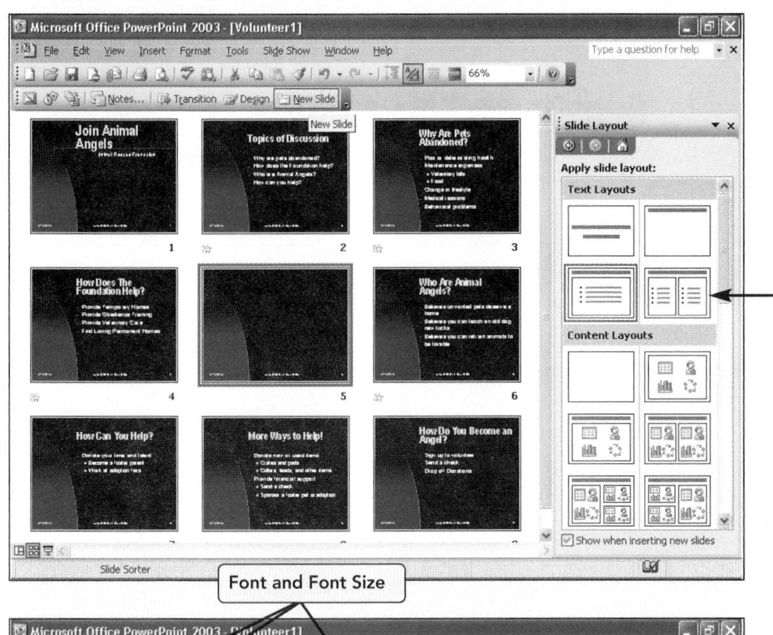

Layout (PP1.43)

The layout controls the way items are arranged on a slide.

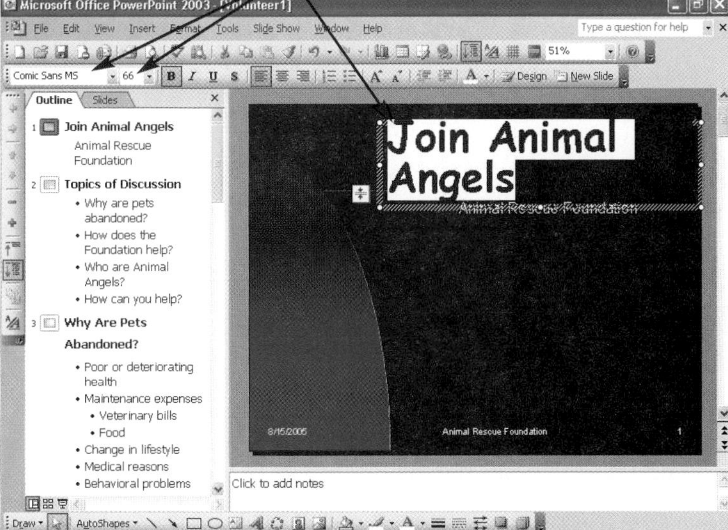

Font and Font Size (PP1.50)

A font is a set of characters with a specific design. Each font has one or more sizes.

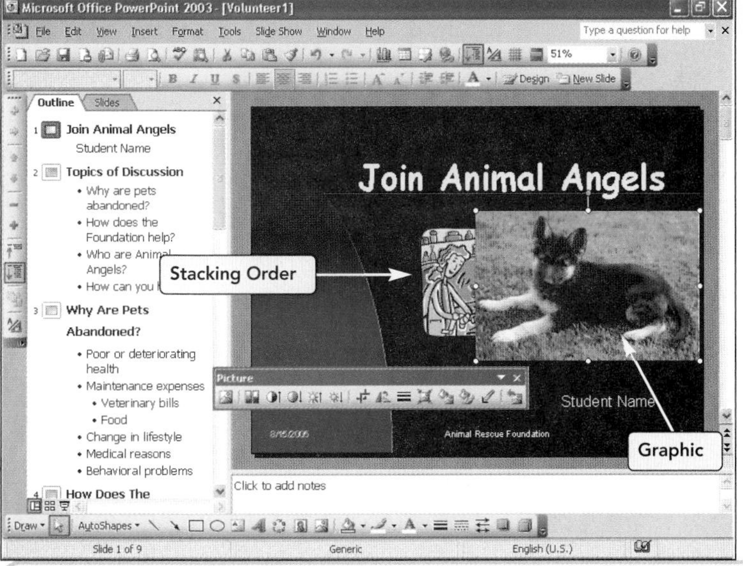

Graphics (PP1.54)

A graphic is a non-text element or object, such as a drawing or picture, that can be added to a slide.

Stacking Order (PP1.60)

Stacking order is the order in which objects are inserted in to different layers of the slide.

LAB 1
Creating a Presentation

key terms

AutoCorrect PP1.19
character formatting PP1.49
clip art PP1.55
current slide PP1.15
custom dictionary PP1.20
default PP1.7
demote PP1.27
drawing object PP1.54
Drawing toolbar PP1.5
embedded object PP1.54
font PP1.50
font size PP1.50
footer PP1.11
format PP1.49
graphic PP1.54
keyword PP1.56
landscape PP1.64
layout PP1.43
main dictionary PP1.20
object PP1.23
Outlining toolbar PP1.5
pane PP1.13
paragraph formatting PP1.49
picture PP1.54
Picture toolbar PP1.59
placeholder PP1.23
point PP1.50
portrait PP1.64
promote PP1.27
sans serif PP1.50
selection rectangle PP1.24
serif PP1.50
sizing handles PP1.45
slide PP1.11
slide show PP1.47
source program PP1.54
spelling checker PP1.20
stacking order PP1.60
template PP1.7
thumbnail PP1.13
typeface PP1.50
view PP1.12
wizard PP1.8
workspace PP1.6

microsoft office specialist skills

The Microsoft Office Specialist certification program is designed to measure your proficiency in performing basic tasks using the Office 2003 applications. Certification demonstrates that you have the skills and provides a valuable industry credential for employment. After completing this lab, you have learned the following Microsoft Office PowerPoint 2003 Specialist skills:

Skill Sets	Skill Standards	Page
Creating Content	Create new presentations from templates	PP1.7
	Insert and edit text-based content	PP1.16
	Insert pictures, shapes, and graphics	PP1.54
Formatting Content	Format text-based content	PP1.49
	Format pictures, shapes, and graphics	PP1.61
Managing and Delivering Presentations	Organize a presentation	PP1.12,1.40–1.45
	Deliver presentations	PP1.47
	Save and publish presentations	PP1.31
	Print slides, outlines, handouts, and speaker notes	PP1.62

command summary

Command	Shortcut Key	Button	Voice	Action
File/New	Ctrl + N			Creates new presentation
File/Open	Ctrl + O		Open File open Open file	Opens existing presentation
File/Close			Close presentation	Closes presentation
File/Save	Ctrl + S		Save	Saves presentation
File/Save As				Saves presentation using new file name and/or location
File/Print Preview			Print preview	Displays preview of file
File/Print	Ctrl + P			Prints presentation
Edit/Undo	Ctrl + Z		Undo	Reverses last action
Edit/Cut	Ctrl + X		Cut	Cuts selection to Clipboard
Edit/Paste	Ctrl + V		Paste	Pastes item from Clipboard
Edit/Select All	Ctrl + A			Selects all objects on a slide or all text in an object, or (in Outline pane) an entire outline
Edit/Delete Slide	Delete			Deletes selected slide
View/Normal			Normal Normal view	Switches to Normal view
View/Slide Sorter			Slide sorter	Switches to Slide Sorter view
View/Slide Show			View show Begin slide show Start slide show Slide show view	Runs slide show

command summary (continued)

Command	Shortcut Key	Button	Voice	Action
Insert/**N**ew Slide	Ctrl + M	New Slide	New slide Insert new slide	Inserts new slide
Insert/**P**icture/**C**lip Art				Opens Clip Organizer and inserts selected clip art
Insert/**P**icture/**F**rom File				Inserts a picture from file on disk
F**o**rmat/**F**ont/**F**ont		Arial		Changes font type
F**o**rmat/**F**ont/**S**ize		18		Changes font size
F**o**rmat/**B**ullets and Numbering/Bulleted				Adds and removes selected bullets
F**o**rmat/Slide **L**ayout				Changes the layout of an existing or new slide
Tools/**S**pelling	F7			Spell-checks presentation

screen identification

1. In the following PowerPoint screen, several items are identified by letters. Enter the correct term for each item in the spaces that follow.

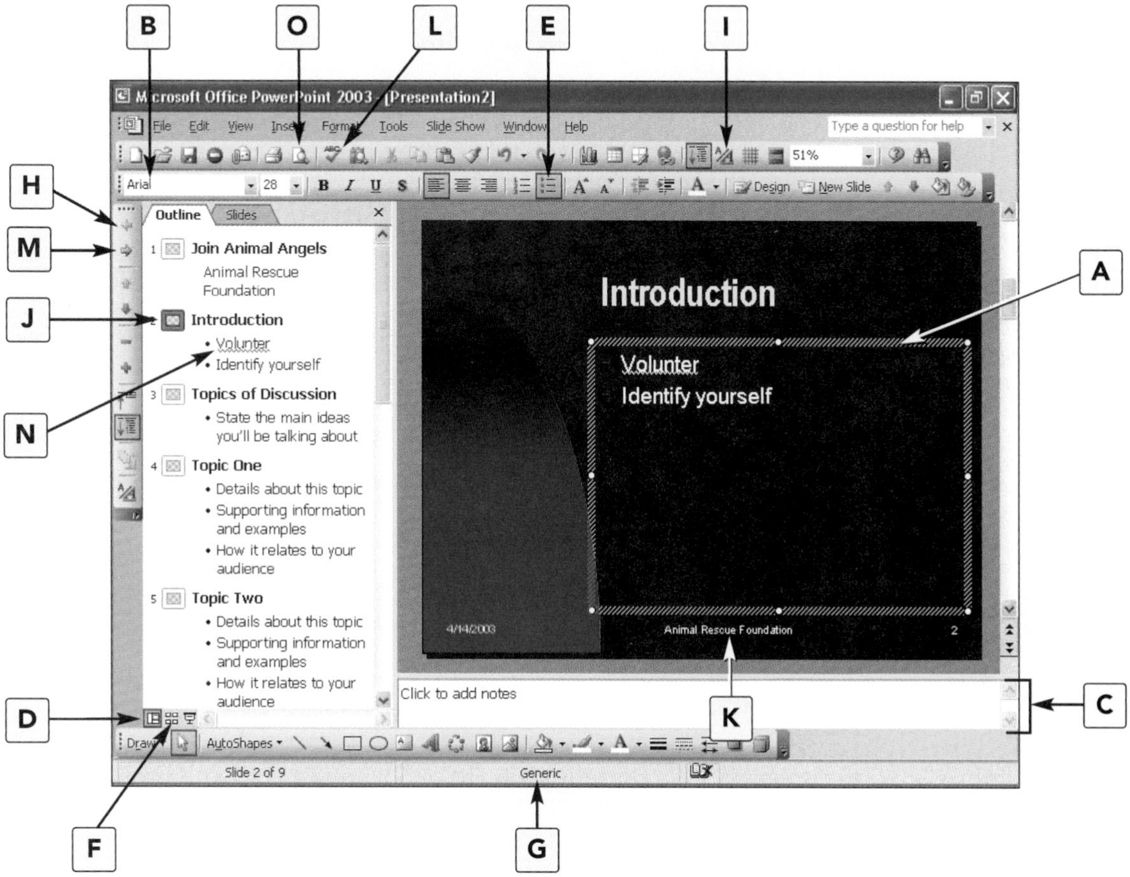

A. ______________
B. ______________
C. ______________
D. ______________
E. ______________
F. ______________
G. ______________
H. ______________
I. ______________
J. ______________
K. ______________
L. ______________
M. ______________
N. ______________
O. ______________

Possible answers for the screen identification are:

Font	Placeholder
Normal view	Show formatting
Slide Sorter	Align left
Notes pane	Bullets
Design template	Spelling
Current slide	Misspelled word
Promotes item	Footer
Demotes item	Print Preview

matching

Match the numbered item with the correct lettered description.

1. formatting	______	**a.**	allows text entry, deletion, selection, and formatting of an object when border appears hatched
2. title slide	______	**b.**	use to view and rearrange all slides
3. slide show	______	**c.**	demotes items in outline
4. [button icon]	______	**d.**	controls the way items are arranged on a slide
5. .ppt	______	**e.**	file of predefined settings used as a pattern to create common types of presentations
6. Slide Sorter view	______	**f.**	displays each slide full screen and in order
7. workspace	______	**g.**	boxes that contain specific types of items or objects
8. template	______	**h.**	default file extension for PowerPoint documents
9. selection rectangle	______	**i.**	first slide in a presentation
10. layout	______	**j.**	large area of the screen where presentations are displayed
	______	**k.**	enhancing the appearance of the slide to make it more readable or attractive

multiple choice

Circle the letter of the correct response.

1. If you want to provide copies of your presentation to the audience showing multiple slides on a page, you would print ______________.
   - **a.** slides
   - **b.** handouts
   - **c.** note pages
   - **d.** outline area

2. If you only have access to an overhead projector, you should create ____________________.
   - **a.** onscreen presentations
   - **b.** Web presentations
   - **c.** black-and-white or color transparencies
   - **d.** all the above

3. The step in the development of a presentation that focuses on determining the length of your speech, the audience, the layout of the room, and the type of audiovisual equipment available is ____________________.
   - **a.** planning
   - **b.** creating
   - **c.** editing
   - **d.** enhancing

4. If you wanted to view the slides as your audience would, you would:
   a. print the notes pages
   b. run the slide show
   c. maximize the PowerPoint application window
   d. close the tabs pane
5. To make your presentation professional and easy to read, you would use a ________ font for the text and a _________ font for the headings.
   a. serif; sans serif
   b. large; small
   c. sans serif; serif
   d. red; black
6. If you want to work on all aspects of your presentation, switch to ____________________ view, which displays the slide pane, outline pane, and note pane.
   a. Slide Sorter
   b. Outline
   c. Slide
   d. Normal
7. When the spelling checker is used, you can create a _______________ dictionary to hold words that you commonly use but are not included in the main dictionary.
   a. custom
   b. official
   c. personal
   d. common
8. Dragging the _______________ sizing handles adjusts both the height and width of the placeholder at the same time.
   a. top
   b. bottom
   c. side
   d. corner
9. A(n)____________________is an onscreen display of your presentation.
   a. outline
   b. handout
   c. slide show
   d. slide
10. Onscreen presentations can be designed specifically for the World Wide Web, where a(n) ______________________ serves as the presentation tool.
   a. overhead projector
   b. browser
   c. white board
   d. computer screen

true/false

Circle the correct answer to the following questions.

1.	A slide is a set of characters with a specific design.	True	False
2.	The suggested maximum number of bullets on a slide is six.	True	False
3.	All drawing objects are inserted into the same layer of the presentation.	True	False
4.	Practicing the delivery of your presentation is the final step in presentation development	True	False
5.	Sans serif fonts have a flair at the base of each letter that visually leads the reader to the next letter.	True	False
6.	The page orientation can be landscape or portrait.	True	False
7.	Graphics are objects, such as charts, drawings, pictures, and scanned photographs, that provide visual interest or clarify data.	True	False
8.	Character formatting features affect selected characters only, while paragraph formatting features affect an entire paragraph.	True	False
9.	A layout contains placeholders for the different items such as bulleted text, titles, charts, and so on.	True	False
10.	Font size is the width of the character and is commonly measured in points.	True	False

fill-in

Complete the following statements by filling in the blanks with the correct terms.

1. __________________ order is the order objects are inserted in the different layers of the slide.
2. An embedded object is edited using the ______________ program.
3. The _____________________ Wizard is a guided approach that helps you determine the content and organization of your presentation through a series of questions.
4. The size of a ______________________ can be changed by dragging its sizing handles.
5. Boxes that are designed to contain specific types of objects such as the slide title, bulleted text, charts, tables, and pictures are called ________________________.
6. The _____________________ toolbar contains buttons that are used to change the appearance or format of the presentation.
7. A ________________ is text or graphics that appears at the bottom of each slide.
8. A _______________ is an individual "page" of your presentation.
9. ________________________________ is a PowerPoint feature that advises you of misspelled words as you add text to a slide and proposes possible corrections.
10. A _________________ is a miniature of a slide.

rating system

★ Easy

★★ Moderate

★★★ Difficult

step-by-step

Triple Crown Presentation ★

1. Logan Thomas works at Adventure Travel Tours. He is working on a presentation about lightweight hiking he will present to a group of interested clients. He has found some new information to add to the presentation. Logan also wants to rearrange several slides and make a few other changes to improve the appearance of the presentation. The handouts of the completed presentation are shown here.

   a. Open the file pp01_Triple Crown. Enter your name in the subtitle on slide 1.

   b. Run the slide show to see what Logan has done so far.

   c. Spell-check the presentation, making the appropriate corrections.

   d. Change the layout of slide 2 to Title, Text, and content. (Hint: Use Format/Slide Layout.) Increase the font size of the bulleted text on slide 2 from 28 to 32 points. Size and position the title, graphic, and text appropriately.

   e. Appropriately size and position the graphic on slide 3.

   f. Insert the picture pp01_Jump on slide 4. Size and position it appropriately.

   g. Move slide 6 before slide 5.

   h. Select slide 4. Open the Outline tab and click at the end of the last bullet under "Why go lightweight?" Press Enter and promote the new bullet twice. Enter the title **Less is More**.

   i. Change the layout of the new slide to Title, Text, and Content. Insert the picture pp01_Stream in the content placeholder.

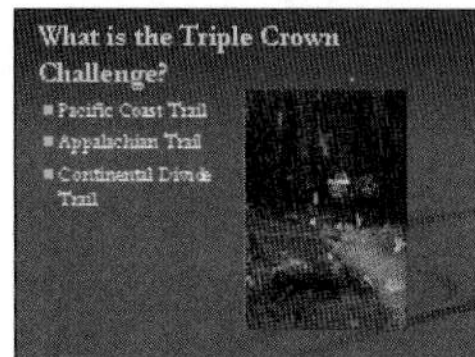

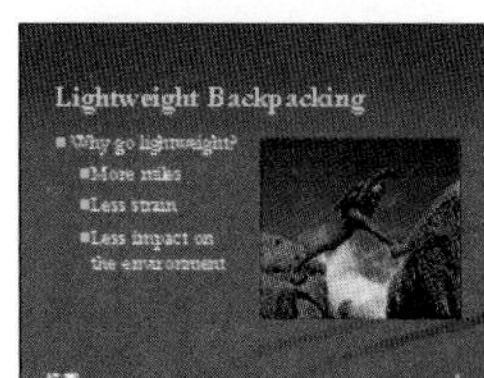

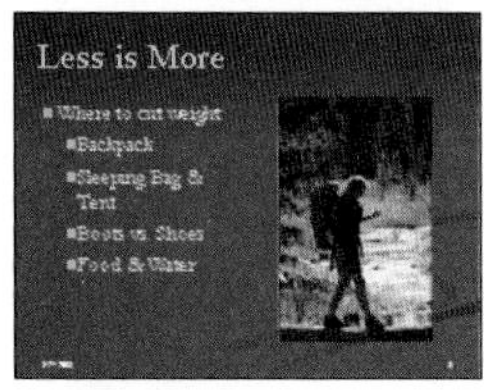

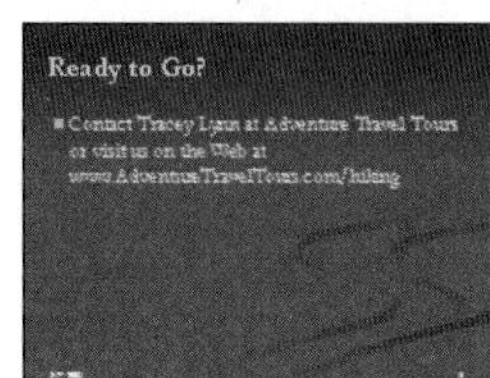

1

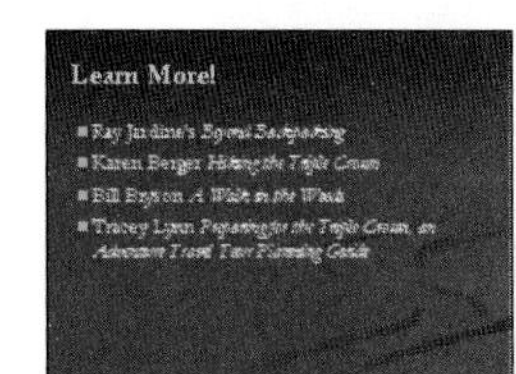

j. Change the layout of slide 7 to Title and Text layout. Add the following text in the text placeholder: **Contact Tracey Lynn at Adventure Travel Tours or visit us on the Web at www.AdventureTravelTours.com/hiking**.

k. Run the slide show.

l. Save the presentation as Triple Crown Presentation. Print the slides as handouts (four per page).

Writing Effective Resumes ★ ★

2. You work for the career services center of a university and you are planning a presentation on how to write effective resumes and cover letters. A coworker has started such a presentation, but has not had time to edit or finalize it. You need to clean it up and enhance it a bit before presenting it. The handouts of the completed presentation are shown here.

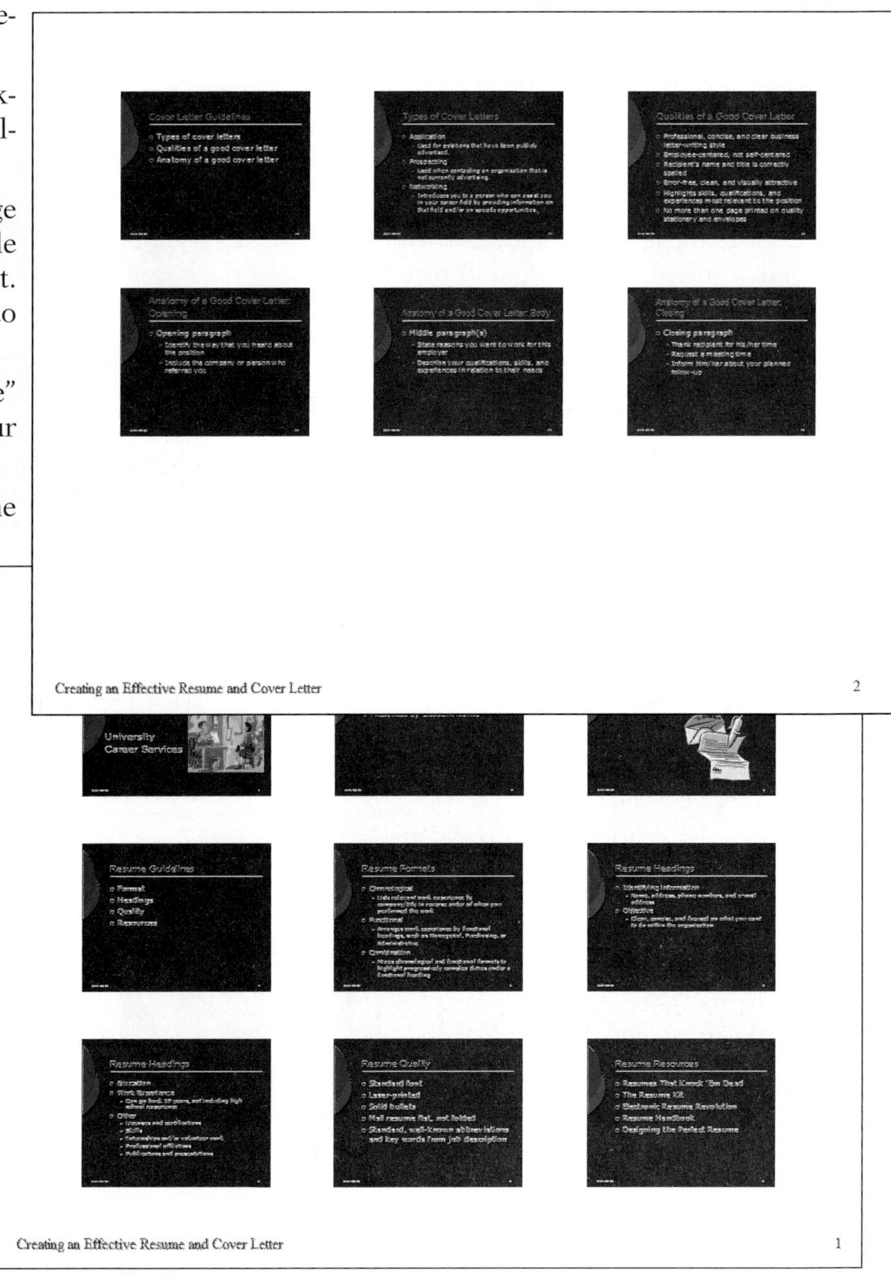

a. Open the PowerPoint presentation pp01_Resume.

b. Run the Spelling Checker and correct any spelling errors.

c. In Normal view, change the font size of the title in the title slide to 44 pt. Increase the subtitle to 36 pt.

d. Replace "Student Name" in slide 2 with your name.

e. On slide 5, capitalize the first word of each bulleted item.

f. Since there is too much text on slide 6, split the slide content into two slides.

g. Reorganize the bulleted items on slide 10 so that "Types of cover letters" is the first item. To match the slide order with the way the topics are now introduced, move slide 13 before slide 11.

h. Break each bulleted item on slide 13 into two or three bullets each as appropriate. Capitalize the first word of each bulleted item. Remove commas and periods at the end of the items. Split the slide content into three slides. Add an appropriate slide title to the slides.

i. On the title slide, insert the pp01_Success clip art. Resize and position it as shown in the example.

j. On slide 3, insert the pp01_Cover Letter clip art below the bulleted list. Position it in the lower right corner of the slide.

k. Save the presentation as Resume1.

l. Run the slide show.

m. Print the slides as handouts (nine per page in landscape orientation) and close the presentation.

Massage Therapy ★ ★

3. Lifestyle Fitness Club is opening a new spa offering personal services that include therapeutic massage. Prior to opening, the club wants to promote the services to the community. The spa manager has asked you create a presentation that can be used as a sales tool with local groups and organizations. You have organized the topics to be presented and located several clip art graphics that will complement the talk. Now you are ready to begin creating the presentation. The handouts of the completed presentation are shown here.

a. Start PowerPoint 2003. Open the New Presentation task pane.

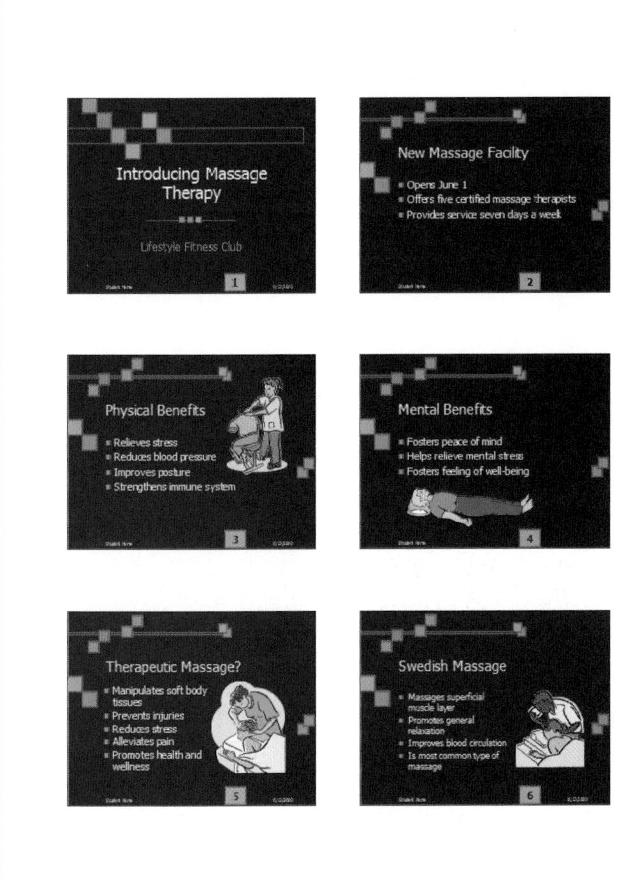

b. Using the AutoContent wizard, select Recommending a Strategy as the type of presentation, and select On-screen as the style of output for the presentation. Enter **Introducing Massage Therapy** in the Presentation Title text box. Enter your name in the footer text box. Keep the other footer options as they are.

c. Replace the owner name, your first name, on the title slide with **Lifestyle Fitness Club**.

d. Delete slide 2.

e. Replace the title and sample bullets on slide 2 with:

Title: **New Massage Facility**

Bullet 1: **Opens May 1**

Bullet 2: **Offers five certified massage therapists**

Bullet 3: **Provides service seven days a week**

Bullet 4: **Call now for an appointment**

f. Replace the title and sample bulleted text on slide 3 with:

Title: **Therapeutic Massage**

Bullet 1: **Manipulates soft body tissues**

Bullet 2: **Prevents injuries**

Bullet 3: **Alleviates pain**

Bullet 4: **Reduces stress**

Bullet 5: **Promotes health and wellness**

g. Change the title of slide 4 to **Reflexology** and replace the sample bullet text with the following bulleted items:

Bullet 1: **Massage points on hands and feet**

Bullet 2: **Points correspond to areas of the body**

Bullet 3: **Entire body affected**

h. Change the title of slide 5 to **Sports Massage Therapy** and include the following bulleted items:

Bullet 1: **Maintenance Massage**

Demoted Bullet 2: **Regular program of massage**

Demoted Bullet 3: **Helps athletes reach optimal performance**

Bullet 4: **Event Massage**

Demoted Bullet 5: **Readies athlete for top performance**

Demoted Bullet 6: **Stimulates circulation**

Bullet 7: **Rehabilitation Massage**

Demoted Bullet 8: **Speeds healing**

Demoted Bullet 9: **Reduces discomfort**

i. Change bullet 1 on slide 2 to **Opens June 1**. Delete bullet 4.

j. Insert a new slide after slide 2 using the Title and Text layout. Add the title **Benefits** and the following bulleted items:

Bullet 1: **Physical**

Demoted Bullet 2: **Relieves stress**

Demoted Bullet 3: **Reduces blood pressure**

Demoted Bullet 4: **Improves posture**

Demoted Bullet 5: **Strengthens immune system**

Bullet 6: **Mental**

Demoted Bullet 7: **Fosters peace of mind**

Demoted Bullet 8: **Helps relieve mental stress**

Demoted Bullet 9: **Fosters a feeling of well-being**

Change the order of bullets 3 and 4 on slide 4.

k. Insert a new slide after slide 5 using the Title and Text layout. Add the title **Shiatsu and Accupressure** and the following bulleted items:

Bullet 1: **Uses system of finger-pressure massage**

Bullet 2: **Based on Asian healing concepts**

Bullet 3: **Treats invisible channels of energy flow**

l. Change the title of slide 8 to **Swedish Massage** and include the following bulleted items:

Bullet 1: **Massages superficial muscle layer**

Bullet 2: **Promotes general relaxation**

Bullet 3: **Improves blood circulation**

Bullet 4: **Is most common type of massage**

m. Split the text on slide 3 between two slides. Title the first slide **Physical Benefits** and the second slide **Mental Benefits**. Delete the first bullet on both slides and promote the remaining bullets.

n. Change the font of the title on the title slide to 48 pt and the subtitle to 32 pt.

o. Insert the graphic pp01_Relaxation on slide 4. Size and position it appropriately.

p. Move slide 9 before slide 6.

q. Insert graphics of your choice to slides 3, 5, and 6. Size and position them appropriately.

r. Spell-check the presentation, making the appropriate changes.

s. Run the slide show.

t. Save the presentation as Massage Therapy.

u. Print the slides as handouts (six per page).

Coffee Product Knowledge ★★★

4. As the manager of the Downtown Internet Café, you want to make a presentation to the other employees about the various blends of coffee that the cafe offers. The purpose of this presentation is to enable employees to answer the many questions that are asked by customers when looking at the Blend of the Day board or choosing the type of coffee beans they want to purchase. The handouts of the completed presentation are shown here.

   a. Start PowerPoint 2003. Open the new Presentation task pane.

   b. Using the AutoContent wizard, select Training as the type of presentation and select Color Overheads as the presentation style. Enter **Coffee Talk** in the Presentation Title text box. Enter your name in the footer text box and keep the other footer settings as they are.

   c. Replace your name in the title slide with **Downtown Internet Cafe**.

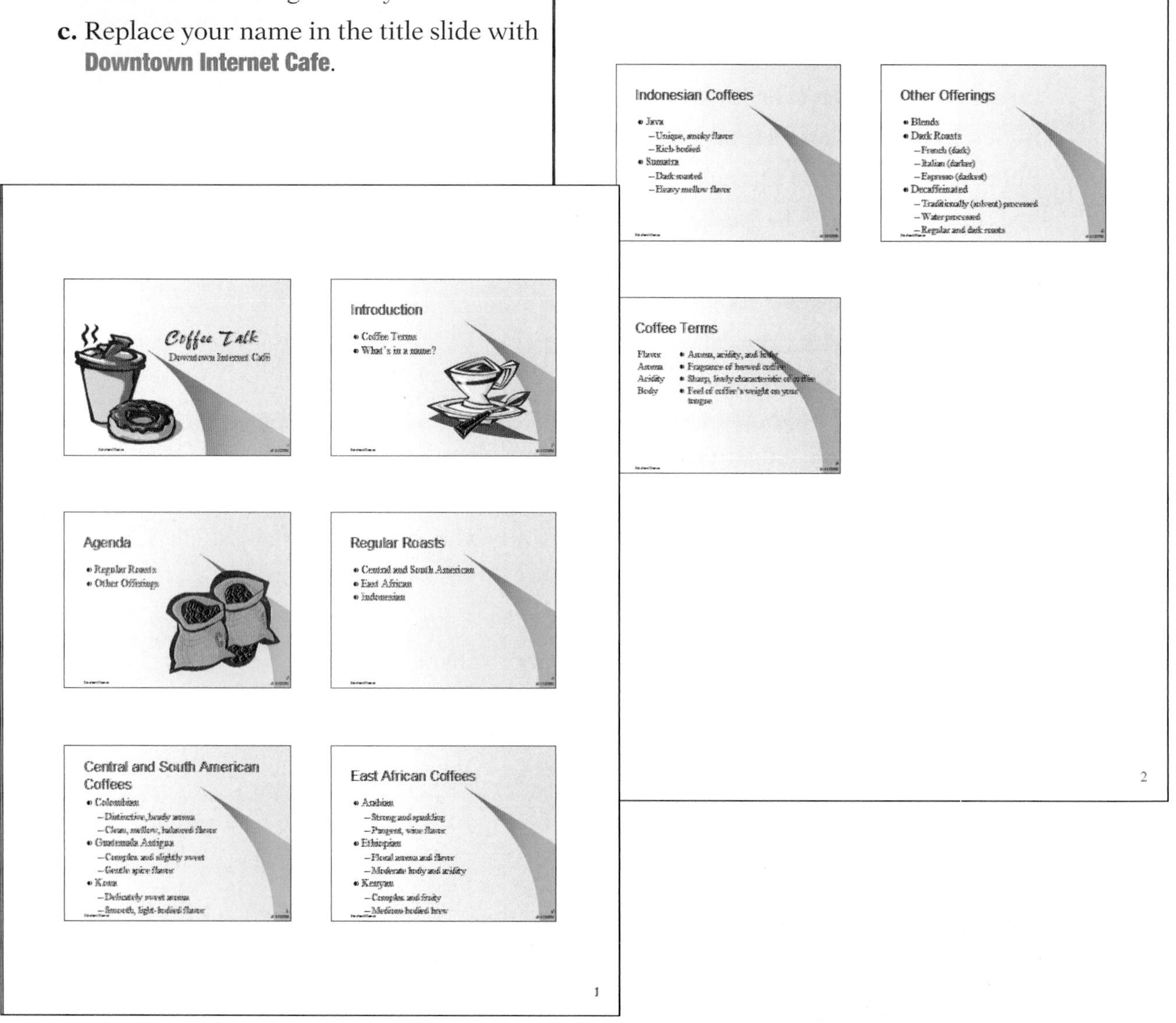

d. Replace the sample bulleted text on slide 2 with the following:

Bullet 1: **What's in a name?**

e. Replace the sample bulleted text on slide 3 with the following:

Bullet 1: **Regular Roasts**

Bullet 2: **Other Offerings**

f. Move slide 4 to the end of the presentation after slide 9.

g. In Normal view, change the title of slide 4 to **Regular Roasts** and replace the sample bulleted text with the following:

Bullet 1: **Central and South American**

Bullet 2: **East African**

Bullet 3: **Indonesian**

h. Change the title of slide 5 to **Central and South American Coffees** and replace the sample bulleted text with the following:

Bullet 1: **Colombian**

Demoted Bullet 2: **Distinctive, heady aroma**

Demoted Bullet 3: **Clean, mellow, balanced flavor**

Bullet 4: **Guatemala Antigua**

Demoted Bullet 5: **Complex and slightly sweet**

Demoted Bullet 6: **Gentle spice flavors**

Bullet 7: **Kona**

Demoted Bullet 8: **Delicately sweet aroma**

Demoted Bullet 9: **Smooth, light-bodied flavor**

i. Change the title of slide 6 to **East African Coffees** and replace the sample bulleted text with the following:

Bullet 1: **Arabian**

Demoted Bullet 2: **Strong and sparkling**

Demoted Bullet 3: **Pungent, wine flavor**

Bullet 4: **Ethiopian**

Demoted Bullet 5: **Floral aroma and flavor**

Demoted Bullet 6: **Moderate body and acidity**

Bullet 7: **Kenyan**

Demoted Bullet 8: **Medium-bodied brew**

Demoted Bullet 9: **Complex and fruity**

j. Change the title of slide 7 to **Indonesian Coffees** and replace the sample bulleted text with the following:

Bullet 1: **Java**

Demoted Bullet 2: **Unique, smoky flavor**

Demoted Bullet 3: **Rich-bodied**

Bullet 4: **Sumatra**

Demoted Bullet 5: **Dark roasted**

Demoted Bullet 6: **Heavy mellow flavor**

k. Change the title of slide 8 to **Other Offerings** and replace the sample bulleted text and graphic with the following:

Bullet 1: **Blends**

Bullet 2: **Dark Roasts**

Demoted Bullet 3: **French (dark)**

Demoted Bullet 4: **Italian (darker)**

Demoted Bullet 5: **Espresso (darkest)**

Bullet 6: **Decaffeinated**

Demoted Bullet 7: **Traditionally (solvent) processed**

Demoted Bullet 8: **Water processed**

Demoted Bullet 9: **Regular and dark roasts**

l. Change the order of the last two demoted bulleted items in slide 6.

m. Add a second bullet to slide 2 with the text **Coffee Terms**.

n. Change the title of slide 9 to **Coffee Terms**. Change the layout to Title and 2-Column Text. (Hint: Use Format/Slide Layout.) Select and delete the graphic. Replace the sample bulleted text with the following in the columns indicated:

Left Column	Right Column
Bullet 1: **Flavor**	**Aroma, acidity, and body**
Bullet 2: **Aroma**	**Fragrance of brewed coffee**
Bullet 3: **Acidity**	**Sharp, lively characteristic of coffee**
Bullet 4: **Body**	**Feel of coffee's weight on your tongue**

o. On slide 9, remove the bullets from the left column. Size and position the column placeholders to align the information in both columns as shown in the example.

p. On the title slide, position the subtitle directly under the title. Change the font and size of the title to improve its appearance.

q. On the title slide, insert the clip art pp01_Logo. Resize and position it in the lower left corner. Move the title and subtitle to the right of the logo.

r. Insert the clip art pp01_Cuppa on slide 2. Appropriately size and position the bulleted items and clip art on the slide.

s. Insert the clip art pp01_Beans on slide 3. Appropriately size and position the clip art on the slide.

t. Run the Spelling Checker and correct any spelling errors.

u. Save the presentation as Coffee.

v. Run the slide show.

w. Print the slides as handouts (six per page).

Job Fair Presentation ★★

5. Jane is preparing for her talk on "Job Fairs" for her Career Club meeting. She has organized the topic to be presented and located several clip art graphics that will complement the talk. She is now ready to begin creating the presentation in PowerPoint. The handouts of the completed presentation are shown here.

   a. Start PowerPoint 2003 and open the new Presentation task pane. Using the AutoContent wizard, select Recommending a Strategy as the type of presentation, and select Color Overheads as the style of output for the presentation. Enter **Making a Job Fair Work for You** in the Presentation Title text box. Enter your name in the footer text box. Keep the other footer options as they are.

   b. Change the font of the title to 48 pts. Replace your name on the title slide with **University Career Club**.

   c. Delete slide 2.

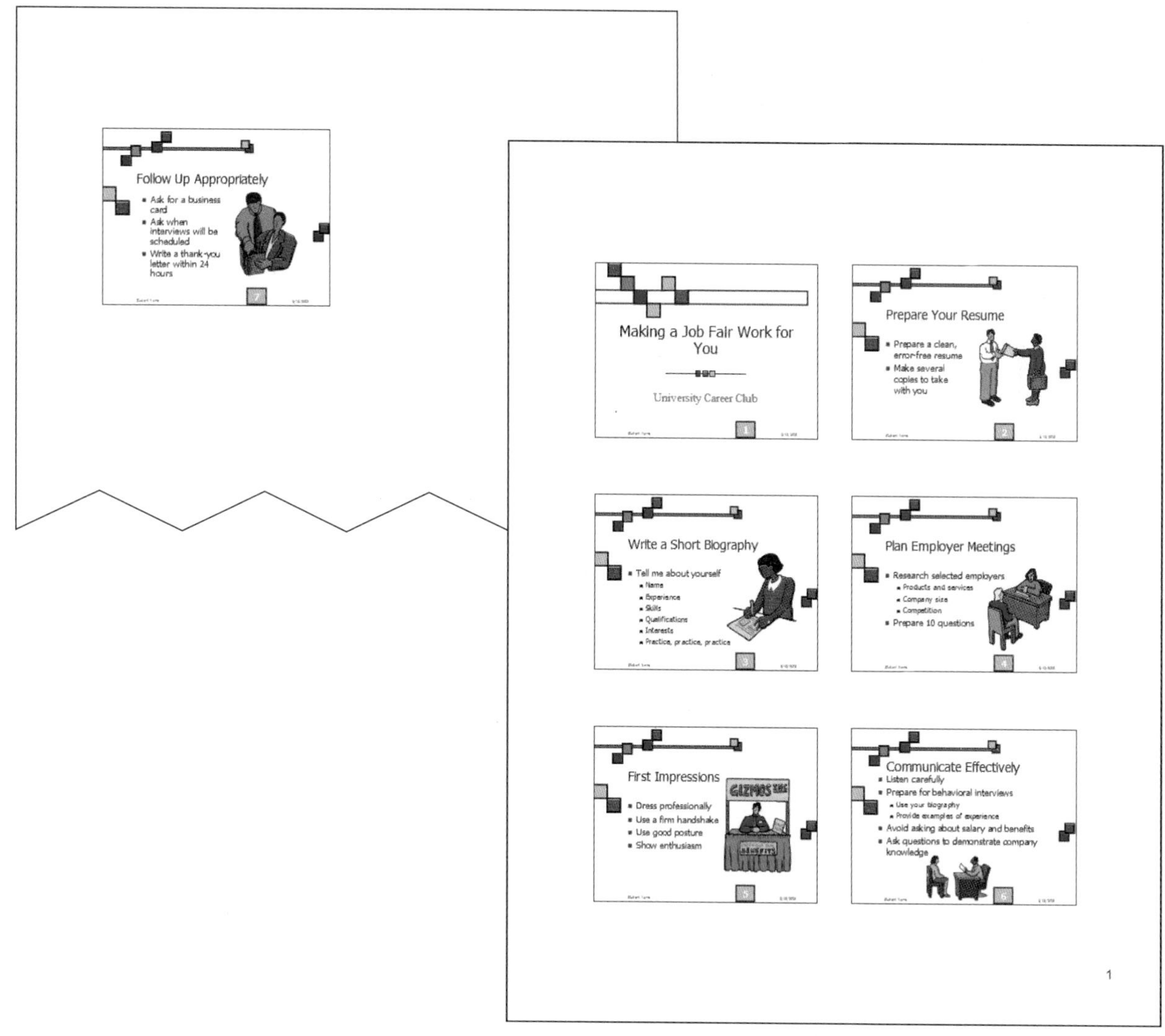

d. Replace the title and sample bulleted text on the new slide 2 with:

Title: **Prepare Your Resume**

Bullet 1: **Prepare a clean, error-free resume**

Bullet 2: **Make several copies to take with you**

e. Replace the title and sample bulleted text in slide 3 with:

Title: **Write a Short Biography**

Bullet 1: **Tell me about yourself**

Demoted Bullet 2: **Name**

Demoted Bullet 3: **Experience**

Demoted Bullet 4: **Skills**

Demoted Bullet 5: **Qualifications**

Demoted Bullet 6: **Interests**

Demoted Bullet 7: **Practice, practice, practice**

f. Replace the title and sample bulleted text in slide 4 with:

Title: **Plan Employer Meetings**

Bullet 1: **Research selected employers**

Demoted Bullet 2: **Products and services**

Demoted Bullet 3: **Company size**

Demoted Bullet 4: **Competition**

Bullet 5: **Prepare 10 questions**

g. Change the title of slide 5 to **Communicate Effectively** and include the following bulleted items:

Bullet 1: **Listen carefully**

Bullet 2: **Prepare for behavioral interviews**

Demoted Bullet 2: **Use your biography**

Demoted Bullet 3: **Provide examples of experience**

Bullet 3: **Avoid asking about salary and benefits**

Bullet 4: **Ask questions to demonstrate company knowledge**

h. Change the title of slide 6 to **First Impressions** and include the following bulleted items:

Bullet 1: **Dress professionally**

Bullet 2: **Use a firm handshake**

Bullet 3: **Use good posture**

Bullet 4: **Show enthusiasm**

i. Insert a new title and text slide after slide 6. Change the title to **Follow Up Appropriately** and include the following bulleted items:

Bullet 1: **Ask for a business card**

Bullet 2: **Ask when interviews will be scheduled**

Bullet 3: **Write a thank-you letter within 24 hours**

j. In Slide Sorter view, move slide 6 before slide 5.

k. Change the font of the subtitle on the title slide to Times New Roman and the size to 36 pt.

l. Insert the following graphics in the slides indicated. Adjust the slide layout as needed. Size and position the graphics appropriately.

Slide 2: pp01_Resume

Slide 3: pp01_Biography

Slide 4: pp01_Meeting

Slide 5: pp01_Booth

Slide 6: pp01_Interview

Slide 7: pp01_Follow Up

m. Run the slide show.

n. Save the presentation as Job Fairs.

o. Print the slides as handouts (six per page).

on your own

Internet Policy Presentation ★

1. You are working in the information technology department at Global Center Corporation. Your manager has asked you to give a presentation on the corporation's Internet policy to the new hire orientation class. Create your presentation in PowerPoint, using the information in the file pp01_InternetPolicy as a resource. Use the AutoContent wizard and the Generic template. Include your name in the footer. When you are done, run the spelling checker, then save your presentation as Internet Policy and print it.

Telephone Training Course ★ ★

2. You are a trainer with Super Software, Inc. You received a memo from your manager alerting you that many of the support personnel are not using proper telephone protocol or obtaining the proper information from the customers who call in. Your manager has asked you to conduct a training class that covers these topics. Using the pp01_Memo data file as a resource, prepare the slides for your class. Use the AutoContent wizard and select an appropriate presentation type. Include your name in the footer. When you are done, save the presentation as Phone Etiquette and print the handouts.

Pet Activities Presentation ★ ★

3. The director of Animal Rescue Foundation has asked you to prepare a presentation that introduces activities people can do with their new adopted pet. Using the pp01_Animals data file as a resource, create an onscreen presentation using the AutoContent wizard. Select an appropriate presentation type. Add clip art, where applicable. Include your name in the footer. When you are done, save the presentation as Pet Activities and print the handouts.

Job Placement Services ★ ★ ★

4. You work at a job placement agency, and you have been asked to do a presentation for new clients that describes the services your company offers and the categories used to list available jobs. Visit a local placement agency or search the Web to gather information about job placement agency services and job listings. Using the AutoContent wizard, select an appropriate presentation type to

create a short presentation. Include your name in the footer. When you are done, save the presentation as Placement Services and print the handouts.

Careers with Animals ★★★

5. You have been volunteering at the Animal Rescue Foundation. The director has asked you to prepare a presentation on careers with animals to present to local schools in hopes that some students will be inspired to volunteer at the foundation. Using the pp01_AnimalCareers data file as a resource, create an onscreen presentation using the AutoContent wizard. Select an appropriate presentation type. Add some clip art where appropriate. Include your name in the footer. When you are done, save the presentation as Careers with Animals and print the handouts.

Modifying and Refining a Presentation

LAB 2

Objectives

After completing this lab, you will know how to:

1. Find and replace text.
2. Create and enhance a table.
3. Modify graphic objects and create a text box.
4. Create and enhance AutoShapes.
5. Change the presentation's design and color scheme.
6. Change slide and title masters.
7. Hide the title slide footer.
8. Duplicate and hide slides.
9. Add animation, sound, transition, and build effects.
10. Control and annotate a slide show.
11. Add speaker notes.
12. Check style consistency.
13. Document a file.
14. Customize print settings.

Case Study

Animal Rescue Foundation

The Animal Rescue Foundation director was very impressed with your first draft of the presentation to recruit volunteers, and asked to see the presentation onscreen. While viewing it together, you explained that you plan to make many more changes to improve the appearance of the presentation. For example, you plan to use a different design background and to include more art and other graphic features to enhance the appearance of the slides. You also explained that you will add more action to the slides using the special effects included with PowerPoint to keep the audience's attention.

The director suggested that you include more information on ways that volunteers can help. Additionally, because the organization has such an excellent adoption rate, the director wants you to include a table to illustrate the success of the adoption program.

Office PowerPoint 2003 gives you the design and production capabilities to create a first-class onscreen presentation. These features include artist-designed layouts and color schemes that give your presentation a professional appearance. In addition, you can add your own personal touches by modifying text attributes, incorporating art or graphics, and including animation to add impact, interest, and excitement to your presentation.

© Ryan McVay/Getty Images

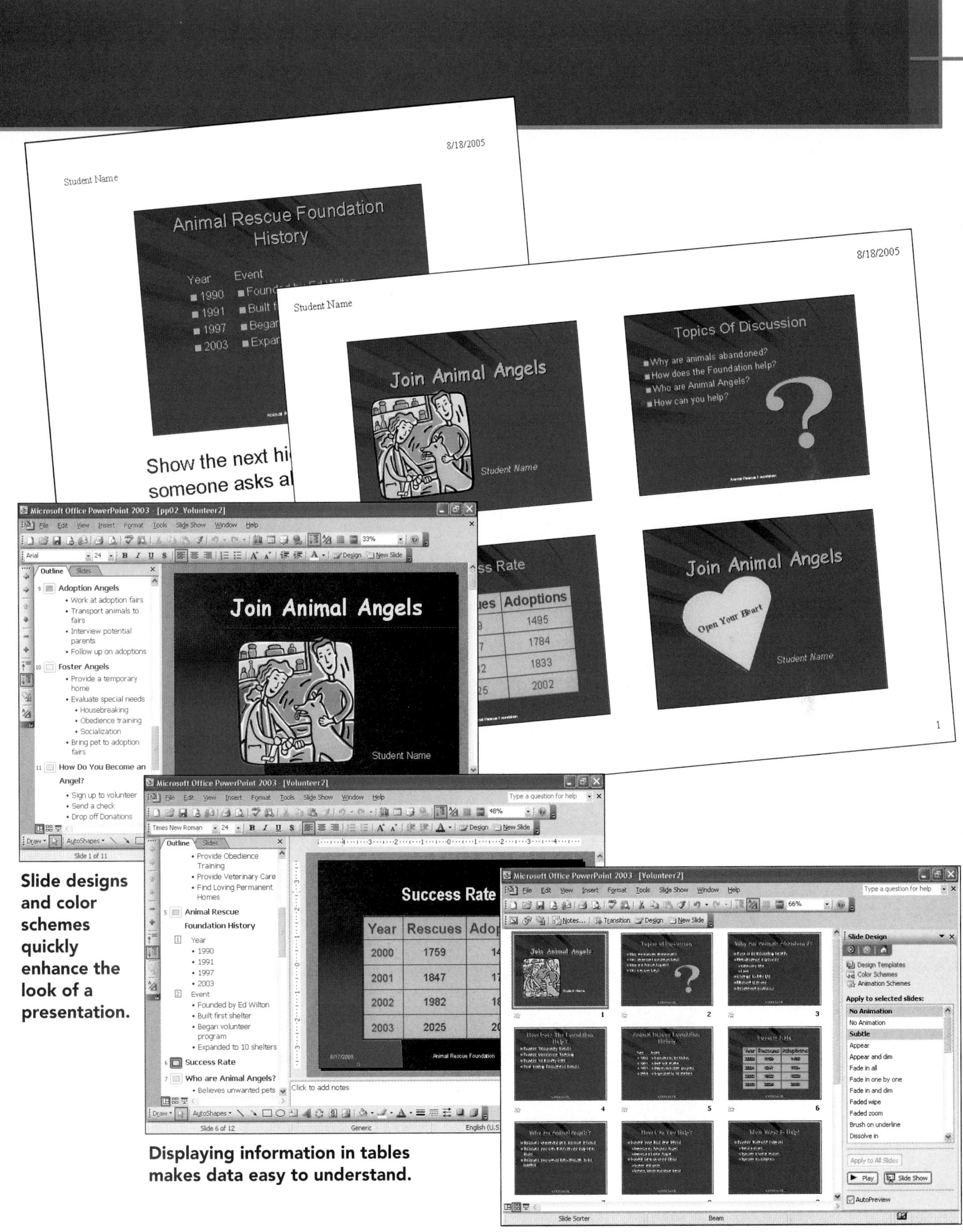

Slide designs and color schemes quickly enhance the look of a presentation.

Displaying information in tables makes data easy to understand.

Slide transitions, builds, and special effects add action to a slide show.

Concept Preview

The following concepts will be introduced in this lab:

1. **Find and Replace** To make editing easier, you can use the Find and Replace feature to find text in a presentation and replace it with other text.
2. **Table** A table is used to organize information into an easy-to-read format of horizontal rows and vertical columns.
3. **Alignment** Alignment controls the position of text entries within a space.
4. **Design Template** A design template is a professionally created slide design that is stored as a file and can be applied to your presentation.
5. **Master** A master is a special slide or page that stores information about the formatting for all slides or pages in a presentation.
6. **Special Effects** Special effects such as animation, sound, slide transitions, and builds are used to enhance the onscreen presentation.

Replacing Text

You have updated the content to include the additional information on ways that volunteers can help the Animal Rescue Foundation. You want to see the revised presentation.

1

- **Start Office PowerPoint 2003.**
- **Open the file** pp02_Volunteer2**.**
- **If necessary, switch to Normal view and close the task pane.**
- **Replace Student Name in slide 1 with your name.**
- **Scroll the Outline tab to view the content of the revised presentation.**

Your screen should be similar to Figure 2.1

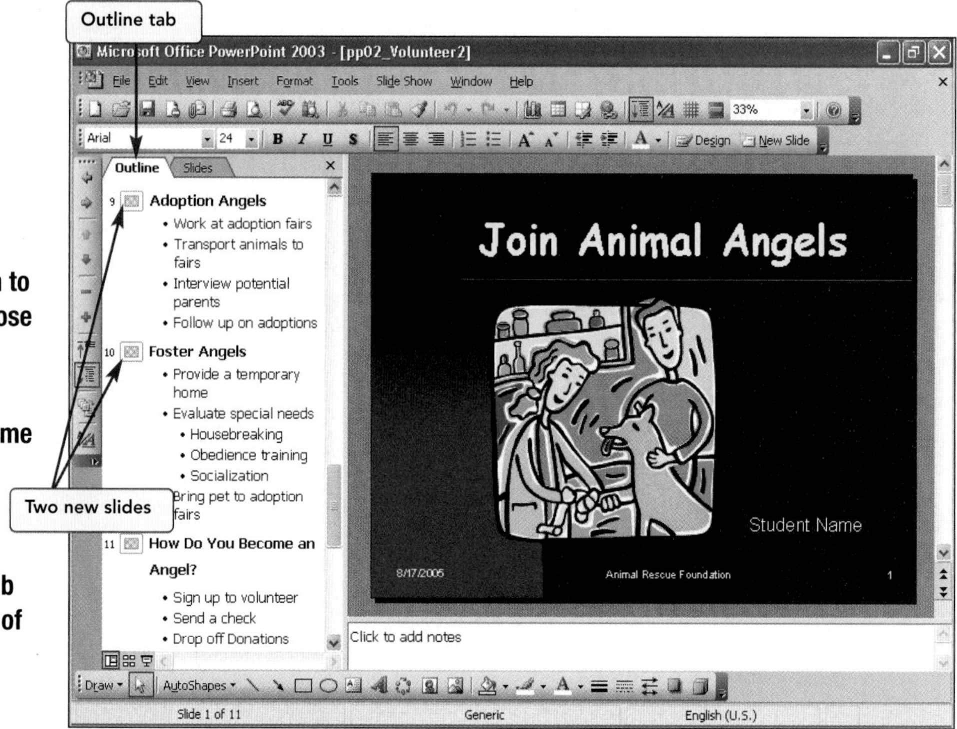

Figure 2.1

You added two new slides, 9 and 10, with more information about the Animal Angels volunteer organization, making the total number of slides in the presentation 11. As you reread the content of the presentation, you decide to edit the text by replacing the word "pet" in many locations with the word "animal."

Concept 1

Find and Replace

1 To make editing easier, you can use the **Find and Replace** feature to find text in a presentation and replace it with other text. For example, suppose you created a lengthy document describing the type of clothing and equipment needed to set up a world-class home gym, and then you decided to change "sneakers" to "athletic shoes." Instead of deleting every occurrence of "sneakers" and typing "athletic shoes," you can use the Find and Replace feature to perform the task automatically.

This feature is fast and accurate; however, use care when replacing so that you do not replace unintended matches.

Using Find and Replace

You want to replace selected occurrences of the word "pet" with "animal" throughout the presentation.

1 • **If necessary, display slide 1.**

• **Choose Edit/Replace.**

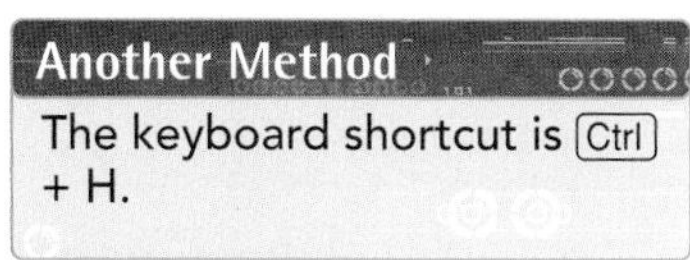

Additional Information

The Edit/Find command locates specified text only.

Your screen should be similar to Figure 2.2

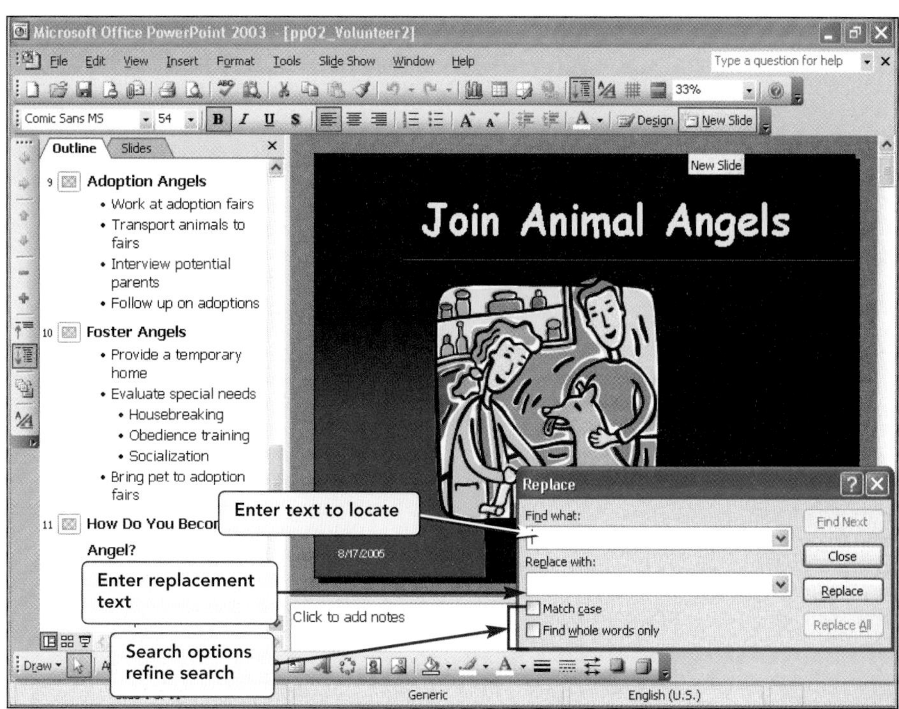

Figure 2.2

In the Find What text box, you enter the text you want to locate. The text you want to replace is entered in the Replace With text box. The replacement text must be entered exactly as you want it to appear in your presentation. The two options described in the following table allow you to refine the procedure that is used to conduct the search.

Option	Effect on Text
Match Case	Distinguishes between uppercase and lowercase characters. When selected, finds only those instances in which the capitalization matches the text you typed in the Find What box.
Find Whole Words Only	Distinguishes between whole and partial words. When selected, locates matches that are whole words and not part of a larger word. For example, finds "cat" only and not "catastrophe" too.

You want to find all occurrences of the complete word "pet" and replace them with the word "animal." You will not use either option because you want to locate all words regardless of case and because you want to find "pet" as well as "pets" in the presentation. You will enter the text to find and replace and begin the search.

2

- **Type pet in the Find What text box.**
- **Pres Tab or click in the Replace with text box.**

Additional Information

After entering the text to find, do not press ←Enter or this will choose Find Next and the search will begin.

- **Type animal in the Replace With text box.**
- **Click Find Next.**
- **If necessary, move the dialog box so you can see the located text.**

Your screen should be similar to Figure 2.3

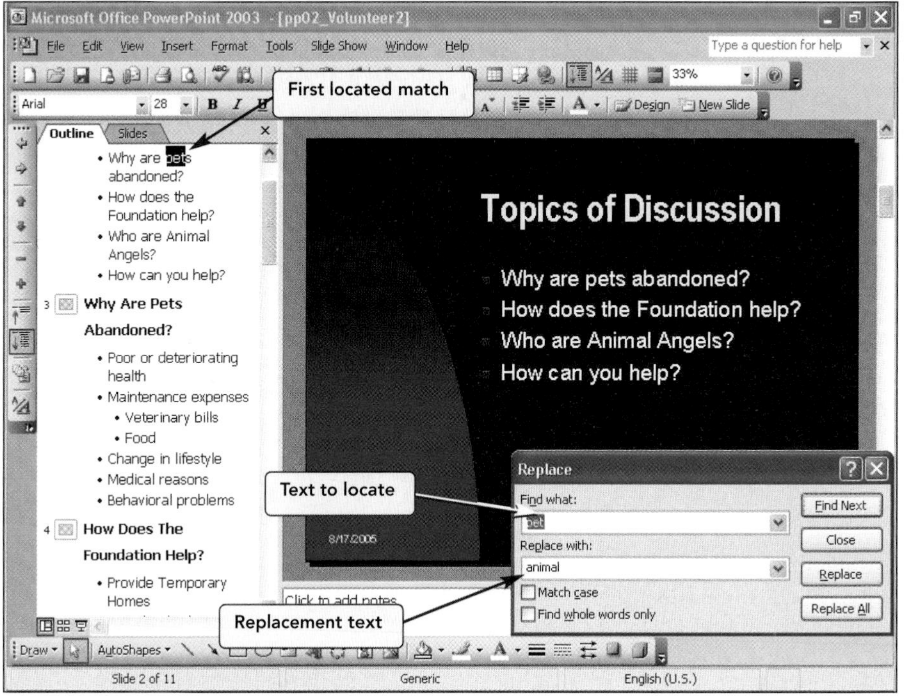

Figure 2.3

Additional Information

Find and Replace will highlight located text in whichever pane is current when the procedure started.

Immediately, the first occurrence of text in the presentation that matches the entry in the Find What text box is located and highlighted in the Outline tab. You will replace the located word in slide 2 with the replacement text.

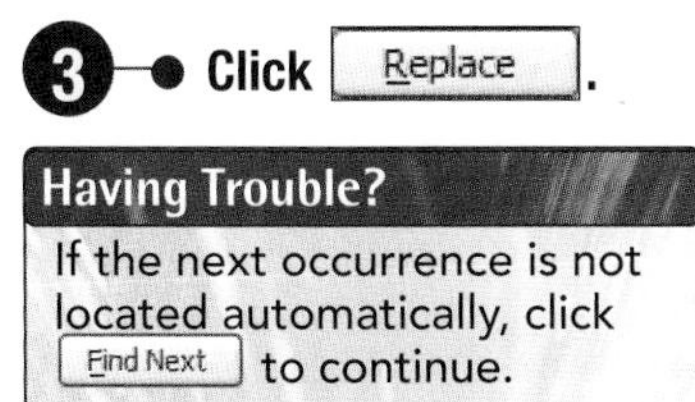

3 Click Replace.

Having Trouble?

If the next occurrence is not located automatically, click Find Next to continue.

Your screen should be similar to Figure 2.4

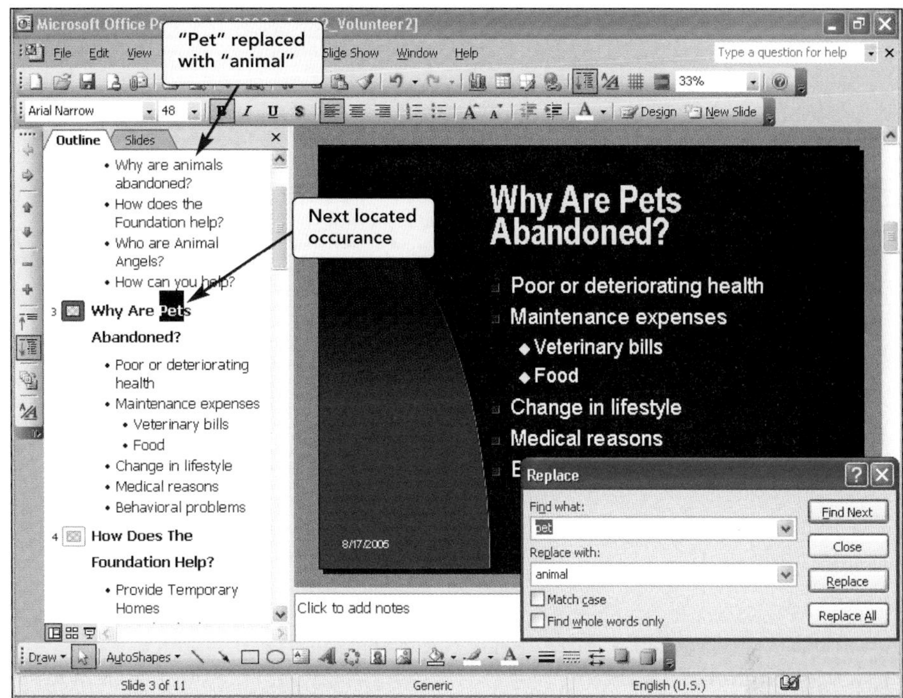

Figure 2.4

The highlighted text is replaced, and the next occurrence of the Find text is located in slide 3. Again, you want to replace this occurrence. As you do, notice the replacement is entered in lowercase even though it is replacing a word that begins with an uppercase character. You will correct this when you have finished using find and replace. If you do not want to replace a word, you can use Find Next to skip to the next occurrence without replacing it. You will continue to respond to the located occurrences.

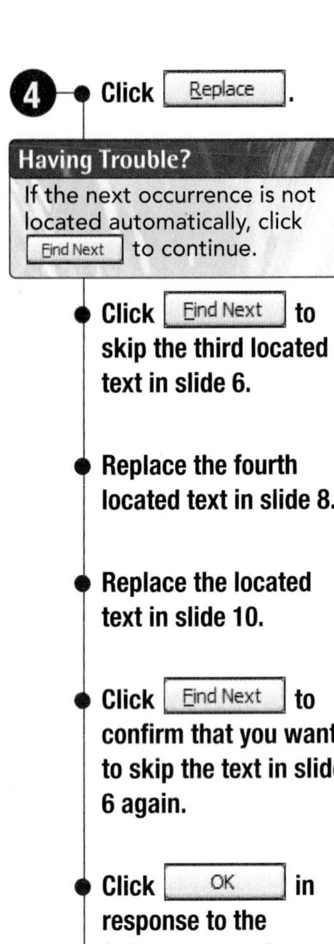

4 Click Replace.

Having Trouble?

If the next occurrence is not located automatically, click Find Next to continue.

- Click Find Next to skip the third located text in slide 6.
- Replace the fourth located text in slide 8.
- Replace the located text in slide 10.
- Click Find Next to confirm that you want to skip the text in slide 6 again.
- Click OK in response to the finished searching dialog box.
- Click Close to close the Replace dialog box.
- Edit the word "animals" to "Animals" in the title of slide 3.
- Save the presentation as **Volunteer2**.

Your screen should be similar to Figure 2.5

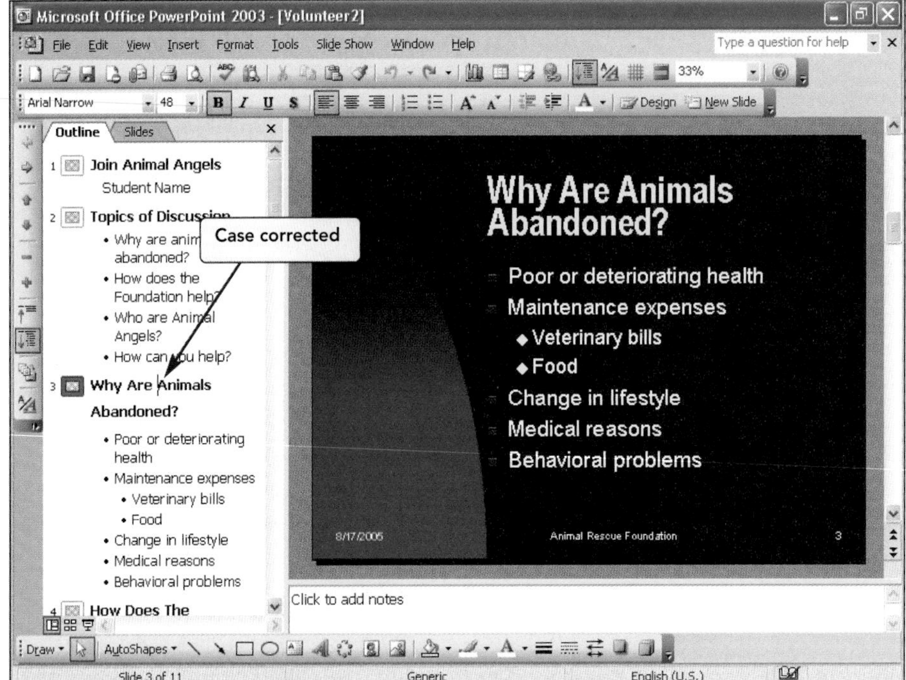

Figure 2.5

As you noticed, when you skip an occurrence, the program rechecks the presentation and asks you to reconfirm your choice before finishing. If you plan to change all occurrences, it is much faster to use the Replace All command button. Exercise care when using Replace All, however, because the search text you specify might be part of another word and you may accidentally replace text you want to keep.

In a similar manner you can find and replace fonts throughout a presentation using Format/Replace Fonts. When using this feature, however, all text throughout the presentation that is in the specified font to find is automatically changed to the selected replacement font.

Creating a Simple Table

During your discussion with the director, he suggested that you add a slide containing data showing the success of the adoption program. The information in this slide will be presented using a table layout.

Concept 2

Table

2 A **table** is used to organize information into an easy-to-read format of horizontal rows and vertical columns. The intersection of a row and column creates a **cell** in which you can enter data or other information. Cells in a table are identified by a letter and number, called a **table reference.** Columns are identified from left to right beginning with the letter A, and rows are numbered from top to bottom beginning with the number 1. The table reference of the top leftmost cell is A1 because it is in the first column (A) and first row (1) of the table. The third cell in column 2 is cell B3. The fourth cell in column 3 is C4.

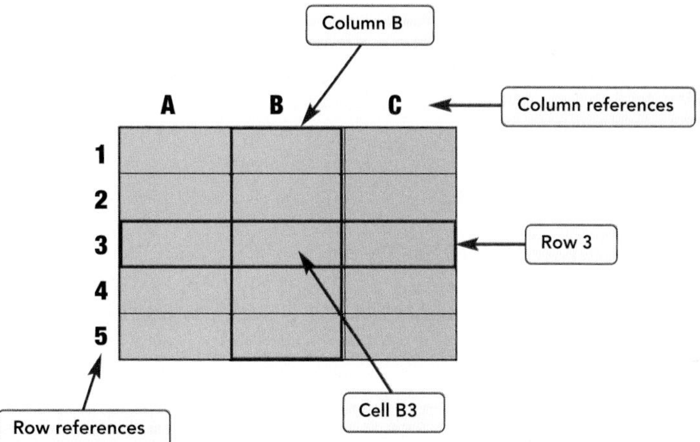

Tables are a very effective method for presenting information. The table layout organizes the information for readers and greatly reduces the number of words they have to read to interpret the data. Use tables whenever you can to make the information in your presentation easier to read.

The table you will create will display columns for the year, and for the number of rescues and adoptions. The rows will display the data for the past four years. Your completed table will be similar to the one shown here.

Year	Rescues	Adoptions
2000	1759	1495
2001	1847	1784
2002	1982	1833
2003	2025	2002

Using the Table Layout

To include this information in the presentation, you will insert a new slide after slide 5. Because this slide will contain a table showing the adoption data, you want to use the table slide layout.

1. **Display slide 5.**
   - **Click** New Slide.
   - **Under the Other Layouts group, click Title and Table.**
   - **Close the Slide Layout task pane.**

   Your screen should be similar to Figure 2.6

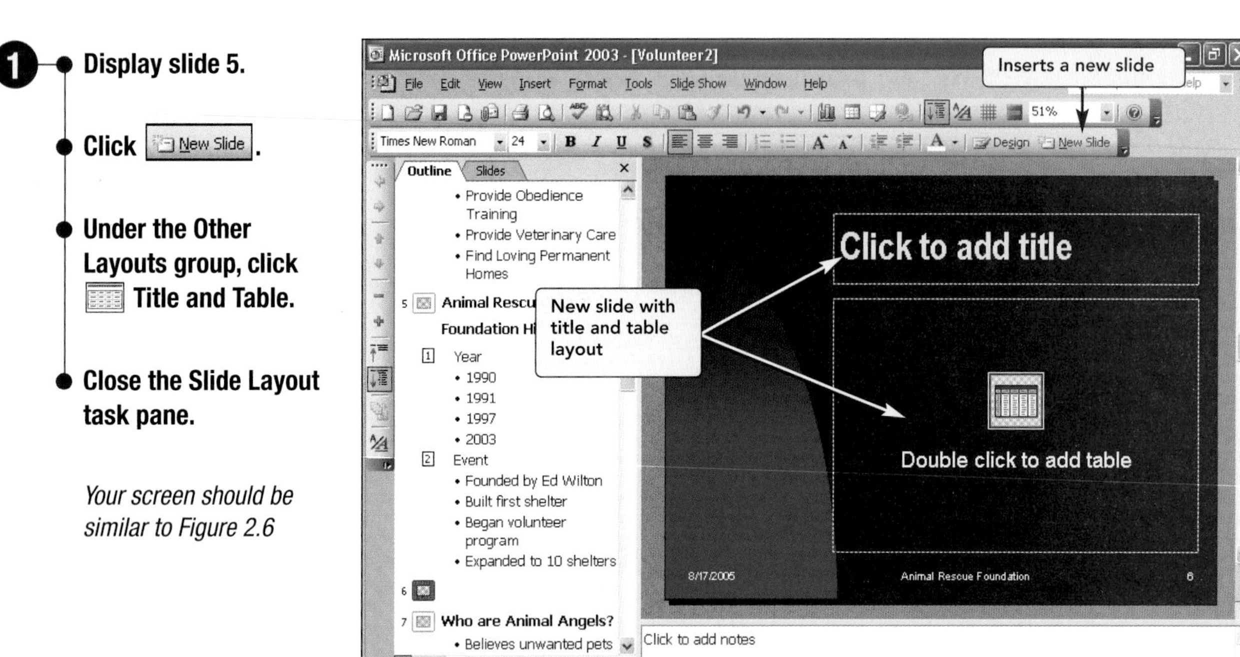

Figure 2.6

A new slide 6 with title and table placeholders is inserted.

Inserting the Table

Next, you want to add a slide title and then create the table to display the number of adoptions and rescues.

1. **Enter the title Success Rate in the title placeholder.**
   - **Double-click the table placeholder.**

   Your screen should be similar to Figure 2.7

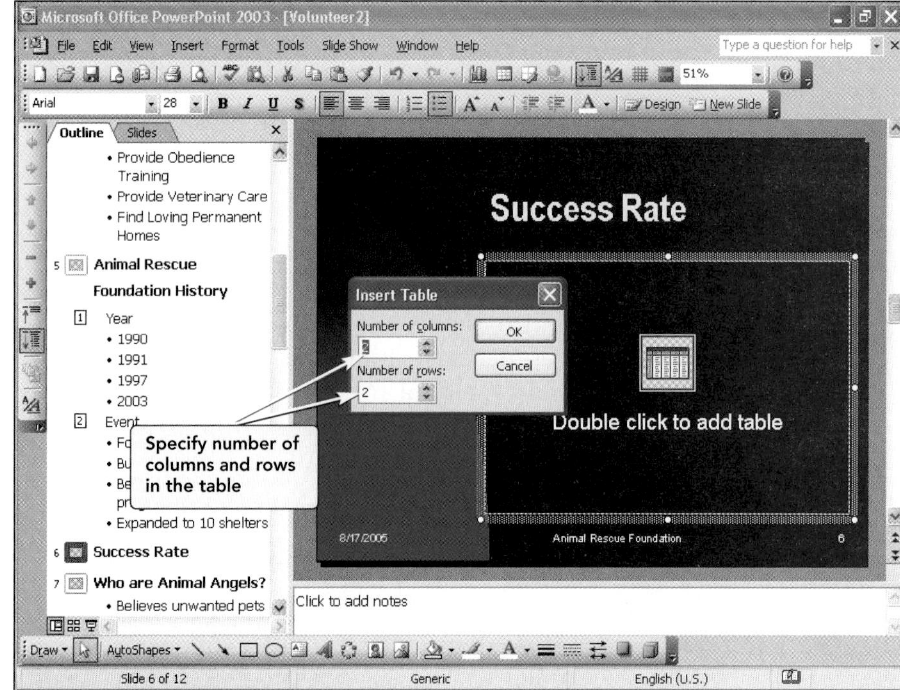

Figure 2.7

In the Insert Table dialog box, you specify the number of rows and columns for the table.

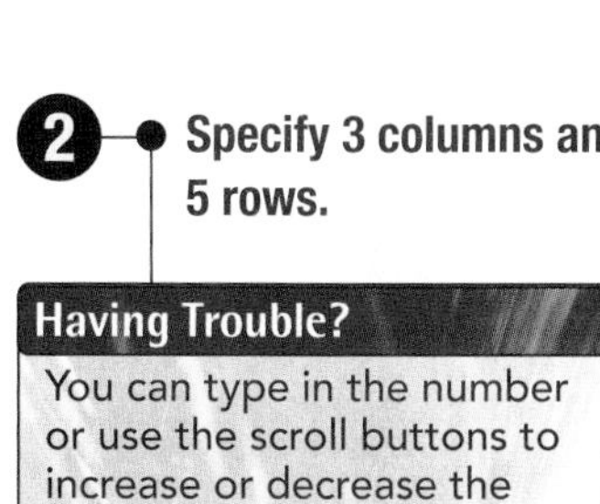

2 • **Specify 3 columns and 5 rows.**

Having Trouble?

You can type in the number or use the scroll buttons to increase or decrease the number.

• **Click** OK.

• **If necessary, move the Tables and Borders toolbar out of the way or dock it below the Formatting toolbar.**

Your screen should be similar to Figure 2.8

Having Trouble?

If the Tables and Borders toolbar is not displayed automatically, open it from the Toolbar shortcut menu.

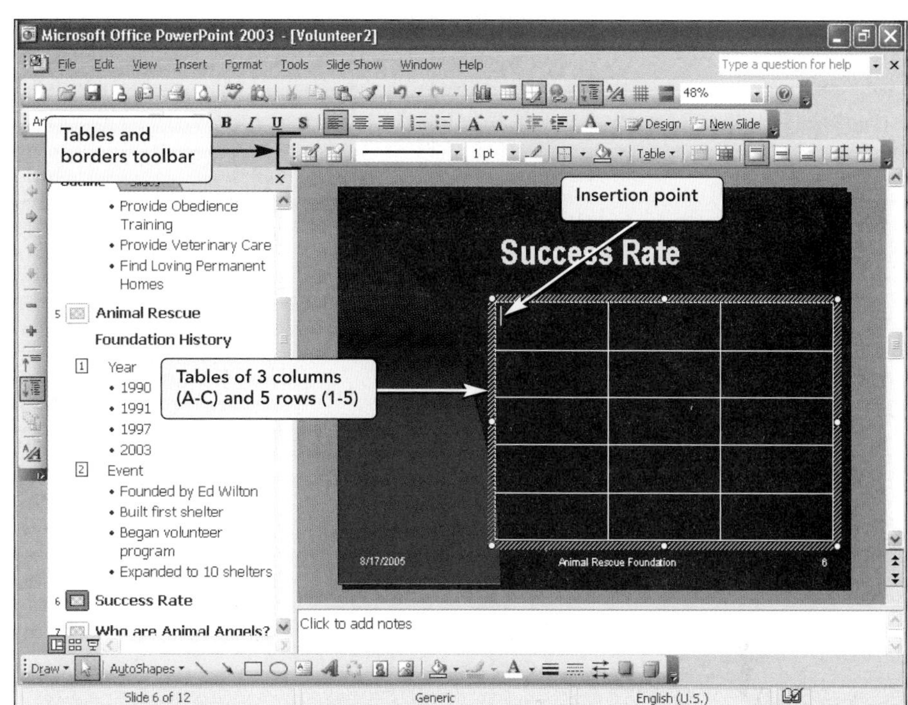

Figure 2.8

A basic table consisting of three columns and five rows is displayed as a selected object. The Tables and Borders toolbar buttons (identified below) are used to modify features associated with tables.

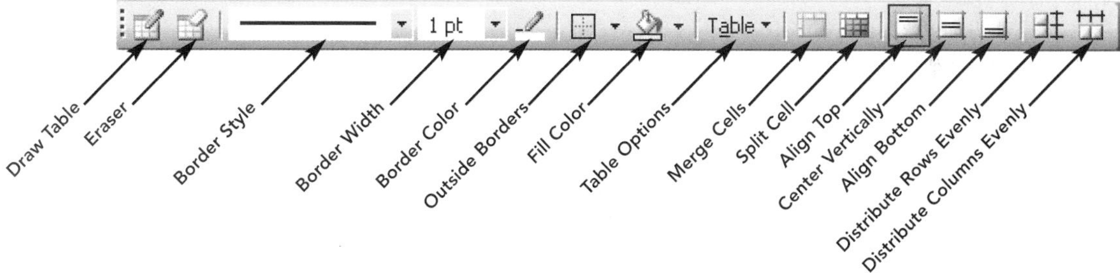

Entering Data in a Table

Now, you can enter the information into the table. The insertion point appears in the top left corner cell, cell A1, ready for you to enter text. To move in a table, click on the cell or use Tab to move to the next cell to the right and Shift + Tab to move to the cell to the left. If you are in the last cell of a row, pressing Tab takes you to the first cell of the next row. You can also use the ↑ and ↓ directional keys to move up or down a row. When you enter a large amount of text in a table, using Tab to move rather than the mouse is easier because your hands are already on the keyboard.

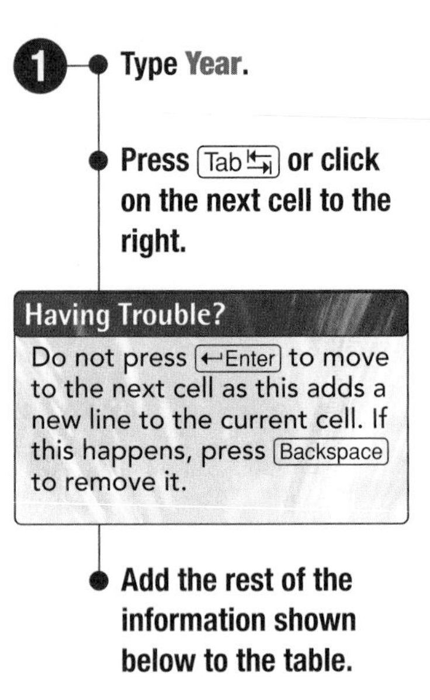

1 **Type Year.**

- **Press Tab or click on the next cell to the right.**

Having Trouble?

Do not press ←Enter to move to the next cell as this adds a new line to the current cell. If this happens, press Backspace to remove it.

- **Add the rest of the information shown below to the table.**

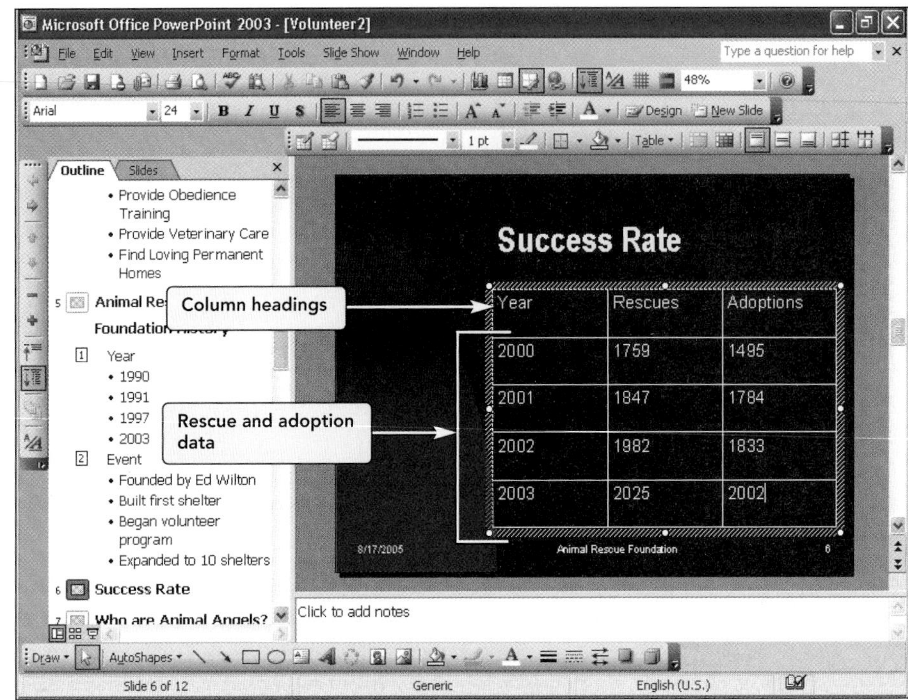

Figure 2.9

	Col. A	Col. B	Col. C
Row 1	Year	Rescues	Adoptions
Row 2	2000	1759	1495
Row 3	2001	1847	1784
Row 4	2002	1982	1833
Row 5	2003	2025	2002

Your screen should be similar to Figure 2.9

Notice that text that is attached to an object, in this case a table, is not displayed in the outline pane.

Applying Text Formats

Additional Information

Many of the Formatting toolbar buttons are toggle buttons, which means that you can click the button to turn on the feature for the selection, and then click it again to remove it from the selection.

Next, you want to improve the table's appearance by formatting the table text. Fonts and font size are two basic text attributes that you have used already. The table below describes some additional text formats and their uses. The Formatting toolbar contains buttons for many of the formatting effects.

Format	Example	Use
Bold, italic	**Bold** *Italic*	Adds emphasis
Underline	Underline	Adds emphasis
Superscript	"To be or not to be."[1]	Used in footnotes and formulas
Subscript	H_2O	Used in formulas
Shadow	Shadow	Adds distinction to titles and headings
Color	Color Color Color	Adds interest

You will increase the font size of the table text and add bold and color.

1

- **Drag to select row 1 containing the column headings and increase the font size to 36 pt.**
- **Click B Bold to bold the selection.**

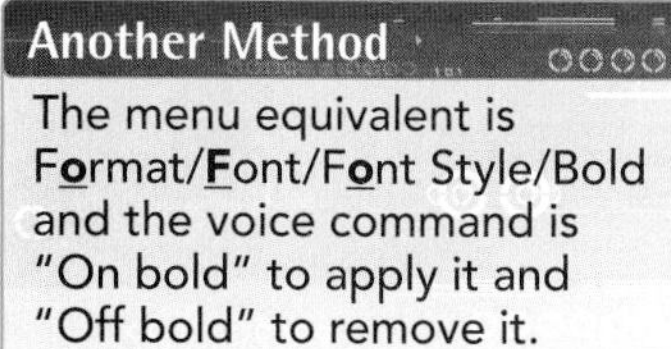

Another Method

The menu equivalent is Format/Font/Font Style/Bold and the voice command is "On bold" to apply it and "Off bold" to remove it.

- **Click A Font Color (in the Formatting or Drawing toolbar).**

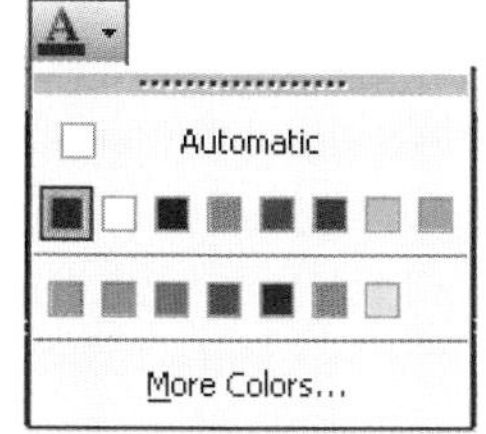

- **Click on the blue color.**

Another Method

The menu equivalent is Format/Font/Color.

- **Select rows 2 through 5 and increase the font size to 28.**

Your screen should be similar to Figure 2.10

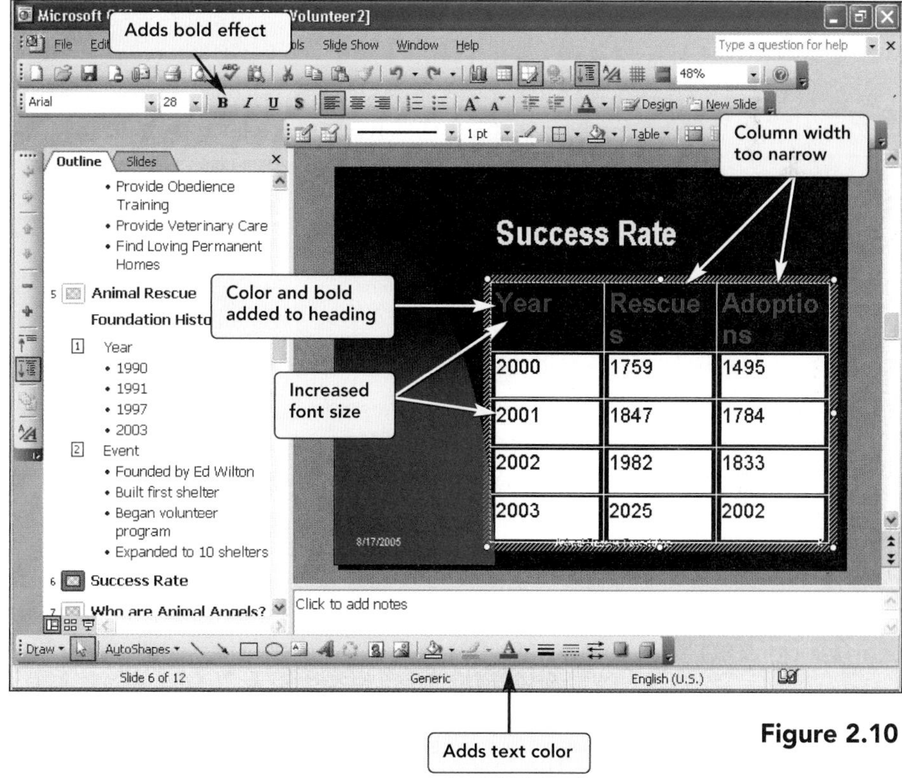

Figure 2.10

Sizing the Table Columns

Because you increased the font size of the headings, two of the headings are too large to display on a single line in the cell space. To correct this problem, you will adjust the size of the columns to fit their contents. To adjust the column width or row height, drag the row and column boundaries. The mouse pointer appears as a when you can size the column and when you can size the row.

1 **Decrease the width of the Year column and then adjust the width of the other two columns as in Figure 2.11.**

Your screen should be similar to Figure 2.11

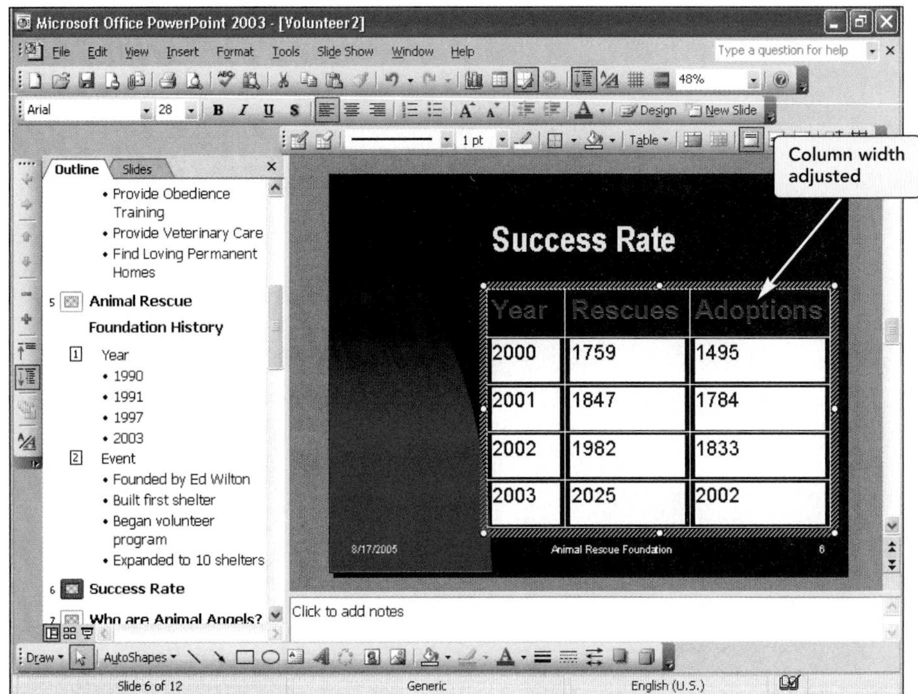

Figure 2.11

Now the column headings easily fit within the cell space.

Aligning Text in Cells

Now that the columns are more appropriately sized, you want to center the text and data in the cells. To do this, you can change the alignment of the text entries.

Concept 3

Alignment

3 **Alignment** controls the position of text entries within a space. You can change the horizontal placement of an entry in a placeholder or a table cell by using one of the four horizontal alignment settings: left, center, right, and justified. You can also align text vertically in a table cell with the top, middle, or bottom of the cell space.

Horizontal Alignment	Effect on Text	Vertical Alignment	Effect on Text
Left	Aligns text against the left edge of the placeholder or cell, leaving the right edge of text, which wraps to another line, ragged.	Top Text	Aligns text at the top of the cell space.
Center	Centers each line of text between the left and right edges of the placeholder or cell.	Middle Text	Aligns text in the middle of the cell space.
Right	Aligns text against the right edge of the placeholder or cell, leaving the left edge of multiple lines ragged.	Bottom Text	Aligns text at the bottom of the cell space.
Justified	Aligns text evenly with both the right and left edges of the placeholder or cell.		

The commands to change horizontal alignment are options under the F**o**rmat/**A**lignment menu. However, using the shortcuts shown below is much quicker.

Alignment	Keyboard Shortcut	Button	Voice
Left	Ctrl + L		Left justify
Center	Ctrl + E		Centered
Right	Ctrl + R		Right justify
Justified	Ctrl + J		

You will center the cell entries both horizontally and vertically in their cell spaces.

1
- **Select the entire contents of the table.**
- **Click Center (on the Formatting toolbar).**
- **Click Center Vertically (on the Tables and Borders toolbar).**

Your screen should be similar to Figure 2.12

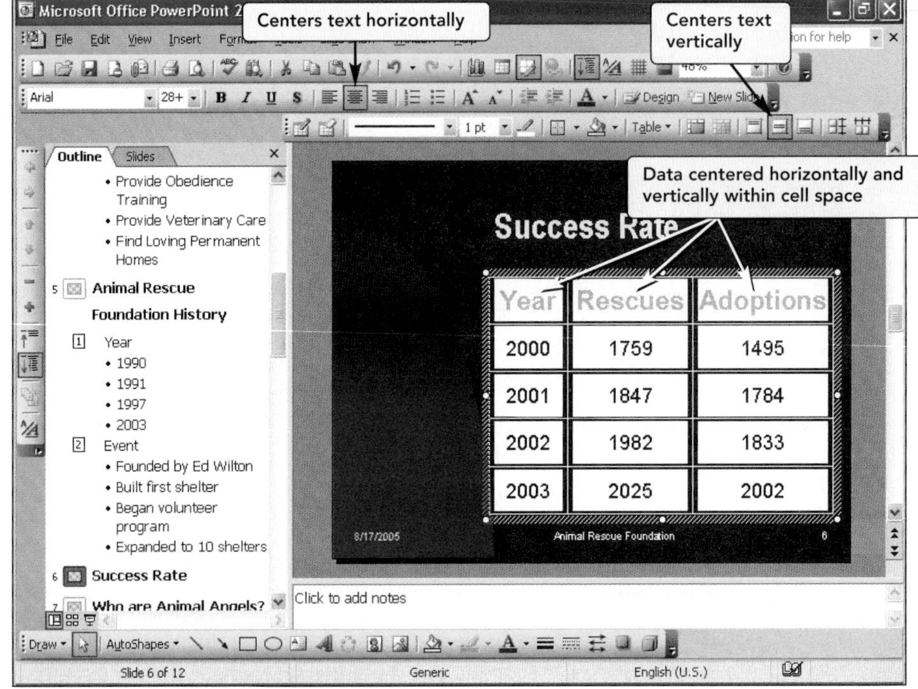

Figure 2.12

Changing the Border Size and Color

Next, you will add a color to the outside border and increase the thickness or weight of the border line. The Tables and Borders toolbar is used to make these enhancements.

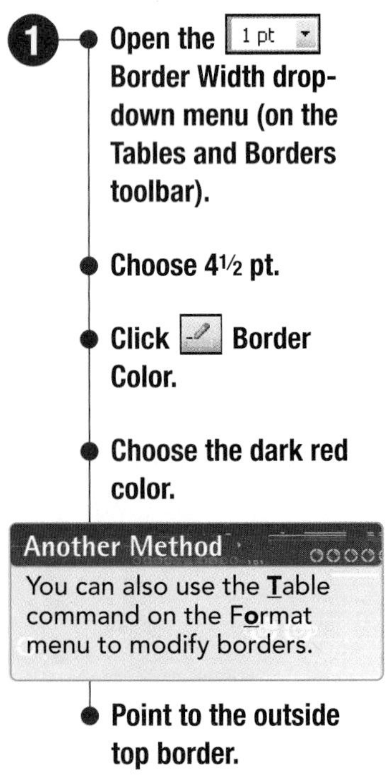

1
- **Open the 1 pt Border Width drop-down menu (on the Tables and Borders toolbar).**
- **Choose 4½ pt.**
- **Click Border Color.**
- **Choose the dark red color.**

Another Method

You can also use the Table command on the Format menu to modify borders.

- **Point to the outside top border.**

Your screen should be similar to Figure 2.13

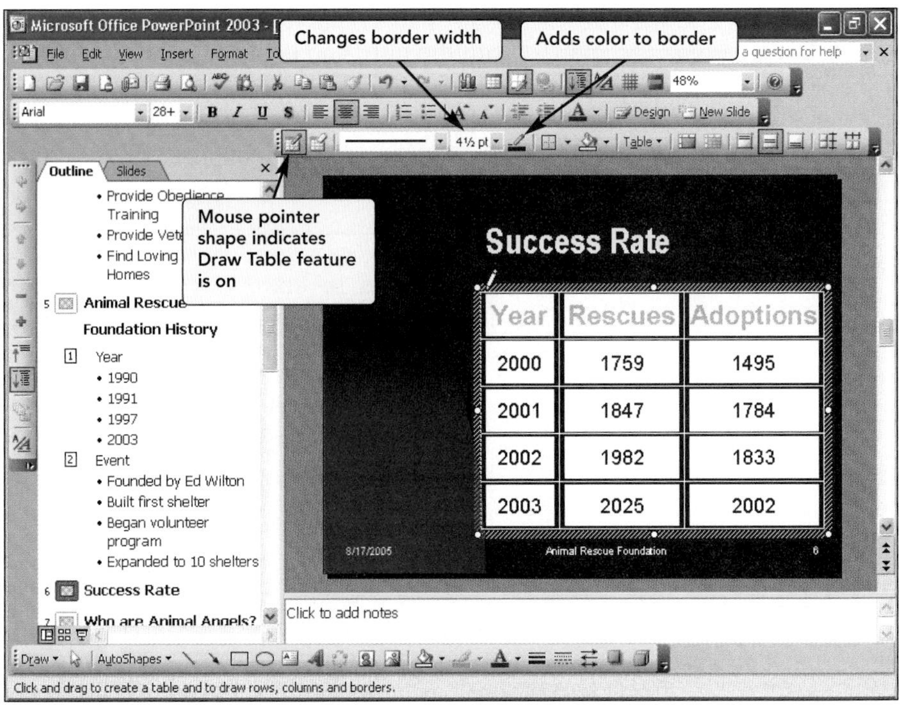

Figure 2.13

The mouse pointer is a ✎ indicating that the Draw Table feature has been turned on. When on, this feature allows you to add row and column lines to an existing table. It is also used to modify the settings associated with the existing lines. You will drag the mouse pointer over the existing outside border to modify it to the new settings you have selected. As you drag, a dotted line identifies the section of the border that will be modified.

2 **Drag along the top border to apply the new settings.**

Having Trouble?

You will need to look carefully to see the dotted line as you drag, as it is difficult to see in the cross-hatch border.

- **In the same manner, apply the new border formats to the remaining three sides of the table.**

- **Click Draw Table to turn off the Draw Table feature.**

- **Click outside the table to deselect it.**

Your screen should be similar to Figure 2.14

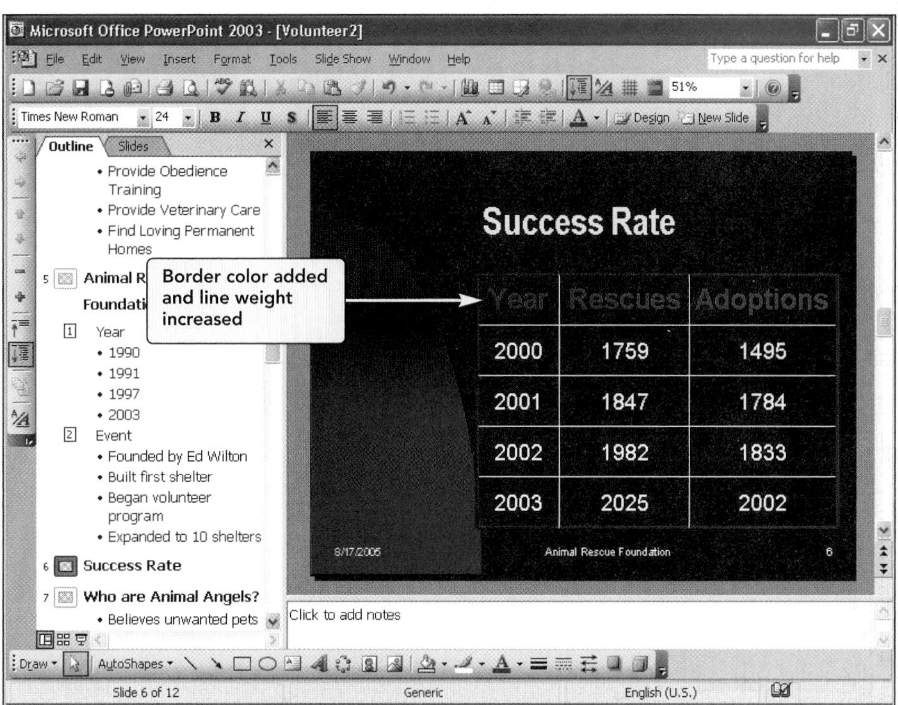

Figure 2.14

The increased weight and color have been applied to the outside border of the table.

Adding Background Fill Color

Finally, you will add a background fill color to the table.

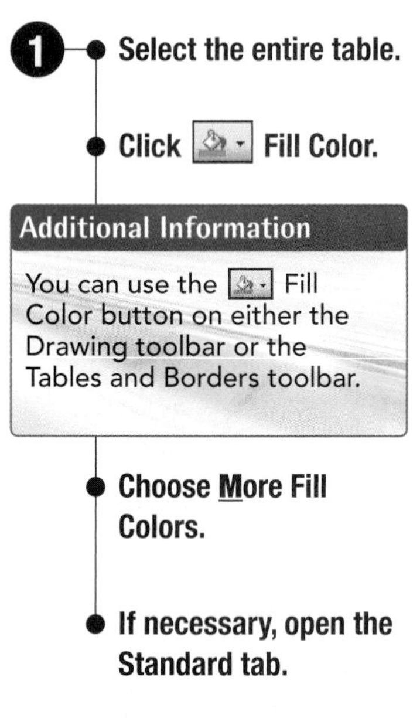

1

- **Select the entire table.**
- **Click Fill Color.**

Additional Information

You can use the Fill Color button on either the Drawing toolbar or the Tables and Borders toolbar.

- **Choose More Fill Colors.**
- **If necessary, open the Standard tab.**

Your screen should be similar to Figure 2.15

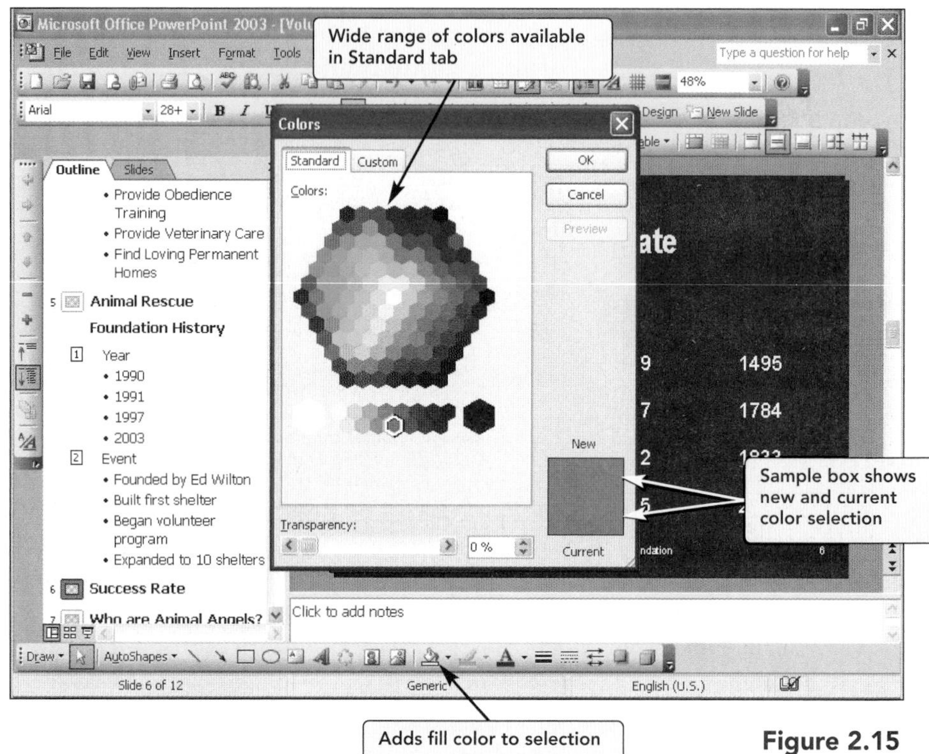

Figure 2.15

From the Standard tab of the Colors dialog box, you can select from a wider range of colors. The current fill color, gray, is selected. The sample box will show the new color you select in the upper half and the current color in the lower half. Because you have not yet selected a new color, only one color is displayed. You want to use a gold color for the table background.

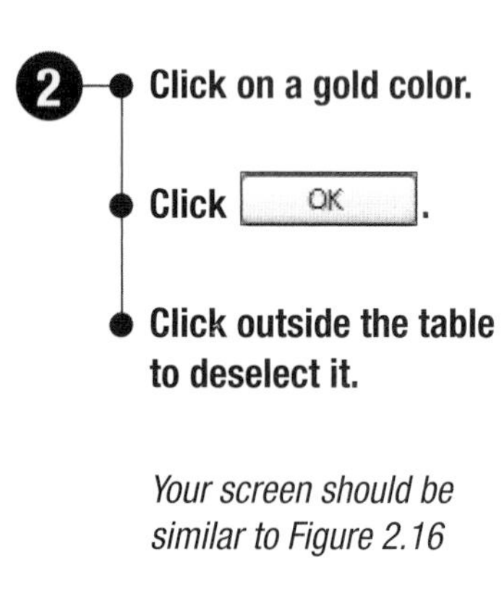

2

- **Click on a gold color.**
- **Click OK.**
- **Click outside the table to deselect it.**

Your screen should be similar to Figure 2.16

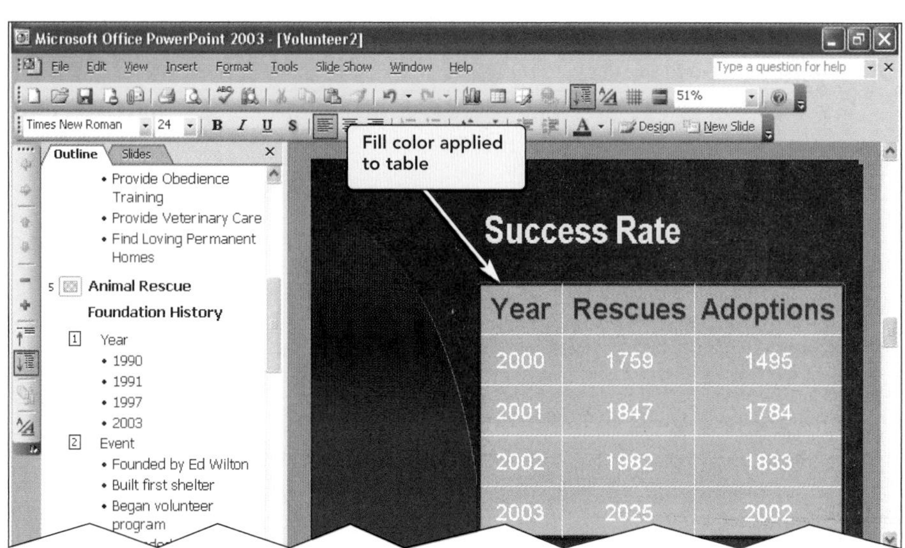

Year	Rescues	Adoptions
2000	1759	1495
2001	1847	1784
2002	1982	1833
2003	2025	2002

Figure 2.16

The new background color makes the data and row and column lines difficult to see. To correct this problem, you will change the color of the lines and data. You will change the interior line color to the same as the outside border color. Because there are many interior table lines, you will use the Format Table dialog box to make this change quickly.

3

- **Change the font color of the years to the same blue as the column headings.**

Additional Information

Because this was the last used font color, you can simply click Font Color to apply the color.

- **Change the font color of the numeric data to a dark color of your choice.**
- **Select the entire table.**
- **Choose Borders and Fill from the table shortcut menu.**

Having Trouble?

Right-click on the table to display the shortcut menu.

Another Method

You can also double-click on the table border to open the Format Table dialog box.

- **Select the red color from the Color drop-down palette.**
- **Click on the two interior table border lines in the diagram.**
- **Click Preview.**
- **If necessary, move the Format table dialog box to see the table.**

Your screen should be similar to Figure 2.17

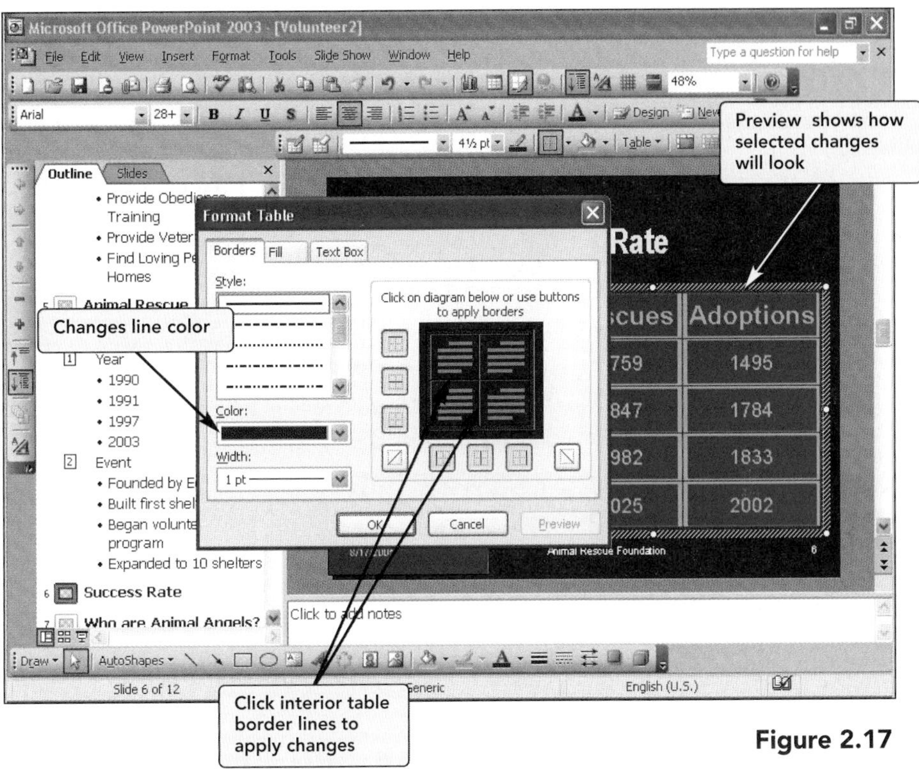

Figure 2.17

All interior table lines in the table in the slide have changed to the selected color. This was faster than changing each interior line color using the Draw Table feature.

4 Click  to apply the settings and close the dialog box.

- Choose **View/Ruler** to display the ruler.

Additional Information

Use the ruler as a guide for placement of objects on the slide.

- Center the table horizontally on the slide as in Figure 2-18.

Having Trouble?

Drag the table placeholder border when the mouse pointer is ✥ to move the table.

Having Trouble?

Align the center sizing handle of the table placeholder with the 0 position on the horizontal ruler.

- Click outside the table to deselect it.
- Save the presentation.

Your screen should be similar to Figure 2.18

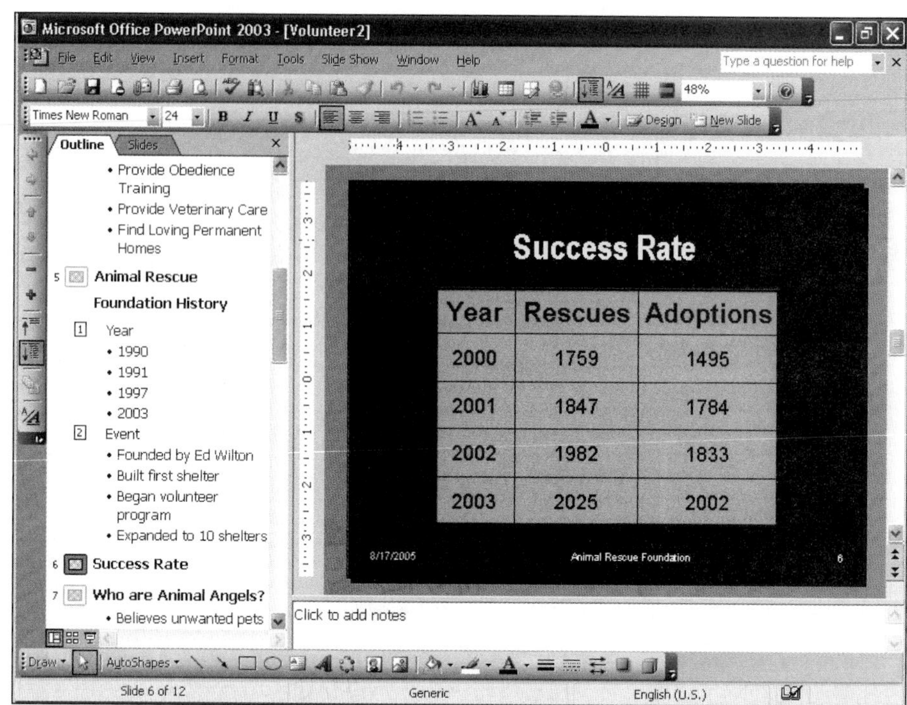

Figure 2.18

The enhancements you added to the table greatly improve its appearance.

Modifying and Creating Graphic Objects

Now you are ready to enhance the presentation by adding several graphics. As you have seen, you can add many ready-made graphics to slides. Many of these can be customized to your needs by changing colors and adding and deleting elements. You can also create your own graphics using the AutoShapes feature.

Changing the Slide Layout

First, you want to add a graphic to slide 2. Before adding the graphic, you will change the slide layout from the bulleted list style to a style that is designed to accommodate text as well as other types of content such as graphics.

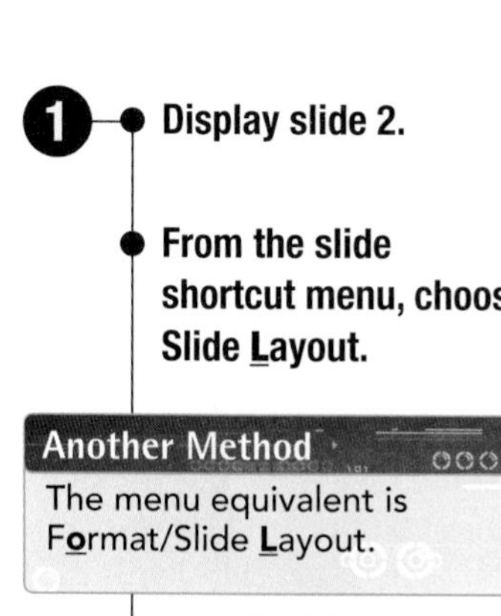

1 **Display slide 2.**

From the slide shortcut menu, choose Slide Layout.

Another Method

The menu equivalent is Format/Slide Layout.

Click Title, Text, and Content (from the Text and Content Layouts category).

Your screen should be similar to Figure 2.19

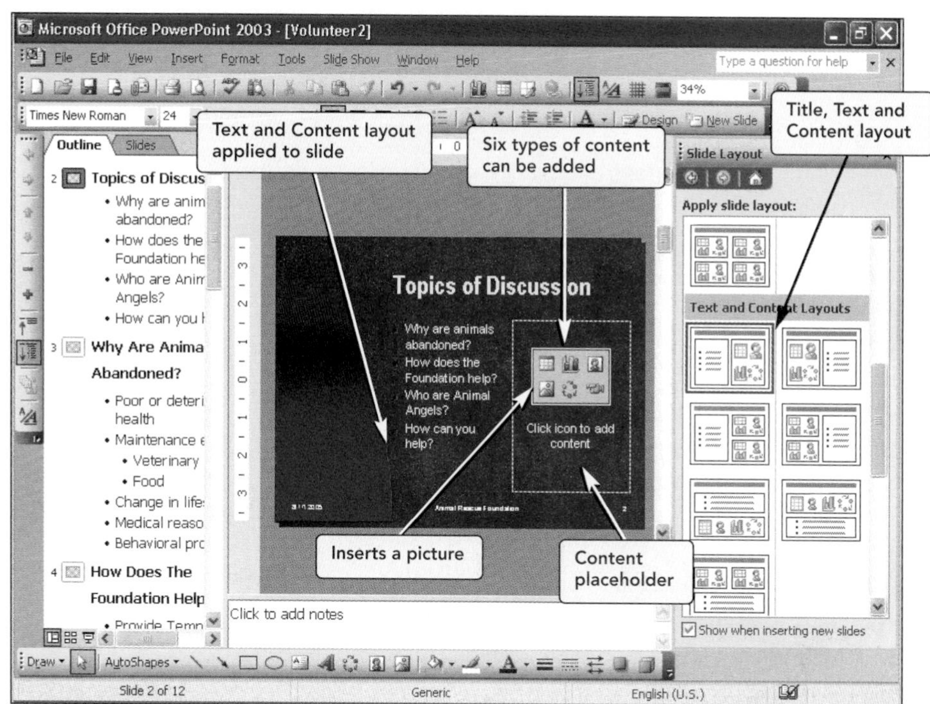

Figure 2.19

A content placeholder was added on the right side of the slide, and the bulleted text placeholder was resized and moved to the left side of the slide. Inside the content placeholder are six icons representing the different types of content that can be inserted. Clicking an icon opens the appropriate feature to add the specified type of content. You will add a clip art graphic of a question mark and then size the placeholder.

2
- Close the Slide Layout task pane.
- Click Insert Picture in the content placeholder.

Additional Information

A ScreenTip identifies the item as you point to it.

- If necessary, change the Look In location to the location containing your data files.
- Locate and select the pp02_Question Mark clip art.
- Click Insert.
- Increase the size of the graphic and position it as in Figure 2.20.

Your screen should be similar to Figure 2.20

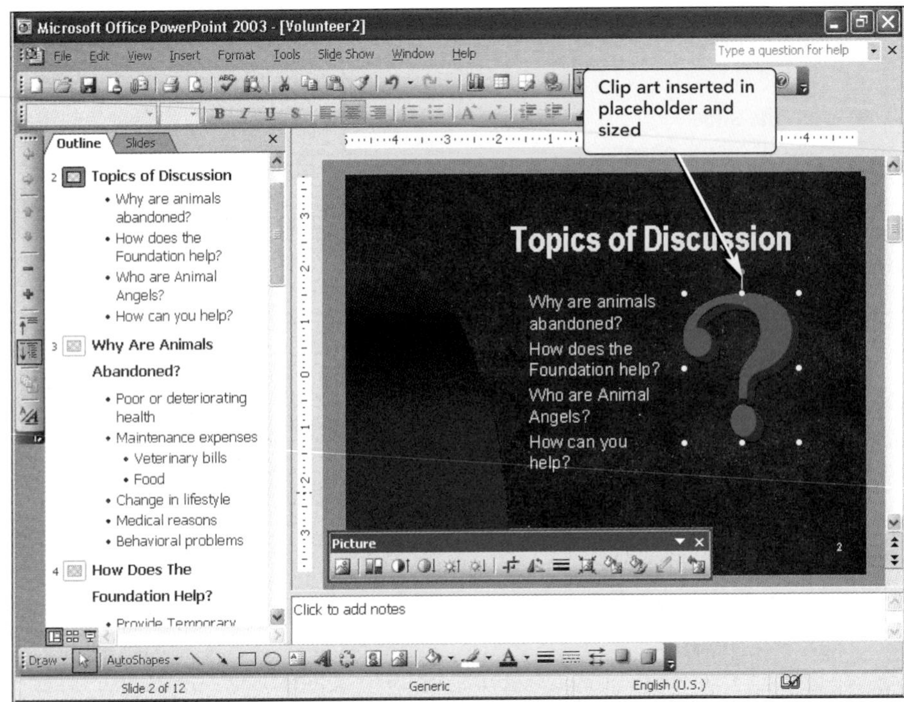

Figure 2.20

Recoloring a Picture

Now you want to change the color of the graphic to a bright gold color.

1

- If necessary, display the Picture toolbar.
- Click Recolor Picture.

Another Method

The menu equivalent is Format/Picture/Recolor.

Your screen should be similar to Figure 2.21

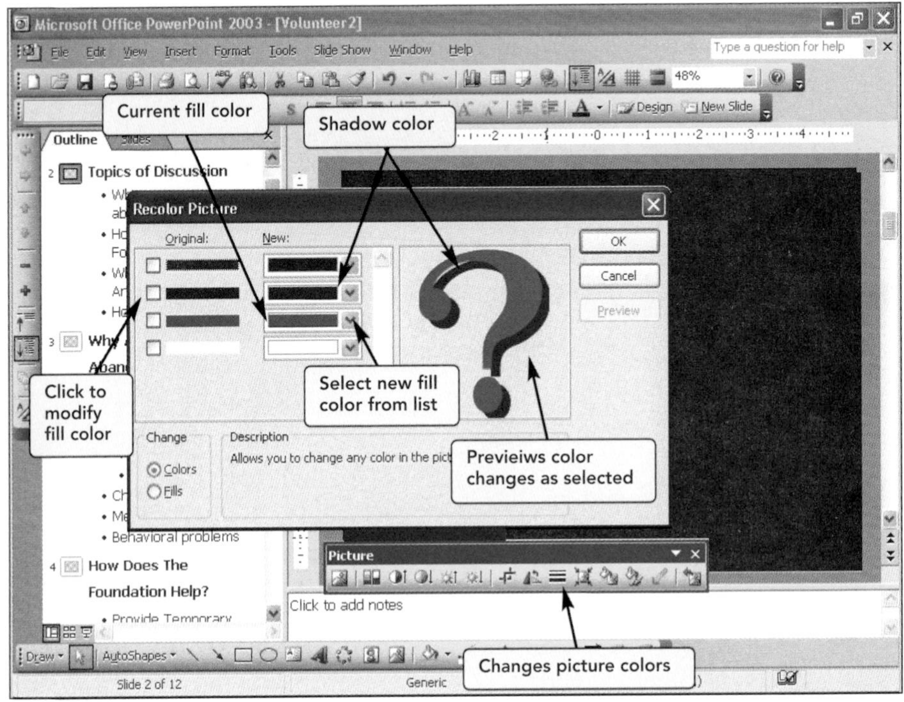

Figure 2.21

The original colors for each component of the picture are listed. Selecting the check box for a component allows you to change the color to a new color. You want to change the light blue color to gold. The preview area reflects your color changes as they are made.

2

- **Select the Original light blue color check box.**
- **Open the New color drop-down menu for the selected component and select gold.**

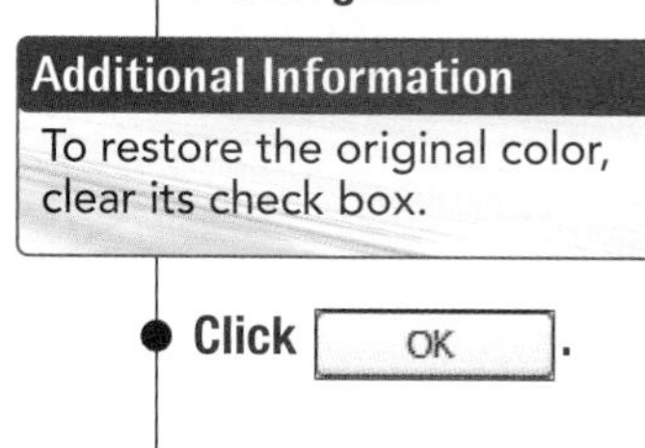

Additional Information

To restore the original color, clear its check box.

- **Click OK.**
- **Deselect the clip art and, if necessary, turn off the Picture toolbar.**

Your screen should be similar to Figure 2.22

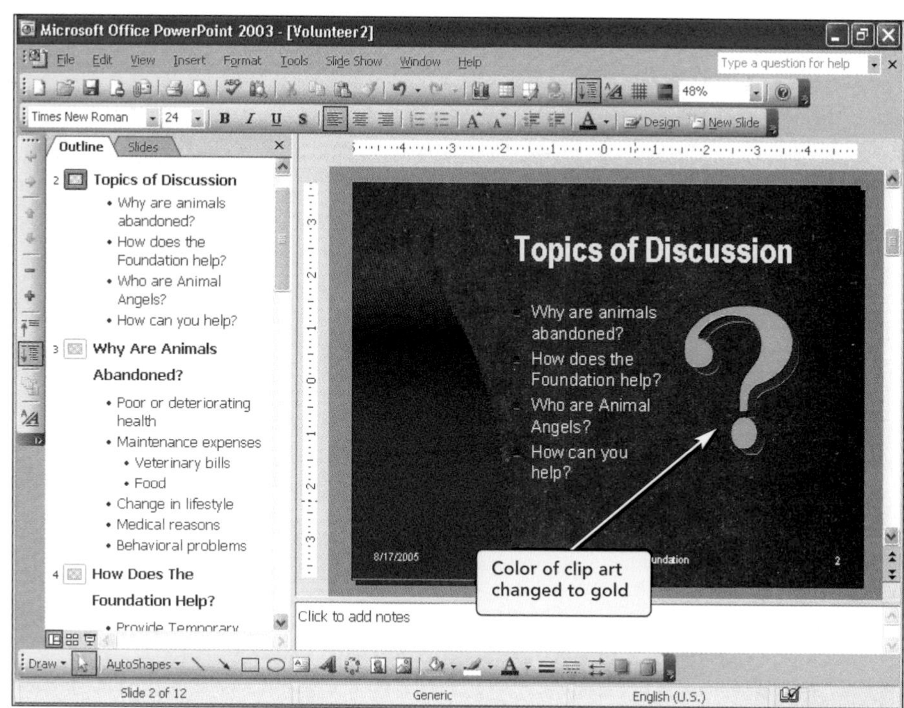

Figure 2.22

The graphic now adds much more color to the slide.

Duplicating a Slide

At the end of the presentation, you want to add a concluding slide. This slide needs to be powerful, because it is your last chance to convince your audience to join Animal Angels. To create the concluding slide, you will duplicate slide 1 and then create a graphic to complement the slide.

Duplicating a slide creates a copy of the selected slide and places it directly after the selected slide. You can duplicate a slide in any view, but in this case you will use the Outline tab in Slide view to duplicate slide 1 and move it to the end of the presentation.

1. Click slide 1 in the Outline tab.
   - Choose **I**nsert/**D**uplicate Slide.
   - Drag slide 2 in the Outline tab to the end of the list of slides.

Another Method

You can also duplicate a slide using the **C**opy and **P**aste commands on the **E**dit menu.

Your screen should be similar to Figure 2.23

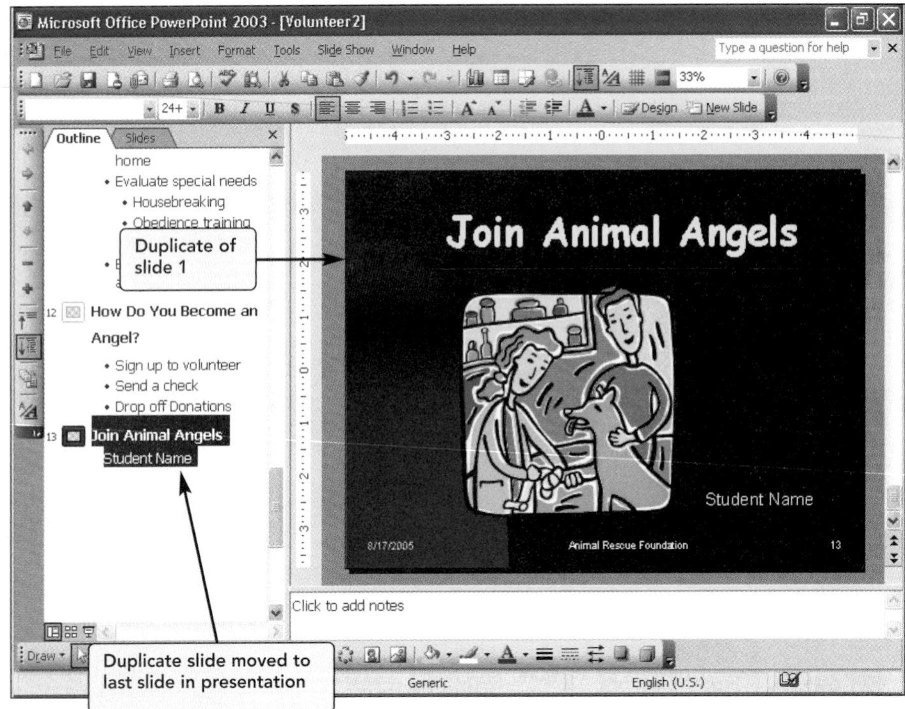

Figure 2.23

Duplicating the slide saved you time because you do not need to redo the changes to the title and subtitle.

Inserting an AutoShape

Additional Information

Most shapes can also be inserted from the Clip Organizer as well.

You want to replace the graphic with another of a heart. To quickly add a shape, you will use one of the ready-made shapes supplied with PowerPoint called **AutoShapes**. These include such basic shapes as rectangles and circles, a variety of lines, block arrows, flowchart symbols, stars and banners, and callouts.

1

- **Select the graphic and press Delete.**
- **Click AutoShapes (in the Drawing toolbar).**

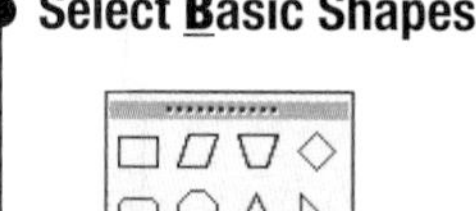

- **Select Basic Shapes.**

- **Click Heart.**
- **In the space on the left side of the slide, click and drag downward and to the right to create the heart.**

Another Method

The menu equivalent is Insert/Picture/AutoShapes.

- **If necessary, size and position the heart as in Figure 2.24.**

Additional Information

An AutoShape can be sized and moved just like any other object.

Another Method

To maintain the height and width proportions of the AutoShape, hold down Shift while you drag.

Your screen should be similar to Figure 2.24

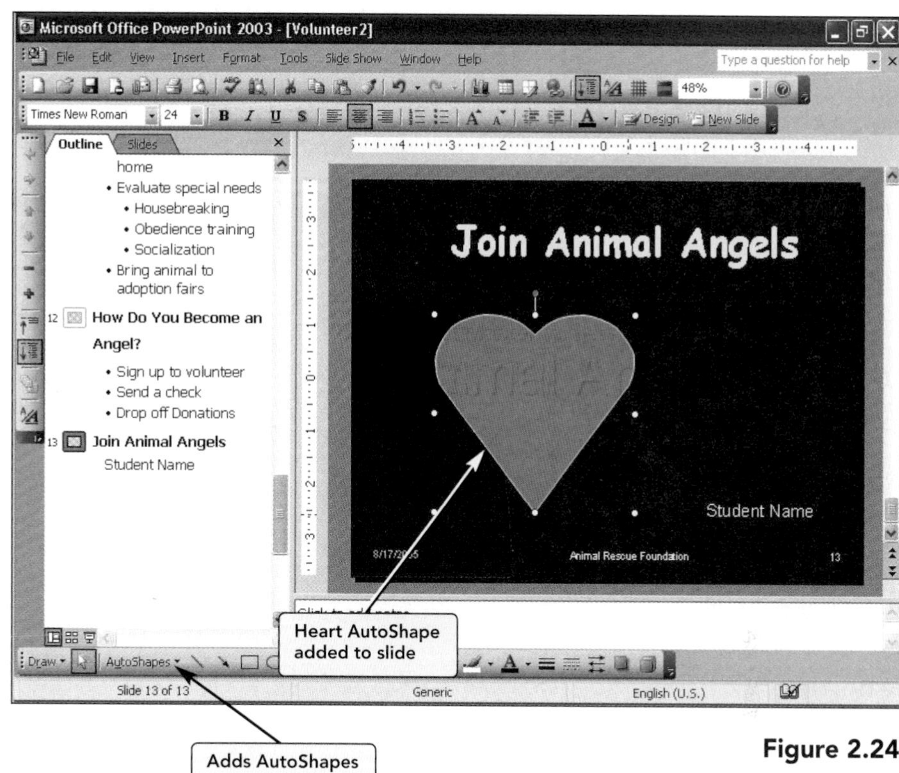

Figure 2.24

Enhancing the AutoShape

Next, you will enhance its appearance by changing the fill color of the heart and adding a shadow behind the heart. Then you will change the color of the shadow. Generally, a darker shade of the object's color for a shadow is very effective.

1 Click Fill Color and select a bright yellow from the Standard Colors palette.

- Click Shadow Style (on the Drawing toolbar).

- Select any shadow style from the pop-up menu.

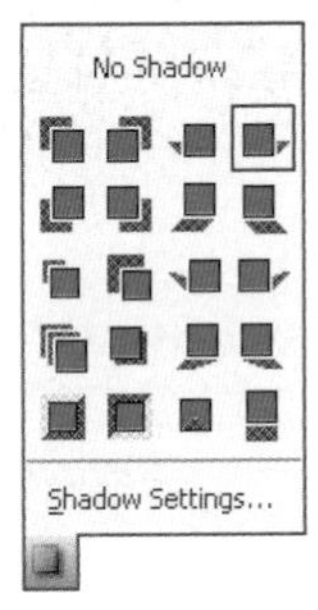

- Click Shadow Style and choose Shadow Settings.

- Click Shadow Color from the Shadow Settings toolbar and select gold.

- Close the Shadow Settings toolbar.

Your screen should be similar to Figure 2.25

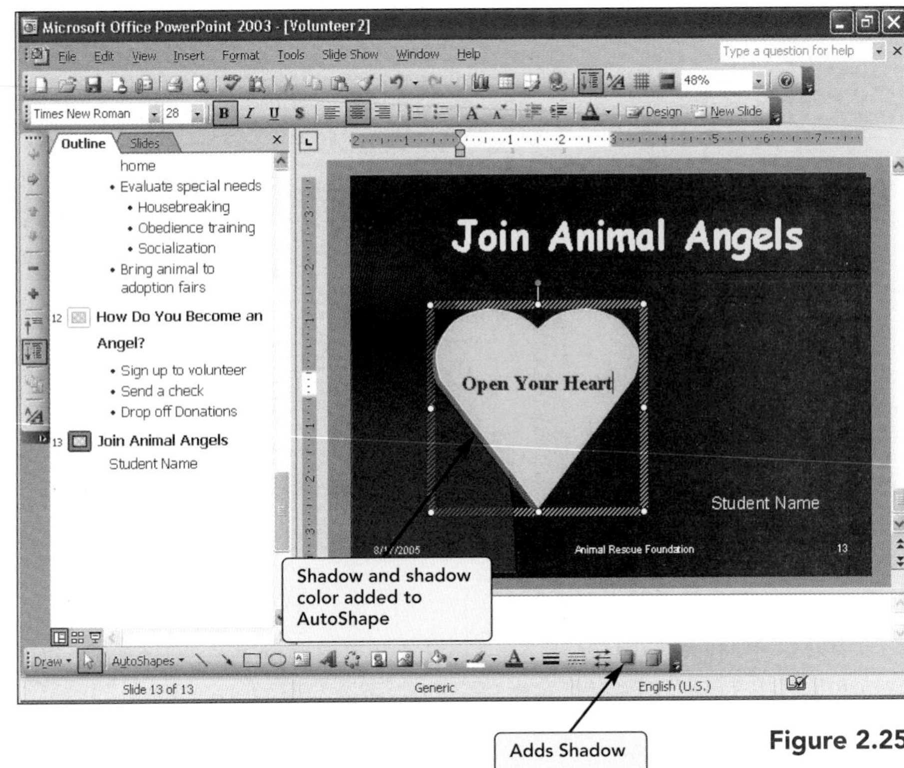

Figure 2.25

The addition of fill color and Shadow effect greatly improves the appearance of the heart.

Adding Text to an AutoShape

Next, you will add text to the heart object. Text can be added to all shapes and becomes part of the shape; when the shape is moved, the text moves with it.

1 Right-click on the AutoShape object to open the shortcut menu, and choose Add Text.

- Click **B** Bold.
- Increase the font size to 28 points.
- Change the font color to blue.
- Type **Open Your Heart**.
- If necessary, adjust the size of the heart to display the text on a single line.

Your screen should be similar to Figure 2.26

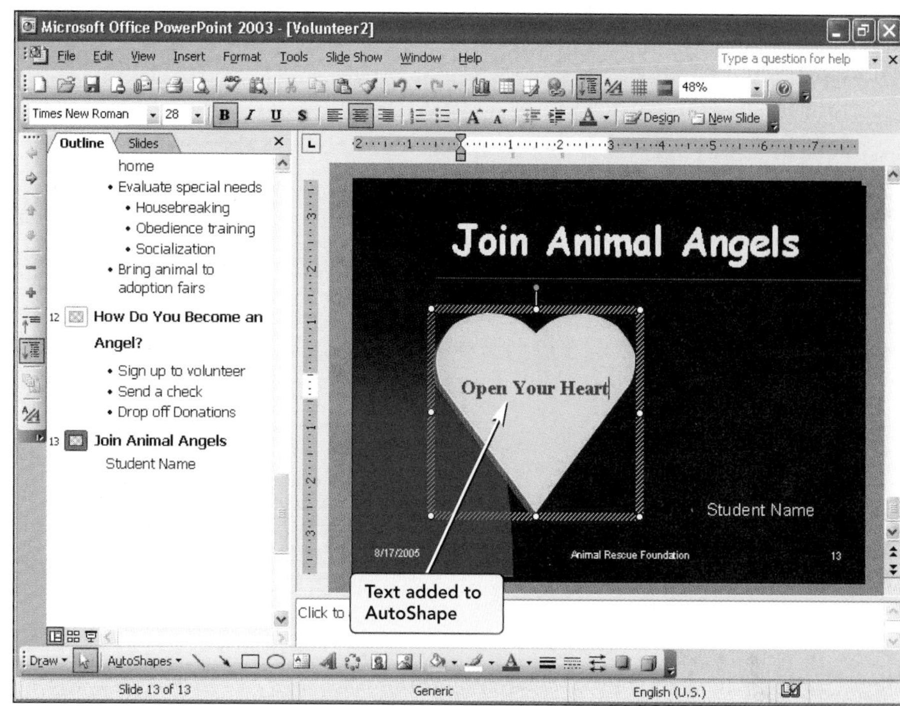

Figure 2.26

Rotating the Object

Additional Information

Holding down ⇧Shift while using the rotate handle rotates the object in 15-degree increments.

Finally, you want to change the angle of the heart. You can rotate an object 90 degrees left or right, or to any other angle. You will change the angle of the heart to the right using the **rotate handle** for the selected object, which allows you to rotate the object to any degree in any direction.

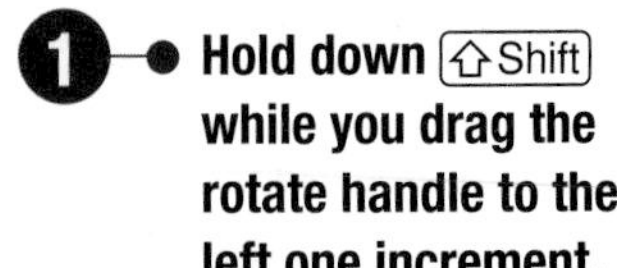

Hold down Shift **while you drag the rotate handle to the left one increment.**

Additional Information

The mouse pointer appears as [rotate pointer] when positioned on the rotate handle.

Your screen should be similar to Figure 2.27

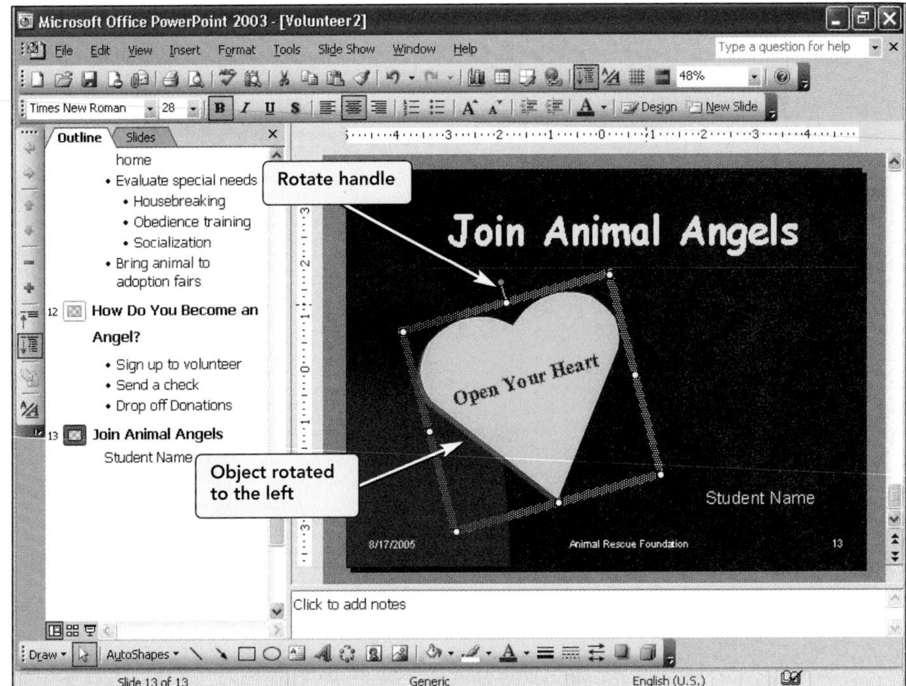

Figure 2.27

The graphic is a nice addition to the final slide of the presentation.

Working with Text Boxes

On slide 12, you want to add the organization's name and address. To make it stand out on the slide, you will put it into a text box. A **text box** is a container for text or graphics. The text box can be moved, resized, and enhanced in other ways to make it stand out from the other text on the slide.

Creating a Text Box

First you create the text box, and then you add the content.

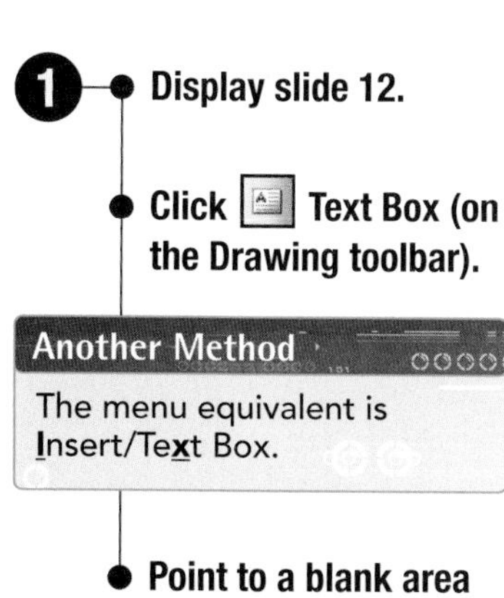

1 ● **Display slide 12.**

● **Click [icon] Text Box (on the Drawing toolbar).**

Another Method

The menu equivalent is Insert/Text Box.

● **Point to a blank area below the bullets and click to create a default size text box.**

Additional Information

Do not drag to create the text box. If you do, it will not resize appropriately when you enter text in the next step.

Your screen should be similar to Figure 2.28

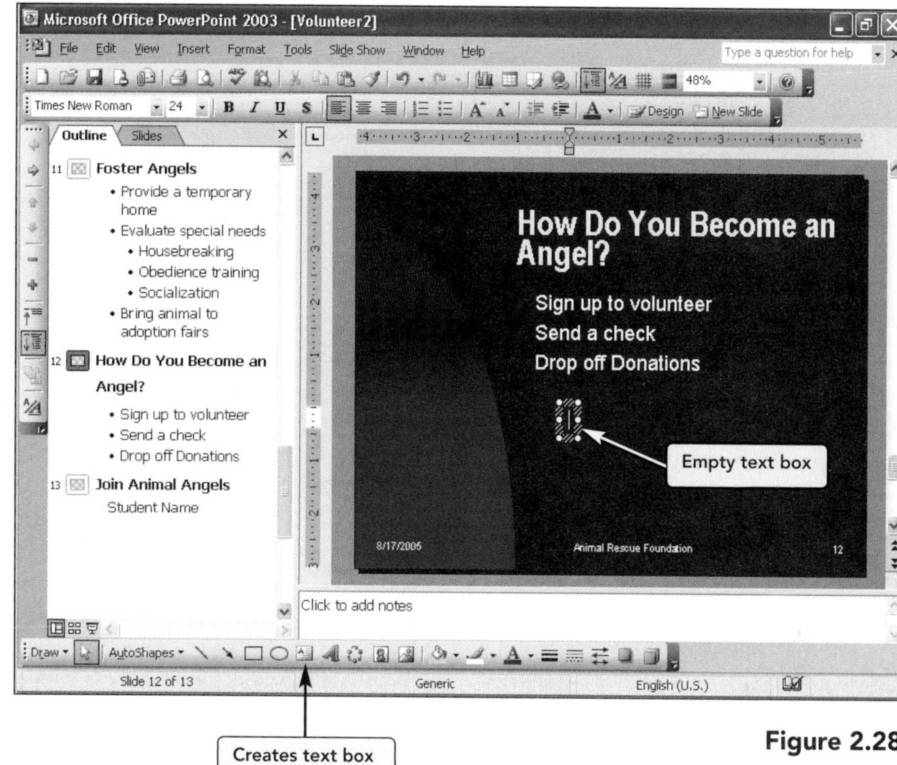

Figure 2.28

The text box is a selected object and is surrounded with a hatched border, indicating you can enter, delete, select, and format the text inside the box.

Adding Text to a Text Box

Additional Information

You could also copy text from another location and paste it into the text box.

The text box displays an insertion point, indicating that it is waiting for you to enter the text. As you type the text in the text box, it will resize automatically as needed to display the entire entry.

1 ● **Type the organization's name and address shown below in the text box. (Press ←Enter at the end of a line.)**

Animal Rescue Foundation

1166 Oak Street

Lakeside, NH 03112

(603) 555-1313

Your screen should be similar to Figure 2.29

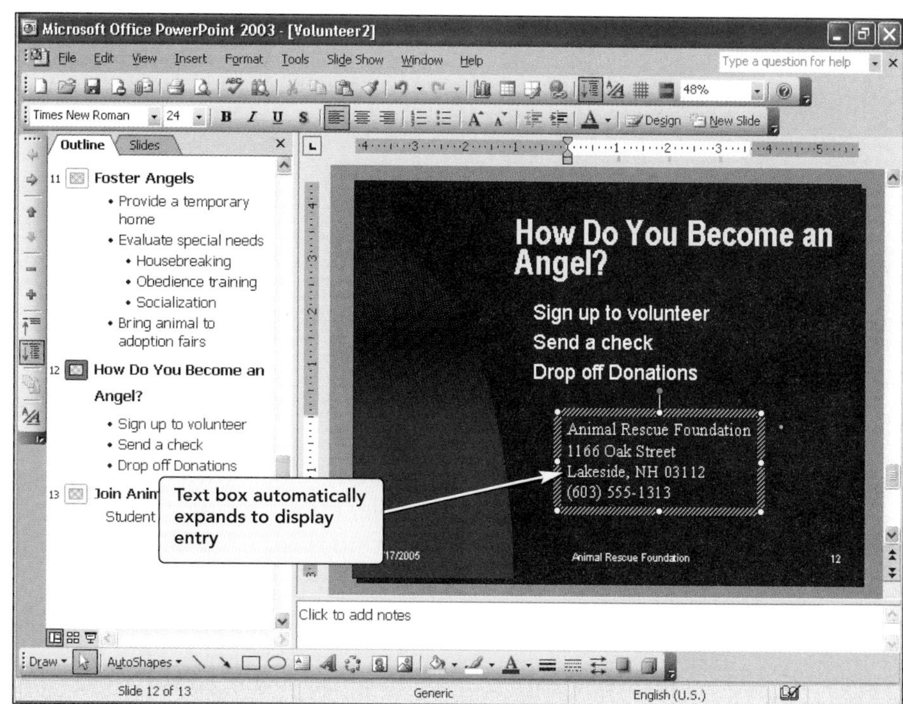

Figure 2.29

Again, because a text box is an object, the content is not displayed in the outline pane.

Enhancing the Text Box

Like any other object, the text box can be sized and moved anywhere on the slide. It can also be enhanced by adding a border, fill color, shadow effect, or a three-dimensional effect to the box. You want to add a border around the box to define the space and add a fill color behind the text.

1
- **Click Line Style (on the Drawing toolbar) and select a style of your choice from the menu.**
- **Click Fill Color and select a color of your choice from the color palette.**
- **If the text does not look good with the fill color you selected, change the text color to a color of your choice.**
- **Position the text box as in Figure 2.30.**
- **Deselect the text box.**
- **Save the presentation.**

Your screen should be similar to Figure 2.30

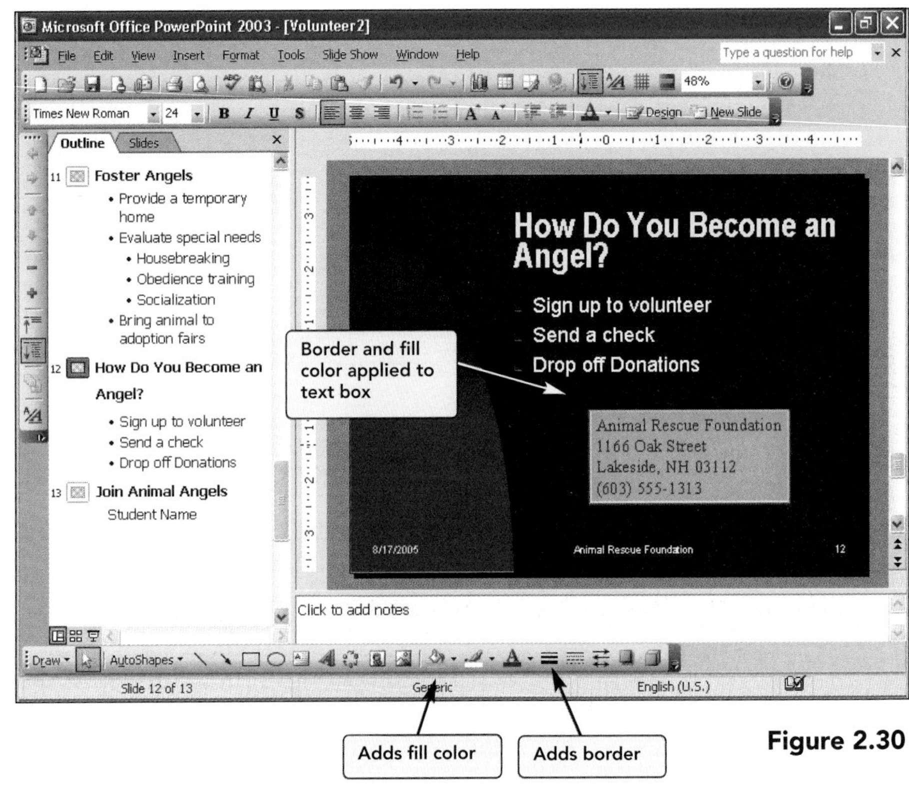

Figure 2.30

The information in the text box now stands out from the other information on the slide.

Changing the Presentation Design

Now you are satisfied with the presentation's basic content and organization. Next you want to change its style and appearance by applying a different design template.

Concept 4

Design Template

4 A **design template** is a professionally created slide design that is stored as a file and can be applied to your presentation. Design templates include features that control the slide color scheme, the type and size of bullets and fonts, placeholder sizes and positions, background designs and fills, and other layout and design elements. PowerPoint provides more than 100 design templates that can be used to quickly give your presentations a professional appearance. Additional design templates are available at the Microsoft Office Template Gallery Web site, or you can create your own custom design templates.

A design template can be applied to all slides or selected slides in a presentation. You can also use more than one type of design template in a single presentation. Use a design template to ensure that your presentation has a professional, consistent look throughout.

Applying a Design Template

A design template can be applied to the entire presentation or to selected slides. You want to change the design template for the entire presentation.

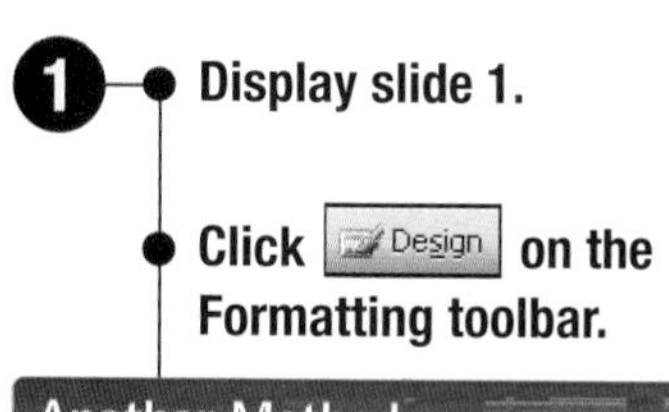

1 **Display slide 1.**

Click Design **on the Formatting toolbar.**

Another Method

The menu equivalent is Format/Slide Design.

Point to the first design preview in the task pane.

Having Trouble?

If your task pane displays large preview images, open any preview's menu and clear the Show Large Previews option.

Your screen should be similar to Figure 2.31

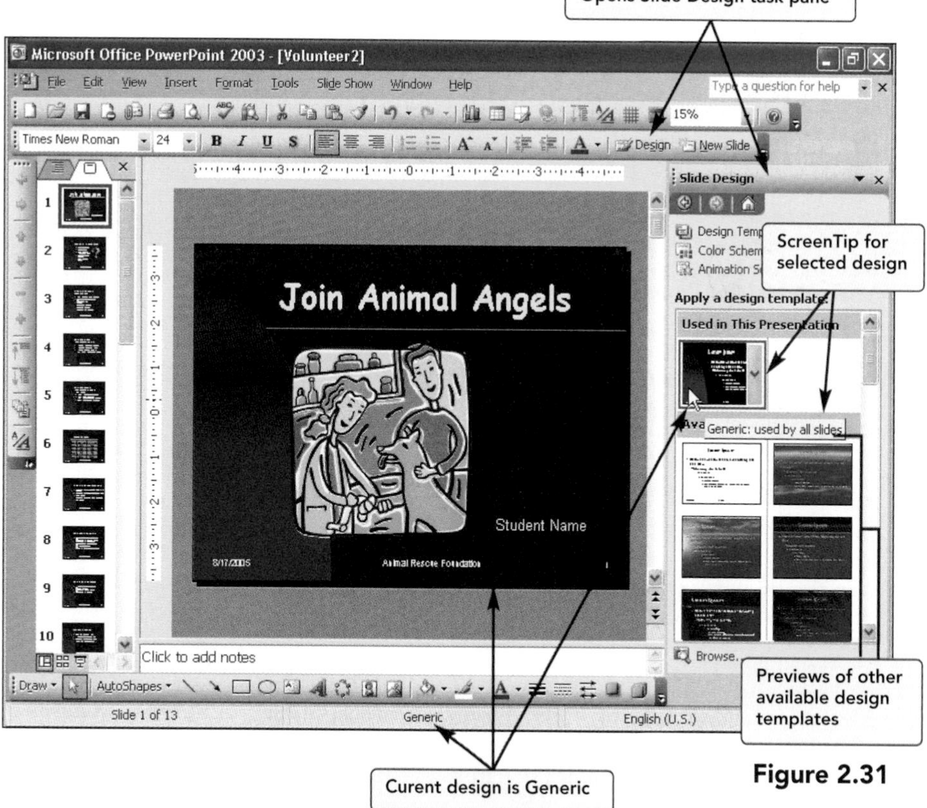

Figure 2.31

Additional Information

Design templates are stored in a file with a .pot file extension.

The Slide Design task pane displays previews of the design templates. The first design preview is the design that is currently used in the presentation. This is the Generic design as identified in the status bar and in the ScreenTip. If other designs were recently used, they appear in the Recently Used section. Previews of other available design templates are displayed in the Available For Use section of the pane.

2 Click Balance in the Available For Use section to see how this design would look.

Your screen should be similar to Figure 2.32

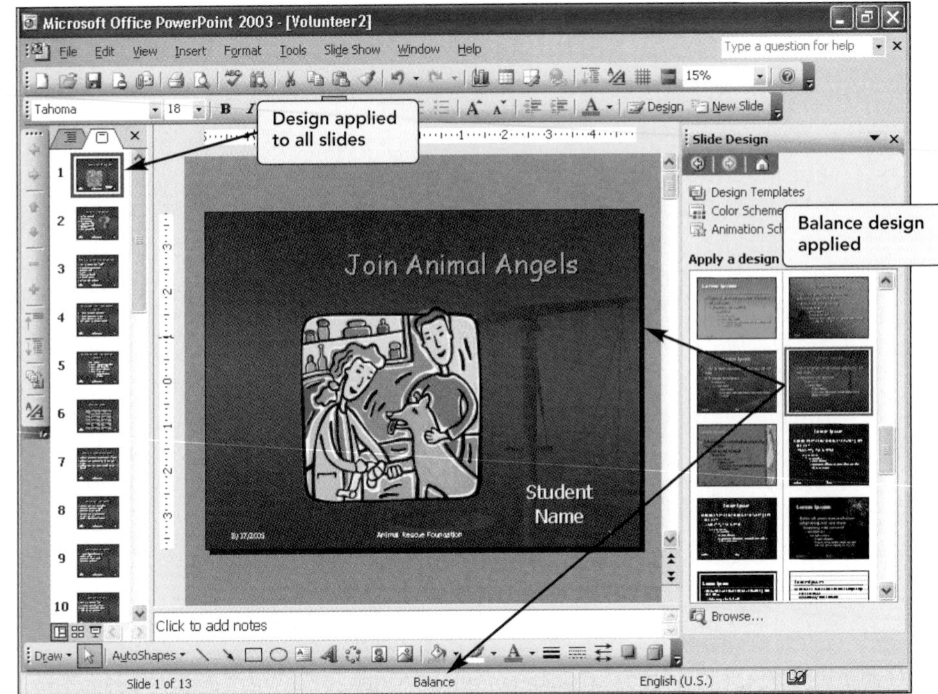

Figure 2.32

Additional Information

To apply a design to selected slides, preselect the slides to apply the design to in the Slide pane, and use the Apply to Selected Slides option from the design preview drop-down menu.

The Balance design template is applied to all slides in the presentation and the status bar displays the name of the current design. As different designs are selected, the previously used designs appear in the Recently Used section.

You will preview several other design templates, and then use the Beam template for the presentation.

3
- Preview several other design templates.
- Choose the Beam template design.

Having Trouble?

If the Beam template design is not available, select a similar design of your choice.

Your screen should be similar to Figure 2.33

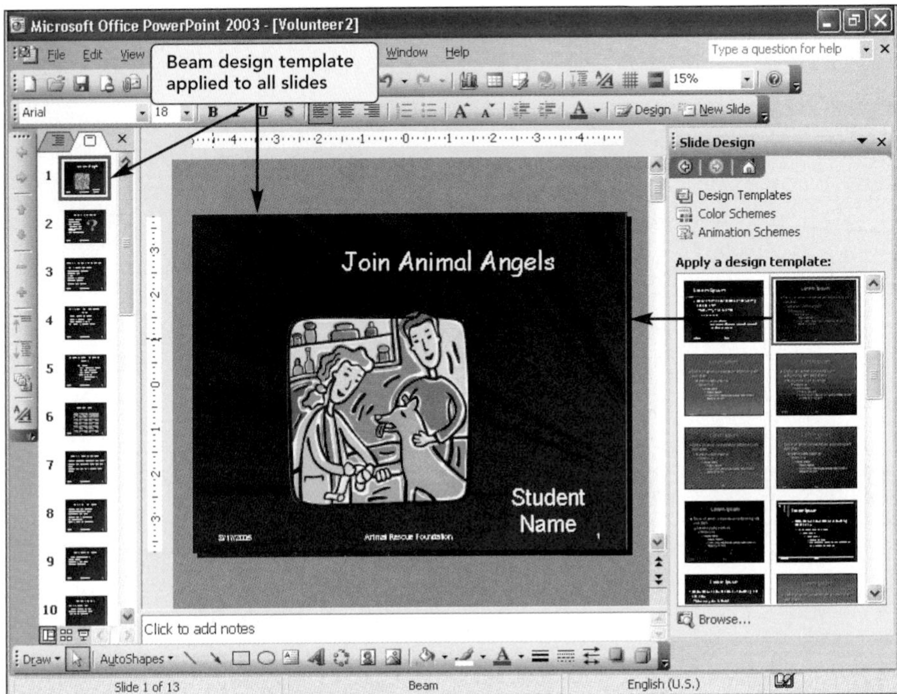

Figure 2.33

The Beam design template has been applied to all slides in the presentation. When a new template design is applied, the text styles, graphics, and colors that are included in the template replace the previous template settings. Consequently, the layout may need to be adjusted. For example, your name may appear on two lines because the font size of the subtitle using this design template is 36 points.

However, if you had made changes to a slide, such as changing the font of the title, these changes are not updated to the new design. In this case, the title is still the Comic Sans MS font you selected, however, its font size has been reduced and it is now too small. You will correct that shortly.

4
- **On the title slide, reduce the subtitle font size to 24 points and, if necessary, size the placeholder to display your name on a single line.**
- **Use the Slide tab to select each slide and check the layout.**
- **Make the adjustments shown in the table below to the indicated slide.**

Your screen should be similar to Figure 2.34

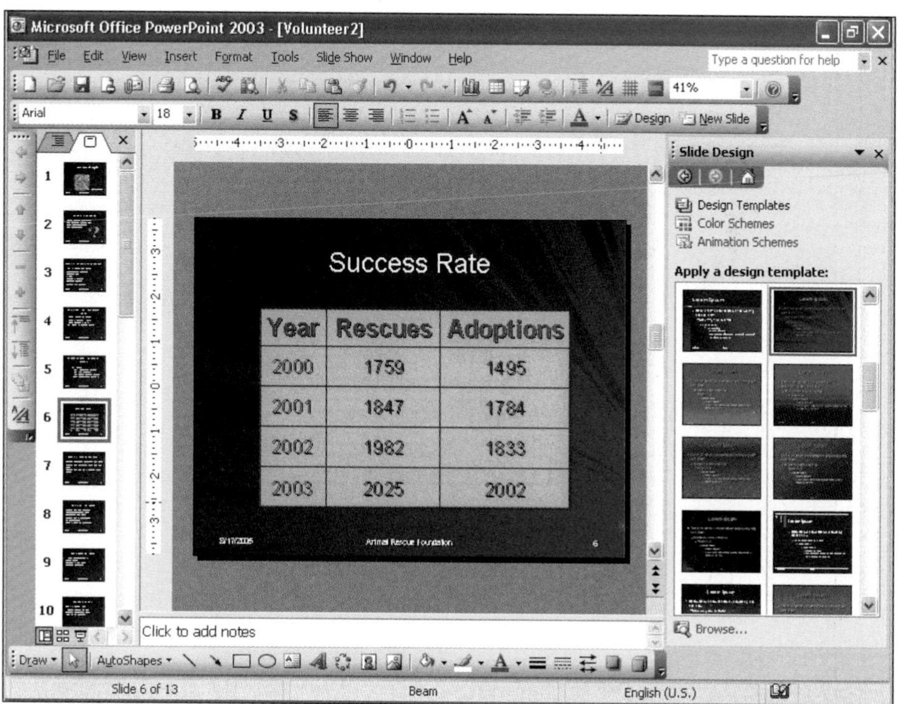

Figure 2.34

Slide	Adjustment
2	Increase the text placeholder width to display each bulleted item on a single line. Move the question mark graphic to the lower right side of the slide.
5	Increase the width of the Event column to display each item on a single line. Center the Year and Event columns on the slide.
6	Adjust the size of the table columns and center the table below the title. If necessary, change the table text colors to coordinate with the new design.

Having Trouble?

If you selected a different design template, you may need to make different adjustments than indicated in the table at left.

Changing the Color Scheme

To make the presentation livelier, you decide to try a different color scheme. Each design template has several alternative color schemes from which you can choose.

1
- **Display slide 1.**
- **Click Color Schemes in the Slide Design task pane.**

Your screen should be similar to Figure 2.35

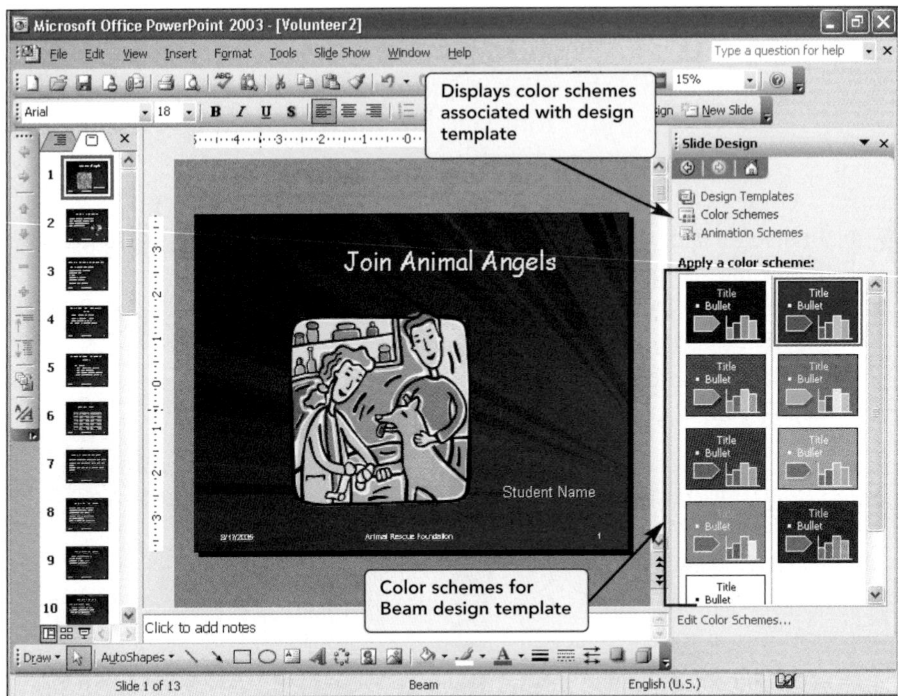

Figure 2.35

The nine color schemes for the Beam design template are displayed in the Slide Design pane. The color scheme with the medium blue background is selected. Each color scheme consists of eight coordinated colors that are applied to different slide elements. Using predefined color schemes gives your presentation a professional and consistent look. You want to see how the dark blue color scheme would look.

2 ● **Select the dark blue color scheme (first column, first row).**

Your screen should be similar to Figure 2.36

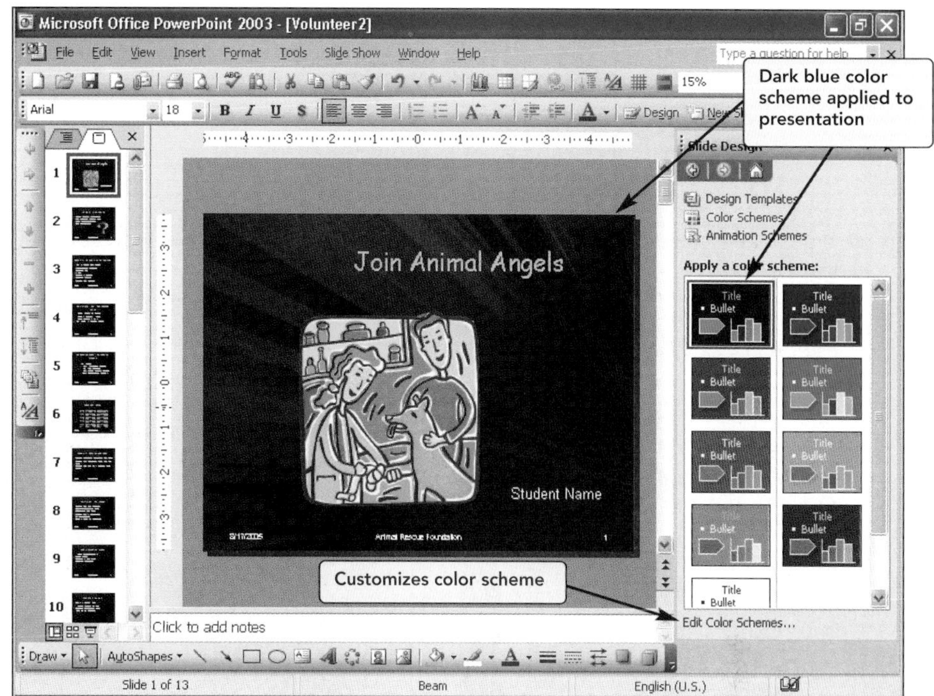

Figure 2.36

The slides display in the selected color scheme. Although you like this color scheme, you think it is a little dark. You can customize color schemes by changing colors associated with the different elements. You will change the background, shadow, and title text colors.

3 ● **Click Edit Color Schemes at the bottom of the Slide Design task pane.**

● **Open the Custom tab, if necessary.**

Your screen should be similar to Figure 2.37

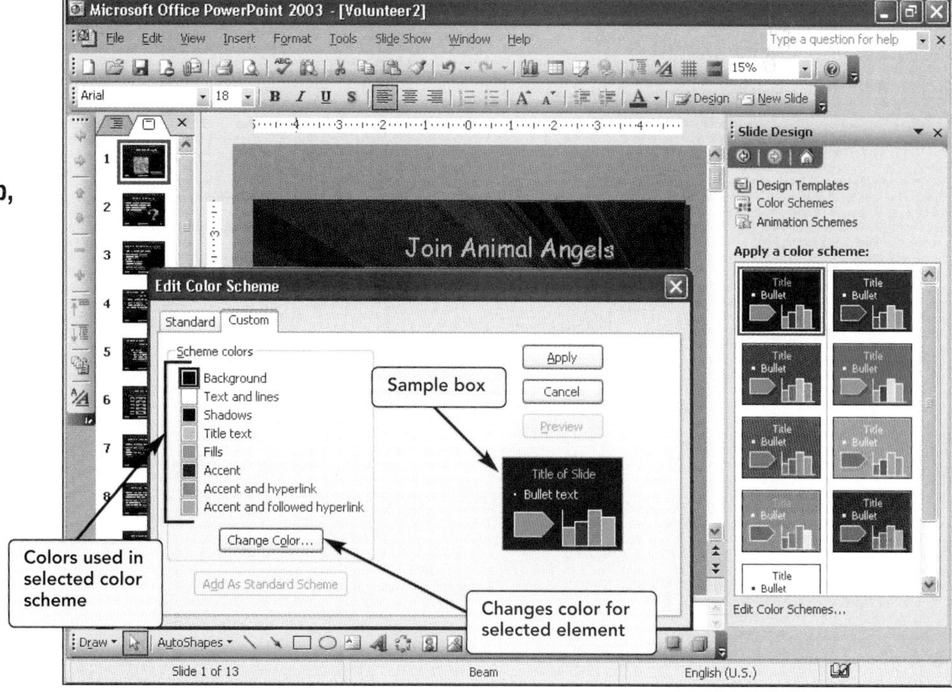

Figure 2.37

The Scheme Colors area of the dialog box shows you the eight colors that are applied to different elements of the template design. The sample box shows where the selected colors are used in a slide. The option to change the background color is selected by default. You will change the color of the background and title first.

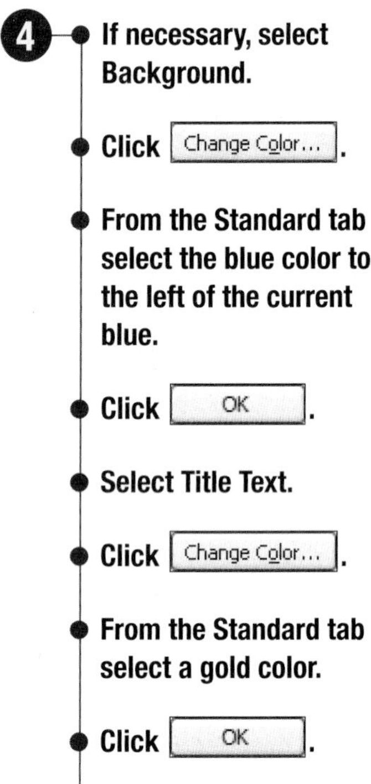

4

- **If necessary, select Background.**
- **Click** Change Color... .
- **From the Standard tab select the blue color to the left of the current blue.**
- **Click** OK .
- **Select Title Text.**
- **Click** Change Color... .
- **From the Standard tab select a gold color.**
- **Click** OK .
- **Click** Preview .
- **Move the Edit Color Scheme dialog box to see more of the slide.**

Your screen should be similar to Figure 2.38

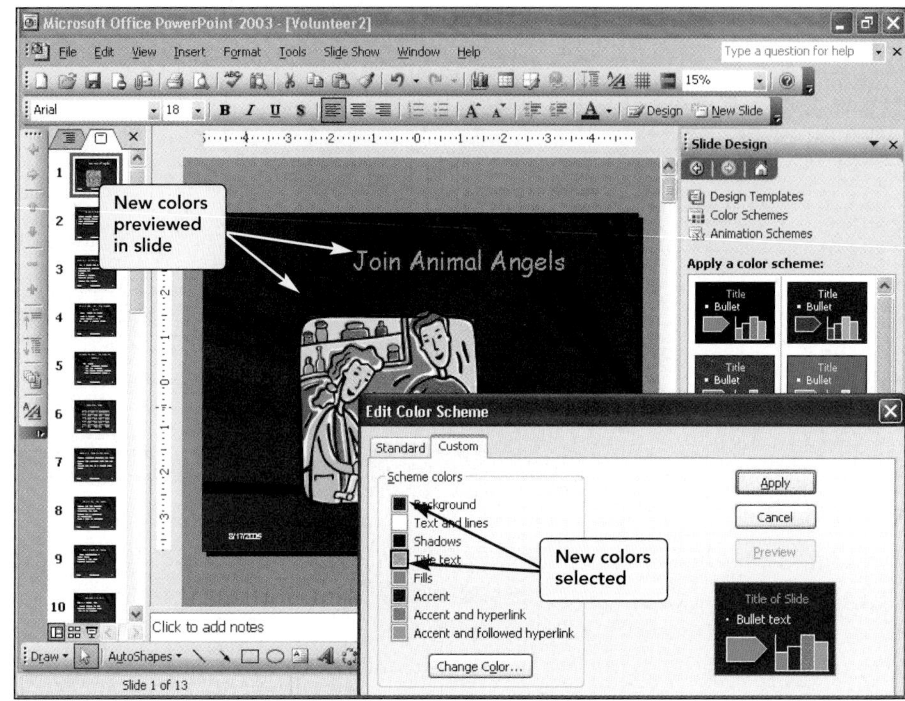

Figure 2.38

The background and title color has changed on all slides in the presentation. Changing the colors has made the slides much brighter. However, you do not like the dark blue used in the shadow color of the beams and will change it to a lighter blue. Because the shadow color is not a standard color found on the Standard color tab, the Custom tab will open automatically. Colors are selected from this tab by dragging the cross-hair to select a color and dragging the slider on the color bar to adjust the brightness.

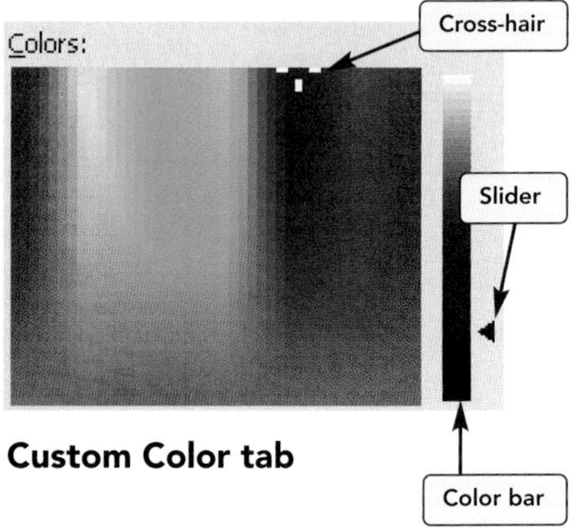

Custom Color tab

5 **Select Shadows and click Change Color... .**

- **Drag the ◂ slider up the color bar to increase the brightness.**

Additional Information

The degrees of red, green, and blue change as you drag the bar. The figures use Red 57, Green 0, and Blue 238.

- **Click OK.**

- **Click Preview.**

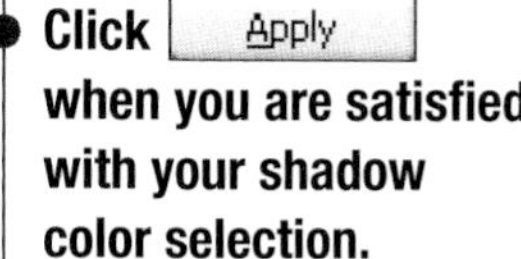

- **Click Apply when you are satisfied with your shadow color selection.**
- **Close the Slide Design pane.**
- **Save the presentation.**

Your screen should be similar to Figure 2.39

Figure 2.39

The new colors give the presentation much more impact. In addition, a new custom color scheme template is added to the available color schemes list in the task pane. This makes it easy to reapply your custom settings in the future.

Working with Master Slides

While viewing the slides, you think the slide appearance could be further improved by changing the bullet design on all slides. Although you can change each slide individually as you did in Lab 1, you can make the change much faster to all the slides by changing the slide master.

Concept 5

Masters

5 A **master** is a special slide or page that stores information about the formatting for all slides or pages in a presentation. There are four key components of a presentation–slides, title slides, speaker notes, and handouts–and each has a master associated with it. The four masters are described below.

Master	Function
Slide Master	Defines the format and placement of title, body, and footer text; bullet styles; background design; and color scheme of each slide in the presentation.
Title Master	Defines the format and placement of titles and text for slides that use the Title Slide layout.
Handout Master	Defines the format and placement of the slide image, text, headers, footers, and other elements that will appear on every handout.
Notes Master	Defines the format and placement of the slide image, note text, headers, footers, and other elements that will appear on all speaker notes.

Any changes you make to a master affect all slides or pages associated with that master. Each design template comes with its own slide master and title master. When you apply a new design template to a presentation, all slides and masters are updated to those of the new design template. Using the master to modify or add elements to a presentation ensures consistency and saves time.

You can create slides that differ from the master by changing the format and placement of elements in the individual slide rather than on the master. For example, when you changed the font settings of the title on the title slide, the slide master was not affected. Only the individual slide changed, making it unique. If you have created a unique slide, the elements you changed on that slide retain their uniqueness even if you later make changes to the slide master. That is the reason that the title font did not change when you changed the design template.

Modifying the Slide Master

You will change the bullet style in the slide master so that all slides in the presentation will be changed.

1 Choose **View/Master/Slide Master.**

Another Method

You also can hold down Shift and click Normal View to display the slide master.

- **If necessary, dock the Slide Master View toolbar below the Formatting toolbar.**

Your screen should be similar to Figure 2.40

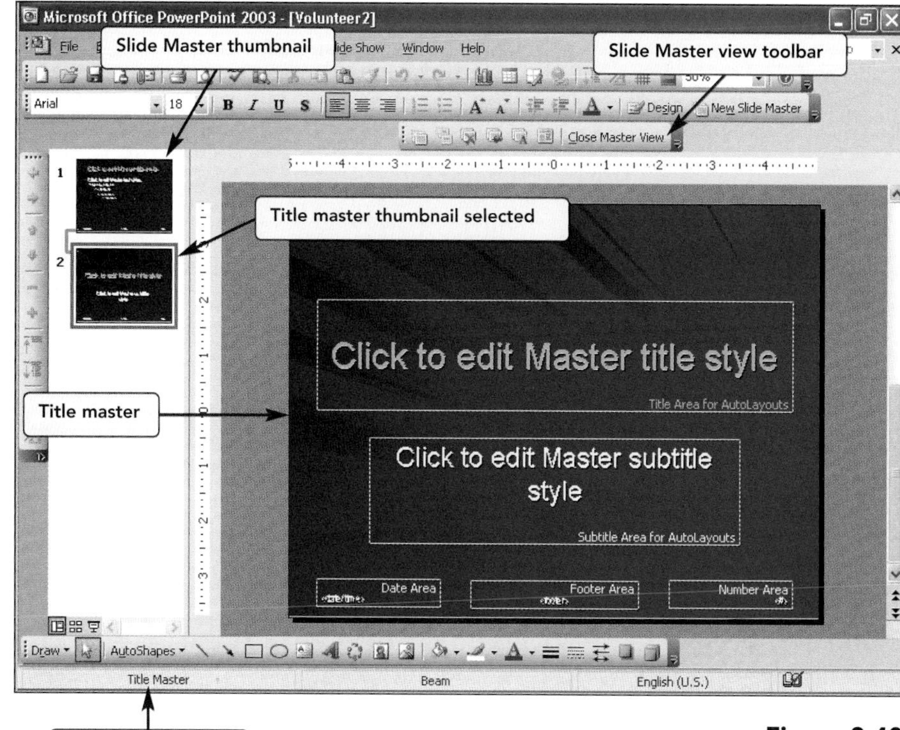

Figure 2.40

Additional Information

Pointing to the master thumbnail displays a ScreenTip that identifies the selected master and the slides where it is used in the presentation.

The view has changed to Master view, and the Slide Master View toolbar is displayed. Thumbnails for both the title master and slide master for the Beam design template appear in the left pane of this view. The second thumbnail for the title master is selected, and the slide pane displays the master for it. The status bar identifies the master you are viewing. You want to make changes to the slide master first.

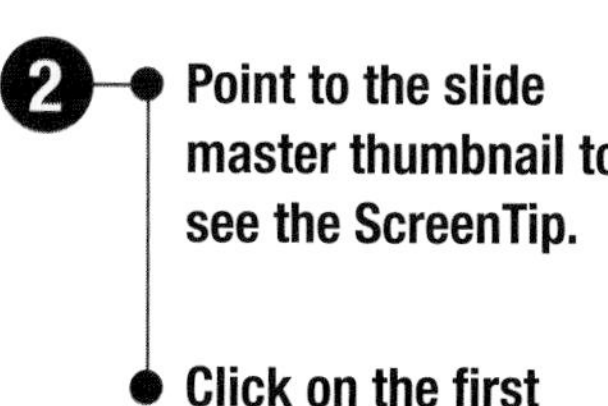

2 **Point to the slide master thumbnail to see the ScreenTip.**

- **Click on the first master thumbnail to select it.**

Your screen should be similar to Figure 2.41

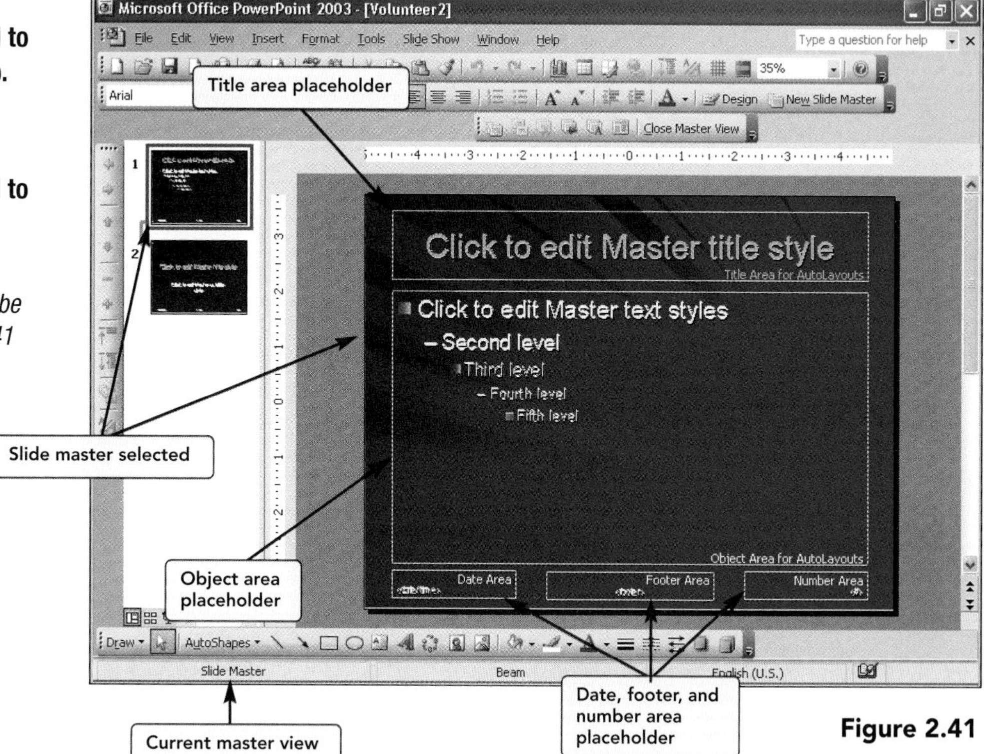

Figure 2.41

The slide master consists of five area placeholders that control the appearance of all slides except a title slide. Each placeholder displays sample text to show you how changes you make in these areas will appear. You make changes to the master slide in the same way that you change any other slide. You will modify the object area placeholder by changing the graphic that is used for the bullet style.

3 **Click the object area to select it.**

Having Trouble?

Do not select an individual item within the object area or the changes will be applied to the item only.

- **Choose Format/Bullets and Numbering.**
- **Click Picture... .**

Your screen should be similar to Figure 2.42

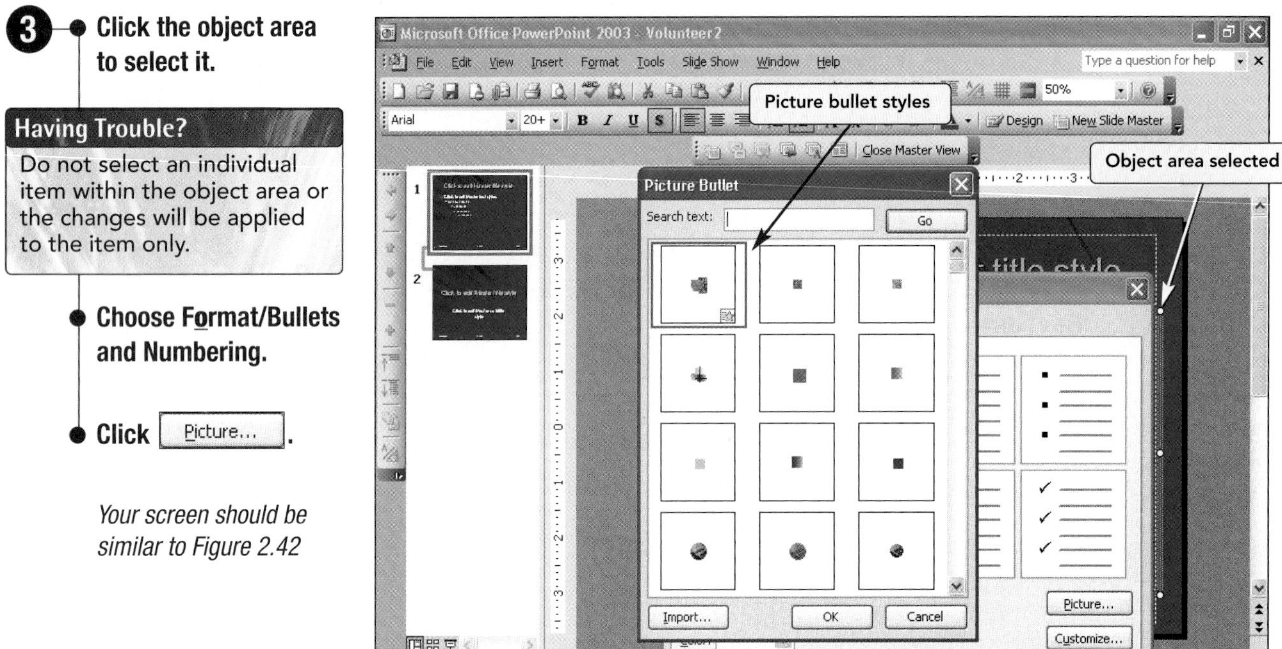

Figure 2.42

From the Picture Bullet dialog box, you select the bullet design you want to use from the bullet styles listed. You will use the square, yellow bullet design.

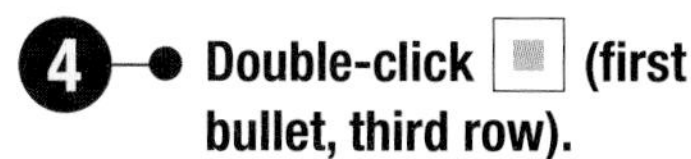

4 Double-click ■ (first bullet, third row).

Having Trouble?

If this bullet style is not available, select another of your choice.

Your screen should be similar to Figure 2.43

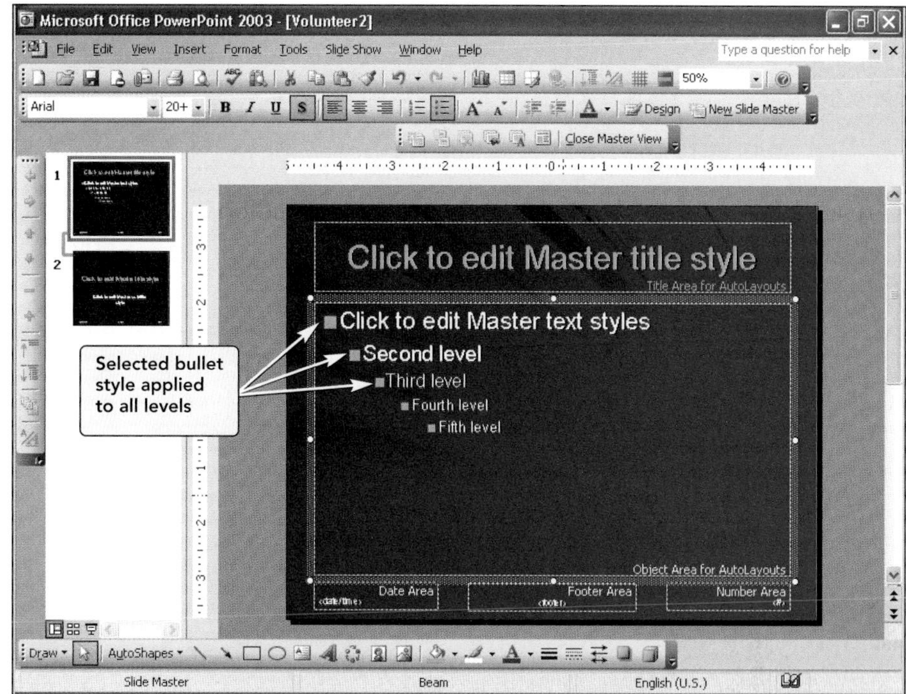

Figure 2.43

Additional Information

You can apply different bullet styles to each level by selecting each level individually.

The selected bullet style has been applied to all levels of items in the object area. Additionally, you decide to delete the date from the footer by deleting the Date Area placeholder.

5 Select the Date Area placeholder.

Press Delete.

Additional Information

You can restore deleted placeholders or add new placeholders to the slide master using Format/Master Layout and selecting the type of placeholder you want to add.

Your screen should be similar to Figure 2.44

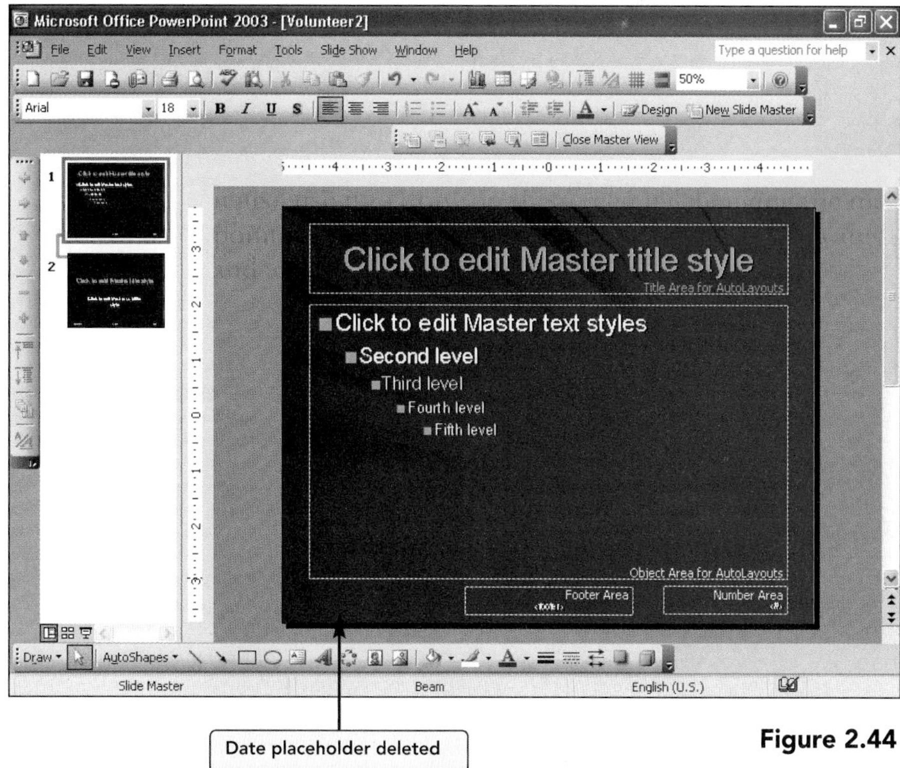

Figure 2.44

Now, you want to see how the changes you have made to the slide master have affected the slides.

6 Click Slide Sorter view.

Your screen should be similar to Figure 2.45

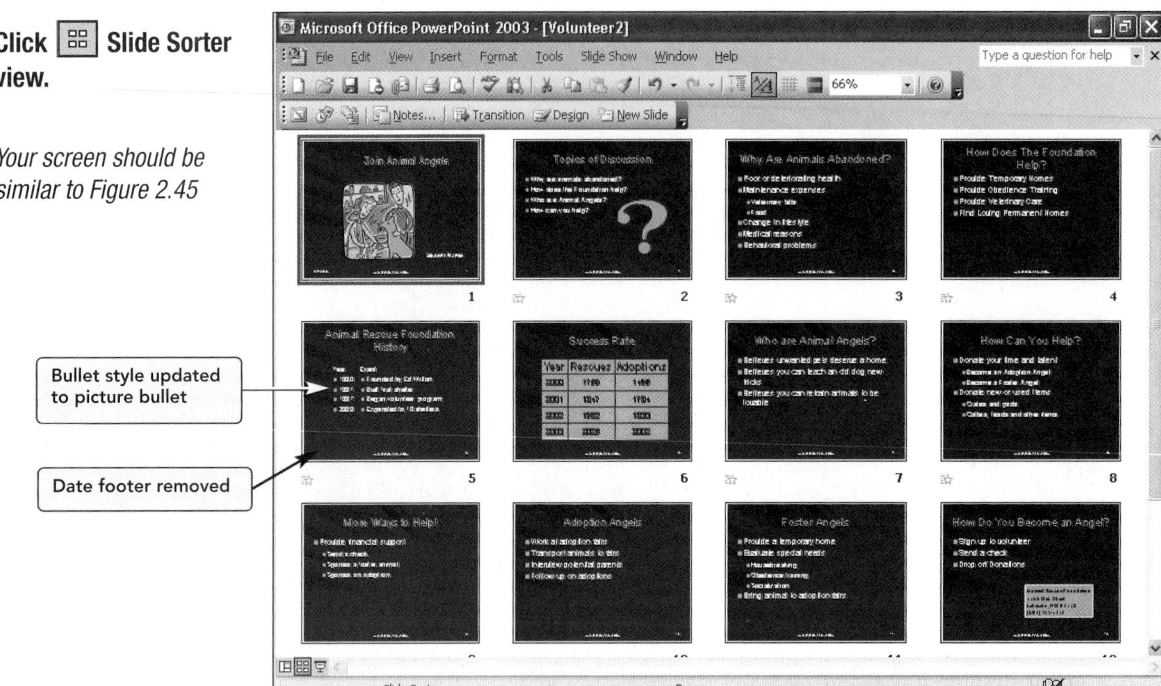

Figure 2.45

You can now see that the change you made to the bullet style in the slide master is reflected in all slides in the presentation. Additionally, none of the slides, except the title slides, displays the date in the footer. Using the slide master allows you to quickly make global changes to your presentation.

Modifying the Title Master

Next you want to enhance the appearance of the two slides that use the title slide layout by changing the title and subtitle.

1 Display slide 1 in Normal view.

Your screen should be similar to Figure 2.46

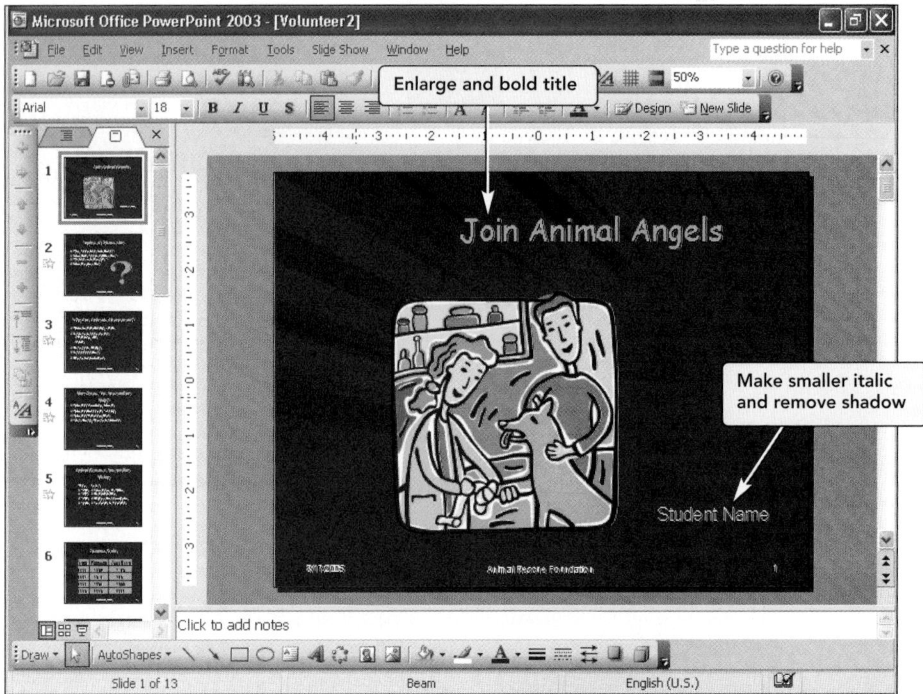

Figure 2.46

Earlier, you changed the font, size, and placement of the title and the placement and font size of the subtitle. Although you still like these changes, you want the title to be larger and the subtitle text smaller and italicized. You also want to remove the shadow from the subtitle.

2

- **Display the Slide Master view.**
- **Display the title master.**
- **Click the master title text placeholder.**

Your screen should be similar to Figure 2.47

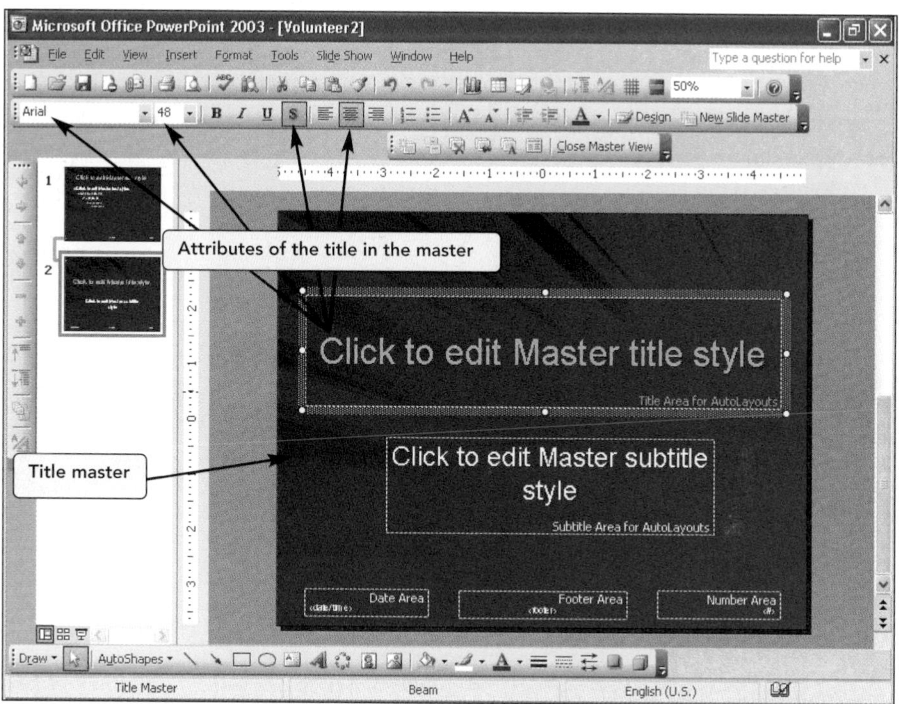

Figure 2.47

Notice that the title master has a slightly different appearance from the title slide in your presentation. This is because you modified the title slide by moving placeholders and changing the font, size, and color, making it a unique slide. The unique changes you made to that slide were not changed when the title master of the Beam design template was applied. The title master attributes reflect the attributes associated with the Beam template, such as the title font of Arial, 48 pt as shown in the toolbar buttons.

3

- **Change the font style to Comic Sans MS.**
- **Increase the font size to 54.**
- **Click B Bold.**
- **Move the title placeholder toward the top of the slide as in Figure 2.48.**
- **Select the subtitle area placeholder.**

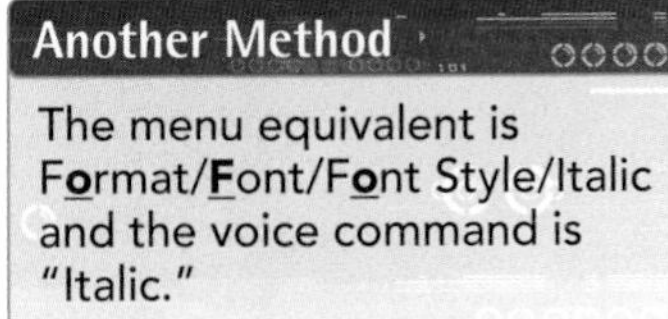

Another Method

The menu equivalent is Format/Font/Font Style/Italic and the voice command is "Italic."

- **Click S Shadow to remove the shadow.**
- **Reduce the font size to 28.**
- **Click I Italic.**
- **Decrease the size of the placeholder and move it to the location shown in Figure 2.48.**

Your screen should be similar to Figure 2.48

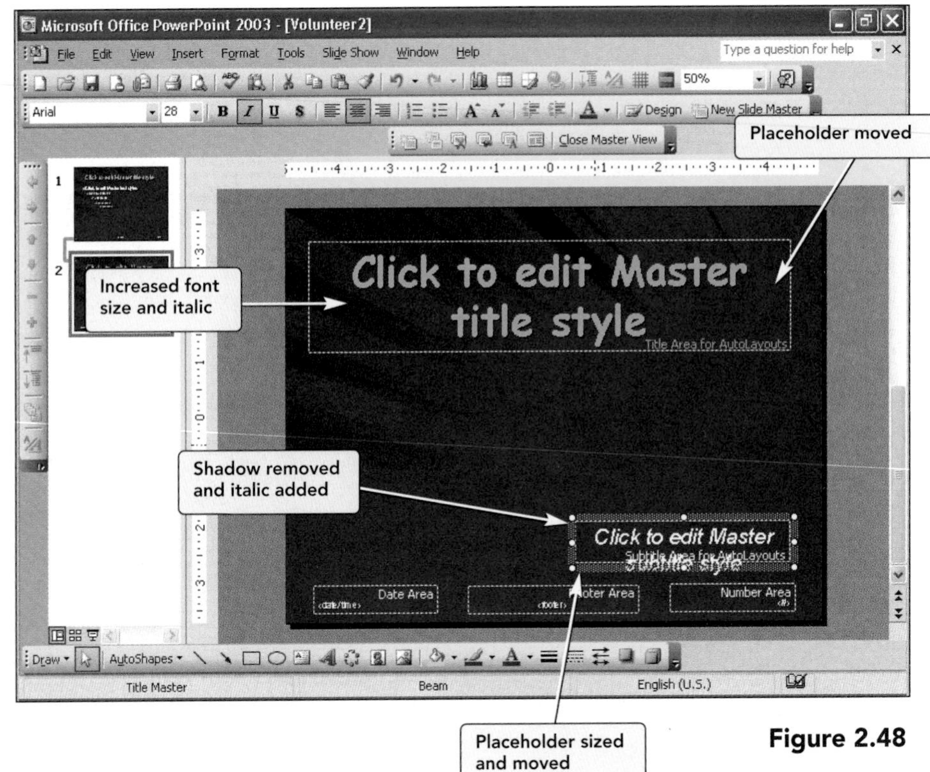

Figure 2.48

You want to see how the title slide looks with the changes you have made.

4 **Switch to Normal view.**

- **Click on the title placeholder.**

Your screen should be similar to Figure 2.49

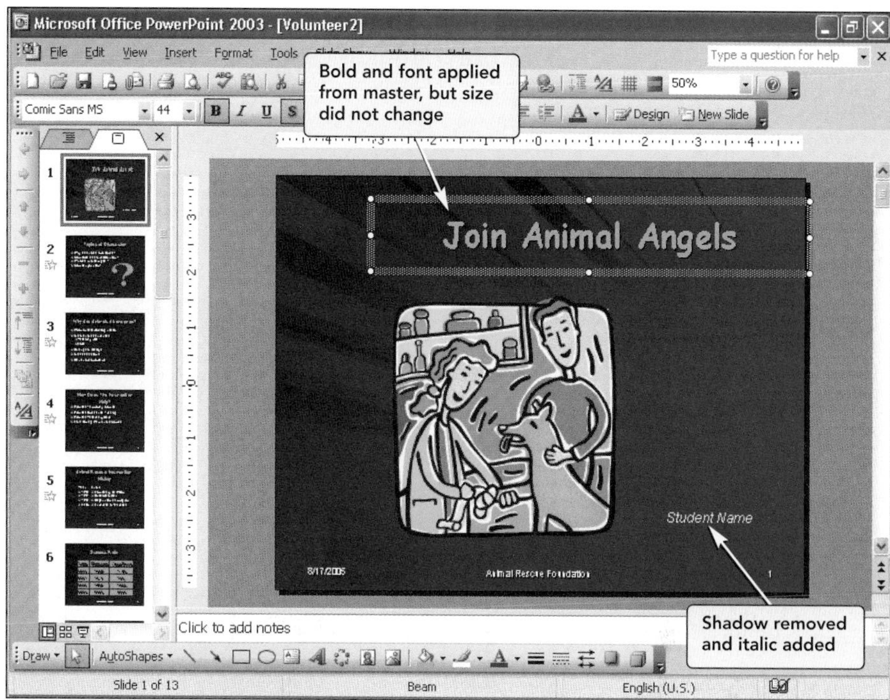

Figure 2.49

Some of the changes you made to the title master were applied to the title slide automatically; however, others were not. This is because the earlier changes you made, such as the font size, made the slide unique. Changes made to an individual slide override the master slide.

Reapplying a Slide Layout

You decide to apply all the settings on the master title slide to the title slides in the presentation. To do this you reapply the slide layout.

1 **Choose Format/Slide Layout.**

- **Point to the Title Slide layout in the Slide Layout task pane.**

- **Click ▾ to open the drop-down menu for the Title Slide layout.**

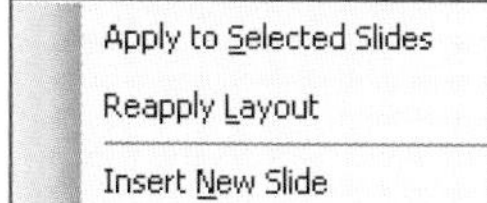

- **Choose Reapply Layout.**

Your screen should be similar to Figure 2.50

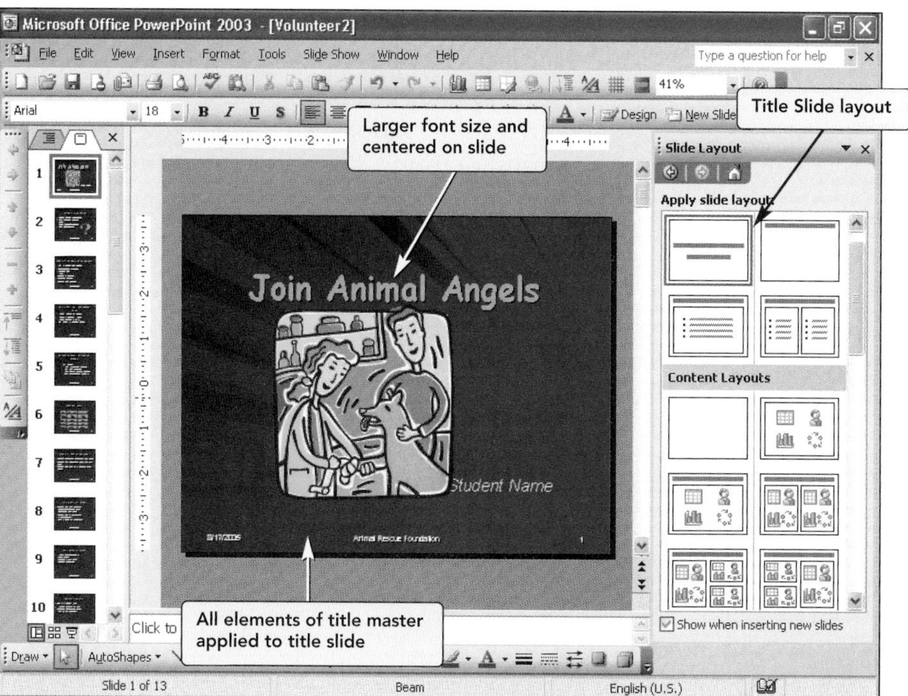

Figure 2.50

All elements of the title master slide have been applied to the title slide. The only adjustment you want to make to slide 1 is to reposition the graphic. Then you will reapply the slide layout to the concluding slide.

2
- **Move the graphic so it does not overlap the subtitle.**
- **Display slide 13 and reapply the Title Slide layout.**
- **Choose View/Ruler to hide the ruler.**
- **Close the Slide Layout task pane.**

Your screen should be similar to Figure 2.51

Figure 2.51

The layout settings have been applied and the concluding slide should not need any adjustments.

Changing and Hiding Footer Text

You would also like to hide the display of the footer information on the title slides and change the information displayed in the other slides. When you created the presentation using the AutoContent Wizard, you specified the information to appear in the footer area for all slides in the presentation. The slide and title masters control the placement and display of the footer information, but they do not control the information that appears in those areas. As you have seen, one way to stop the footer information from appearing, is to delete the footer placeholder from the master. Alternatively, you can change or turn off the display of selected footer information or hide the footer in title slides only.

1. **Choose View/Header and Footer.**
   - **Open the Slide tab, if necessary.**

Your screen should be similar to Figure 2.52

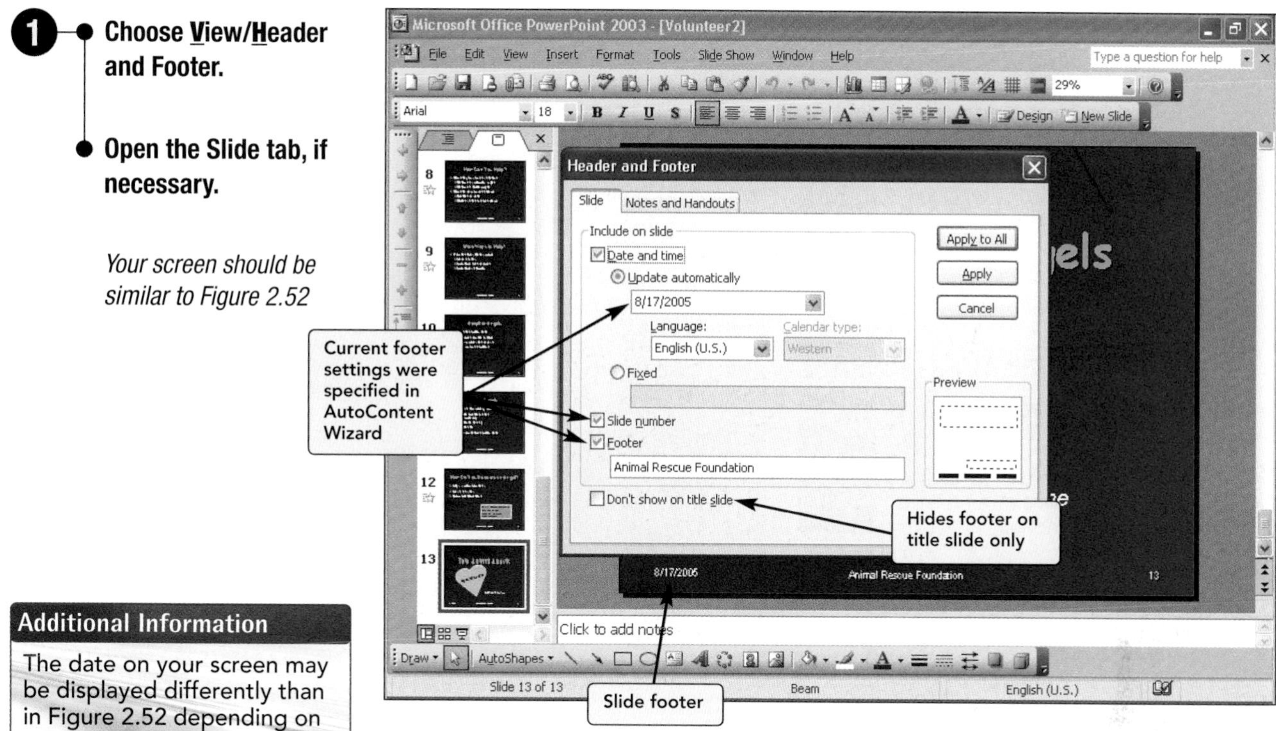

Figure 2.52

Additional Information

The date on your screen may be displayed differently than in Figure 2.52 depending on your Windows settings.

The Date and Time option is selected, and the date is set to update automatically using the current system date whenever the presentation is opened. However, because you deleted the Date area placeholder from the slide master, this information is not displayed on all (except title slides). You can also change this option to enter a fixed date that will not change.

Because the slide number option is selected, the slide number is displayed in the Number area placeholder on each slide. The text you entered, "Animal Rescue Foundation," appears in the footer text box and is displayed in the Footer area placeholder. You want to turn off the display of the slide number. Also, you do not want to display any footer information on the title slides, and will select the option to hide it.

2 • **Click Slide Number to deselect this option.**

• **Select Don't show on title Slide.**

• **Click Apply to All.**

• **Save the presentation.**

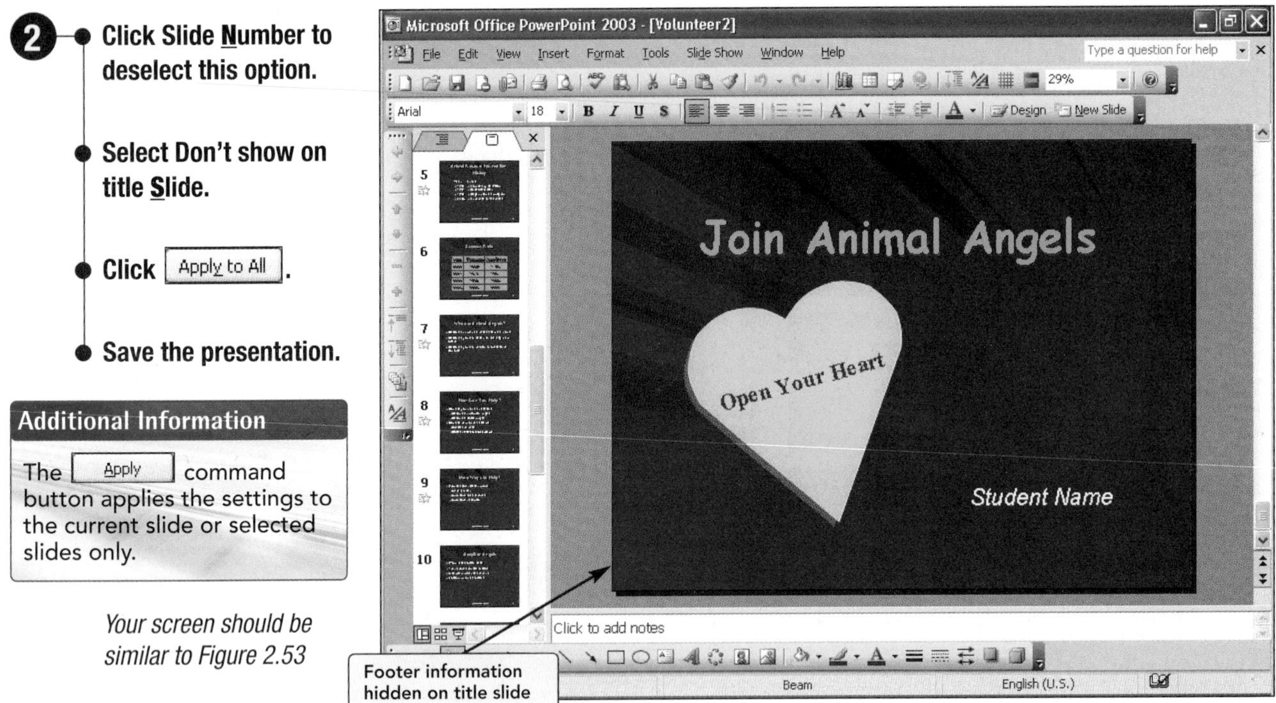

Your screen should be similar to Figure 2.53

Figure 2.53

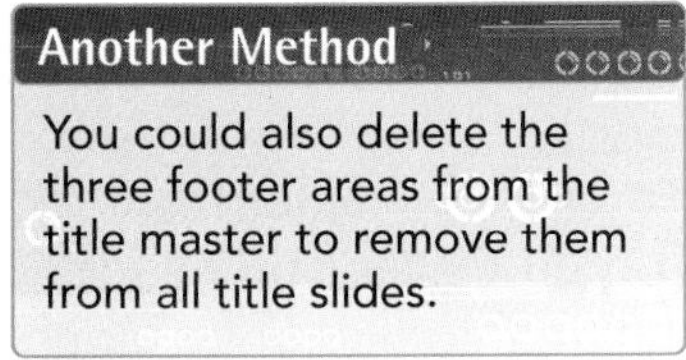

Additional Information

The Apply command button applies the settings to the current slide or selected slides only.

Another Method

You could also delete the three footer areas from the title master to remove them from all title slides.

No footer information is displayed on the concluding slide which uses the title slide layout. As you run the slide show next, you will also see that the footer does not display on the first slide. Additionally, the only footer information that appears on all other slides is the name of the organization because you deleted the Date area placeholder and deselected the slide number footer option.

3 • **Run the slide show beginning with slide 1.**

• **Click on each slide to advance through the presentation.**

You think the presentation looks quite good, but you have several changes in mind to make it more interesting.

Note: If you are ending your session now, save the presentation and exit PowerPoint. When you begin again, open this file.

Using Special Effects

You decide to use some of PowerPoint's special effects to enhance the onscreen presentation.

Concept 6

Special Effects

6 **Special effects** such as animation, sound, slide transitions, and builds are used to enhance an onscreen presentation.

Animation adds action to text and graphics so they move around on the screen. You can assign sounds to further enhance the effect.

Transitions control the way that the display changes as you move from one slide to the next during a presentation. You can select from many different transition choices. You may choose Dissolve for your title slide to give it an added flair. After that you could use Wipe Right for all the slides until the next to the last, and then use Dissolve again to end the show. As with any special effect, use slide transitions carefully.

Builds are used to display each bullet point, text, paragraph, or graphic independently of the other text or objects on the slide. You set up the way you want each element to appear (to fly in from the left, for instance) and whether you want the other elements already on the slide to dim or shimmer when a new element is added. For example, because your audience is used to reading from left to right, you could design your build slides so the bullet points fly in from the left. Then, when you want to emphasize a point, bring a bullet point in from the right. That change grabs the audience's attention.

When you present a slide show, the content of your presentation should take center stage. You want the special effects you use, such as animation, builds, and transitions, to help emphasize the main points in your presentation—not draw the audience's attention to the special effects.

Animating an Object and Adding Sound Effects

You will begin by adding animation and sound to the AutoShape object on the final slide.

1 **Display slide 13.**

From the heart AutoShape's shortcut menu select Custom Animation.

The menu equivalent is Sli**d**e Show/Custo**m** Animation.

Your screen should be similar to Figure 2.54

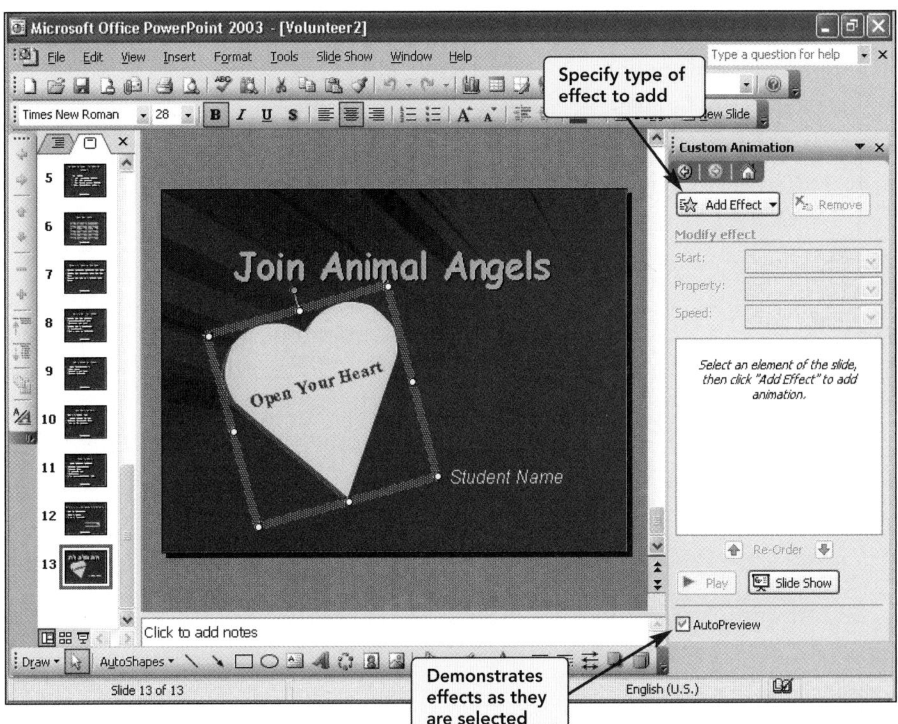

Figure 2.54

The Custom Animation task pane is used to assign animations and sound to objects on the slide. As you add animated items to a slide, each item is numbered. The number determines the order in which they display. A non-printing numbered tag appears on the slide near each animated item that correlates to the effects in the list.

You will animate the AutoShape object only. As you make selections, the Custom Animation list box will display the selected settings for the object and the effect will be demonstrated in the slide.

2 **If necessary, select the AutoPreview option.**

- **Click** **, select Entrance, and choose 5, Fly In.**

> **Having Trouble?**
> If Fly In is not available on the drop-down menu, select More Effects and select it from the dialog box.

- **From the Direction drop-down menu, select From Left.**
- **From the Speed drop-down menu, select Medium.**
- **Display the** 1 Heart 3: Open Y... **drop-down menu and select Effect Options.**

Your screen should be similar to Figure 2.55

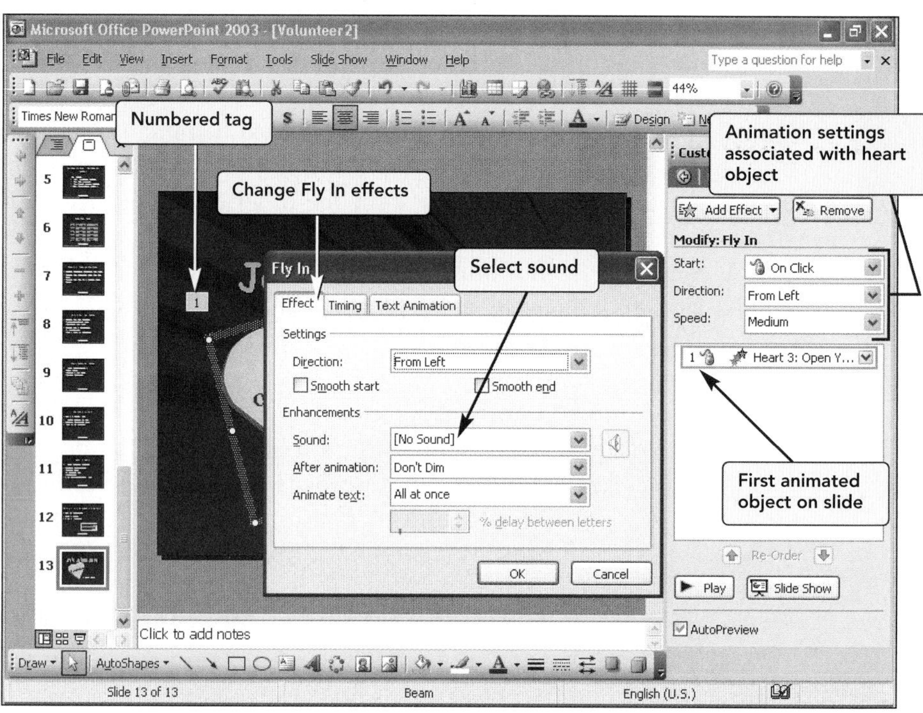

Figure 2.55

The list box in the task pane displays information about the first animated object on the slide. The numbered tag near the AutoShape identifies the animated object. The tag does not display when the slide show is run.

The Fly In dialog box includes the setting you already specified for the direction of the effect. You want to include a sound with the fly-in effect.

3 From the Sound drop-down menu, choose Chime.

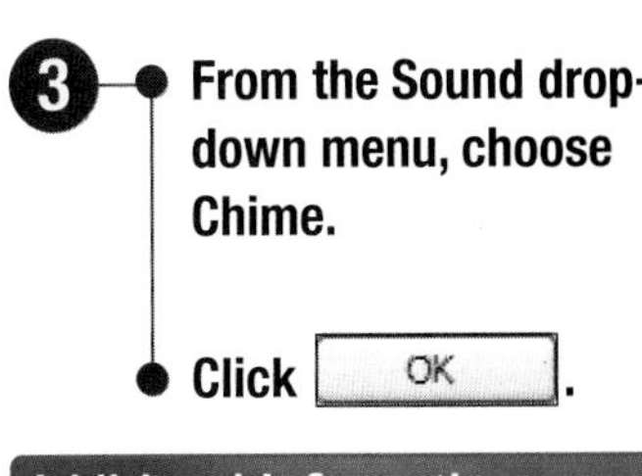

Click OK.

Additional Information

You must have a speaker and a sound card to hear the sound.

Your screen should be similar to Figure 2.56

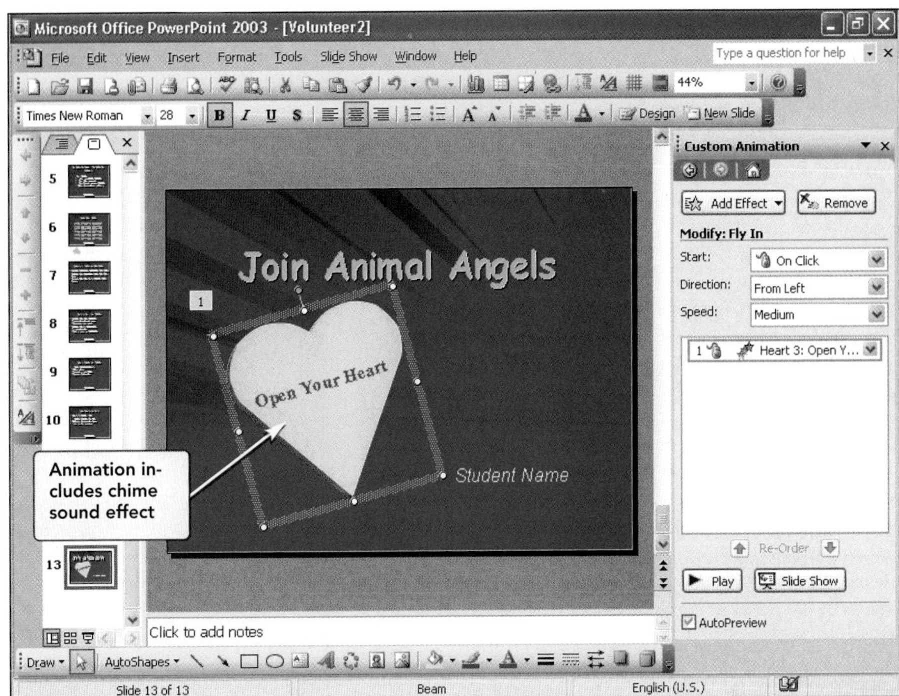

Figure 2.56

The heart appeared using the fly-in effect, and the chime sound played as it will when the slide show is run.

Adding Transition Effects

Next, you want to add a transition effect to all the slides. Although you can add transitions in Normal view, you will use Slide Sorter view because it has its own toolbar that makes it easy to perform many different tasks in this view.

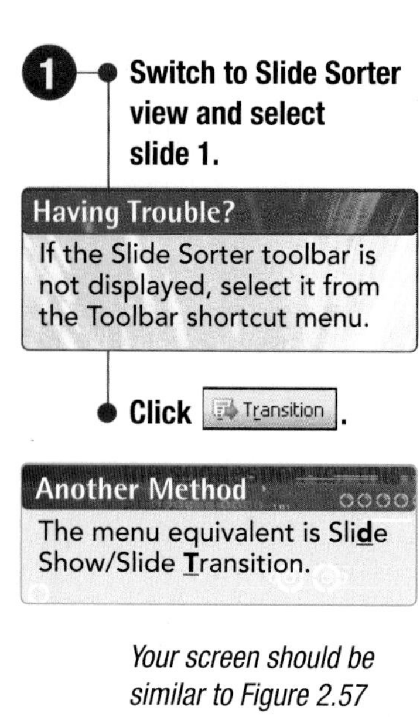

1 **Switch to Slide Sorter view and select slide 1.**

Having Trouble?

If the Slide Sorter toolbar is not displayed, select it from the Toolbar shortcut menu.

Click Transition.

Another Method

The menu equivalent is Slide Show/Slide Transition.

Your screen should be similar to Figure 2.57

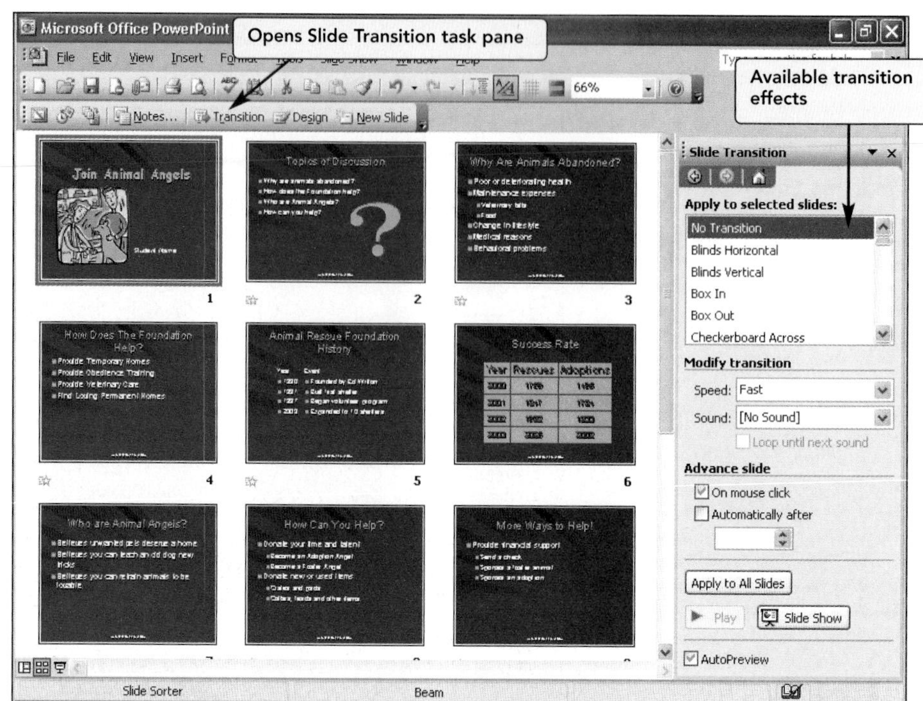

Figure 2.57

Additional Information

When AutoPreview is not on, you need to click Play to see the effect.

In the Slide Transition task pane, the list box displays the names of the transition effects that can be used on the slides. Currently, No Transition is selected, because the current slide does not include a transition effect. Because the AutoPreview option is selected, as you select a transition effect, the effect is displayed in the current slide. You can also replay the transition effect by clicking Play.

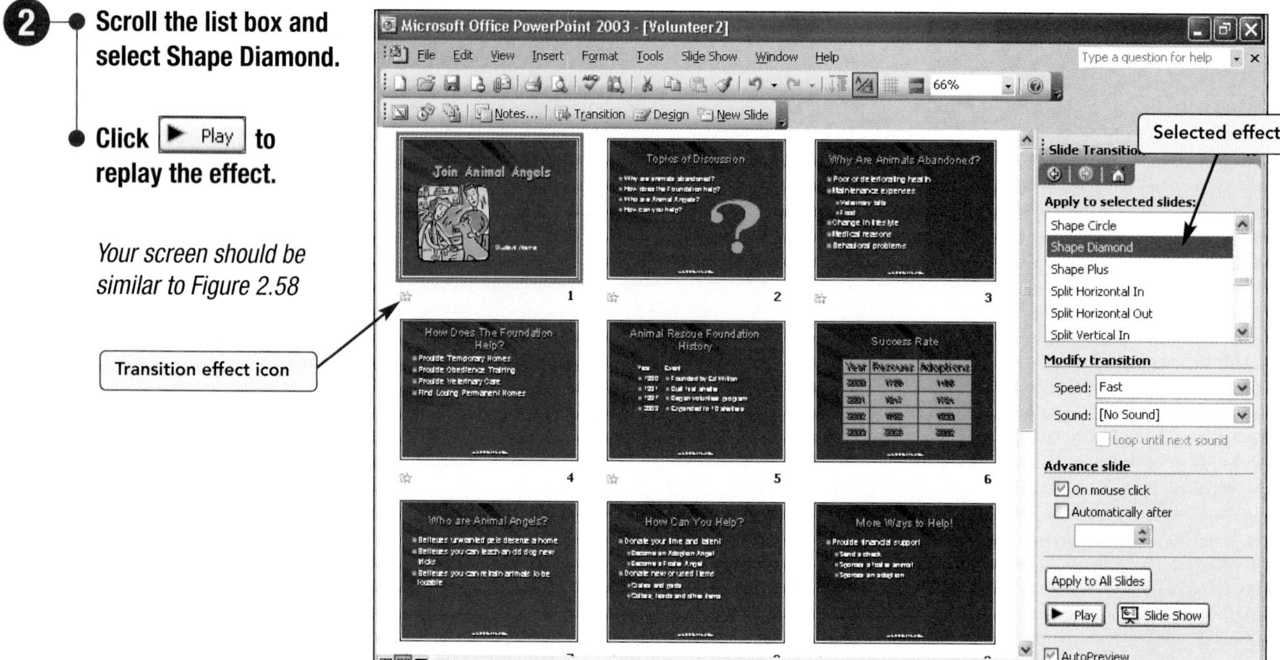

2 **Scroll the list box and select Shape Diamond.**

Click Play **to replay the effect.**

Your screen should be similar to Figure 2.58

Figure 2.58

A preview of the selected transition effect is displayed on the current slide, and a [transition icon] transition icon is displayed below slide 1. This indicates that a transition effect has been applied to the slide. Several other slides in the presentation also display a transition effect icon. This is because the AutoContent Wizard automatically used the Cut transition effect on all slides, except the title slide, that were added when the presentation was created originally.

You like the way the transition effects work and decide to use the Random Transition effect, which will randomly select different transition effects, on all the slides. You will select and change all the slides at once.

3

- **Choose Random Transition (last option in list).**
- **Click Apply to All Slides.**
- **Close the Slide Transition pane.**

Your screen should be similar to Figure 2.59

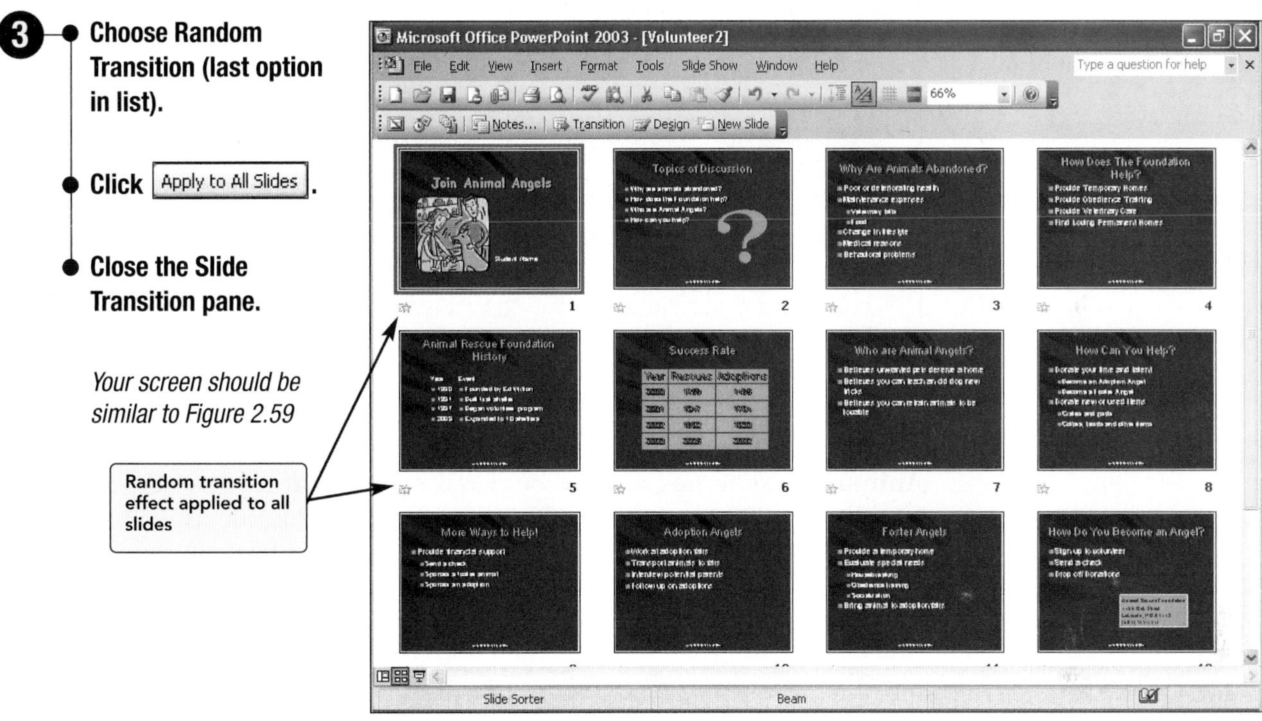

Figure 2.59

The transition icon appears below each slide, indicating that a transition effect has been applied to all slides.

4

- **Save the presentation.**
- **Run the slide show from the beginning to see the different transition effects.**

Adding Build Effects

The next effect you want to add to the slides is a build effect that will display progressively each bullet on a slide. When a build is applied to a slide, the slide initially shows only the title. The bulleted text appears as the presentation proceeds. A build slide can also include different build transition effects, which are similar to slide transition effects. The effect is applied to the bulleted text as it is displayed on the slide.

1 Click .

Click Animation Schemes from the Slide Design task pane.

Additional Information

You can use the Animation Schemes and Custom Animation commands on the Slide Show menu to add sound build effects. To use this option, you must be in Normal view.

Your screen should be similar to Figure 2.60

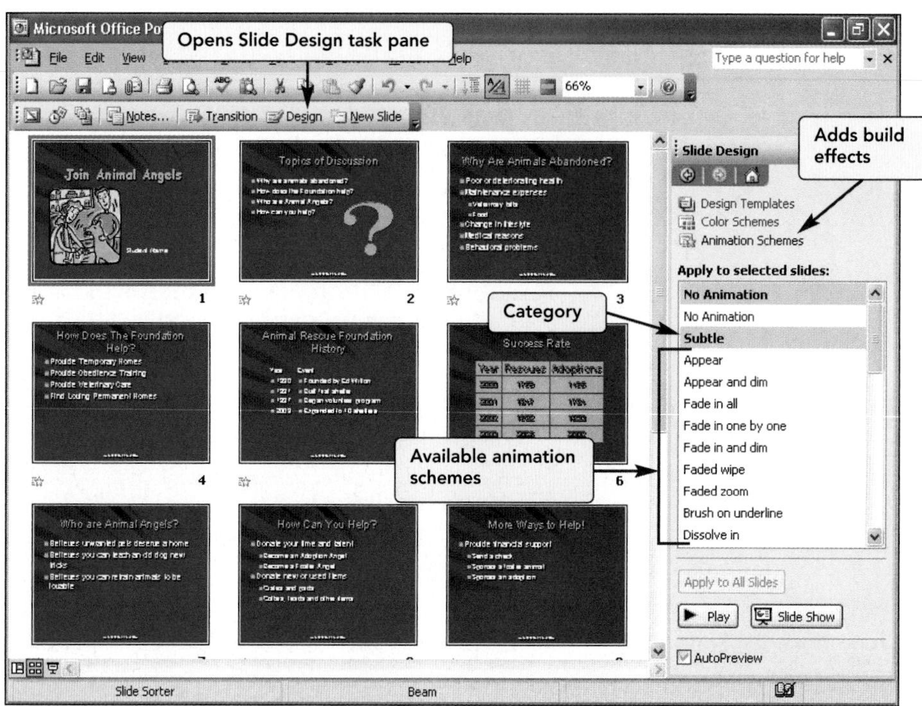

Figure 2.60

The Slide Design task pane displays a list of animation schemes. **Animation schemes** are preset visual effects that can be added to slide text. Each scheme usually includes an effect for the title as well as for the bulleted items. Some schemes include a slide transition effect as well. The schemes are divided into three categories: Subtle, Moderate, and Exciting.

Additional Information

Pointing to a scheme name displays a description of the effects in a ScreenTip.

You will use two different build effects in the presentation. The two title slides will use one build effect and all other slides except slides 5 and 6 will use another effect. You do not want slides 5 and 6 to have any build effects because they are tables and the content is not conducive to this type of animation.

2

- If necessary, select AutoPreview to turn on this feature.
- Make slide 2 the current slide and select a few animation schemes to see how they look.
- Select Wipe from the Subtle category.
- Click Apply to All Slides.
- Select slides 5 and 6.

Having Trouble?

You can select and deselect multiple slides by holding down Ctrl while making your selection.

- Select No Animation from the No Animation category.
- Select slides 1 and 13.
- Select the Big Title effect from the Exciting category.
- Select slide 1 and click [Slide Show button] to start Slide Show.
- Click on the slide to display the subtitle.

Your screen should be similar to Figure 2.61

Figure 2.61

The first slide is displayed using the Wedge transition effect and Big Title animation, but the subtitle did not display until you clicked on the slide. When a build is applied to a slide, the body items are displayed only when you click or use any of the procedures to advance to the next slide. This allows the presenter to focus the audience's attention and to control the pace of the presentation.

Controlling the Slide Show

As much as you would like to control a presentation completely, the presence of an audience usually causes the presentation to change course. PowerPoint has several ways to control a slide show during the presentation. Before presenting a slide show, you should rehearse the presentation. To help with this aspect of the presentation, PowerPoint includes a Rehearse Timings option on the Slide Show menu that records the time you spend on each slide as you practice your narration. If your computer is set up with a microphone, you could even record your narration with the Record Narration option.

Navigating in a Slide Show

Running the slide show and practicing how to control the slide show help you to have a smooth presentation. For example, if someone has a question about a previous slide, you can go backward and redisplay it. You will try out some of the features you can use while running the slide show.

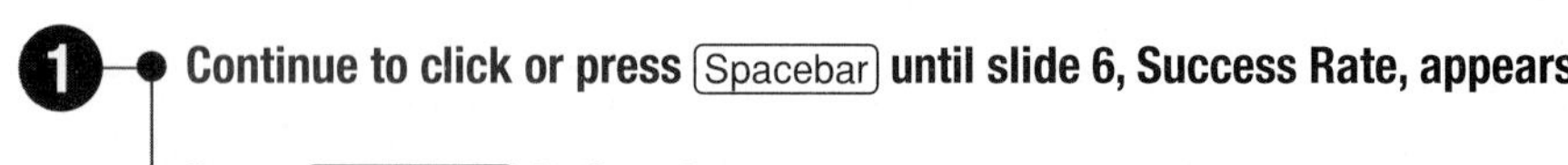

1 **Continue to click or press Spacebar until slide 6, Success Rate, appears.**

Press Backspace (2 times).

Additional Information

You can return to the first slide in the presentation by holding down both mouse buttons for two seconds.

You returned the onscreen presentation to slide 4, but now, because the audience has already viewed slides 5 and 6, you want to advance to slide 7. To go to a specific slide number, you type the slide number and press ←Enter.

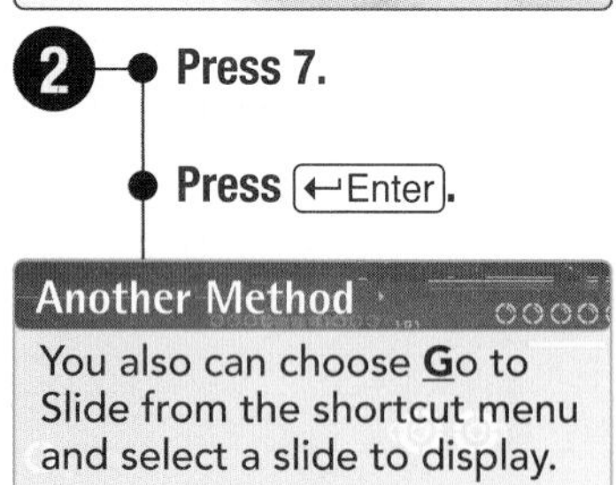

2 **Press 7.**

Press ←Enter.

Another Method

You also can choose Go to Slide from the shortcut menu and select a slide to display.

Click 3 times to display the three bulleted items.

Additional Information

You can also white out the screen by pressing W or using Screen/White Screen on the shortcut menu.

Slide 7, Who are Animal Angels?, is displayed. Sometimes a question from an audience member can interrupt the flow of the presentation. If this happens to you, you can black out the screen to focus attention onto your response.

3 **Press B.**

Another Method

The menu equivalent is Screen/Black Screen on the shortcut menu.

The screen goes to black while you address the topic. When you are ready to resume the presentation, you can bring the slide back.

4 **Click, or press B.**

Adding Freehand Annotations

During your presentation, you may want to point to an important word, underline an important point, or draw checkmarks next to items that you have covered. To do this, you can use the mouse pointer during the presentation. When you move the mouse, the mouse pointer appears and the Slide Show toolbar is displayed in the lower left corner of the screen.

1 **Move the mouse on your desktop.**

Your screen should be similar to Figure 2.62

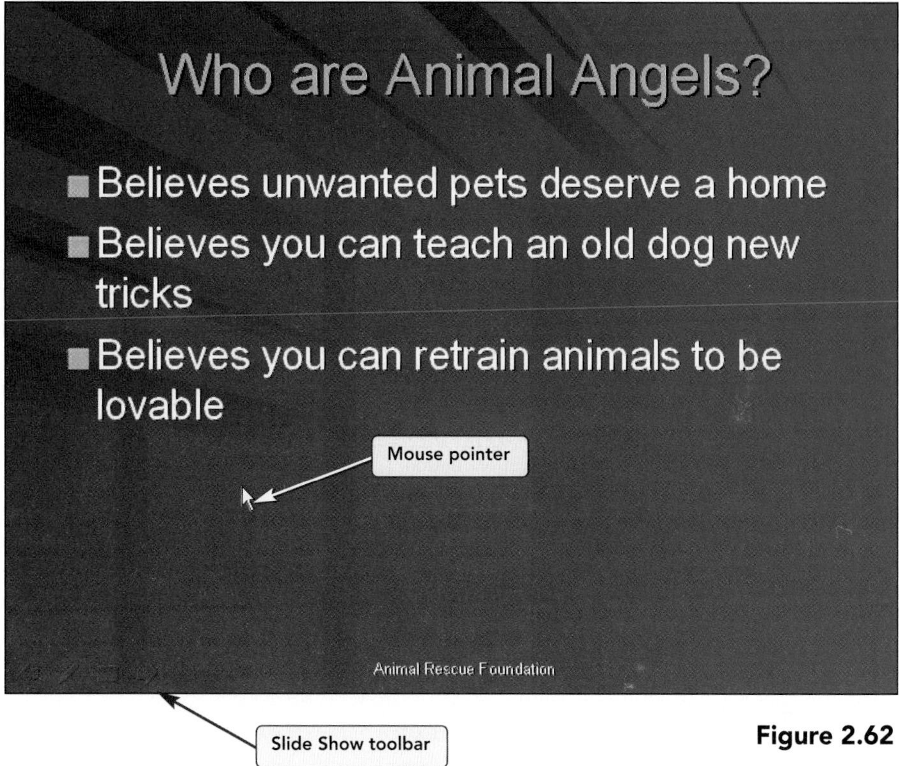

Figure 2.62

The mouse pointer in its current shape can be used to point to items on the slide. You can also use it to draw on the screen by changing the mouse pointer to a ballpoint pen, felt tip pen, or highlighter, which activates the associated freehand annotation feature.

2 Click [button] to display the Pointer options menu.

Another Method

You can also select Pointer Options from the shortcut menu.

Your screen should be similar to Figure 2.63

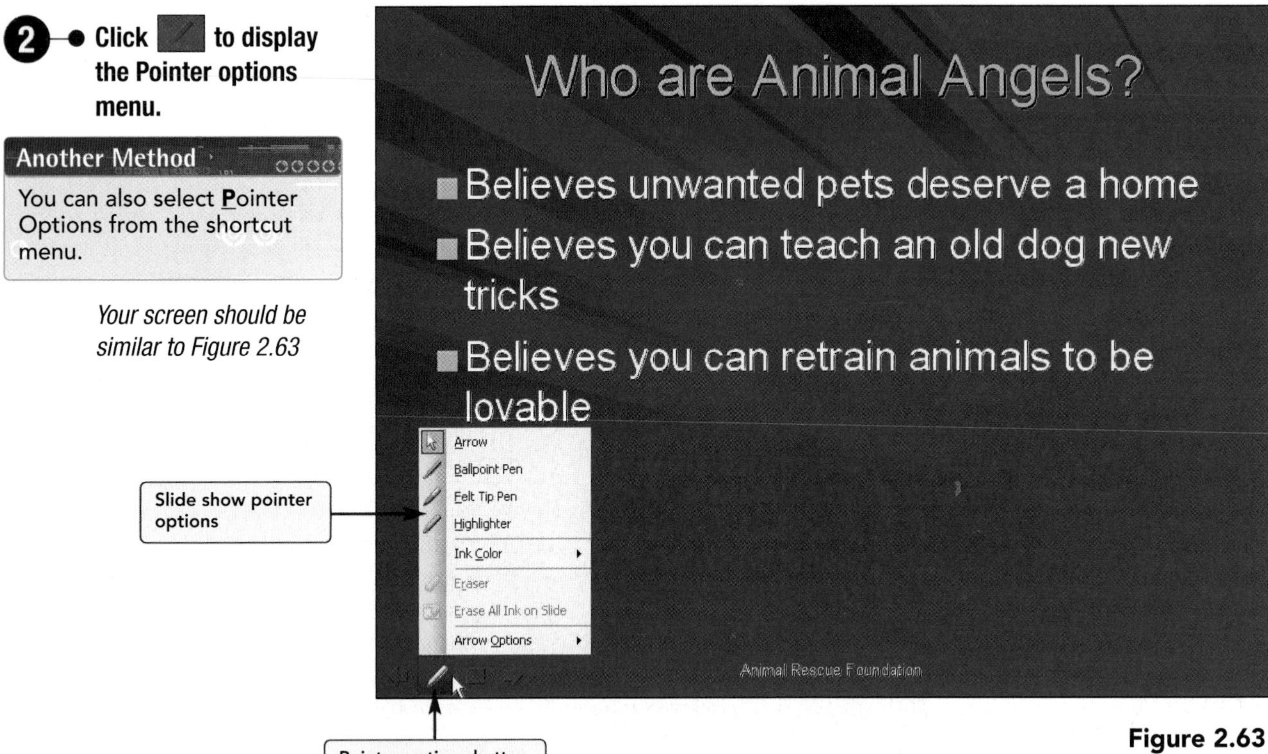

Figure 2.63

The mouse pointer and arrow options are described in the following table.

Pointer Options	Effect
Arrow	Displays the mouse pointer as an arrow.
Ballpoint Pen	Changes the mouse pointer to a diamond shape and turns on ballpoint pen annotation.
Felt Tip Pen	Changes the mouse pointer to a circle shape and turns on felt tip pen annotation.
Highlighter	Changes the mouse pointer to a bar shape and turns on highlighter.
Ink Color	Displays a color palette to select a color for the annotation tool.
Eraser	Erases selected annotations.
Erase All Ink on Slide	Removes all annotations from the slide.
Arrow Options	**(These options apply only if Arrow is selected.)**
Automatic	Hides the mouse pointer if it is not moved for 15 seconds. It reappears when you move the mouse. This is the default setting.
Visible	Displays the mouse pointer as an arrow and does not hide it.
Hidden	Hides the mouse pointer until another pointer option is selected.

You will try out several of the freehand annotation features to see how they work. To draw, you select the pen style and then drag the pen pointer in the direction you want to draw.

3 **Choose Felt Tip Pen.**

Additional Information

The mouse pointer changes shape depending upon the selected annotation tool.

- **Drag the dot pointer until a circle is drawn around the word "teach."**
- **Choose Highlighter from the Pointer options menu and highlight the word "retrain."**
- **Choose Ballpoint Pen from the Pointer options menu.**

Another Method

You can also use Ctrl + P to display the Ballpoint pen.

- **Choose Ink Color from the Pointer options menu and select gold.**

Additional Information

The Automatic ink color setting determines the default color to use for annotations based upon the slide design colors.

- **In the first bulleted item, draw a caret after the word "a" and write the word "good" above the line.**

Your screen should be similar to Figure 2.64

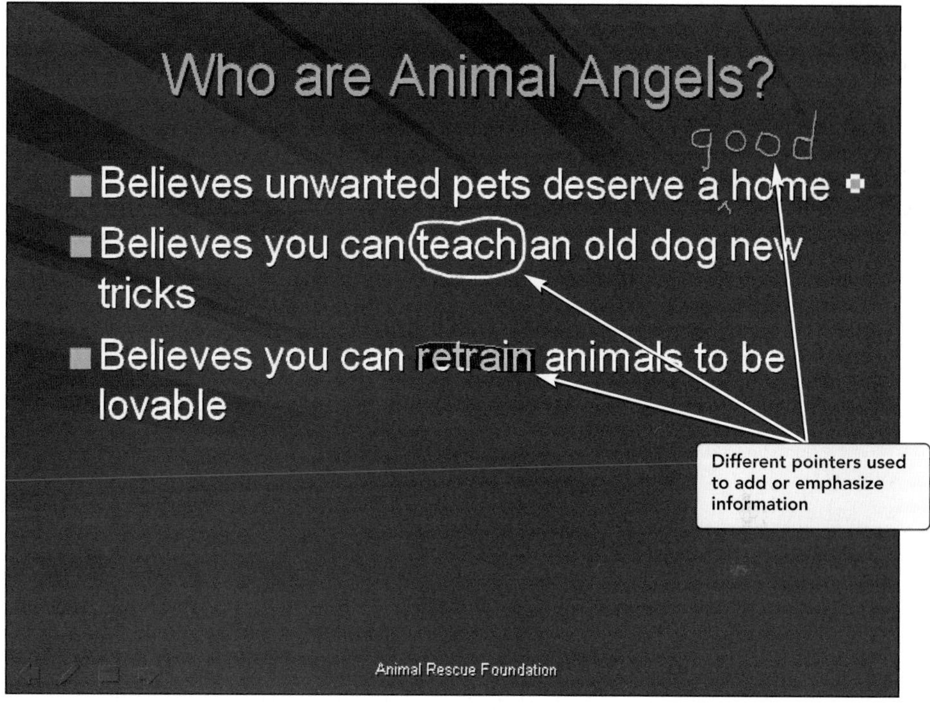

Figure 2.64

4 • Practice using the freehand annotator to draw any shapes you want on the slide.

• To erase the annotations, select Erase All Ink on Slide from the Pointer options menu.

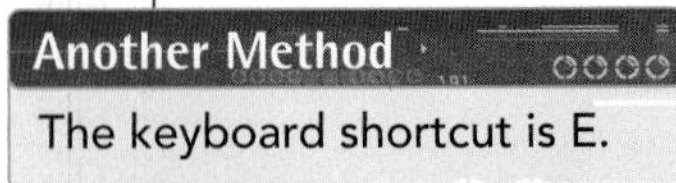

• To turn off freehand annotation, select Arrow from the Pointer options menu.

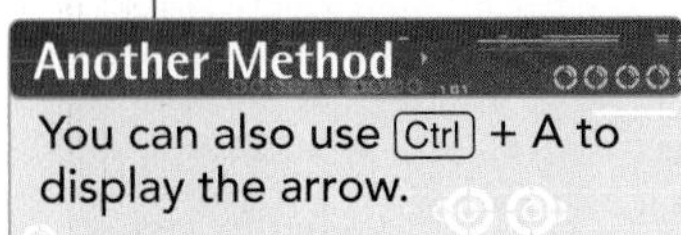

• Press Esc to end the slide show.

• Close the task pane.

If you do not erase annotations before ending the presentation, you are prompted to keep or discard the annotations when you end the slide show. If you keep the annotations they are saved to the slides and will appear as part of the slide during a presentation.

Hiding Slides

As you reconsider the presentation, you decide to show the Success Rate slide only if someone asks about this information. To do this, you will hide the slide.

1 • Select slide 6.

• Click Hide Slide.

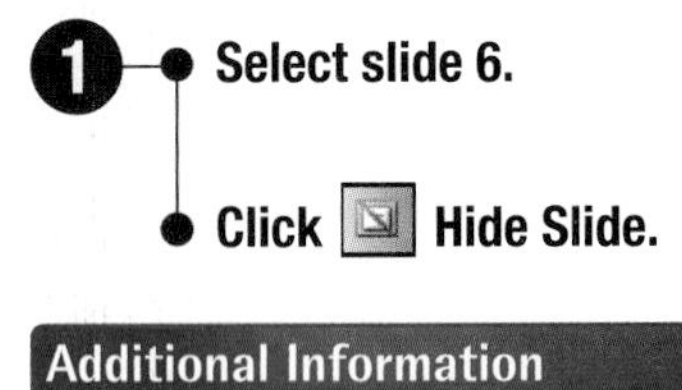

Your screen should be similar to Figure 2.65

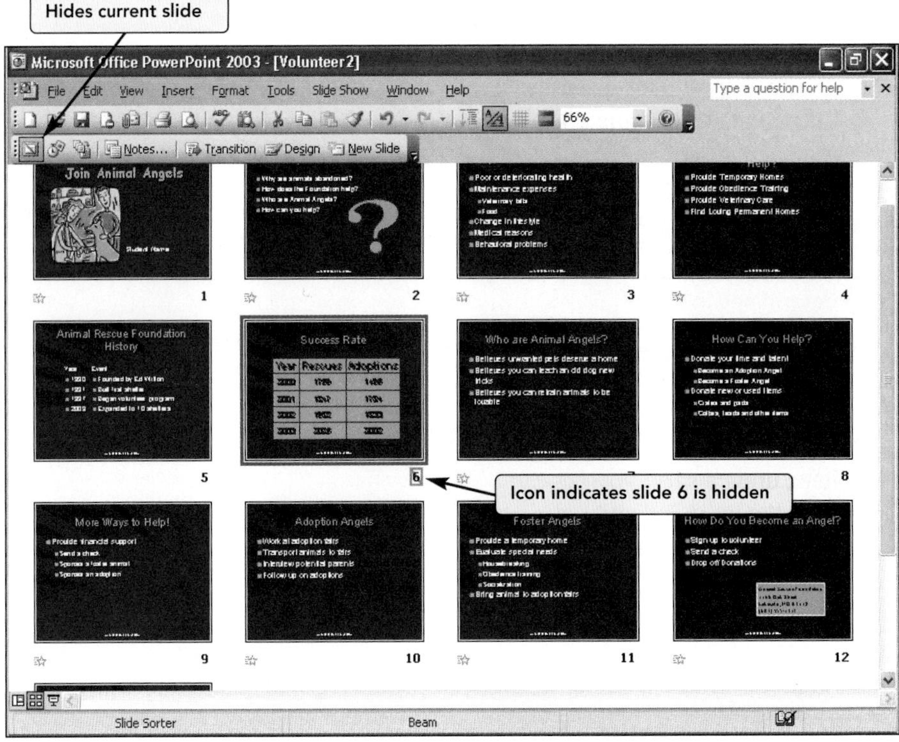

Figure 2.65

Notice that the slide number for slide 6 is surrounded by a box with a slash drawn through it which indicates that the slide is hidden. Next, you will run the slide show to see how hidden slides work. You will begin the show at the slide before the hidden slide.

2
- **Select slide 5.**
- **Click [icon] to run the slide show from the current slide.**
- **Click to display the next slide, which should be Who Are Animal Angels?**

Your screen should be similar to Figure 2.66

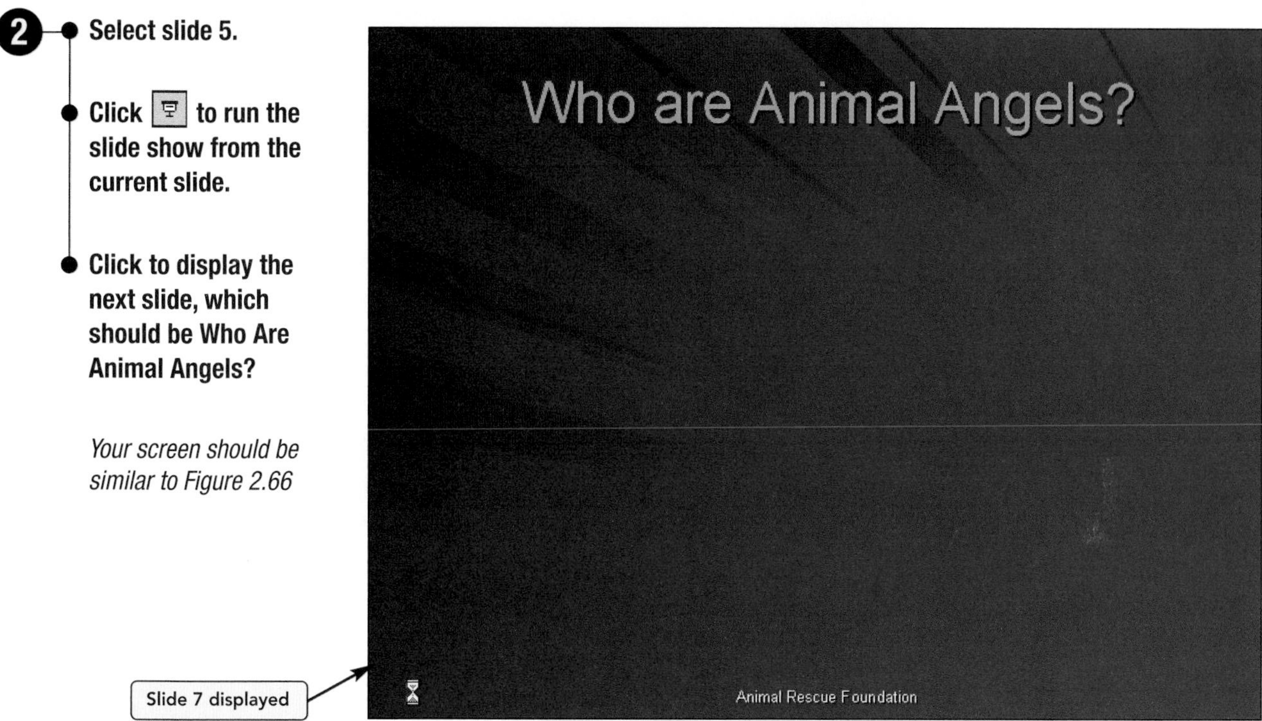

Figure 2.66

Slide 6 was not displayed because it is hidden. To show how to display a hidden slide, you will return to slide 5 and then display slide 6.

3 • Press [Page Up] twice to display slide 5 again.

• Press H to see slide 6.

Your screen should be similar to Figure 2.67

Another Method

You can also use Go to Slide on the shortcut menu to display a hidden slide.

Figure 2.67

Adding Speaker Notes

When making your presentation, there are some critical points you want to be sure to discuss. To help you remember the important points, you can add notes to a slide and then print the **notes pages**. These pages display the notes below a small version of the slide they accompany. You can create notes pages for some or all of the slides in a presentation. You decide to add speaker notes on slide 5 to remind you about the hidden slide.

1 Press Esc to end the slide show.

Display slide 5 in Normal view.

Click in the notes pane.

Type **Show the next hidden slide if someone asks about adoption rates.**.

Additional Information

You can enlarge the notes area by dragging the pane divider line.

Your screen should be similar to Figure 2.68

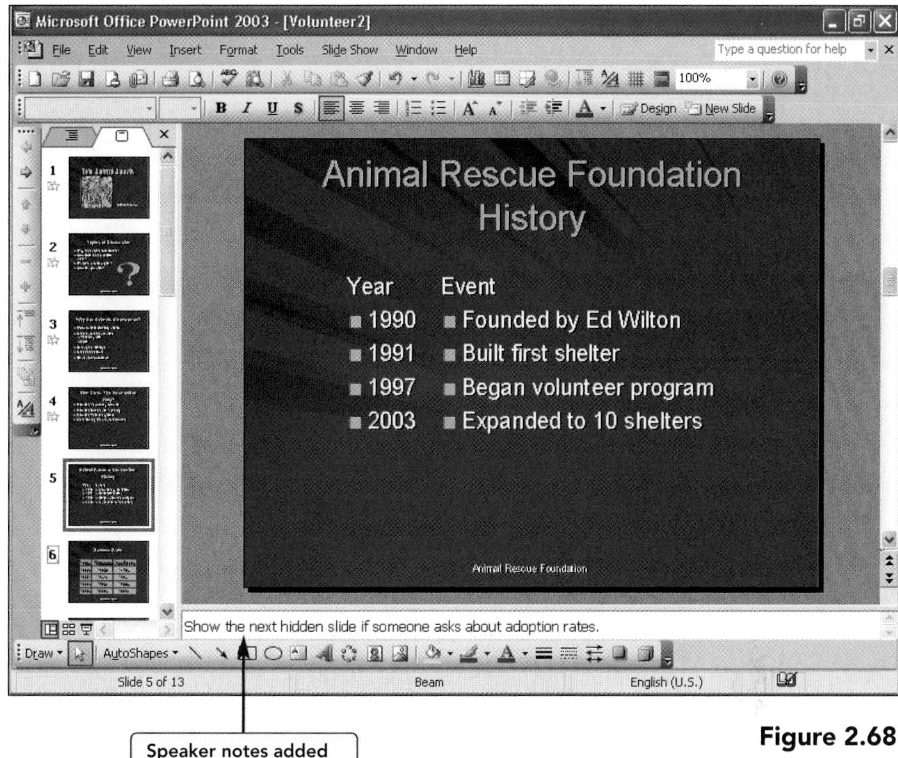

Figure 2.68

You want to preview the notes page to check its appearence before it is printed.

2 Choose **View/Notes Page**.

Your screen should be similar to Figure 2.69

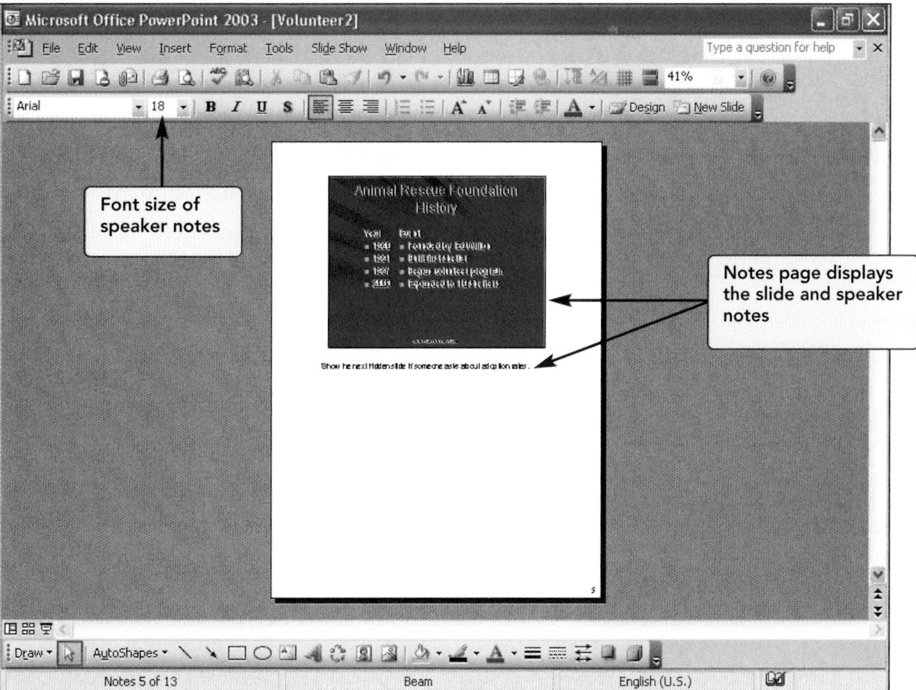

Figure 2.69

The notes pages display the notes you added below the slide that the note accompanies.

To make the speaker notes easy to read in a dimly lit room while you are making the presentation, you will increase the font size of the notes text.

3

- **Click on the note text to select the placeholder.**
- **Select the note text.**
- **Increase the font size to 24.**

Your screen should be similar to Figure 2.70

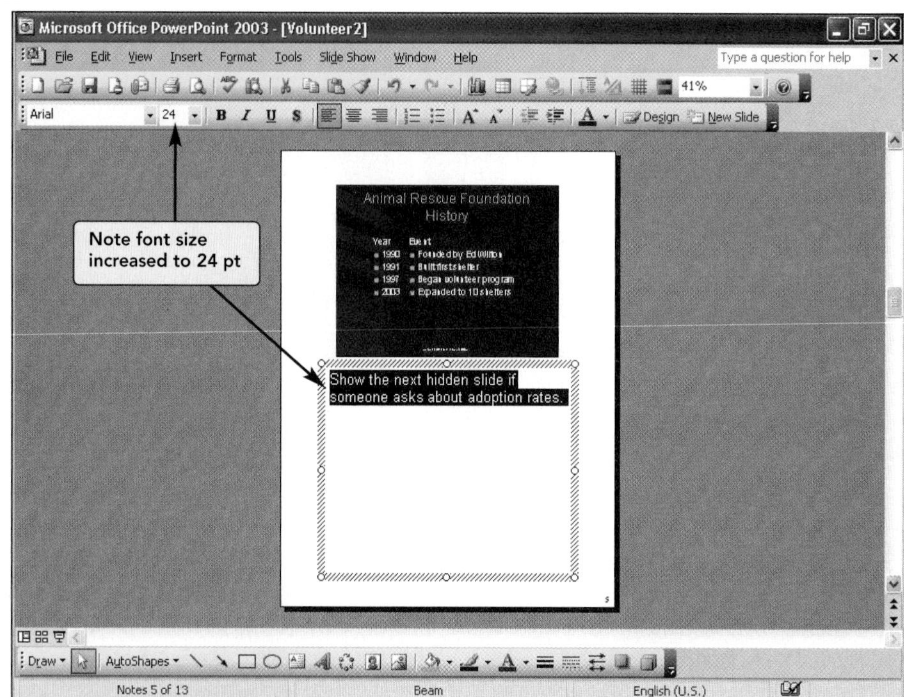

Figure 2.70

Checking Style

Having Trouble?

If your school has disabled the Office Assistant, you will not be able to complete this section.

You want to make a final check of the presentation for consistency and style. To help with this, you can use the **style check** feature which checks for consistency in punctuation and capitalization as well as for visual elements such as the maximum number of bulleted items in a list. To use this feature, you need to turn it on and set the options to check. Additionally, the Office Assistant feature must be on, otherwise you will not be notified about located style inconsistencies.

1

- **Display slide 1 in Normal view.**
- **Choose Tools/Options.**
- **Open the Spelling and Style tab and select Check Style.**
- **If prompted, click Enable Assistant to turn on the Office Assistant.**
- **Click Style Options... .**

Your screen should be similar to Figure 2.71

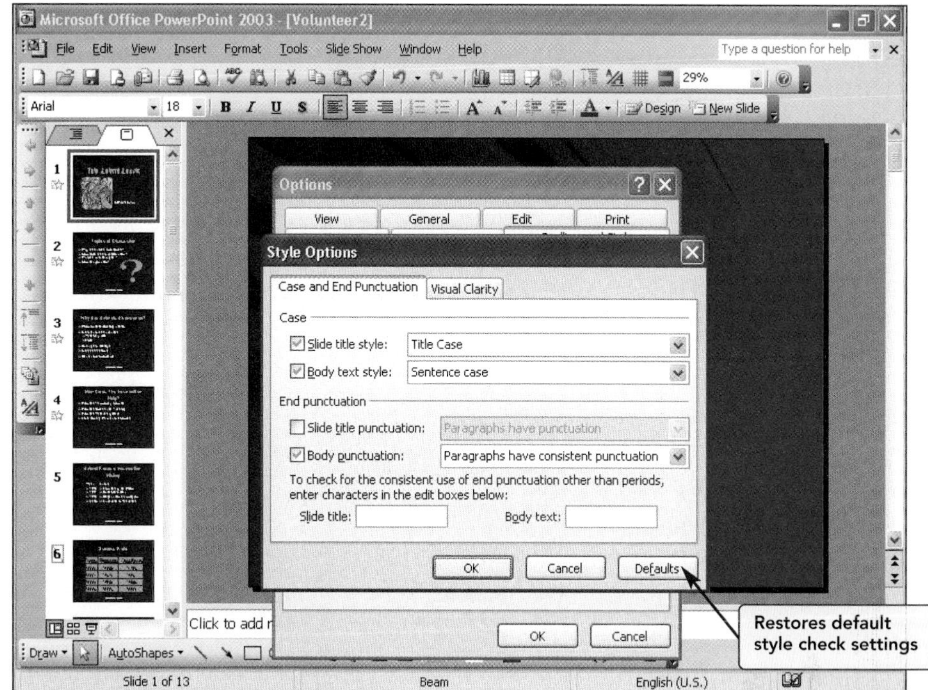

Figure 2.71

Additional Information

You can turn on/off options and change the default settings by selecting from the option's drop-down menu.

The Case and End Punctuation tab provides options that allow you to control the kind of style check used for capitalization and punctuation. The default style rule is to use title case (first letter of most words is capitalized) for slide titles and sentence case (only the first word is capitalized) for body text. Additionally, style checking looks for consistent use of end punctuation in body text.

You want to use the default settings for the style check.

2

- **If necessary, click Defaults to use the default settings as shown in Figure 2.71.**
- **Open the Visual Clarity tab.**
- **If necessary, select all the options.**

Your screen should be similar to Figure 2.72

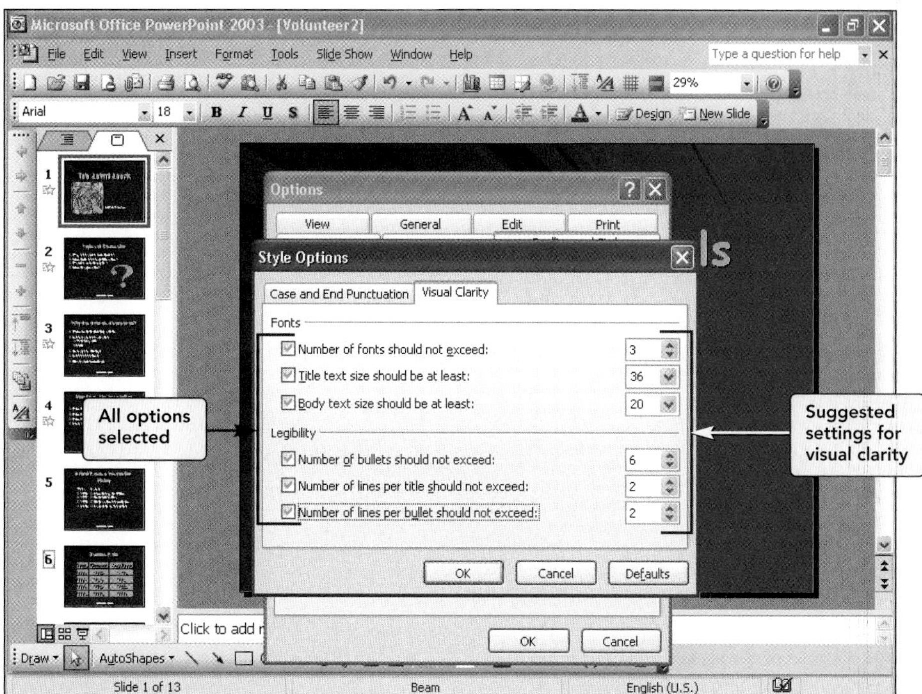

Figure 2.72

When a style check is made, each slide is examined for visual clarity. The default settings use guidelines for proper slide design: the font size is large, the number of fonts used is small, and the amount of text on a slide is limited. For example, the maximum number of bullets per slide is six and number of lines per bullet is two. All these settings help you adhere to good slide design.

The style check feature is active only when the Office Assistant is displayed. As you display each slide in Normal view, the style is evaluated. It displays a next to the placeholder area in any slides in which it detects a potential problem.

3

- **Click** 

2 times.
- **Click on the slide pane of slide 1 to activate the pane.**
- **Because no problems were identified in slide 1, click in the scroll bar to display slide 2.**

Having Trouble?

If you advance to the next slide using the Slides tab, you must click on the slide pane each time to activate it and evaluate the style.

- **Click on the .**
- **Move the Assistant character to the right side of the screen.**

Your screen should be similar to Figure 2.73

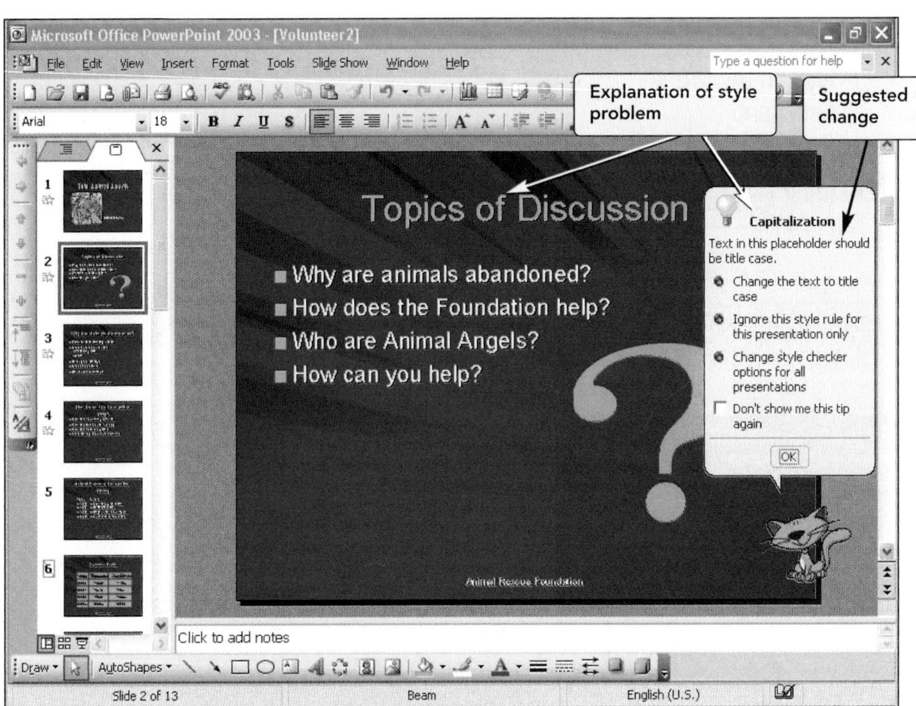

Figure 2.73

Having Trouble?

Your Assistant character may be different from the character shown here.

The Assistant displays an explanation of the problem it has located. In this case, because each word in the title is not capitalized, the title case rule has been violated. You will use the suggestion to correct the title case. As soon as you respond to the style checker, the correction is made and the next located potential problem is identified.

4 • Choose "Change the text to title case."

• Click on the 💡 next to the object area placeholder.

Your screen should be similar to Figure 2.74

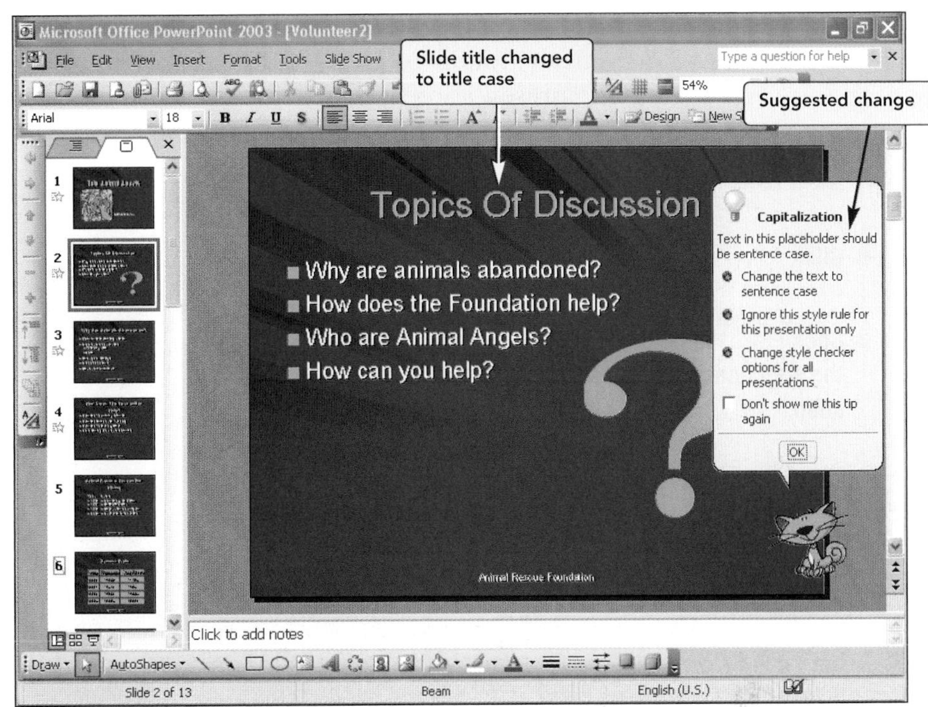

Figure 2.74

The title case is corrected and a second lightbulb appears indicating that another style problem has been identified. The suggested style change is to change the bulleted items to sentence case for body text.

5 • Choose "Change the text to sentence case."

Your screen should be similar to Figure 2.75

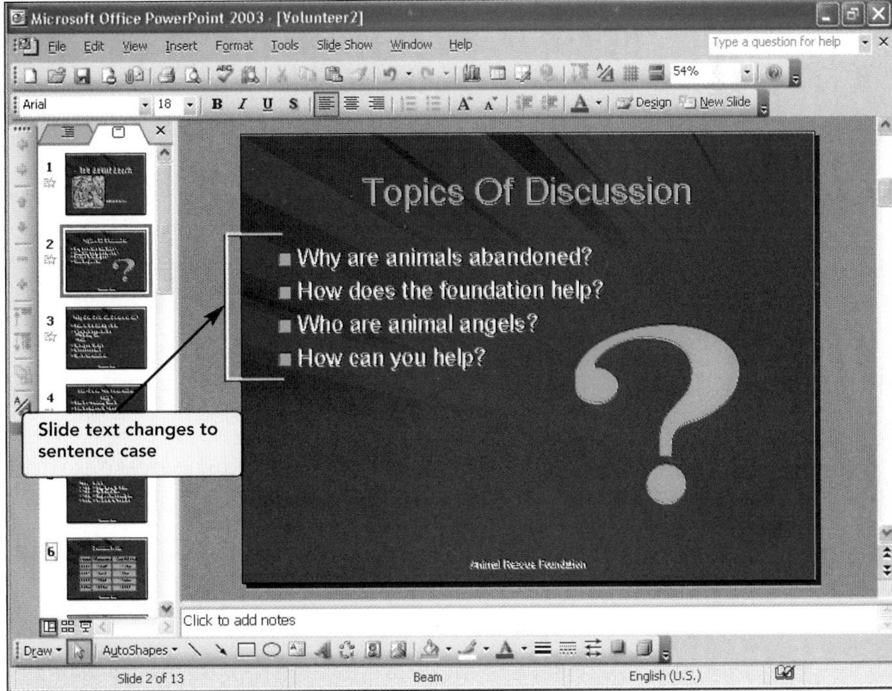

Figure 2.75

Making this change, however, changed proper names, such as the name of the volunteer organization, to lowercase. In this case, you do not want to keep this change. You will undo the change and skip the style check suggestion to clear it. Then you will continue checking the rest of the presentation.

6 **Click Undo.**

- **Click .**
- **Click OK to ignore the suggestion for this slide.**
- **Continue checking the style on the remaining slides in the presentation, making the changes shown in the table below Figure 2.76.**

Your screen should be similar to Figure 2.76

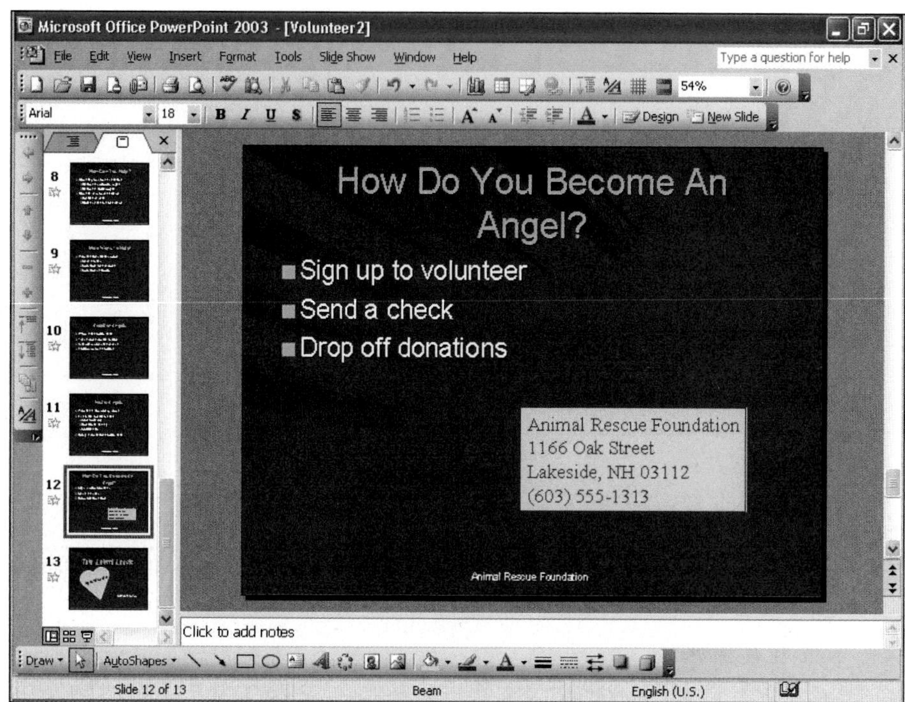

Figure 2.76

Slide	Adjustment
4	Change the text to sentence case.
5	Click OK to ignore changes for this slide.
7	Change the text to title case.
8	Click OK to ignore change for this slide.
9	Change the text to title case.
12	Change the text to title case. Change the text to sentence case.

Now that you have checked the presentation, you will turn off this feature.

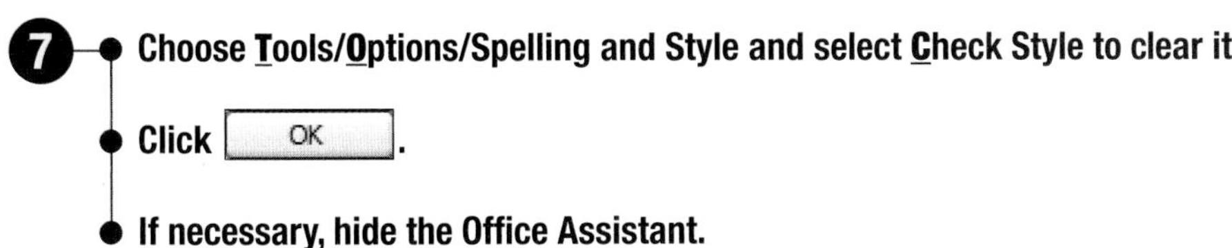

7

- **Choose Tools/Options/Spelling and Style and select Check Style to clear it.**
- **Click OK.**
- **If necessary, hide the Office Assistant.**

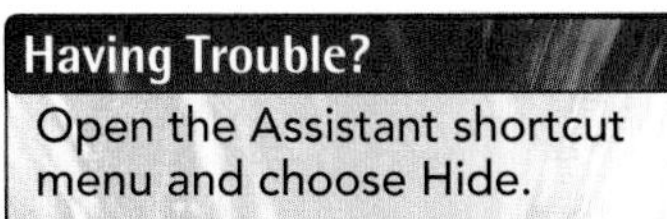

Having Trouble?

Open the Assistant shortcut menu and choose Hide.

Documenting a File

Before saving the completed presentation, you want to include file documentation with the file when it is saved.

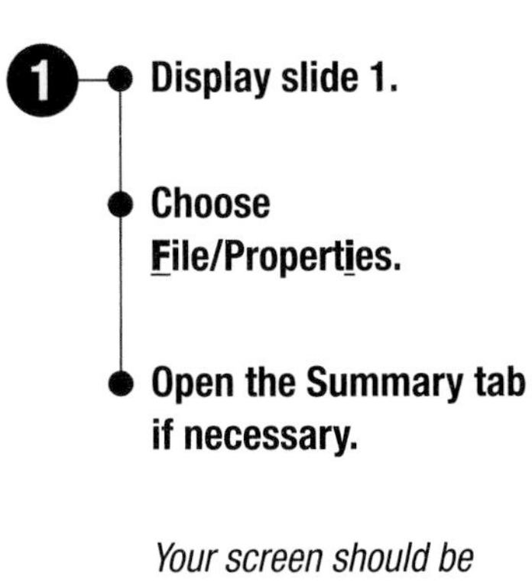

1

- **Display slide 1.**
- **Choose File/Properties.**
- **Open the Summary tab if necessary.**

Your screen should be similar to Figure 2.77

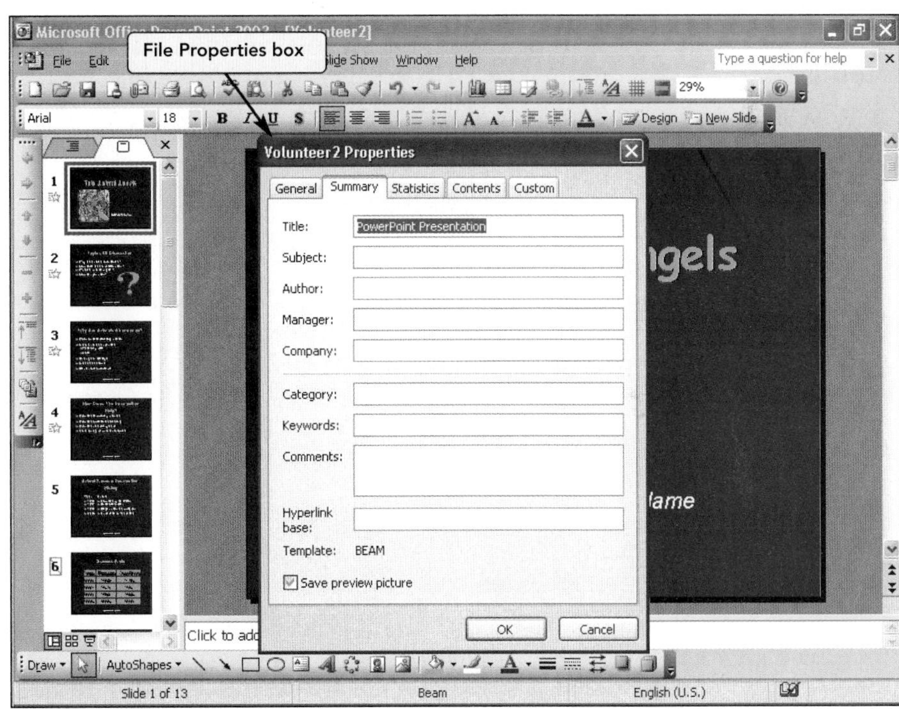

Figure 2.77

The Summary tab text boxes are used for the following:

Option	Action
Title	Enter the presentation title. This title can be longer and more descriptive than the presentation file name.
Subject	Enter a description of the presentation's content.
Author	Enter the name of the presentation's author. By default this is the name entered when PowerPoint was installed.
Manager	Enter the name of your manager.
Company	Enter the name of your company.
Category	Enter the name of a higher-level category under which you can group similar types of presentations.
Keywords	Enter words that you associate with the presentation so the Find File command can be used.
Comments	Enter any comments you feel are appropriate for the presentation.
Hyperlink base	Enter the path or URL that you want to use for all hyperlinks in the document.
Template	Identifies the template that is attached to the file.
Save Preview Picture	Saves a picture of the first slide with the file to display in the Open dialog box.

2

- **In the title text box, enter Animal Angels.**
- **In the subject text box, enter Volunteer recruitment.**
- **In the Author text box, enter your name.**
- **If necessary, select "Save preview picture."**

Your screen should be similar to Figure 2.78

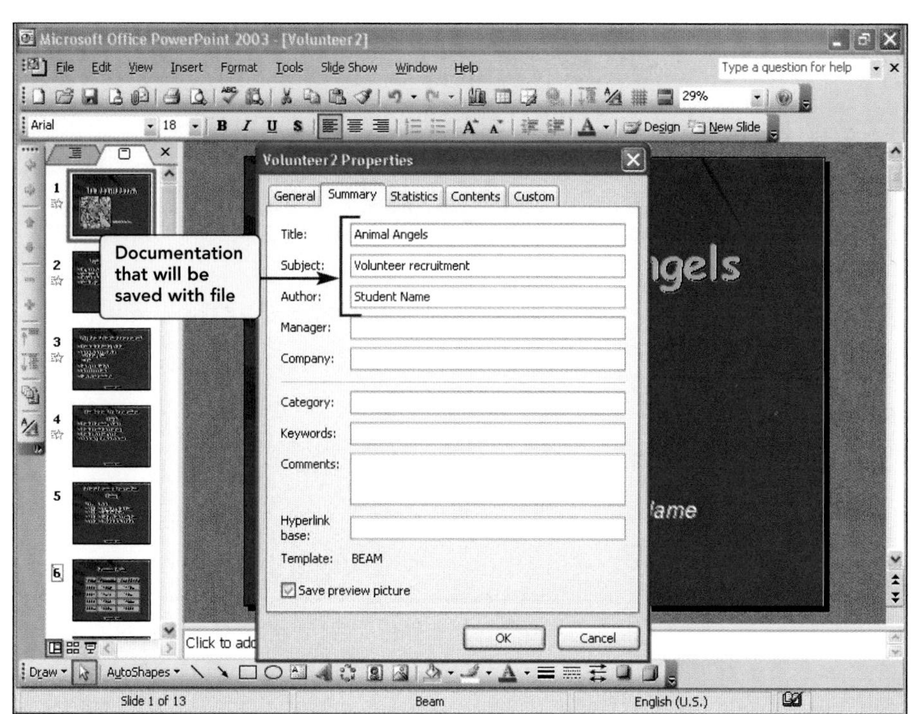

Figure 2.78

3 Click OK.

- Save the presentation.

Customizing Print Settings

You have created both slides and notes pages for the presentation. Now you want to print the notes page and some of the slides. Customizing the print settings by selecting specific slides to print and scaling the size of the slides to fill the page are a few of the ways to make your printed output look more professional.

Printing Selected Slides

First you will print the notes page for the slide on which you entered note text.

1 Choose **File/Print.**

- If necessary, select the printer.
- From the Print Range section, select Slides.
- Type 5 in the Slides text box.
- From the Print What drop-down list box, select Notes Pages.
- If necessary, select Grayscale from the Color/Grayscale drop-down list box.
- Click Preview.

Your screen should be similar to Figure 2.79

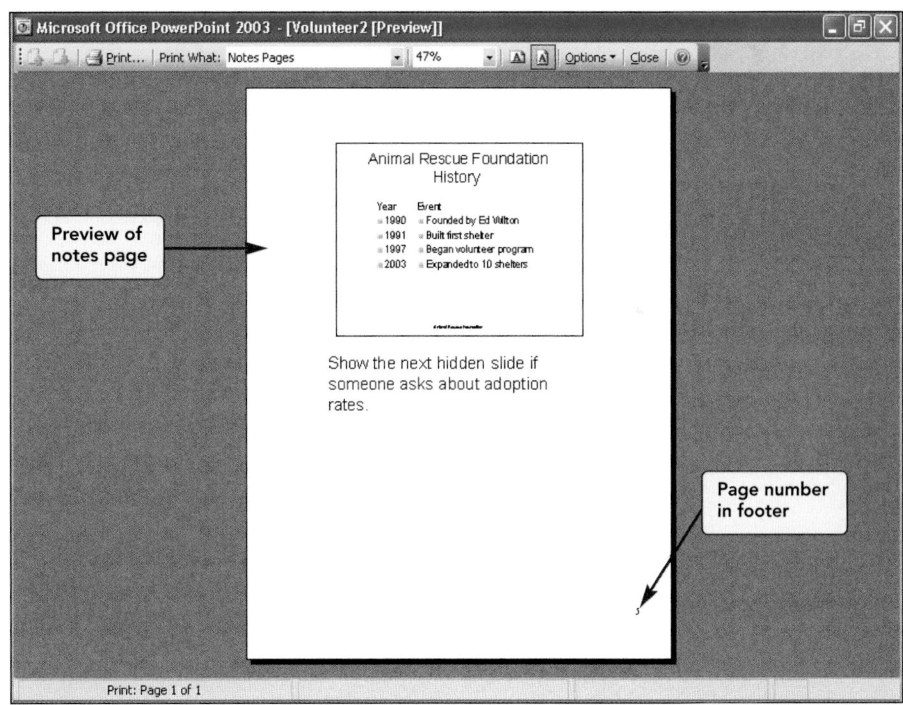

Figure 2.79

The notes page is displayed in portrait orientation as it will appear when printed.

Adding Headers and Footers to Notes and Handouts

Currently, the only information that appears in the footer of the notes page is the page number. You want to include the date and your name in the header of the notes and handouts.

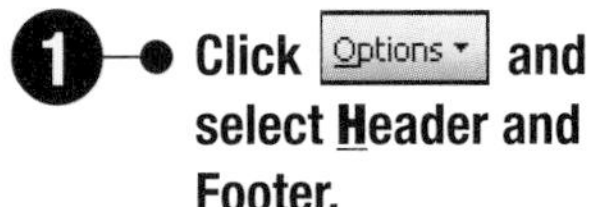

Click Options and select Header and Footer.

Your screen should be similar to Figure 2.80

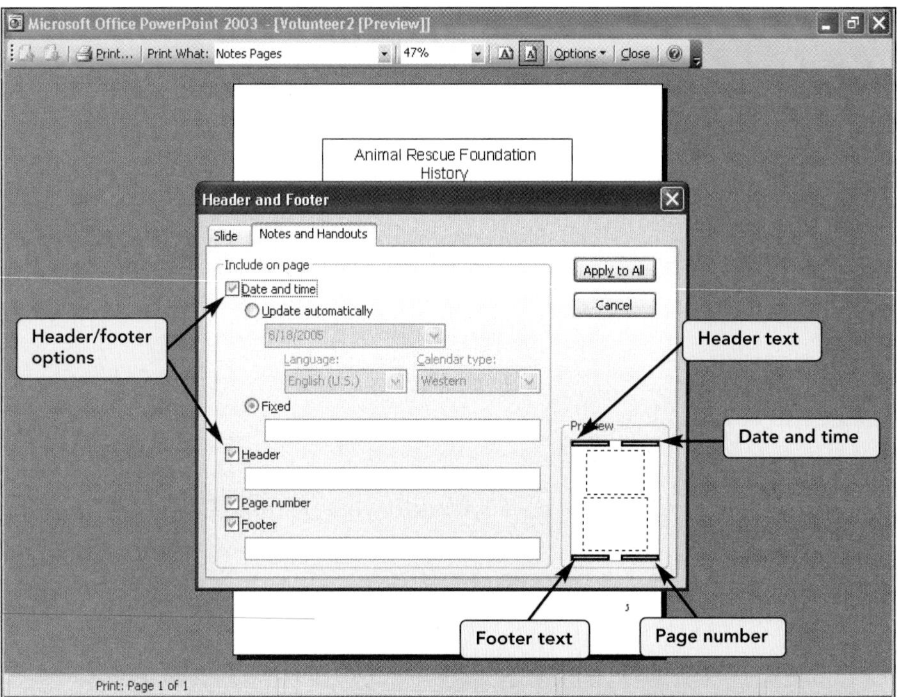

Figure 2.80

As in slides, you can display date and time information and footer text. In addition, on notes and handouts, you can include header text and a page number. The preview area identifies the four areas where this information will appear and identifies the currently selected areas in bold. The header option is selected, but because it does not include text, nothing is displayed.

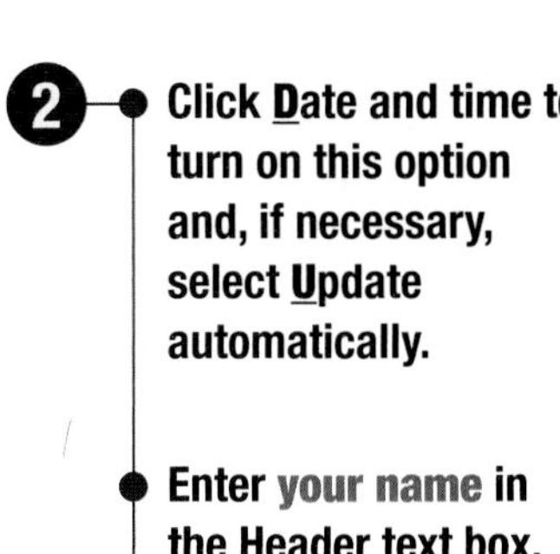

2 • **Click Date and time to turn on this option and, if necessary, select Update automatically.**

• **Enter your name in the Header text box.**

• **Click Apply to All.**

Your screen should be similar to Figure 2.81

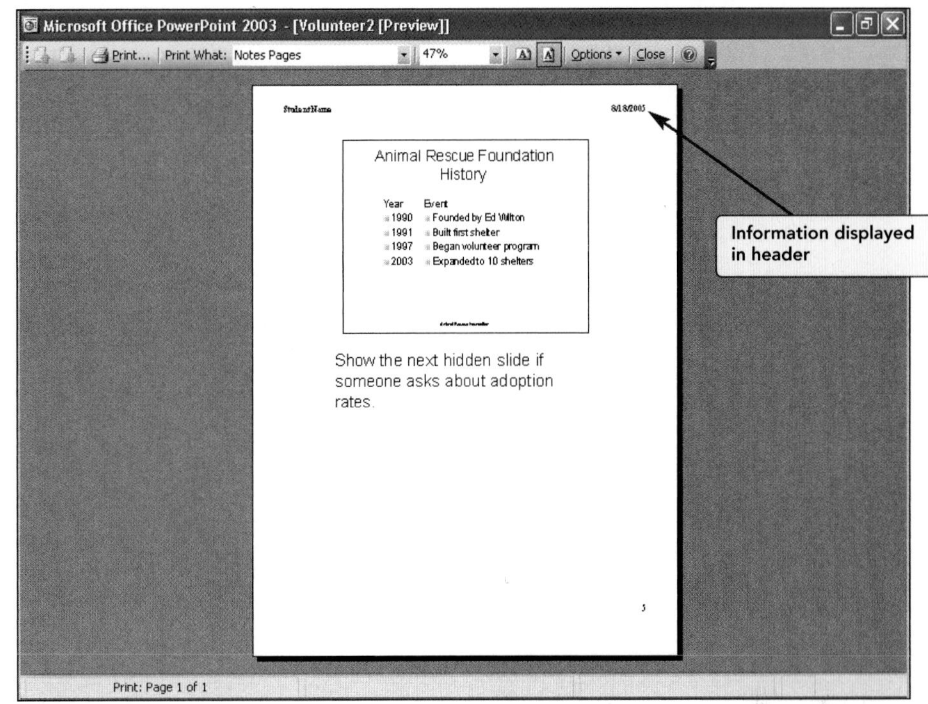

Figure 2.81

The information is displayed in the header as specified.

3 • **Click Print....**

• **Click OK to print the specified Notes page.**

Scaling Slides

Next you will print a few selected slides to be used as handouts. You will change the orientation to landscape and scale the slides to fit the paper size.

1 Click [Print...].

- In the Slides text box, type **1, 2, 6, 13.**
- Specify Handouts as the component to print and 4 slides per page.
- Click [Preview].
- Click [landscape button] to change to landscape orientation.
- Click [Options] and select Scale to Fit Paper.

Your screen should be similar to Figure 2.82

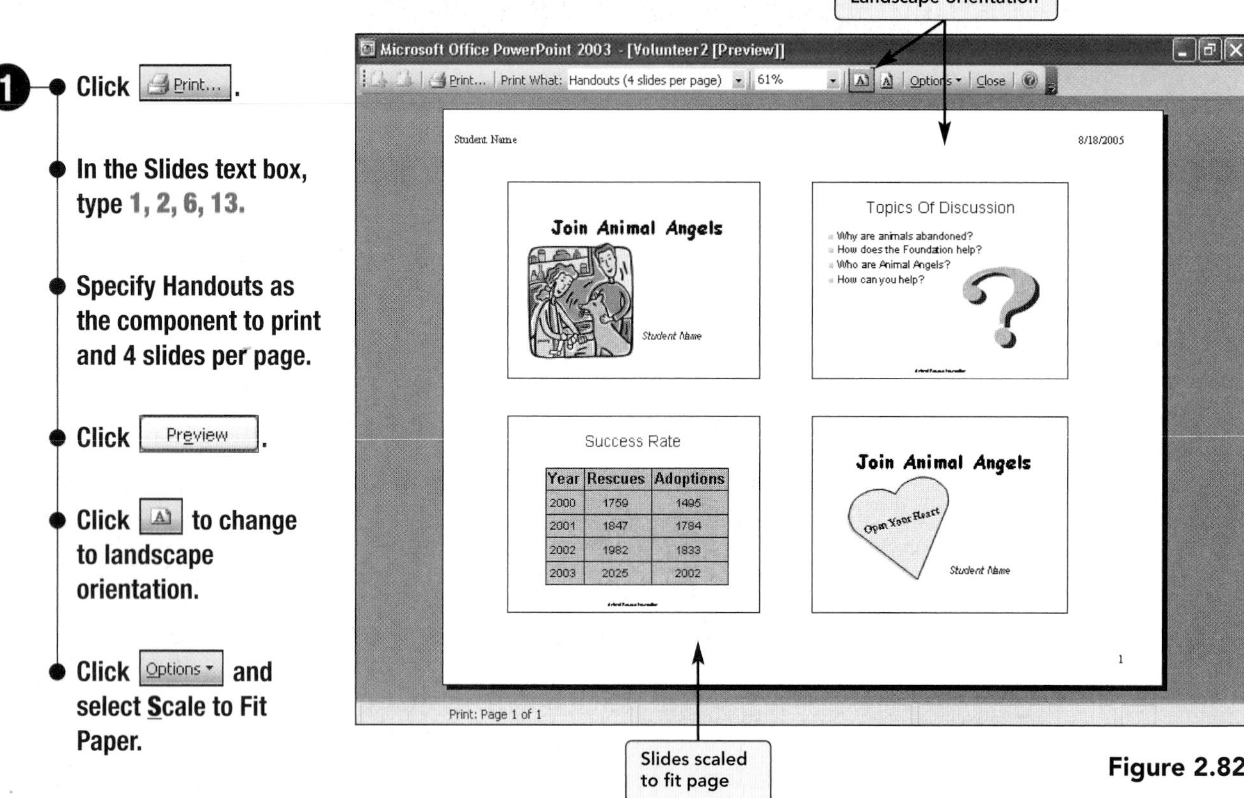

Figure 2.82

The four selected slides are displayed in landscape orientation and the slide images were sized as large as possible to fill the page.

2 Print the handout.

- Close the Print Preview window.
- Save the completed presentation.
- Exit PowerPoint.

The view you are in when you save the file is the view that will be displayed when the file is opened. The print settings are also saved with the file.

Focus on Careers

EXPLORE YOUR CAREER OPTIONS

Marketing Communications Specialist

Are you interested in technology? Could you explain it in words and pictures? Marketing Communications Specialists assist sales and marketing management with communications media and advertising materials that represent the company's products and services to customers. In high-tech industries, you will take information from scientists and engineers and use PowerPoint to transform the data into eye-catching presentations that communicate effectively. You may also create brochures, develop Web sites, create videos, and write speeches. If you thrive in a fast-paced and high-energy environment and work well under the pressure of deadlines, then this job may be for you. Typically a bachelor's degree in journalism, advertising, or communications is desirable. The salary can range from $35,000 to $85,000, depending on the industry.

LAB 2
Modifying and Refining a Presentation

Find and Replace (PP2.5)

To make editing easier, you can use the Find and Replace feature to find text in a presentation and replace it with other text as directed.

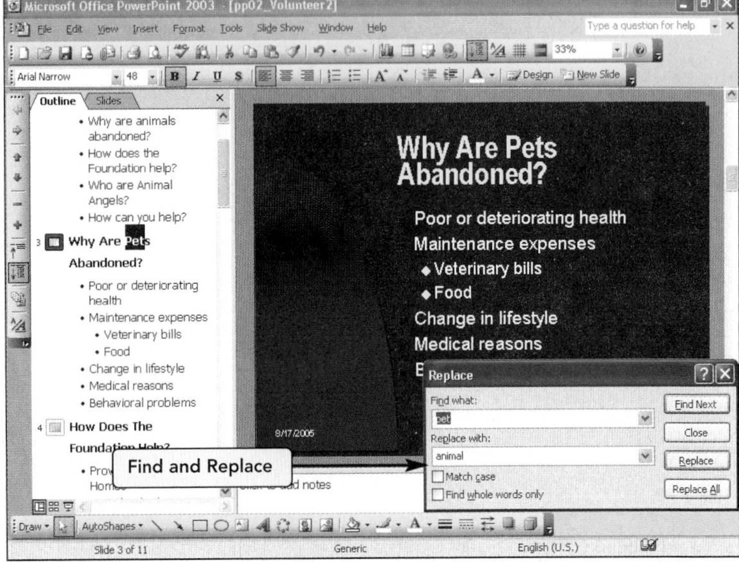

Table (PP2.9)

A table is used to organize information into an easy-to-read format of horizontal rows and vertical columns.

Alignment (PP2.15)

Alignment controls how text entries are positioned within a space.

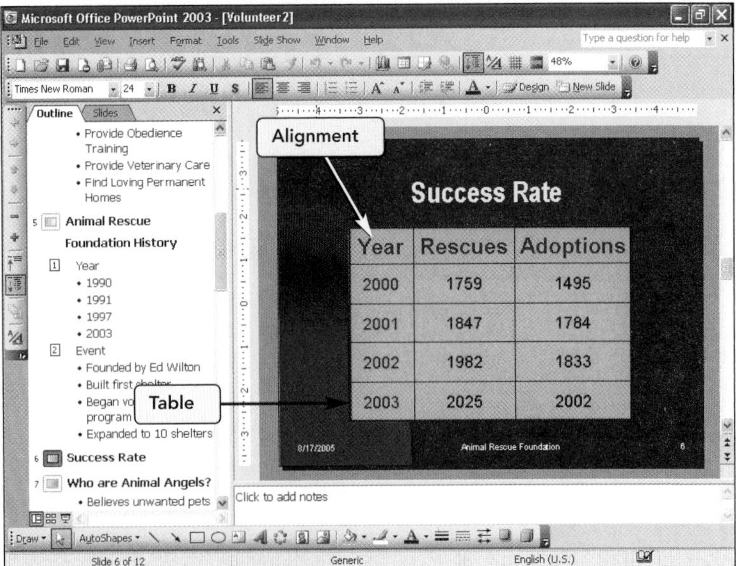

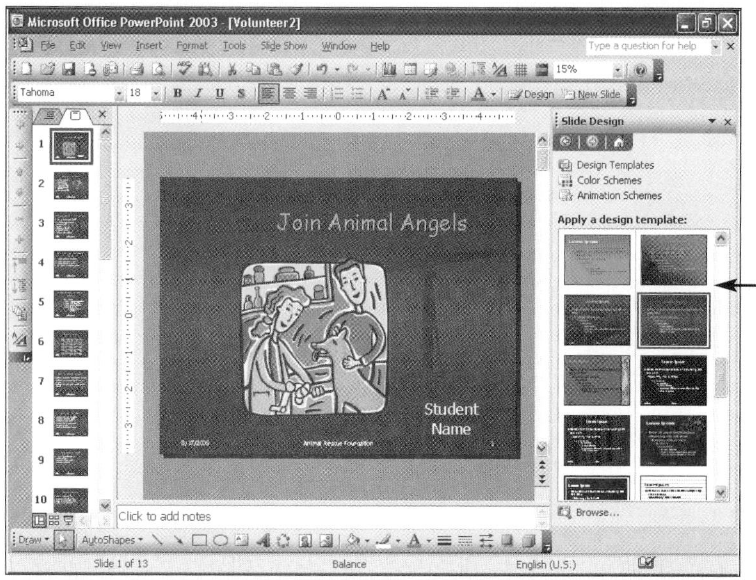

Design Template (PP2.31)

A design template is a professionally created slide design that is stored as a file and can be applied to a presentation.

Design template

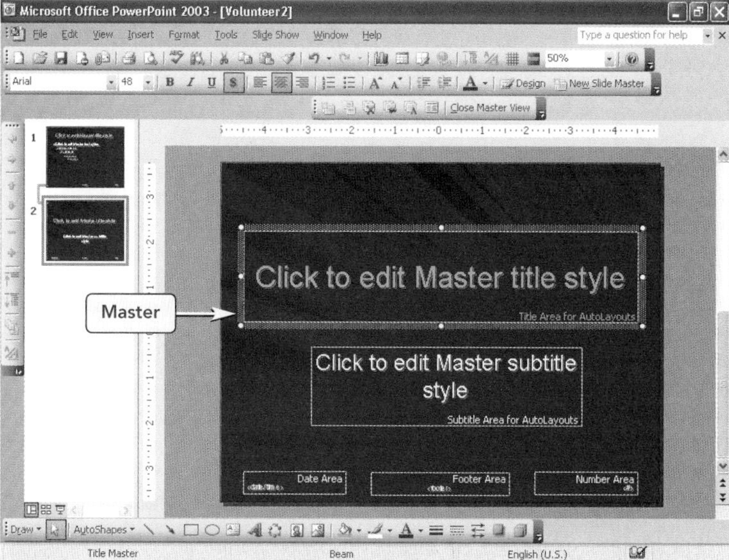

Master

Master (PP2.38)

A master is a special slide or page that stores information about the formatting for all slides in a presentation.

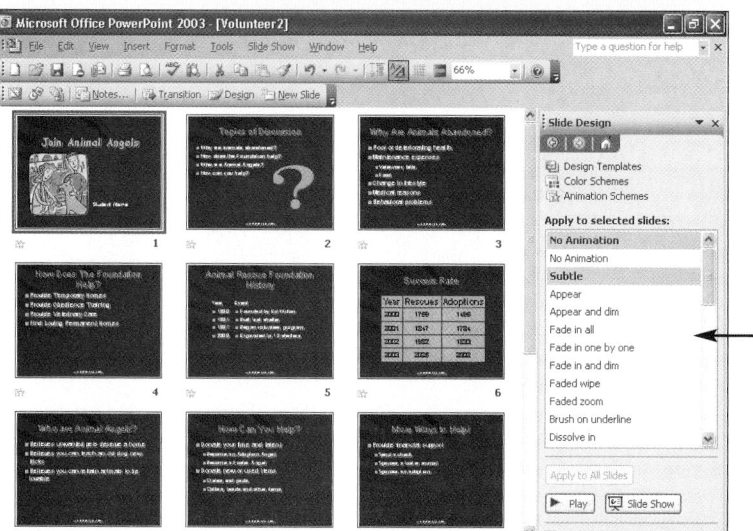

Special Effects (PP2.49)

Special effects such as animation, sound, slide transitions, and builds are used to enhance the onscreen presentation.

Special effects

LAB 2 Modifying and Refining a Presentation

key terms

microsoft office specialist skills

The Microsoft Office Specialist certification program is designed to measure your proficiency in performing basic tasks using the Office 2003 applications. Certification demonstrates that you have the skills and provides a valuable industry credential for employment. After completing this lab, you have learned the following Microsoft Office PowerPoint 2003 Specialist skills:

Skill Sets	Skill Standards	Page
Creating Content	Insert and edit text-based content	PP2.5
	Insert tables, charts, and diagrams	PP2.9
	Insert pictures, shapes, and graphics	PP2.22, 2.24
Formatting Content	Format text-based content	PP2.13, 2.15
	Format pictures, shapes, and graphics	PP2.22, 2.25
	Format slides	PP2.31, 2.33, 2.72
	Apply animation schemes	PP2.54
	Apply slide transitions	PP2.51
	Work with masters	PP2.38
Managing and Delivering Presentations	Organize a presentation	PP2.23, 2.63
	Set up slide shows for delivery	PP2.60
	Deliver presentations	PP2.56
	Save and publish presentations	PP2.8
	Print slides, outlines, handouts, and speaker notes	PP2.71

command summary

Command	Shortcut Key	Button	Voice	Action
File/Properties				Displays statistics and stores information about presentation
Edit/Find	Ctrl + F			Finds specified text
Edit/Replace	Ctrl + H			Replaces located text with specified replacement text
View/Notes Page				Displays notes page view
View/Master/Slide Master	Shift +			Displays slide master for presentation
View/Ruler				Displays or hides ruler
View/Header and Footer				Specifies information that appears as headers and footers on slides, notes, outlines, and handout pages
Insert/Duplicate Slide				Inserts duplicate of current slide
Insert/Picture/AutoShapes				Inserts selected AutoShape object
Insert/Text Box				Adds a text box
Format/Font/Font Style/Bold	Ctrl + B	B	On bold	Adds bold effect to selection
Format/Font/Font Style/Italic	Ctrl + I	I	Italic	Adds italic effect to selection
Format/Font/Color		A		Adds color to selection
Format/Alignment	Ctrl + L		Left justify	Aligns text in a cell or placeholder to left, center, right, or justified
	Ctrl + E		Centered	
	Ctrl + R		Right justify	
	Ctrl + J			

Command	Shortcut Key	Button	Voice	Action
F**o**rmat/Slide **D**esign		Design		Changes appearance of slide by applying a different design template
F**o**rmat/**R**eplace Fonts				Finds specified font and replaces it with another
F**o**rmat/P**i**cture/R**e**color				Changes color of a picture
F**o**rmat/**M**aster Layout				Selects placeholder to be added
F**o**rmat/**T**able				Changes table border and fill color
Tools/**O**ptions/Spelling and Style				Sets spelling and style options
Sli**d**e Show/Custo**m** Animation				Applies custom animation
Sli**d**e Show/Slide **T**ransition		Transition		Adds transition effects
Sli**d**e Show/**H**ide Slide				Hides selected slide
Slide Show Pointer Options Menu				
Arrow	Ctrl + A			Changes pointer to arrow and turns off freehand annotation
Ballpoint Pen	Ctrl + P			Changes pointer to ballpoint pen and turns on freehand annotation
Felt Tip Pen				Changes pointer to felt tip pen and turns on freehand annotation
Highlighter				Changes pointer to a highlighter
Ink **C**olor				Shows color palette for annotation tool
E**r**aser	Ctrl + E			Changes pointer to eraser
Erase all Ink on Slide	E			Removes all annotations from slide
Slide Show Screen Options Menu				
Go to Slide				Displays specified slide
S**c**reen/**B**lack Screen	B			Blacks out screen
S**c**reen/**W**hite Screen	W			Whites out screen

matching

Match the numbered item with the correct lettered description.

1. transition	_____	**a.** indicates a transition effect has been applied to the slide
2. [icon]	_____	**b.** ready-made shapes, such as block arrows, stars and banners, and callouts
3. design template	_____	**c.** special slide that controls format for the title slide only
4. slide master	_____	**d.** indicates the slide is hidden
5. build	_____	**e.** printed output that displays a slide and its related notes
6. [icon]	_____	**f.** controls the way one slide appears on the screen and the next appears
7. table	_____	**g.** defines the background design, text format, and placeholder placement for each slide
8. Esc	_____	**h.** professionally created slide design that can be applied to a presentation
9. AutoShapes	_____	**i.** ends the slide show and displays the slide last viewed as the current slide
10. notes pages	_____	**j.** special effect that controls how bulleted points appear during the slide show
	_____	**k.** displays information in a row and column format

multiple choice

Circle the letter of the correct response.

1. If you wanted to display a black slide during a presentation, you would press ____________.
   - **a.** H
   - **b.** U
   - **c.** B
   - **d.** E
2. If you wanted to add a company logo on each slide in your presentation, you would place it on the ____________________________.
   - **a.** handout
   - **b.** notes page
   - **c.** outline slide
   - **d.** master

3. To substitute one word for another in a presentation, you would use the ______________ command on the Edit menu.
   a. Find
   b. Locate
   c. Replace
   d. Duplicate
4. To proportionally size an AutoShape, graphic, or picture, hold down ____________________ while you drag.
   a. Ctrl
   b. Alt
   c. ⇧Shift
   d. Ctrl + Alt
5. To display bullets on a slide one at a time, you would apply a(n) _______________________ .
   a. build
   b. transition
   c. animation
   d. motion
6. To ensure that your presentation has a professional, consistent look throughout, use a(n) _________________________.
   a. slide layout
   b. design template
   c. animation scheme
   d. transition
7. Using a __________________ to modify or add elements to a presentation ensures consistency and saves time.
   a. design template
   b. slide layout
   c. table
   d. master
8. Slide transitions and build slides are ______________ that are used to enhance the onscreen presentation.
   a. animations
   b. slide masters
   c. graphics
   d. special effects
9. If you want to display information in columns and rows, you would create a(n) ________________.
   a. table
   b. text box
   c. slide layout
   d. AutoShape
10. To help you remember the important points during a presentation, you can add comments to slides and print ______________.
   a. notes pages
   b. slide handouts
   c. preview handouts
   d. handouts

true/false

Circle the correct answer to the following questions.

1.	Builds control the way that the display changes as you move from one slide to another during a presentation.	True	False
2.	Style checking looks for consistency in punctuation and capitalization.	True	False
3.	Alignment controls the position of text entries in a placeholder.	True	False
4.	Masters are professionally created slide designs that can be applied to your presentation.	True	False
5.	An AutoShape is an object that can be enhanced using drawing tools and menu commands.	True	False
6.	A handout master defines the format and placement of the slide image, text, headers, footers, and other elements that are to appear on every slide in the presentation.	True	False
7.	A title master defines the format and placement of titles and text for slides that use the title layout.	True	False
8.	Transitions are used to display each bullet point, text, paragraph, or graphic independently of the other text or objects on the slide.	True	False
9.	An AutoShape is a container for text or graphics.	True	False
10.	A master is a special slide or page on which the formatting for all slides or pages in your presentation is defined.	True	False

fill-in

Complete the following statements by filling in the blanks with the correct terms.

1. The ______________ master controls format, placement, and all elements that are to appear on every audience handout.
2. The ______________ feature checks the presentation for consistency in punctuation and capitalization.
3. ______________ add action to text and graphics so they move on the screen.
4. A ______________ is made up of rows and columns of cells that you can fill with text and graphics.
5. A ____________________ is a container for text or graphics.
6. Alignment controls the position of text entries within a ______________________ or ____________.
7. ______________ are used to define where text and graphics appear on a slide.
8. ______________ display each bullet point, text, paragraph, or graphic independently of the other text or objects on the slide.

9. ______________________ are professionally created slide designs that can be applied to your presentation.

10. The ______________ slide is a special slide on which the formatting for all slides in your presentation is defined.

rating system
★ Easy
★★ Moderate
★★★ Difficult

step-by-step

Enhancing a College Recruiting Presentation ★

1. Bonnie is the Assistant Director of New Admissions at Arizona State University. Part of her job is to make recruiting presentations at community colleges and local high schools about the University. She has already created the introductory portion of the presentation and needs to reorganize the topics and make the presentation more visually appealing. Several slides of the modified presentation are shown here:

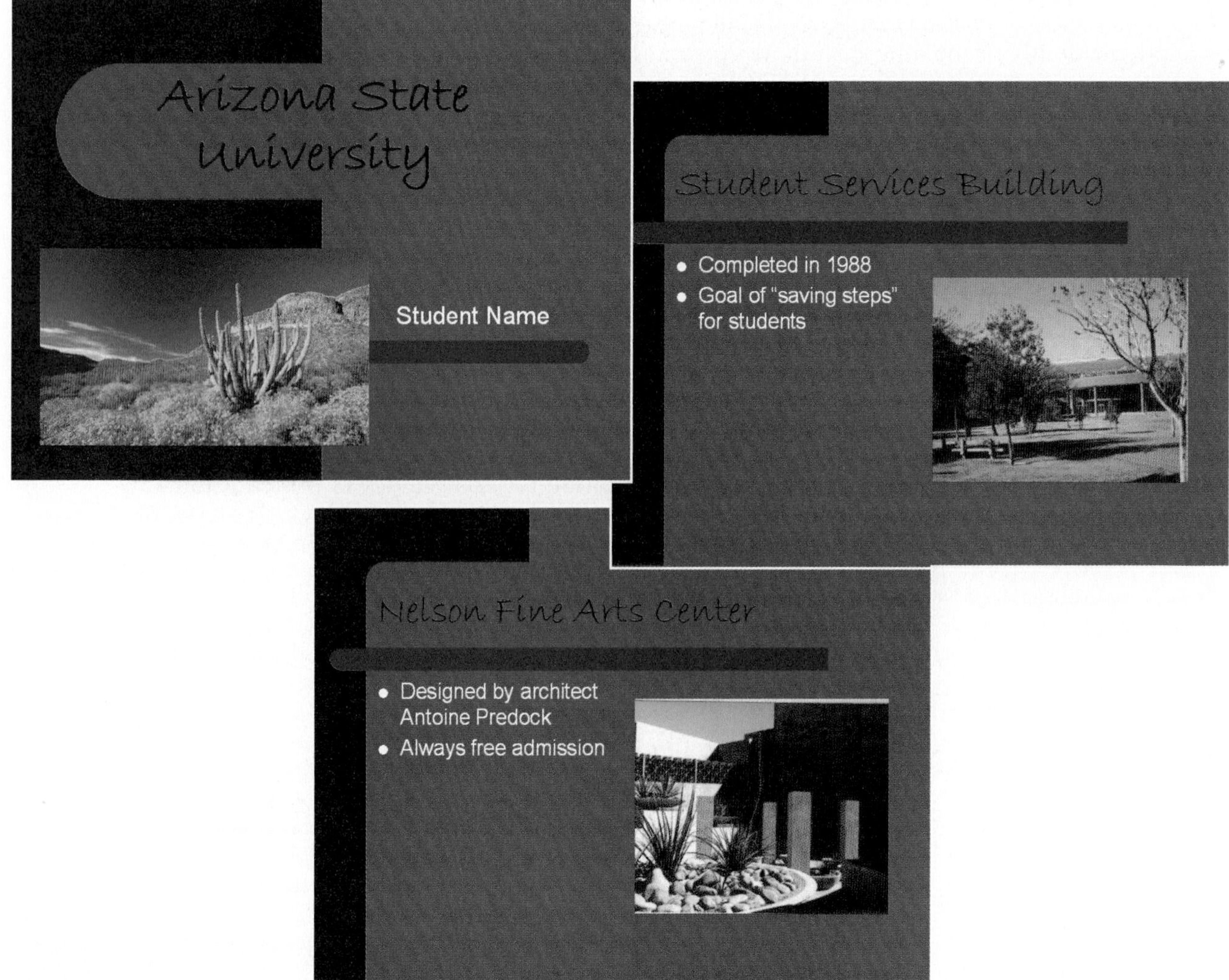

a. Open the file pp02_ASU Presentation.

b. Run the slide show to see what Bonnie has done so far.

c. Spell-check the presentation, making the appropriate corrections.

d. Move slide 5 before slide 3.

e. Move slide 5 before slide 4.

f. Use the Find and Replace command to locate all the occurrences of "Arizona State University" and replace them with **ASU** on all slides except the first and second slides.

g. Enter your name as the subtitle in slide 1. Insert the picture pp02_Arizona on the title slide. Size the picture and position the placeholders on the slide appropriately.

h. Demote all the bulleted items on slides 8 and 9 except the first item.

i. Apply a new presentation design of your choice to the presentation. Apply a new slide color scheme. Modify the font of the titles using the title and slide masters.

j. Duplicate slide 1 and move the duplicate to the end of the presentation. Delete the graphic. Replace your name with **Apply Now!**. Apply the Change Font Size custom animation Emphasis effect at a slow speed. Increase the font to a larger size.

k. Bonnie would like to add some pictures of the buildings at the end of the presentation. Switch to Slide Sorter view and select slides 12, 13, and 14. Apply the Title, Text and Content layout. Insert the picture pp02_Student Services in slide 12, the picture pp02_Library in slide 13, and the picture pp02_Fine Arts in slide 14.

l. Check the style of the presentation and make any changes you feel are appropriate. Turn the style check feature off when you are done.

m. Add a Wave custom animation at a medium speed and the Applause sound to the title text on the title slide.

n. Apply the Strips build effect at a medium speed in a Right Down direction to slides 3 through 7, 10, and 11.

o. Run the slide show.

p. Add file documentation and save the presentation as ASU Presentation1. Print slides 1, 2, and 12–15 as handouts (six per page).

Completing the Massage Therapy Presentation ★ ★

2. To complete this problem, you must have completed Step-by-Step Exercise 3 in Lab 1. You have completed the first draft of the presentation on therapeutic massage, but still have some information to add. Additionally, you want to make the presentation look better using many of the PowerPoint design and slide show presentation features. Several slides of the modified presentation are shown here:

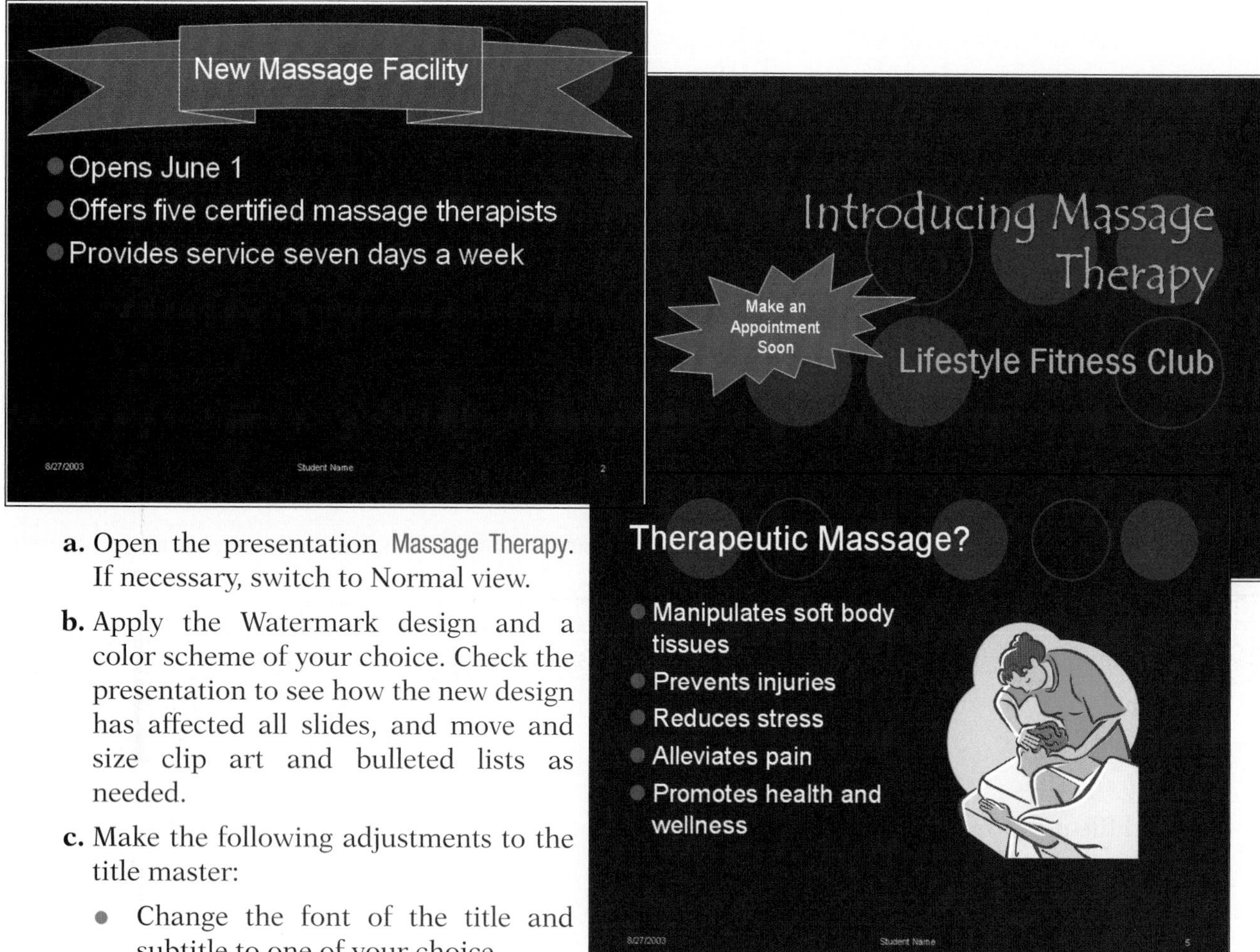

a. Open the presentation Massage Therapy. If necessary, switch to Normal view.

b. Apply the Watermark design and a color scheme of your choice. Check the presentation to see how the new design has affected all slides, and move and size clip art and bulleted lists as needed.

c. Make the following adjustments to the title master:

- Change the font of the title and subtitle to one of your choice.
- Change the font color of the title and subtitle to colors of your choice. Add a shadow.

d. On slide 2, replace the slide title with an AutoShape of your choice. Add the text **New Massage Facility** to the AutoShape. Add a medium speed Dissolve In or Out custom animation to the AutoShape. Add a medium speed Fly In custom animation to the bulleted list.

e. Duplicate the title slide and move it to the end of the presentation. Add an AutoShape to this slide that includes the text **Make an Appointment Soon**. Format the object and text appropriately. Move the title and subtitle to accommodate the drawing object.

f. Select an animation scheme of your choice to add transition and build effects to all the slides. Run the slide show.

g. Add the following note to slide 5 in a point size of 18:

Basically, all massages are therapeutic.

h. Add the following note to slide 10 in a point size of 18:

Ask if there are any questions. Pass out brochures.

i. Style-check the presentation and make any necessary changes. Turn off the style-check option when you are done.

j. Add file documentation and save the completed presentation as **Massage Therapy2**.

k. Print the notes page for slide 10. Print slides 1, 5, and 6 as handouts with three slides per page.

Enhancing the Job Fairs Presentation ★ ★

3. To complete this problem, you must have completed Step-by-Step Exercise 5 in Lab 1. Tim has completed the first draft of the presentation for Job Fairs, but he still has some information he wants to add to the presentation. Additionally, he wants to make the presentation look better using many of the PowerPoint design and slide show presentation features. Several slides of the modified presentation are shown here:

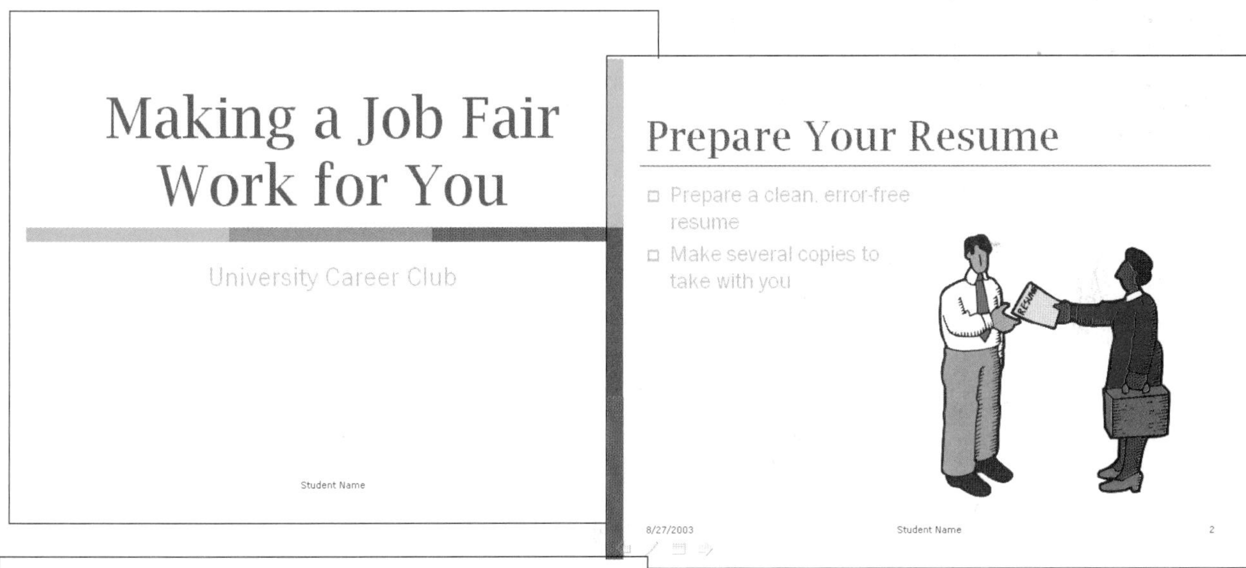

a. Open the presentation Job Fairs. If necessary, switch to Normal view.

b. Change the design template to Levels. Change the color scheme to a color of your choice.

c. Change to Slide Sorter view and check the slide layouts. Make the following adjustments:

- Slide master:
  - — Delete the Date area and Number area placeholders.
  - — Change the font of the title to one of your choice. Increase the font size. Change the font color to a color of your choice.
- Title master:
  - — Change the text color of the subtitle to a color of your choice, bold it, and change it to a font of your choice.

d. Check the slide layouts again in Slide Sorter view and fix the placement and size of the placeholders and pictures as needed.

e. Apply a custom animation to the clip art and bulleted list on slide 3 and add sound effects of your choice.

f. Duplicate the title slide and move it to the end of the presentation. Add a drawing object to this slide that includes the text **Good Luck!**. Format the object and text appropriately.

g. Select an animation scheme of your choice to add transition and build effects to all the slides. Run the slide show.

h. Add the following note to slide 3 in a point size of 18:

You must be able to give a short biography when asked "Tell me about yourself." Practice until you can tell the story smoothly.

i. Style-check the presentation and make any necessary changes. Turn off the style-check feature when you are done.

j. Add file documentation and save the completed presentation as Job Fairs2.

k. Print the notes page for slide 3. Print slides 1, 2, 6, and 8 as handouts with four slides per page.

Enhancing the Triple Crown Presentation ★ ★ ★

4. To complete this problem, you must have completed Step-by-Step Exercise 1 in Lab 1. Logan's work on the Triple Crown Presentation was well received by his supervisor. She would like to see some additional information included in the presentation, including a table of upcoming qualifying hikes. Several of the slides from his updated presentation are shown here:

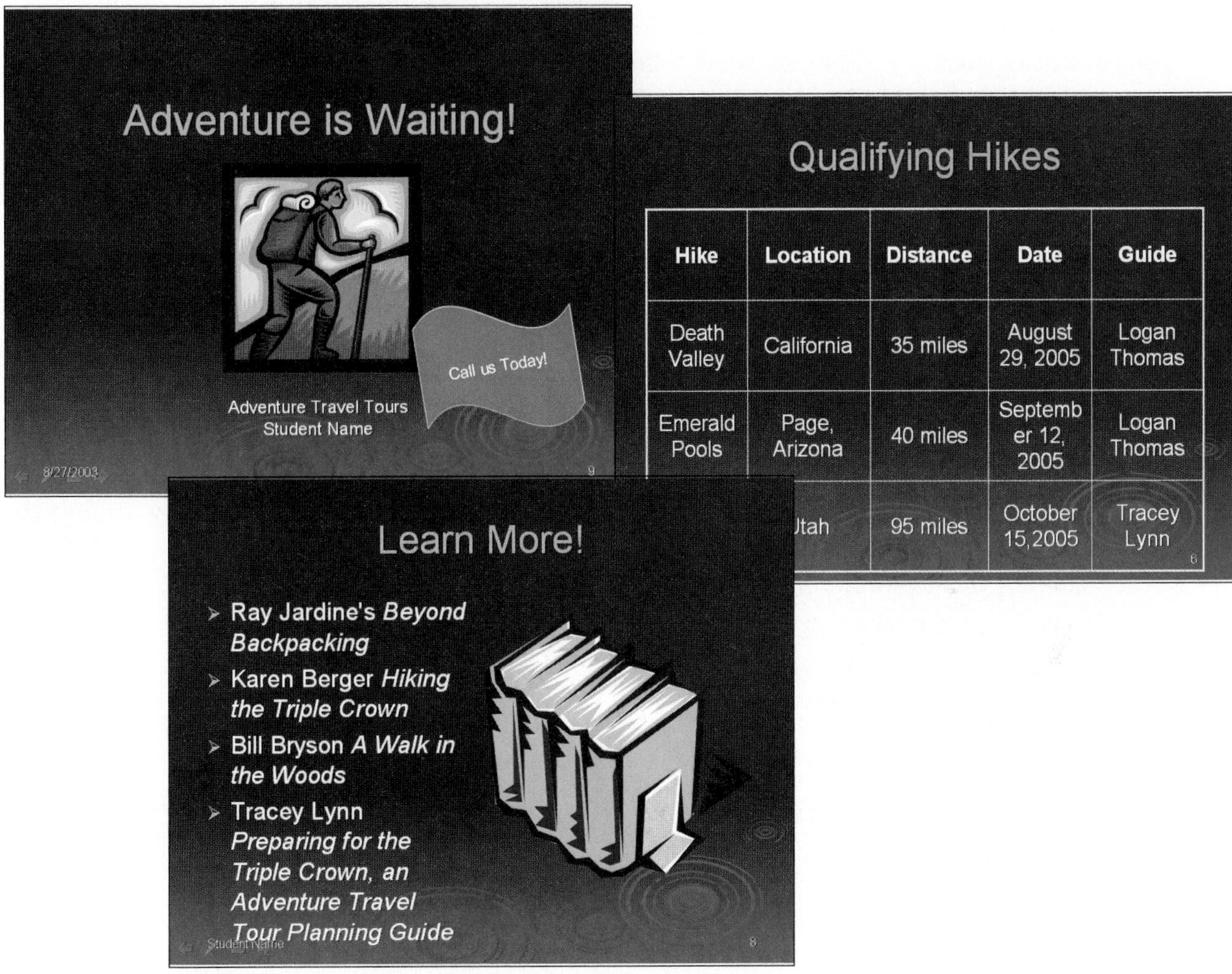

a. Open the file Triple Crown Presentation.

b. Apply a new presentation design and color scheme of your choice to the presentation. Check the presentation to see how the new design has affected all the slides, and move and size graphics and bulleted lists as needed.

c. Modify the text color of the titles using the title and slide masters.

d. Insert a Title and Table slide after slide 6, with 5 columns and 4 rows. Enter the title **Qualifying Hikes**. Enter the following information in the table:

Hike	Location	Distance	Date	Guide
Death Valley	California	35 miles	August 29, 2005	Logan Thomas
Paria Canyon	Page, Arizona	40 miles	September 12, 2005	Logan Thomas
Bryce to Zion	Utah	95 miles	October 15, 2005	Tracey Lynn

e. Size and position the table as shown in the example. Add bold to the table headings. Change the column and row size as needed. Center the table contents vertically and horizontally.

f. Change the border color to one of your choice.

g. Change the layout of slide 6 to Title, Text, and Content. Insert the clip art graphic pp02_Read. Change the coloring of the books from brown and tan to blue.

h. Duplicate slide 1 and place the copy at the end of the presentation. Change the title to **Adventure is Waiting!**.

i. Add a footer that contains your name left-aligned and the slide number right-aligned.

j. Add an AutoShape of your choice to the final slide with the text: **Call us Today!**.

k. Use the Find and Replace command to replace all occurrences of Paria Canyon with **Emerald Pools**.

l. Add the following information to the file properties:

Title: **Triple Crown Presentation2**

Subject: **Lightweight Backpacking Tours**

Author: **Student Name**

Company: **Adventure Travel Tours**

m. Save the file as Triple Crown Presentation2. Print slides 1, 6, 7, and 9 as a handout with all four slides on one page.

Enhancing the Coffee Presentation ★ ★ ★

5. To complete this problem, you must have completed Step-by-Step Exercise 4 in Lab 1. Evan, the owner of the Downtown Internet Cafe, was so impressed with your presentation on coffee that he has decided to run it periodically throughout the day on a large screen in the cafe so customers can see it as well. To "spiff it up," he wants you to convert it to an onscreen presentation with more graphics as well as other design and animation effects. Several slides of the modified presentation are shown here:

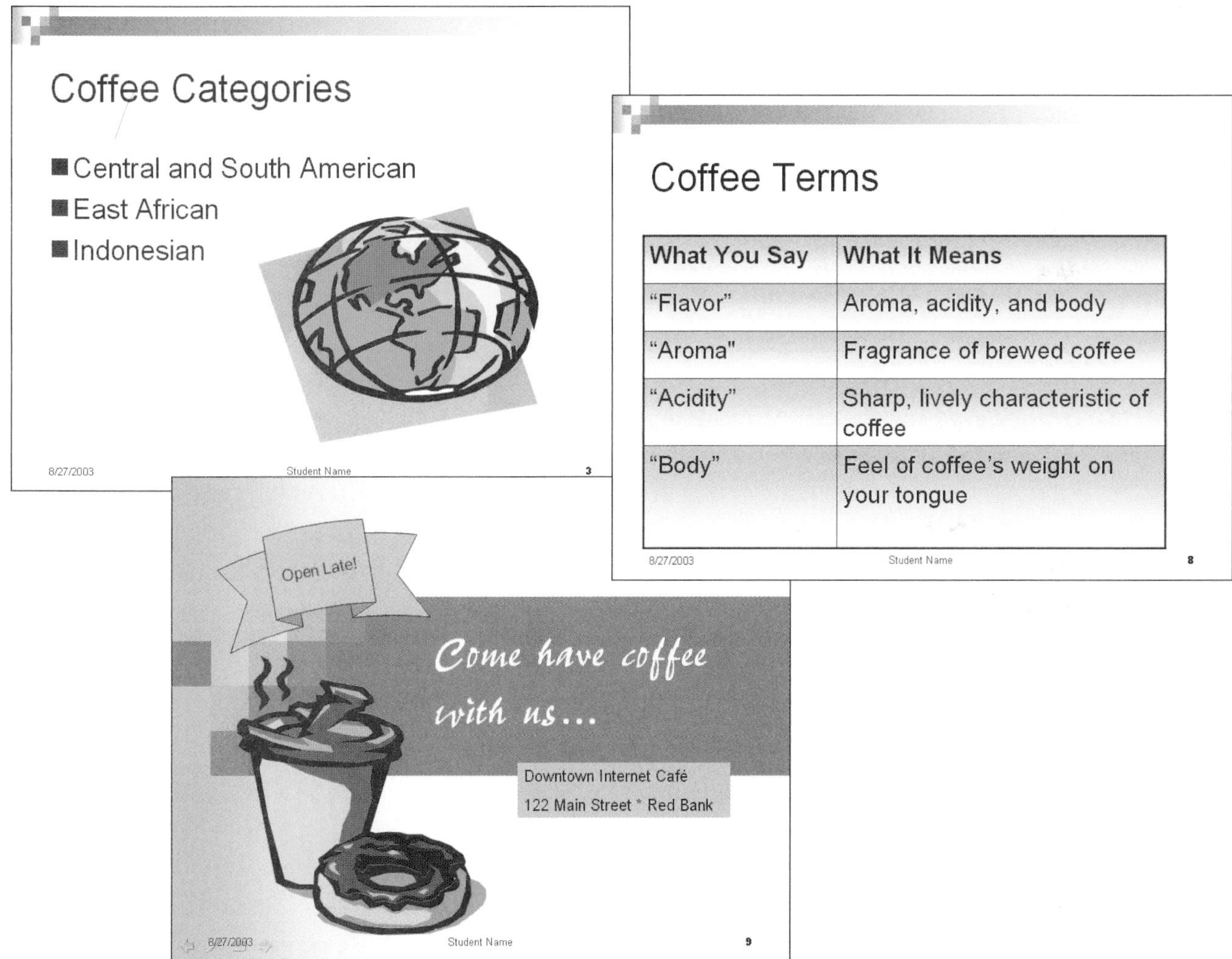

a. Open the file Coffee.

b. Use the Replace feature to replace both instances of the term "Regular Roasts" with **Coffee Categories**. Do the same to replace both instances of the term "Other Offerings" with **Coffee Types**.

c. Change the design template to Pixel or a design of your choice. Select a color scheme of your choice. Check the presentation to see how the new design has affected all slides, and move and size clip art and bulleted lists as needed.

d. Use the slide master to change the font color of all first-level bullet text to a different color.

e. Apply a custom animation and sound of your choice to the coffee cup clip art on slide 2.

f. Change the title of slide 3 to **What's Brewing?**. Delete the clip art.

g. Copy the clip art from slide 2 to slide 3 and size and position it appropriately. Add a third bullet to slide 3 with the text: **Coffee Terms**. Delete slide 2.

h. Insert the graphic pp02_Globe on slide 3. Recolor the background of the picture with colors that match the slide design.

i. Change the title "Central and South American Coffee" on slide 4 to **Coffees from the Americas**.

j. Insert a new slide with a table format after slide 7. Enter the title, **Coffee Terms**. Create the table with 2 columns and 5 rows. Enter **What You Say** as the first column heading and **What It Means** as the second column heading. Copy the terms and definitions from slide 9 into the table. Change the font size of the text as needed. Bold the column headings and put quotation marks around the terms. Center-align the What You Say column. Size the columns and table appropriately. Add a fill color to the table.

k. Delete slide 9.

l. Duplicate the title slide and move the duplicate to the end of the presentation. Change the title to **Come have coffee with us . . .** and delete the subtitle text. Delete the subtitle placeholder.

m. Add the following information in a text box on slide 9:

Downtown Internet Cafe

122 Main Street * Red Bank

n. Add a fill color and border to the text box.

o. Insert an AutoShape of your choice on the last slide with the text **Open Late!**.

p. Check the presentation style and make any necessary changes. Turn off the style-check feature when you are done.

q. Set the slide transition to automatically advance after 10 seconds. Run the slide show.

r. Add file documentation information and save the completed presentation as Coffee Show.

s. Print slides 1, 2, 8, and 9 as handouts, four per page.

on your own

Successful Interview Techniques ★

1. You work at an employment agency and your manager has asked you to create an onscreen presentation about interview techniques. This presentation will be loaded on all the computers that your company makes available to clients for online job searches, and instructions on how to run the presentation will be posted at each workstation. Select a presentation design that you like and create the presentation using the following notes for reference. Add clip art and build effects where applicable. Add your name to the footer on each slide except the title slide. Set the slide transition so that it automatically advances after an appropriate length of time (long enough for the person viewing the presentation to read each slide's contents). Save the presentation as Interview Techniques. Print all slides of your presentation, six per page.
   - Before a job interview, you should thoroughly research the company (use the library or the Web). For example, what is one event that occurred in the company within the last five years?
   - During the interview, demonstrate your expertise, using a consultant's style of communicating. Create open and clear communication, and effectively respond to open-ended questions. Examples of open-ended questions are: "Tell me about yourself." "What makes you stand out?" "What are your greatest weaknesses?" You should also be ready to answer questions about why you are interviewing with the company and how and where you fit within their organization. You must be prepared to handle both spoken and unspoken objections. And finally, you must justify your salary requirements; don't just negotiate them.

Enhancing the Animal Careers Presentation ★

2. To finish creating the basic Careers with Animals presentation that you began in Lab 1, On Your Own Exercise 5, turn it into an onscreen presentation with a custom design, clip art, sound, transitions, and builds so it will hold your audience's interest. Add speaker notes and rehearse the presentation. When you are done, save the presentation as Animal Careers2, print the presentation as handouts, and print the notes pages for slides containing notes only.

Explaining Fad Diets ★ ★

3. You have been asked to give a lunchbox presentation at the LifeStyle Fitness Club on fad diets. You plan to first describe all fad diets and then end with a summary of the benefits of eating according to the USDA's Food Pyramid and proper exercise. Do some research on the Web to obtain a list of fad diets, including a brief description, pros, and cons. Select an appropriate slide design and include some graphics to liven up the presentation. Add a table that includes some of your data. Include your name in the footer. When you are done, save the presentation as Fad Diets and print the handouts.

Enhancing the Internet Policy Presentation ★ ★ ★

4. After completing the Internet Policy presentation in Lab 1, On Your Own Exercise 1, you decide it needs a bit more sprucing up. First of all, it would be more impressive as an onscreen presentation with a custom design. You also want to add some information about personal computing security. Do some research on the Web to find some helpful tips on protecting personal privacy and safeguarding your computer. Also, add some animated clip art pictures, non-standard bullets, builds, and

transitions to help liven up the content. Make these and any other changes that you think would enhance the presentation. Add a table and check the style consistency of the presentation. Add appropriate documentation to the file. When you are done, save it as Internet Policy2, print the presentation as handouts, and print the notes pages for slides containing notes only.

Sharing Favorite Vacation Spots ★★★

5. You and your fellow Getaway Travel Club members have decided that each of you should do a presentation on your favorite vacation spot (one you have already been to or one you would like to go to). Pick a location and do some research on the Web and/or visit a local travel agency to get information about your chosen destination. Create a presentation using a custom design and include clip art, animation, sounds, transitions, and build effects to make the presentation more interesting. Include your name as a footer or subtitle on at least one slide. Create and enhance a table. Use speaker notes if necessary to remind yourself of additional information you want to relay that is not included in the slides. Add appropriate documentation to the file. Run the slide show and practice your presentation, then save as Travel Favorites and print your presentation and notes pages.

Working Together 1: Copying, Embedding, and Linking Between Applications

Case Study

Animal Rescue Foundation

The director of the Animal Rescue Foundation has reviewed the PowerPoint presentation you created and has asked you to include a chart showing the adoption success rate that was created using Excel. Additionally, the director has provided a list of dates for the upcoming volunteer orientation meetings that he feels would be good content for another slide.

Frequently you will find that you want to include information that was created using a word processor, spreadsheet, or database application in your slide show. As you will see, you can easily share information between applications, saving you both time and effort by eliminating the need to recreate information that is available in another application. You will learn how to share information between applications while you create the new slides. The new slides containing information from Word and Excel are shown here.

Note: The Working Together section assumes that you already know how to use Office Word and Excel 2003 and that you have completed Lab 2 of PowerPoint. You will need the file Volunteer2, which you saved at the end of Lab 2 of PowerPoint. If this file is not available, use ppwt1_Volunteer2.

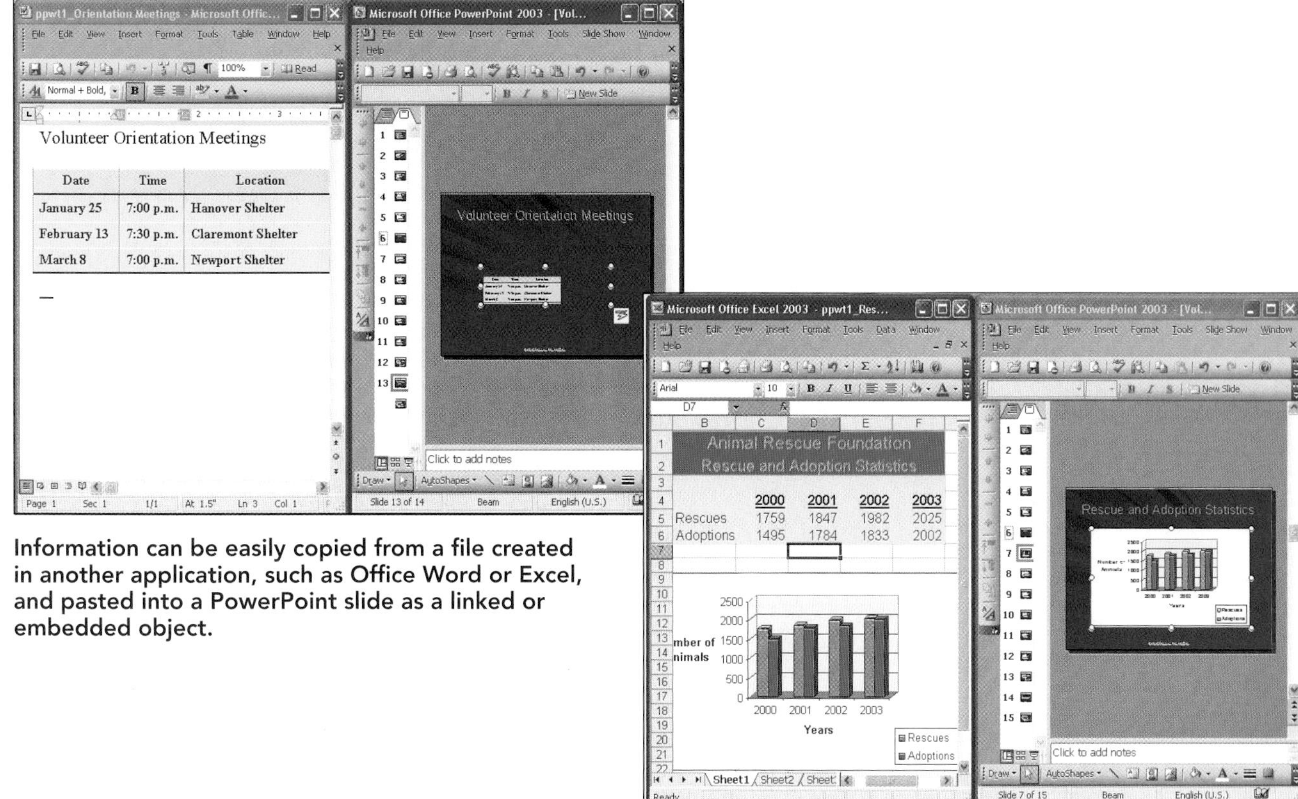

Information can be easily copied from a file created in another application, such as Office Word or Excel, and pasted into a PowerPoint slide as a linked or embedded object.

Copying Between Applications

The orientation meeting information has already been entered in a document using Word. All the Microsoft Office System applications have a common user interface, such as similar commands and menu structures. In addition to these obvious features, they have been designed to work together, making it easy to share and exchange information between applications.

Rather than retype the list of orientation meeting dates provided by the director, you will copy it from the Word document into the presentation. You can also use the same commands and procedures to copy information from PowerPoint or other Office applications into Word.

Copying from Word to a PowerPoint Slide

First, you need to modify the PowerPoint presentation to include a new slide for the orientation meeting dates.

1

- **Start Office PowerPoint 2003.**
- **Open the presentation** Volunteer2 **(saved at the end of Lab 2).**
- **Insert a new slide using the Title Only layout after slide 12.**
- **Close the Slide Layout task pane.**
- **Display the new slide in Normal view.**

Your screen should be similar to Figure 1

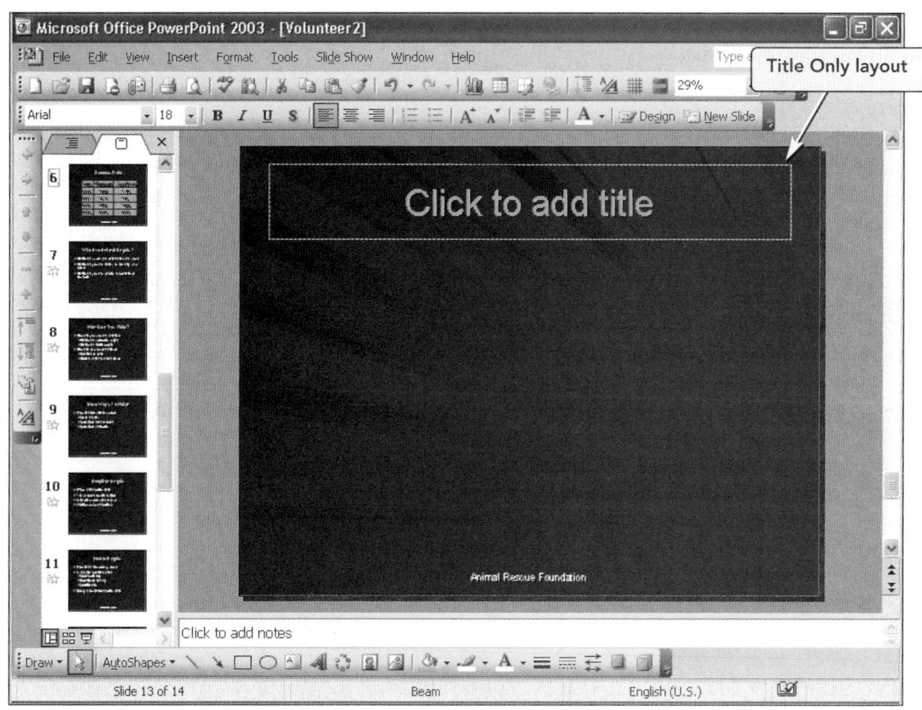

Figure 1

To copy the information from the Word document file into the PowerPoint presentation, you need to open the Word document.

2

- **Start Office Word 2003.**
- **Open the document** ppwt1_Orientation Meetings**.**

Your screen should be similar to Figure 2

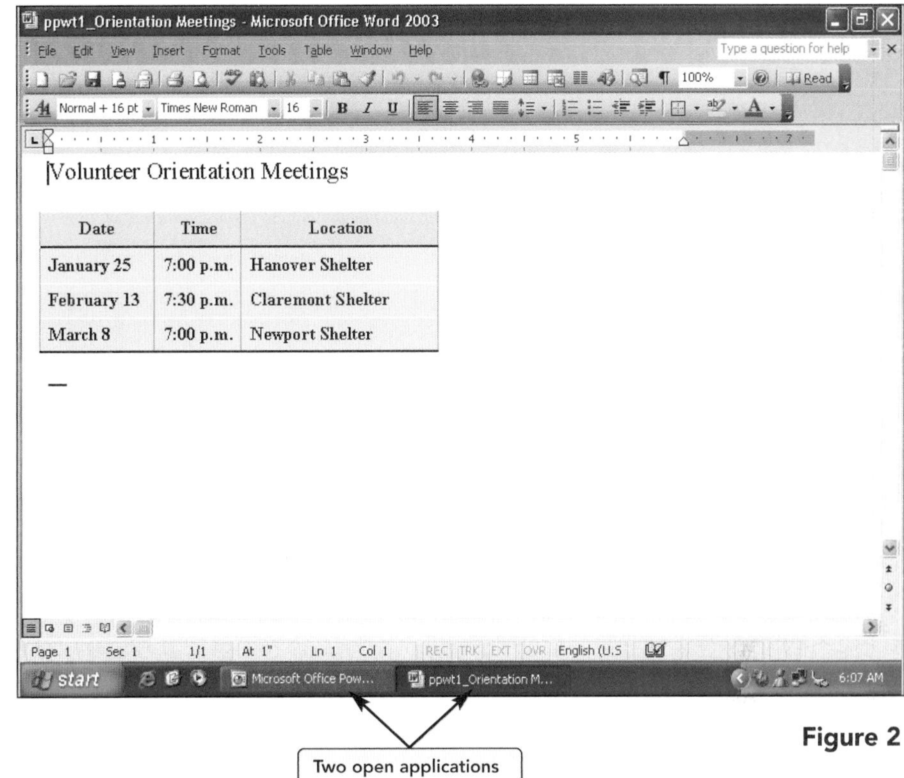

Figure 2

There are now two open applications, Word and PowerPoint. PowerPoint is open in a window behind the Word application window. Both application buttons are displayed in the taskbar. There are also two open files, Orientation Meetings in Word and Volunteer2 in PowerPoint. Word is the active application, and Orientation Meetings is the active file. To make it easier to work with two applications, you will tile the windows to view both on the screen at the same time.

3

- **Right-click on a blank area of the taskbar to open the shortcut menu.**
- **Select Tile Windows Vertically**
- **Click on the Word document window to make it active.**

Your screen should be similar to Figure 3

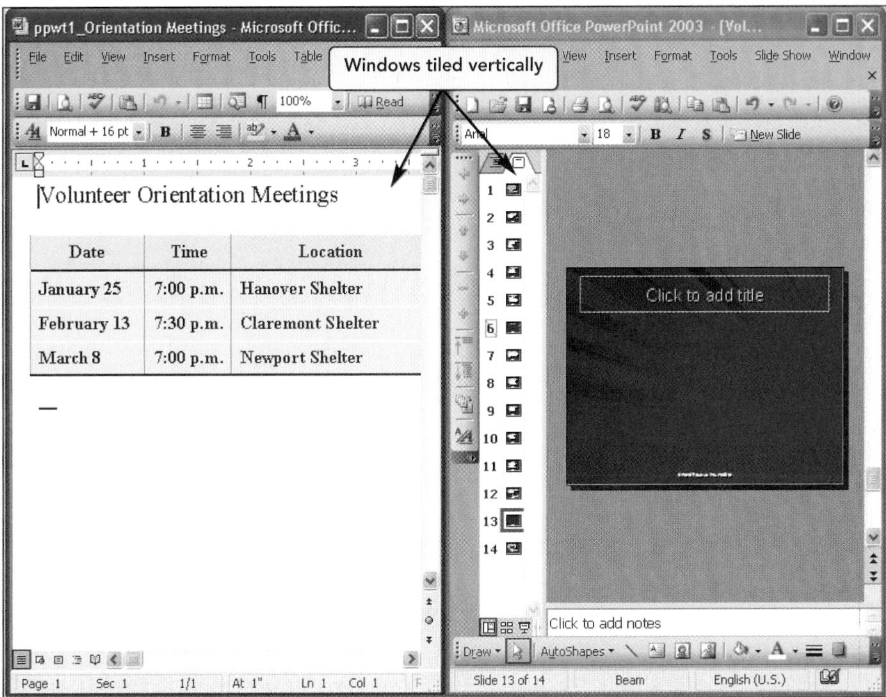

Figure 3

First, you will copy the title from the Word document into the title placeholder of the slide. While using the Office Word and PowerPoint applications, you have learned how to use cut, copy, and paste to move or copy information within the same document. You can also perform these same operations between documents in the same application and between documents in different applications. The information is pasted in a format that the application can edit, if possible.

4

- **Select the title "Volunteer Orientation Meetings."**
- **Drag the selection using the right mouse button to the title placeholder in the slide.**

Having Trouble?

If you drag using the left mouse button, the selection is moved instead of copied.

- **From the shortcut menu, select Copy.**

Another Method

You could also use Copy and Paste to copy the title to the slide.

- **Click on the slide to deselect the placeholder.**

Your screen should be similar to Figure 4

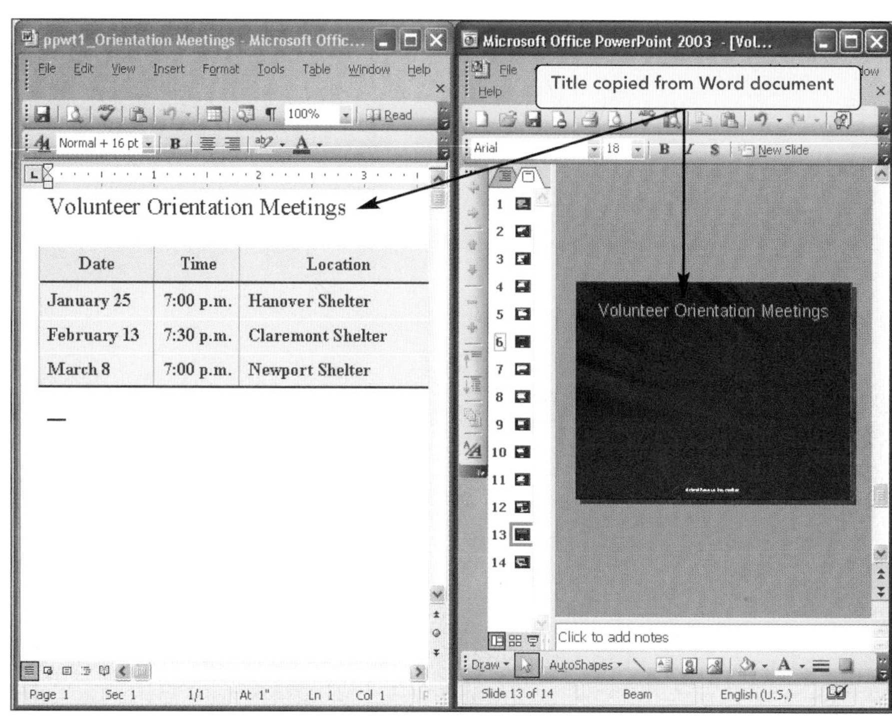

Figure 4

The title has been copied into the slide and can be edited and manipulated within PowerPoint. The formats associated with the slide master are applied to the copied text. If the copied text included formatting, such as color, it would override the slide master settings, just as if you formatted a slide individually to make it unique.

Embedding a Word Table in a PowerPoint Slide

Next you want to display the table of orientation dates below the title in the slide. You will copy and embed the table in the slide. As you have seen, an object that is embedded is stored in the file that it is inserted into, called the **destination file**, and becomes part of that file. The embedded object can then be edited using features from the source program, the program in which it was created. Since the embedded object is part of the destination file, modifying it does not affect the original file called the **source file**.

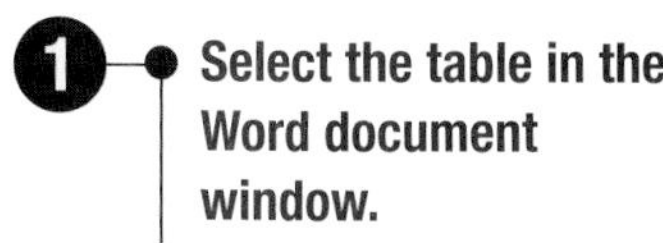

1 **Select the table in the Word document window.**

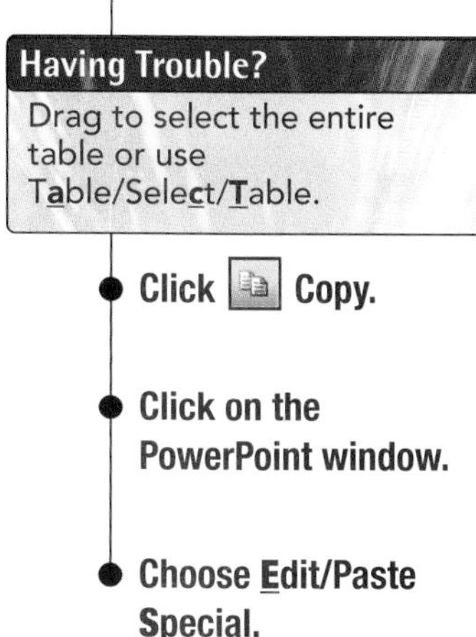

Having Trouble?

Drag to select the entire table or use Table/Select/Table.

- **Click Copy.**
- **Click on the PowerPoint window.**
- **Choose Edit/Paste Special.**

Your screen should be similar to Figure 5

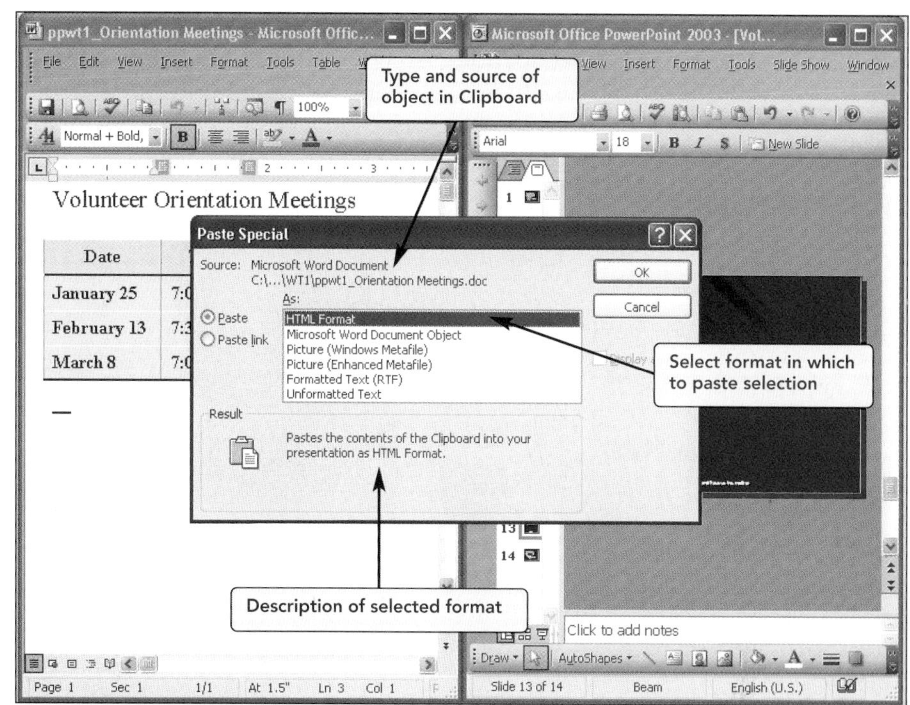

Figure 5

The Paste Special dialog box displays the type of object contained in the Clipboard and its location in the Source area. From the As list box, you select the type of format in which you want the object inserted into the destination file. The default option inserts the copy in HTML (HyperText Markup Language) format. The Result area describes the effect of your selections. In this case, you want the object inserted as a Word Document Object.

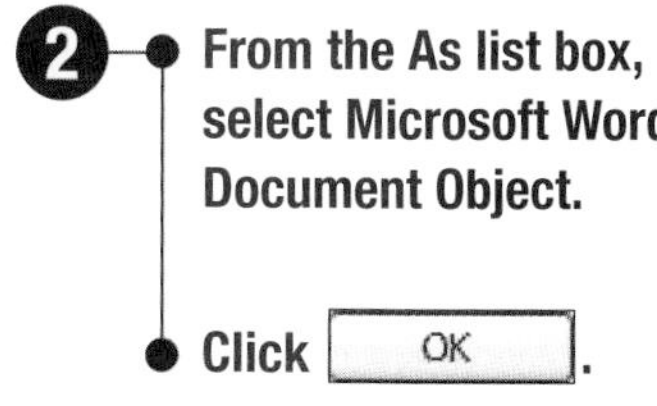

2 **From the As list box, select Microsoft Word Document Object.**

- **Click OK.**

Your screen should be similar to Figure 6

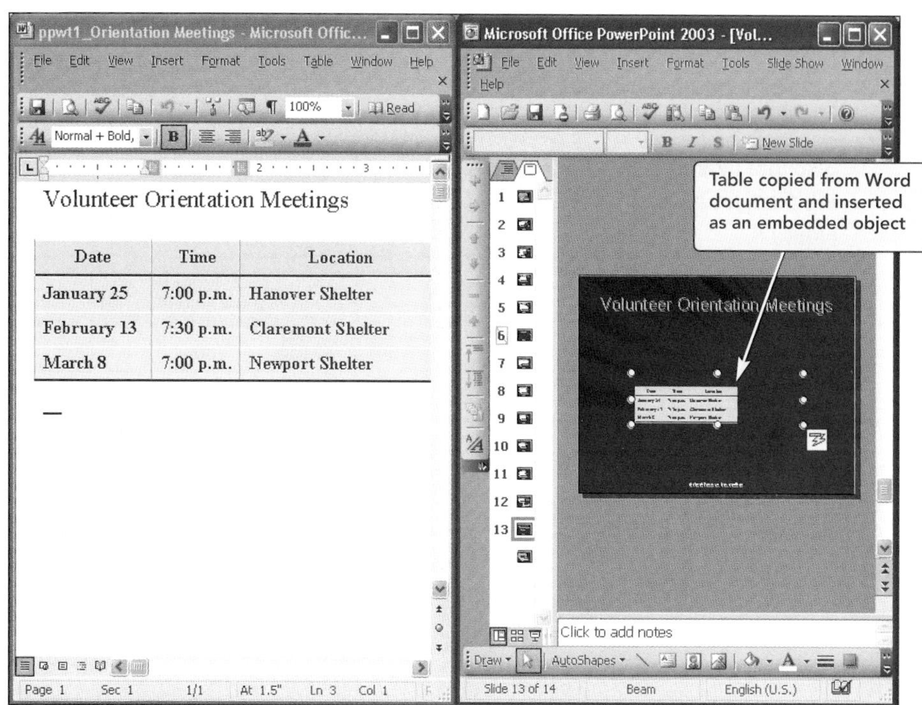

Figure 6

The table, including the table formatting, is copied into the slide as an embedded object that can be manipulated using the Picture toolbar. You will trim or crop the object so that the object size is the same size as the table. Then you will increase the size of the object and position it in the slide.

3

- **Choose Undo Tile from the taskbar shortcut menu.**
- **If necessary, maximize the PowerPoint window and select the table.**
- **Display the Picture toolbar.**
- **Click Crop.**
- **Position the cropping tool over a corner crop mark and drag inward to reduce the size of the object to the same size as the table.**

Your screen should be similar to Figure 7

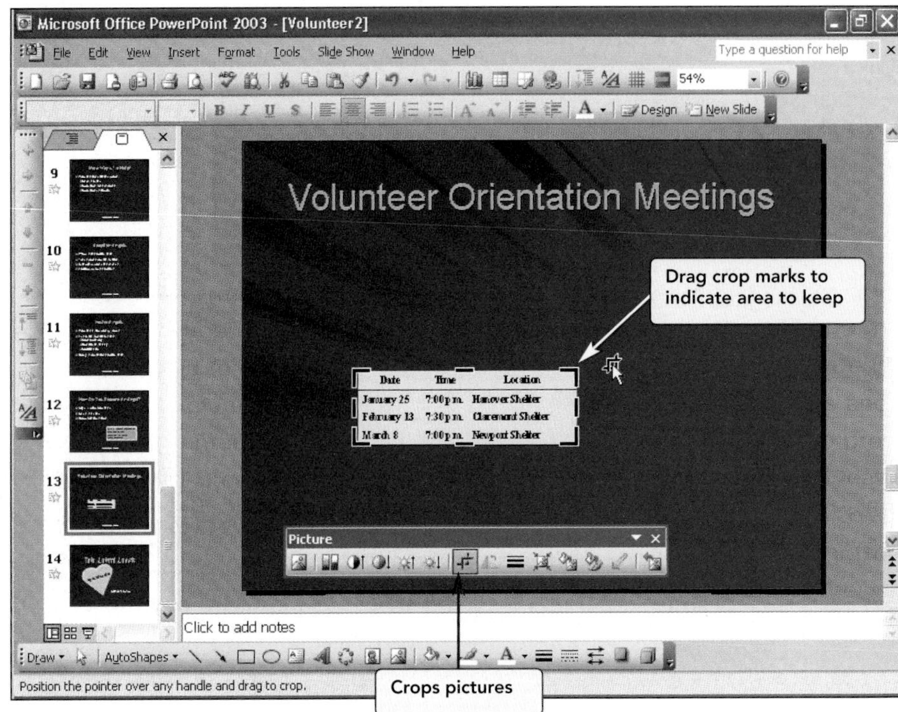

Figure 7

4

- **Click Crop to turn off the cropping tool.**
- **Size and move the table object as in Figure 8.**
- **Deselect the object.**
- **Close the Picture toolbar.**

Your screen should be similar to Figure 8

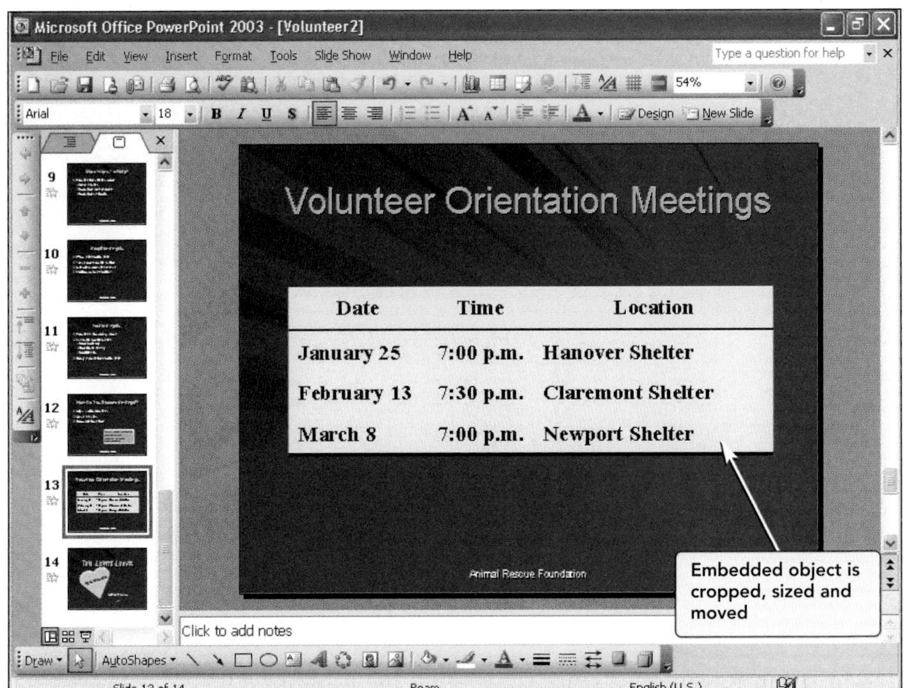

Figure 8

Editing an Embedded Object

As you look at the table, you decide you want to change the appearance of the text in the headings. To do this, you will edit the embedded object using the source program.

Word menus and toolbar

1 Double-click the table.

Another Method

The menu equivalent is <u>E</u>dit/Document <u>O</u>bject/<u>E</u>dit.

Your screen should be similar to Figure 9

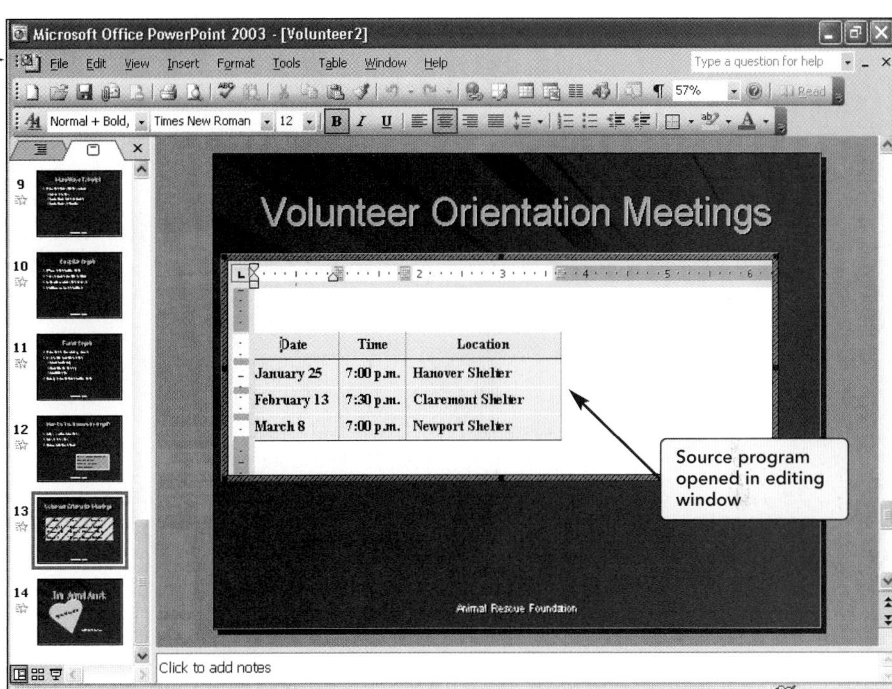

Figure 9

Additional Information

The user must have the source program on their system to be able to open and edit an embedded object.

The source program, in this case Word, is opened. The Word menus and toolbars replace some of the menus and toolbars in the PowerPoint application window. The embedded object is displayed in an editing window. Now, you can use the Word commands to edit the object.

2 • **Change the font color of the three headings to blue.**

• **Left-align the three headings.**

• **Close the source program by clicking anywhere outside the object.**

Your screen should be similar to Figure 10

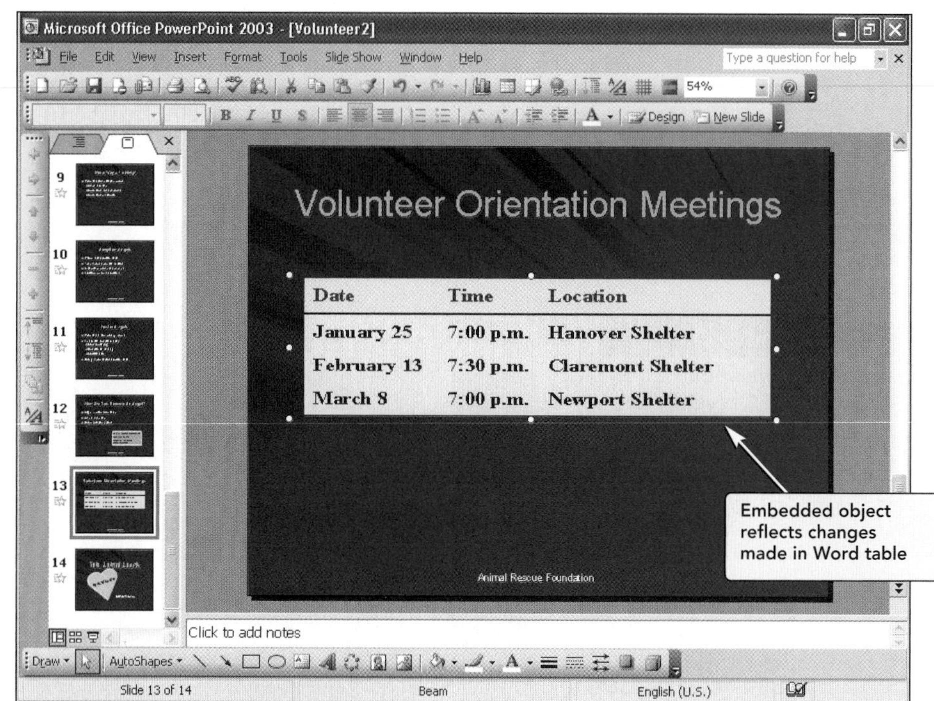

Figure 10

The embedded object in the PowerPoint slide is updated to reflect the changes you made in the Word table.

3 • **Click** Orientation Meetings ... **in the taskbar to switch to the Word application.**

• **Deselect the table and notice that the source file has not been affected by the changes you made to the embedded object.**

• **Exit Word.**

Linking Between Applications

Next you want to copy the chart of the rescue and adoption data into the presentation. You will insert the chart object into the slide as a **linked object**, which is another way to insert information created in one application into a document created by another application. With a linked object, the actual data is stored in the source file (the document in which it was created). A graphic representation or picture of the data is displayed in the destination file (the document in which the object is inserted). A connection between the information in the destination file to the source file is established by creating a link. The link contains references to the location of the source file and the selection within the document that is linked to the destination file.

When changes are made in the source file that affect the linked object, the changes are automatically reflected in the destination file when it is opened. This connection is called a **live link**. When you create linked objects, the date and time on your machine should be accurate. This is because the program refers to the date of the source file to determine whether updates are needed when you open the destination file.

Linking an Excel Chart to a PowerPoint Presentation

The chart of the rescue and adoption data will be inserted into another new slide following slide 6.

1

- **Insert a new slide following slide 6, using the Title Only layout.**
- **Close the Slide Layout task pane.**
- **Start Office Excel 2003 and open the workbook** ppwt1_RescueData **from your data files.**
- **Tile the application windows vertically.**

Your screen should be similar to Figure 11

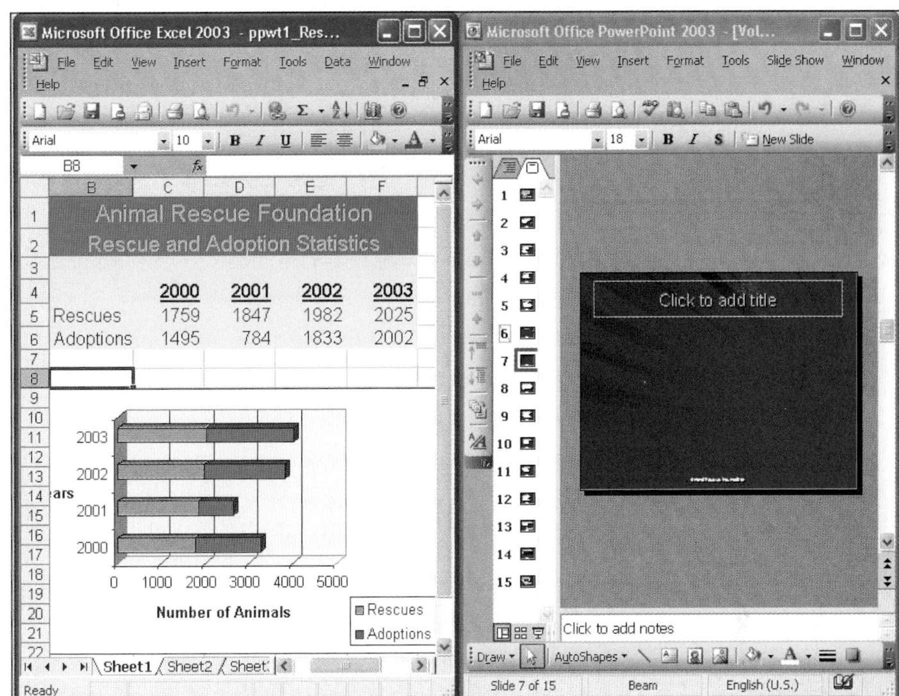

Figure 11

The worksheet contains the rescue and adoption data for the past four years as well as a column chart of the data. Again, you have two open applications, PowerPoint and Excel. Next you will copy the second title line from the worksheet into the slide title placeholder.

- **Select cell B2.**
- **Click**  **Copy.**
- **Select the Title placeholder in the slide.**
- **Choose Edit/Paste Special and select Formatted Text (RTF).**
- **Click** **.**
- **Remove the extra blank lines below the title and the extra space at the end of the title.**
- **If necessary, size the placeholder and position the title appropriately on the slide.**
- **Click on the slide to deselect the placeholder.**

Your screen should be similar to Figure 12

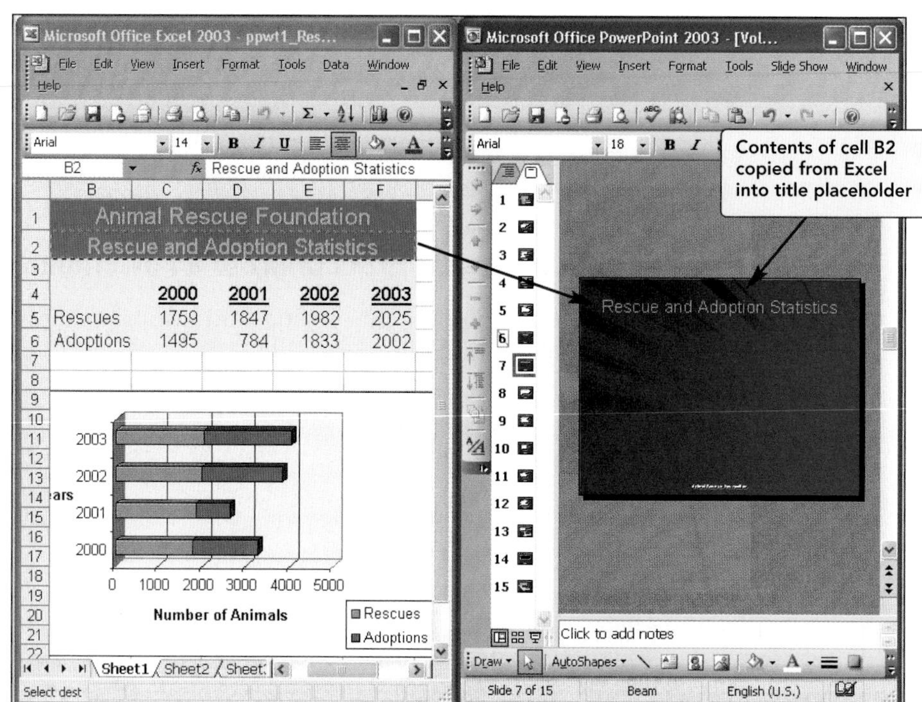

Figure 12

Now, you are ready to copy the chart. By making the chart a linked object, it will be updated automatically if the source file is edited.

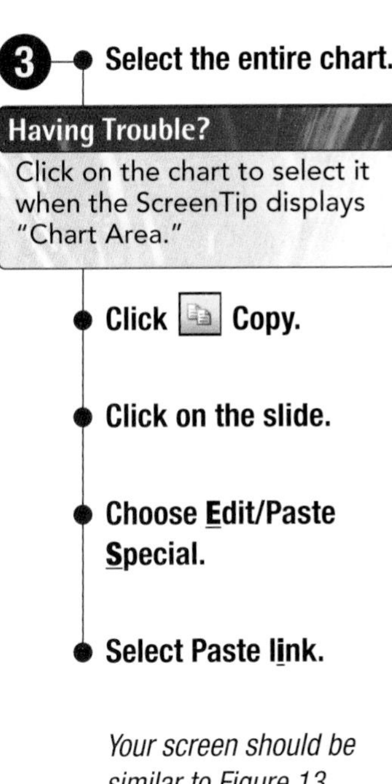

3 • **Select the entire chart.**

Having Trouble?

Click on the chart to select it when the ScreenTip displays "Chart Area."

• **Click Copy.**

• **Click on the slide.**

• **Choose Edit/Paste Special.**

• **Select Paste link.**

Your screen should be similar to Figure 13

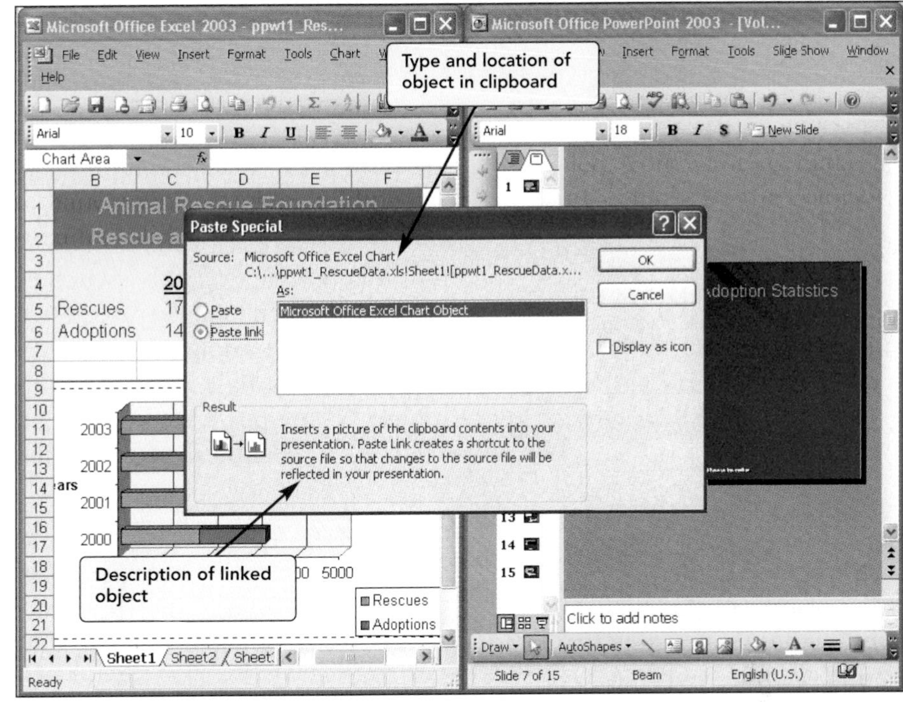

Figure 13

Again, from the As list box, you select the type of format in which you want the object inserted into the destination file. The only available option for this object is as a Microsoft Excel Chart Object. The Result area describes the effect of your selections. In this case, the object will be inserted as a picture, and a link will be created to the chart in the source file. Selecting the Display as Icon option changes the display of the object from a picture to an icon. Double-clicking the icon displays the object picture. The default selections are appropriate.

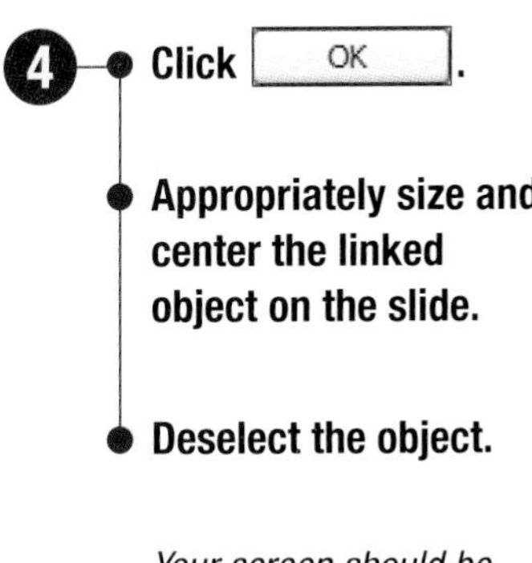

4 • **Click OK.**

• **Appropriately size and center the linked object on the slide.**

• **Deselect the object.**

Your screen should be similar to Figure 14

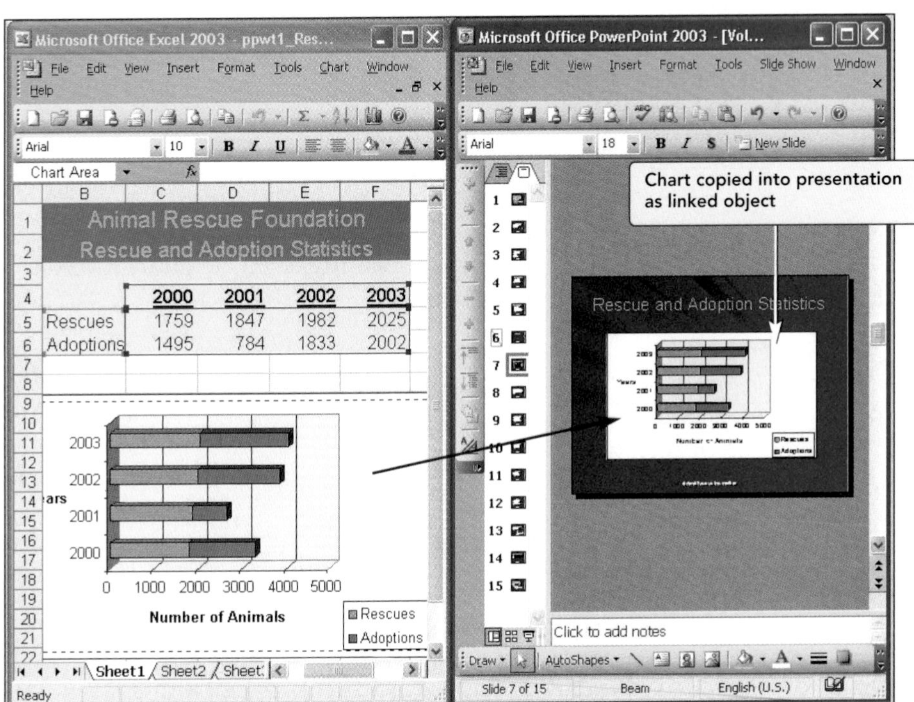

Figure 14

Updating a Linked Object

While looking at the chart in the slide, you decide to change the chart type from a column chart to a bar chart. You believe that a bar chart will show the trends more clearly. You also notice the adoption data for 2001 looks very low. After checking the original information, you see that the wrong value was entered in the worksheet and that it should be 1784.

To make these changes, you need to switch back to Excel. Double-clicking on a linked object quickly switches to the open source file. If the source file is not open, it opens the file for you. If the application is not started, it both starts the application and opens the source file.

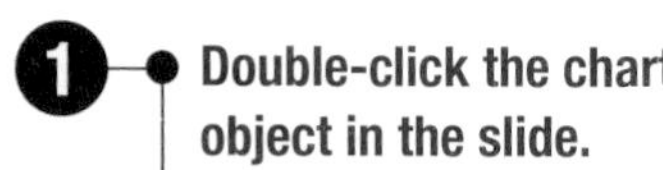

1. **Double-click the chart object in the slide.**

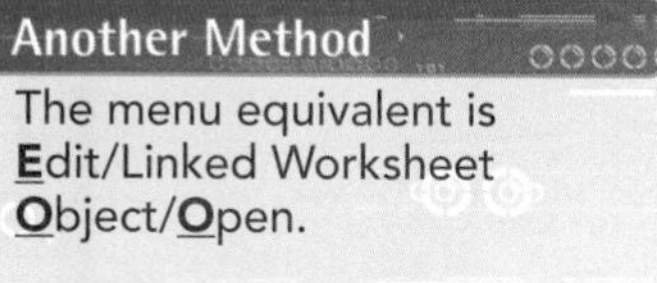

- **In Excel, right click on one of the columns in the chart and select Chart Type.**

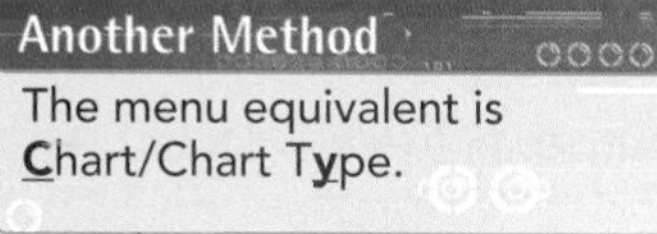

- **Select Column.**
- **Select Clustered column with a 3-D visual effect.**
- **Click OK.**
- **Edit the value in cell D6 to 1784.**

Your screen should be similar to Figure 15

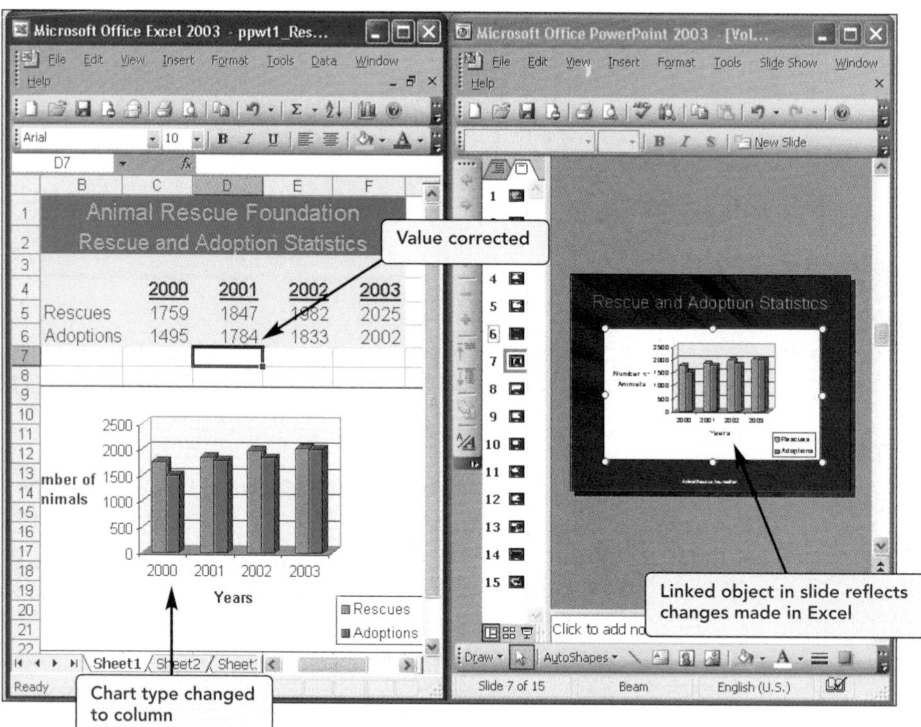

Figure 15

The chart in both applications has changed to a bar chart, and the chart data series has been updated to reflect the change in data. This is because any changes you make in the chart in Excel will be automatically reflected in the linked chart in the slide.

2 • **Untile the application windows.**

• **Save the revised Excel workbook as RescueData Linked.**

• **Exit Excel.**

• **If necessary, maximize the PowerPoint window.**

Editing Links

Whenever a document is opened that contains links, the application looks for the source file and automatically updates the linked objects. If there are many links, updating can take a lot of time. Additionally, if you move the source file to another location, or perform other operations that may interfere with the link, your link will not work. To help with situations like these, you can edit the settings associated with links. You will look at how to do this, though you will not actually edit the settings.

1 • **If necessary, select the chart object.**

• **Choose Edit/Links.**

Your screen should be similar to Figure 16

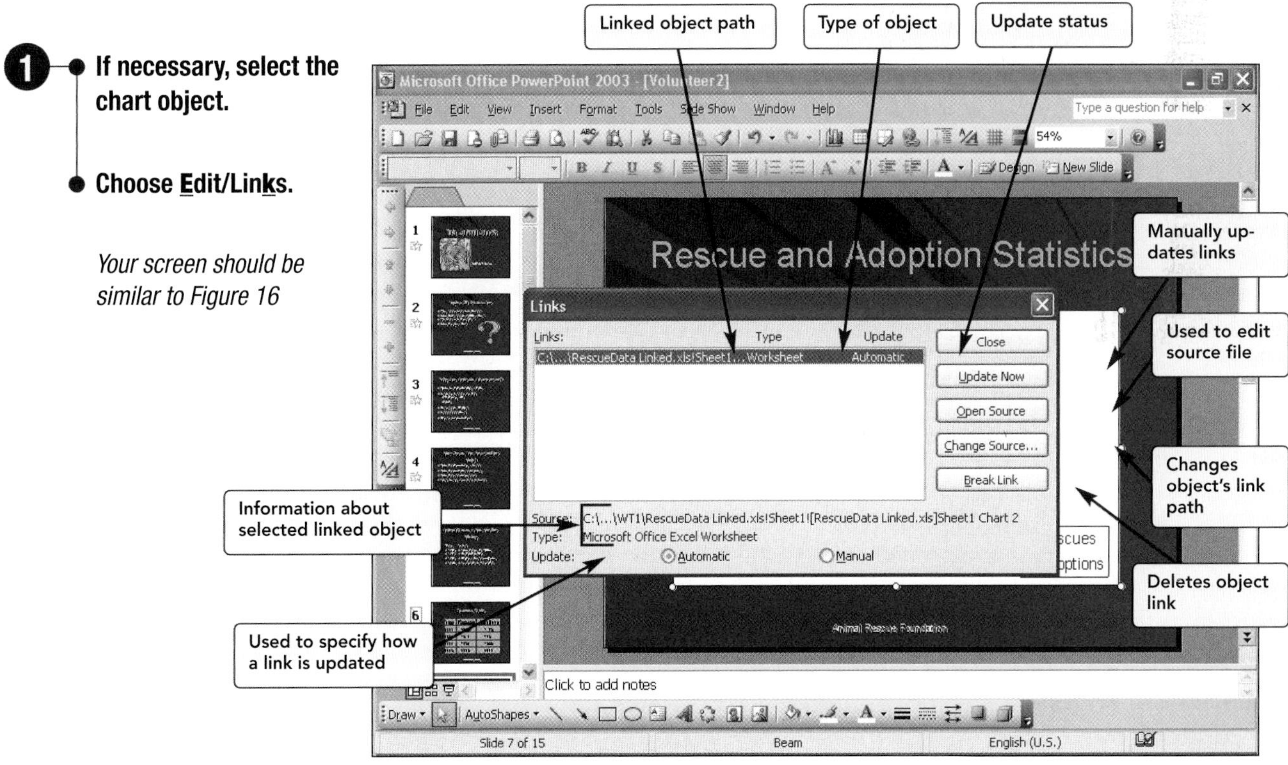

Figure 16

The Links dialog box list box displays information about all links in the document. This includes the path and name of the source file, the range of linked cells or object name, the type of file, and the update status. Below the list box the details for the selected link are displayed. The other options in this dialog box are described in the table on the next page.

Option	Effect
Automatic	Updates the linked object whenever the destination document is opened or the source file changes. This is the default.
Manual	The destination document is not automatically updated, and you must use the Update Now command button to update the link.
Locked	Prevents a linked object from being updated.
Open Source	Opens the source document for the selected link.
Change Source	Used to modify the path to the source document.
Break Link	Breaks the connection between the source document and the active document.

You do not want to make any changes to the link.

Linking documents is a very handy feature, particularly in documents whose information is updated frequently. If you include a linked object in a document that you are giving to another person, make sure the user has access to the source file and application. Otherwise the links will not operate correctly.

Printing Selected Slides

Next, you will print the two new slides.

1

- **Switch to Slide Sorter view and select slides 7 and 14.**
- **Use View/Header and Footer to modify the slide footer to display your name on slides 7 and 14 only.**

Having Trouble?

Select the slides you want to modify, use the command, and click Apply to apply the new footer to the selected slides only.

- **Choose File/Print.**
- **If necessary, select the printer.**
- **Select Selection as the print range.**
- **Specify Slides as the type of output.**
- **Preview the output and change the print to grayscale if necessary.**
- **Print the slides.**
- **Save the PowerPoint presentation as** Volunteer2 Linked **and exit PowerPoint.**

Your printed output should be similar to that shown here.

Rescue and Adoption Statistics

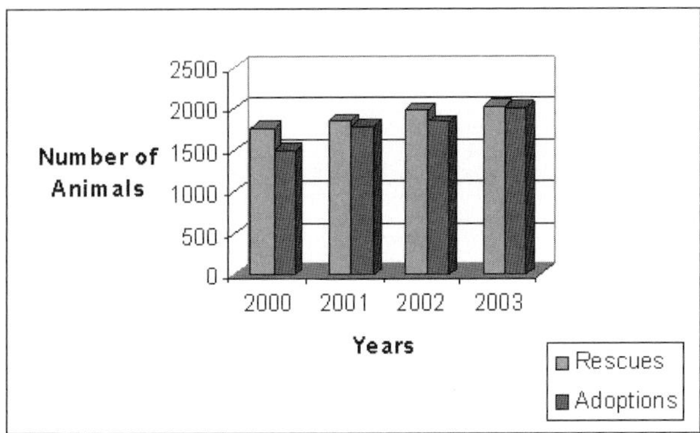

Student Name

Volunteer Orientation Meetings

Date	Time	Location
January 25	7:00 p.m.	Hanover Shelter
February 13	7:30 p.m.	Claremont Shelter
March 8	7:00 p.m.	Newport Shelter

Student Name

WORKING TOGETHER 1

Copying, Embedding, and Linking Between Applications

key terms

destination file PPWT1.4
linked object PPWT1.8
live link PPWT1.9
source file PPWT1.4

microsoft office specialist skills

The Microsoft Office Specialist certification program is designed to measure your proficiency in performing basic tasks using the Office 2003 applications. Certification demonstrates that you have the skills and provides a valuable industry credential for employment. After completing this lab, you have learned the following Microsoft Office PowerPoint 2003 Specialist skills:

Skill Sets	Skill Standards	Page
Creating Content	Insert and edit text based content	PPWT1.2
	Insert objects	PPWT1.11
Managing and Delivering Presentations	Organize a presentation	PPWT1.2, 1.9
	Print slides, outlines, handouts, and speaker notes	PPWT1.14

command summary

Command	Action
Edit/Paste Special/ <Object>	Inserts an item from Clipboard as an embedded object
Edit/Paste Special/Paste Link	Inserts an item from Clipboard as a linked object
Edit/Links	Changes settings associated with linked objects
Edit/Linked Worksheet Object/Open	Opens source application of linked object
Edit/Document Object/Edit	Opens source application of embedded object

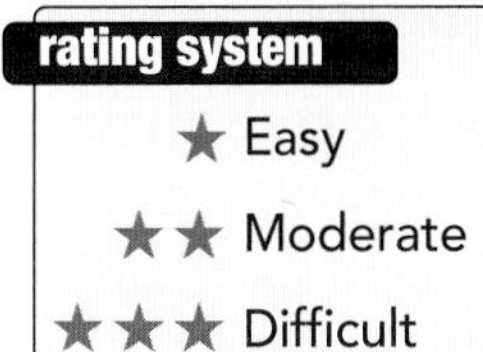

step-by-step

Embedding a Table of Massage Prices ★

1. To complete this problem, you must have completed Step-by-Step Exercise 2 in Lab 2. The Massage Therapy presentation is almost complete. You just need to add some information to the presentation about the prices. This information is already in a Word document as a table. You will copy and embed it into a new slide. The completed slide is shown here.

- **a.** Start Word and open the document ppwt1_MassagePrices.
- **b.** Start PowerPoint and open the Massage Therapy2 presentation.
- **c.** Add a new slide after slide 9 using the Title Only layout.
- **d.** Copy the title from the Word document into the slide title placeholder.
- **e.** Copy the table into the slide as an embedded object. Exit Word.
- **f.** Size and position the object on the slide appropriately.
- **g.** Edit the table to increase the font size as needed.
- **h.** Change the fill color of the table to match the slide design.
- **i.** Save the presentation as Massage Therapy3.
- **j.** Print the new slide.

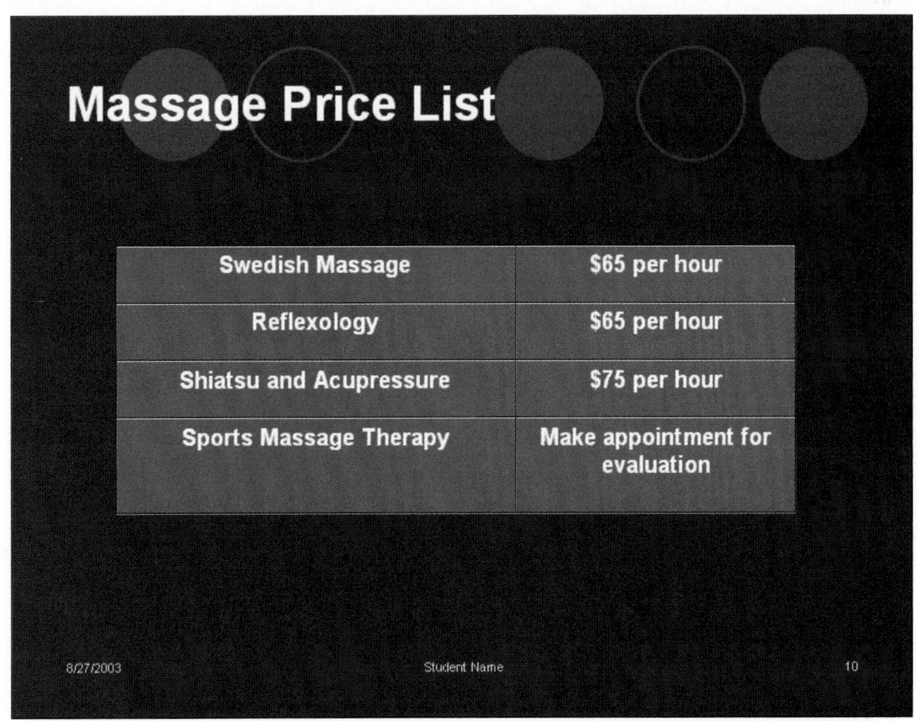

Linking a Table of Coffee Prices ★ ★

2. To complete this problem, you must have completed Step-by-Step Exercise 4 in Lab 2. Evan, owner of the Downtown Internet Cafe, wants you to include information about special prices on coffee beans in the coffee slide show you created. You will link the coffee price information to the presentation, because the prices change frequently with market conditions and good buys. The completed slide is shown here.

   a. Start Word and open the document ppwt1_CoffeePrices.

   b. Start PowerPoint and open the presentation Coffee Show.

   c. Add a new slide at the end of the presentation using the Title Only layout.

   d. Enter the slide title **. . . Or Take Some Home**.

   e. Copy the table of prices into the slide as a linked object.

   f. Copy the text "Roast Coffee Specials" from the Word document into a text box on the slide. Apply a new font color and increase the font size.

   g. Size and position the objects appropriately.

   h. In the Word document, change the price of Kona to **$14.95**.

   i. Save the Word document as Coffee Prices Linked. Exit Word.

   j. Save the PowerPoint presentation as Coffee Show Linked.

   k. Print the new slide.

...Or Take Some Home

Roast Coffee Specials		
Coffee	**Description**	**Cost/Pound**
Columbian Blend	**Classic body and aroma**	**$8.50**
Kona	**Smooth, light bodied**	**$14.95**
Ethiopian	**Floral aroma and flavor**	**$12.00**
Sumatra	**Dark roasted**	**$7.95**

8/27/2003 Student Name 10

Linking a Worksheet on Forest Use ★ ★ ★

3. To complete this problem, you must have completed Step-by-Step Exercise 4 of Lab 2. Logan has found some interesting data on the increase in Americans hiking and wants to include this information in his lecture presentation. The completed slide is shown here.

a. Start PowerPoint and open the Triple Crown Presentation2 presentation.

b. Start Excel and open the ppwt1_Forest Use worksheet.

c. Add a new slide after slide 6 using the Title Only layout.

d. Enter the title **Most Popular Forest Activities**.

e. Copy the worksheet range A2 through B6 as a linked object into slide 7. Size and position it appropriately.

f. You notice that the percentage for hiking in the year 2002 seems low. After checking the original source, you see you entered the value incorrectly. In Excel, change the value in cell B5 to **36.4%**.

g. Copy the text in cell A8 and paste it into the Notes for slide 7.

h. Save the worksheet as Forest Use Linked. Exit Excel.

i. Save the presentation as Triple Crown Presentation3.

j. Print the new slide.

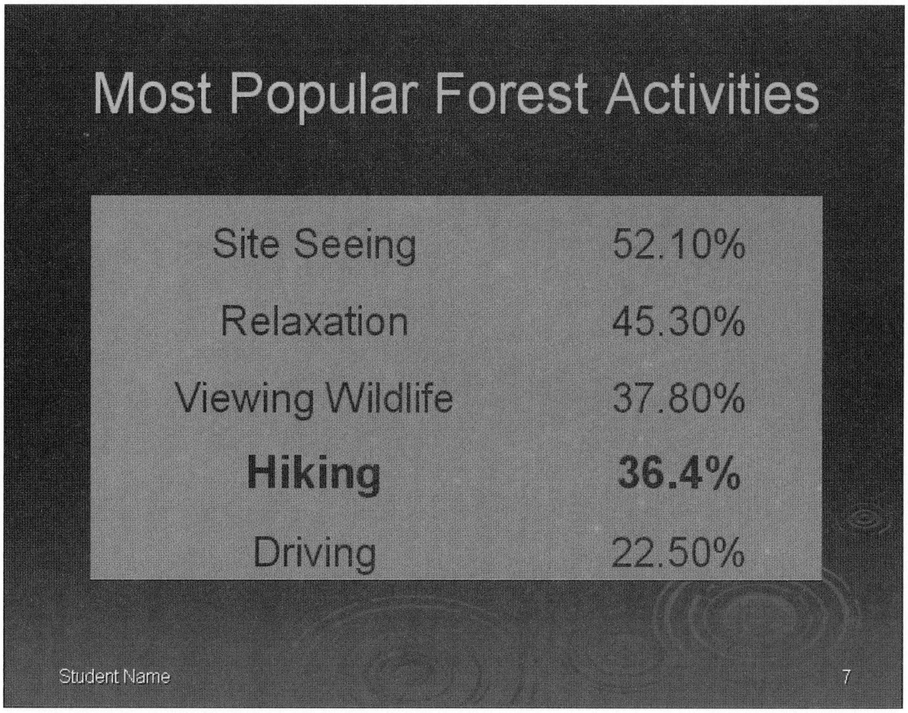

Most Popular Forest Activities

Activity	Percentage
Site Seeing	52.10%
Relaxation	45.30%
Viewing Wildlife	37.80%
Hiking	**36.4%**
Driving	22.50%

Student Name 7

Using Advanced Presentation Features

LAB 3

Objectives

After completing this lab, you will know how to:

1. Create a new presentation from existing slides.
2. Create a numbered list.
3. Use Format Painter.
4. Create a custom background.
5. Change the design template.
6. Zoom slides.
7. Modify objects and change stacking order.
8. Wrap text in an object.
9. Group, ungroup, and align objects.
10. Create and modify a chart.
11. Create and modify an organization chart.
12. Export a presentation outline to Word.
13. E-mail a presentation.
14. Rehearse timings.
15. Package a presentation for a CD.
16. Prepare overheads or 35mm slides.

Case Study

Animal Rescue Foundation

The volunteer recruitment presentation you created for the Animal Rescue Foundation was a huge success. Now the agency director has asked you to create a presentation to use during new volunteer orientation programs. To create this presentation, you will modify and expand the recruitment presentation. This will include creating a new slide that presents an overview of the orientation, and another slide showing the organization of the agency. In addition, you plan to make the presentation more interesting by adding customized clip art and a custom background.

To help with these enhancements, PowerPoint 2003 includes several tools, such as graphs and organization charts that are designed to help present data. You will also use several Drawing tool features to customize a clip art graphic to enhance the presentation. Several slides from the completed presentation are shown here.

Ryan McVay/Corbis

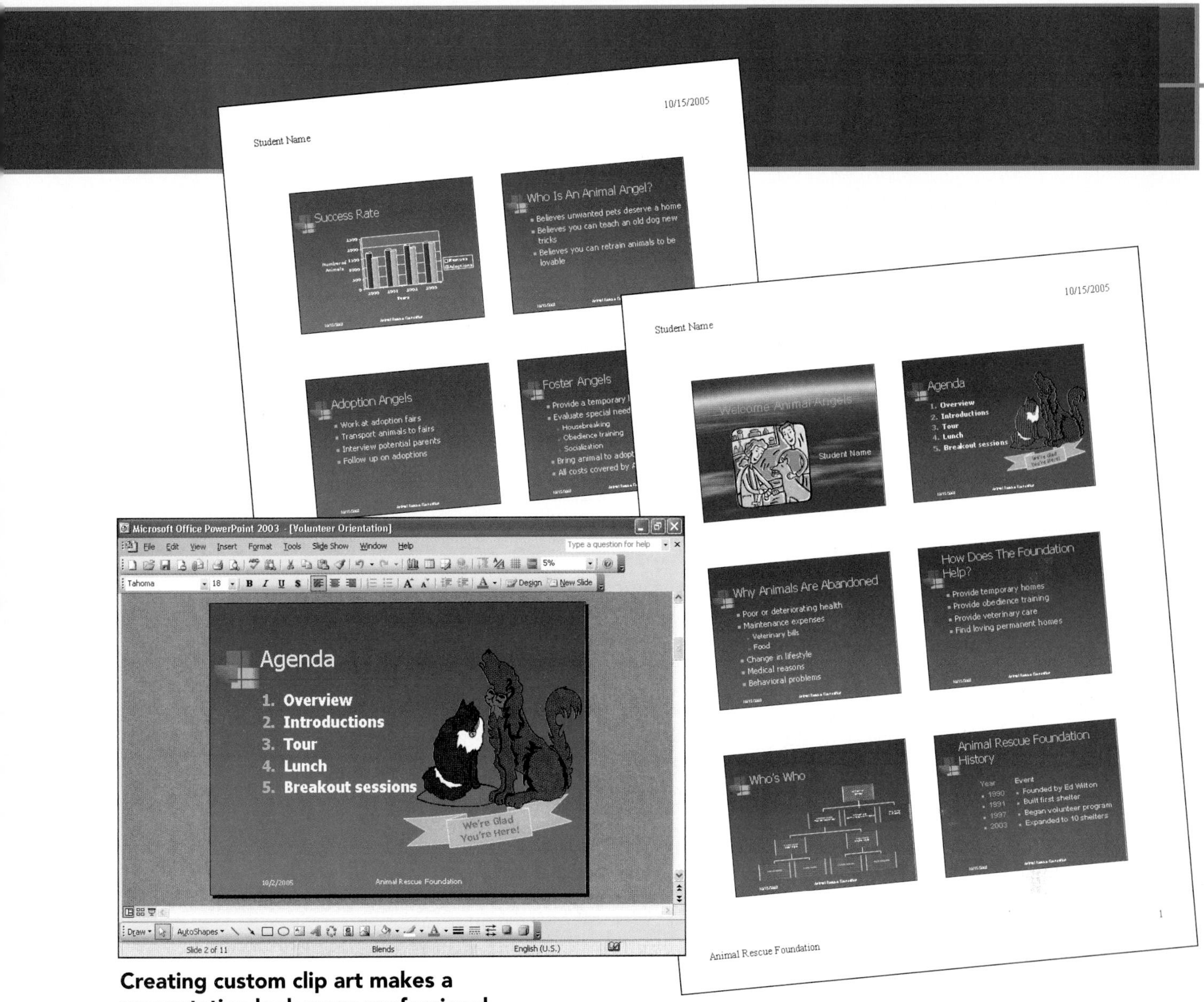

Creating custom clip art makes a presentation look more professional.

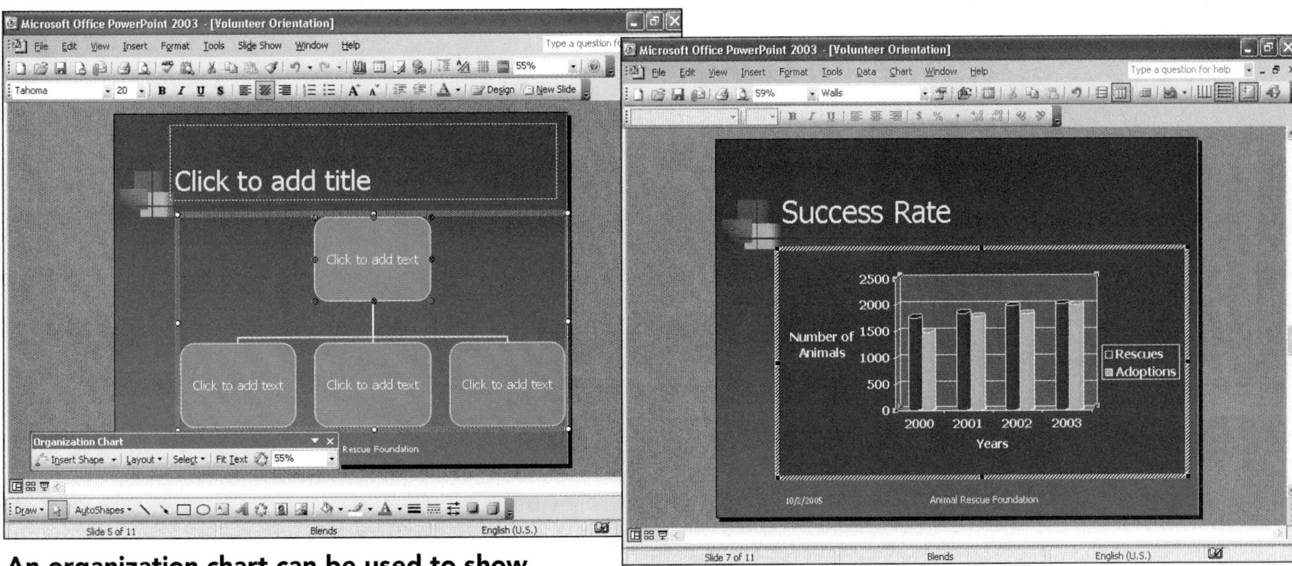

An organization chart can be used to show the hierarchy of an organization.

A graphic representation of table data as a chart makes data easier easier to understand.

Concept Preview

The following concepts will be introduced in this lab:

1. **Group** A group is two or more objects that are treated as a single object.
2. **Object Alignment** Object alignment refers to the position of objects relative to each other by their left, right, top, or bottom edges; or horizontally by their centers or vertically by their middles; or in relation to the entire slide.
3. **Chart** A chart is a visual representation of numeric data that is used to help an audience grasp the impact of your data more quickly.
4. **Collect and Paste** The collect and paste feature is used to store multiple copied items in the Office Clipboard and then paste one or more of the items into another location or document.
5. **Organization Chart** An organization chart is a map of a group, which usually includes people, but can include any items that have a hierarchical relationship.

Creating a New Presentation from Existing Slides

You worked very hard developing the content and layout for the volunteer recruitment presentation. Now you need to create a new presentation to be used during the volunteer orientation meeting. Much of the material in the volunteer recruitment presentation can also be used in the volunteer orientation presentation. To make the task of creating the new presentation easier, you will use the existing presentation, modify it to fit your needs, and save it as a new presentation. You have already made a few changes to the presentation. You changed the design and removed a few slides that you will not need in the orientation presentation.

1 Start Office PowerPoint 2003.

- Open the file pp03_Recruitment.
- If necessary, maximize the window and switch to Normal view.
- Change the title of slide 1 to **Welcome Animal Angels**.
- Replace Student Name on slide 1 with **your name**.
- Look at each of the slides to see the changes that have been made.
- Delete slide 10.
- Display slide 1 again.

Your screen should be similar to Figure 3.1

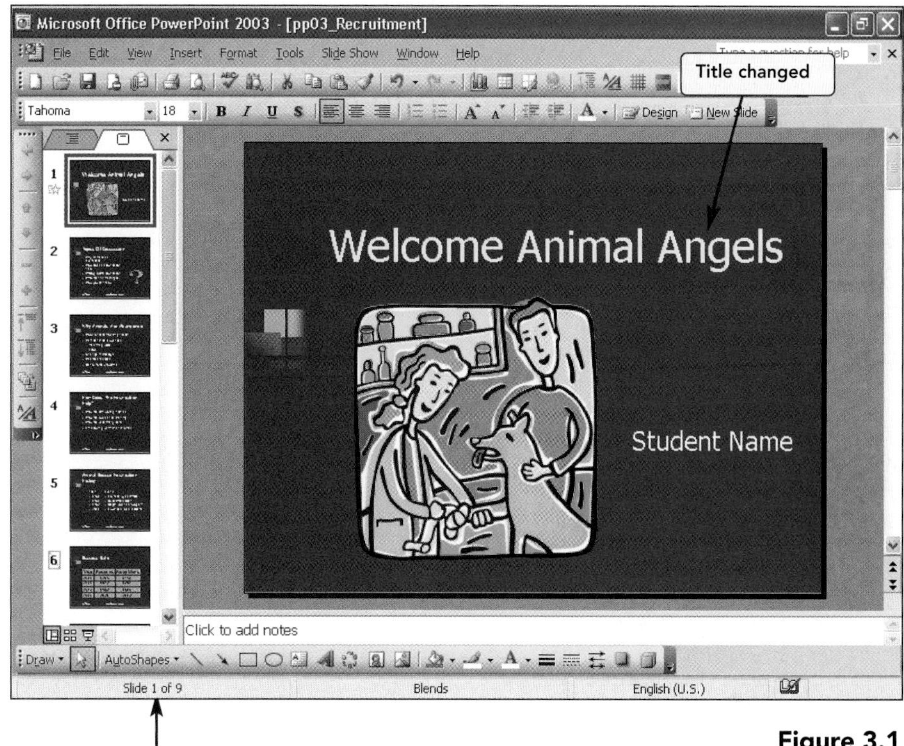

Figure 3.1

Copying Slides from Another Presentation

Now you want to replace the ending slide you just deleted with a slide from another presentation you have been working on. To do this, you will copy the slide from the other presentation into the volunteer orientation presentation.

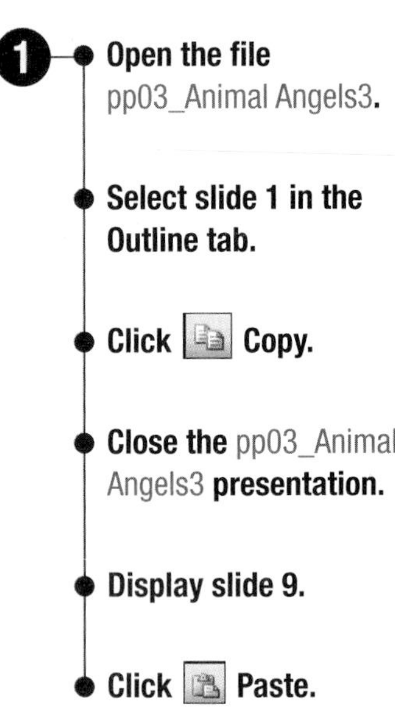

1
- **Open the file** pp03_Animal Angels3**.**
- **Select slide 1 in the Outline tab.**
- **Click Copy.**
- **Close the** pp03_Animal Angels3 **presentation.**
- **Display slide 9.**
- **Click Paste.**

Your screen should be similar to Figure 3.2

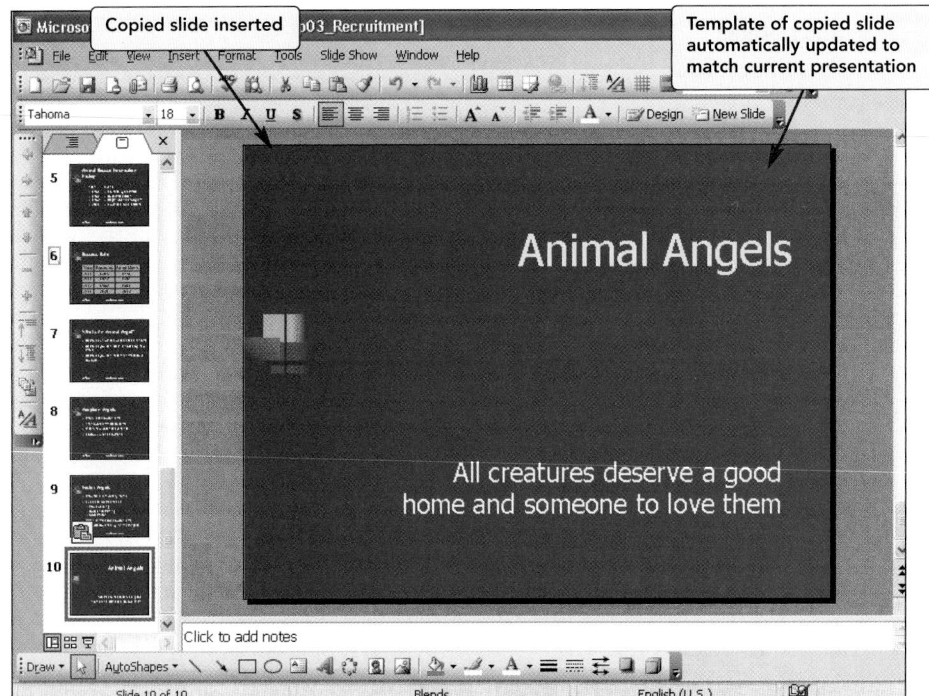

Figure 3.2

The copied slide is inserted into the presentation after the current slide. In addition, the slide template of the copied slide is updated automatically to match that of the current presentation.

Saving the New Presentation

Before you make any additional changes, you will save the file as a new presentation.

1
- **Modify the title of slide 10 to Thank You for Joining Animal Angels.**
- **Save the revised presentation as** Volunteer Orientation**.**

Your screen should be similar to Figure 3.3

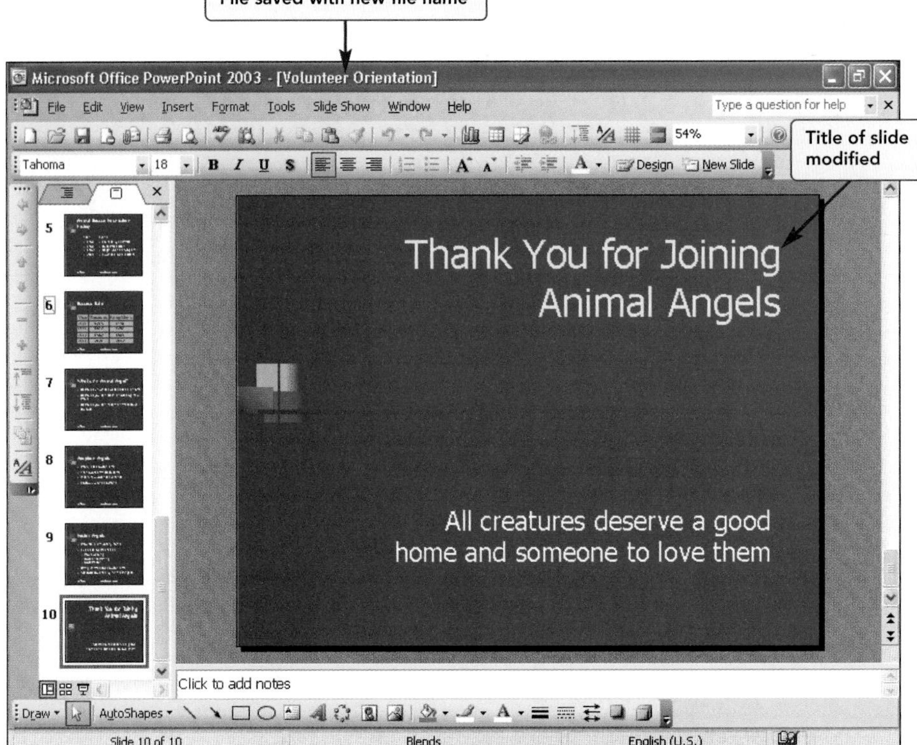

Figure 3.3

By modifying an existing presentation and saving it as a new presentation, you have saved a lot of time in the creation of your new presentation.

Enhancing the New Presentation

Now that the basic presentation is assembled, you want to make some enhancements, such as adding an agenda slide, changing the color of text on a few slides, and adding some more content.

Creating a Numbered List

First you want to change the second slide, which shows the topics of discussion, to a slide showing the agenda for the orientation. Since the agenda shows a sequential order of events, you want to use a numbered list rather than bullets.

1

- **Change the title of slide 2 to Agenda.**
- **Select the five bulleted items.**
- **Type the text for the following five bulleted items:**

  Overview

  Introductions

  Tour

  Lunch

  Breakout sessions

- **Select the five bulleted items on slide 2.**
- **Click Numbering.**

Your screen should be similar to Figure 3.4.

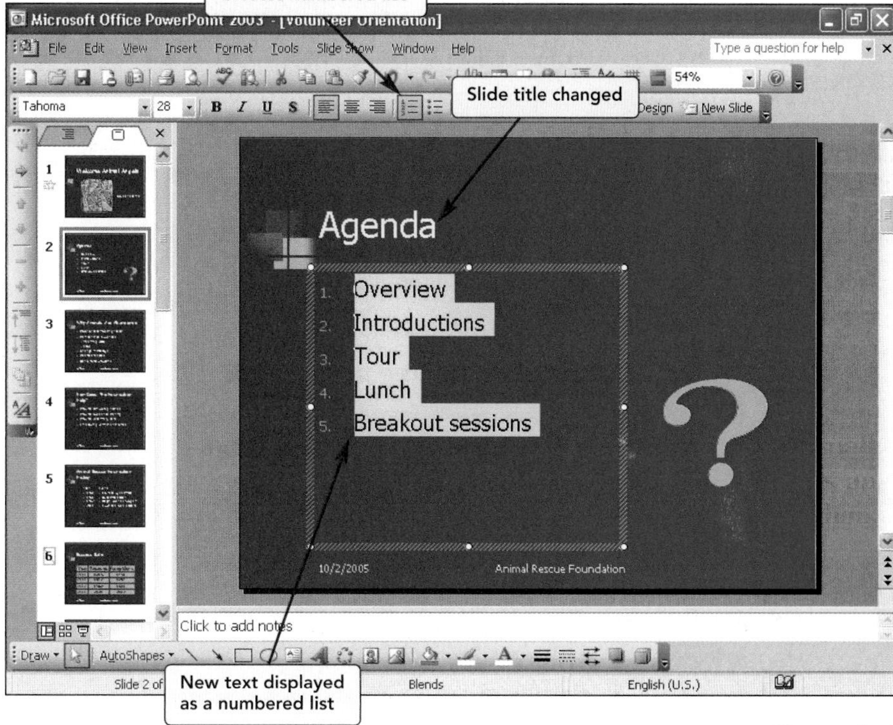

Figure 3.4

Another Method

You can also change a bulleted list to a numbered list by typing. To do this, press Backspace to remove the bullet at the beginning of the line, type 1, A, a, I, or i followed by a period or closing parenthesis, type the text, and then press ←Enter to start a new line. The next line is automatically numbered using the same style.

The bullets have been replaced with numbers, indicating a sequential order of events.

You would also like to change the size of the numbers so they will stand out more on the slide.

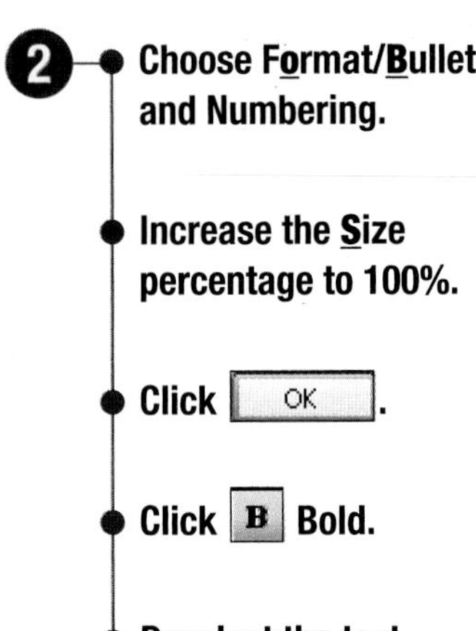

2

- **Choose Format/Bullets and Numbering.**
- **Increase the Size percentage to 100%.**
- **Click OK.**
- **Click B Bold.**
- **Deselect the text.**

Your screen should be similar to Figure 3.5

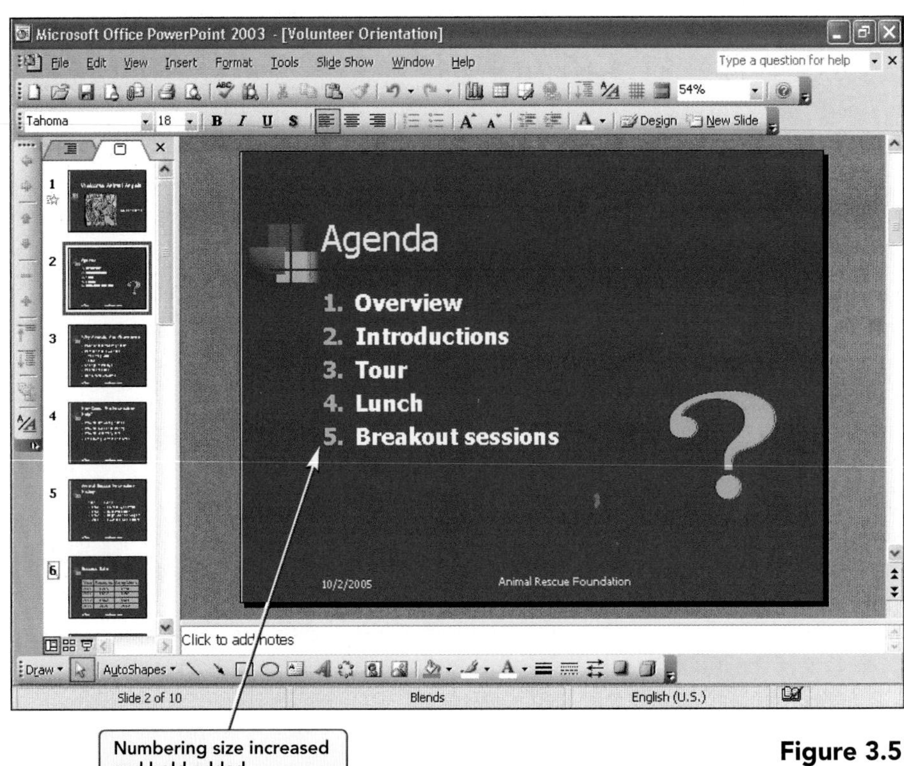

Figure 3.5

Additional Information

The Numbered tab of the Bullets and Numbering dialog box also allows you to select from several other numbering styles as well as specify a starting number.

The numbers have changed to the size you selected and now stand out more from the text.

Using Format Painter

You decide that slide 5, which shows the history of the Animal Rescue Foundation, could benefit from the addition of a little more color. To help you quickly apply the same formats to multiple selections, you will use the **Format Painter** tool. This feature applies the formats associated with the current selection to new selections. If the selection is a paragraph, the formatting is applied to entire paragraphs. If the selection is a character, it is applied to a word or selection you specify.

1 • **Display slide 5.**

• **Select the word "Year" in the slide.**

• **Change the font to Arial, bold, and the font color to gold.**

• **Double-click Format Painter.**

• **Click 1990.**

Additional Information

Single-clicking Format Painter applies the format to one selection, whereas double-clicking allows you to apply the format multiple times.

Additional Information

When the Format Painter feature is on, the mouse pointer appears as .

Your screen should be similar to Figure 3.6

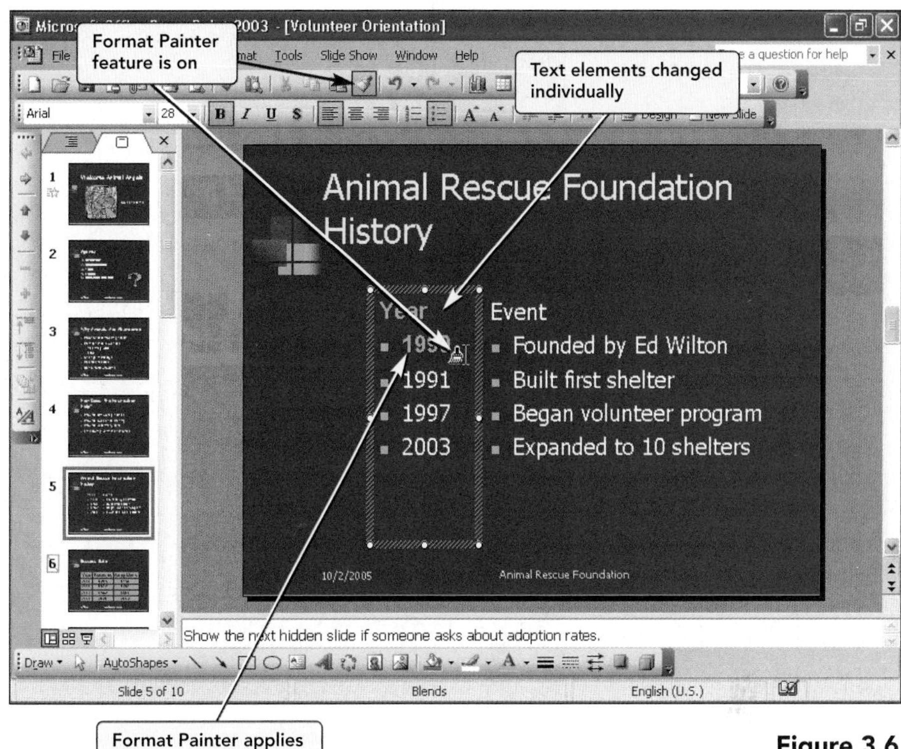

Figure 3.6

The text automatically changed to the same font settings associated with the selection when you turned on Format Painter. In one single click, you quickly applied three formats.

2

- **Use Format Painter to format the remaining three years.**
- **Click Format Painter to turn off the feature.**
- **Change "Event" to Arial and bold.**
- **Use Format Painter to change all the event text to match the heading.**
- **Turn off Format Painter.**

- **Deselect the text.**
- **Size the placeholder so each bullet is on one line.**

Your screen should be similar to Figure 3.7

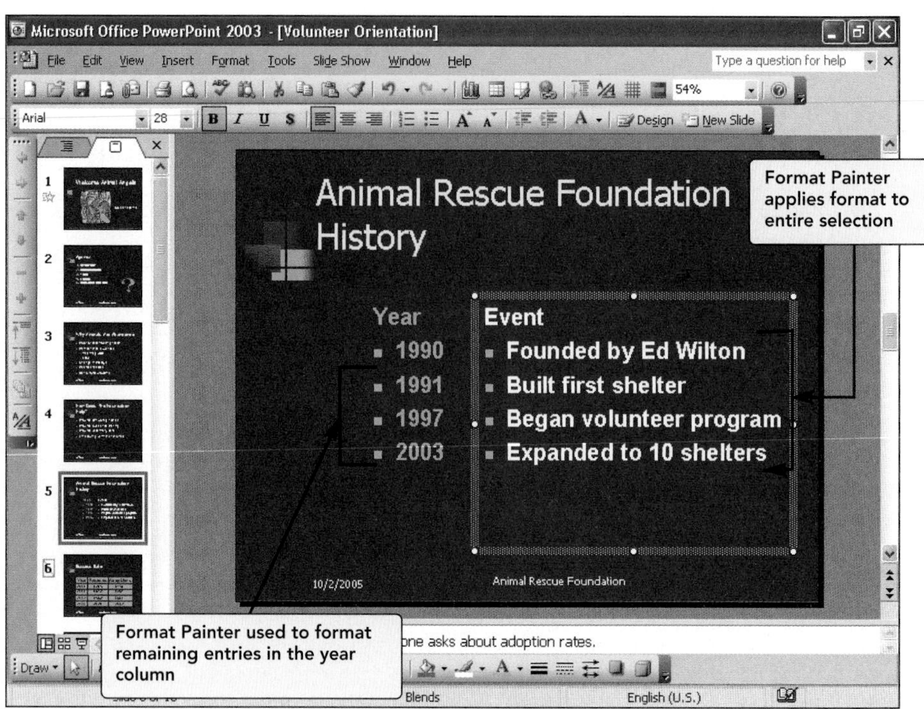

Figure 3.7

Modifying the Design Template

Although you like the template design you selected for this presentation, you think the presentation design would benefit by adding a little variety. To do this, you decide to change the appearance of several of the slides by changing the slide background and using a different design template.

Creating a Custom Background

As you look at the slides you decide you want to add a more interesting background. You will do this by adding a gradient color to the background.

1 Choose Format/ Background.

- Select Fill Effects from the Background Fill color drop-down list.
- Open the Gradient tab and select Two colors.
- From the Color 1 drop-down list, select the dark blue color from the top row.
- From the Color 2 drop-down menu, select More Colors.
- Select a lighter blue color from the Standard color palette and click OK.
- From the Shading styles area, select Horizontal and click OK.

Your screen should be similar to Figure 3.8

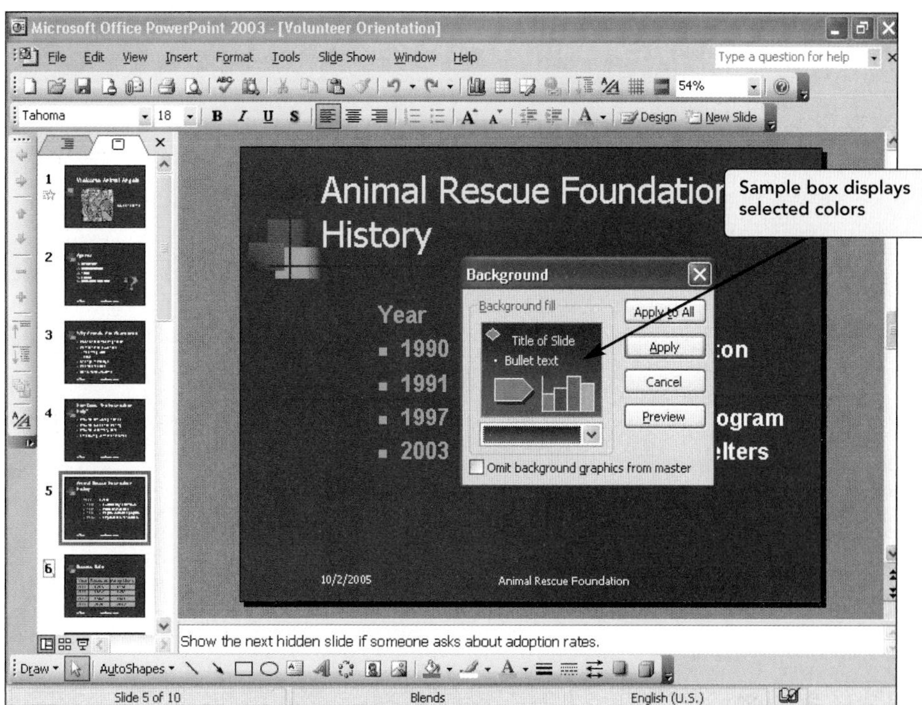

Figure 3.8

The selected colors in the gradient shading style you selected are displayed in the Sample box so you can see how it will look on the slide.

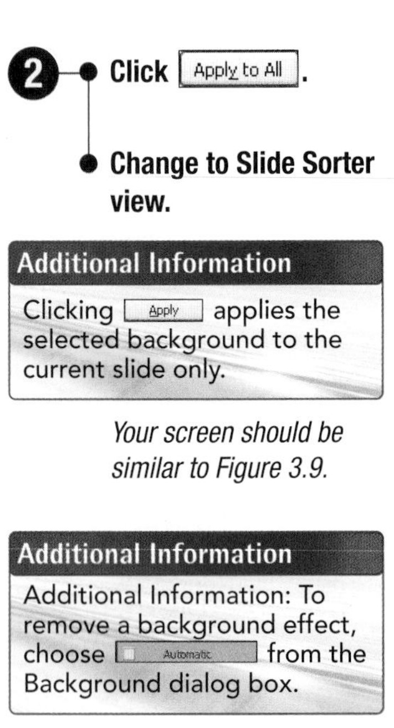

2 Click Apply to All.

- Change to Slide Sorter view.

Additional Information

Clicking Apply applies the selected background to the current slide only.

Your screen should be similar to Figure 3.9.

Additional Information

Additional Information: To remove a background effect, choose Automatic from the Background dialog box.

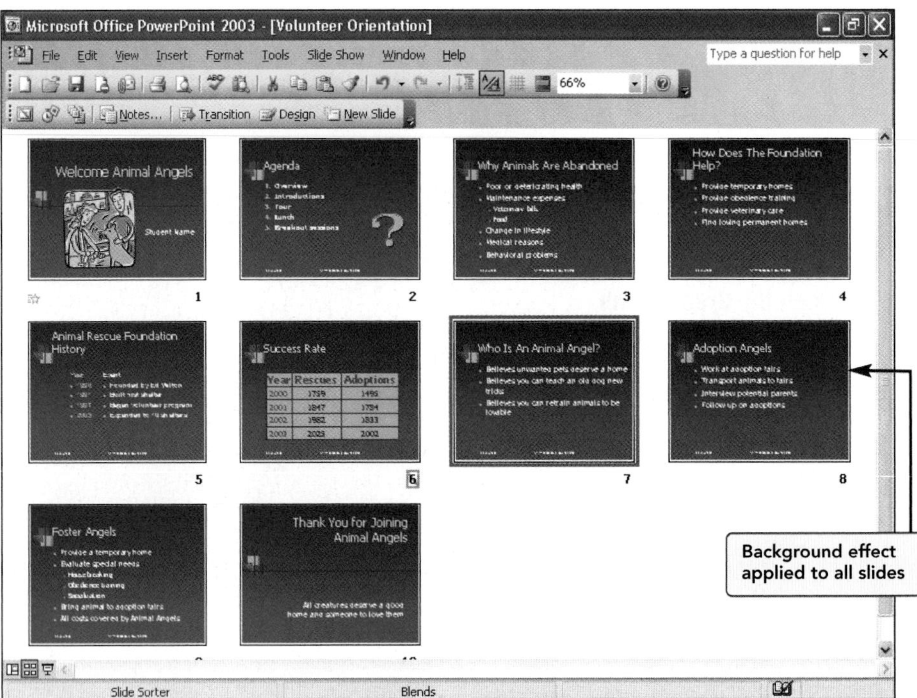

Figure 3.9

The gradient style background adds interest to the slides.

Applying a Slide Master to Selected Slides

Next you want to change the design template for the first and last slides in the presentation to another template. Design templates can be applied to selected slides as well as to an entire presentation.

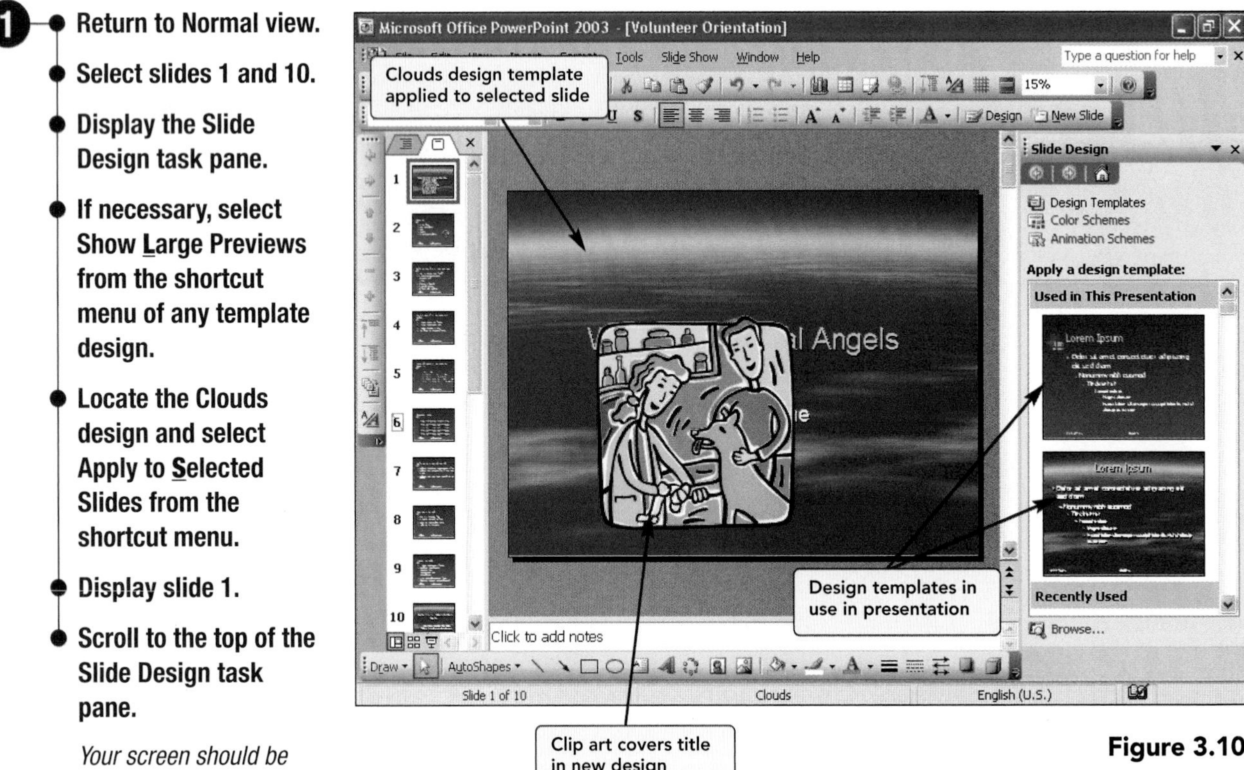

1 Return to Normal view.

- Select slides 1 and 10.
- Display the Slide Design task pane.
- If necessary, select Show Large Previews from the shortcut menu of any template design.
- Locate the Clouds design and select Apply to Selected Slides from the shortcut menu.
- Display slide 1.
- Scroll to the top of the Slide Design task pane.

Your screen should be similar to Figure 3.10

Figure 3.10

The Used in This Presentation section of the Slide Design task pane displays thumbnails for both design templates in use. As you can see by looking at slide 1, you need to make some changes to the title slide arrangement. You will make these changes to the slide title master.

2 **Display Slide Master view.**

Point to the title slide master of the Clouds design (thumbnail 4).

Your screen should be similar to Figure 3.11

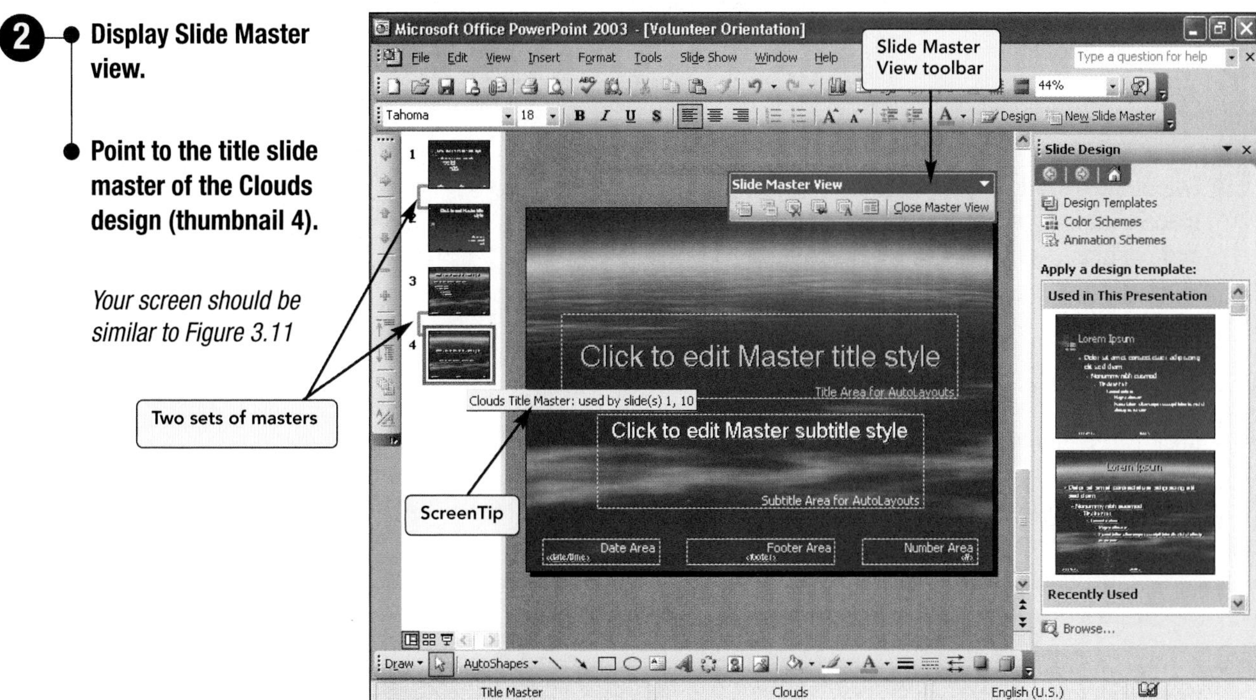

Figure 3.11

Because you are using two different slide designs in the presentation, there are two sets of masters, one for each design. Pointing to a slide master thumbnail displays a ScreenTip showing the design name and the slides in the presentation that use that template. Using menu commands and buttons on the Slide Master View toolbar, you can add, duplicate, rename, and delete masters. You can also preserve a master, which protects it from being deleted automatically in certain cases by PowerPoint.

You will modify the title master of the Clouds design and then you will rename it Sky.

3

- **Select the title placeholder and change the font color to dark gold and 48 pt.**
- **Move the title placeholder to the position shown in Figure 3.12.**
- **Select the subtitle placeholder and size and position it as in Figure 3.12.**
- **Right-align the subtitle text.**
- **Click Rename Master.**
- **Replace the existing name with Sky and click Rename.**
- **Point to the Sky thumbnail in the Slide Design task pane.**

Your screen should be similar to Figure 3.12

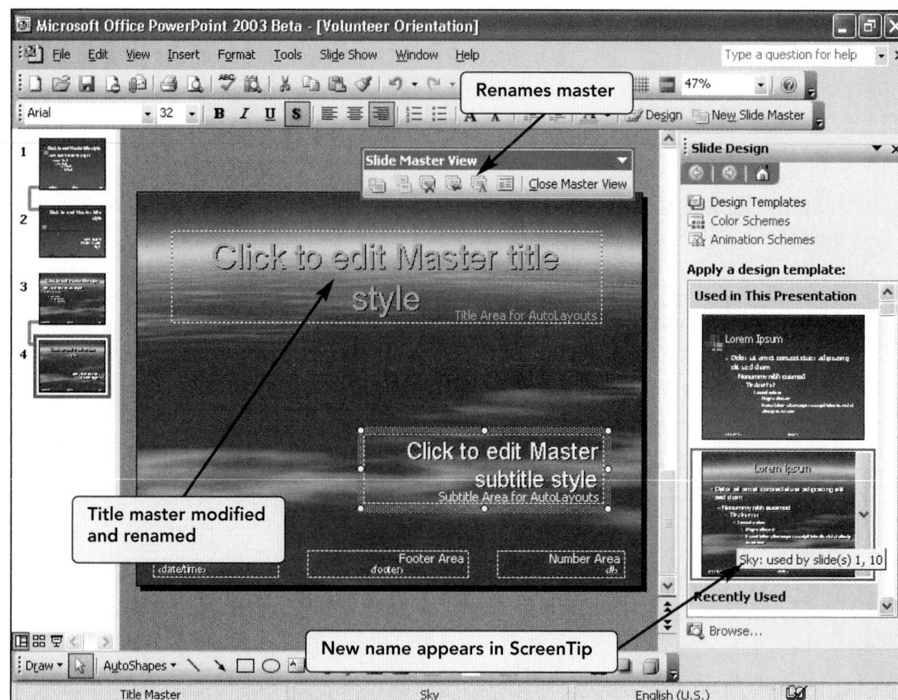

Figure 3.12

The new name appears in the ScreenTip.

4

- **Close Slide Master view.**
- **If necessary, reapply the slide layout.**

Having Trouble?

Use Format/Slide Layout and select Reapply Layout from the Title Slide layout shortcut menu.

- **Close the task pane and change to Slide Sorter view.**

Your screen should be similar to Figure 3.13

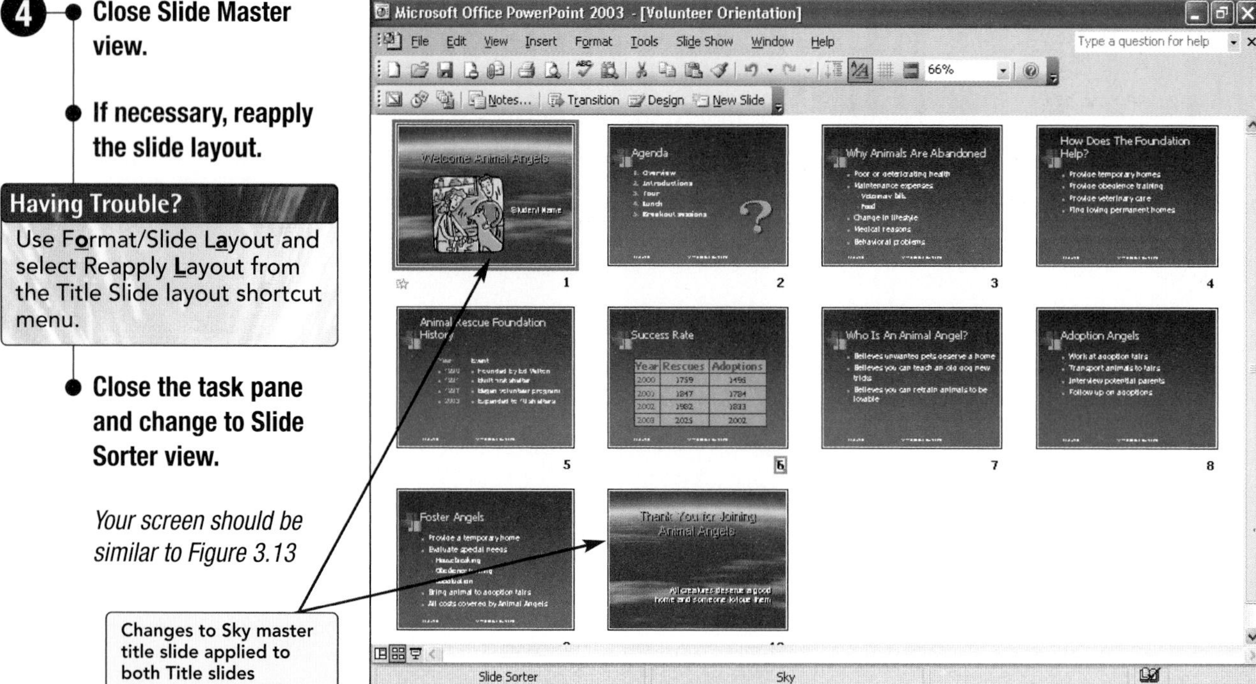

Figure 3.13

The changes you made to the master title slide are displayed in the two title slides in the presentation. In order to make changes throughout your presentation, you must make design changes to both pairs of masters.

Adding a Picture Background

Finally, you decide to use a different slide background for the last slide in the presentation. You will use a picture of a sunrise in place of the clouds.

1

- **Display slide 10 in Normal view.**
- **Choose Format/Background**
- **Select Fill Effects from the Background Fill color drop-down list.**
- **Open the Picture tab.**
- **Click Select Picture... .**
- **Change the location to the location of your data files and select** pp03_Sunrise**.**
- **Click Insert .**
- **Click OK .**
- **Select Omit background graphics from master.**
- **Click Apply .**
- **Change to Slide Sorter view.**
- **Save the presentation.**

Your screen should be similar to Figure 3.14

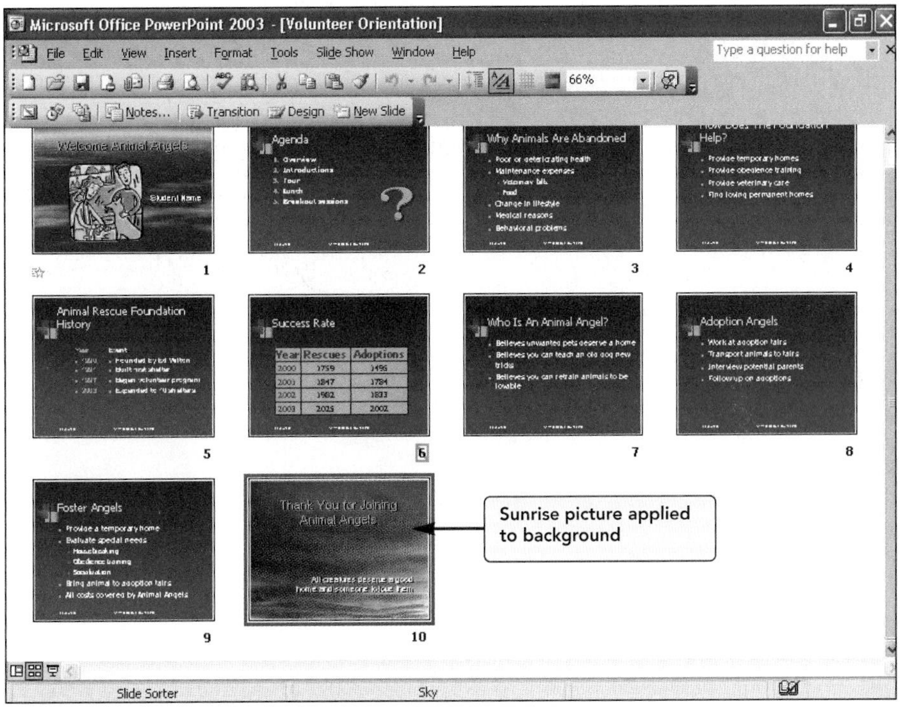

Sunrise picture applied to background

Figure 3.14

The sunrise background has been applied to the selected slide only.

Customizing Graphics

You want to replace the question mark clip art on the Agenda slide with a graphic of a cat and a dog. You were unable to find a graphic of a cat and dog together that you liked, so you decide to create a custom graphic from two separate graphics. You will do this by opening and modifying the graphics individually, then grouping them into one object.

Concept 1

Group

1 A **group** is two or more objects that are treated as a single object. Many clip art pictures are composed of several different elements that are grouped together. This allows you to easily move, resize, flip, or rotate all pieces of the group as a single unit. Features or **attributes**, such as line or fill color, associated with all objects in the group can also be changed at one time.

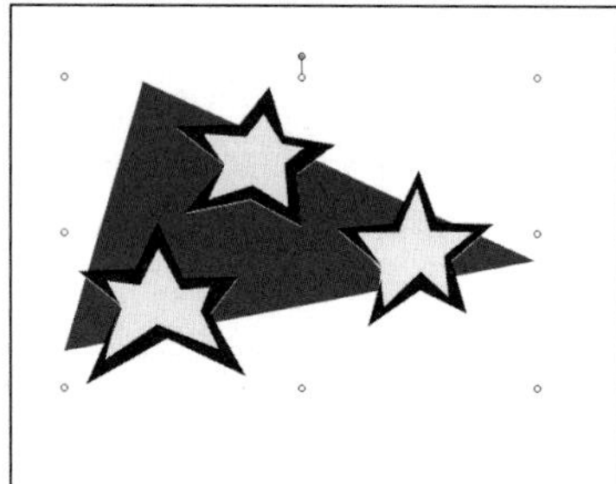

Grouped

Ungrouped

Sometimes you may want to ungroup the parts of an object so that the individual parts can be manipulated independently. Other times you may want to combine several objects to create your own graphic object that better suits your needs.

First you need to delete the existing clip art and placeholder. Then you will insert, position, and modify the new picture.

1

- **Display slide 2 in Normal view.**
- **Delete the question mark graphic and the clip art placeholder.**
- **Insert the graphic file** pp03_Cat **from your data file location.**
- **Move it to the right of the numbered list.**

Your screen should be similar to Figure 3.15

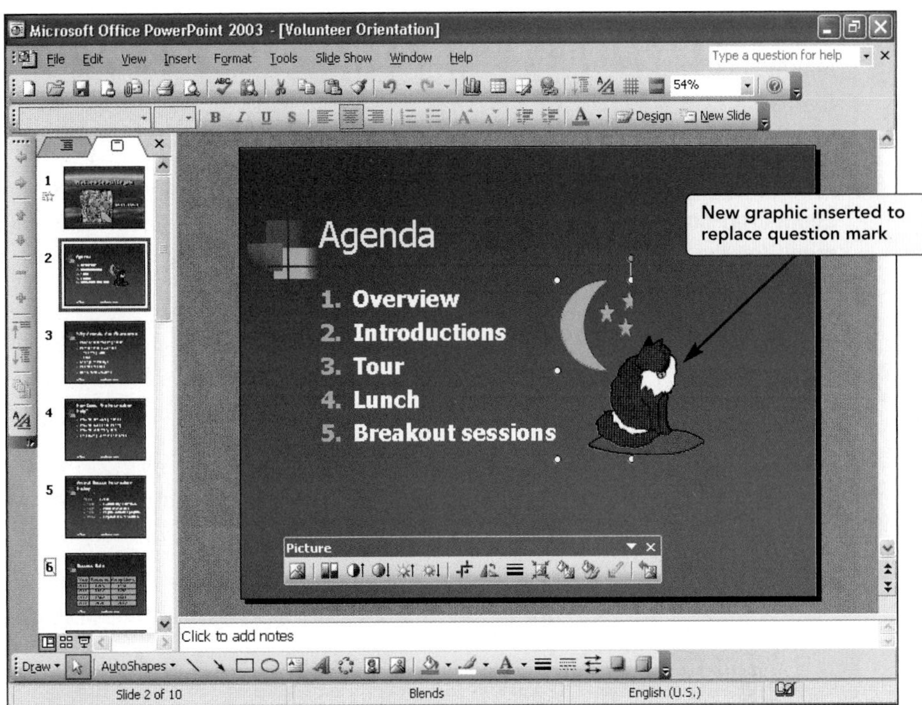

Figure 3.15

The cat graphic is made up of several elements grouped together.

Zooming the Slide

To make complex graphics easier to work with, you can turn off the display of panes and increase the magnification of the slide. In Normal view the slide is sized by default to fit within the pane and is about 60 percent of full (100 percent) size. You can increase the onscreen display size up to four times normal display (400 percent) or reduce the size to 33 percent. Changing the Zoom percentage only affects the onscreen display of the slide; it does not change the actual font or object sizes.

1 **Close the tabs pane and the Outlining toolbar.**

Open the 55% Zoom drop-down menu (on the Standard toolbar) and choose 100%.

Another Method

The menu equivalent is View/Zoom.

Your screen should be similar to Figure 3.16

Figure 3.16

The slide display is increased to 100 percent, and the entire slide is now too large to fully display in the window. The graphic is much larger, and as you make changes to the graphic, you will be able to more easily select different parts of the object.

You want to modify the graphic first by changing the color of the pillow below the cat. You can customize graphics by adding and deleting pieces of the graphic, changing the fill and line colors, and otherwise editing the graphic using features on the Drawing toolbar. However, to do this, the graphic must be a drawing object.

Converting Graphics to Drawing Objects

Because this is an imported graphic (it was not originally created within PowerPoint using the Drawing features), it first needs to be converted to a drawing object that can be manipulated using features included within PowerPoint.

1. **Click anywhere outside the graphic to deselect all the elements.**

- **Click on the moon to select the object.**
- **Press Delete.**
- **In the same manner, delete the stars.**

> **Additional Information**
> Select multiple objects by holding down Ctrl while clicking on each object.

Your screen should be similar to Figure 3.20

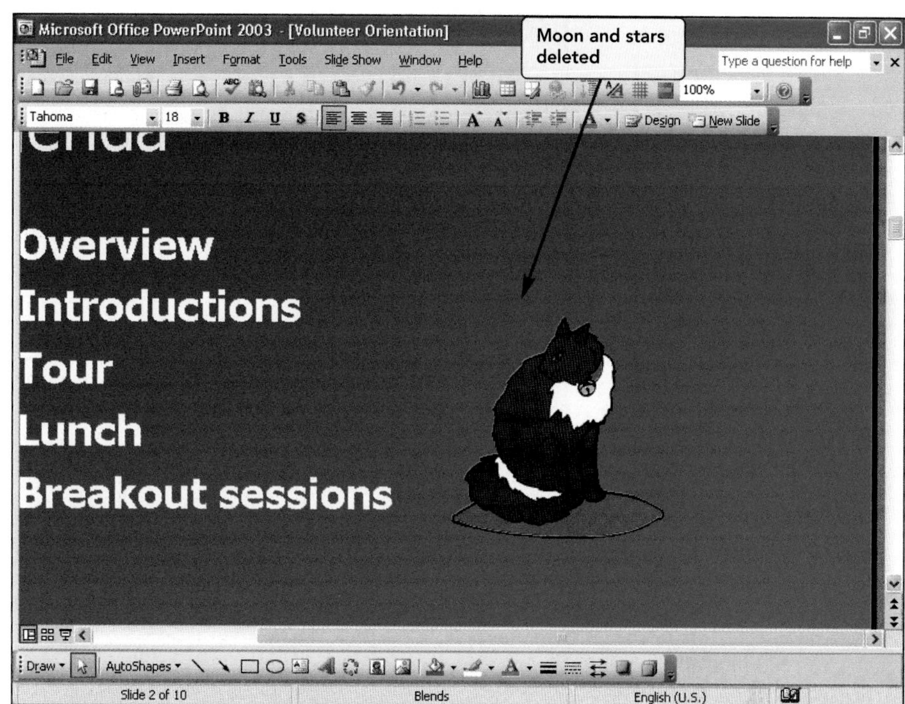

> **Additional Information**
> The graphic was made by starting with a black outline of the entire image filled with black, and then overlaying colored pieces to construct the cat. Because of this construction, certain areas of the graphic cannot be deleted.

> **Additional Information**
> The graphic does not need to be ungrouped to select and modify separate parts using features on the Drawing toolbar.

The moon and stars are deleted.

Regrouping Objects

You think the graphic looks a lot better now. Next you will add a graphic of a dog to the slide and combine it with the cat graphic. You will regroup the parts of the cat graphic again and then insert the picture of the dog.

1

- **Click near the cat to select the entire cat graphic.**
- **Choose Grouping/ Regroup from the shortcut menu.**

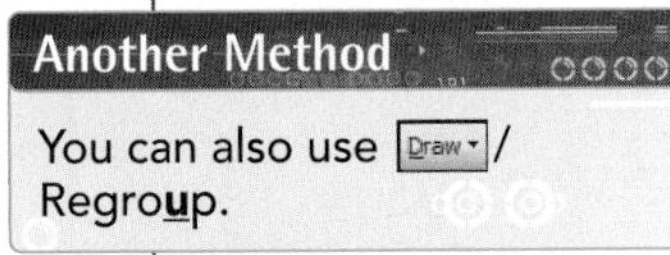

Another Method

You can also use Draw/ Regroup.

- **Open the Zoom drop-down menu and choose Fit.**
- **Insert the picture** pp03_Dog **from your data file location.**
- **Move and size the object as in Figure 3.21.**

Your screen should be similar to Figure 3.21

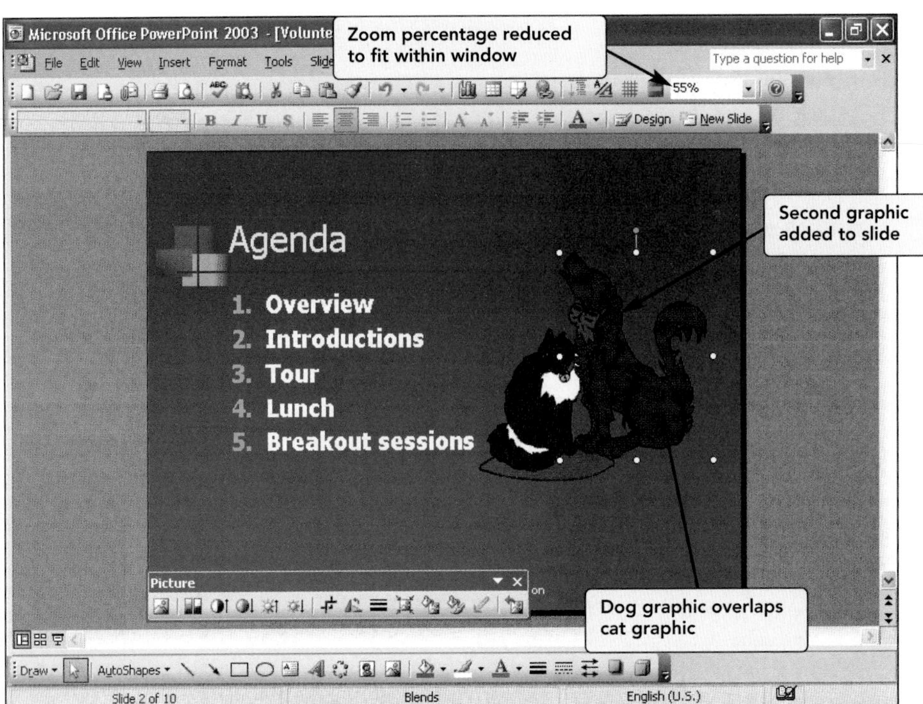

Figure 3.21

Did you notice when you moved the cat object, that all the objects in the group were identified and moved as a group? In contrast, when you moved and sized the dog object, because it has not been converted to a drawing object yet, separate parts were not identified as it was manipulated.

Changing the Stacking Order

Notice the dog graphic overlaps the cat graphic. This is because as each new object is added to a slide, it is added to a separate drawing layer that stacks on top of the previous layer.

Now you want to see if the graphic would look better if the dog object were behind the cat. To change the order of these two objects, you will send the dog object to the back of the stack.

1

- **If necessary, select the dog graphic.**
- **Click Draw and choose Order/Send to Back.**
- **Size and position the graphics as in Figure 3.22.**

Additional Information

The Bring Forward and Send Backward options move the objects forward or backward in the stack one layer at a time.

Your screen should be similar to Figure 3.22

Figure 3.22

The dog is now behind the cat.

Aligning Objects

Next you want to align the dog and cat so that the bottoms of the graphics are even. Although you can position objects on your slides visually by dragging to the approximate location, you can make your slides appear more professional by using tools in PowerPoint to precisely align and position objects.

Concept 2

Object Alignment

2 **Object alignment** refers to the position of objects relative to each other by their left, right, top, or bottom edges; or horizontally by their centers or vertically by their middles; or in relation to the entire slide.

There are several methods for aligning objects. You can align objects to a **grid**, a set of intersecting lines that form small squares on the slide. The grid is not displayed by default, but whenever you move, resize, or draw an object, the object's corners automatically "snap" to the nearest intersection of the grid. You can display the grid to help align objects more accurately. You can also snap an object to other shapes so that new objects align themselves with the pre-existing shapes. The grid lines run through the vertical and horizontal edges of other shapes, and the new shape aligns with the closest intersection of that grid.

Another way to align an object is to use a guide. A **guide** is a line, either vertical or horizontal, that you position on the slide. When an object is close to the guide, the object's center or corner (whichever is closer) snaps to the guide.

A third way to align objects is to other objects. For example, you can align the centers or the left edges of two objects. Using this method allows you to precisely align the edges or tops of selected shapes. At least two objects must be selected to align them.

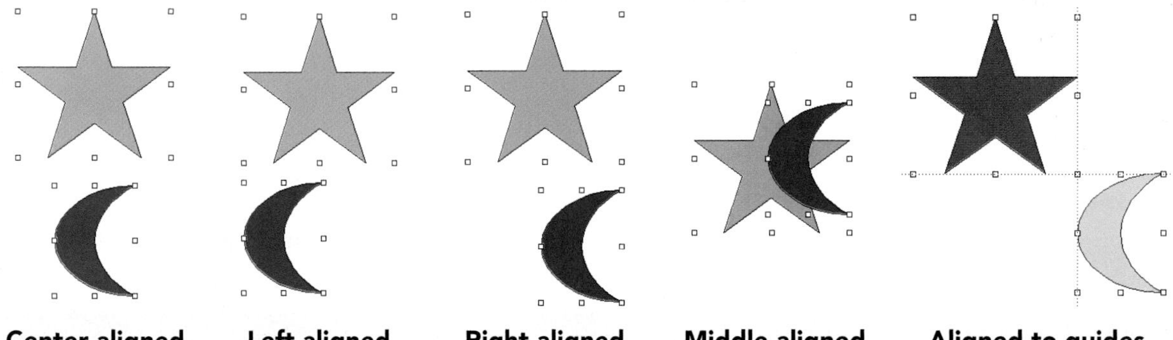

Center aligned **Left aligned** **Right aligned** **Middle aligned** **Aligned to guides**

Objects can also be aligned relative to the slide as a whole, such as to the top or side of a slide. Objects can further be arranged or distributed so that they are an equal distance from each other vertically, horizontally, or in relation to the entire slide. You must have at least three objects selected to distribute them.

You will display the slide gridlines and then evenly position the bottoms of the two graphics.

1 • **Click Show/Hide Grid.**

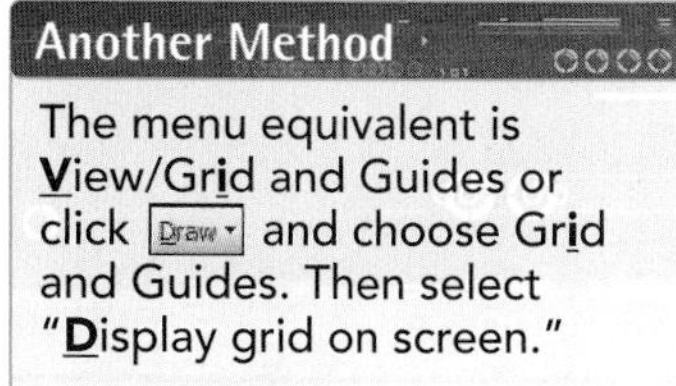

Another Method

The menu equivalent is View/Grid and Guides or click Draw and choose Grid and Guides. Then select "Display grid on screen."

Your screen should be similar to Figure 3.23

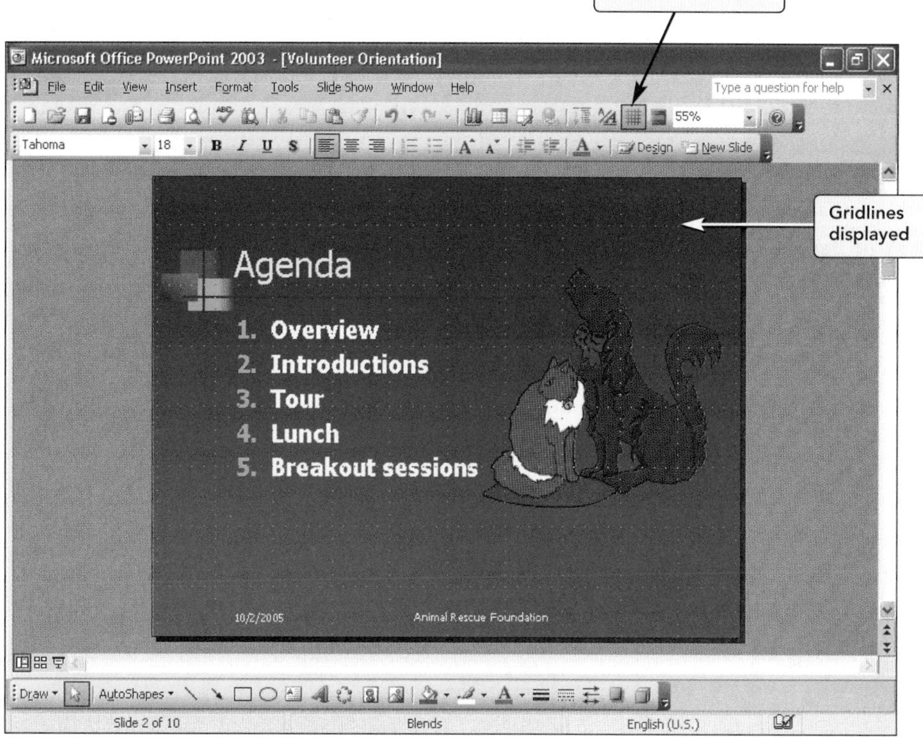

Figure 3.23

All slides in the presentation display a grid consisting of a crosshatch pattern of lines. Now you can easily align the bottom of the graphics.

2 • **Align both graphics evenly with the horizontal gridline that runs below the fifth bulleted item.**

• **Position the dog graphic just to the right of the cat and bring it to the front of the cat.**

Additional Information

To override the snap-to settings, hold down Alt as you drag an object.

Your screen should be similar to Figure 3.24

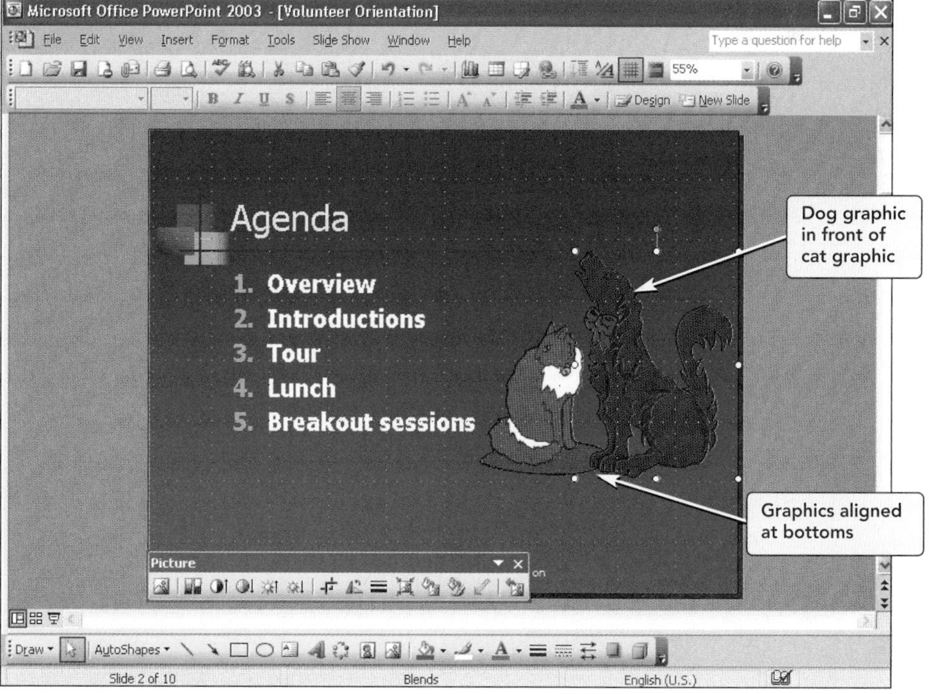

Figure 3.24

As you moved the objects, they automatically snapped to the nearest grid-line when you released the mouse button.

Grouping Objects

Now you want to combine the two graphics into one by grouping them, and then you will size them appropriately on the slide.

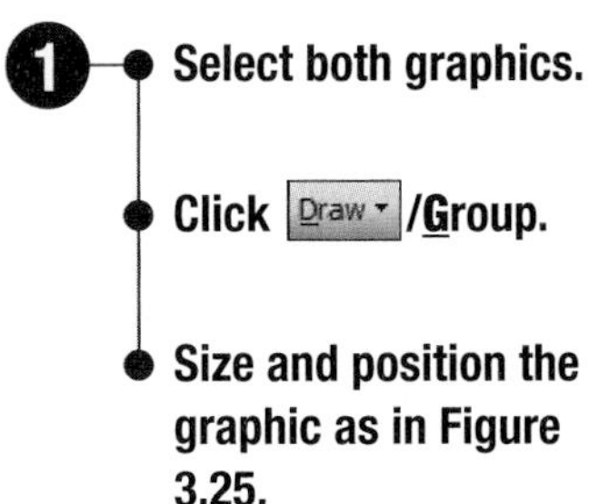

Your screen should be similar to Figure 3.25

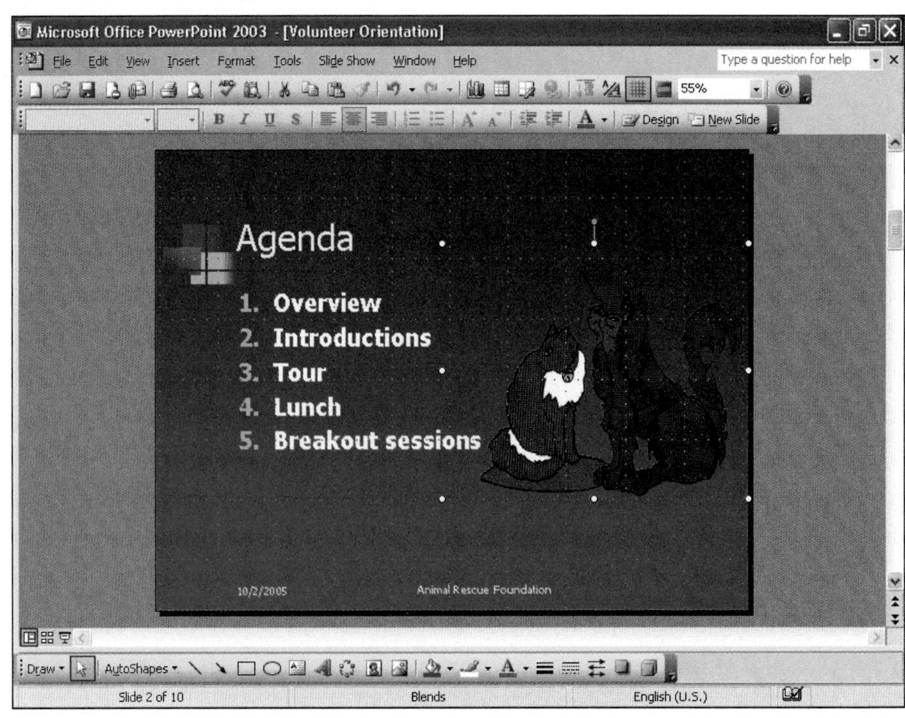

Figure 3.25

Additional Information

To select an object within a grouped object, select the group first, then click on the object you want to select.

Because the objects are grouped, they size and move as a single object. You could also change features associated with all objects in the group at once, such as changing the fill or line color of all objects. Even when objects are grouped, you can still select an object within a group and modify it individually without ungrouping the object.

Wrapping Text in an Object

Below the graphic, you decide to add a banner that welcomes the volunteers.

1 Create a Curved Down Ribbon AutoShape banner below the graphic as shown in Figure 3.26.

- Change the fill color to gold.
- Right-click on the object and choose Add Text from the shortcut menu.
- Type **We're Glad You're Here!**.
- Change the font color to the same color as the pillow and apply bold.
- Click outside the AutoShape to turn off text editing.

Your screen should be similar to Figure 3.26

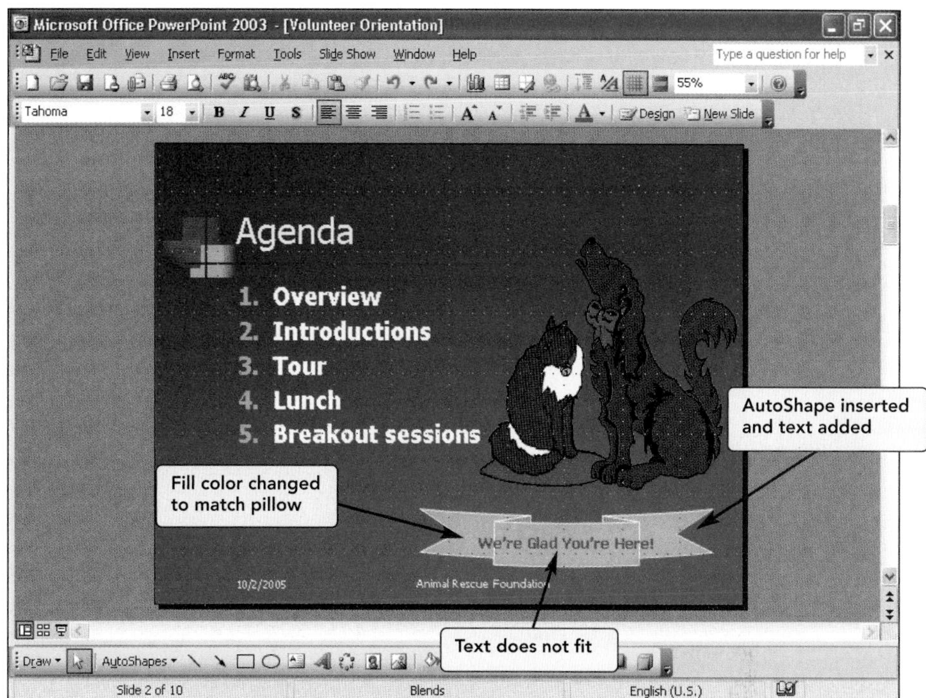

Figure 3.26

Notice that the text does not fit inside the center of the graphic. Although you could manually increase the size of the banner to fit the text, you would rather wrap the text in the AutoShape and then resize the banner to fit the text.

2 • **Choose Format AutoShape from the object's shortcut menu.**

Another Method

The menu equivalent is Format/AutoShape.

- **Open the Text Box tab.**
- **Select Word wrap text in AutoShape.**
- **Select Resize AutoShape to fit text.**
- **Click OK.**
- **Size, position, and rotate the AutoShape as shown in Figure 3.27.**
- **Move the AutoShape behind the animal graphic object.**

Your screen should be similar to Figure 3.27

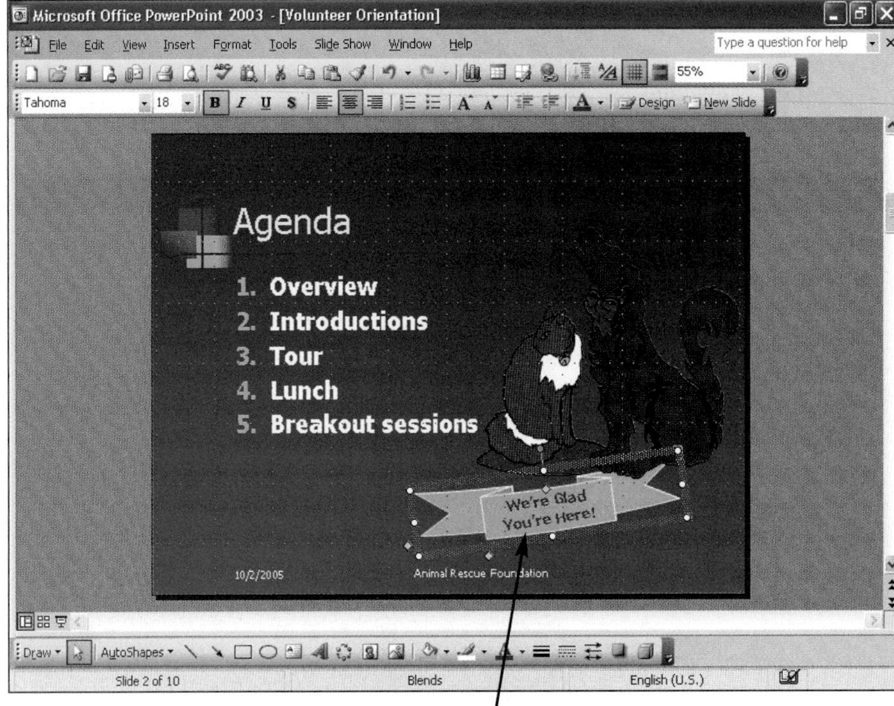

Figure 3.27

The text wraps to a second line and the size of the AutoShape has adjusted to fully display the two lines of text.

Centering Objects

Next you want to center the banner below the graphic. You will align the centers of the two objects and then group them into one object.

1

- **Select both the banner and the animal graphic.**
- **Click Draw and choose Align or Distribute/Align Center.**

Having Trouble?

Make sure the Relative to Slide option is not selected. If it is, using Align Center will align the object with the center of the slide, not the other object.

- **Group the two objects together.**
- **Position the grouped object as in figure 3.28.**
- **Click on the slide to deselect the grouped object.**
- **Click [gridlines button] to turn off the display of gridlines.**
- **Save the presentation.**

Your screen should be similar to Figure 3.28

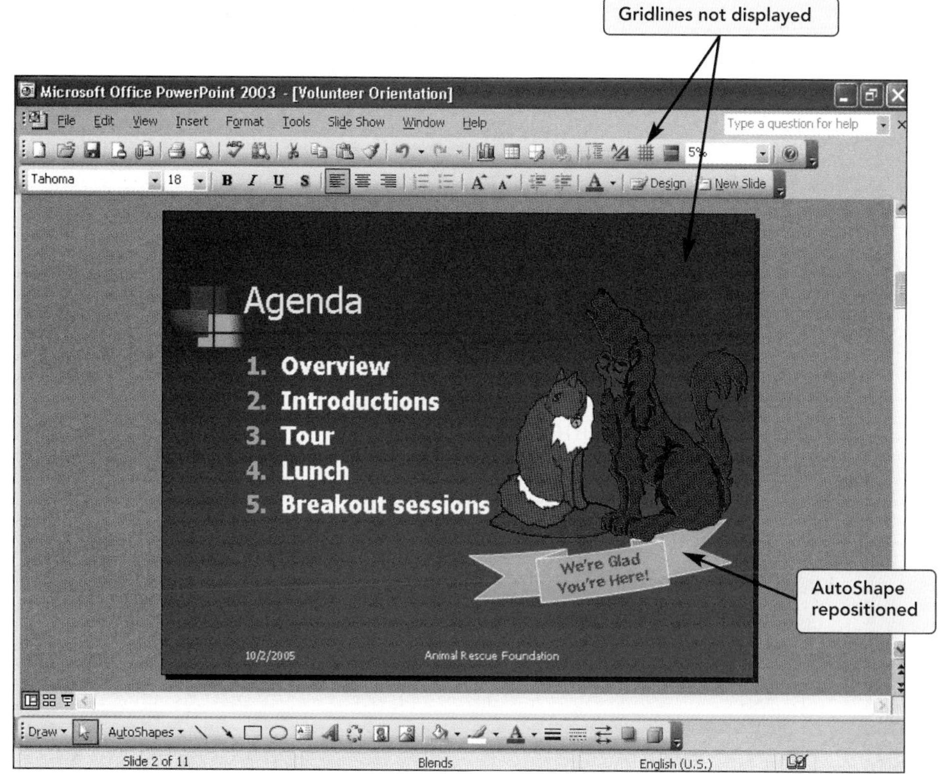

Figure 3.28

Creating a Chart Slide

The next change you want to make is to show the adoption success rate data in slide 5 as a chart rather than a table.

Concept 3

Chart

3 A **chart**, also called a **graph**, is a visual representation of numeric data. When you are presenting data to an audience, they will grasp the impact of your data more quickly if you present it as a chart. PowerPoint 2003 includes a separate program, Microsoft Graph, designed to help you create 14 types of charts with many different formats for each type.

Each type of chart represents the data differently and has a different purpose. It is important to select the type of chart that will provide the right emphasis to support your presentations. The basic chart types are described below.

Type of Chart	Description
Area	Shows the relative importance of a value over time by emphasizing the area under the curve created by each data series.
Bar	Displays categories vertically and values horizontally, placing more emphasis on comparisons and less on time. Stacked-bar charts show the relationship of individual items to a whole by stacking bars on top of one another.
Column	Similar to a bar chart, except categories are organized horizontally and values vertically. Shows data changes over time or comparison among items.
Line	Shows changes in data over time, emphasizing time and rate of change rather than the amount of change.
Pie	Shows the relationship of each value in a data series to the series as a whole. Each slice of the pie represents a single value in a data series.

Most charts are made up of several basic parts as identified and described below.

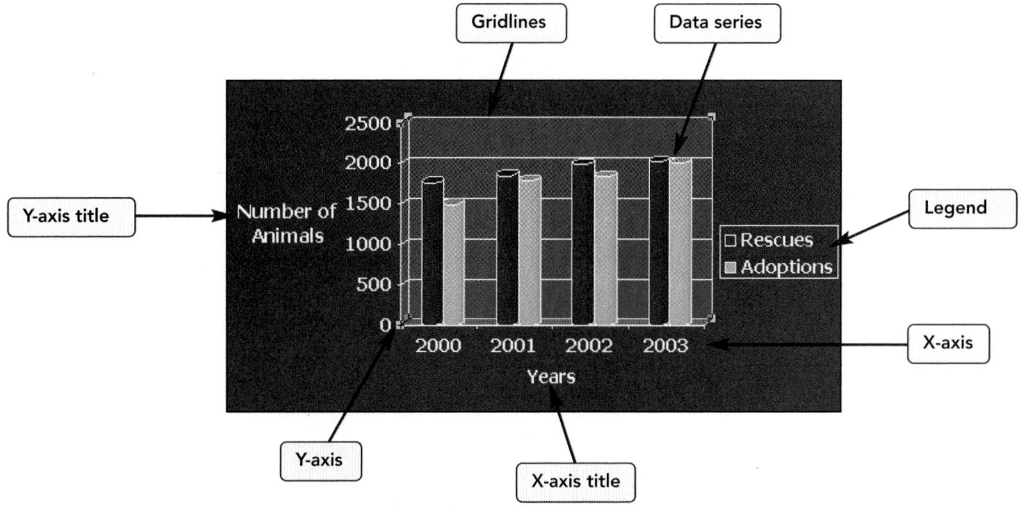

Part	Description
X axis	The bottom boundary of the chart, also called the **category axis**, is used to label the data being charted; the label may be, for example, a point in time or a category.
Y axis	The left boundary of the chart, also called the **value axis**, is a numbered scale whose numbers are determined by the data used in the chart. Each line or bar in a chart represents a data value. In pie charts there are no axes. Instead, the data that is charted is displayed as slices in a circle or pie.
Data Series	Each group of related data that is plotted in a chart.
Legend	A box containing a brief description identifying the patterns or colors assigned to the data series in a chart.
Titles	Descriptive text used to explain the contents of the chart.

You will create the chart in a new slide following the slide containing the table of data on success rates. PowerPoint includes a special slide layout for charts which contains a placeholder that opens the Graph application.

1 Switch to Slide Sorter view.

- Insert a new slide in Title and Chart slide layout after slide 6.

Another Method

You can also use Insert/Chart or click to add a chart object to a slide.

- Double-click on slide 7.
- Choose View/Normal (Restore Panes).
- If necessary, display the Slides tab.

Your screen should be similar to Figure 3.29

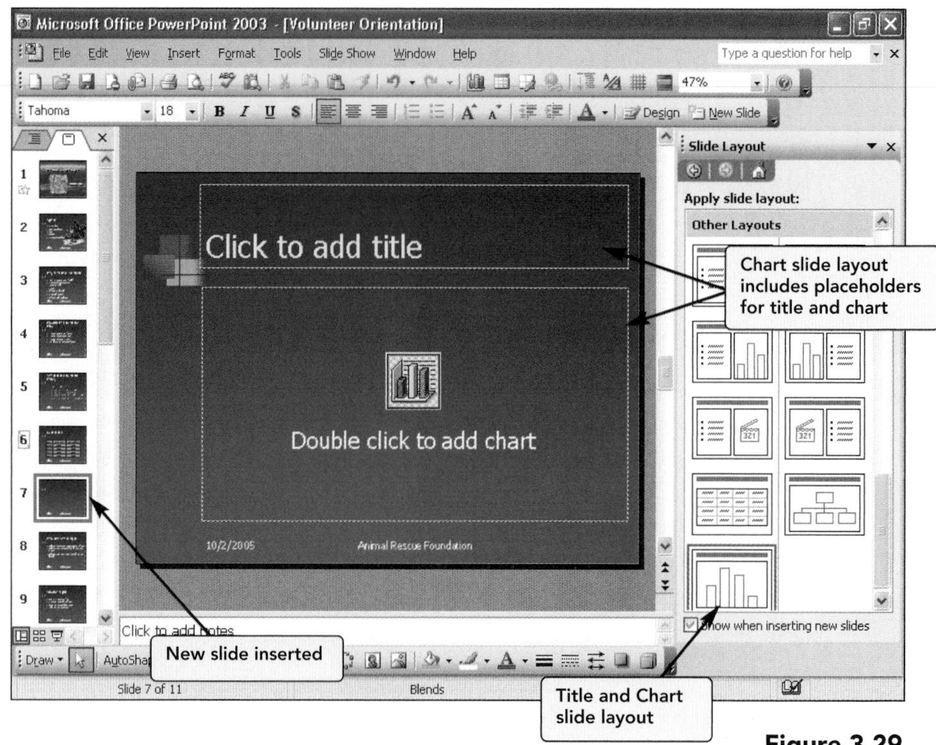

Figure 3.29

Copying Data to the Office Clipboard

The chart slide layout includes a placeholder for the title and another placeholder for the chart. When you double-click on the chart placeholder, the Microsoft Graph application will open and you will be asked to enter the data you want to chart. Because this data is already contained in the table in slide 6, you will copy the data from the table into the chart. You will also copy the title text from slide 6 into the chart slide. You could copy and paste the selections one after the other, or you can use the Office Clipboard to collect multiple items and paste them as needed.

Concept 4

Collect and Paste

4 The **collect and paste** feature is used to store multiple copied items in the Office Clipboard and then paste one or more of the items into another location or document. For example, you could copy a chart from Excel and a paragraph from Word, then switch to PowerPoint and copy the two stored items into a slide in one easy step. This saves you from having to switch back and forth between documents and applications multiple times.

The Office Clipboard and the system Clipboard are similar, but separate, features. The major difference is that the Office Clipboard can hold up to 24 items, whereas the system Clipboard holds only a single item. The last item you copy to the Office Clipboard is always copied to the system Clipboard. When you use the Office Clipboard, you can select from the stored items to paste in any order.

The Office Clipboard is available in all Office 2003 applications, and is accessed through the Clipboard task pane. Once the Clipboard task pane is opened, it is available for use in any program, including non-Office programs. In some programs where the Cut, Copy, and Paste commands are not available, or in non-Office programs, the Clipboard task pane is not visible but it is still operational. You can copy from any program that provides copy and cut capabilities, but you can only paste into Word, Excel, Access, PowerPoint, and Outlook.

First you will copy the slide title text from slide 6 to the Office Clipboard.

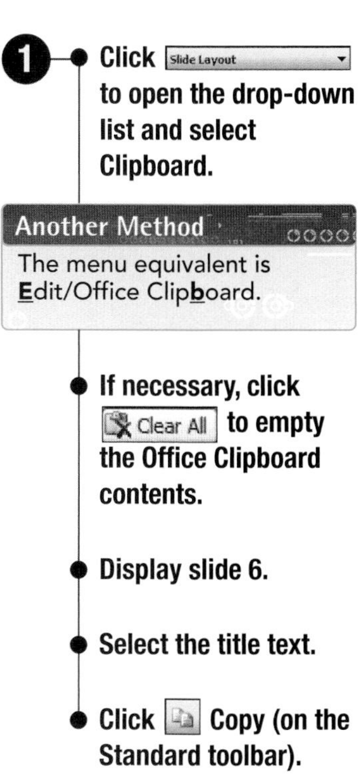

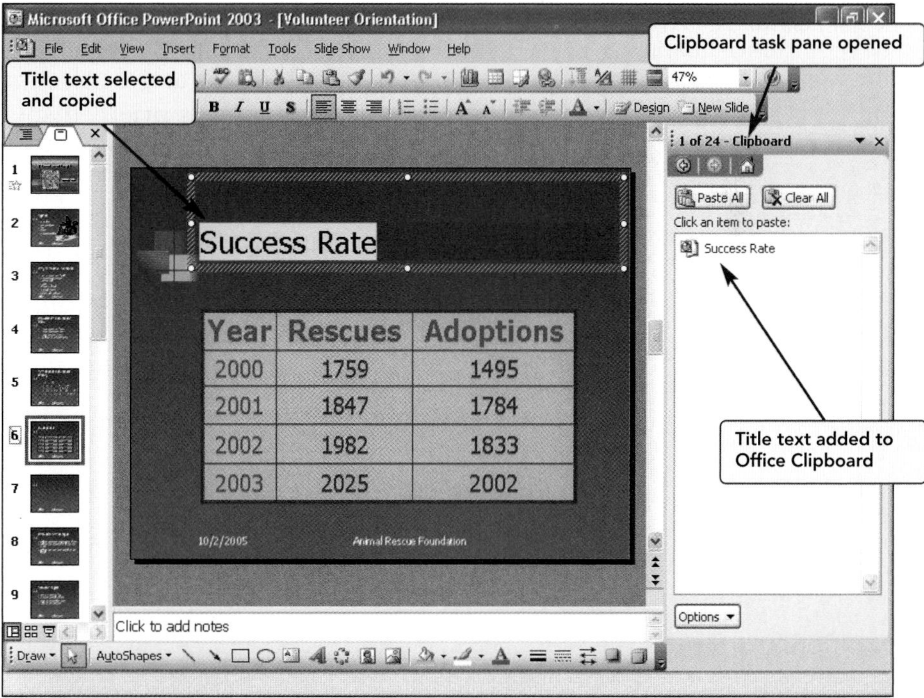

Figure 3.30

The Clipboard task pane displays a PowerPoint icon representing the copied item and the first few lines of the copied selection. Next you will copy the contents of the table into the Office Clipboard. As items are copied, they are added sequentially to the Office Clipboard with the last copied item at the top of the list.

2 **Drag to select the entire contents of the table.**

Click Copy.

Your screen should be similar to Figure 3.31

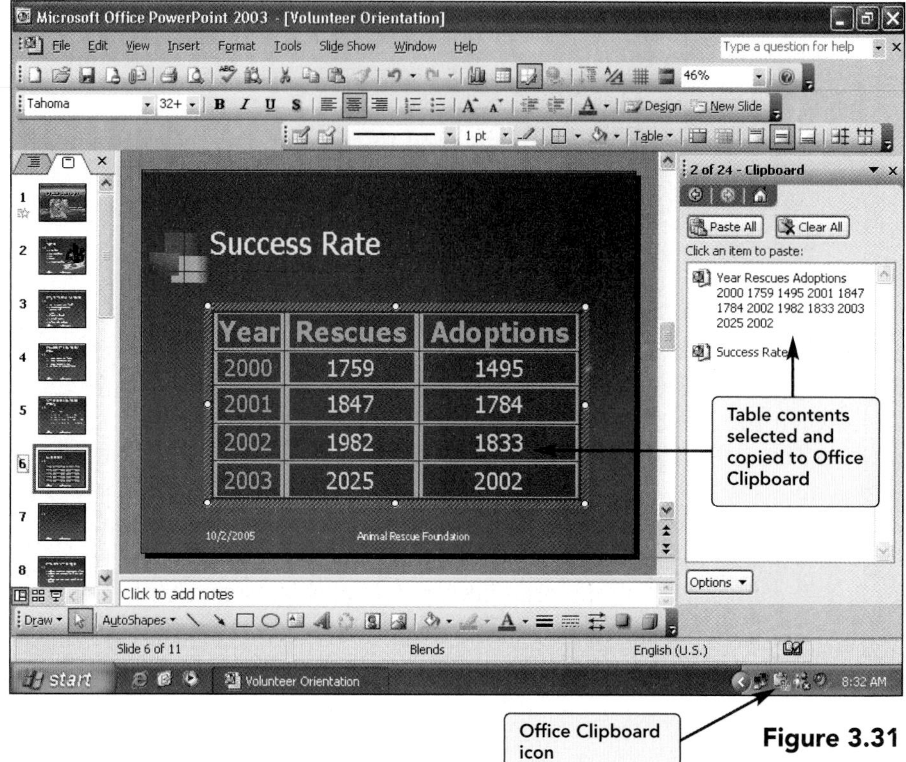

Figure 3.31

Additional Information

The Office Clipboard is automatically activated if you copy or cut two different items consecutively in the same program; if you copy one item, paste the item and then copy another item in the same program; or if you copy one item twice in succession.

The Office Clipboard now contains two PowerPoint document icons, one for each copied item. The Office Clipboard icon appears in the taskbar to show that the Clipboard is active. Also, as the selection is copied, the taskbar briefly displays a ScreenTip indicating that 1 out of a possible 24 items was collected.

1 of 24 - Clipboard
Item collected.

Specifying the Chart Data

Now you are ready to start the Microsoft Graph application and use the table data to create the chart.

1

- **Display slide 7.**
- **Close the Tabs pane.**
- **Double-click [icon] in the placeholder.**
- **If necessary, display the toolbar on two rows.**

Your screen should be similar to Figure 3.32

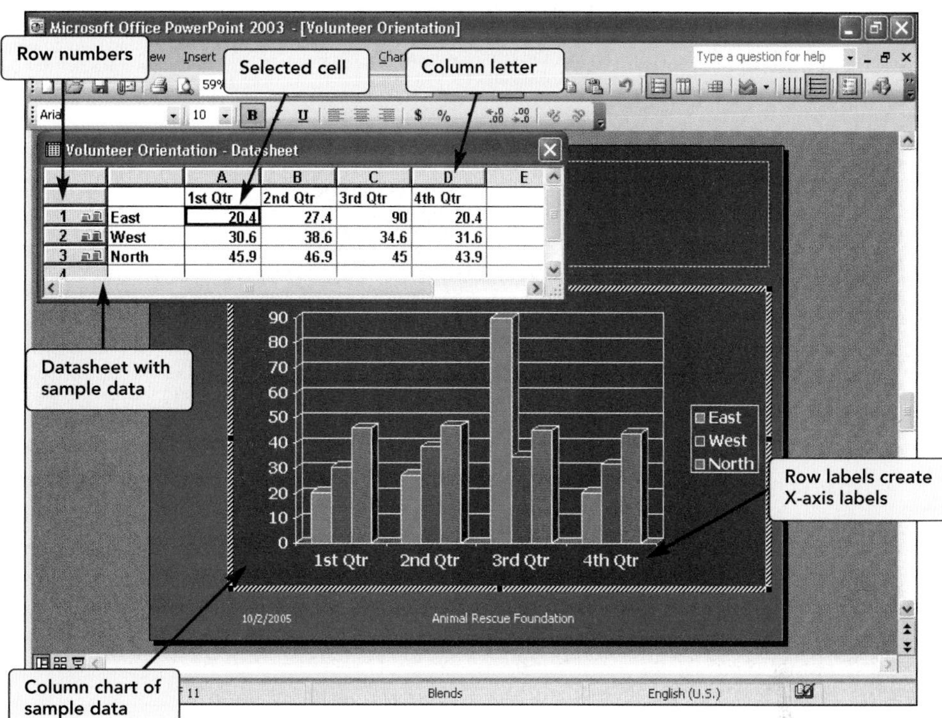

		A	B	C	D	E
		1st Qtr	2nd Qtr	3rd Qtr	4th Qtr	
1	East	20.4	27.4	90	20.4	
2	West	30.6	38.6	34.6	31.6	
3	North	45.9	46.9	45	43.9	

Figure 3.32

The Microsoft Graph program is activated and a column chart using the sample data from the datasheet is displayed in the slide. In addition, a datasheet containing sample data is displayed in the Datasheet window. A **datasheet** is a table consisting of rows and columns. As in a table, the intersection of a row and column creates a cell in which text or data is entered. Notice that the datasheet displays the column letters A through E and row numbers 1 through 4. Each cell has a unique name consisting of a column letter followed by a row number. For example, cell A1 is the intersection of column A and row 1. The cell that is surrounded by the border is the selected cell and is the cell you can work in.

In addition to displaying sample data, the datasheet also contains placeholders for the column labels, which are used as the legend in the chart, and for the row labels, which are used as X-axis labels.

You need to replace the sample data in the datasheet with the data you copied from slide 6. Unfortunately, because the Graph application is running, the Clipboard task pane is not displayed. However, because the table data was the last item copied to the Clipboard, you can simply click [icon] Paste in the Standard toolbar to insert the last copied item from the system Clipboard into the datasheet.

2 • **Click in the gray cell in the top left corner of the Datasheet window to select the entire datasheet.**

• **Click Paste.**

• **Click OK in response to the advisory dialog box.**

Your screen should be similar to Figure 3.33

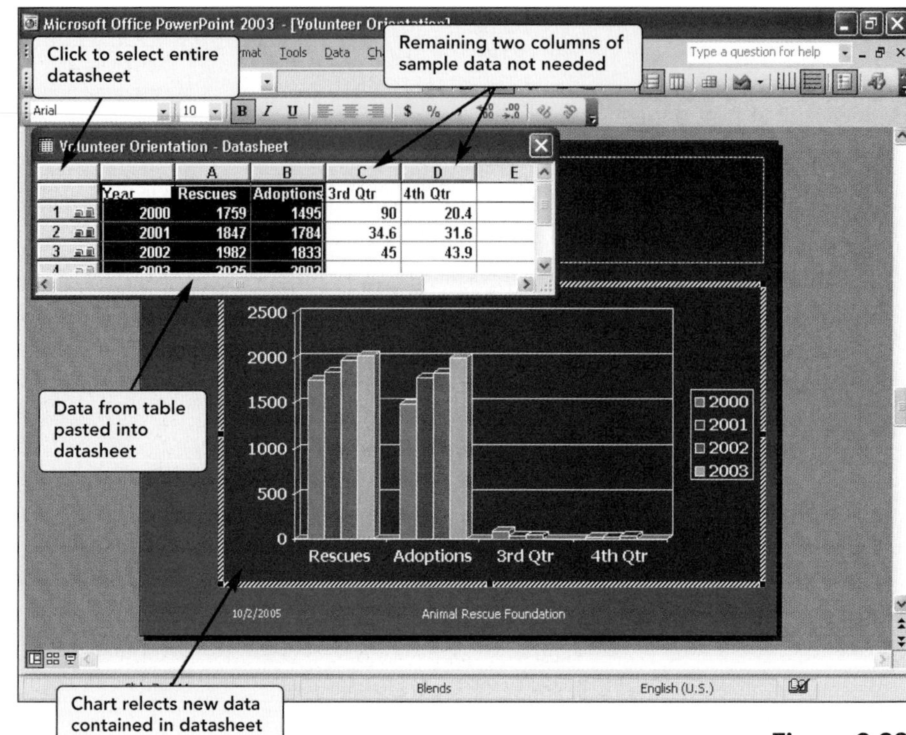

Figure 3.33

The datasheet is updated and displays the data from the table. The chart also reflects the change in data. Finally, you need to remove the remaining two columns of sample data.

3 • **Drag over the column letters C and D to select both columns.**

• **Press Delete.**

Your screen should be similar to Figure 3.34

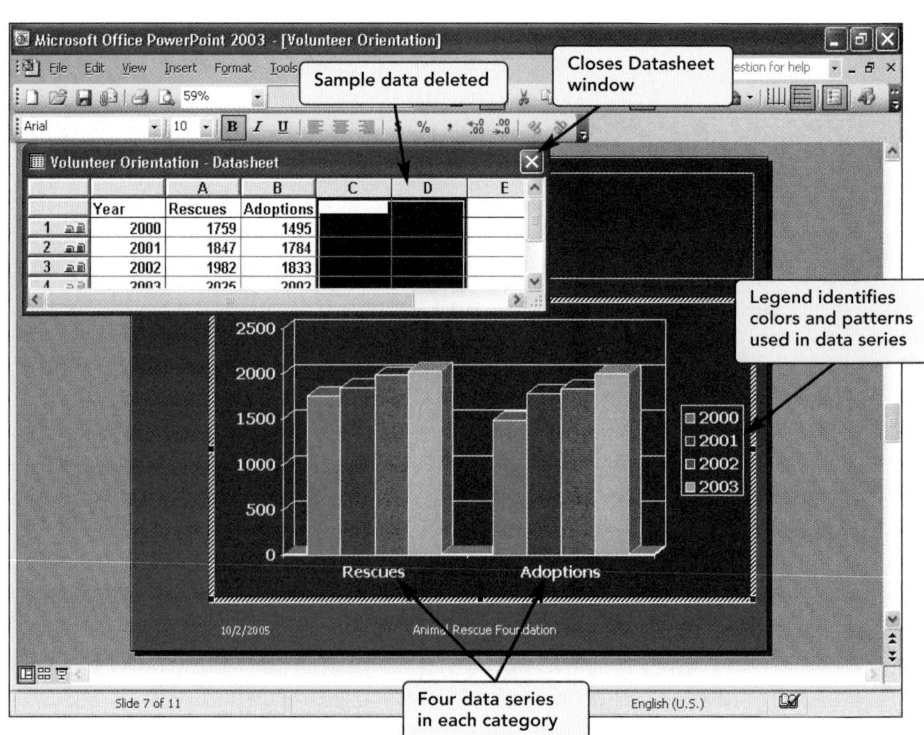

Figure 3.34

Each data series has a unique color or pattern assigned to it to identify the different series. The legend identifies the color or pattern associated with each data series. As you can see, the values and text in the chart are directly linked to the datasheet, and any changes you make in the datasheet are automatically reflected in the chart.

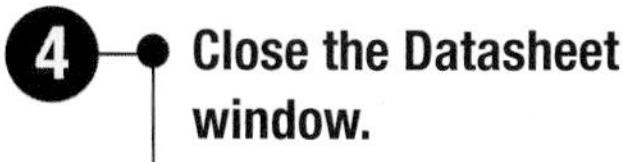

4 **Close the Datasheet window.**

Another Method

You can also click View Datasheet to hide and display the Datasheet window at any time.

- **Click on the slide outside the chart.**

Your screen should be similar to Figure 3.35

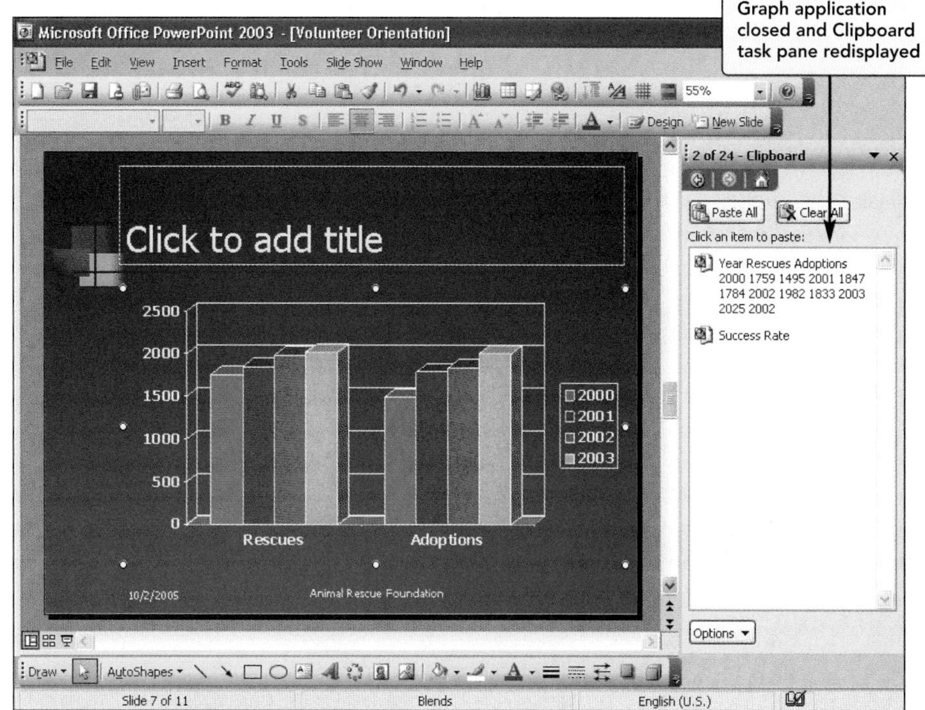

Figure 3.35

The Graph application is closed, and because the PowerPoint application is active again, the Office Clipboard task pane is displayed. Before modifying the chart, you will copy the title from the Office Clipboard into the slide.

5

- **Click in the chart title placeholder.**
- **Click on the Success Rate icon in the Clipboard task pane.**
- **Click Clear All to clear the contents of the Office Clipboard.**
- **Close the Clipboard task pane.**

Your screen should be similar to Figure 3.36

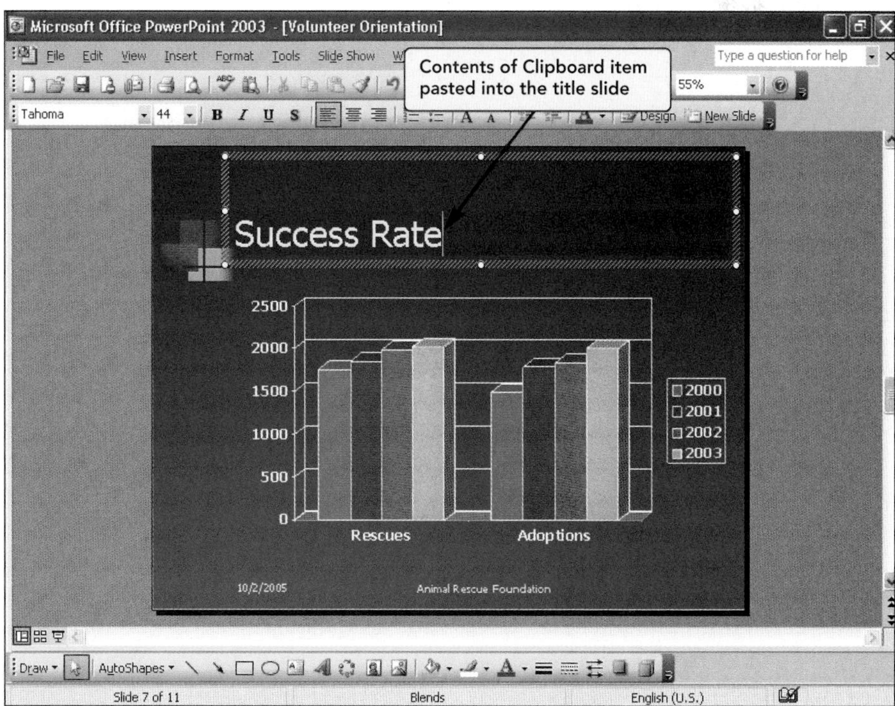

Figure 3.36

The contents of the first copied item are pasted from the Office Clipboard into the title of the slide.

Modifying Chart Data

As you look at the chart, you decide you want to change it so that the data is displayed based on the columns of data (years), not the rows of data (Rescue and Adoption categories), which is the default. To modify the chart, you need to activate the Graph application again. Then you can use the features on the Graph menu and toolbar to edit the chart.

1 **Double-click the chart object to open it for editing.**

Another Method

You can also use Chart Object/Edit from the chart objects shortcut menu.

Click By Column.

Another Method

The menu equivalent is Data/Series in Columns.

Your screen should be similar to Figure 3.37

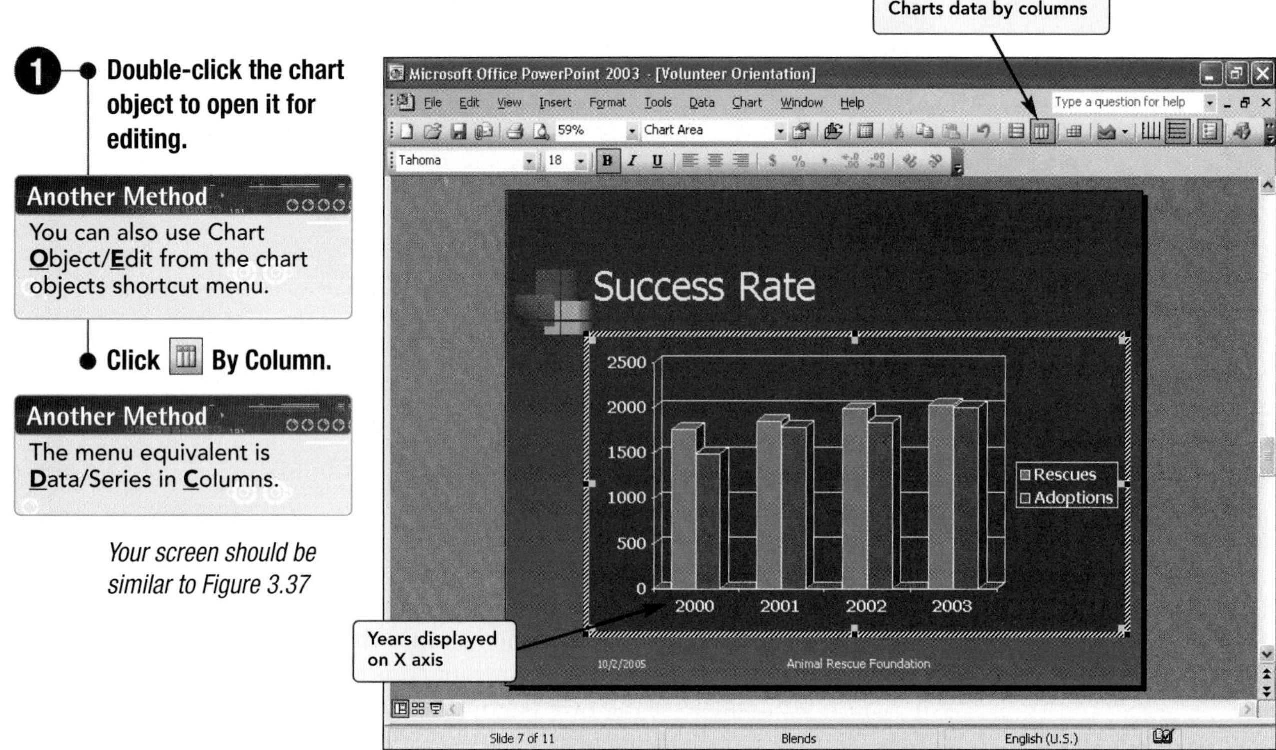

Figure 3.37

The years are now displayed along the X axis. The chart now shows the increasing success rate for adoptions and rescues over time more clearly.

Adding Axis Titles

Next you want to add labels along the axes to clarify the information in the chart.

1. **Choose Chart/Chart Options.**
   - **If necessary, open the Titles tab.**

Your screen should be similar to Figure 3.38

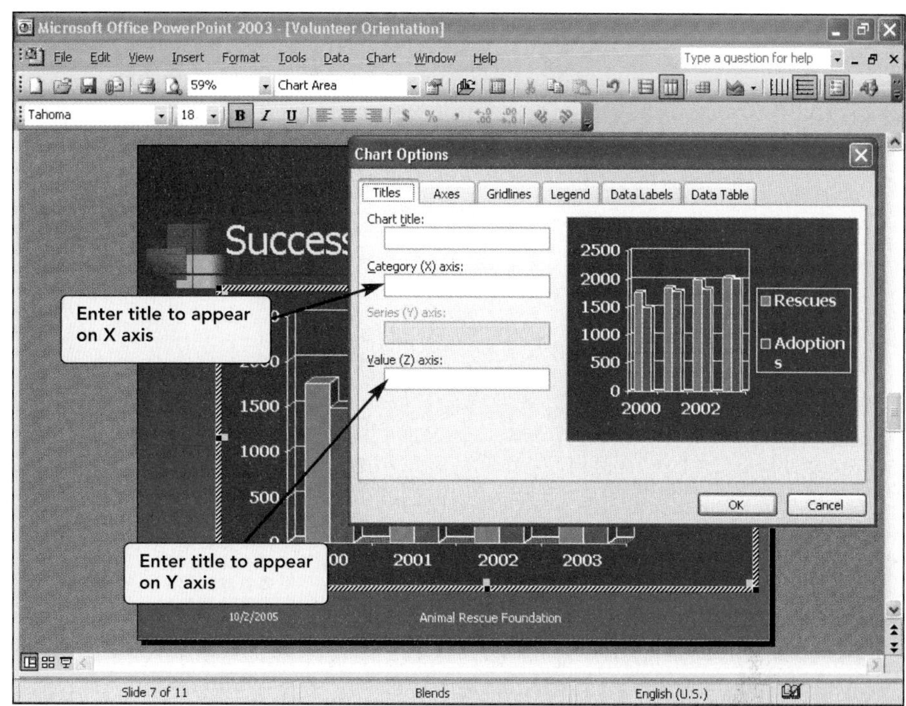

Figure 3.38

The Chart Options dialog box is used to add features to a chart, including titles, legends, and gridlines, that make it easier to understand the data in the chart. You will add titles along the two axis lines.

2. **Type Years in the Category (X) Axis text box.**
   - **Type Number of Animals in the Value (Z) Axis text box.**

Additional Information

Because this is a three-dimensional chart, a Z axis is used to display the values.

   - **Click OK.**

Your screen should be similar to Figure 3.39

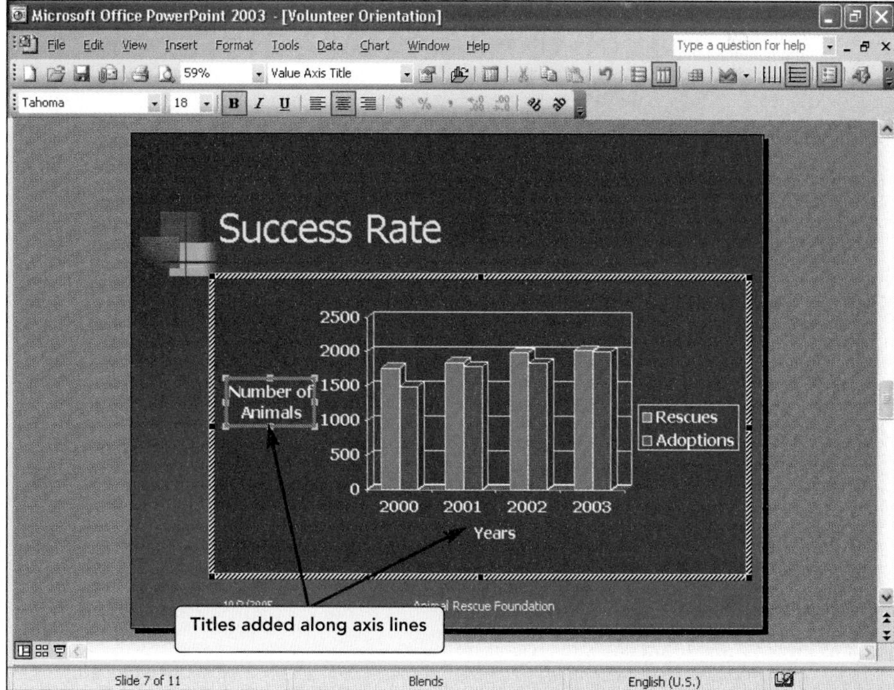

Figure 3.39

The labels you entered appear along the appropriate axes.

Changing Chart Formats

Next you want to change the color and appearance of the data series to give them more visual interest.

1 **Click on any one of the Adoptions (purple) columns to select all the columns for that data series.**

- **Click Format Data Series.**

Another Method

The menu equivalent is Format/Selected Data Series, and the keyboard equivalent is Ctrl + 1. You can also double-click the chart element or choose Format Data Series from the shortcut menu.

- **If necessary, open the Patterns tab.**

Your screen should be similar to Figure 3.40

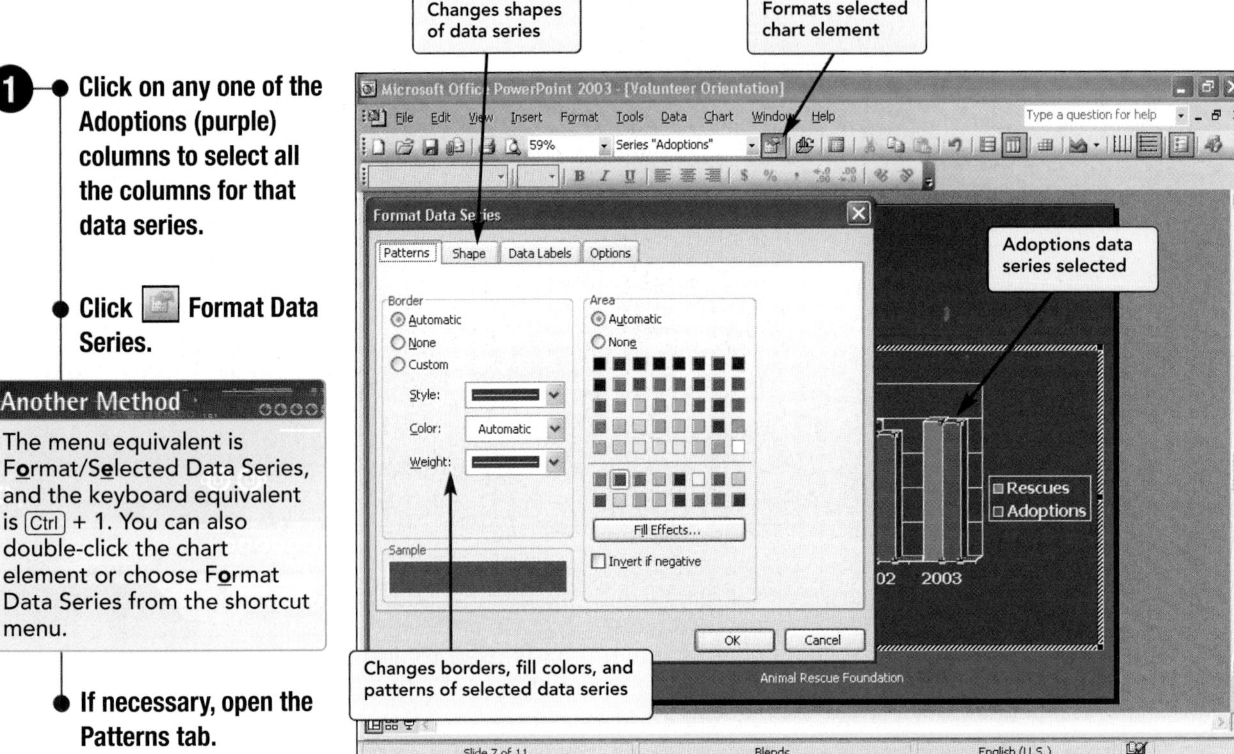

Figure 3.40

The Format Data Series dialog box is used to modify the appearance of the selected data series. The default chart colors are colors associated with the presentation design template. You want to change the color and shape of the bars. From the Patterns tab, you can select different borders and fill colors and patterns. The Shape tab is used to select different chart series shapes. You will change the color to gold and the shape to a cylinder.

2 From the Area color palette, select a dark gold color.

- Open the Shape tab.
- Select the cylinder shape, 4.
- Click OK.
- Deselect the data series.

Your screen should be similar to Figure 3.41

Additional Information

You can also change other elements of the chart, such as the background and text color, gridlines, and scale.

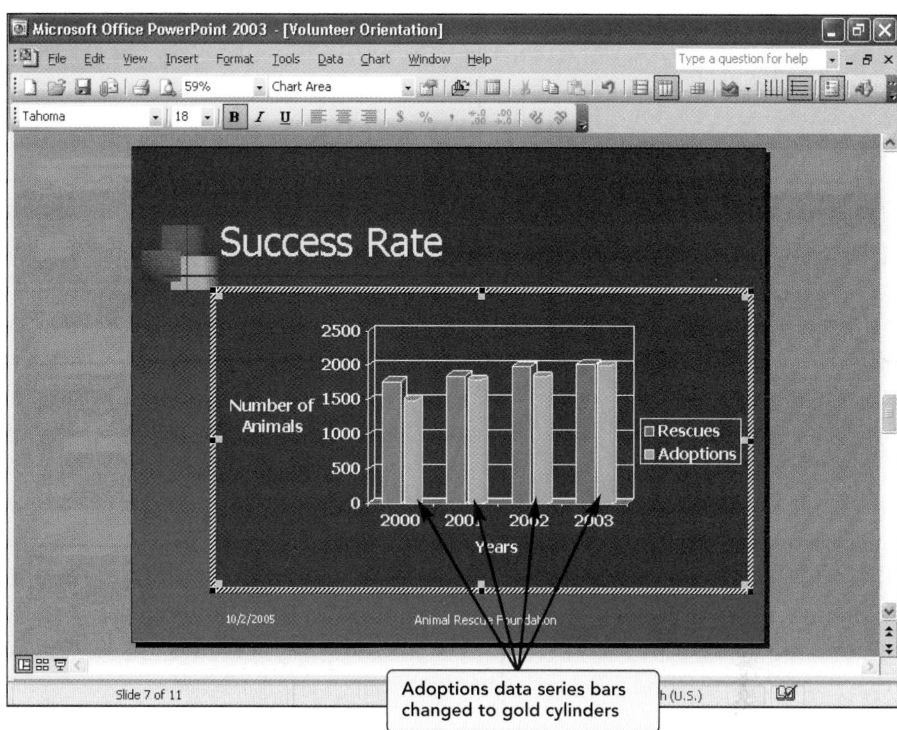

Figure 3.41

The four Adoptions data series bars have changed to a dark gold cylinder shape.

3 Change the Rescues data series in the same way, using a color of your choice and the same cylinder shape.

Your screen should be similar to Figure 3.42

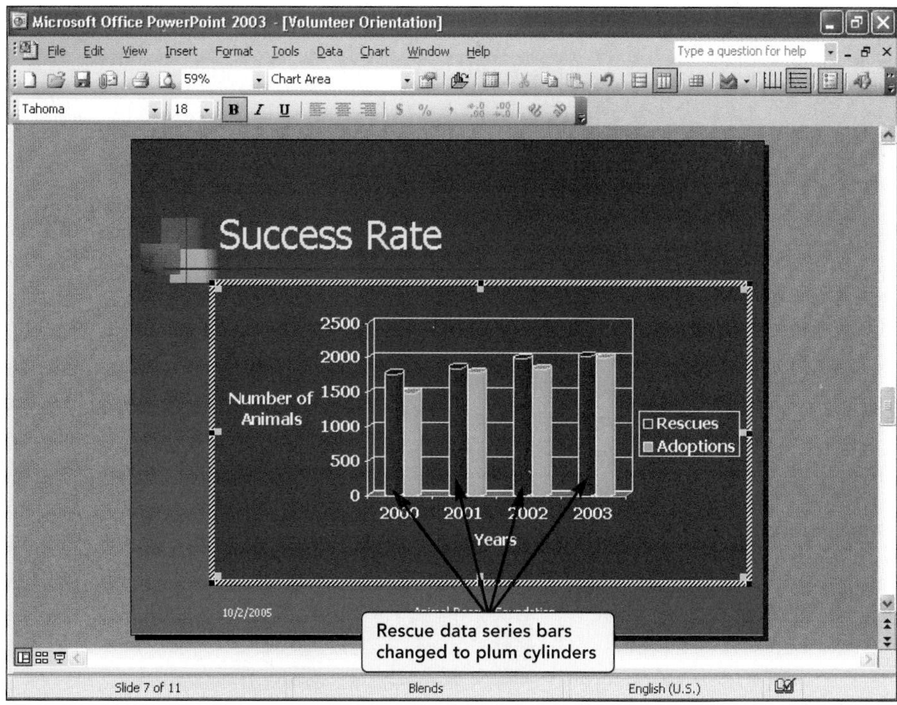

Figure 3.42

Next you want to add color to the chart walls.

4 Double-click on the background behind the data series.

Additional Information

The mouse pointer displays "Walls" in a ScreenTip.

- Select a lighter blue color from the Area color palette.
- Click OK.

Your screen should be similar to Figure 3.43

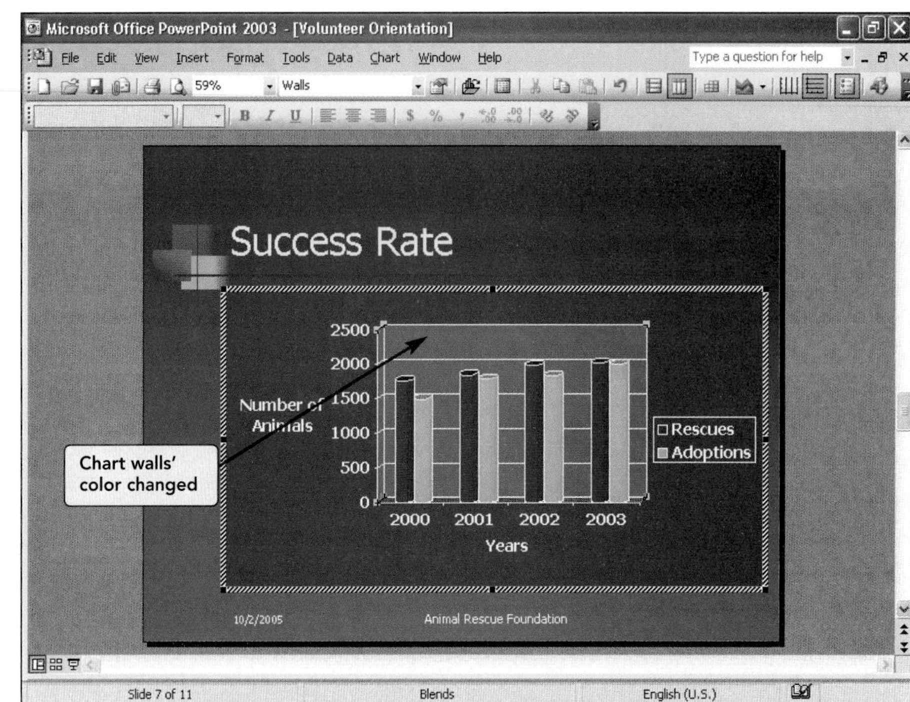

Figure 3.43

The chart is now much more attractive and more meaningful. Now that the success rate is represented in a chart, you decide to delete the slide containing the same information in table layout.

5 Click outside the chart to close the Graph application.

- Switch to Slide Sorter view.
- Delete slide 6.
- Save the presentation.

Your screen should be similar to Figure 3.44

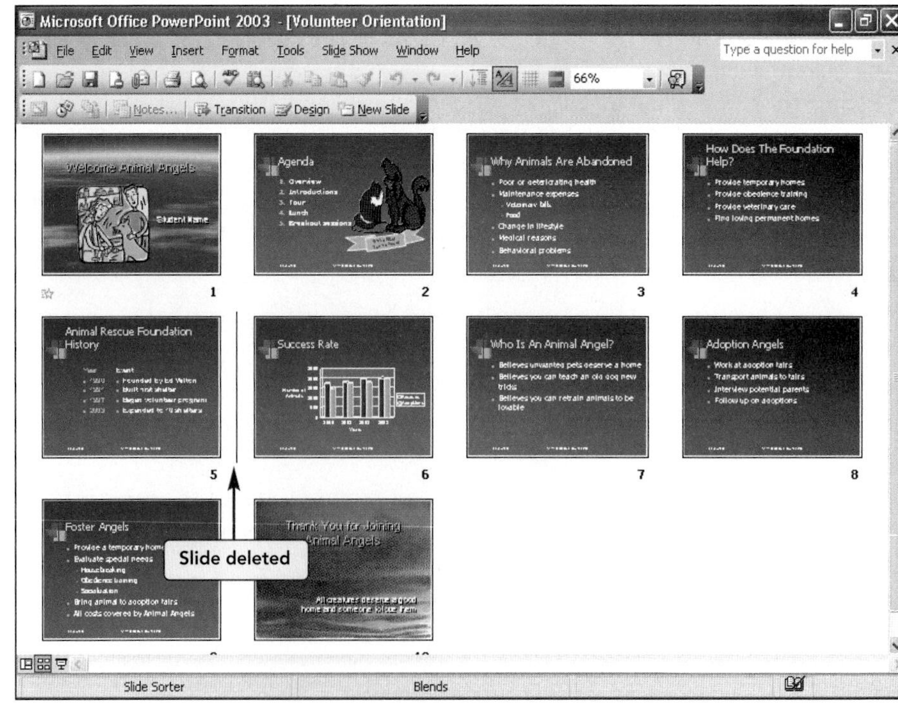

Figure 3.44

Creating an Organization Chart

To provide the volunteers with an overview of the structure of the Animal Rescue Foundation organization, you want to include an organization chart in the presentation.

Concept 5

Organization Chart

5 An **organization chart** is a map of a group, which usually includes people, but can include any items that have a hierarchical relationship. A **hierarchy** shows ranking, such as reporting structures within a department in a business. PowerPoint 2003 includes a separate application called Microsoft Organization Chart that is designed to help you quickly create organization charts.

There are several different styles of organization charts from which you can choose, depending on how you would like to display the hierarchy and how much room you have on your slide. A basic organization chart is shown below. All organization charts consist of different levels that represent the hierarchy. A **level** is all the boxes at the same hierarchical position regardless of the boxes each reports to. The topmost box in the organization chart is at level 1. All boxes that report directly to it are at level 2. Those boxes reporting to a level 2 box are at level 3, and so forth. An organization chart can have up to 50 levels.

The **manager box** is the top-level box of a group. **Subordinate boxes** report to the manager box. **Co-worker boxes** are boxes that have the same manager. Co-workers form a group. A **group** consists of all the boxes reporting to the same manager, excluding assistant boxes. **Assistant boxes** represent administrative or managerial assistants to a manager. A **branch** is a box and all the boxes that report to it.

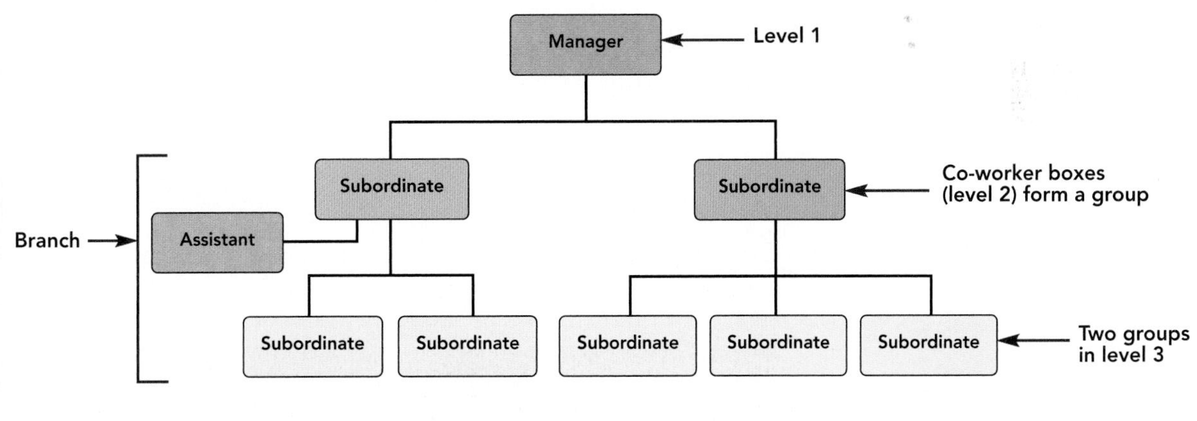

You will add a new slide following slide 4 to display the organization chart. Just as when creating a chart of data, there is a special slide layout for organization charts with a placeholder that opens the Organization Chart application.

1

- **Insert a new slide after slide 4 using the Title and Diagram or Organization Chart slide layout.**
- **Close the Slide Layout task pane.**
- **Double-click slide 5.**
- **Double-click [icon] in the organization chart placeholder.**

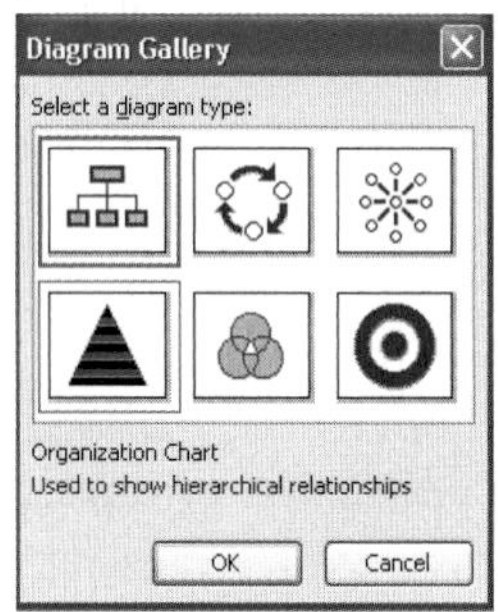

- **Double-click [icon] Organization Chart in the Diagram Gallery dialog box.**

Your screen should be similar to Figure 3.45

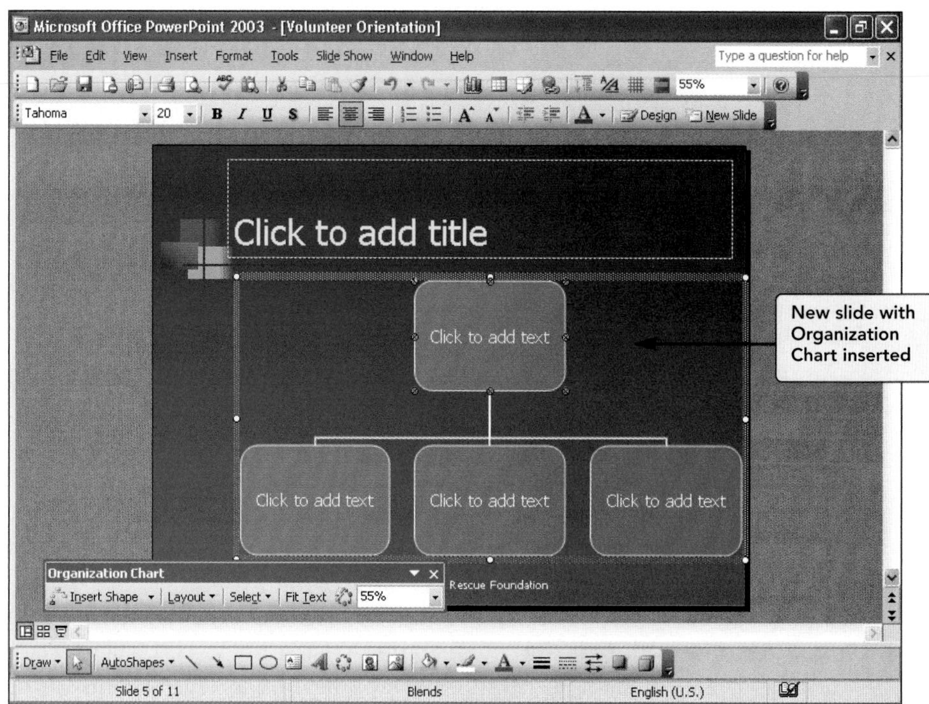

Figure 3.45

The Organization Chart toolbar contains the commands and tools to create and edit the organization chart.

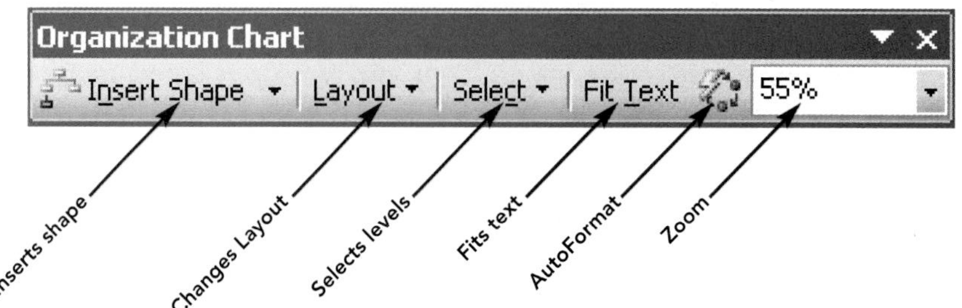

When you create a new organization chart, a chart containing four boxes (the default) is displayed. To enter information into a box, you type over the placeholder text. The top box in the organization chart is already selected. You will enter the name of the director of the Animal Rescue Foundation in the top-level box. You will also increase the zoom to make it easier to see the text in the boxes.

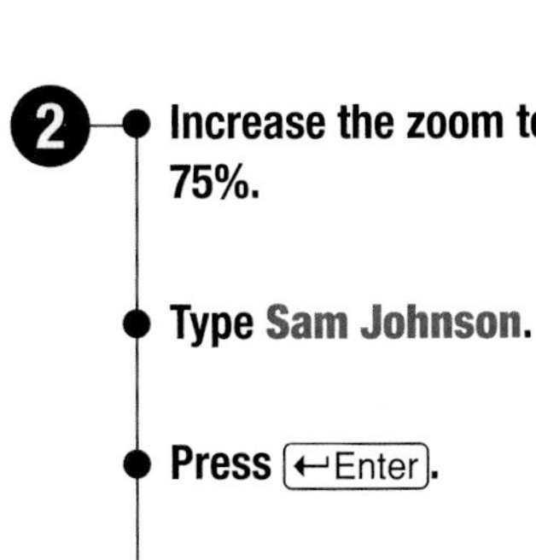

2 Increase the zoom to 75%.

- Type **Sam Johnson.**
- Press ←Enter.
- Type **Director.**
- Click on the organization chart background.

Your screen should be similar to Figure 3.46

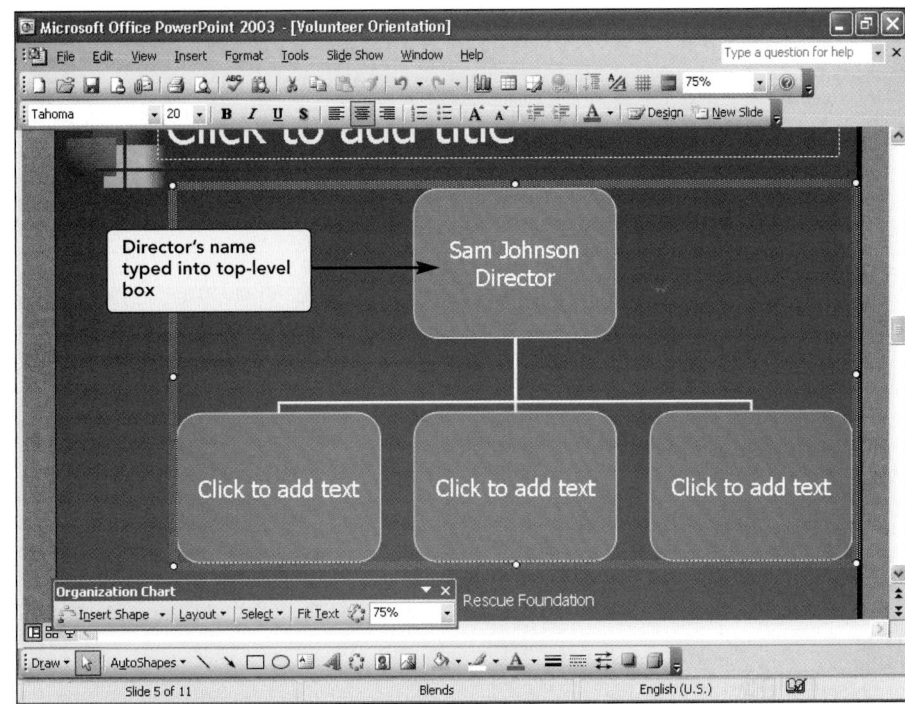

Figure 3.46

Next, you will add text to the other boxes. As you do, because some of the entries are too large to fit in the box, they will overlap. To fix this, you will size the text to fit within the box.

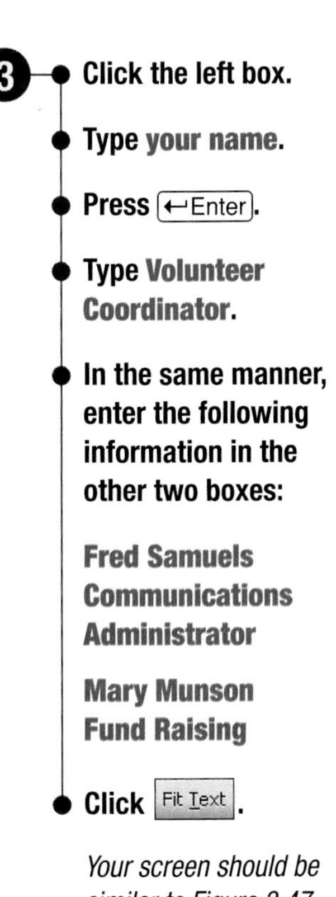

3 Click the left box.

- Type **your name.**
- Press ←Enter.
- Type **Volunteer Coordinator.**
- In the same manner, enter the following information in the other two boxes:

  Fred Samuels
  Communications Administrator

  Mary Munson
  Fund Raising

- Click Fit Text.

Your screen should be similar to Figure 3.47

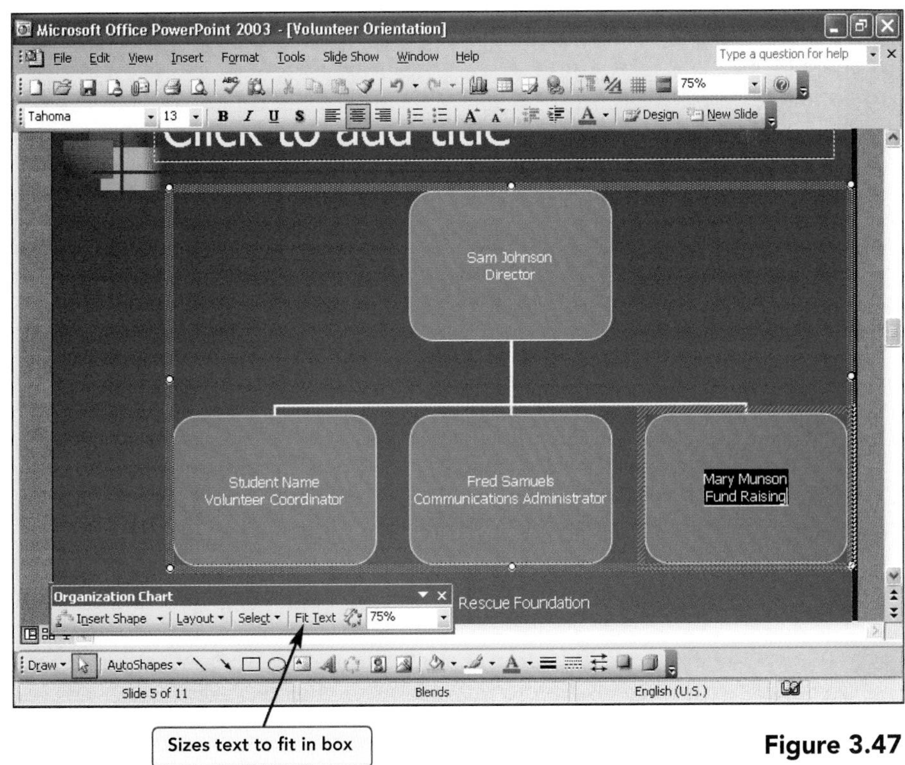

Figure 3.47

The font size of the text was reduced in all the boxes to the size needed to display the largest entry in the boxes.

Adding Boxes

Since this orientation is for volunteers, you are going to expand only the Volunteer Coordinator section of the organization chart. To add a box, you first select the type of box to add and then select the box to link it to. You will add two subordinate boxes for the two people who report directly to you.

1
- **Click the Volunteer Coordinator box.**
- **Open the Insert Shape drop-down menu and select Subordinate.**
- **Click the new subordinate box.**
- **Type Martin Crane.**
- **Press ←Enter.**
- **Type Foster Angels.**
- **Click on the chart background.**

Your screen should be similar to Figure 3.48

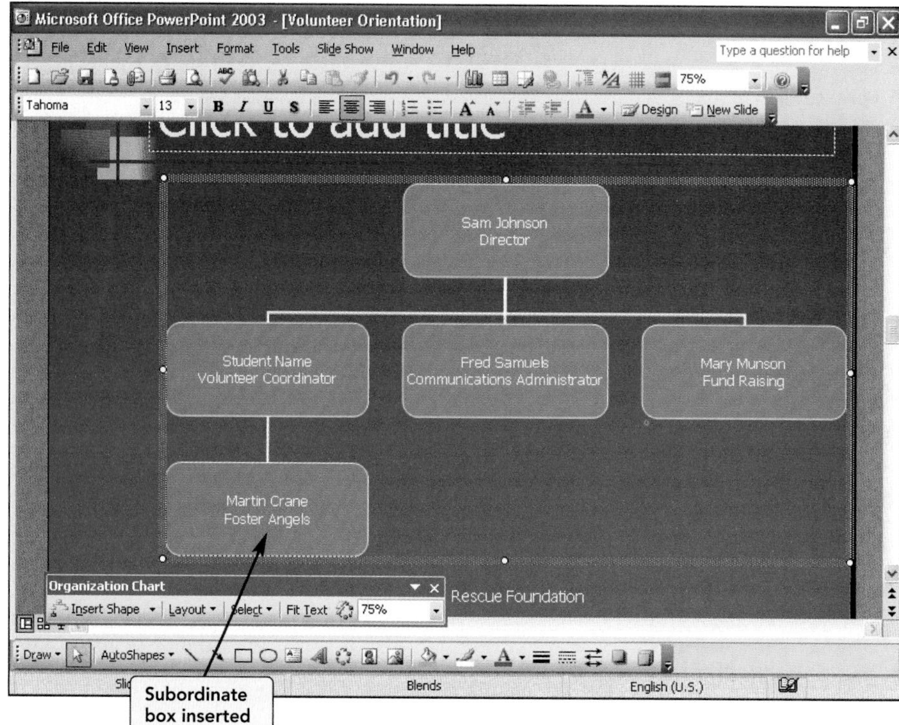

Figure 3.48

The new box appears in the same color background as the existing boxes. Next you will add a co-worker box next to Martin Crane.

2 • **Click on Martin Crane's box.**

• **Open the Insert Shape drop-down menu and select Coworker.**

• **Click the new co-worker box.**

• **Type Peg Ludwig.**

• **Press ←Enter.**

• **Type Adoption Angels.**

• **Click on the chart background.**

Your screen should be similar to Figure 3.49

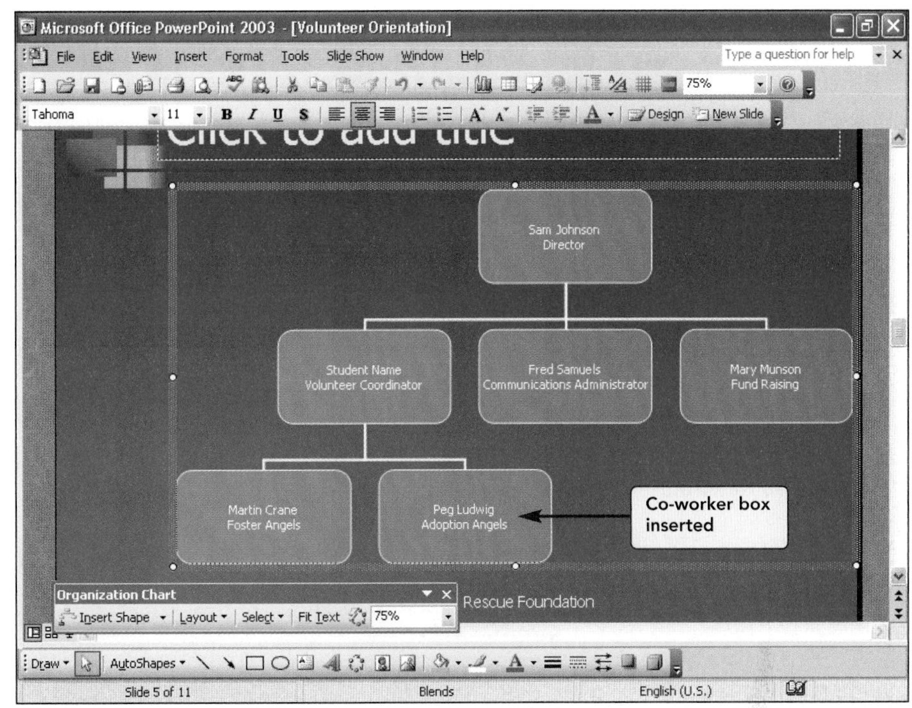

Figure 3.49

Enhancing the Organization Chart

To make the organization chart more interesting, you decide to change the appearance of the boxes, text, and lines. You could select each element individually and make changes, but PowerPoint includes an AutoFormat option that provides prepackaged styles.

1 • **Click AutoFormat.**

Your screen should be similar to Figure 3.50

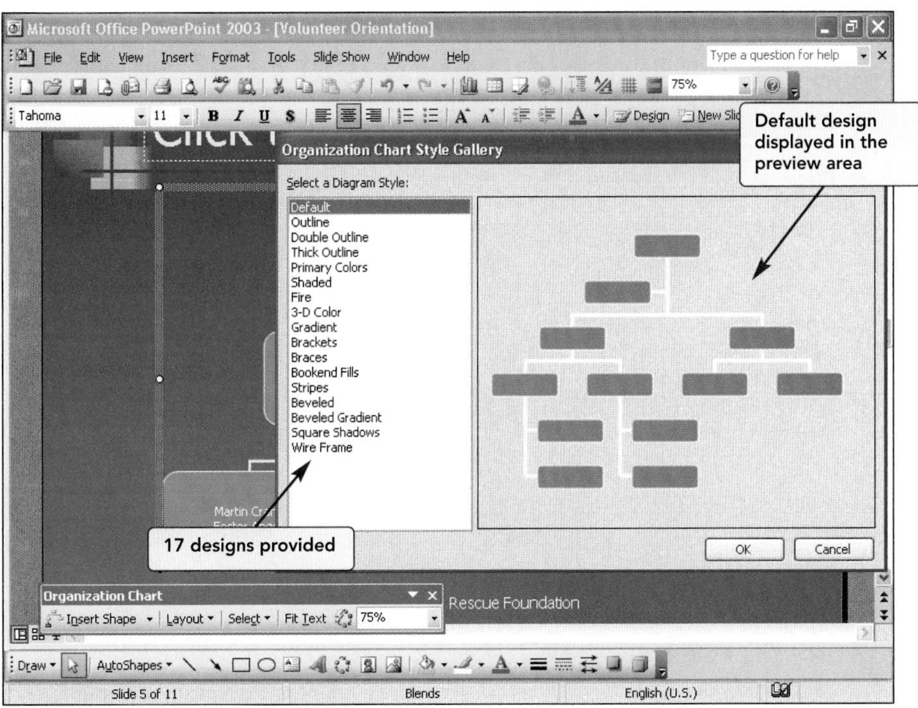

Figure 3.50

From the Organization Chart Style Gallery dialog box, you can select from 17 designs. The selected design, Default, is displayed in the preview area.

2

- **Select several diagram styles and preview the samples.**
- **Choose Bookend Fills.**
- **Click OK.**

Your screen should be similar to Figure 3.51

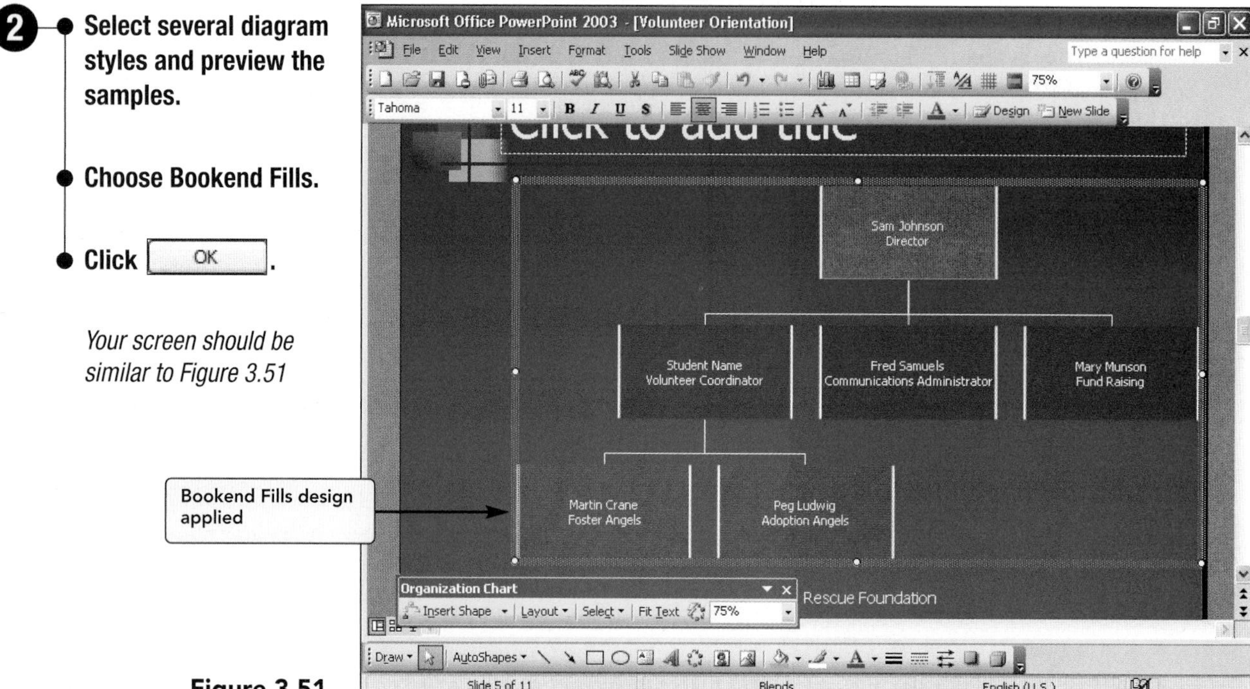

Figure 3.51

The final enhancement is to make the Volunteer branch of the organization chart stand out, so you decide to color and bold the names in the boxes.

3

- **Click on the Volunteer Coordinator box to select it and drag to select your name.**
- **Click B Bold.**
- **Click S Shadow.**
- **Click A Font Color and select gold.**
- **Use Format Painter to apply the same formats to the names in the two boxes below yours.**
- **Turn off Format Painter and click on the chart background.**

Your screen should be similar to Figure 3.52

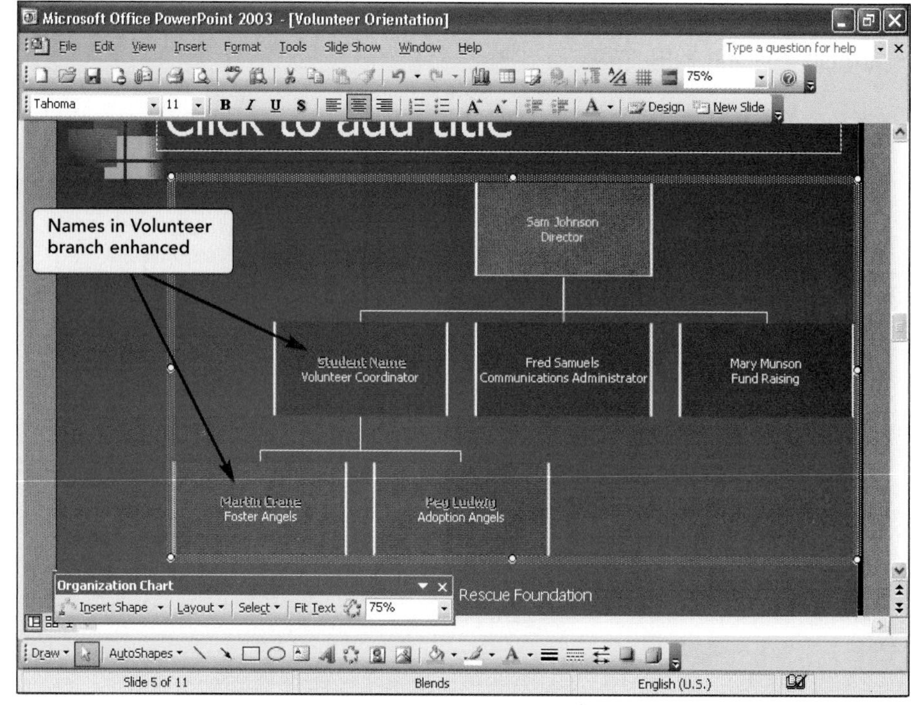

Figure 3.52

Changing the Organization Chart Layout

You also decide to add to the chart the names of the volunteer assistants who work for the coordinators.

1 **Add two subordinate boxes under Martin Crane and enter the names Susan Allison and Maria Garcia.**

Additional Information

Clicking Insert Shape will insert the default shape of Subordinate.

- **In a similar manner, under Peg Ludwig add two subordinate boxes and enter the names Jamul Johnson and Kaye Benjamin.**
- **Change the font color to gold and bold in the new boxes.**

Your screen should be similar to Figure 3.53

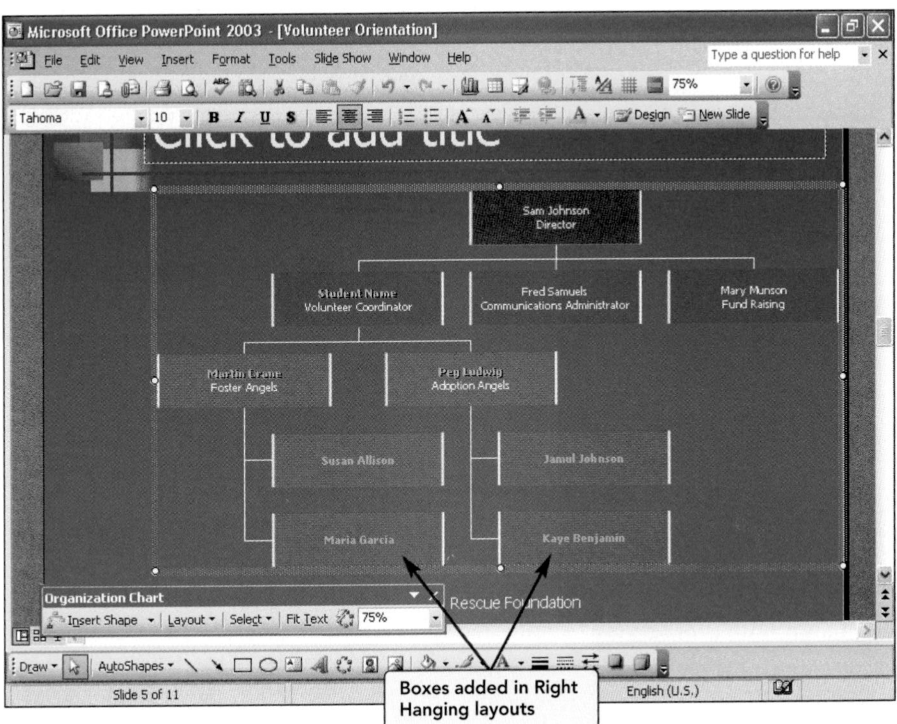

Figure 3.53

PowerPoint automatically adds the new subordinate boxes in a Right Hanging layout. You want to change the arrangement of the boxes. You can change the arrangement of the entire organization chart or only selected levels. You will rearrange the co-worker boxes to appear in the Standard layout to match the rest of the chart. To change a level, select the level above the level whose layout you want to change.

2

- **Click the box for Martin Crane.**
- **Open the Layout drop-down menu and choose Standard.**
- **In a similar manner, change the layout for the boxes beneath Peg Ludwig.**
- **Click on the slide background.**
- **Return the zoom to Fit.**

Your screen should be similar to Figure 3.54

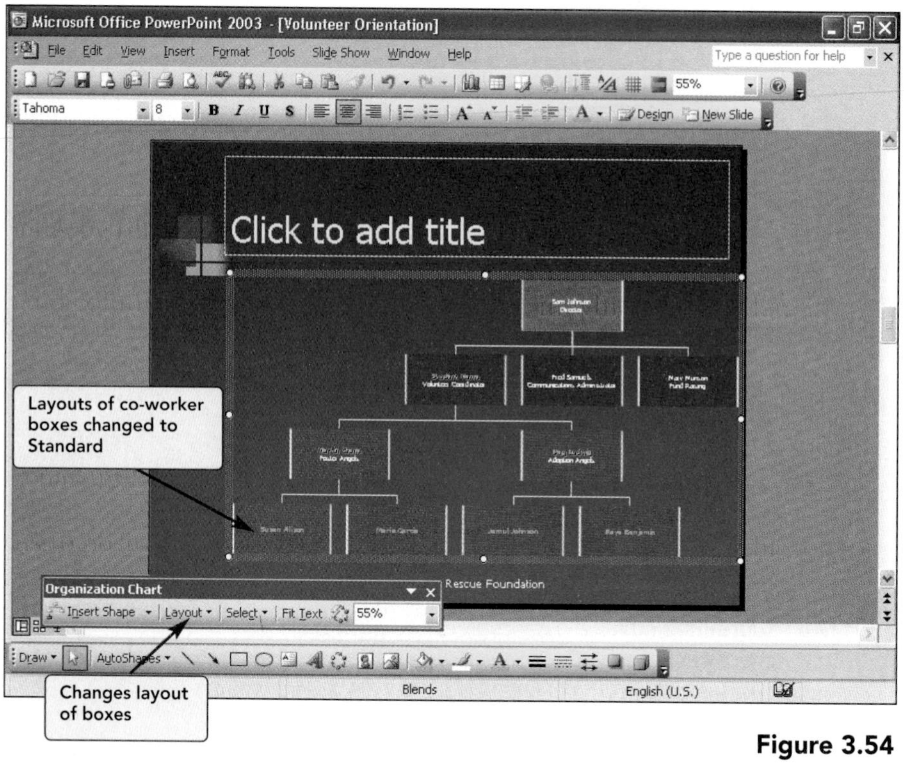

Figure 3.54

Additional Information

You can click on the chart to reopen the Organization Chart application to further modify the chart at any time.

The last step is to add the title.

3 Type **Who's Who** as the slide title.

- **Save the presentation.**
- **Choose View/Normal (Restore Panes).**

Your screen should be similar to Figure 3.55

4 To see how all the changes you have made to the presentation look, run the presentation beginning with slide 1.

- **Print the presentation as handouts in portrait orientation, six per page.**

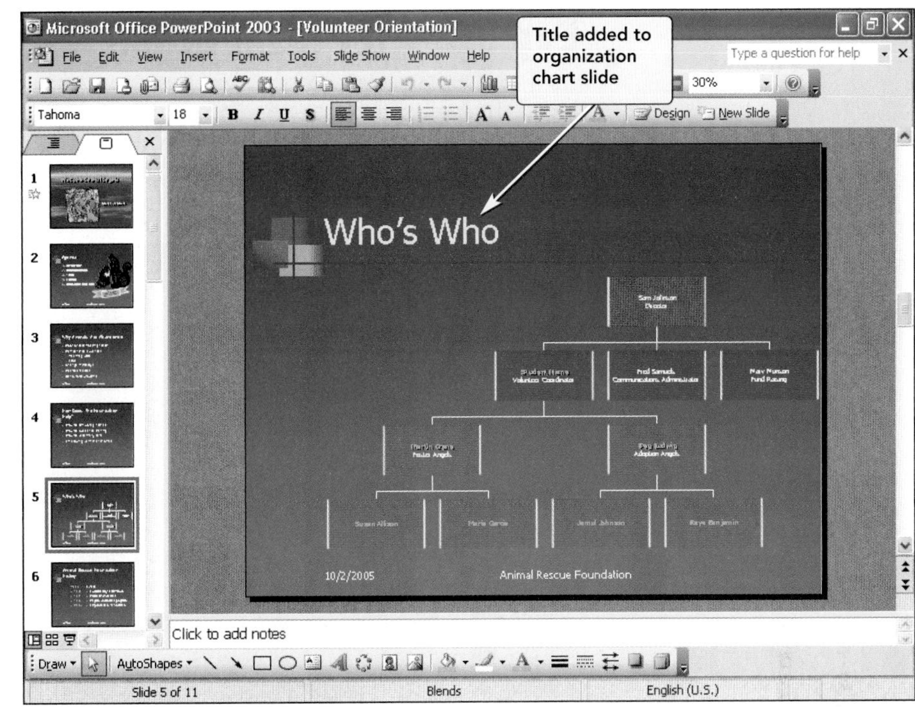

Figure 3.55

Your handouts will be similar to those shown here.

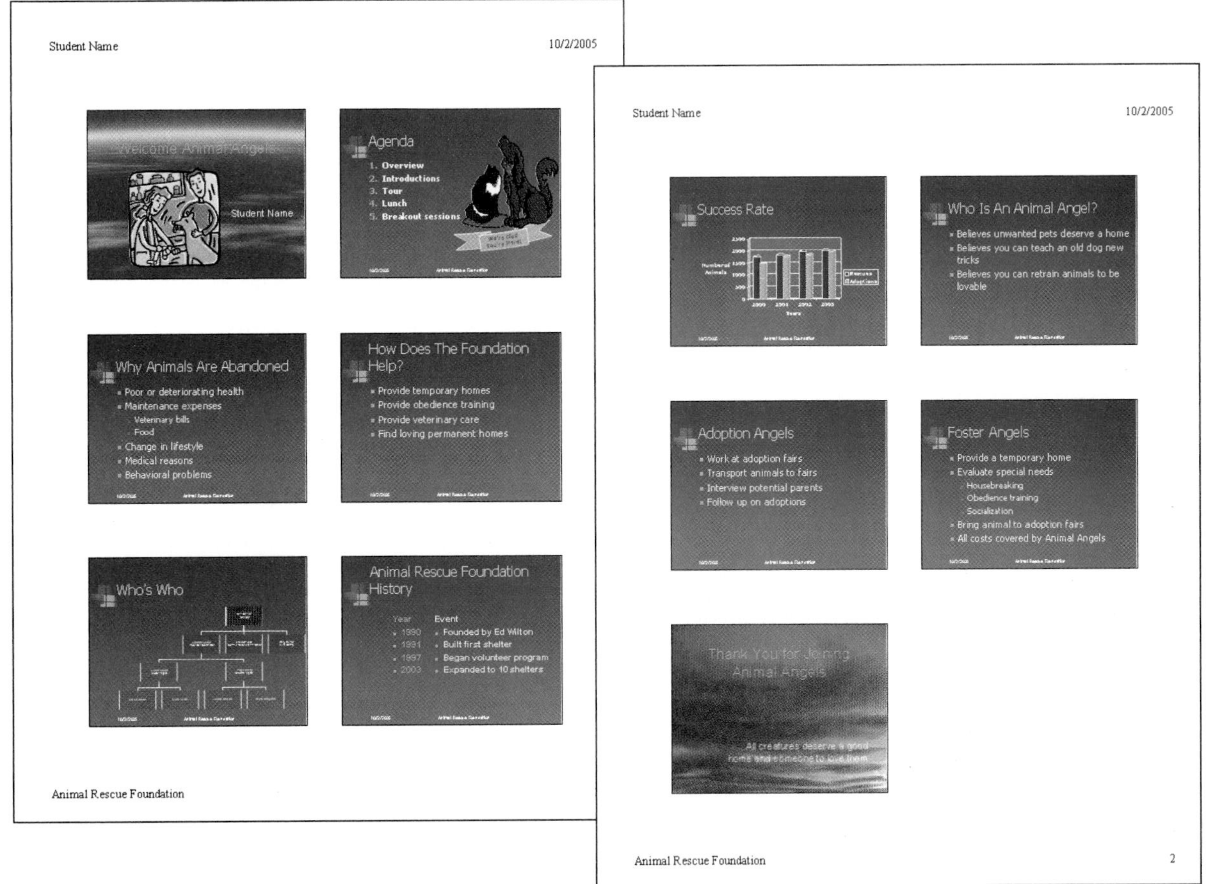

Exporting a Presentation Outline to Word

Now that the presentation is nearly complete, you need to send a copy of the text portion of the presentation to the director for approval. To do this quickly, you can save the text of the presentation to a text file.

1 **Choose File/Send to/Microsoft Office Word.**

Your screen should be similar to Figure 3.56

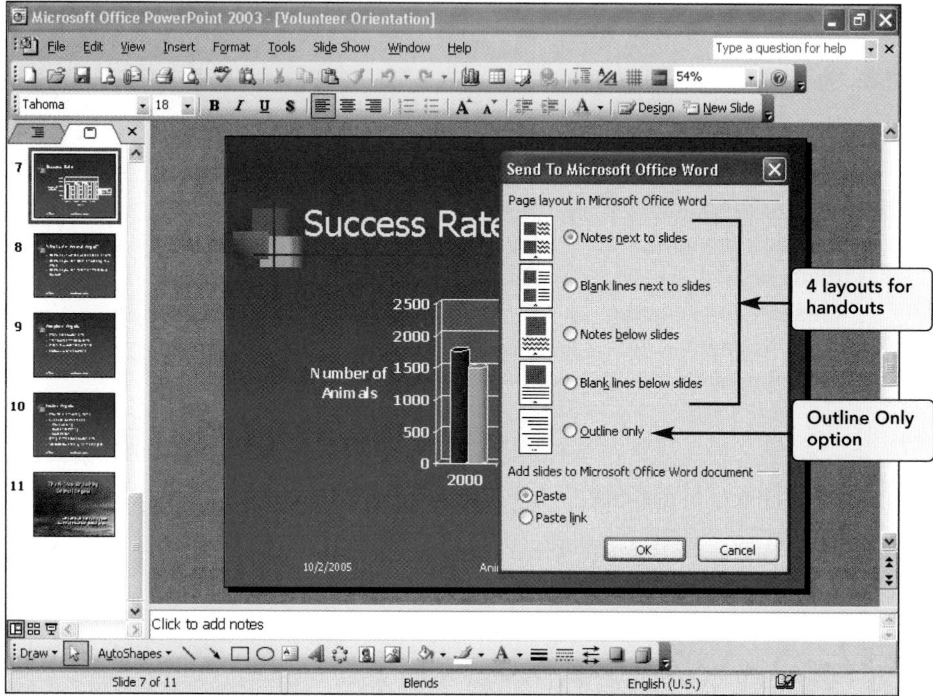

Figure 3.56

From the dialog box, you can select from four layouts for handouts, or you can create a document containing the outline only. If you choose a handout layout, you can also choose to include the slides in the handouts or just provide links to the slides. You want to create a Word document of just the outline of the presentation.

2 Select Outline Only.

Click 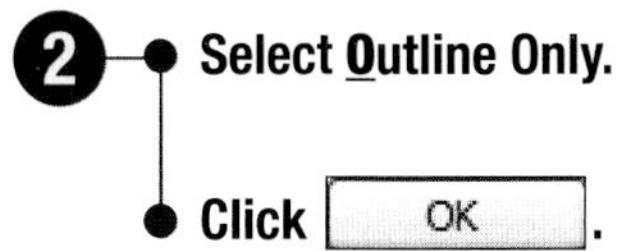.

Your screen should be similar to Figure 3.57

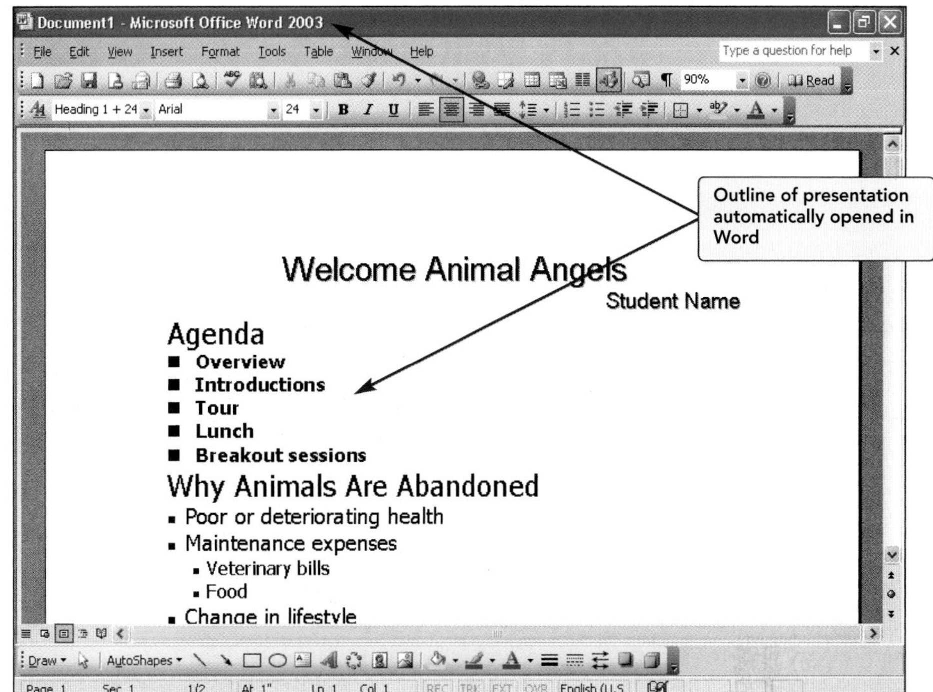

Figure 3.57

Word opens and displays the outline for the presentation.

3 **Scroll through the document to review the outline.**

Save the document as Orientation Outline **with a Word document (.doc) file type.**

Print the outline and exit Word.

E-mailing a Presentation

The director has asked you to send a copy of the presentation for review by e-mail. To do this, you will send the presentation as an attachment to an e-mail message. An **attachment** is a copy of a file that is included with an e-mail message. The attached file can then be opened by the recipient using the application in which it was created.

1 **Click E-mail.**

Having Trouble?

If you do not have an e-mail program installed, the button is not displayed and you will need to skip this section.

- **If necessary, click OK in the Choose Profile dialog box.**

Another Method

The menu equivalent is File/Send to/Mail Recipient (as Attachment).

Your screen should look similar to Figure 3.58

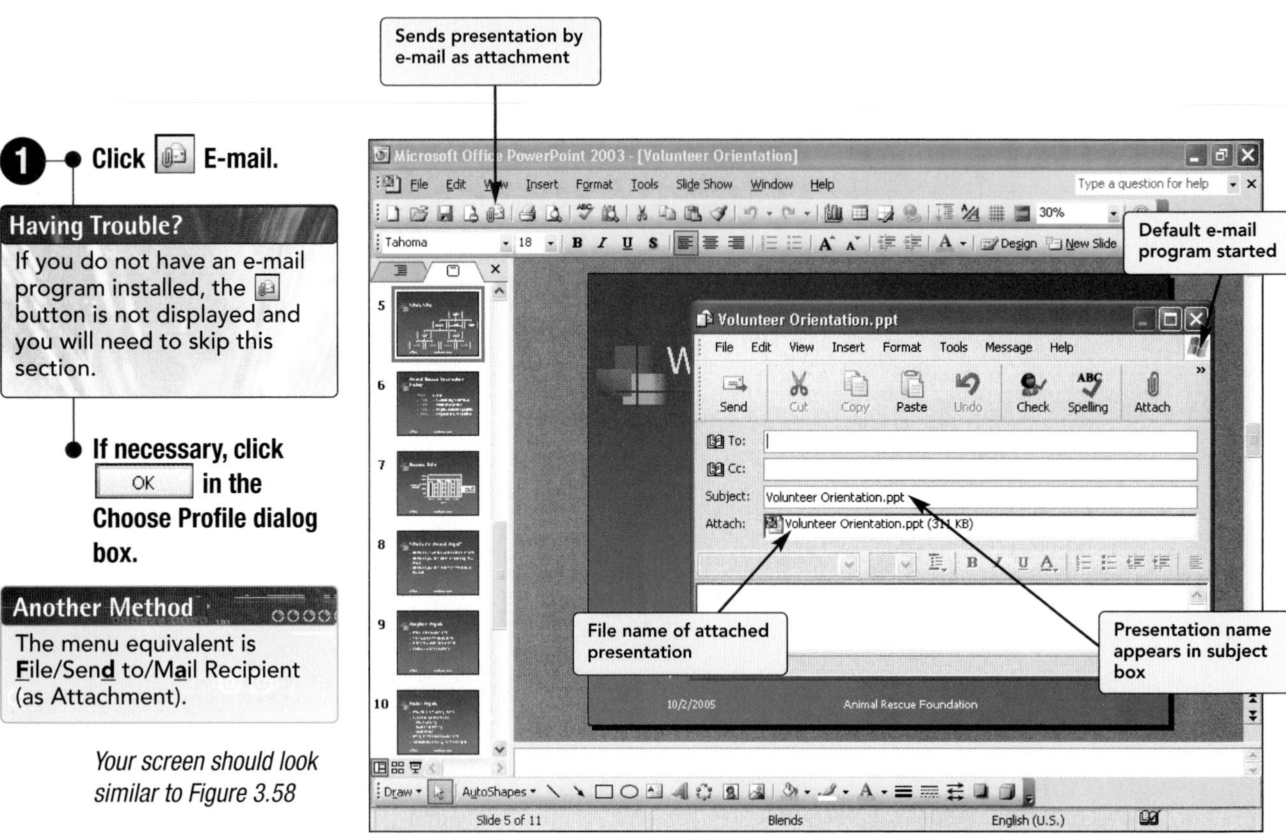

Figure 3.58

Having Trouble?

If your default e-mail program is other than Outlook Express, your e-mail window will look slightly different.

Additional Information

To send an e-mail message to multiple recipients, separate the e-mail addresses with semicolons.

The default e-mail program on your system is started, and a new message window is displayed.

You need to specify the recipient's e-mail address, the e-mail address of anyone you want to send a courtesy copy of this message to (CC:), and the subject and body of the message. You can use the toolbar buttons to select recipient names from your e-mail address book, attach a file to the message, set the message priority (high, normal, or low priority), include a follow-up message flag, and set other e-mail options. The file name of the presentation appears in the Subject box. The Attach box also displays the file name of the presentation file that will be sent with the e-mail message.

2 • **Enter the e-mail address of the person you want to send the message to in the To box.**

Additional Information

Your instructor will provide the e-mail address to use. For example, if you have a personal e-mail address, your instructor may want you to use it for this exercise.

• **Enter the following in the message text area: Attached is the presentation I have been working on for the new volunteer orientation meeting. Please let me know if you have any suggestions..**

• **Press ←Enter twice and type your name.**

Your screen should look similar to Figure 3.59

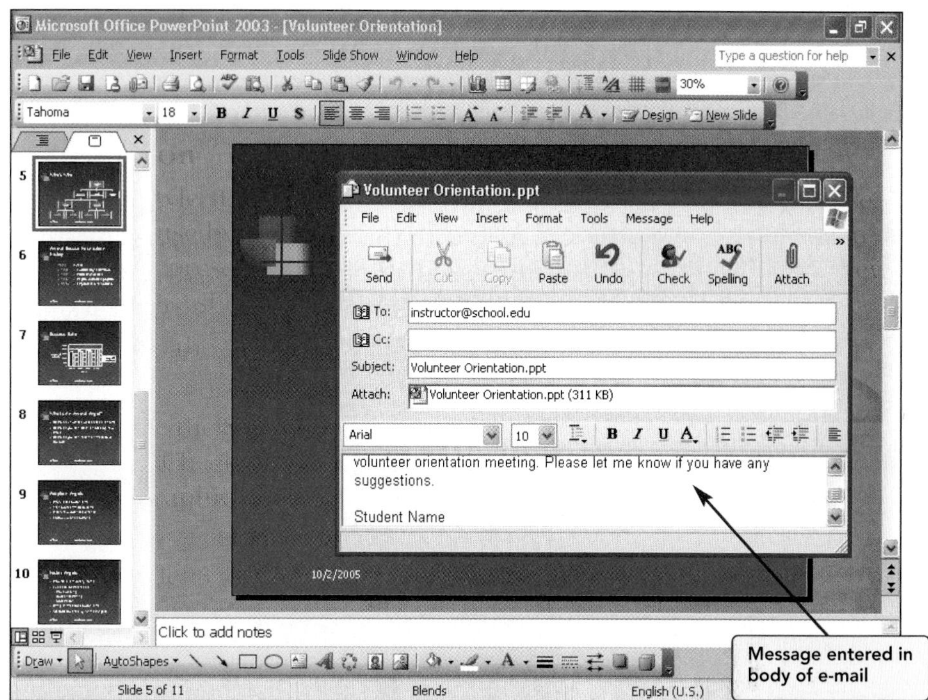

Figure 3.59

You are now ready to send the e-mail message. If you have an Internet connection, you could click Send to send the e-mail message. Instead, you will save it to be sent at a later time.

3 • **Choose File/Save As and save the message as Volunteer Presentation to the location where you save your files.**

• **Close the e-mail window.**

• **If necessary, click No in response to the prompt to send the message.**

When the message is sent, the recipient can open the attachment and view the presentation using PowerPoint.

Delivering Presentations

Typically presentations are delivered by connecting a computer to a projector to display the slides on a large screen. Before delivering a presentation, it is important to rehearse it so that you are well prepared and at ease with both the equipment and the materials. It is best to rehearse in a setting as close as possible to the real situation with a small audience who will give you honest feedback. Since most presentations are allotted a set amount of time, as part of the rehearsal you may also want to keep track of the time spent on each slide and the total time of the presentation.

Rehearsing Timing

Additional Information

If your computer has a microphone, you could even record your narration using Slide Show/Record Narration.

To help with this aspect of the presentation, PowerPoint includes a timing feature that records the length of time spent on each slide and the total presentation time while you are rehearsing. If the presentation runs either too long or too short, you can quickly see which slides you are spending too much or too little time on and adjust the presentation accordingly.

1 **Choose Slide Show/Rehearse Timings.**

Your screen should be similar to Figure 3.60

Figure 3.60

The Rehearsal toolbar appears and starts a clock to time your delivery. The button advances to the next step in the show and the will pause the timing. You can also return to the previous slide to repeat the rehearsal and apply new timings to the slide using the button on the toolbar.

Normally you would read your narration aloud while you rehearse the timing. For this exercise, think about what you would say for each slide. The toolbar will record the time for each slide. When you reach the end of the presentation, a message box displays the total time for the presentation.

2

- **Advance through the slide show as you would during the actual presentation.**
- **Click Yes to keep the slide timings.**
- **Save the presentation.**

Your screen should be similar to Figure 3.61

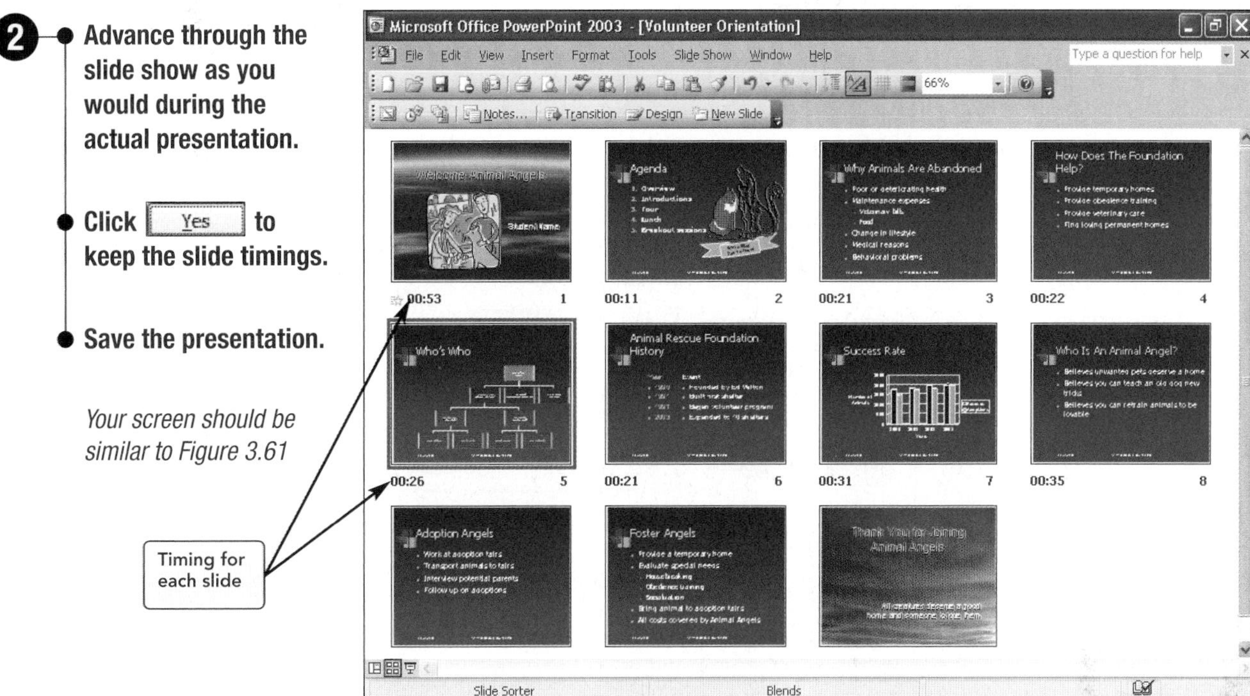

Figure 3.61

The presentation is displayed in Slide Sorter view, showing the timing for each slide. Now that you can see the individual timings, you can easily see where you are spending too little or too much time.

You can also preset timings for each slide, and the slides will be advanced automatically for you during the presentation. To turn on this feature use Sli**d**e Show/**S**et Up Show and select the **U**sing Timings option to advance slides.

Packaging Presentations for a CD

Finally, you are going to use the Package for CD feature to create an archive folder of your presentations. The Package for CD feature allows you to package your presentations and all of the supporting files to a folder, which can be copied to a CD. Viewers can then automatically run your presentations from the CD. The updated Microsoft Office PowerPoint Viewer is included on the CD so the viewer does not have to have PowerPoint installed on their PC to view your presentation.

1 Choose File/Package for CD.

Your screen should be similar to Figure 3.62

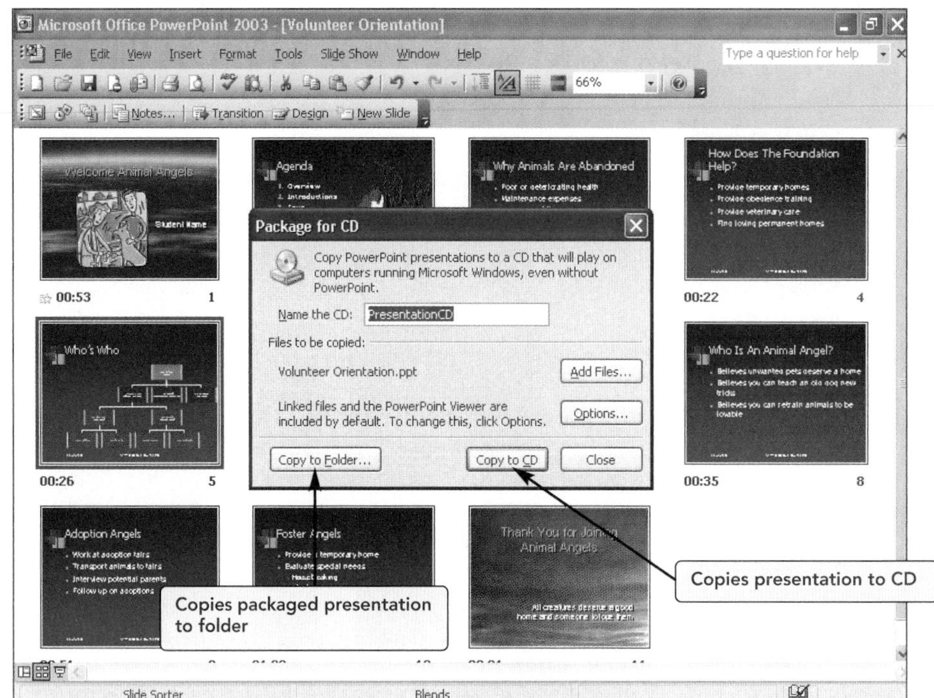

Figure 3.62

The Volunteer Orientation presentation is automatically added to the list for the CD. You also want to include the Animal Angels presentation on the CD.

2 Click Add Files... **.**

Select the file pp03_Animal Angels3.ppt **from your data file location.**

Click Add **.**

Your screen should be similar to Figure 3.63

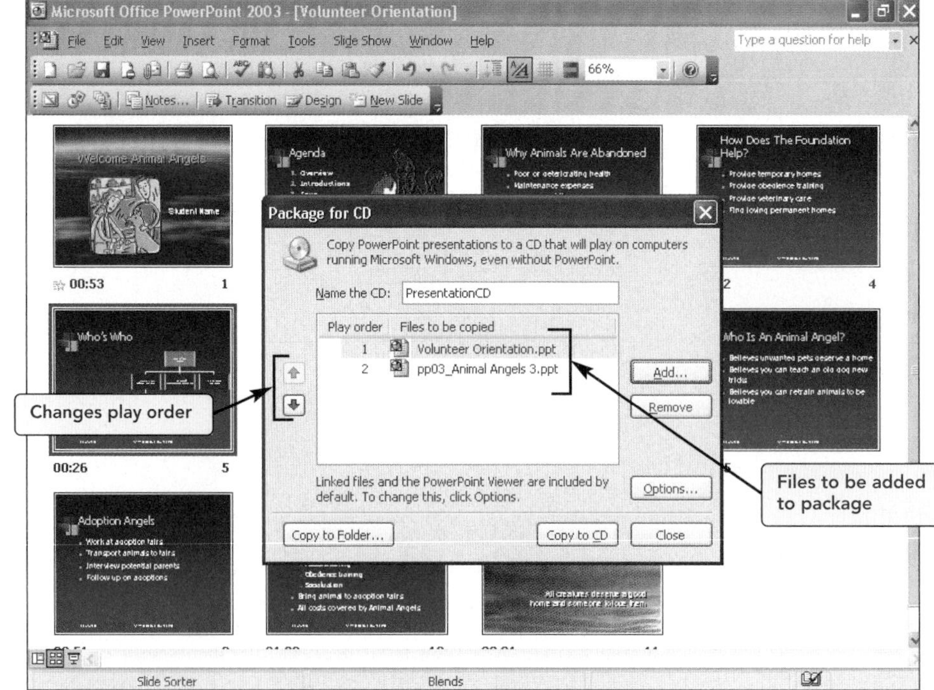

Figure 3.63

Additional Information

You could also copy the files directly to a CD at this point using Copy to CD.

Currently the Volunteer Orientation presentation will play before the Animal Angels presentation. You want to reverse the order, then copy the presentations to a folder.

3

- Click [↓] to move the Volunteer Orientation presentation down the play list.
- Click Copy to Folder... .
- Name the folder OrientationCD.
- Change the location to the location where you save your files.
- Click OK .
- When the files are finished copying, click Close .
- Exit PowerPoint.

When you are ready to create the CD, all you would need to do is copy the OrientationCD folder to the CD.

Preparing Overheads and 35mm Slides

If you are unsure of the availability of a data projector, you may want to convert the presentation to overheads or 35mm slides. To create overheads, you print your presentation as black-and-white or color transparencies, using transparencies in the printer instead of paper. Be sure to order the type of transparency that is appropriate for your printer.

You can also transform your electronic slides to 35mm slides by contacting a local service bureau. Follow their instructions for sending the presentation.

Focus on Careers

EXPLORE YOUR CAREER OPTIONS

Training Specialist

In today's job market, learning new skills is the only way to keep current with ever-changing technology. A training specialist in a corporate environment is responsible for teaching employees how to do their jobs, which usually involves computer training. Training Specialists use PowerPoint to create materials for their lectures, and can automate the presentations and package to a CD to send to employees at remote locations. The position of training specialist usually requires a college degree and commands salaries from $35,000 to $75,000 depending on experience and skill.

LAB 3
Using Advanced Presentation Features

Group (PP3.16)

A group is two or more objects that are treated as a single object.

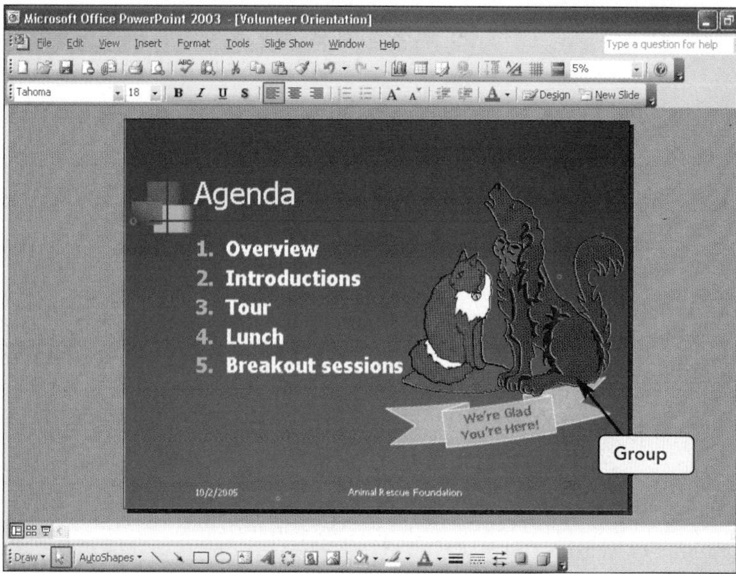

Object Alignment (PP3.24)

Object alignment refers to the position of objects relative to each other by their left, right, top, or bottom edges; or horizontally by their centers or vertically by their middles; or in relation to the entire slide.

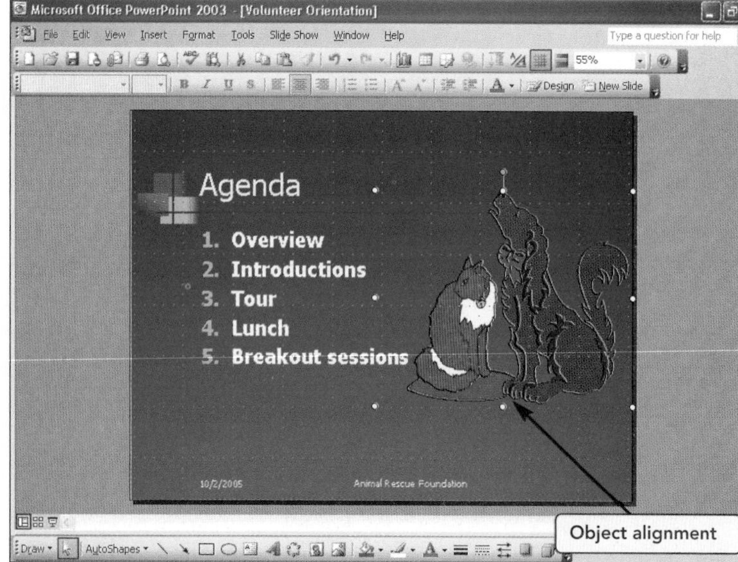

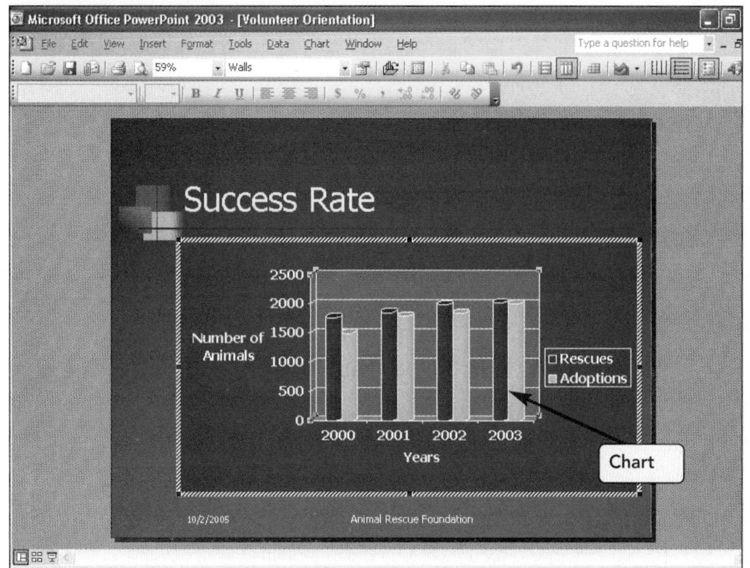

Chart (PP3.30)

A chart is a visual representation of numeric data that is used to help an audience grasp the impact of your data more quickly.

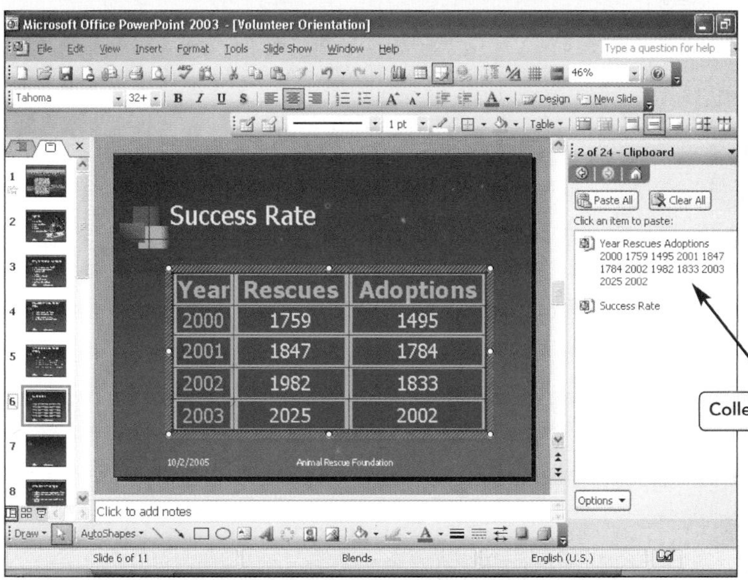

Year	Rescues	Adoptions
2000	1759	1495
2001	1847	1784
2002	1982	1833
2003	2025	2002

Collect and Paste (PP3.33)

The Collect and paste feature is used to store multiple copied items in the Office Clipboard and then paste one or more of the items into another location or document.

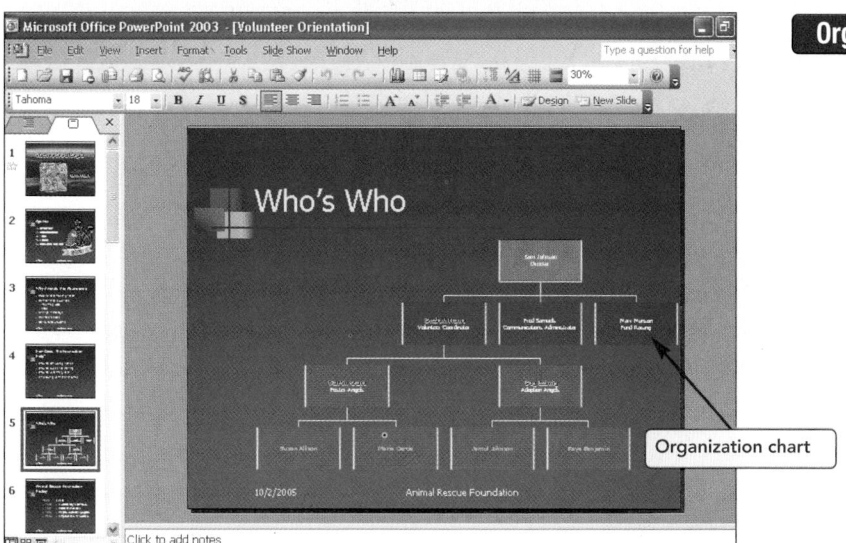

Organization Chart (PP3.43)

An organization chart is a map of a group, which usually includes people, but can include any items that have a hierarchical relationship.

LAB 3

Using Advanced Presentation Features

key terms

microsoft office specialist skills

The Microsoft Office Specialist certification program is designed to measure your proficiency in performing basic tasks using the Office System applications. Certification demonstrates that you have the skills and provides a valuable industry credential for employment. After completing this lab, you have learned the following Microsoft Office PowerPoint 2003 Specialist skills:

Skill Sets	Skill Standard	Page
Creating Content	Insert and edit text-based content	PP3.5
	Insert tables, charts, and diagrams	PP3.30,3.43
	Insert pictures, shapes, and graphics	PP3.16,3.26
Formatting Content	Format text-based content	PP3.8
	Format pictures, shapes, and graphics	PP3.19,3.23,3.28
	Format slides	PP3.10
	Work with masters	PP3.13
Managing and Delivering Presentations	Organize a presentation	PP3.5,3.24,3.44
	Rehearse timing	PP3.56
	Prepare presentations for remote delivery	PP3.57
	Export a presentation to another Microsoft Office program	PP3.52

command summary

Command	Shortcut Key	Button	Voice	Action
File/Pac**k**age for CD				Saves presentation and all supporting files to a folder for use on a CD
File/Sen**d** To/Microsoft Office **W**ord				Exports text of presentation to Word
File/Sen**d** To/M**a**il Recipient (as Attachment)				Sends presentation or selected slide as an e-mail attachment
Edit/Office Clip**b**oard				Opens Clipboard task pane
View/Gr**i**d and Guides				Displays guidelines that help align objects
View/**Z**oom		45%		Changes size of onscreen display of slide
Insert/C**h**art				Adds a chart object to a slide
F**o**rmat/**B**ullets and Numbering				Creates bulleted or numbered lists
F**o**rmat/Bac**k**ground				Applies colors, patterns, or pictures to a slide background
F**o**rmat/Aut**o**Shape				Changes characteristics of an AutoShape
Sli**d**e Show/**S**et Up Show/**U**sing Timings				Sets up slide show to advance automatic calls by preset timings
Sli**d**e Show/**R**ehearse Timings				Starts slide show and sets timings for slide
Sli**d**e Show/Record **N**arration				Records Narration while rehearsing the presentation
Draw/**G**roup				Groups objects together

command summary

Command	Shortcut Key	Button	Voice	Action
Draw/**U**ngroup				Ungroups objects
Draw/Regro**u**p				Groups objects together again that were previously ungrouped
Draw/O**r**der/Send to Bac**k**				Sends object to bottom of stack
Draw/Grid and Guides/ Display grid on screen				Displays or hides grid lines
Draw/**A**lign or Distribute				Aligns or distributes objects
Chart				
F**o**rmat/S**e**lected Data Series	Ctrl + 1			Applies patterns, shapes, and other formats to selected data series
Data/Series in **C**olumns				Arranges chart based on columns in Datasheet window
Chart/Chart **O**ptions				Adds and modifies chart options such as titles, legends, and gridlines
Organization Chart				
Insert Shape/**S**ubordinate				Adds a box below selected box
Insert Shape/**C**o-worker				Adds a box at same level as selected box
Insert Shape/**S**tandard				Applies Standard layout to selected boxes
				Applies selected design to boxes of organization chart

matching

Match the numbered item with the correct lettered description.

1. [icon]	_______	**a.** two or more objects treated as a single object
2. legend	_______	**b.** shows ranking within a department
3. titles	_______	**c.** descriptive text used to explain the content of a chart
4. grid	_______	**d.** used to convert text to a bulleted list
5. data series	_______	**e.** series of lines used to position objects on a slide
6. attachment	_______	**f.** intersection of a row and column in a table
7. group	_______	**g.** description of patterns or colors in a data series
8. [icon]	_______	**h.** visual representation of numeric data
9. hierarchy	_______	**i.** applies multiple formats to the selected text
10. chart	_______	**j.** group of related data plotted in the chart
	_______	**k.** file copied along with an e-mail message

true/false

Circle the correct answer to the following statements.

1.	Many clip art pictures are composed of several different elements that are grouped together.	True	False
2.	You can move objects up or down within a stack using the Group button on the Drawing toolbar.	True	False
3.	You can align objects to a grid, a set of intersecting lines that form small squares on the slide.	True	False
4.	To make changes throughout a presentation you must make changes to all pairs of masters.	True	False
5.	You must have at least three objects selected to distribute them.	True	False
6.	Column charts show data changes over time or comparison among items.	True	False
7.	The system Clipboard holds up to 24 items.	True	False
8.	All organization charts consist of different levels that represent the hierarchy.	True	False
9.	A branch is all the boxes at the same level regardless of the boxes each reports to.	True	False
10.	The Package for CD feature allows the viewer to automatically run your presentations from the CD.	True	False

fill-in

Complete the following statements by filling in the blanks with the correct terms.

1. The intersection of a row and column creates a(n) ______________ in which text or data is entered.
2. A(n) _____________ is a box and all the boxes that report to it.
3. The table used to create a chart in PowerPoint is called a ________________.
4. __________________ means to position objects relative to each other by their left, right, top, or bottom edges.
5. A(n) _______________ presentation can be opened and viewed from an e-mail.
6. A(n) _________ chart emphasizes the area under the curve.
7. The ______ or category axis contains the labels of the data being charted.
8. The __________ identifies the patterns or colors assigned to data in a chart.
9. _______________ boxes have the same manager.
10. Changing the ____________ percentage only affects the onscreen display of the slide; it does not change the actual font or object size.

multiple choice

Circle the letter of the correct response to the questions below.

1. To work with separate parts of a graphic, you must ______________ the elements.
   - **a.** regroup
   - **b.** bring it to front
   - **c.** select
   - **d.** ungroup
2. If you wanted to align objects to a vertical or horizontal line, you would turn on the __________________.
   - **a.** grid
   - **b.** align gauge
   - **c.** guide
   - **d.** form gauge

3. If you needed to create a chart that shows the relationship of each value in the data series to the series as a whole, you would select the ________ chart.
   a. line
   b. pie
   c. column
   d. bar

4. PowerPoint documents can be ______________ to Microsoft Word.
   a. imported
   b. extracted
   c. exported
   d. moved

5. __________________ is the capability of a program to store multiple copied items in the Office Clipboard and then paste one or more of the items into another location or document.
   a. Collecting and pasting
   b. Copying and pasting
   c. Collecting and storing
   d. Duplicating and inserting

6. A(n) ____________________ chart can include any items that have a hierarchical relationship.
   a. pie
   b. organization
   c. bar
   d. area

7. The _____________ ensures that as each object is added to the slide, it is added to the top layer.
   a. stacking order
   b. grouping order
   c. object alignment
   d. branching

8. When an object is close to the ____________, the center or corner snaps to the line.
   a. center
   b. align gauge
   c. guide
   d. form gauge

9. The ______________ is the top-level box of a group.
   a. co-worker box
   b. manager box
   c. subordinate box
   d. branch

10. Features or _________________, such as line or fill color, associated with objects in a group can be changed.
   a. properties
   b. qualities
   c. elements
   d. attributes

rating system

★ Easy

★★ Moderate

★★★ Difficult

step-by-step

Employee Morale Presentation ★

1. Chirag Shah works in the personnel department of a manufacturing company. Chirag has recently been studying the ways that employee morale can affect production levels and employee job satisfaction. Chirag has been asked to hold a meeting with department managers to suggest methods that can be used to improve employee morale. He has already started a PowerPoint presentation to accompany his talk, but still needs to make several changes and enhancements to the presentation. Several slides of the completed presentation are shown here.

   a. Start PowerPoint and open the presentation pp03_Employee Motivation. Replace the Student Name placeholder with your name.

   b. Change the design layout on slide 5 to Title, Text, and Content. Insert the graphic pp03_Motivation on slide 5. Size and place the clip art to the right of the text.

   c. Convert the five demoted bullets on slide 3 to a numbered list. Change the color of the numbers.

   d. Demote the last three bullets on slide 5. Add a callout AutoShape containing the words **You're doing a good job, Thanks!** Bold the text in the AutoShape. Position the AutoShape appropriately on the slide.

   e. Insert the clip art of pp03_Success on slide 1. Size and position the clip art appropriately. Ungroup the clip art and delete the tan color from the roof of the building. Regroup the clip art.

   f. Change the design template of the presentation to one of your choice. Change the slide zoom to 100%. Adjust the text and graphics on the slides as needed.

   g. Save the presentation as Employee Motivation2. Print the presentation as handouts, six slides per page.

   h. Export the presentation outline to Word. Save the Word document as Motivation Outline using the Word document file type (.doc). Print the outline.

Employee Motivation

Student Name

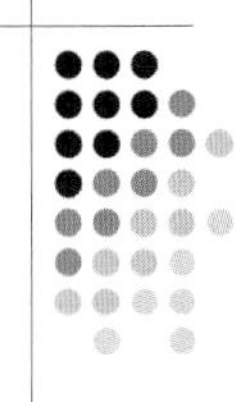

Topics for Discussion

- The following have been suggested:
  1. Flexibility
  2. Positive feedback
  3. Expert input
  4. Sharing the wealth
  5. Creating a team

Positive Feedback

- Talk with employees one-on-one weekly
- Acknowledge jobs well done publicly
  - in person
  - in monthly staff meeting
  - in company newsletter

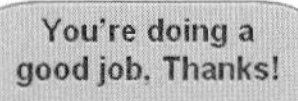

Traveling with Your Dog ★ ★

2. The Animal Rescue Foundation has asked you to help them create a presentation to inform the community about traveling with dogs. The presentation is partially completed, and you have been asked to enhance it so that it can be used at an upcoming meeting. Several slides of the completed presentation are shown here.

   a. Start PowerPoint and open the pp03_Doggie Travel presentation. Enter your name on the first slide in place of Student Name.

   b. Change the layout of slide 2 to Title and 2 Content. Insert the file pp03_Auto in the placeholder.

   c. Modify the clip art by changing the turquoise strip to the left of the car to green.

   d. On slide 2 enhance the column headings in the table by applying fill and text colors, increasing the row height, and vertically and horizontally centering the data. Bold all the text in the table.

   e. Increase the font size of the text in the first placeholder on slide 6 to 24.

   f. Insert a Title and Chart slide after slide 4. Delete the data in the datasheet. Copy the slide title and data (exclude the Total column and row) from slide 2. Paste the data into the chart datasheet on slide 5. Make the chart as large as possible and enhance it using the Microsoft Graph features. Paste the slide title you copied into the title for the chart slide.

   g. The travel tips have a duplicated slide. Delete slide 8. Apply a numbered list to the lists on slides 8 and 9. Set the numbering on slide 9 to begin at 5.

   h. Create an AutoShape of your choice on the last slide. Add the text **TRAVEL WITH YOUR DOG** in the AutoShape. Word wrap and resize the AutoShape to fit the text.

   i. Change the fill color to complement the slide. Increase the text size and bold the text. Resize the AutoShape if needed.

   j. Save the presentation as Doggie Travel Tips. E-mail the presentation to your instructor. Print the presentation as handouts with six slides per page.

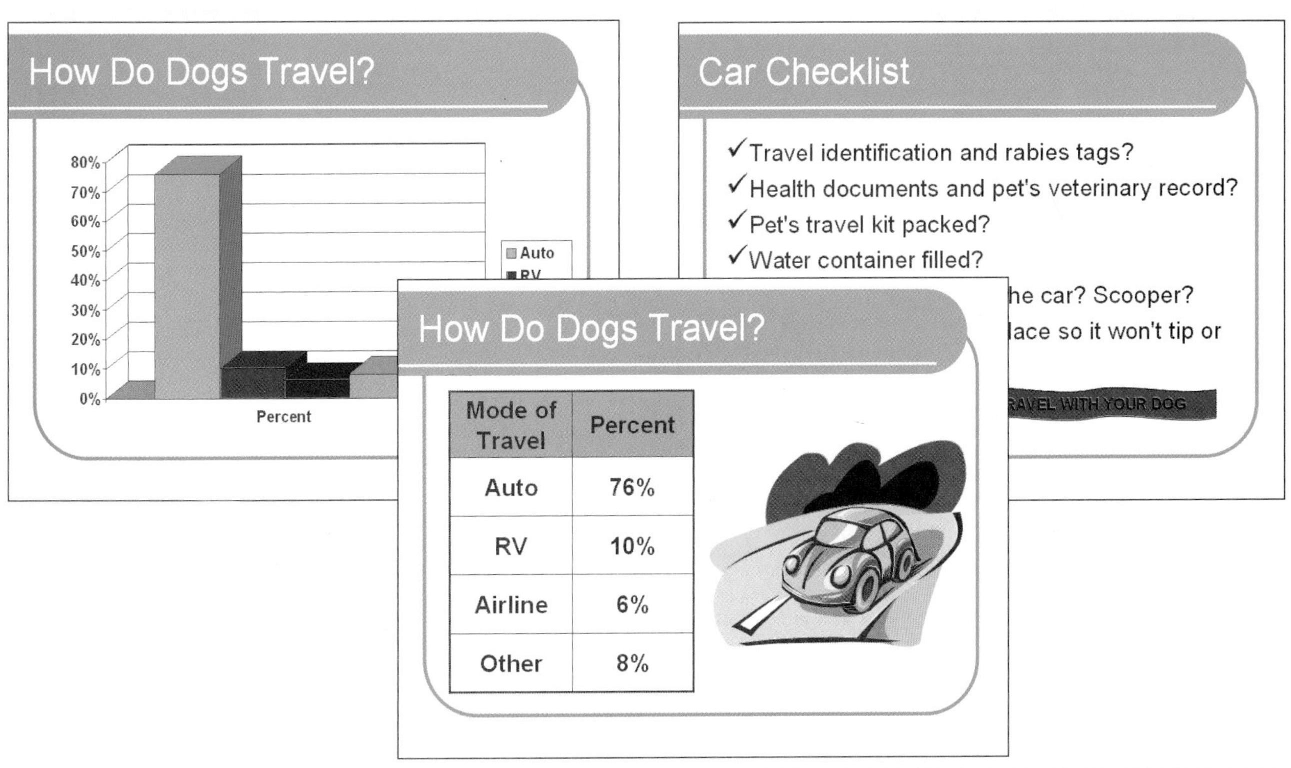

Soccer Presentation ★ ★

3. You are the assistant coach for the girl's varsity soccer team at Valley High School. You are busy preparing for the upcoming team tryouts and need to finish a presentation you will make to the athletes before tryouts begin. You need to make several changes to the presentation, including a chart of the coaching staff. Several slides of the completed presentation are shown here.

   a. Start PowerPoint and open the file pp03_Valley Soccer.

   b. Change the slide zoom to 100%.

   c. Create a numbered list with the bulleted text on slide 2.

   d. Change the design template to Default Design. Insert the image pp03_Futbol on slide 1. Select slides 2 through 6. Insert the background image pp03_Varsity on these slides.

   e. Add red fill color to the title text box on slide 2. Use the Format Painter to add this color to all of the title text boxes on slides 3 through 6.

   f. Insert a new slide after slide 3 using the organization chart layout. Add an organization chart with the title **Coaching Staff**. Enter **Heather Mills, Head Coach** in the top-level box. Enter the following information into the other chart boxes:

      Caroline Harrison, Assistant Coach (second level)

      Molly Hernandez, Assistant Coach (second level)

      Patricia Gardeta, Volunteer Assistant Coach (second level)

   g. Add word wrap to the text in the Gardeta AutoShape. Add the Fire AutoFormat to the diagram.

   h. Add the date to the footer of the title slide. Adjust the formatting of the slides as needed.

   i. Save the presentation as Valley Soccer Presentation. Print the presentation with six slides per page. Rehearse the timing of the presentation.

   j. Export the presentation outline to Word. Save the outline in Word as Soccer Outline. E-mail the presentation to your instructor.

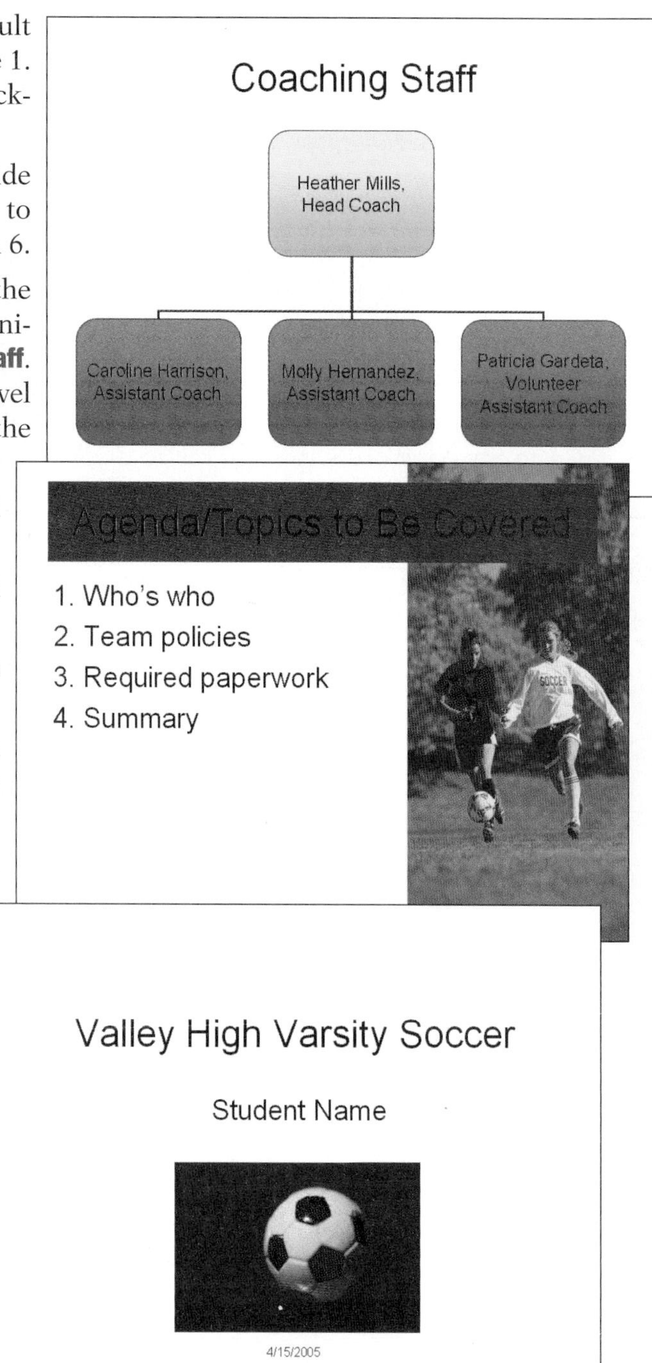

Nutrition and Exercise Presentation ★★★

4. Annette Ramirez is the new Lifestyle Fitness Club nutritionist. She would like to use the presentation on exercise currently in use by the Club to discuss the benefits of a nutrition plan. She has asked you to modify the current presentation to include some nutrition information. Several slides of the completed presentation are shown here.

   a. Start PowerPoint and open the file pp03_Exercise.
   b. Change the zoom to 100%. Change the Slide Design to one of your choice. Check all slides and adjust the text and graphics as needed throughout.
   c. Change the bulleted list on slide 3 to a numbered list. Change the color of the numbered list to blue.
   d. Use Format Painter to change the bulleted list on slide 4 to a numbered list matching slide 3.
   e. Change the title on slide 1 to **Fitness and Nutrition**.
   f. Change the title on slide 2 to **What Exercise and Nutrition Can Do for You**.
   g. Select and group the three images on slide 1.
   h. Change the layout of slide 6 to Title, Text, and Content. Delete the clip art placeholder. Size and position the image to fit the slide.
   i. Change the appearance of the table on slide 9 by using text colors, adjusting row heights, and vertically and horizontally centering the labels.
   j. Circuit Training has been changed to Advanced Step. Adjust the entries accordingly.
   k. Open the Excel file pp03_Fitness Trends. Using the Office Clipboard, copy the two title lines and then copy the worksheet data. Exit Excel.
   l. Insert a new slide after slide 10 using the chart layout. Paste the worksheet data into the chart datasheet. Paste the title from Excel into the slide title placeholder. Size the title text appropriately.
   m. Delete the border line around the legend. Modify the chart using the features you learned in the lab.

n. On the last slide, delete the text box and the subtitle placeholder. Create an AutoShape in a shape of your choice and add the text **Make it part of your life!**

o. Word wrap and size the AutoShape text. Change the fill color to match the colors on the slide. Adjust the text size and color as appropriate.

p. Insert the file pp03_LFC Logo. Ungroup the graphic. Remove the white border around each of the images (see the example). Size and position the graphic to the left of the title on slide 11.

q. Save the presentation as Fitness and Nutrition. Export the outline to Word. Save the Word file as Fitness and Nutrition Outline. Rehearse the timing of the presentation.

r. Print the outline. Print the presentation as handouts with six slides per page.

s. E-mail the presentation to your instructor.

Future Job Statistics ★★★

Continuing Exercises

5. Your presentation on Job Fairs has really turned out well (Exercise 5 of Lab 2). You did some additional research on the Department of Labor's Web site and found the projected number of college-level jobs in 2008. You think this new data will fit nicely into the presentation as a chart. Several slides of the completed presentation are shown here.

a. Open the PowerPoint file JobFairs2.

b. Change the slide zoom to 100%.

c. On slide 7 change the bullets to numbers. Change the color of the numbers to red.

d. Use the Format Painter to change the text on slide 5 to a red numbered list.

e. Insert the image pp03_Hurry on slide 1 as the background.

f. Change the color of the woman's dress on slide 2 to gold. Regroup the image.

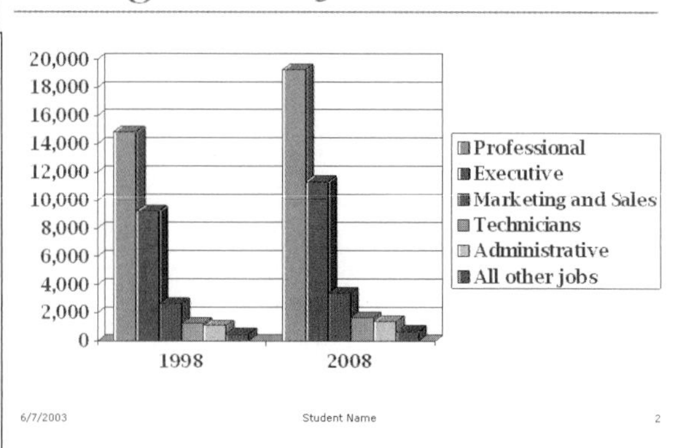

g. Insert a new Title and Chart slide after slide 1. Title the slide **College-Level Jobs**. Insert a 3-D bar chart and enter the following data into the datasheet:

Occupational Group	1998	2008
Professional	14,860	19,250
Executive	9,200	11,320
Marketing and Sales	2,640	3,400
Technicians	1,250	1,690
Administrative	1,090	1,390
All other jobs	510	690

h. Delete the clip art on slide 6 and insert the image pp03_Jobs. Adjust the image appropriately. Rehearse the timing of the presentation.

i. Save your completed presentation as JobFairs3. Print the presentation as handouts with six slides per page.

j. E-mail the presentation to your instructor. Export the presentation to Word as an Outline. Save the document as Jobs Outline.

j. Package the presentation for CD in a folder named Jobs.

on your own

Family Reunion Presentation ★

1. Your family is holding a reunion in your home town this year. They have heard all about your new computer skills, and one of your aunts has requested you put on a presentation following the welcome dinner. Using the skills you have learned so far, create a presentation that includes an organization chart for your family tree, photos you have scanned, family anecdotes, and graphics. Save your presentation as Family Reunion and print it with six slides per page. Consider e-mailing your completed work to a family member.

Lifeguard Orientation ★

2. As part of your job as Head Lifeguard at the local pool, you have been asked to create a presentation for the new lifeguard training seminar. Use the data provided in pp03_Lifegaurd to create a presentation on pool safety. Use the skills you have learned in the lab to include a numbered list of steps on water safety. Create an organization chart to explain the chain of command. Format the slides as you like. Save your presentation as Lifeguard Presentation. Print the slides.

Updating the Travel Presentation ★ ★

3. Your fellow Getaway Travel Club members are really excited about choosing the club's upcoming summer trip. Your presentation to the club went very well (Lab 2, On Your Own 5), and your locale was chosen to be among the finalists to present to the club officers. If chosen, your presentation will be placed on the club's Web site. You need to do more research on your locale to include the costs

associated with the trip. You decide that the data would be easier to understand and more convincing if it were presented in chart form. Using your file Travel Favorites, modify the presentation. Create charts for the costs you researched. Update your information on the key tourist attractions with better graphics. Save your updated presentation as Travel Favorites2. Prepare the presentation for CD. Export the presentation to Word as an outline and print the slides.

Storyland Fairytale Presentation ★ ★ ★

4. You work in a children's bookstore called Storyland. The owner has asked you to put together a presentation that highlights some of the more popular titles available at the store. The presentation will be used as part of new employee orientation. Your completed presentation should include a chart that tracks sales, a numbered list that includes sales tips, a custom background, modified graphics, and an organization chart. Save your presentation as Storyland Orientation. Prepare overheads of the presentation and e-mail your presentation to your instructor.

Preventing Network Infection Presentation ★ ★ ★

5. Your computer survey class requires you to do a research project on computer viruses and worms. Do some research on the Web to learn more about viruses and worms and how companies and schools are protecting their networks from infection. Create a PowerPoint presentation that includes the features, products, and methodologies you have learned about. Search the Web for appropriate clip art images that you can group or ungroup as necessary to enhance your slides. If appropriate data is available, create a chart that displays the increase in viruses reported over the last five years. Include your name and the current date in a footer on the slides. Save your presentation as Preventing Network Infection. Export the slides to Word as an outline. Print the outline and six-slides-per-page handouts.

Creating a Presentation for a Kiosk and the Web

LAB 4

Objectives

After completing this lab, you will know how to:

1. Create a presentation from a design template
2. Import text from other sources.
3. Insert slides from another presentation.
4. Create a complex table.
5. Add animated graphics.
6. Create and modify a WordArt object.
7. Add sound.
8. Set up a self-running presentation.
9. Create custom shows.
10. Create an agenda slide.
11. Add hyperlinks and action buttons.
12. Publish a presentation on the Web.
13. Create a design template.

Case Study

Animal Rescue Foundation

The director of the Animal Rescue Foundation has asked you to create a presentation promoting the organization that will run on a kiosk in the local shopping mall. This presentation needs to capture the attention of passers-by in a very busy area. Two ways to capture attention are to add animation and sound. You will add several different animation and sound features to your presentation, along with music that will play throughout the entire presentation. At the end, the presentation will loop back to the first slide and continue playing.

You also want to publish this presentation on the Animal Rescue Foundation's Web site. PowerPoint 2003 will automatically convert a presentation to a format that runs on the Web. Since you want to give the viewer a means to navigate through the presentation, you will add navigation buttons that go forward and back through the slides. You will also add a home page that contains links to key slides in the presentation. The completed self-running presentation and Web page are shown here.

© Getty Images

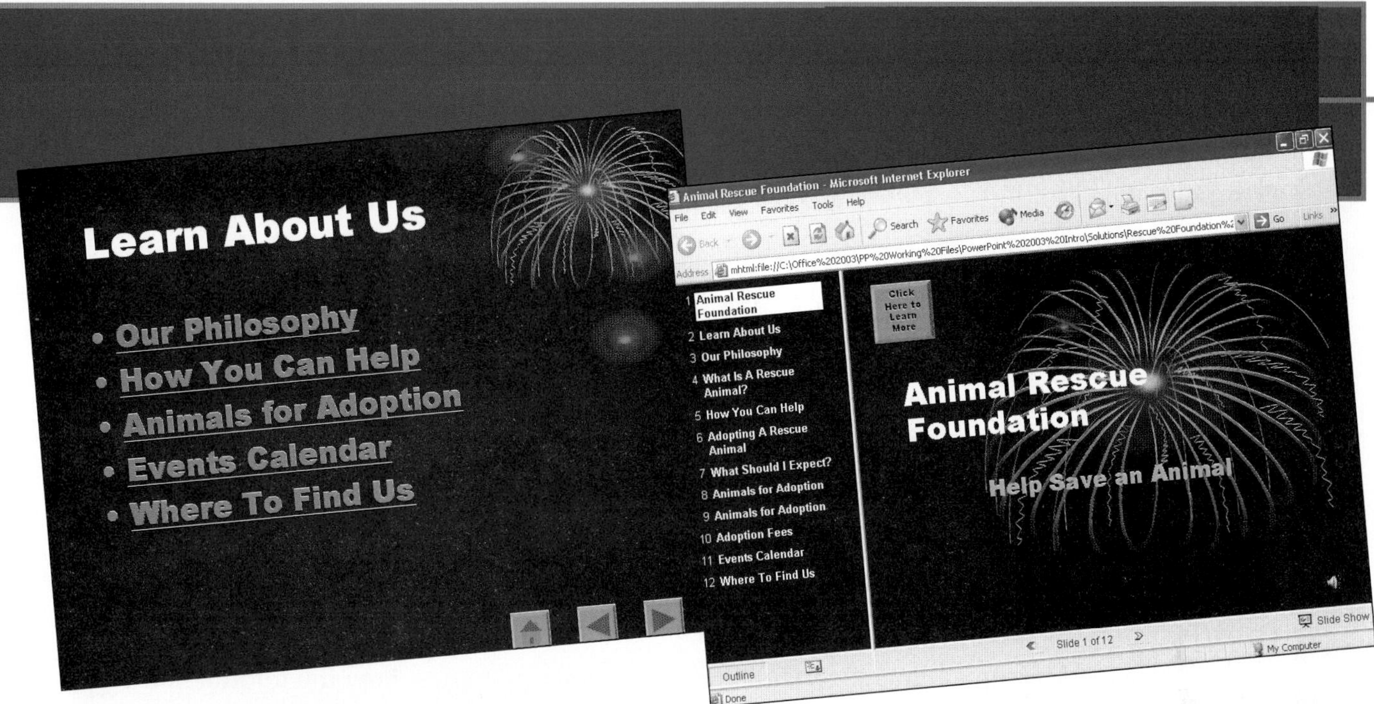

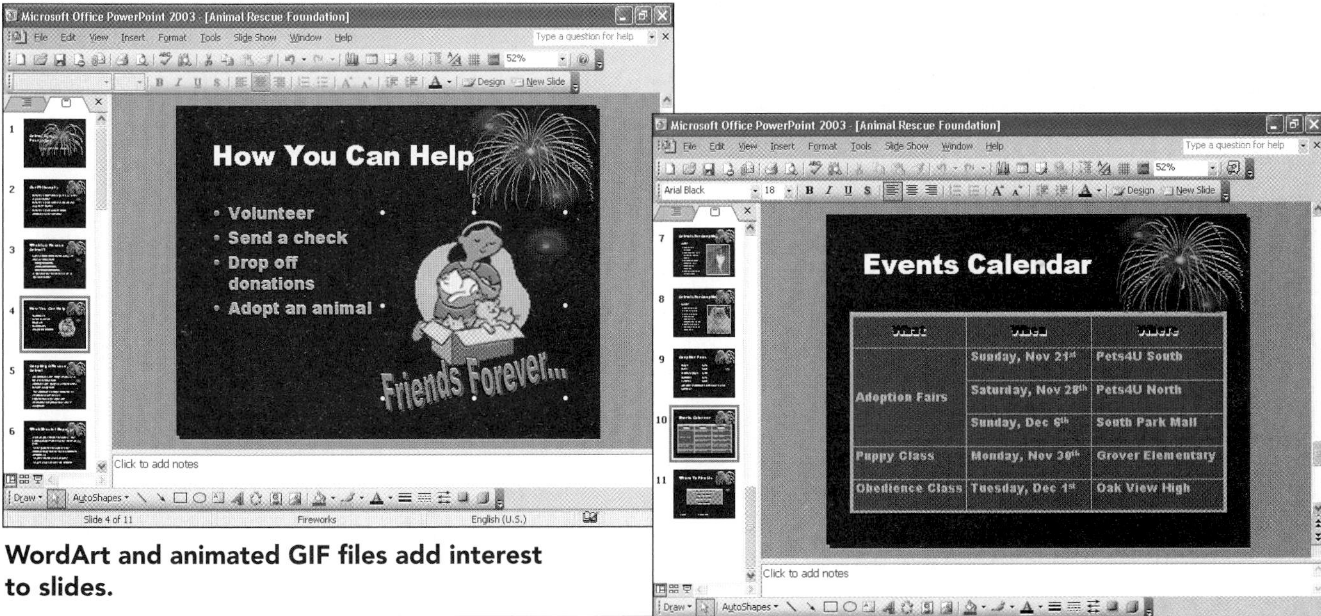

WordArt and animated GIF files add interest to slides.

Using tables makes information easier to read.

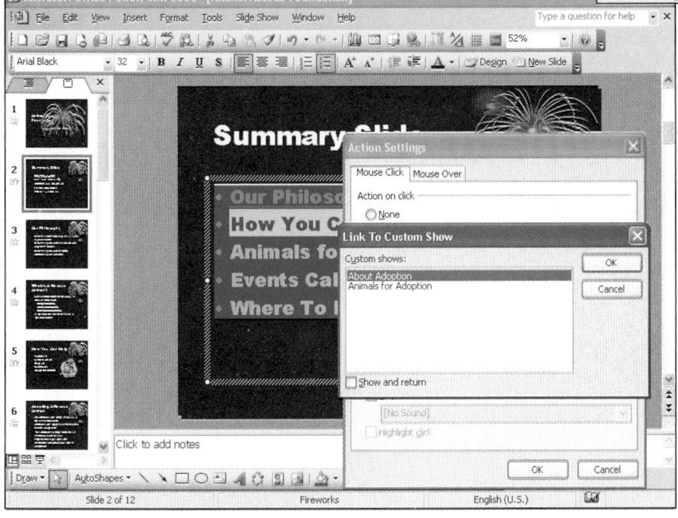

Creating a summary slide with hyperlinks adds custom navigation to a presentation.

Concept Preview

The following concepts will be introduced in this lab:

1. **Animated GIF** An animated GIF file is a type of graphic file that has motion.
2. **WordArt** The WordArt feature is used to enhance slides by changing the shape of text, adding 3-D effects, and changing the alignment of text on a line.
3. **Sound and Movie Files** Almost all PCs today are equipped with multimedia capabilities, which means they can play the most commonly used sound and movie files.
4. **Custom Show** A custom show is a presentation that runs within a presentation.
5. **Hyperlinks** Hyperlinks provide a quick way to jump to other slides, custom shows, presentations, objects, e-mail addresses, or Web pages.
6. **Action Buttons** Action buttons consist of shapes, such as right- and left-facing arrows, that are used to navigate through a presentation.
7. **Hypertext Markup Language** All Web pages are written using a programming language called Hypertext Markup Language (HTML). HTML commands control how the information on a page, such as font colors and size, is displayed.

Creating a Presentation from Multiple Sources

Often, as you are developing a presentation, you will have information from a variety of sources, such as text from a Word document or slides from other presentations. You can easily incorporate this information into a presentation without having to recreate it again.

Creating a New Presentation from a Design Template

When you first start PowerPoint 2003, a blank new presentation in the default template design is open. Because you have already decided to use the Fireworks design template for the new presentation, you will create a new presentation using this design first.

1. Start PowerPoint 2003.
   - Choose Create a New Presentation from the Getting Started task pane.

Additional Information

Clicking New on the Standard toolbar opens a new blank presentation in the Default Design template and the Slide Layout task pane.

   - Choose From Design Template.
   - If necessary, select Show Large Previews from the Slide Design task pane shortcut menu.
   - Click on the Fireworks design template to apply it to the presentation.

Your screen should be similar to Figure 4.1

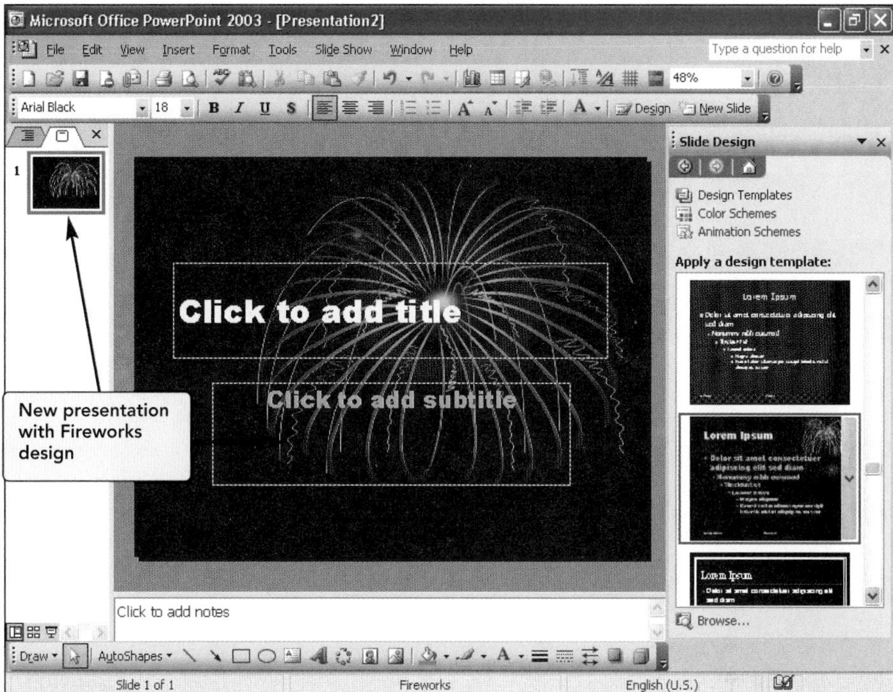

Figure 4.1

Additional Information

Each unnamed presentation you open during a session is assigned a number.

The default presentation is closed and a new presentation (Presentation2) consisting of one slide in the Fireworks design is displayed. Now you are ready to add content to the presentation.

2 Close the Slide Design task pane.

- Type **Animal Rescue Foundation** in the title text box.
- Type **Help Save an Animal** in the subtitle text box.

Your screen should be similar to Figure 4.2

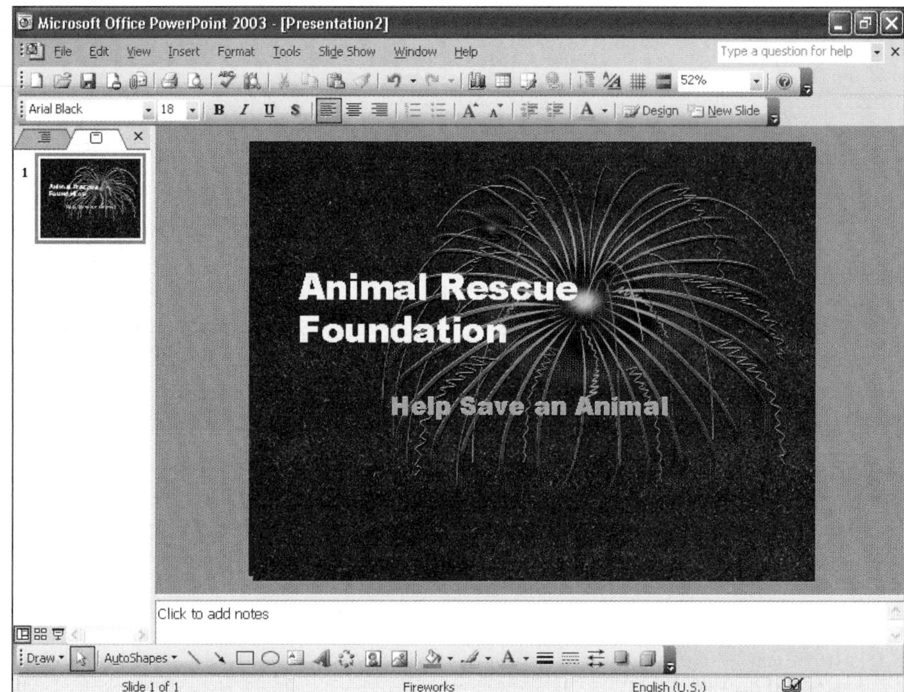

Figure 4.2

Before you can add additional text, you need to add slides to the presentation.

Inserting Text from a Word Document

Additional Information

Text created in other word processing programs can also be used to create a new presentation. The text files that PowerPoint can import are Word (.doc), Rich Text Format (.rft), Plain Text Format (.txt), or HTML (.htm) files.

Additional Information

In Word, if you apply Outline Numbering styles to the outline text, save the file as a Rich Text Format (rtf) file before importing it to PowerPoint. This removes the Numbering style so that outline numbers do not appear on the slide, but maintains the heading style.

You have already started developing the content for the promotional presentation by creating an outline in Word. Instead of retyping this information, you will insert slides containing the text for the presentation by importing the outline. For best results, the document you want to import should be formatted using heading styles so PowerPoint can easily convert the file content to slides. PowerPoint uses the heading levels to determine the slide title and levels for the slide body text. If heading levels are not available, PowerPoint determines these features from the paragraph indentations.

Additionally, you have another document that contains information about specific animals that are available for adoption. You will use the information from both of these documents to quickly create the new presentation.

As you created the outline in Outline view in Word, heading styles were automatically applied. Now all you have to do is import the outline into PowerPoint.

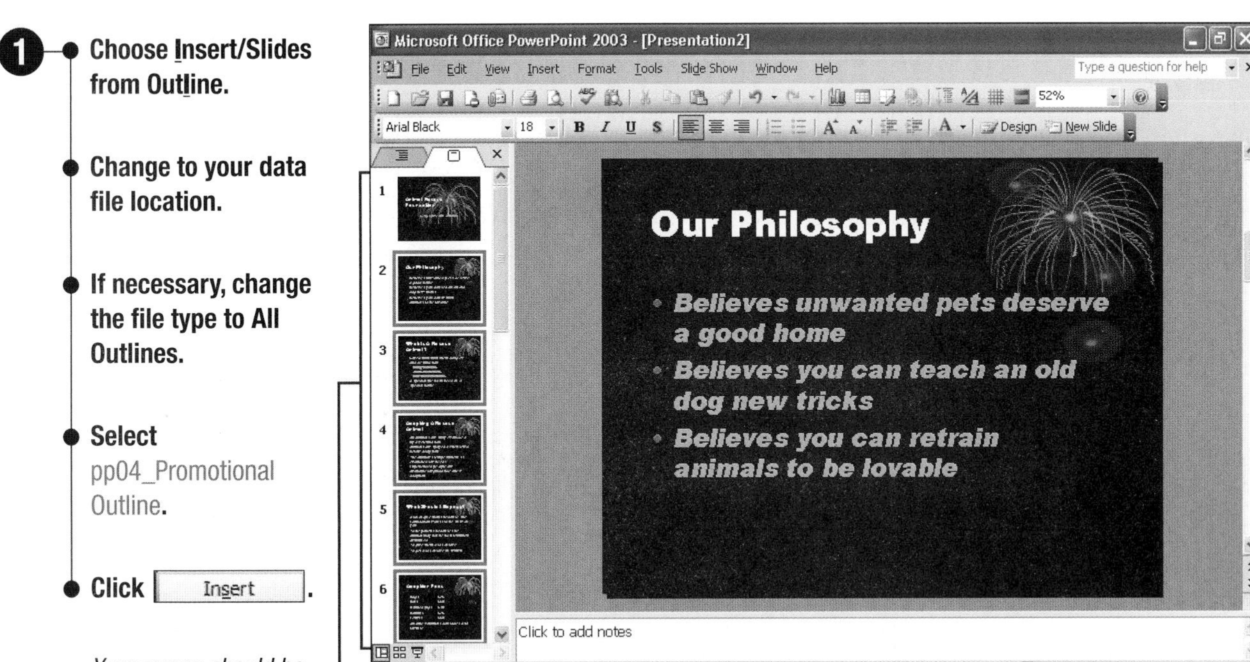

Figure 4.3

Another Method

You can create a presentation directly from within Word using File/Send to/Microsoft PowerPoint.

The outline text is imported into the blank presentation and inserted as separate slides. Each level 1 heading appears as an individual slide title. Text formatted as a level 2 heading is a main body text point, a level 3 heading is a second-level body text point, and so on.

Now you want to add the information about the animals available for adoption.

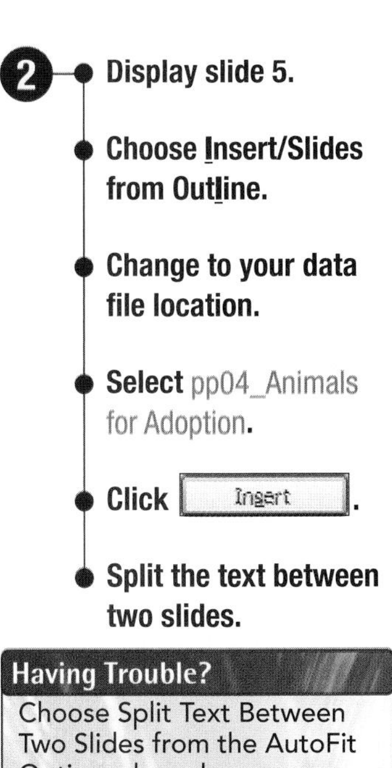

Having Trouble?

Choose Split Text Between Two Slides from the AutoFit Options drop-down menu.

Your screen should be similar to Figure 4.4

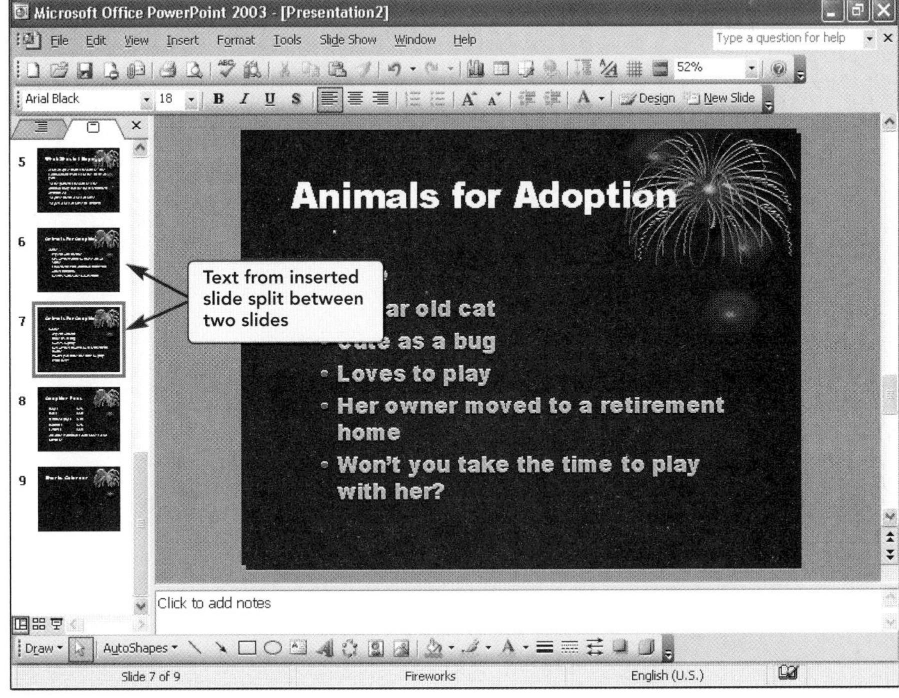

Figure 4.4

Slides 6 and 7 now contain the information about the animals currently available for adoption.

Inserting Slides from Another Presentation

Next you want to add two more slides to the presentation. To save time, you will insert slides that have already been created in another presentation into your current presentation. First you will add a slide after slide 3.

1.
- **Display slide 3.**
- **Choose Insert/Slides from Files.**
- **Open the Find Presentation tab, if necessary.**

Your screen should be similar to Figure 4.5

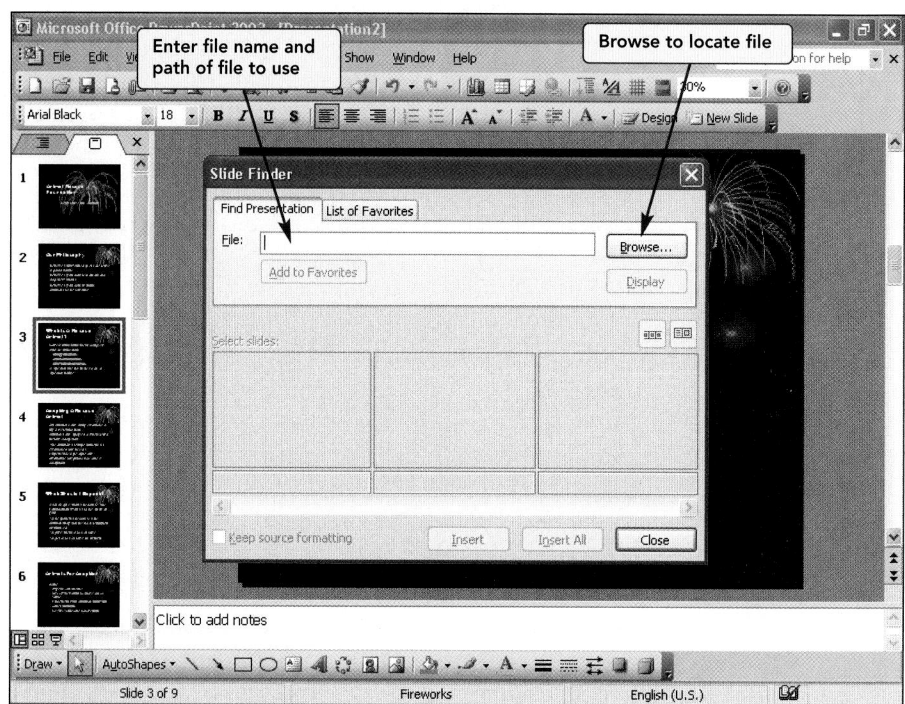

Figure 4.5

The Slide Finder dialog box is used to locate the presentation file containing the slides you want to copy into your current presentation. You can enter the file name and path directly in the File text box, or use the Browse... button to locate and select the file just as you would when opening an existing presentation.

2 • **Click** Browse... .

• **Change the Look In location to the location of your data files.**

• **Select** pp04_Foundation Introduction.

• **Click** Open .

Your screen should be similar to Figure 4.6

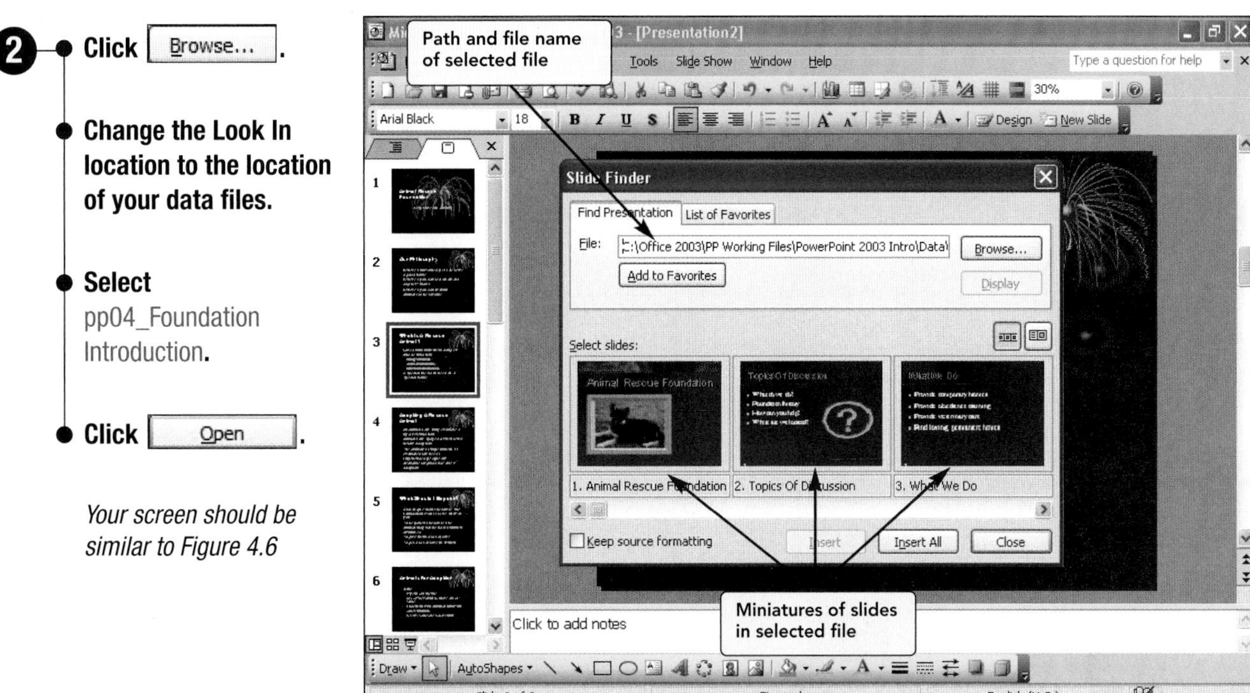

Figure 4.6

Additional Information

Click 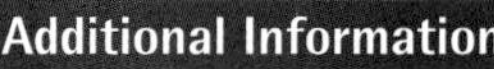 to switch to horizontal format and to switch to list format.

The path and file name of the selected file are displayed in the File text box. In addition, miniatures of the slides in the presentation are displayed in the Select Slides area. You can view the slides in two different formats: horizontal or list. Horizontal format displays a miniature of each slide side by side with the slide title below each slide. This is the default view. List format displays the titles of all slides in the presentation in a list and a preview of the selected slide.

3 • **Scroll the slides to the right and select slide 5, How You Can Help.**

• **Click** Insert .

Your screen should be similar to Figure 4.7

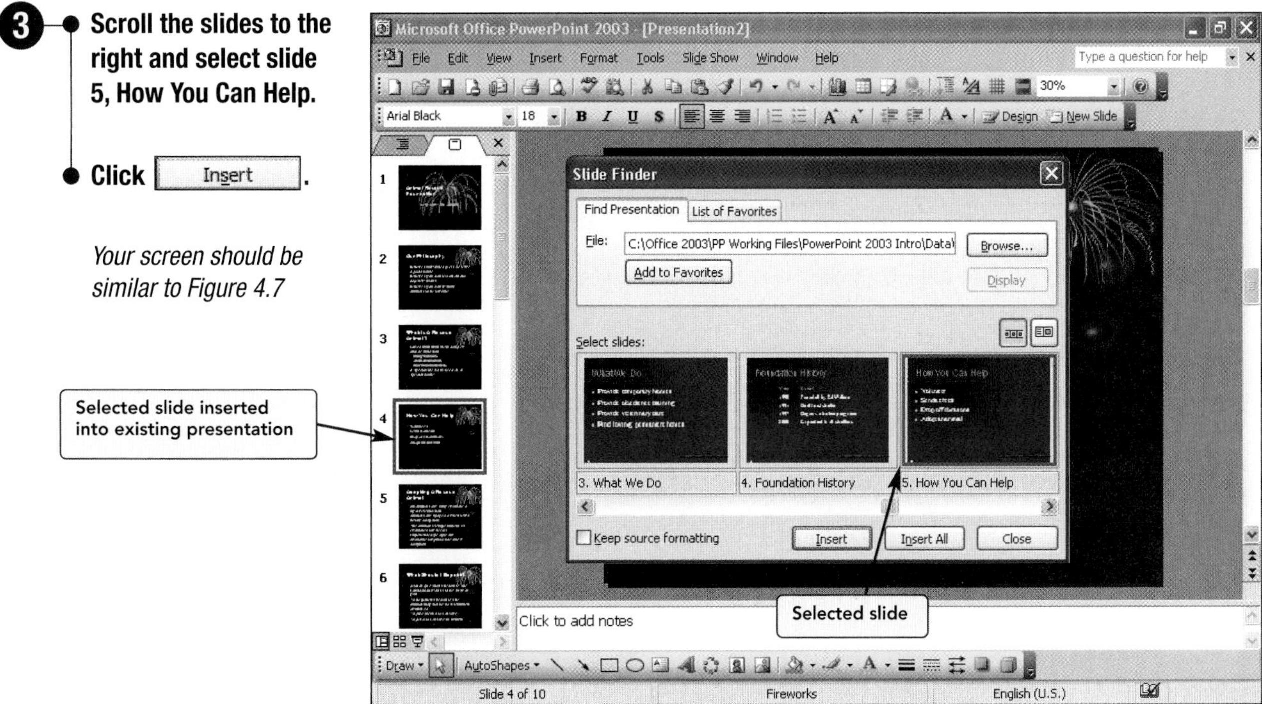

Figure 4.7

The selected slide from the Foundation Introduction presentation file is inserted into the new presentation and the template design is applied to the slide. Next you will insert the last slide from the Foundation Introduction presentation as the ending slide (11) of the new presentation.

4

- **Select slide 10 in the Slide tab.**
- **Click on slide 5 from the Select Slides area of the dialog box to deselect it.**

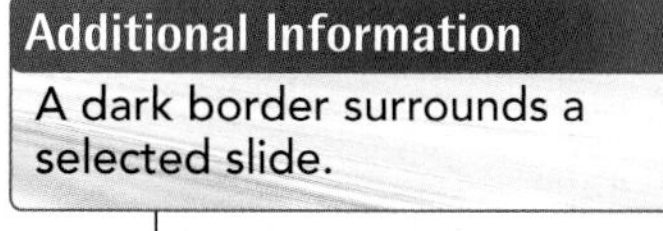

- **Click on slide 6 from the Select Slides area of the dialog box to select it.**
- **Click** Insert.
- **Click** Close.

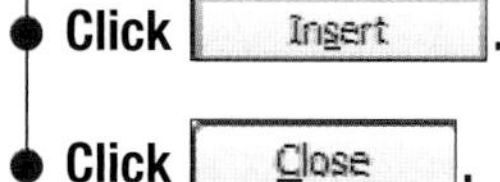

Your screen should be similar to Figure 4.8

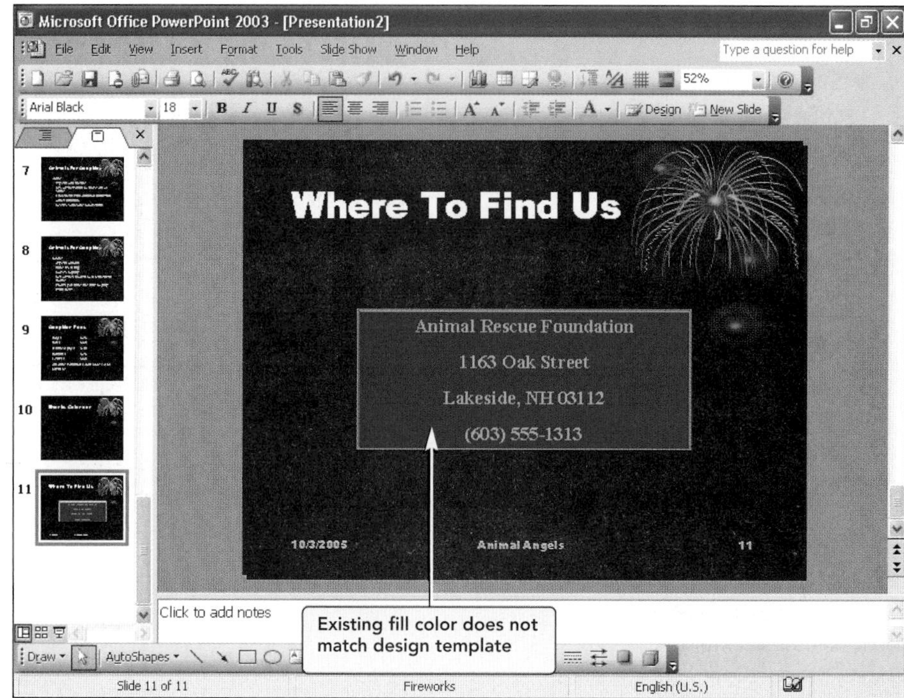

Figure 4.8

Now that all the slides you need have been added to the presentation, you need to make a few design adjustments. First you need to change the fill and font color of the text box to coordinate with the template colors.

5

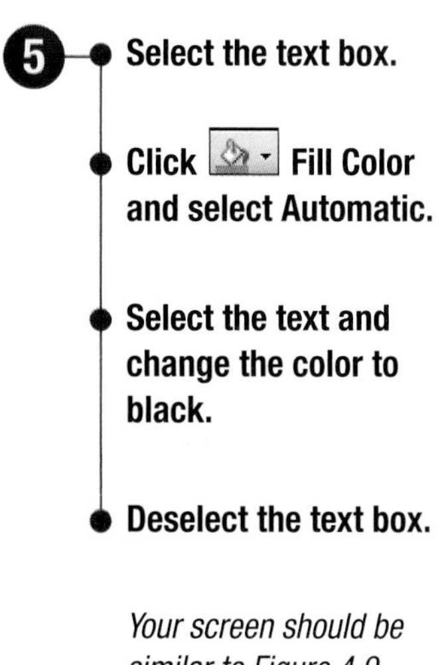

- **Select the text box.**
- **Click** Fill Color **and select Automatic.**
- **Select the text and change the color to black.**
- **Deselect the text box.**

Your screen should be similar to Figure 4.9

Figure 4.9

Next, make the following changes to the slides specified.

6

- **Change the slide layout of slide 7 to the Title, Text, and Content.**
- **Insert the picture file** pp04_Jake **from your data files on slide 7.**
- **Appropriately size and position the picture.**
- **Add a 6 pt dark gold border around the picture.**

Having Trouble?

Use Line Style and Line Color on the Drawing toolbar.

Your screen should be similar to Figure 4.10

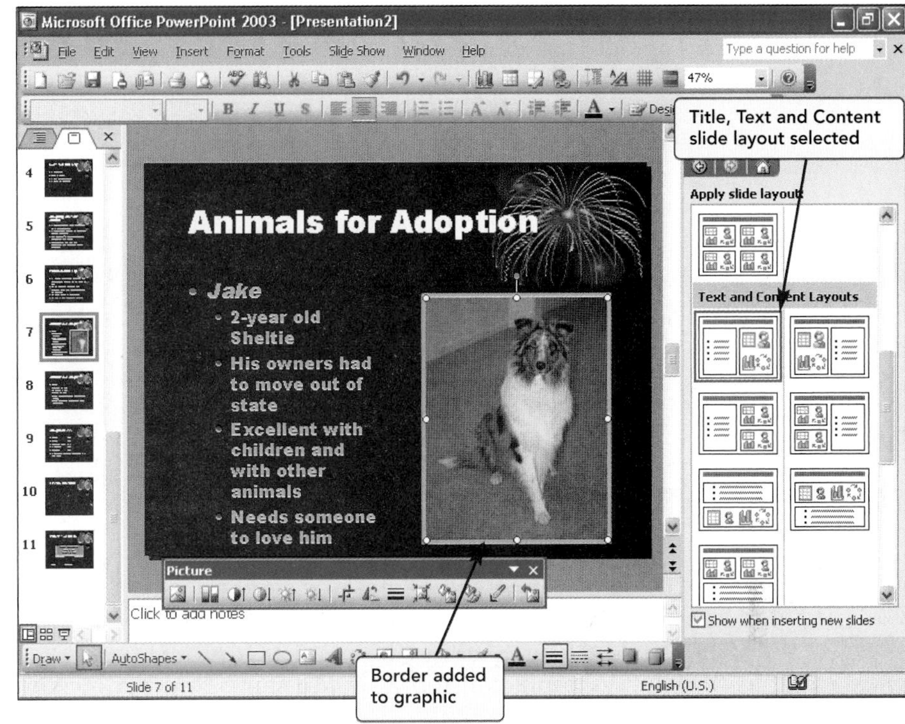

Figure 4.10

The addition of the graphic adds much more impact to the slide.

7

- **Repeat the same steps to add the picture file** pp04_Sadie **from your data files to slide 8.**
- **Change to Slide Sorter view.**
- **Run the slide show from the beginning to see how all the changes you have made so far look.**
- **Save the presentation as** Animal Rescue Foundation**.**

Your screen should be similar to Figure 4.11

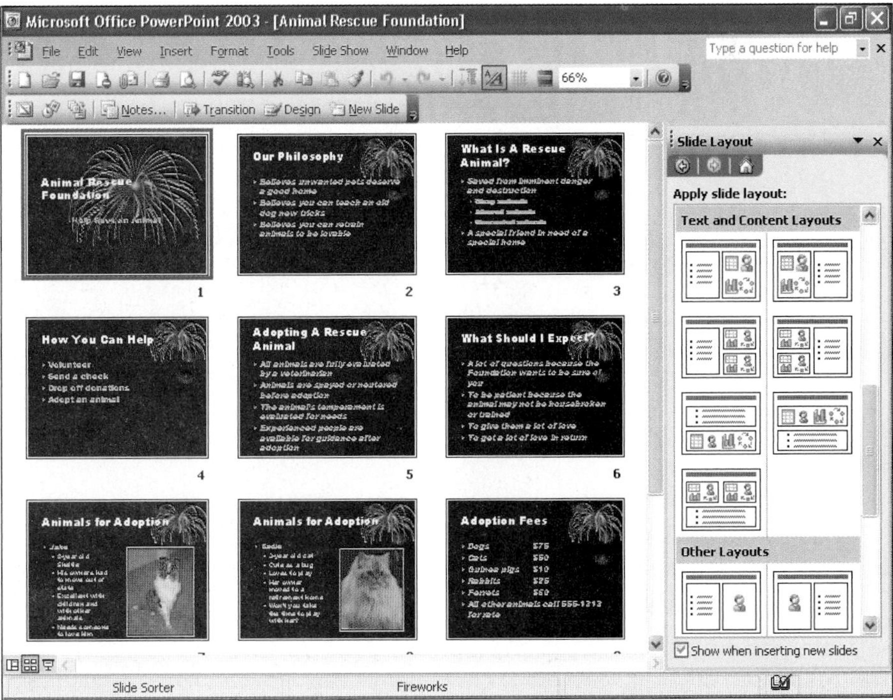

Figure 4.11

Creating a Complex Table

Next you want to add a calendar of events in a table format. The table will display the type, date, and location of the event. Your completed table will be similar to the one shown below.

[illegible]	[illegible]	[illegible]
Adoption Fairs	Sunday, Nov 21st	Pets4U South
	Saturday, Nov 28th	Pets4U North
	Sunday, Dec 6th	South Park Mall
Puppy Class	Monday, Nov 30th	Grover Elementary
Obedience Class	Tuesday, Dec 1st	Oak View High

PowerPoint includes several different methods that you can use to create tables. One method is to apply the Table slide layout to a slide. You used this method to create a simple table in Lab 2. Another method uses the Insert/Table command or the Insert Table button to create a simple table consisting of the same number of rows and columns. Finally, Draw Table can be used to create any type of table, but is most useful for creating complex tables that contain cells of different heights or a varying number of columns per row. You will use the Draw Table feature to create this table.

1

- **Display slide 10, Events Calendar in Normal view.**
- **Apply the Title Only slide layout.**
- **Close the Slide Layout task pane.**
- **Click Tables and Borders.**
- **If necessary, dock the Tables and Borders toolbar below the Formatting toolbar.**

Your screen should be similar to Figure 4.12

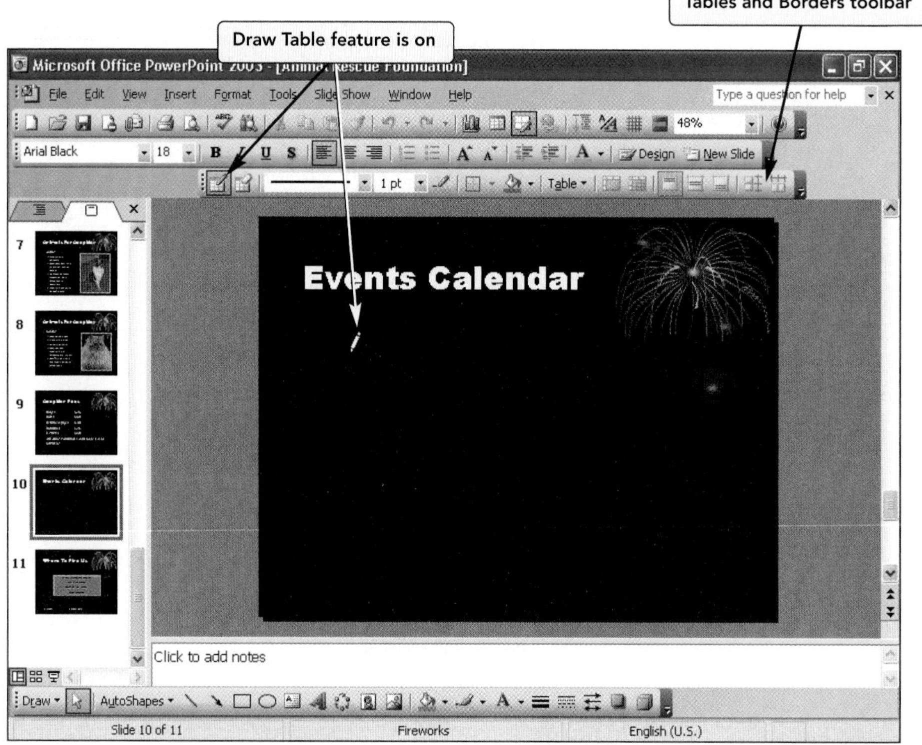

Figure 4.12

The Tables and Borders toolbar appears, and the mouse pointer changes to a pen when positioned on the slide. This indicates the Draw Table feature is on.

Using Draw Table to create a table is similar to the way you would use a pen to draw a table. First you define the outer table boundary by dragging diagonally to the size you want. Then you drag to create the column and row lines. A dotted line appears to show the boundary or lines you are creating as you drag. When creating row or column lines, drag from the beginning boundary to the end to extend the line the distance you want.

You will use Draw Table to create the table boundary and columns and rows. As you do, refer to Figure 4.13 for guidance. When creating a table using this feature, it is also helpful to display the ruler so you can more accurately draw the table lines.

2
- **Choose View/Ruler to display the ruler.**
- **Drag downward and to the right to create an outer table boundary of approximately 3.5 inches by 7.5 inches.**
- **Add two vertical column lines at positions 2.5 and 5.5 on the ruler.**
- **Draw five horizontal lines to create the rows as shown in Figure 4.13. (Lines 2 and 3 begin at the end of the first column.)**

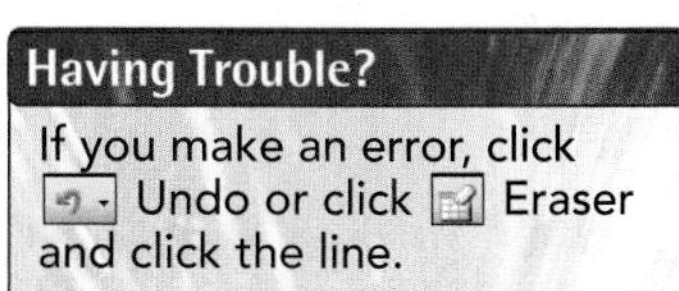

Having Trouble?

If you make an error, click Undo or click Eraser and click the line.

Your screen should be similar to Figure 4.13

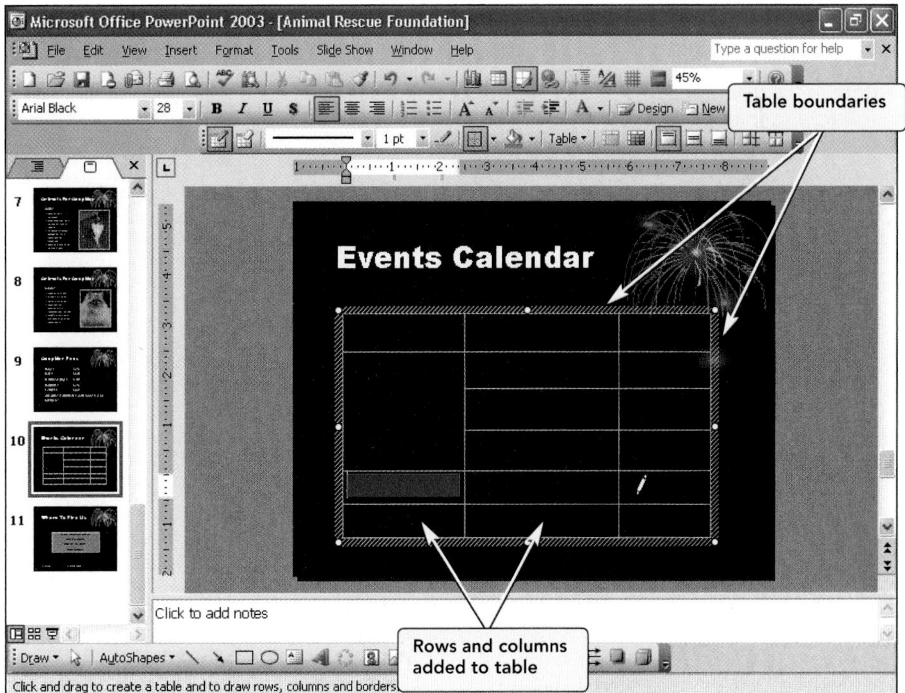

Figure 4.13

Do not be concerned if your table is not exactly like that in Figure 4.13. You will adjust the table lines shortly.

Now you are ready to enter the information into the table. As you enter the text, the cells will automatically increase in size to accommodate the entries and the text will wrap in the cells.

3 **Click Draw Table to turn off the Draw Table feature.**

Another Method

Typing in any cell will also turn off Draw Table.

- **Enter the data shown at right.**

	Col A	Col B	Col C
Row 1	**What**	**When**	**Where**
Row 2	**Adoption Fairs**	**Saturday, Nov 21st**	**Pets4U South**
Row 3		**Saturday, Nov 28th**	**Pets4U North**
Row 4		**Sunday, Dec 6th**	**South Park Mall**
Row 5	**Puppy Class**	**Monday, Nov 30th**	**Grover Elementary**
Row 6	**Obedience Class**	**Tuesday, Dec 1st**	**Oak View High**

Additional Information

You can copy and edit similar table entries to save time.

Additional Information

The "st" and "th" following the date will automatically change to superscript as soon as you enter a space after the word.

Your screen should be similar to Figure 4.14

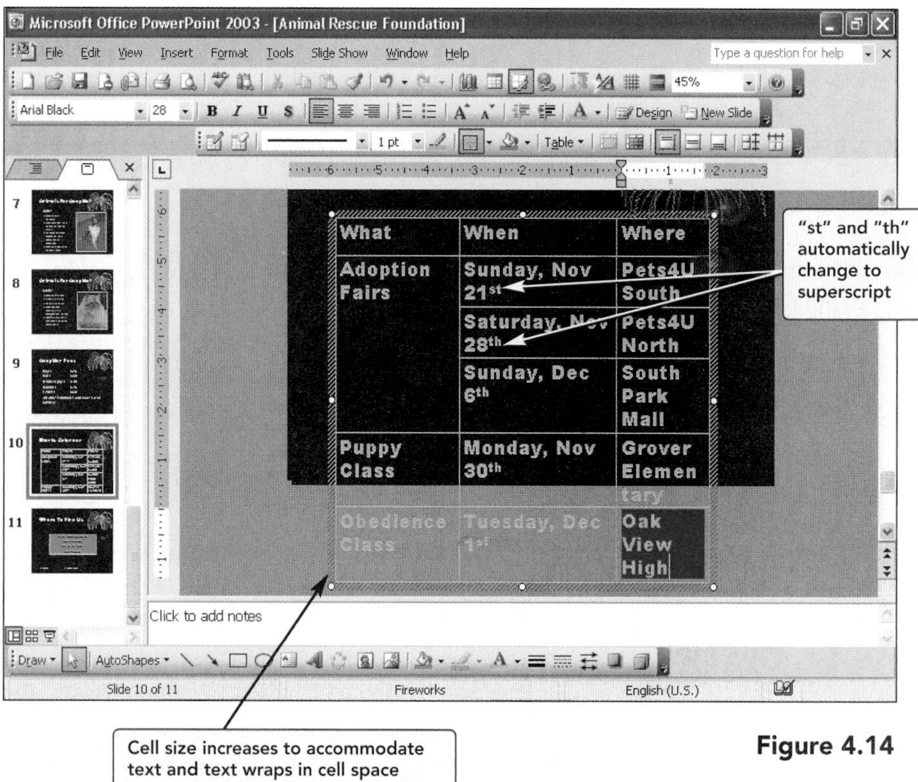

Figure 4.14

Because the table size has increased to accommodate the information in the table, it is too large to fit on the slide. You will fix this by making the font size of the text in the table smaller.

Enhancing the Table

Additional Information

Many commands for working with tables are available by clicking Table on the Tables and Borders toolbar.

Next you need to adjust the size of the text, size the columns and rows appropriately, and add other enhancements to the table. As you continue to modify the table, the contents of many cells can be selected and changed at the same time. The following table describes how to select different areas of a table.

Area to Select	Procedure
Cell	Drag across the contents of the cell.
Row	Drag across the row. Use Table ▾/Select Row.
Column	Drag down the column. Use Table ▾/Select Column.
Multiple cells, rows, or columns	Drag through the cells, rows, or columns. Select the first cell, row, or column, and hold down ⇧Shift while clicking on another cell, row, or column.
Contents of next cell	Press Tab ↹.
Contents of previous cell	Press ⇧Shift + Tab ↹.
Entire table	Drag through all the cells. Use Table ▾/Select Table. Click the crosshatched table border.

Additional Information

A dotted table border indicates the entire table and all its contents are selected.

First you will reduce the size of the text. You could do this by selecting a point size from the drop-down list. Another way, however, is to decrease the size by units.

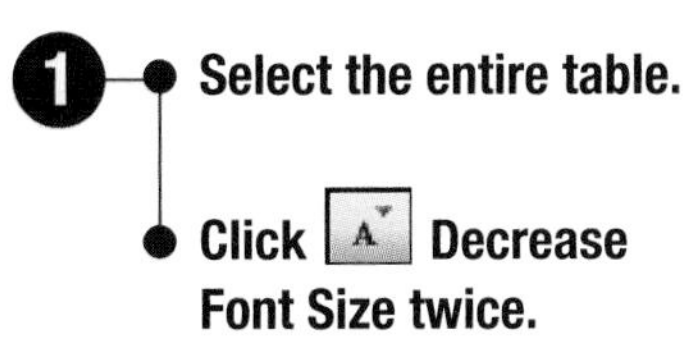

1 **Select the entire table.**

Click A Decrease Font Size twice.

Having Trouble?

Clicking A increases the fonts size by units.

Your screen should be similar to Figure 4.15

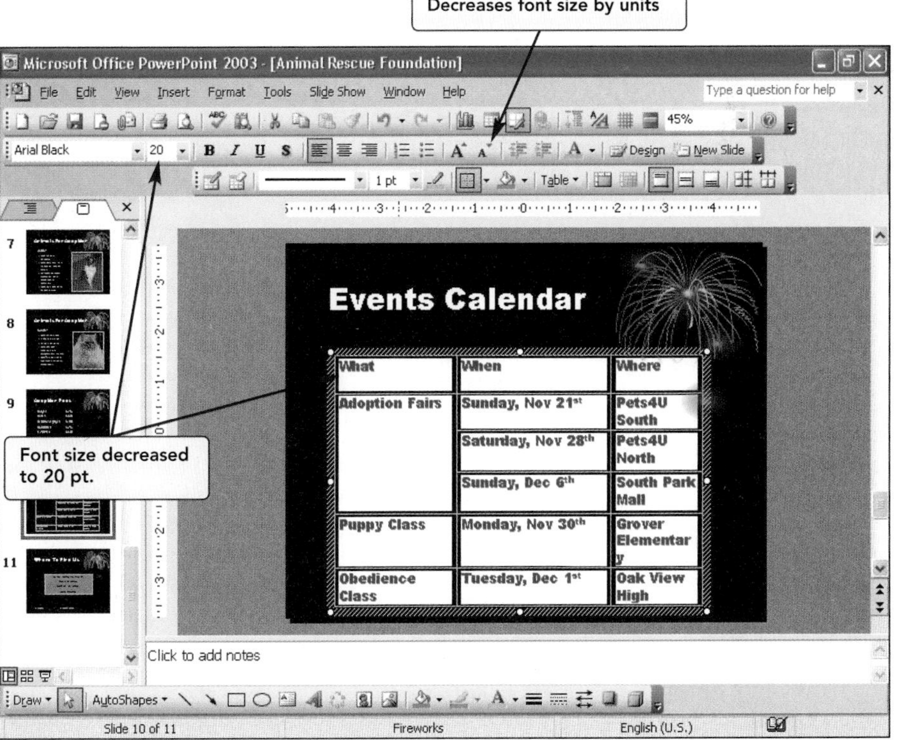

Figure 4.15

The font size has quickly been reduced by two units, and at 20 points the table now fits in the slide. Next, you will adjust the column widths so that the cell contents will display on a single line.

2

- **Point to the right border of column A and drag to increase or decrease the column width until the information in the What column just fits on a single line.**
- **In the same manner, adjust the When and Where column widths as needed to display the cell contents on a single line.**

Having Trouble?

You may need to increase the size of the entire table to display the cell contents on a single line.

- **Position the table as in Figure 4.16.**

Your screen should be similar to Figure 4.16

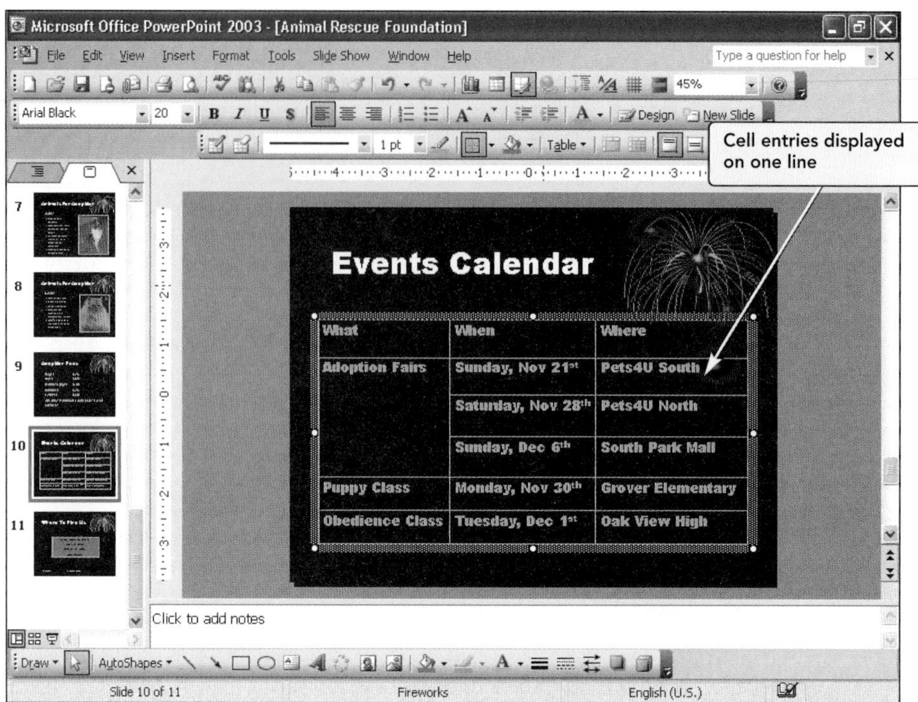

Figure 4.16

You also want to adjust the heights of the rows so they are all the same and center the text in several cells.

3

- **Select the table.**
- **Click Distribute Rows Evenly (in the Tables and Borders toolbar).**
- **Select row 1 and click Center and Center Vertically to change the orientation of the text in the row to centered horizontally and vertically.**
- **Click to center vertically the text "Adoption Fairs" in row 2 of column A.**

Your screen should be similar to Figure 4.17

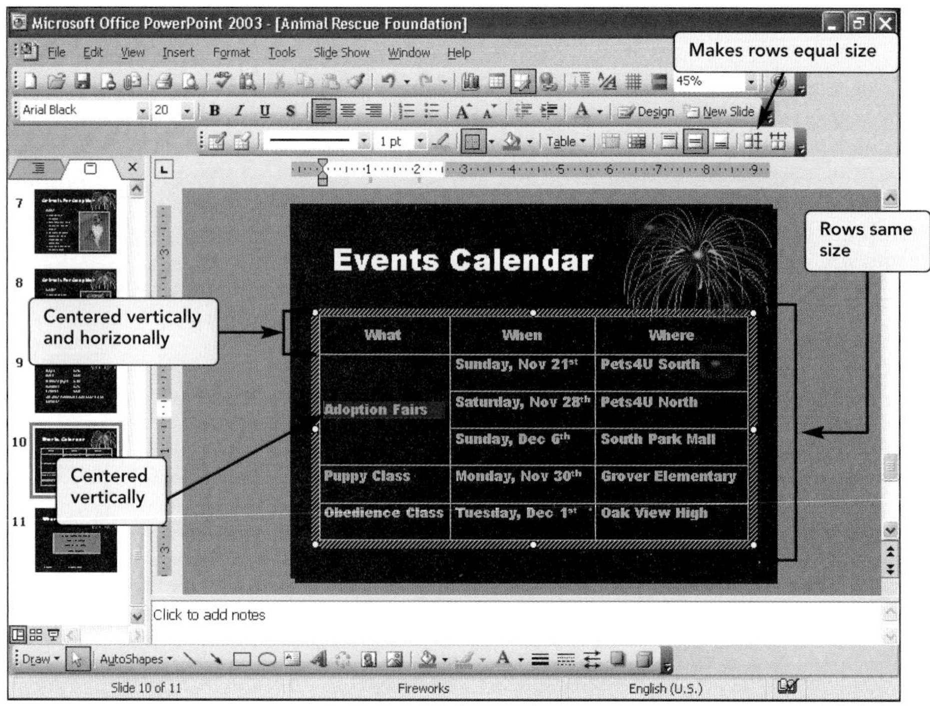

Figure 4.17

Next you will add some color to the table.

4

- **Select the entire table and apply a fill color of your choice to the selection.**
- **Select row 1 and change the text to an appropriate color, bold, and shadowed.**

Your screen should be similar to Figure 4.18

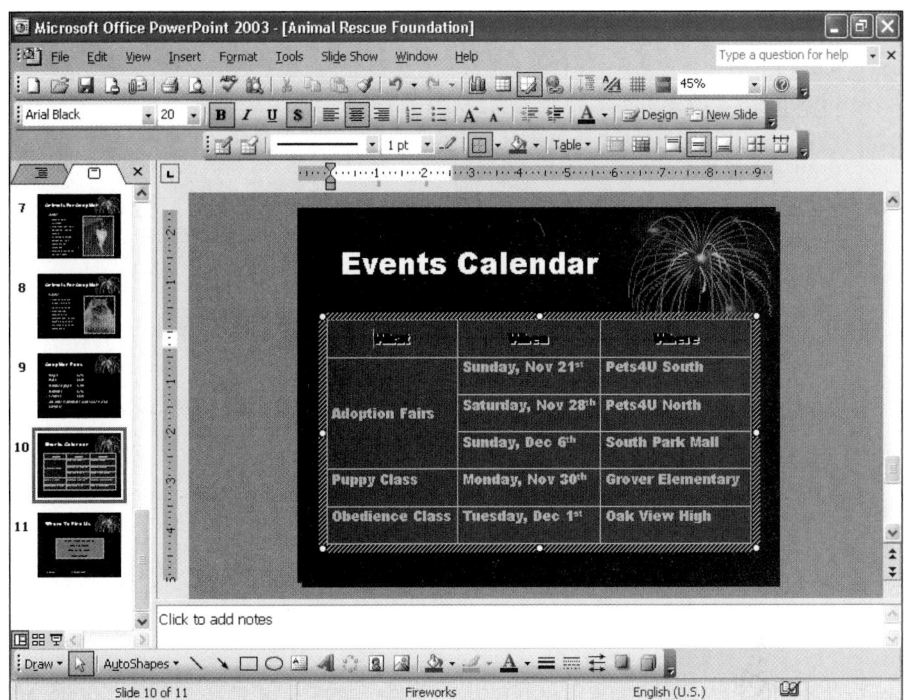

Figure 4.18

The final enhancement is to make the table border wider and a different color.

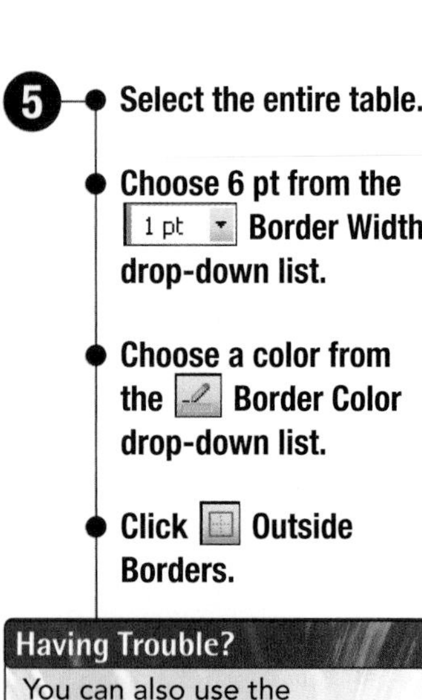

5 Select the entire table.

- Choose 6 pt from the 1 pt Border Width drop-down list.
- Choose a color from the Border Color drop-down list.
- Click Outside Borders.

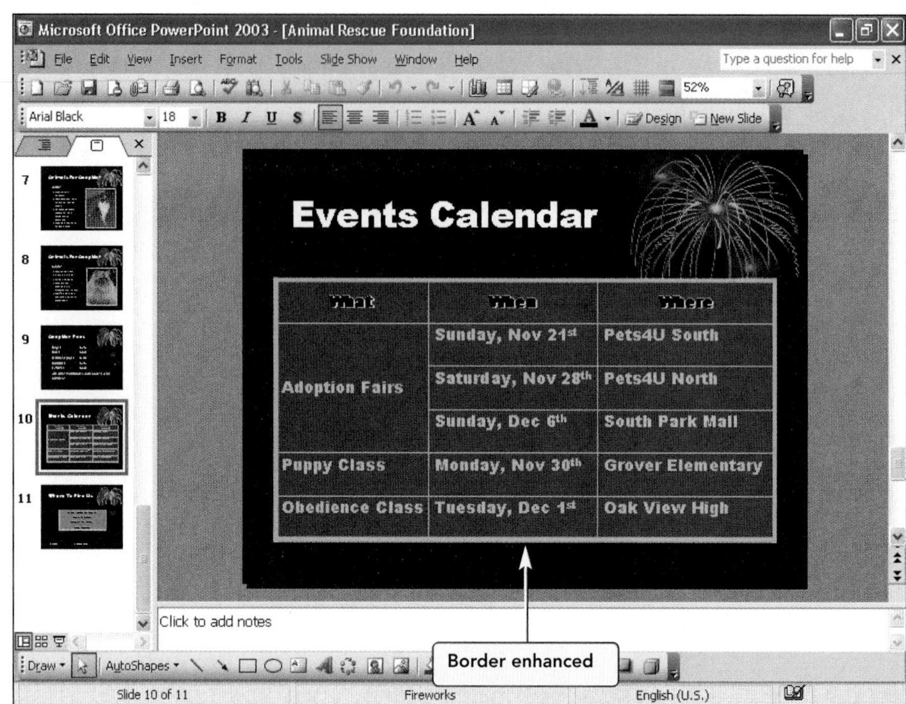

Figure 4.19

Having Trouble?

You can also use the Format/Table command or /Borders and Fill to add, change, and remove borders and fills.

- Turn off Draw Table and click outside the table to deselect it.
- Close the Tables and Borders toolbar.
- Turn off the display of the ruler.
- Save the presentation.

Your screen should be similar to Figure 4.19

The table displays the information in an attractive and easy-to-read manner.

Adding Interest to the Presentation

Although you like the look of the Fireworks template, you feel it is rather static for a kiosk presentation and want to add some action to the presentation. You will do this by adding an animated picture and graphic text to a slide.

Adding Animated Graphics

First, you want to enhance the How You Can Help slide by adding a graphic from an animated GIF file.

Concept 1

Animated GIF

1 An **animated GIF** file is a type of graphic file that has motion. It consists of a series of GIF (Graphic Interchange Format) images that are displayed in rapid succession to produce an animated effect. They are commonly used on Web pages and can also be incorporated into PowerPoint presentations.

When an animated GIF file is inserted into a PowerPoint slide, it does not display action until you run the presentation. If you save the presentation as a Web page and view it in a browser, the animated GIF files run as soon as you view the page containing the graphic.

You cannot modify an animated graphic image using the features in the Picture toolbar. If you want to make changes to the graphic, such as changing the fill color or border, you need to use an animated GIF editing program.

You want to add an animated graphic that will really capture the attention of viewers.

1
- **Display slide 4 in Normal view.**
- **Apply the Title, Text, and Content slide layout to the slide.**
- **Click Insert Picture.**
- **Specify your data file location and select** pp04_Adoptions.
- **Click Insert.**

Additional Information

The Microsoft Clips Online Web site includes many animated graphics in the Motion category.

- **Size and position the graphic as shown in Figure 4.20.**

Your screen should be similar to Figure 4.20

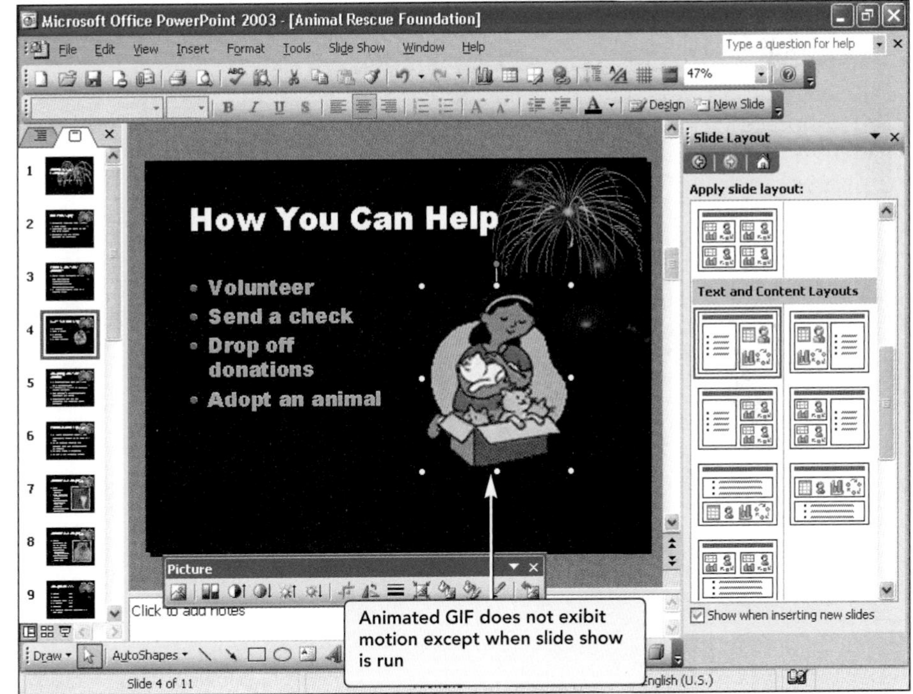

Figure 4.20

The graphic will not exhibit motion until you run the slide show.

2
- **Display the slide in Slide Show view to see the animation.**
- **Press Esc to stop the slide show.**

Creating a WordArt Object

You also want to add graphic text to the slide to further enhance the slide. You will add the phrase "Friends Forever" below the picture. To make this phrase unique and more interesting, you will enter it using the WordArt feature.

Concept 2

WordArt

2 The **WordArt** feature is used to enhance slides by changing the shape of text, adding 3-D effects, and changing the alignment of text on a line. You can also rotate, flip, and skew WordArt text. The text that is added to a slide using WordArt is a graphic object that can be edited, sized, or moved to any location on the slide.

Use WordArt to add a special touch to your presentations, but limit its use to a single element on a slide. You want the WordArt to capture the viewer's attention. Here are some examples of WordArt.

You will create a WordArt object for the text to appear below the animated graphic.

1

- **If necessary, deselect the graphic.**
- **Close the Slide Layout task pane.**
- **Click Insert WordArt.**

Your screen should be similar to Figure 4.21

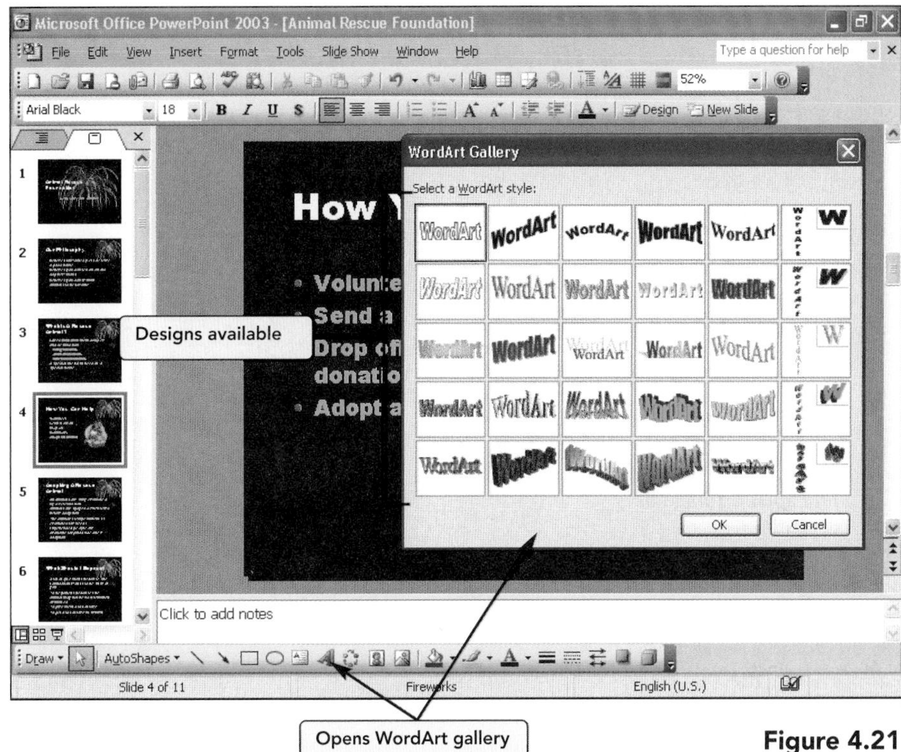

Figure 4.21

The first step is to select one of the 30 styles or designs of WordArt from the WordArt Gallery dialog box. These styles are just a starting point. As you will see, you can alter the appearance of the style by selecting a different color, shape, and special effect.

2

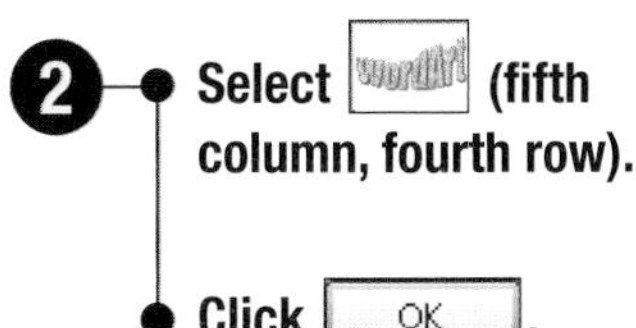

- **Select (fifth column, fourth row).**
- **Click OK.**

Your screen should be similar to Figure 4.22

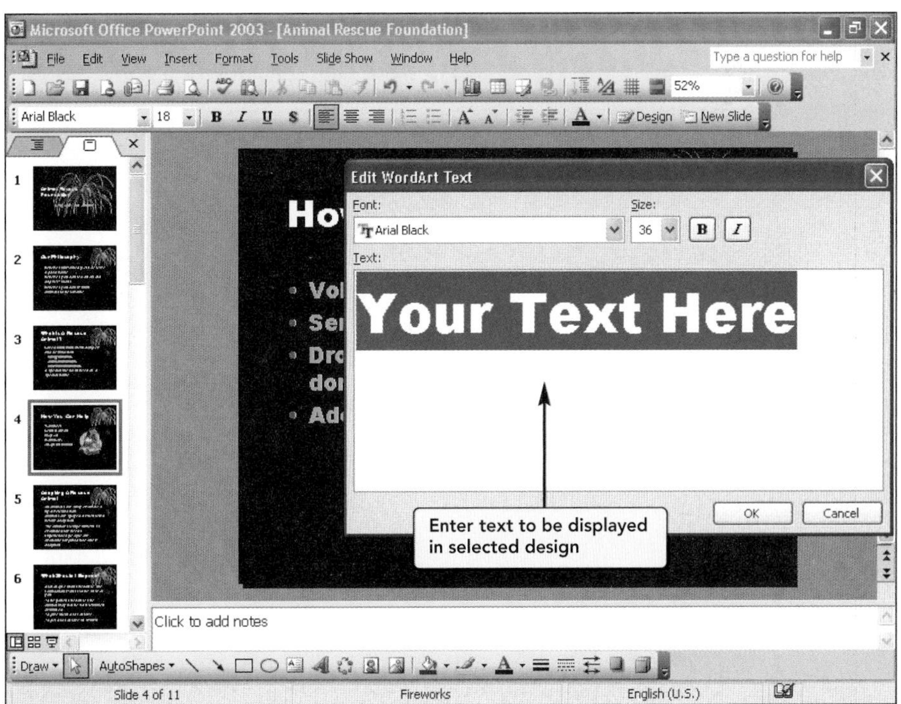

Figure 4.22

Next, in the Edit WordArt Text dialog box, you need to enter the text you want displayed using the selected WordArt design.

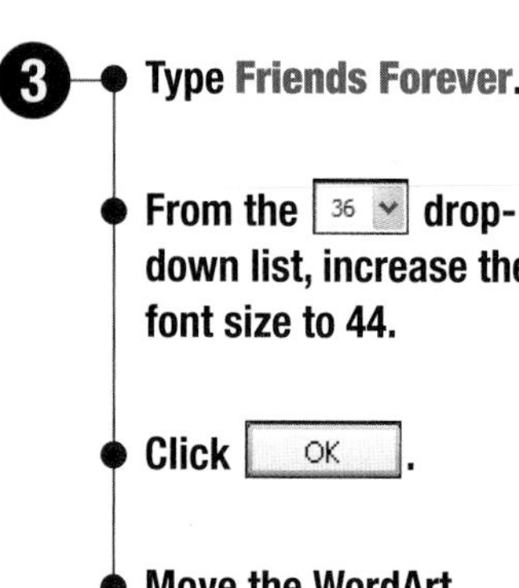

3 Type **Friends Forever**.

- From the 36 drop-down list, increase the font size to 44.
- Click OK.
- Move the WordArt object to the position shown in Figure 4.23.

Your screen should be similar to Figure 4.23

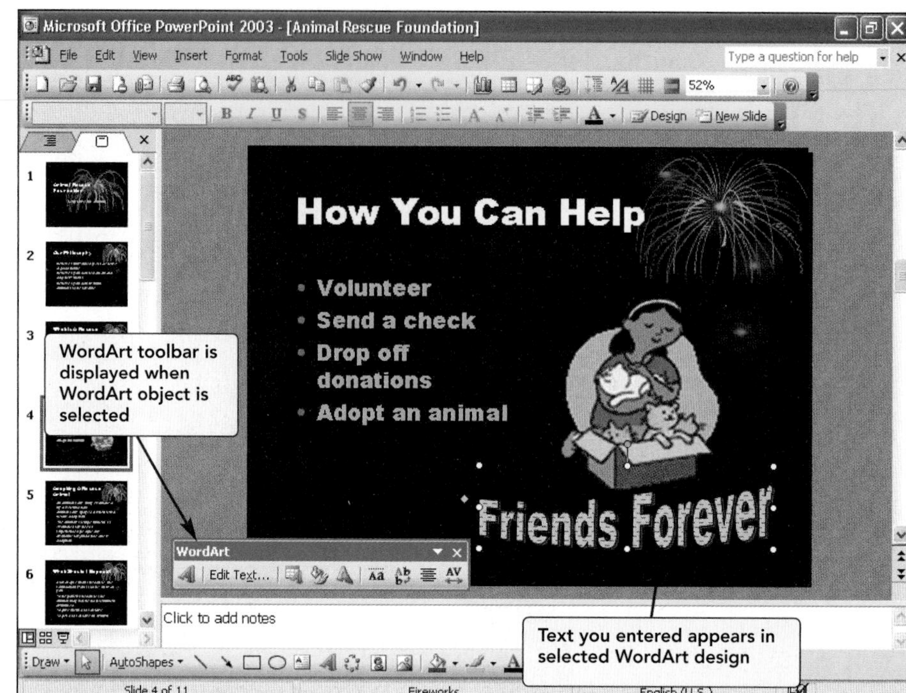

Figure 4.23

Now the text you entered is displayed in the selected WordArt style on the slide. The handles surrounding the WordArt object indicate that it is selected. Whenever a WordArt object is selected, the WordArt toolbar is displayed. The WordArt toolbar buttons (identified below) are used to modify the WordArt.

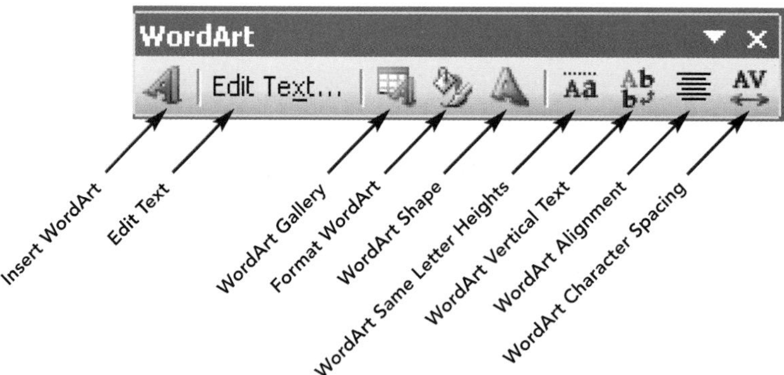

Editing WordArt Text

As you look at the WordArt, you decide that you want to add an ellipsis following the text to lead the reader to the next slide. The text can be entirely changed or simply edited, as you will do.

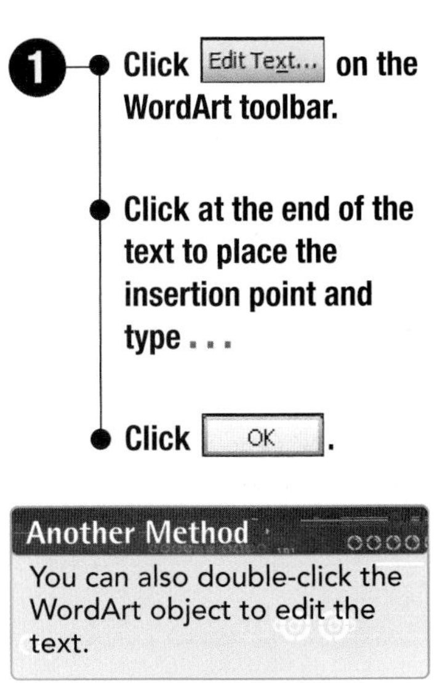

Another Method

You can also double-click the WordArt object to edit the text.

Your screen should be similar to Figure 4.24

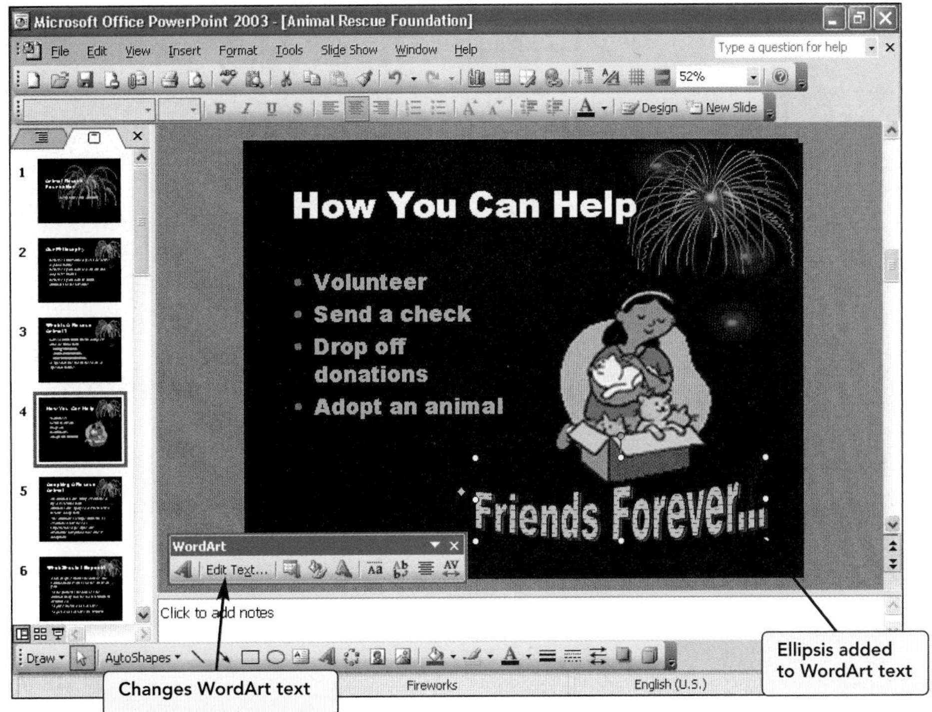

Figure 4.24

The change you made to the text in the Edit WordArt Text dialog box appears in the WordArt object.

Enhancing a WordArt Object

Now you want to change the appearance of the WordArt object to make it more interesting. First you will change the shape of the object.

1 Click WordArt Shape.

Choose Double Wave 2 (eighth column, third row).

Your screen should be similar to Figure 4.25

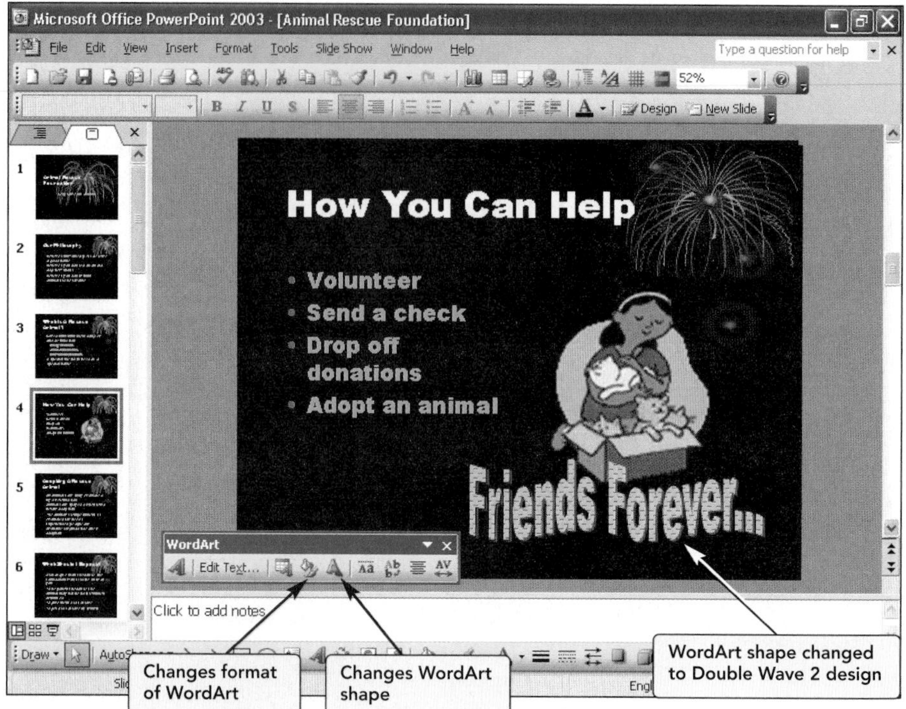

Figure 4.25

Next you want to change the color of the WordArt characters so they match the color scheme of the design template.

2 Click Format WordArt.

Open the Colors and Lines tab.

Your screen should be similar to Figure 4.26

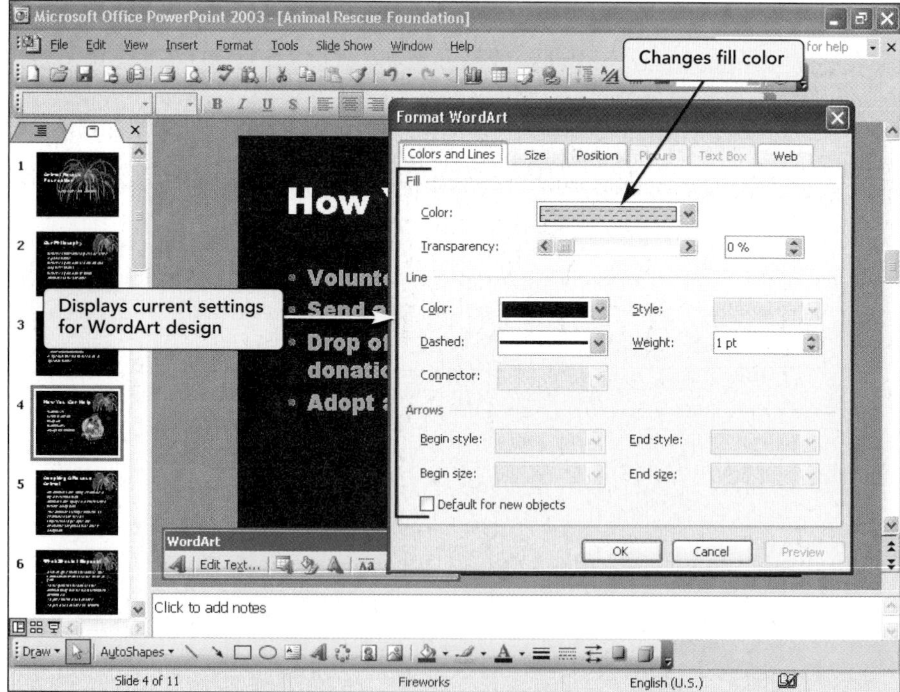

Figure 4.26

The Format WordArt dialog box shows the color and line settings for the selected WordArt design style. You want to change the colors to complement the color scheme of the design template.

3 ● **Open the Fill Color drop-down list box.**

● **Select the orange color of the slide color scheme from the color palette.**

● **Click OK.**

Your screen should be similar to Figure 4.27

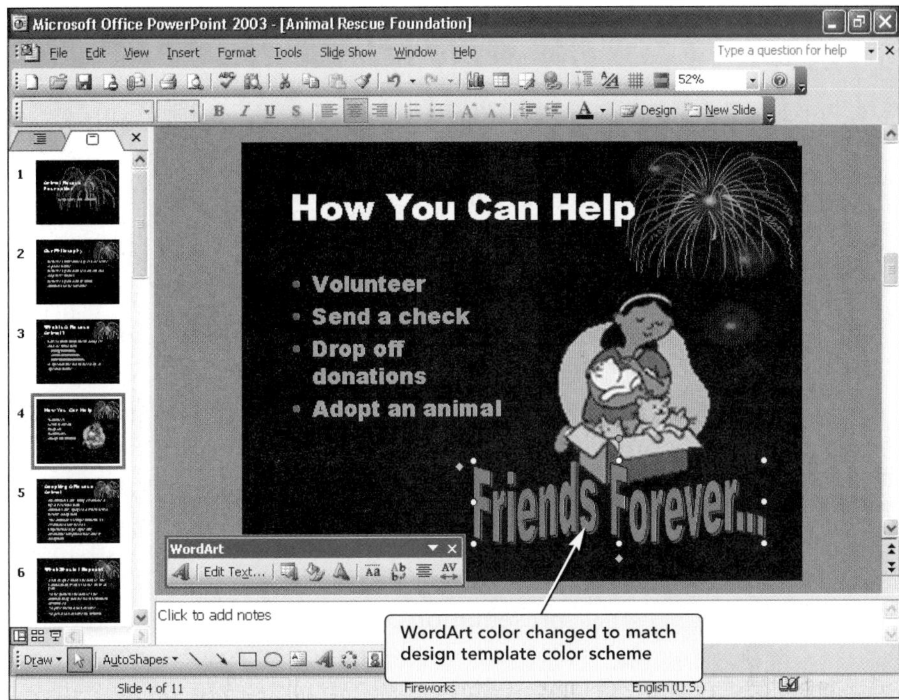

Figure 4.27

The selected fill color is used to fill the object. The last changes you want to make are to decrease the size of the WordArt object and to rotate the object to appear at an angle across the lower corner of the slide.

4 ● **Drag the sizing handles to decrease the WordArt object size to that shown in Figure 4.28.**

● **Move the rotate handle slightly to the left to slant the text to the right.**

Having Trouble?

Drag the green rotate handle to rotate the object.

● **Position the object as in Figure 4.28.**

● **Group the two objects.**

Your screen should be similar to Figure 4.28

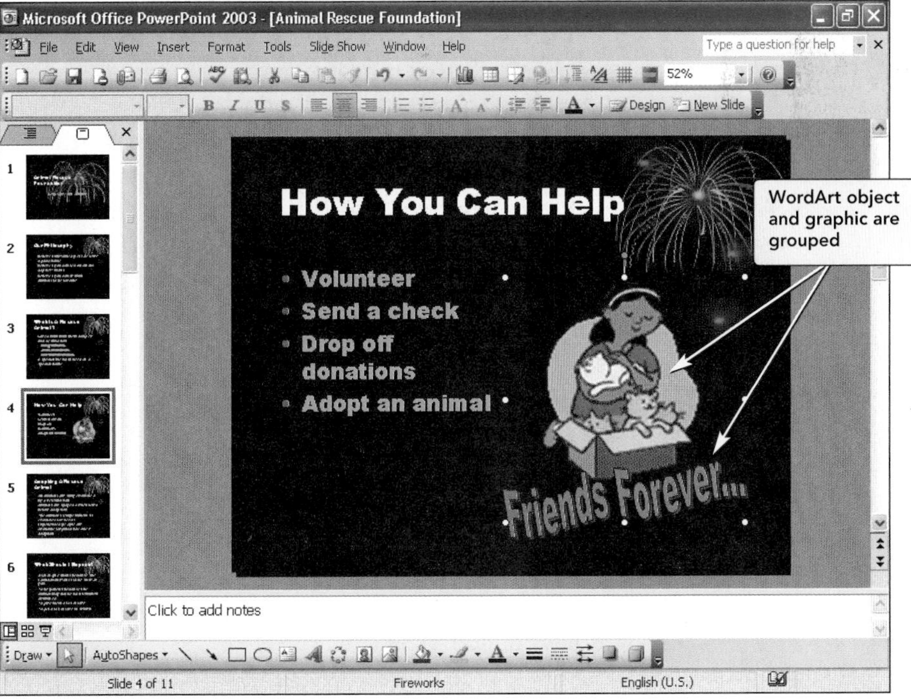

Figure 4.28

Now that you are finished enhancing the WordArt object, you want to see how it will look full screen.

5

- **Click [Slide Show icon] Slide Show.**
- **Press (Esc) and click outside the WordArt object to deselect it.**
- **If necessary, close the WordArt toolbar.**
- **Save the presentation.**

Setting Up a Presentation for a Kiosk

Additional Information

When recording a voice narration, you need a sound card and a microphone. Use Slide Show/Record Narration. The slide show runs while you speak into the microphone. Once the slide show is complete, you can choose to save the timings along with the narration.

A presentation that is designed to run unattended on a kiosk has several special requirements. Because there is no one available while the slide show is running to clarify content and answer questions, you could record a narration to accompany the presentation. However, you feel the presentation content is both clear and complete and you decide to simply include background music to attract attention and to make the presentation more enjoyable as it runs. Next, you need to add slide transitions and to specify how long to display a slide before advancing to the next slide. Finally, you need to set up the presentation to be self-running.

Adding Sound

Now that the content of the slides is complete, you want to add some background sound to the presentation as it is playing on the kiosk. There are several ways to add sound to a presentation. You can add discreet sounds that play when you click on an icon or automatically when the slide displays. You can play music from a file or a CD that runs continuously throughout the presentation. You can record a narration for your presentation; this, however, will override any other sounds you have programmed into it. You can also incorporate movie clips into a presentation.

Concept 3

Sound and Movie Files

3 Almost all PCs today are equipped with multimedia capabilities, which means they can play the most commonly used sound and movie files. A **sound file** is a type of file that plays sounds or music, and a **movie file** plays a motion picture with sound. This table lists the most common sound and movie file types.

Format	File Extension
Waveform-audio	.wav
Musical Instrument Digital Interface	.mid
Video for Windows	.avi
Moving Picture	.mpeg
Quick Time for Windows	.mov

WAV files are typically used for sounds, while MIDI files are typically used for music. Most sound cards are capable of playing MIDI files, but because these files were developed for synthesizers, you will not hear the true sound quality through a PC sound card.

AVI files do not require any special hardware or software to run, but they produce the lowest quality video. Both MPEG and MOV files produce better quality video, but both require special software, and MPEG requires special hardware.

When you choose to run a presentation on the Web, choose file types that are most commonly used. If you cannot control the computer on which your presentation will run, limit your audio to WAV files and your video to AVI files.

Additional Information

To play a CD, use Insert/Movies and Sounds/Play CD Audio Track.

For your kiosk, you want music to play continuously while the presentation runs. You could play tracks from a CD if the PC in the kiosk had a CD-ROM drive. You decide to use a short sound clip of music.

1 • **Display slide 1.**

• **Choose Insert/Movies and Sounds/Sound from File.**

• **Select** pp04_Doggie **from your data file location.**

Additional Information

The Windows Media folder contains many short sound files.

• **Click** OK.

• **Click** Automatically **to confirm that you want the sound to play automatically.**

• **Move the sound icon** to the lower right corner of the slide.

Your screen should be similar to Figure 4.29

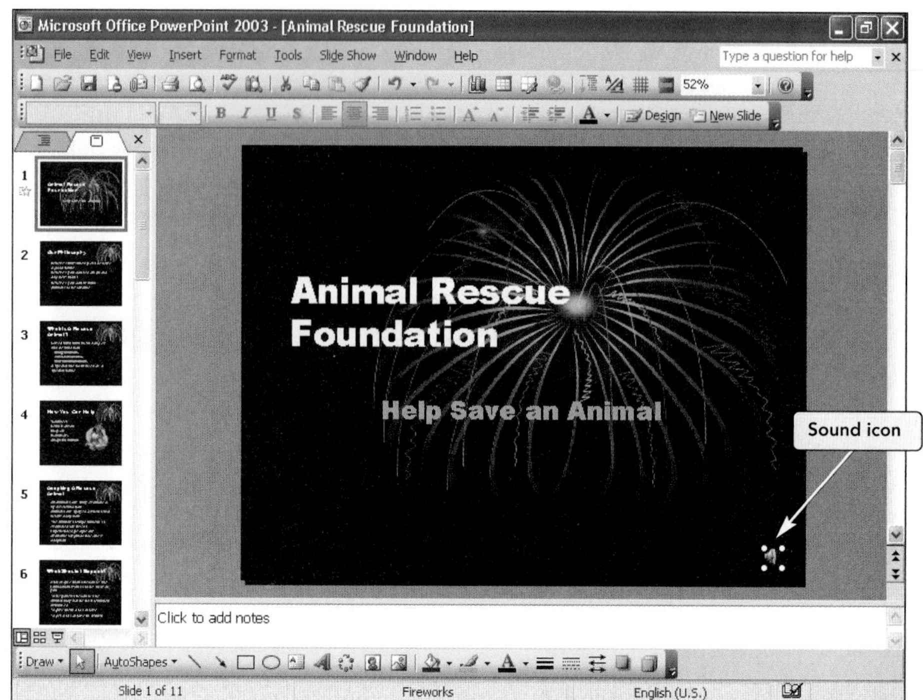

Figure 4.29

Now that you have added the music, you need to program how to play it during the slide show. You want the music to play continuously while the slide show runs.

2 • **Choose Slide Show/Custom Animation.**

• **Open the** pp04_Doggie **drop-down list in the Custom Animation task pane.**

• **Choose Effect Options.**

• **If necessary, open the Effect tab.**

Your screen should be similar to Figure 4.30

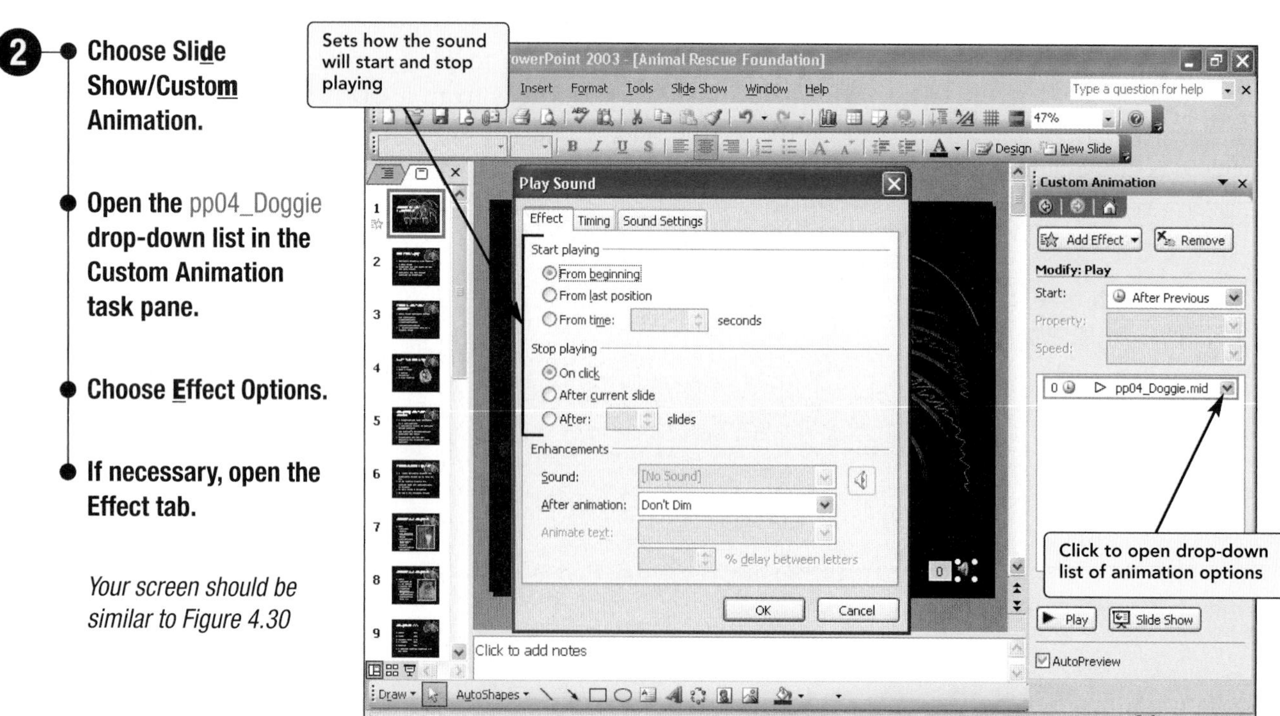

Figure 4.30

For each object on a slide, you can assign effects such as animation to the media element and control the order and timing. You want the music to start playing from the beginning of the presentation and to stop after the last slide (11). In addition, because the sound file is only 15 seconds long, you need to loop or repeat the sound so it will play the length of the presentation.

3
- **Under Stop Playing, select After, enter 11 in the text box, and click OK.**
- **Right click the sound icon and choose Edit Sound Object.**
- **Select Loop until stopped and and click OK.**
- **Run the slide show from the beginning.**

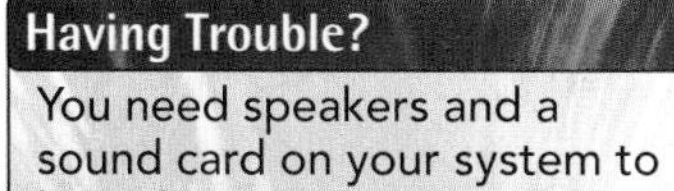

Having Trouble?

You need speakers and a sound card on your system to hear the sound.

Another Method

You can also preview the sound in Normal view by double-clicking the sound icon.

The music played continuously as you moved from slide to slide and stopped at the end of the presentation.

Adding Slide Transitions

You also want the slide show to display different transition effects as it runs and to automatically advance to the next slide after a set time has elapsed.

- **Switch to Slide Sorter view.**
- **Select all the slides.**
- **Click Transition.**
- **Choose Random Transition at Medium speed as the effect.**
- **Select Automatically After.**
- **Change the timing to advance the slides automatically every 7 seconds.**
- **Click Apply to All Slides.**

Your screen should be similar to Figure 4.31

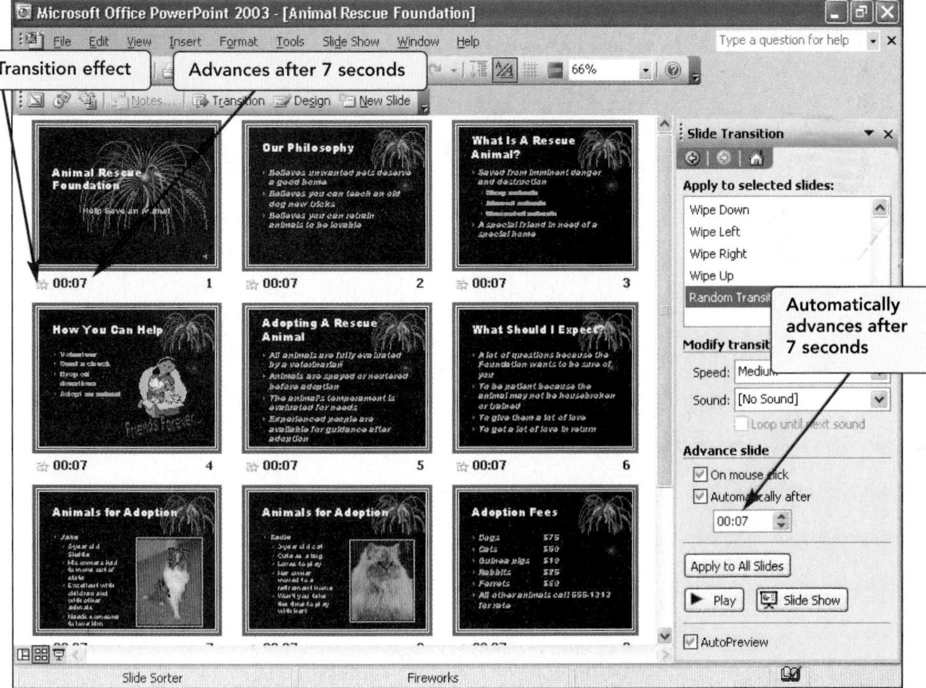

Figure 4.31

Making the Presentation Self-Running

Now you will make the slide show self-running so that it will restart automatically when it has finished.

1 **Close the Slide Transition task pane.**

Choose Slide Show/Set Up Show.

Your screen should be similar to Figure 4.32

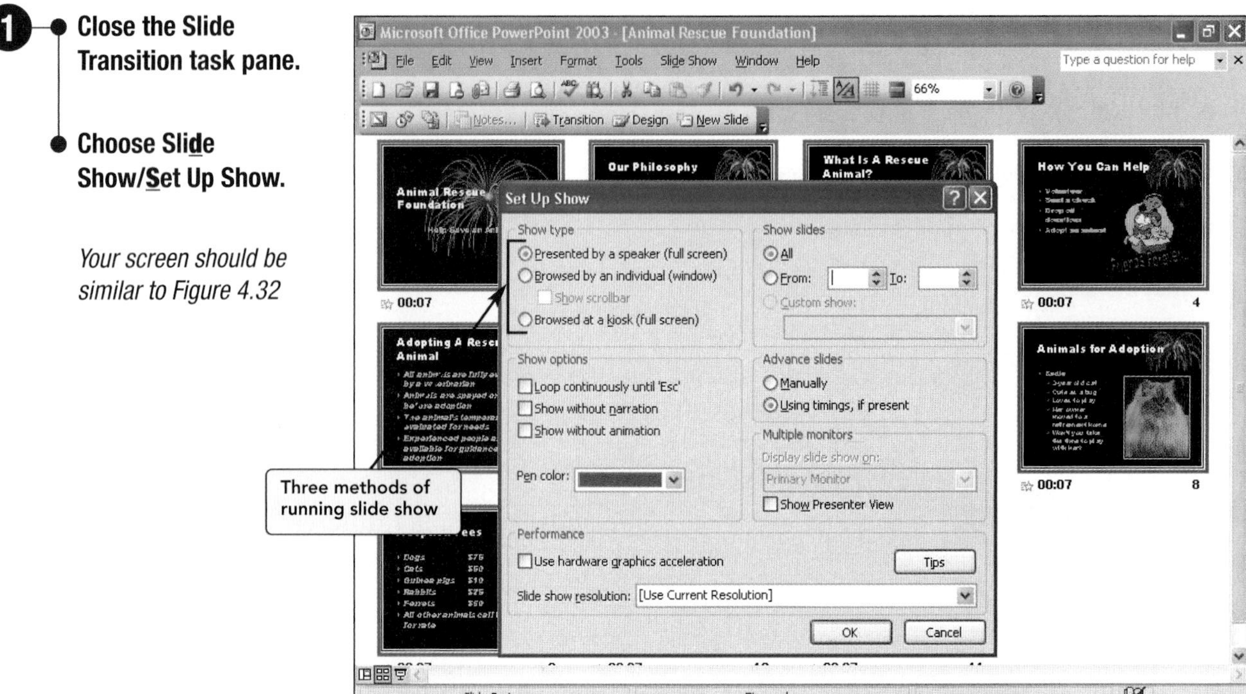

Figure 4.32

The Set Up Show dialog box allows you to choose from three ways of running a show. The first option, Presented by a Speaker, is the default and most frequently used style. As you have seen, this method requires that a speaker run the presentation. The second option, Browsed by an Individual, is used when one person views the presentation in a small window over an intranet (a network within an organization) or on a Web page. The third option, Browsed at a Kiosk, is the option you will use to create a self-running presentation that is displayed full screen. You can run the entire presentation or selected slides. The presentation will automatically play at full screen and restart automatically.

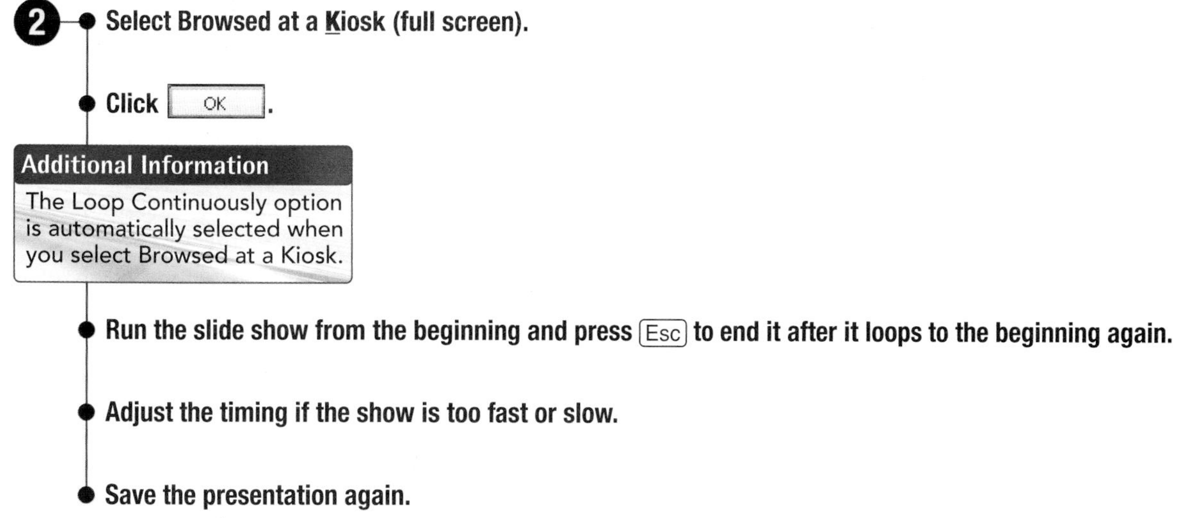

2

- **Select Browsed at a Kiosk (full screen).**
- **Click OK.**

Additional Information

The Loop Continuously option is automatically selected when you select Browsed at a Kiosk.

- **Run the slide show from the beginning and press Esc to end it after it loops to the beginning again.**
- **Adjust the timing if the show is too fast or slow.**
- **Save the presentation again.**

To deliver the presentation to the mall directors to run on the kiosks, you will package the presentation for CD.

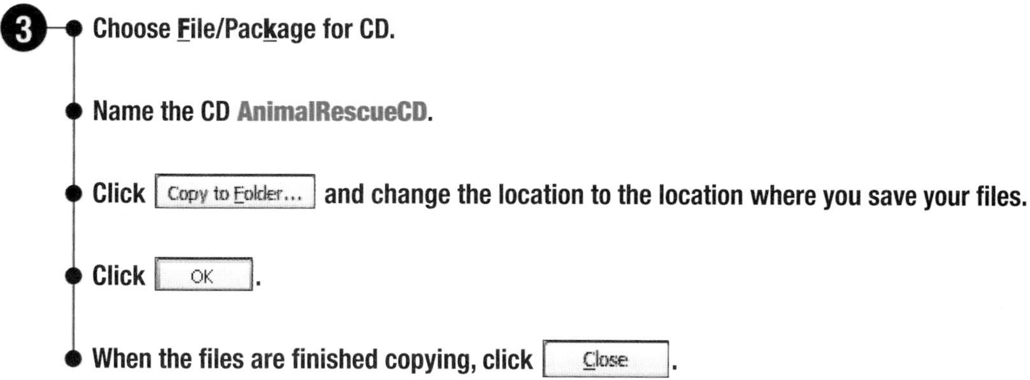

3

- **Choose File/Package for CD.**
- **Name the CD AnimalRescueCD.**
- **Click Copy to Folder... and change the location to the location where you save your files.**
- **Click OK.**
- **When the files are finished copying, click Close.**

Setting Up the Presentation for Browsing

The Animal Rescue Foundation main shelter has a computer in the lobby that they want to use to show this same presentation. Rather than have the presentation loop continuously, you want to change it to a presentation that can be run by an individual using mouse control. This gives viewers the ability to control the slide show and go back to review a slide immediately or go forward more quickly to see other slides. To add this capability, you will create several custom shows and add hyperlinks and navigation controls to the presentation.

Creating Custom Shows

First you will group some slides into custom shows.

Concept 4

Custom Show

4 A **custom show** is a presentation that runs within a presentation. For example, you may have one presentation that you need to give to two different groups. The overview slides are the same for both groups, but there are a few slides that are specific to each group. Rather than create two separate presentations, you can include all the slides in your main presentation and then group the specific slides into two custom shows that run after the overview slides. While you are running the slide show, you can jump to the specific custom show that you created for that audience.

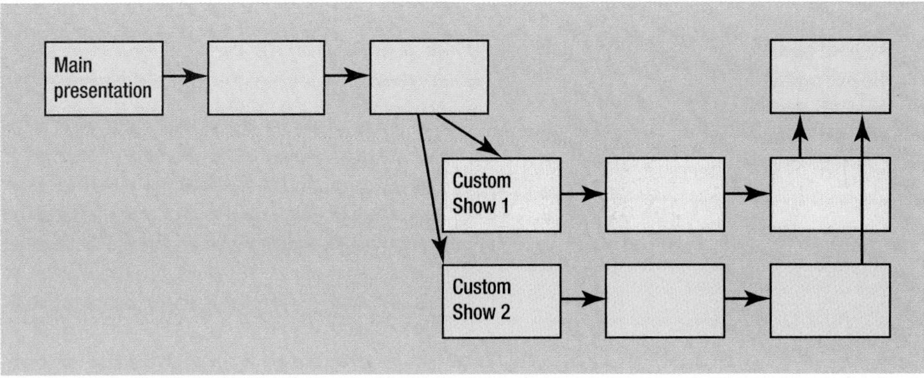

You are going to create two custom shows within your presentation. One custom show will run the slides that describe adopting rescue animals. The other custom show will run the slides that describe the animals that are available for adoption.

1
- **Choose Slide Show/Custom Shows.**
- **Click New... .**

Your screen should be similar to Figure 4.33

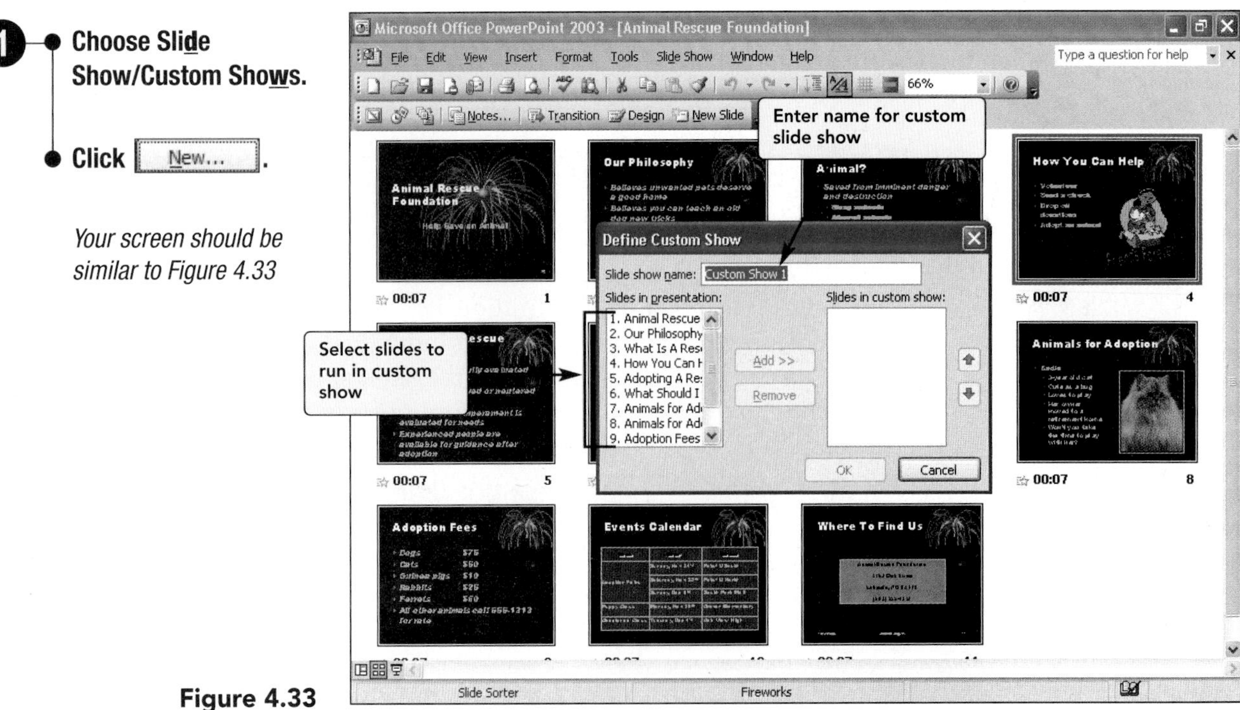

Figure 4.33

In the Define Custom Show dialog box, you name the custom show and select the slides that will run within the show. All the slides in a custom show must also be in the main presentation.

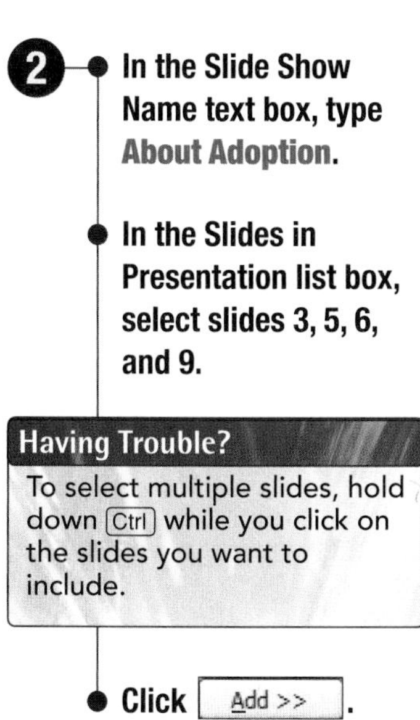

2

- **In the Slide Show Name text box, type About Adoption.**
- **In the Slides in Presentation list box, select slides 3, 5, 6, and 9.**

Having Trouble?

To select multiple slides, hold down Ctrl while you click on the slides you want to include.

- **Click Add >>.**

Your screen should be similar to Figure 4.34

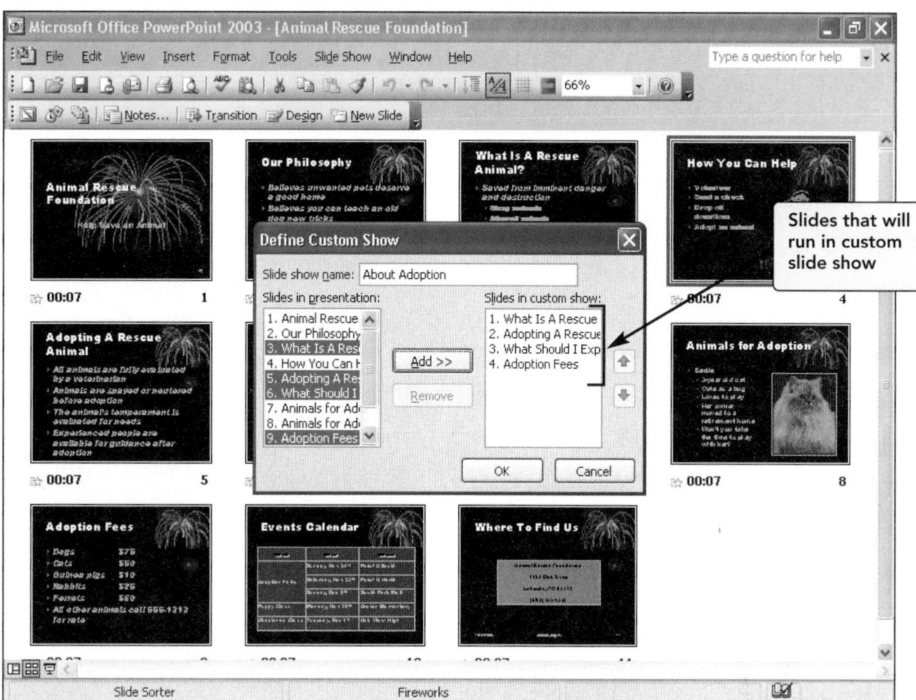

Figure 4.34

Next you want to make slide 2 in the custom show, slide 1. To change the order of the slides in the custom show, select a slide in the Slides in Custom Show list box, and then click one of the arrows to move the slide up or down the list. This will not change the order of the slides in the main presentation.

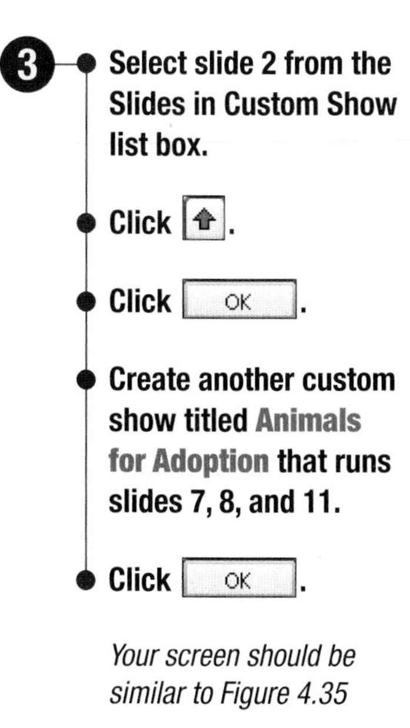

3

- **Select slide 2 from the Slides in Custom Show list box.**
- **Click ⬆.**
- **Click OK.**
- **Create another custom show titled Animals for Adoption that runs slides 7, 8, and 11.**
- **Click OK.**

Your screen should be similar to Figure 4.35

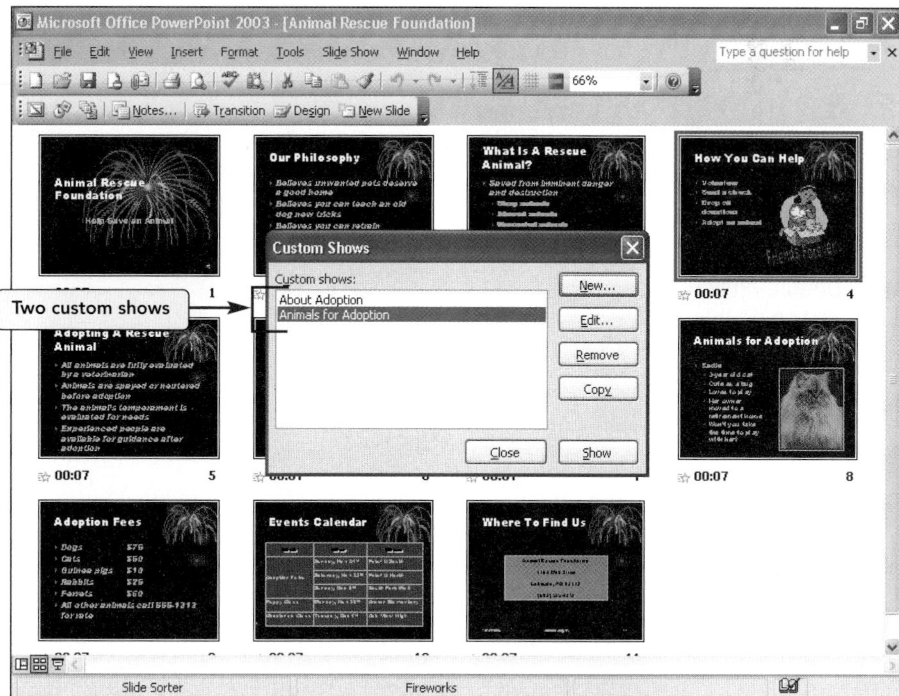

Figure 4.35

The name of the second custom show is added to the Custom Shows list. Now you will see how the About Adoption custom show runs.

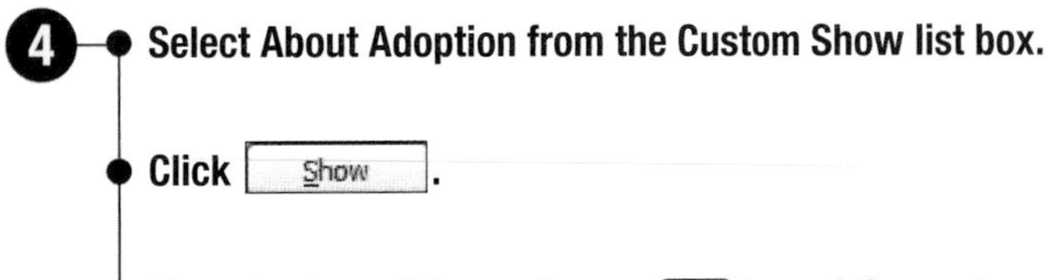

4 Select About Adoption from the Custom Show list box.

- Click Show.
- View the four slides and press Esc to end the custom show.

The custom show plays in a continual loop and does not play the sound. The sound only plays if you start the presentation from slide 1.

Creating an Agenda Slide

Now that you have created the custom shows, you will create an agenda slide to use as a starting point for the entire presentation. An agenda slide contains a list of items or main topics from the presentation. Viewers can then make a selection from the list, and the presentation will jump directly to the slide containing the selected topic or a custom presentation will automatically run. When the custom show is finished, the presentation returns to the agenda slide.

An agenda slide is created from a summary slide consisting of a bulleted list of agenda items. A **summary slide** is created automatically from slides in the presentation whose titles you want to appear as agenda items.

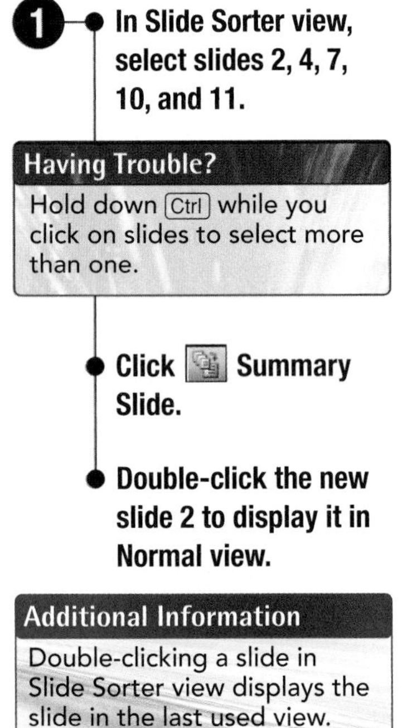

1 In Slide Sorter view, select slides 2, 4, 7, 10, and 11.

Having Trouble?

Hold down Ctrl while you click on slides to select more than one.

- Click Summary Slide.
- Double-click the new slide 2 to display it in Normal view.

Additional Information

Double-clicking a slide in Slide Sorter view displays the slide in the last used view.

Your screen should be similar to Figure 4.36

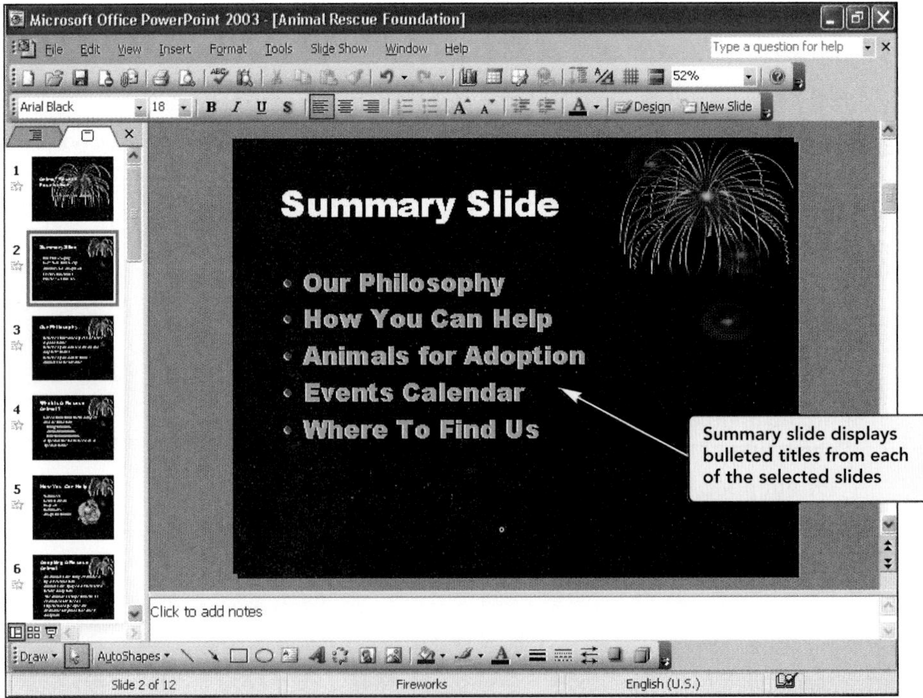

Figure 4.36

A new slide titled Summary Slide appears as slide 2. The summary slide is always inserted in front of the slide containing the first selected item. The slide contains bulleted titles from each of the selected slides.

Adding Hyperlinks

The next step in creating an agenda slide is to create a hyperlink from each bulleted item to its corresponding slide or custom show.

Concept 5

Hyperlinks

5 **Hyperlinks** provide a quick way to jump to other slides, custom shows, presentations, objects, e-mail addresses, or Web pages. You can assign the hyperlink to text or to any object, including pictures, tables, clip art, and graphs. You can jump to sites on your own system or network as well as to sites on the Internet and the Web. The user jumps to the referenced location by clicking on the hyperlink.

1
- **Select the first bulleted item.**
- **Choose Slide Show/Action Settings.**
- **If necessary, open the Mouse Click tab.**

Your screen should be similar to Figure 4.37

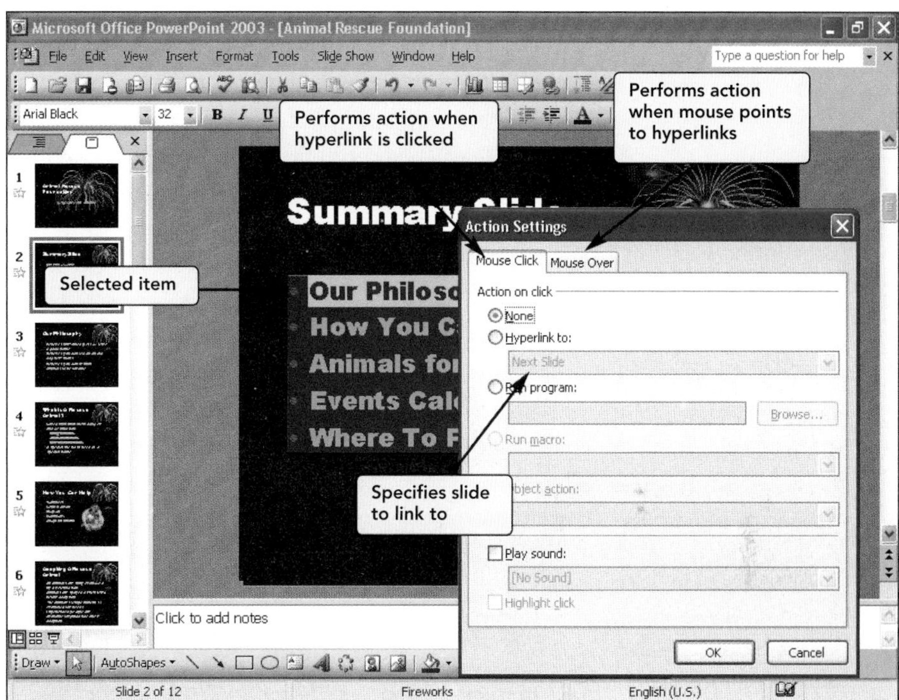

Figure 4.37

The two tabs in the Action Settings dialog box allow you to specify the action that is needed to activate the hyperlink. Mouse Click performs an action when the viewer clicks the hyperlink, and Mouse Over performs the action when the mouse pointer rests or passes over the hyperlink. Within each tab you specify the type of action you want to perform: jump to another location using a hyperlink, play a sound, or run a program or macro. Generally, it is best to use Mouse Click for hyperlinks so that you do not accidentally go to a location because you passed the mouse pointer over the hyperlink. Mouse Over is commonly used to play sounds or to highlight an object.

The first bulleted item will be a hyperlink to the next slide in the presentation. This is the default hyperlink selection.

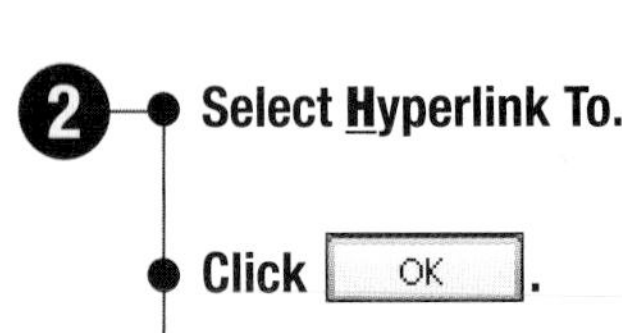

2 Select **H**yperlink To.

Click OK.

Click outside the hyperlink to clear the selection.

Your screen should be similar to Figure 4.38

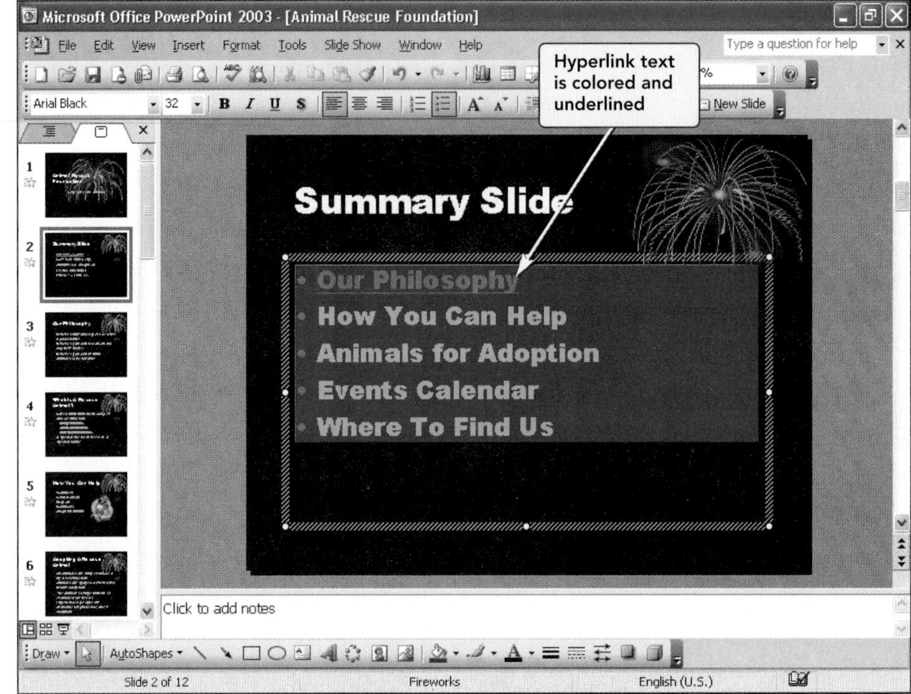

Figure 4.38

The hyperlink text appears underlined and in color. The color of the hyperlink text is determined by the presentation's color scheme.

The second bulleted item will be a hyperlink to the About Adoption custom show. You want the custom show to run and then return to the slide containing the hyperlink.

3 Select the text in the second bulleted item.

Choose Sli**d**e Show/**A**ction Settings.

Select **H**yperlink To.

From the Hyperlink To drop-down list, select Custom Show.

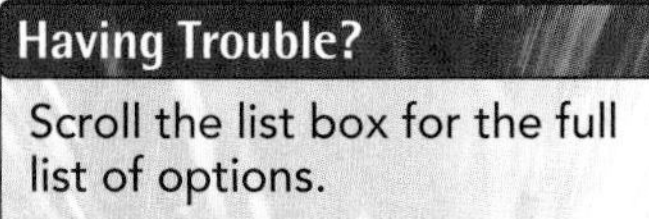

Having Trouble?

Scroll the list box for the full list of options.

Your screen should be similar to Figure 4.39

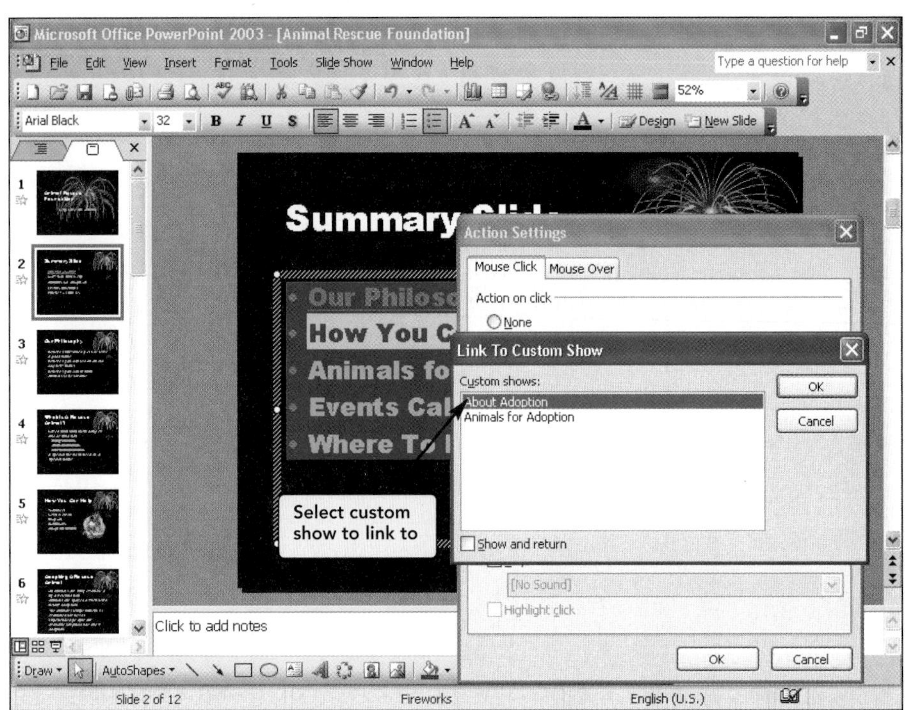

Figure 4.39

From the Link To Custom Show dialog box, you select the custom show to which you want to create a hyperlink.

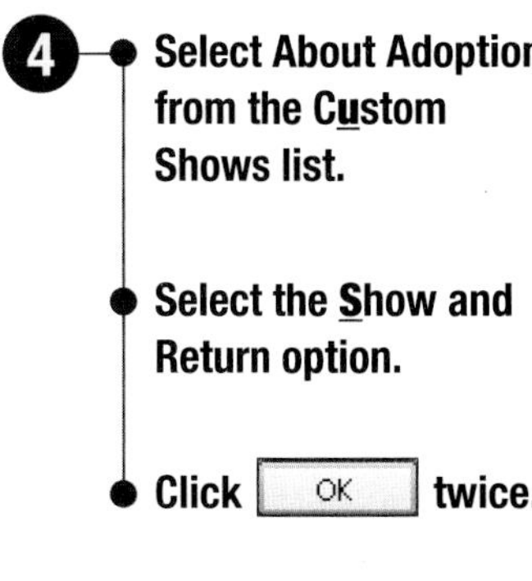

4

- **Select About Adoption from the Custom Shows list.**
- **Select the Show and Return option.**
- **Click OK twice.**

Your screen should be similar to Figure 4.40

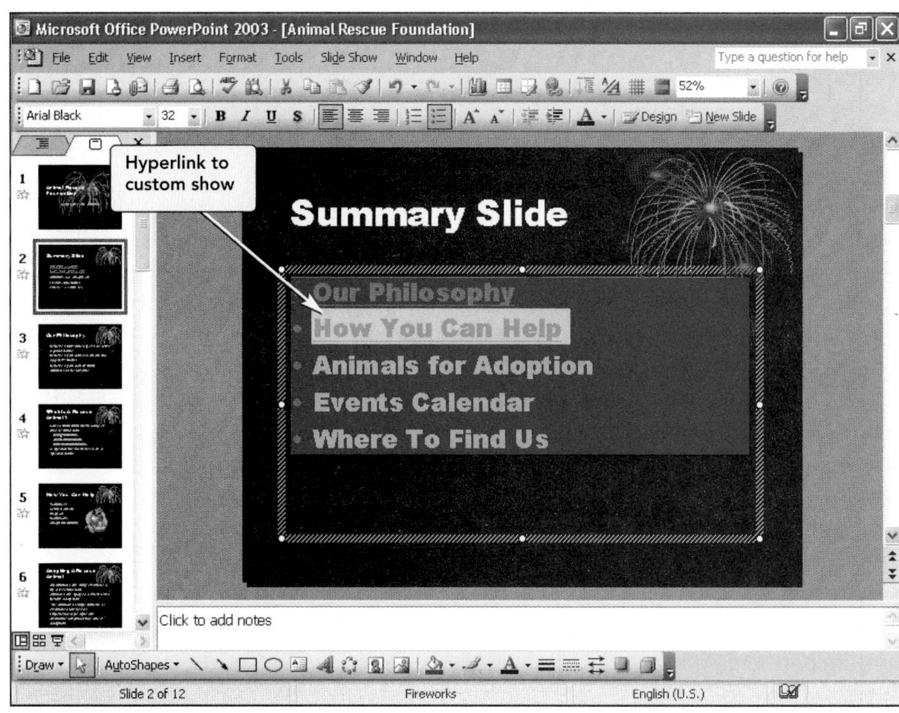

Figure 4.40

When the second bulleted item is selected, it will start the custom show. Now you need to add links for the remaining three items. The third bulleted item will be a hyperlink to the custom show named Animals for Adoption. The fourth and fifth will be to slides of the same name.

5

- **Link the third bulleted item to the Animals for Adoption custom show, selecting the Show and Return option.**
- **To link the fourth item, select Slide as the Hyperlink To option and select slide 11.**
- **To link the fifth item, select Slide as the Hyperlink To option and select slide 12.**
- **Change the title of the agenda slide to Learn About Us.**
- **Click outside the title to deselect it.**

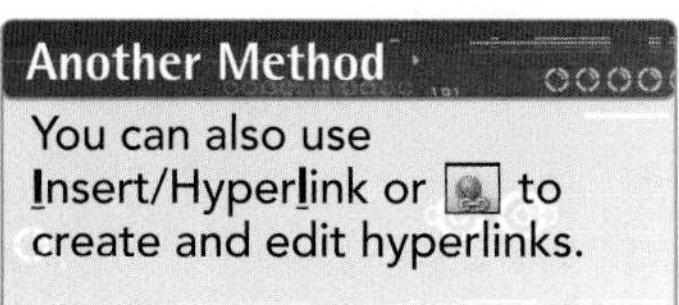

Your screen should be similar to Figure 4.41

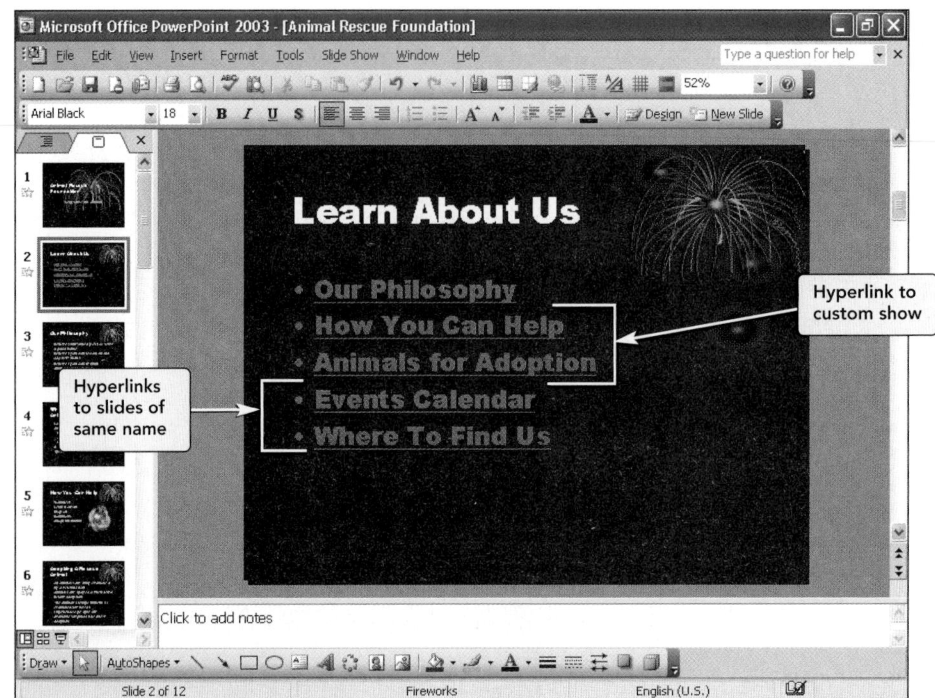

Figure 4.41

The addition of hyperlinks makes the summary slide an agenda slide, which can be used to jump to the selected topic.

Using Hyperlinks

Next you want to try out one of the hyperlinks to see how they work. To activate the hyperlinks, you need to run the slide show.

1 • **Run the slide show beginning with slide 2.**

Having Trouble?

To run the slide show starting from the current slide, click [icon]. Using Sli**d**e Show/**V**iew Show or F5 begins the presentation at slide 1.

Additional Information

The mouse pointer shape changes to a [hand] when pointing to a hyperlink.

• **Click on the Animals for Adoption hyperlink.**

Your screen should be similar to Figure 4.42

Figure 4.42

The slide show jumps to the first slide of the custom show and begins running the custom show.

2 • **When the custom show loops again to the first slide, press Esc to end the custom show and display the agenda slide.**

• **Press Esc to end the slide show presentation.**

• **Save the presentation as** Rescue Foundation Self Running**.**

Additional Information

The color of a selected hyperlink is different from those that have not been selected. This color change identifies those links that have already been viewed.

Adding Action Buttons

To help the viewer navigate through the presentation, you decide to add action buttons to the slides.

Concept 6

Action Buttons

6 PowerPoint includes special objects called **action buttons** that can be inserted in a presentation and assigned a hyperlink. Action buttons consist of shapes, such as right- and left-facing arrows, that are used to navigate through a presentation. They are designed specifically for self-running presentations and presentations that run on a company network or the Web. Action buttons perform their associated action when you click on them or pass the mouse over them.

You have decided to have the first slide display continuously until the viewer clicks on a button to start the presentation. Once in the presentation, each slide will have a home button that will take the viewer back to the agenda slide, a forward button that will go to the next slide, and a backward button that will return to the previous slide.

1
- **Display slide 1 in Normal view.**
- **Choose Slide Show/Action Buttons.**

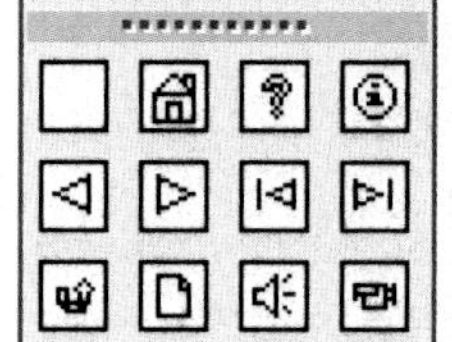

- **Click ☐ Custom (first column, first row).**
- **In the upper left corner of the slide, drag to create a button that is approximately 1 inch by 1 inch.**
- **In the Mouse Click tab of the Action Settings dialog box, make the button a hyperlink to the next slide.**
- **Click** **.**

Your screen should be similar to Figure 4.43

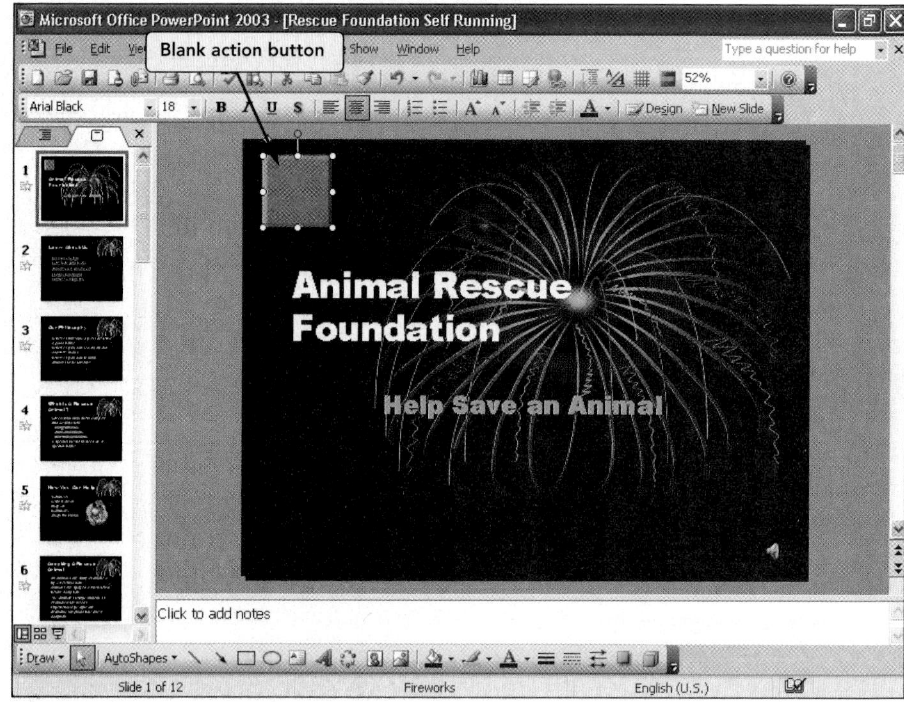

Figure 4.43

Next you need to add text to the button that contains the instructions for the viewer. You add button text just as you add text to a text box.

2

- **Right-click on the button and choose Add Text from the shortcut menu.**
- **Type Click Here to Learn More.**
- **Right-click on the button and choose Format AutoShape.**
- **Open the Text Box tab.**
- **Select Word wrap text in AutoShape.**
- **Select Resize AutoShape to fit text.**
- **Click OK.**
- **Change the text color to black and the font size to 14.**
- **Click outside the action button to deselect it.**

Your screen should be similar to Figure 4.44

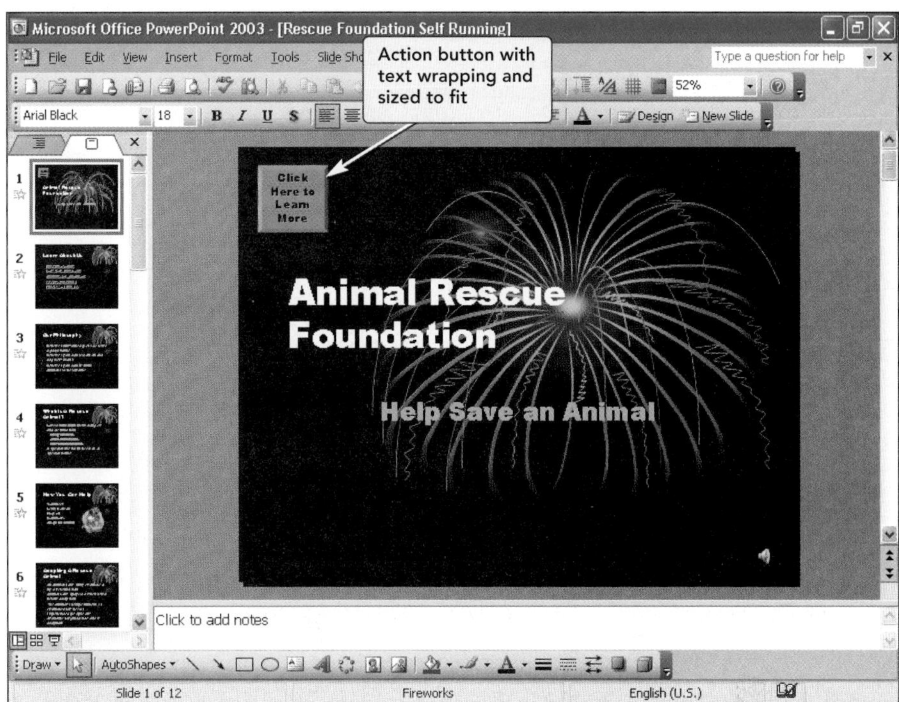

Figure 4.44

You will follow the same procedure to add three other buttons to the slides: home, forward, and backward. These buttons are predesigned, and contain icons that represent the action they perform. Therefore, you do not need to add text to the button. Since you want these buttons to appear on all slides other than title slides, you will add them to the Slide Master.

3 **Switch to Slide Master view and display the Slide Master.**

Having Trouble?

In Slide Master view, two slides appear in the Slide tab. Be sure to modify the Slide Master and not the Title Master.

- **Delete the three footer object boxes.**
- **Choose Slide Show/Action Buttons.**
- **Click Home (second column, first row).**
- **Click in the lower right of the footer area to create a default size button.**
- **Add a hyperlink to slide 2, the agenda slide.**
- **Click OK twice.**

Your screen should be similar to Figure 4.45

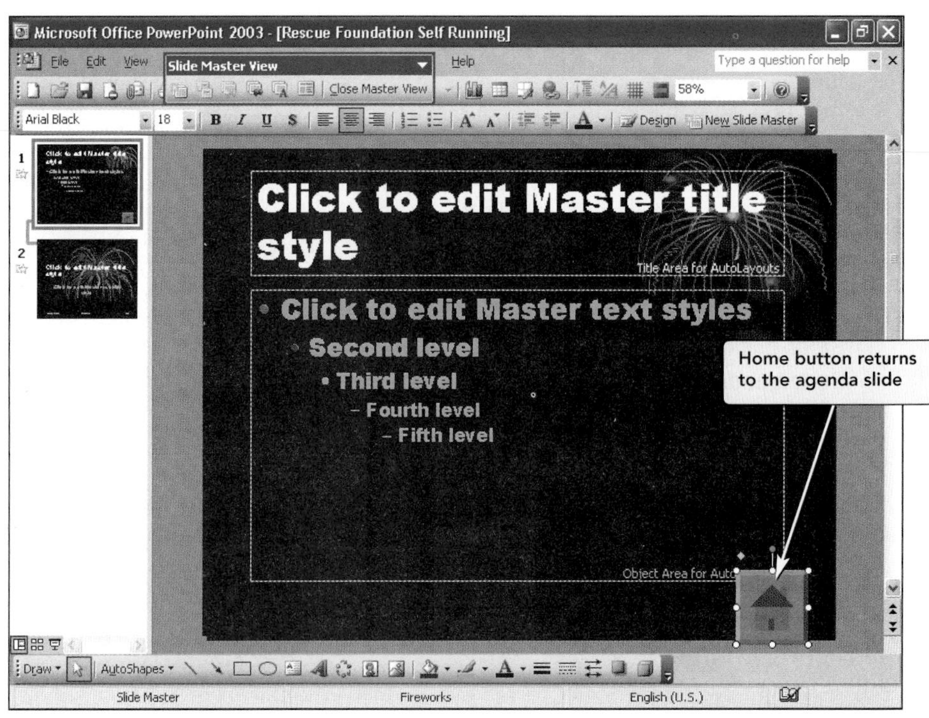

Figure 4.45

Changing the Button Size

Now you want to reduce the size of the button by about half. In addition to changing the size of an object by dragging to an approximate size, you can change the size by entering an exact measurement for the object's height and width or by entering a percentage value to increase or decrease the object from its original size. Since you want to make the object about half its original size, you will reduce it by 50 percent.

1. - Choose **Format/AutoShape**.
   - Open the Size tab.
   - Under Scale enter 50% in both the **Height** and **Width** boxes.
   - Click OK.
   - Move the button to the location shown in Figure 4.46.

Additional Information

If the slide miniature is displayed, you can see how the button looks on the current slide.

Your screen should be similar to Figure 4.46

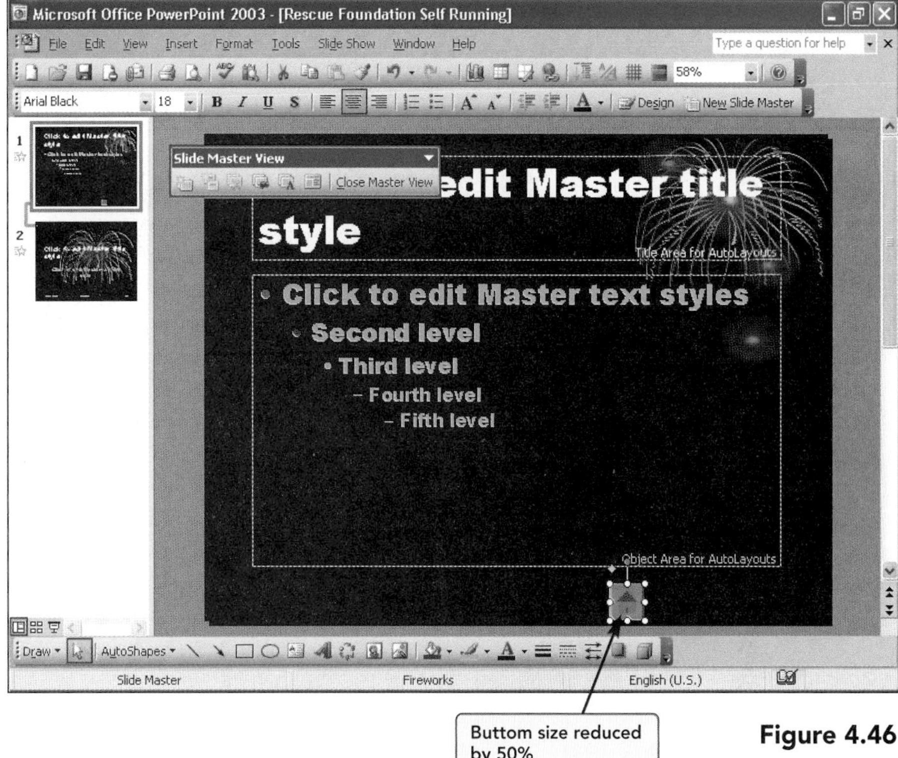

Figure 4.46

Now you will add the forward and back buttons.

2. - To the right of the home button, add a default size Back or Previous button that hyperlinks to the previous slide.
   - To the right of the back button, add a default size Forward or Next button that hyperlinks to the next slide.
   - Select the two new buttons and reduce their size by 50 percent.

Your screen should be similar to Figure 4.47

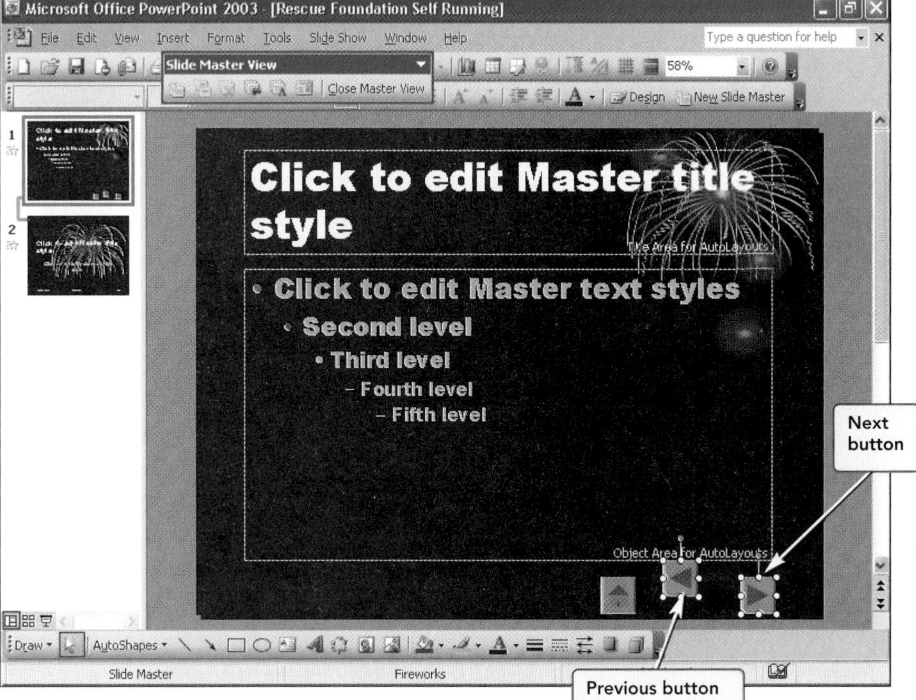

Figure 4.47

Finally, you want to position and align the three buttons.

3 — **Select the three buttons.**

- **Click Draw and choose Align or Distribute/Align Top.**
- **Click Draw and choose Align or Distribute/Distribute Horizontally.**

Your screen should be similar to Figure 4.48

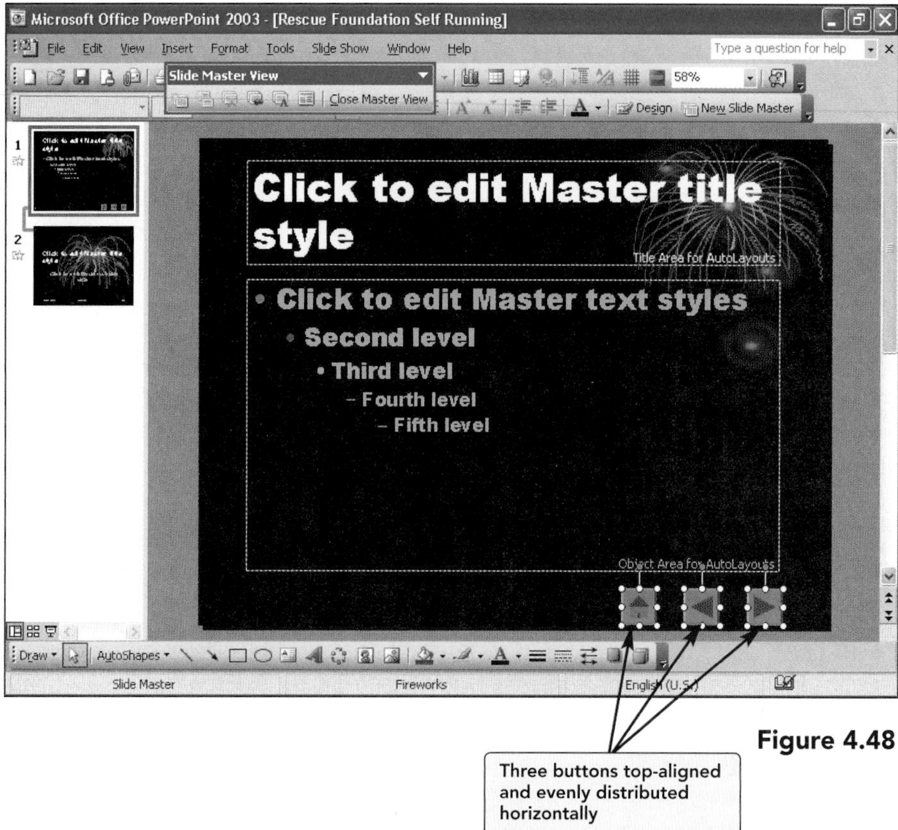

Figure 4.48

Additional Information

The outside buttons do not move; only the middle button moves to equalize the spacing.

The three buttons are evenly aligned with the top of the buttons and are an equal distance apart horizontally. Because the buttons were added to the slide master, they will appear in the same location on each slide in the presentation. You want to check the slides to make sure the buttons do not interfere with any of the text or graphics on the slides.

4 — **Switch to Slide Sorter view.**

- **Make any necessary adjustments to objects on the slides so they do not overlap the buttons.**

Your screen should be similar to Figure 4.49

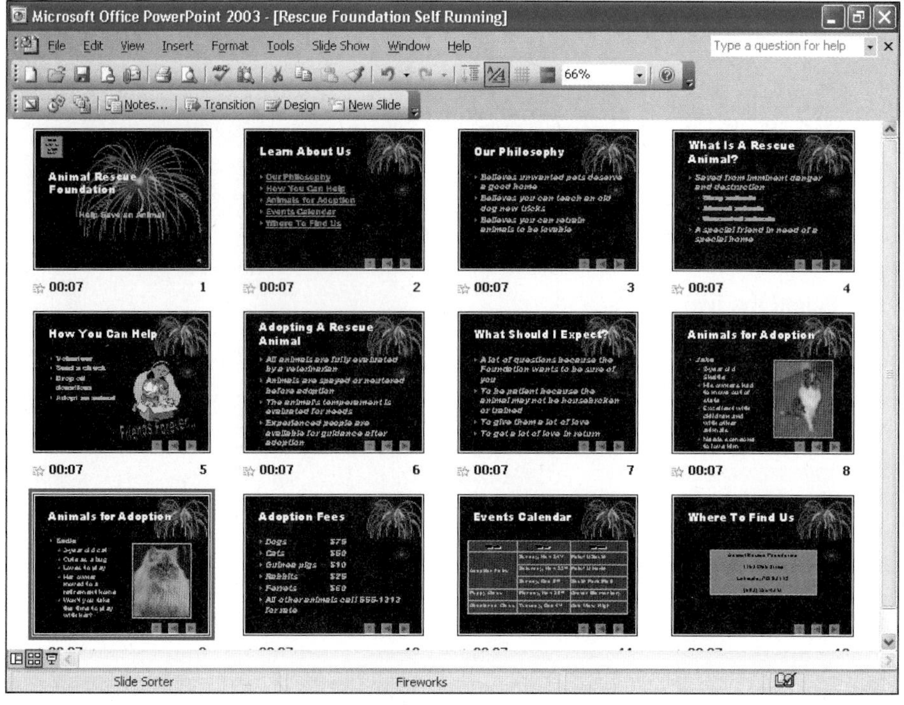

Figure 4.49

Using Action Buttons

Now you are ready to run the revised presentation using the buttons. First you will turn off the features that make the presentation run continuously and change the music to play longer while the presentation is running.

1

- **In Slide Sorter view, select all slides.**
- **Open the Slide Transition task pane.**
- **Clear the Automatically After option.**
- **Click Apply to All Slides.**
- **In Normal view, select the sound object on slide 1.**
- **Open the Custom Animation task pane.**
- **Open the pp04_Doggie drop-down list and select Effect Options.**
- **Increase the number of slides to stop playing after to 25.**
- **Click OK.**
- **Close the task pane and save the presentation.**
- **Run the slide show beginning at slide 1 and practice using the buttons.**

Your screen should be similar to Figure 4.50

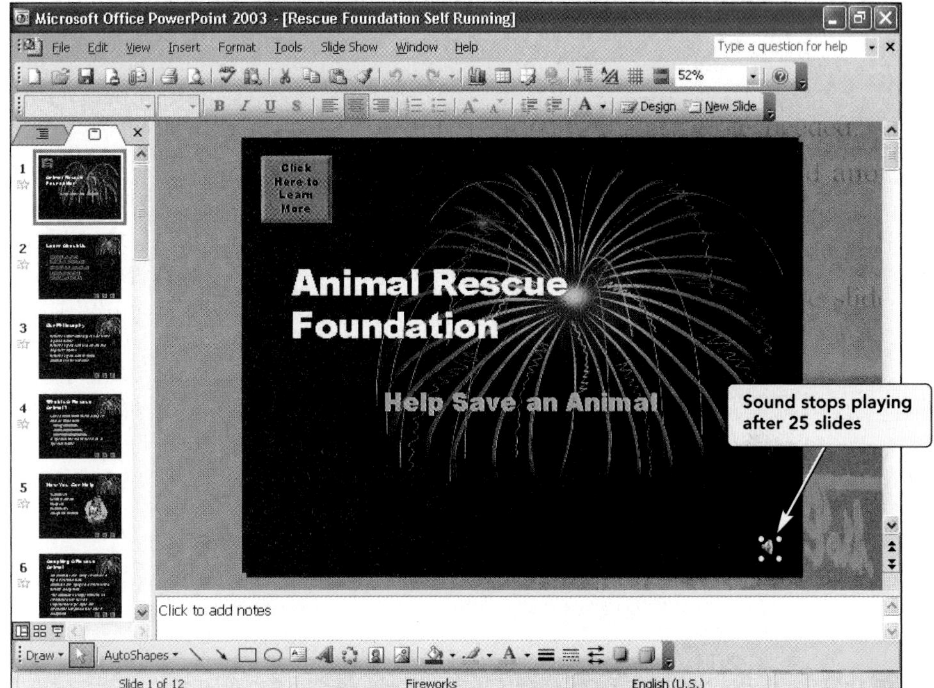

Figure 4.50

Publishing a Presentation on the Web

You want to publish or save a copy of the presentation file for use on the World Wide Web (WWW). Publishing a file saves the file in Hypertext Markup Language (HTML) format.

Concept 7

Hypertext Markup Language

7 All Web pages are written using a programming language called **Hypertext Markup Language (HTML)**. HTML commands control how the information on a page, such as font colors and size, is displayed. HTML also allows users to click on highlighted text or images and jump to other locations on the same page, to other pages in the same site, or to other sites and locations on the Web altogether.

HTML commands are interpreted by the browser software program you are using to access the WWW. A **browser** is a program that connects you to remote computers and displays the Web pages you request. The computer that stores the Web pages and sends them to a browser when requested is called the **server**.

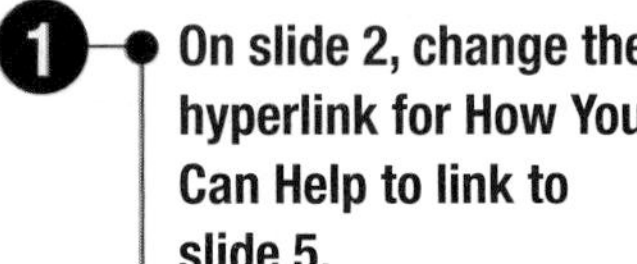

Custom shows do not run in a Web browser, so before you publish the presentation, you first need to change the two hyperlinks to the custom shows to links to the first slide in the sequence. Most other features, including transitions and sound, will run in newer versions of browser programs.

1
- **On slide 2, change the hyperlink for How You Can Help to link to slide 5.**
- **Change the Animals for Adoption hyperlink to link to slide 8.**

Saving the presentation as a Single-File Web Page

Now that the presentation is ready for Web delivery, you can save it as a Web page. You can save a presentation in two ways:

- Web Page—Saves the presentation as a Web page and creates an associated folder that contains supporting files such as bullets, background textures, and graphics.
- Single-File Web Page—Saves the presentation as a Web page that integrates all supporting information, including graphics and other files, into a single file.

You will save the presentation to a single-file Web page, which is the default file type.

1 • **Choose File/Save as Web Page.**

• **Specify the location to save the file.**

• **Enter the file name Rescue Foundation Web.**

Your screen should be similar to Figure 4.51

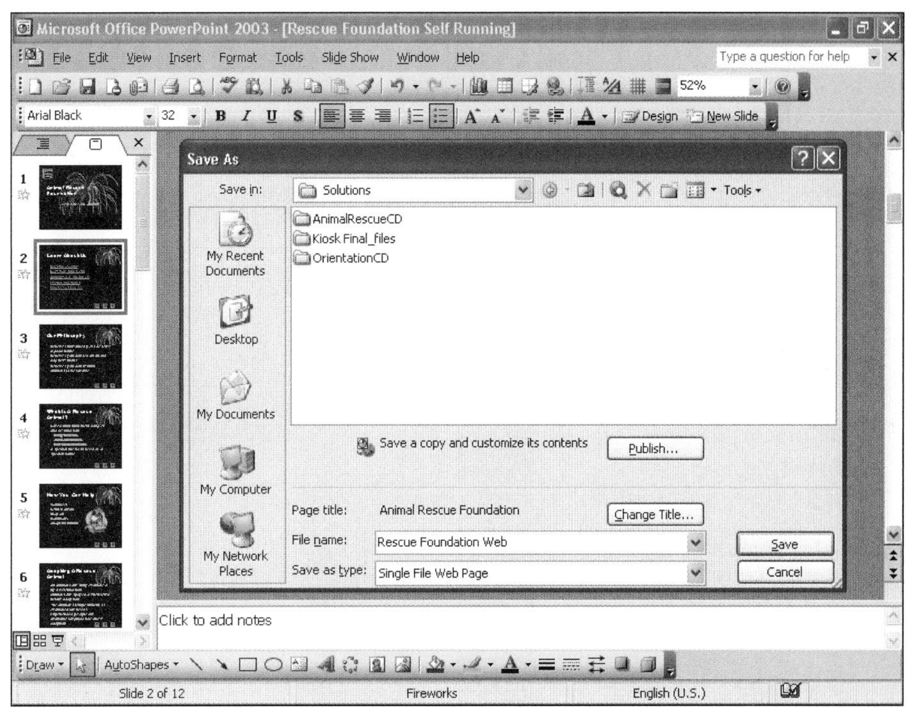

Figure 4.51

Additional Information

Clicking Change Title... allows you to specify a different page title.

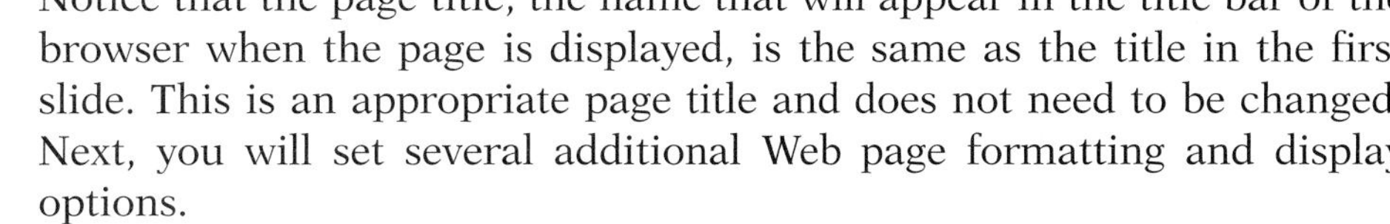

Notice that the page title, the name that will appear in the title bar of the browser when the page is displayed, is the same as the title in the first slide. This is an appropriate page title and does not need to be changed. Next, you will set several additional Web page formatting and display options.

2 • **Click Publish.**

Your screen should be similar to Figure 4.52

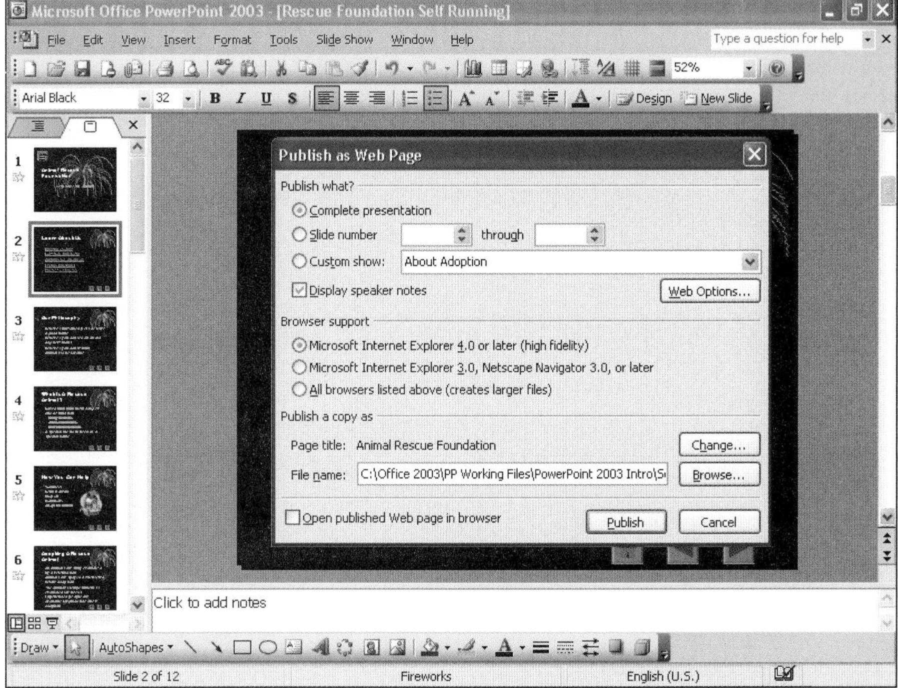

Figure 4.52

In the Publish as Web Page dialog box, you can specify the slides you want to publish under Publish What, and optimize the Web page for a particular browser or browser version under Browser support. The default settings, Complete Presentation and Microsoft Internet Explorer 4.0 or later, are appropriate for your needs. You do want to specify some additional Web options.

3 **Click Web Options... .**

In the General tab, select Show slide animation while browsing.

Your screen should be similar to Figure 4.53

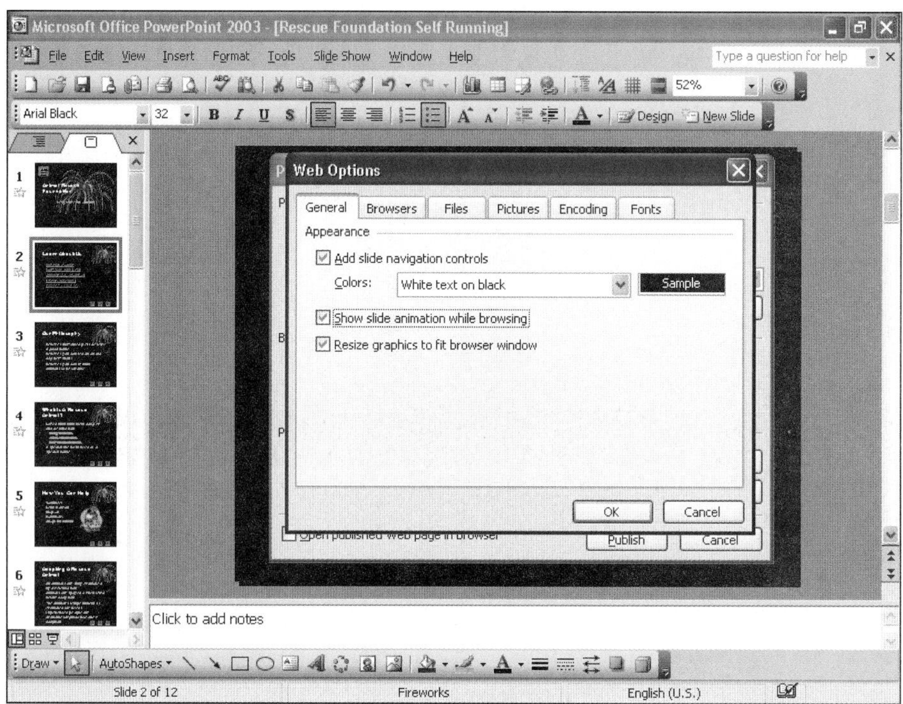

Figure 4.53

The three Appearance options on the General tab should be selected. The Add Slide Navigation Controls option will display a table of contents listing that can be used to navigate the presentation. The Resize Graphics to Fit Browser Window option automatically sizes the slides to fit the browser window.

4
- **Click OK.**
- **To immediately see how your published Web presentation looks in your browser after you publish it, select Open published Web page in browser.**
- **Click Publish.**
- **If necessary, maximize the browser window.**

Additional Information

You can also use File/Web Page Preview to open your presentation in a Web browser.

Your screen should be similar to Figure 4.54

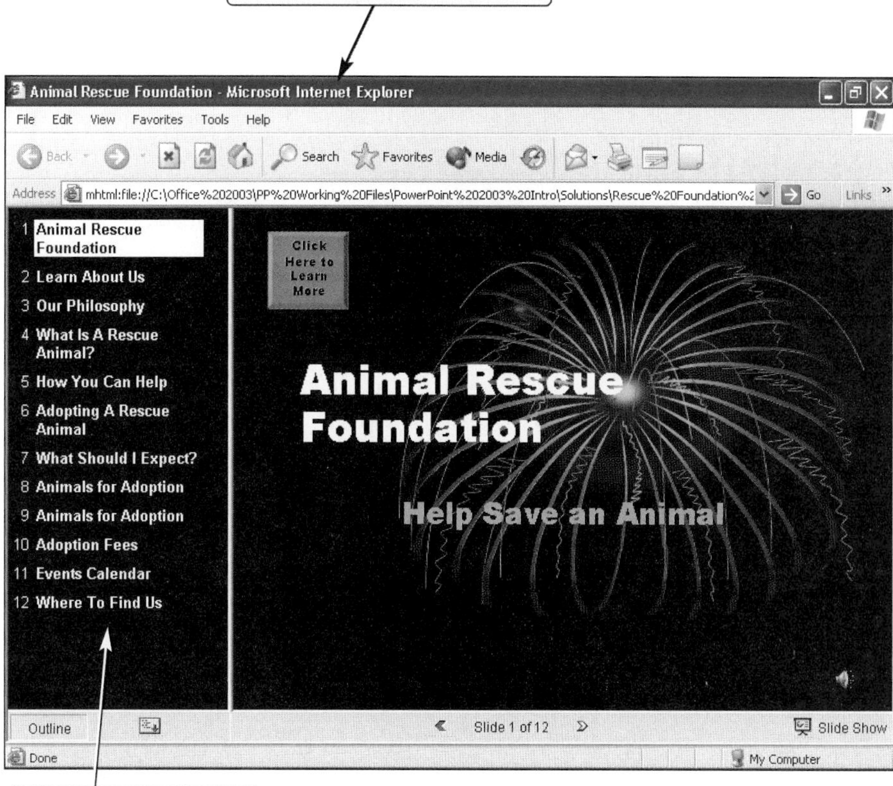

Figure 4.54

Additional Information

A Single-File Web Page file type has a file extension of MHTML.

The file is converted to an HTML document and saved as a Single-File Web Page file type. This file contains all the elements on the page, such as images and hyperlinks, and all supporting files, such as those for bullets, graphics, and background. Any graphics that were added to the page that were not already JPEG or GIF files are converted to that format.

The browser on your system is loaded offline, and the page you created is displayed in the browser window. The left side of the window displays a table of contents listing consisting of the slide titles. Clicking on a title will display the associated slide on the right side.

Navigating a Web Presentation

To navigate through the presentation, you can use the table of contents list, the action buttons, or the agenda slide hyperlinks.

1
- **Try out the various methods of navigation in the presentation.**
- **When you are finished, click ✕ Close to exit the browser.**
- **Preview slides 2, 5, and 11 as handouts, three per page.**
- **Include a header on the handout that displays the current date and your name.**

Your screen should be similar to Figure 4.55

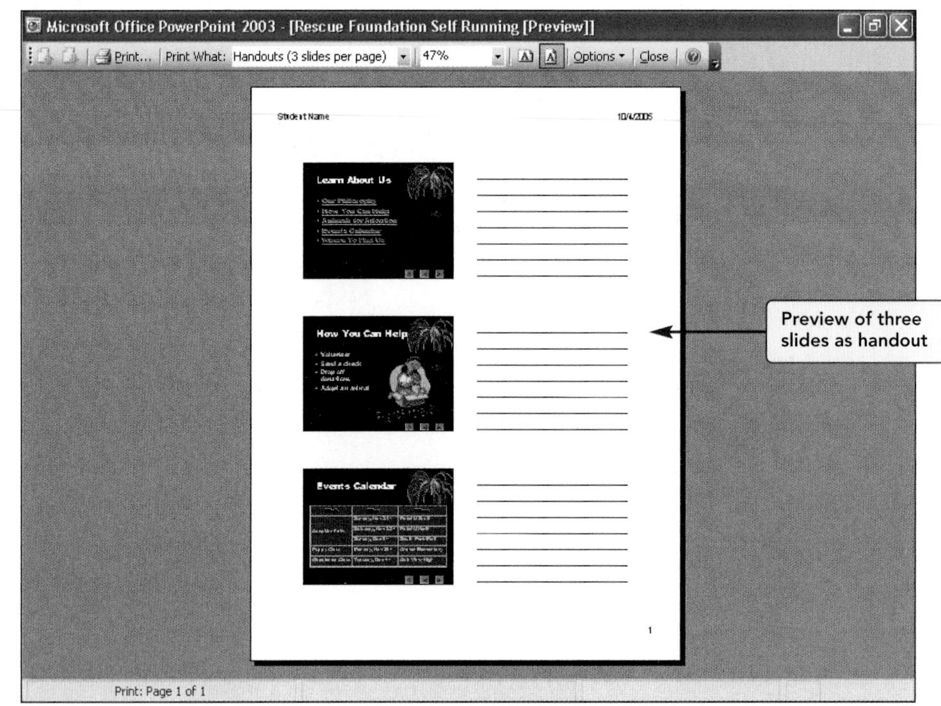

Figure 4.55

2
- **Print the handout.**
- **Close the Print Preview window.**
- **Save the presentation.**

Saving a Presentation as a Design Template

Finally, you decide to save the first two slides of your presentation as a design template so you can quickly create another presentation that already contains the navigation items you added.

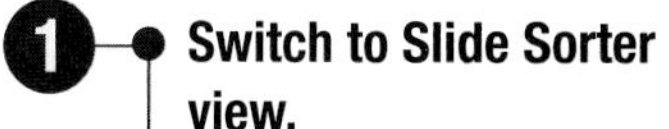

1 **Switch to Slide Sorter view.**

- **Delete slides 3 through 12.**
- **Choose File/Save As.**
- **From the Save As Type box, select Design Template.**
- **Change the file location to the location of your solution files.**
- **Enter the file name Self Running.**

Your screen should be similar to Figure 4.56

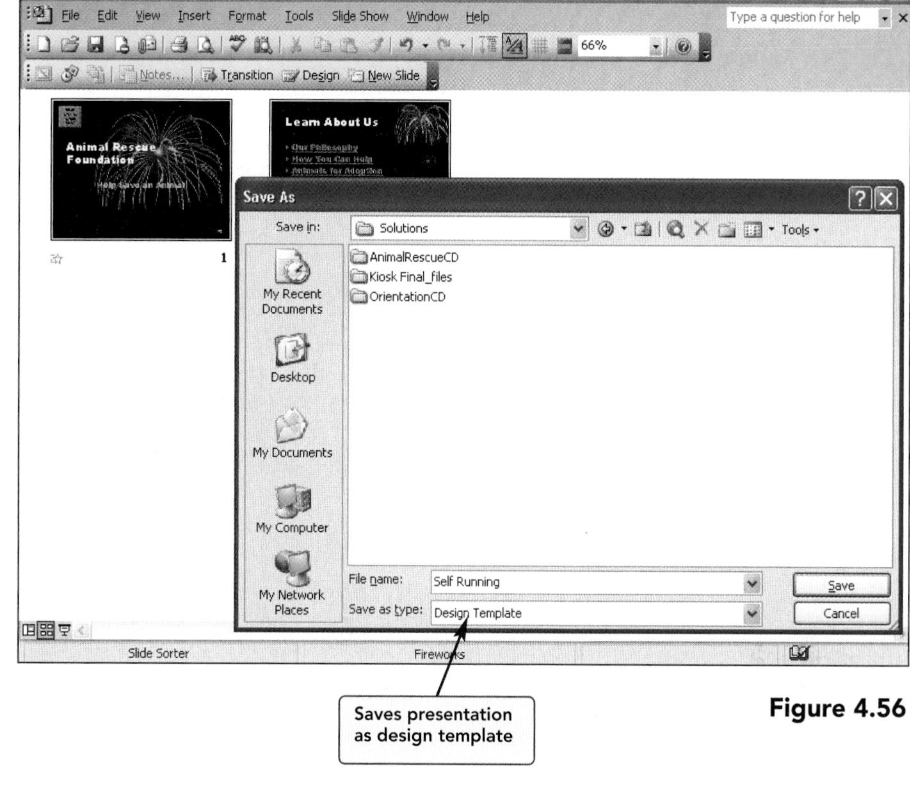

Figure 4.56

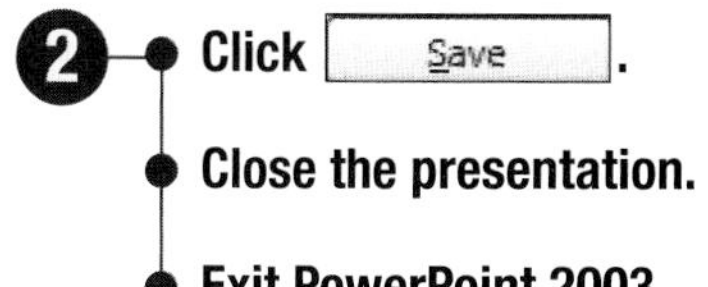

2 **Click Save.**

- **Close the presentation.**
- **Exit PowerPoint 2003.**

The default location to save a design template is the Template folder on your computer's hard drive. Saving it to this location will display the template name in the list of templates in the task pane. However, because you are saving it to your solution file location, it will not display in the template list.

The presentation is saved with a .pot file extension in your solution file folder and can be opened and modified to a new presentation. Because the extension is a template extension, when you save the modified presentation you will be prompted to give it a new file name, thereby preserving the template file for future use.

Focus on Careers

EXPLORE YOUR CAREER OPTIONS

Public Relations Specialists

Informing the general public of an organization's policies, activities, and accomplishments is an important part of a public relations specialist's job. In addition to radio, print, and televised media, PowerPoint can be used to create presentations that can be viewed in public places, such as a kiosk or on the Web. The position of public relations specialist usually requires a college degree and commands salaries from $39,000 to over $75,000 depending on experience and skill.

LAB 4
Creating a Presentation for a Kiosk and the Web

Animated GIF (PP4.19)

An animated GIF file is a type of graphic file that has motion.

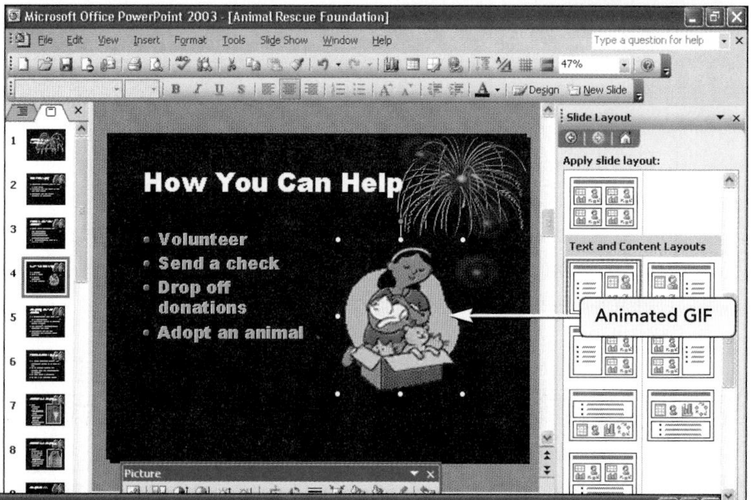

WordArt (PP4.20)

The WordArt feature is used to enhance slides by changing the shape of text, adding 3-D effects, and changing the alignment of text on a line.

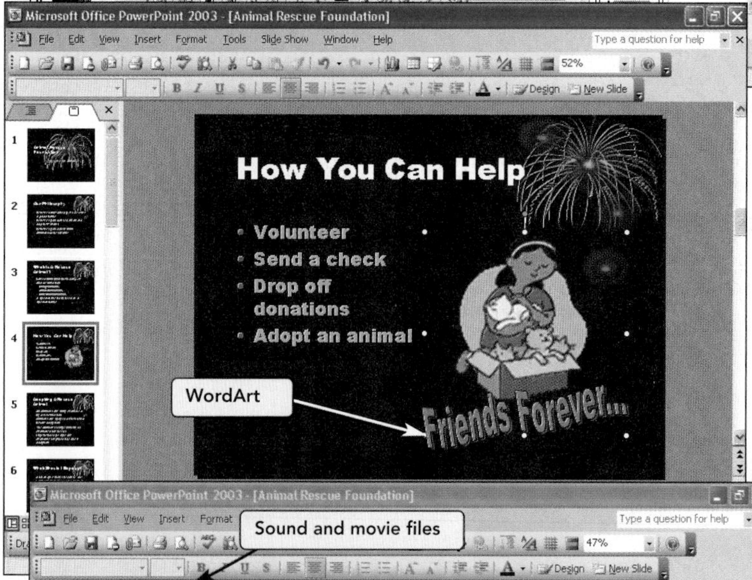

Sound and Movie Files (PP4.27)

Almost all PCs today are equipped with multimedia capabilities, which means they can play the most commonly used sound and movie files.

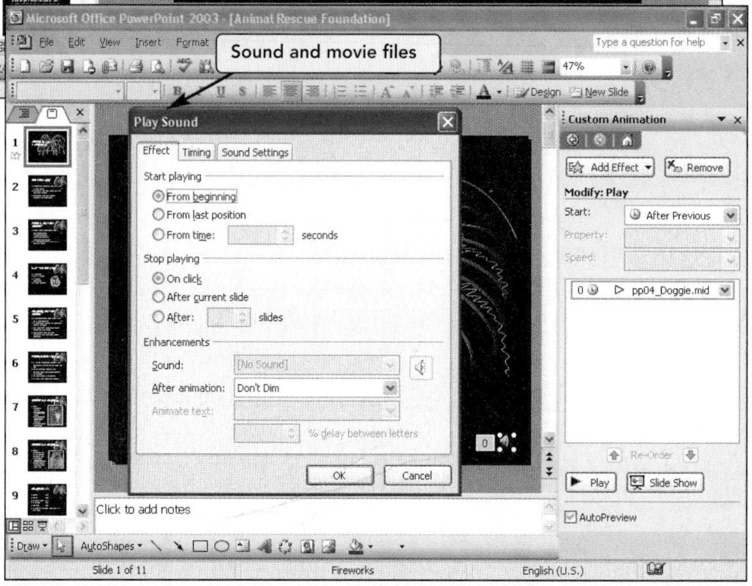

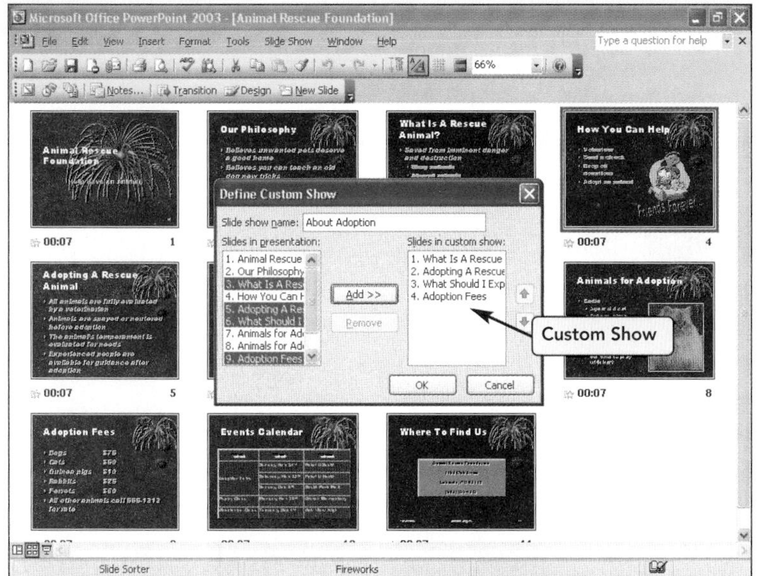

Custom Show (PP4.32)

A custom show is a presentation that runs within a presentation.

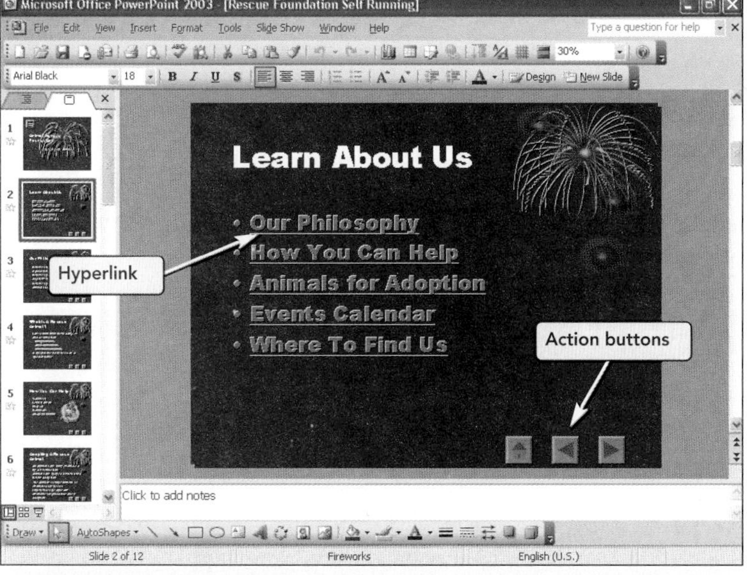

Hyperlink (PP4.35)

Hyperlinks provide a quick way to jump to other slides, custom shows, presentations, objects, e-mail addresses, or Web pages.

Action Buttons (PP4.40)

Action buttons consist of shapes, such as right- and left-facing arrows, that are used to navigate through a presentation.

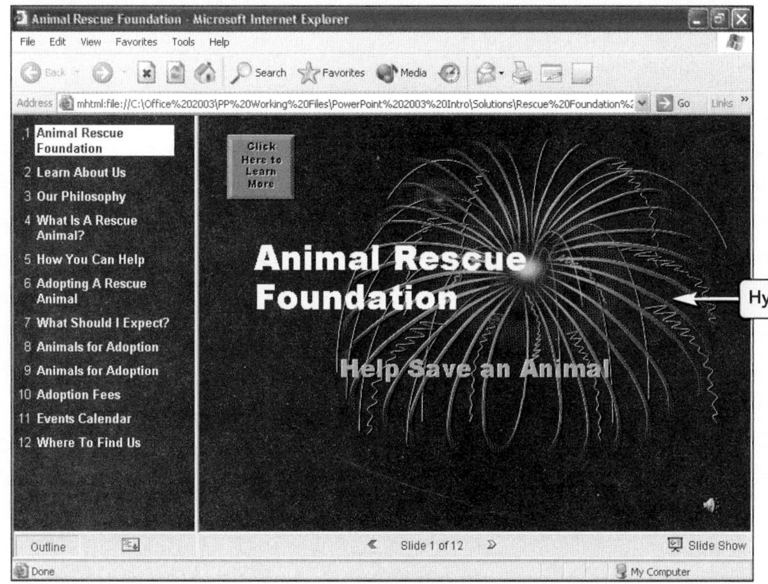

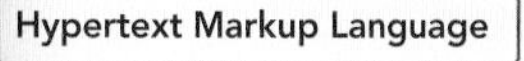

Hypertext Markup Language (PP4.46)

All Web pages are written using a programming language called Hypertext Markup Language (HTML). HTML commands control how the information on a page, such as font colors and size, is displayed.

LAB 4

key terms

action button PP4.40
animated GIF PP4.19
browser PP4.46
custom show PP4.32
hyperlink PP4.35
Hypertext Markup Language (HTML) PP4.46
publish PP4.45
server PP4.46
summary slide PP4.34
WordArt PP4.20

microsoft office specialist skills

The Microsoft Office Specialist certification program is designed to measure your proficiency in performing basic tasks using the Office System applications. Certification demonstrates that you have the skills and provides a valuable industry credential for employment. After completing this lab, you have learned the following Microsoft Office PowerPoint 2003 Specialist skills:

Skill Sets	Skill Standard	Page
Creating Content	Create new presentations from templates	PP4.4
	Insert and edit text-based content	PP4.6
	Insert tables, charts, and diagrams	PP4.12
	Insert pictures, shapes, and graphics	PP4.20
	Insert objects	PP4.26
Formatting Content	Apply slide transitions	PP4.29
	Customize slide templates	PP4.50
Managing and Delivering Presentations	Organize a presentation	PP4.7
	Set up slide shows for delivery	PP4.31,4.39
	Prepare presentations for remote delivery	PP4.31
	Save and publish presentations	PP4.45

command summary

Command	Button	Voice	Action
File/Save as Web Page			Publishes presentation on Web
Insert/Slides from Files			Inserts selected slides from another presentation
Insert/Slides from Outline			Creates slides from outline text
Insert/Movies and Sounds/ Sound from File			Inserts sound or movie files into selected slide
Insert/Movies and Sounds/ Play CD Audio Track			Plays a CD
Insert/Table			Inserts a table consisting of the specified number of rows and columns
Insert/Hyperlink			Creates a hyperlink
Format/AutoShape/Size			Changes size and scale of selected AutoShape
Format/Table			Formats borders and fill color of selected table
Slide Show/Set Up Show			Sets up presentation to run for specific situations
Slide Show/Custom Shows			Creates presentations within a presentation
Slide Show/Action Buttons			Adds navigation buttons to a slide
Slide Show/Action Settings			Specifies action that is needed to activate hyperlinks
Slide Show/Custom Animation			Adds motion and determines how sound is played

matching

Match the numbered item with the correct lettered description.

1. agenda slide	_____	**a.**	vertically centers cell contents
2. server	_____	**b.**	combination of multiple images that appear to move
3. .mpeg	_____	**c.**	creates a home action button
4. [icon]	_____	**d.**	a single-file Web page file type
5. action buttons	_____	**e.**	moving picture file extension
6. [icon]	_____	**f.**	contains a list of items or main topics from the presentation
7. custom show	_____	**g.**	computer that stores Web pages and sends them to a browser
8. hyperlink	_____	**h.**	shapes that are used to navigate through a presentation
9. .WAV	_____	**i.**	allows user to jump to a new location in the presentation
10. animated GIF	_____	**j.**	presentation that runs within another presentation
11. .MHTML			

multiple choice

Circle the letter of the correct response to the questions below.

1. The feature that is used to enhance your presentation by changing the shape of text, adding 3-D effects, and changing the alignment of text is called _______________.
   a. TextArt
   b. WordArt
   c. DrawShape
   d. WordWrap

2. A(n) _______________ is a presentation that runs within a presentation.
   a. custom show
   b. moving picture
   c. hyperlink
   d. agenda slide

3. If you do not have control over what computer your presentation will run on, use _______ and _________ files for audio and video.
   a. WAV, MPEG
   b. MIDI, AVI
   c. WAV, AVI
   d. MIDI, MOV

4. The ______________ feature is most useful for creating complex tables that contain cells of different heights or varying number of columns per row.
   a. Insert Table
   b. Draw Table
   c. Table Slide Layout
   d. Create Table

5. __________ control(s) how the information on a Web page is displayed.
   a. Formatting
   b. Browsers
   c. HTML commands
   d. Servers

6. A(n) _________________ file is a type of graphic file that has motion.
   a. animated GIF.
   b. moving graphic
   c. static GIF
   d. animated WAV

7. A(n) ____________________ loops back to the beginning slide and allows users to select what parts of the presentation they want to view.
   a. special show
   b. continuous show
   c. custom show
   d. agenda show

8. ___________________ provide a quick way to jump to other slides or Web pages.
   a. Action buttons
   b. Text links
   c. Hyperlinks
   d. Hypertext commands

9. Pages on the Web are written using the _______________ programming language.
   a. WWW
   b. HTML
   c. MPMC
   d. HMCL

10. A _________________ is a program that displays Web pages.
    a. viewer
    b. browser
    c. server
    d. control

true/false

Check the correct answer to the following statements.

1.	A presentation can be created from a Word outline document.	True	False
2.	WordArt is used to enhance predrawn images.	True	False
3.	Individual slides from one presentation can be inserted into another presentation.	True	False
4.	Animated images only move when the slide show is run.	True	False
5.	When a table is created in PowerPoint, it must have an equal number of columns and rows.	True	False
6.	Movies can be inserted into a PowerPoint presentation.	True	False
7.	When a presentation is run on a kiosk, it must have user interaction to repeat itself.	True	False
8.	A unique show runs a presentation within a presentation.	True	False
9.	An agenda slide can be linked to other slides in the presentation.	True	False
10.	Action buttons can be added to the slide master and appear on all slides in the presentation.	True	False

fill-in

Complete the following statements by filling in the blanks with the correct terms.

1. Text that is added to a slide using ________________ is a graphic object that can be edited, sized, or moved to any location on the slide.
2. When a(n) ____________ file is inserted into a PowerPoint slide, it does not display action until you run the presentation.
3. ______ files are typically used for sounds, and ________ files are typically used for music.
4. The programming language used on the Web is called ___________________.
5. ___________ files do not require any special hardware but they produce the lowest quality video.
6. When a custom show is finished, the presentation returns to the ______________.
7. A(n) ________________ is a presentation within a presentation.
8. A(n) _________________ slide is created from the titles of the selected slides.
9. ______________ buttons can be added to a presentation to move to other slides in the presentation.
10. ______________ provide a quick way to jump to other locations in a presentation.

rating system

★ Easy

★★ Moderate

★★★ Difficult

step-by-step

Betty's Birds Kiosk ★

1. You work at Betty's Birds, and are in charge of new customer orientation. Betty has requested that you create a kiosk presentation that will run in the store and help customers choose the right pet bird. Some of the completed slides are shown here.

   a. Open PowerPoint 2003. Create a new presentation using the Echo design template. Change the color scheme with the teal background choice.

   b. Add the title **Betty's Birds** and the subtitle **Your First Bird** to slide 1.

   c. Insert the graphic pp04_Birds to the right of the subtitle.

   d. Import text from the file pp04_Bird Outline. View the new slides and adjust the text as needed.

   e. Insert the graphic pp04_Dancing Parrot on slide 8.

   f. Insert a new Title Only slide at the end of the presentation. Insert the title **Betty's Birds**. Create a WordArt object with the text **Thank You** in a font of your choice. Position the WordArt object in the lower right corner of the slide.

   g. Search for the bird sound file pp04_Parrot Talk and insert it on slide 1 with the automatic play option selected.

   h. Add clip art of your choice to slides 3 and 9.

   i. Create an agenda slide as slide 2 with hyperlinks to the appropriate slides.

   j. Add home, next, and previous action buttons to the slide master that link to the agenda slide, next, and previous slides.

   k. Save the presentation as a Web page named Betty's Birds.

   l. Delete all slides except the first and last slides. Save the presentation as a template named Birds.

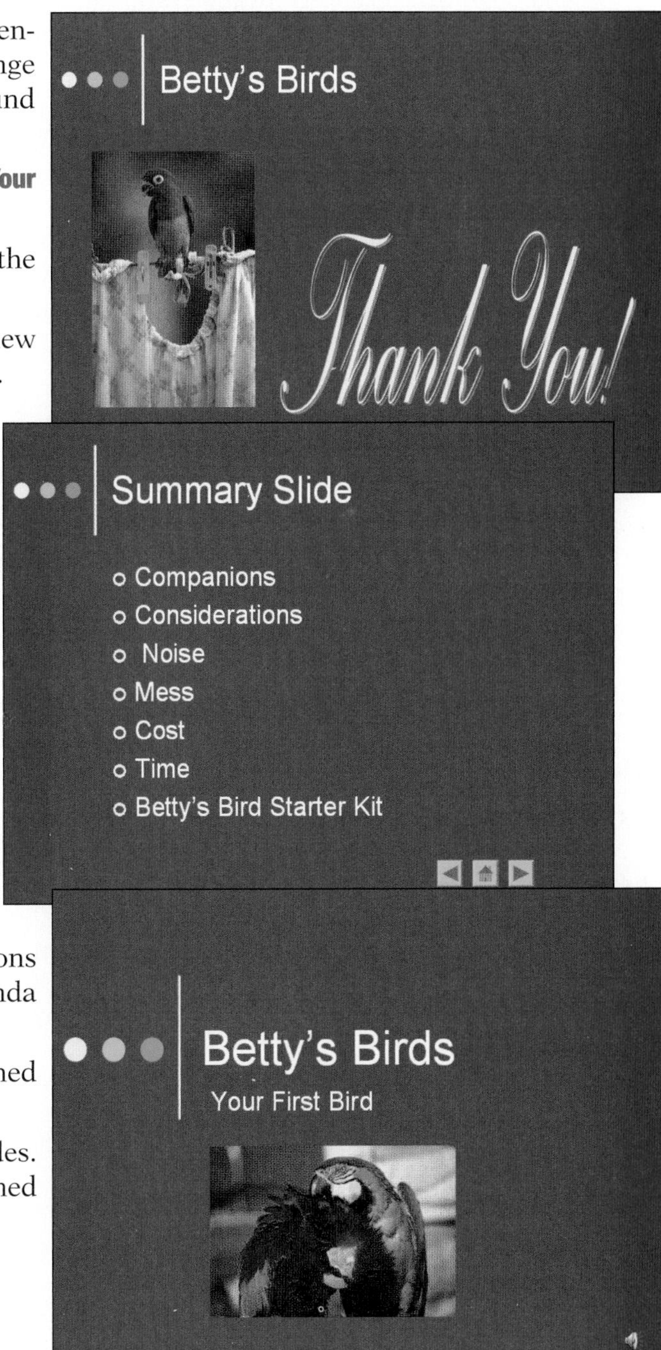

Anthology Cinema Web Presentation ★ ★

2. You work at Anthology Cinema in the media and customer relations department. You have been asked to create a presentation about the summer movie matinees that will run on the company's Web site. Some of the completed slides from your presentation are shown here.

   a. Open PowerPoint 2003. Create a new presentation using the Glass Layers design template. Change the color scheme to the light orange background choice.

   b. Add the title **Saturday Matinee** and the subtitle **Thrill-a-Minute Movies** to slide 1.

   c. Insert the graphic pp04_Anthology Logo on slide 1. Center the logo on the slide and adjust the title and subtitle as shown in the example.

   d. Import text from the file pp04_Anthology Outline. View the new slides and adjust the text as needed.

   e. Change the layout of slide 5 to Title, Text, and Content. Insert the graphic pp04_Popcorn in the placeholder. Adjust the size of the image to fill the slide. View the slide show to see the animation.

   f. Insert a new slide at the end of the presentation with a Blank layout. Create a WordArt object with the text **Visit us soon!** in a font of your choice. Change the WordArt shape to Arch Up. Insert the graphic pp04_Ticket below the WordArt object.

   g. Create a WordArt object with the text **Anthology Cinema** in the same font as the first WordArt object. Change the WordArt shape to Arch Down.

   h. Add the sound file pp04_Film and select the automatic start option.

   i. Preview slides 1, 5, and 6 as handouts, three per page.

   j. Save the presentation as a Web page named Anthology Cinema Web Presentation.

Adventure Travel Tours ★ ★

3. Adventure Travel Tours would like to create more business in their student travel division. You have been asked to create a Web presentation that highlights the Student Abroad Tour and gives advice to potential clients on what to expect from the trip. Some of the completed slides are shown here.

   a. Start PowerPoint and open the file pp04_Europe. Include your name on the title slide. Insert the graphic pp04_Champs Elysees in the lower left corner of slide 1. Adjust slide layout as needed.

   b. Create two custom slide shows, one titled **Food** that displays slides 5 through 8, and another titled **Favorite Places** that displays slides 7 and 10.

   c. Create a summary slide that includes slides 3 through 11. Title the slide **Topics**.

   d. Add Mouse Click hyperlinks from each item on the agenda slide to the appropriate slide or custom slide show (Jambon & Fromage links to the Food custom show).

   e. Insert the graphic pp04_Dinner on slide 6 and adjust the layout as required.

   f. Add home, back, and forward action buttons to the slide master. The home button should return to the agenda slide. Size and position the buttons appropriately. Reposition any text or graphics in the presentation as needed.

   g. Set the slides to advance automatically after 10 seconds with slow transition. Set the presentation to run on a kiosk as a continuous loop.

   h. Insert an audio of your choice to run while the presentation runs.

   i. Insert the animated graphic pp04_Train on slide 11.

   j. Add a WordArt object with the text **Off the Beaten Path** in a font of your choice on slide 8. Apply the Wave 2 shape. Position the WordArt object over the upper left corner of the photo.

   k. Run the slide show and test all the hyperlinks. Edit any slides as necessary.

   l. Save the presentation as a Web page named Europe Web Presentation. Print the presentation with six slides per page.

   m. Turn off the automatic advance setting and remove the audio. Redo the two hyperlinks that linked to custom shows to link to the appropriate slides. Preview the Web page and run the presentation.

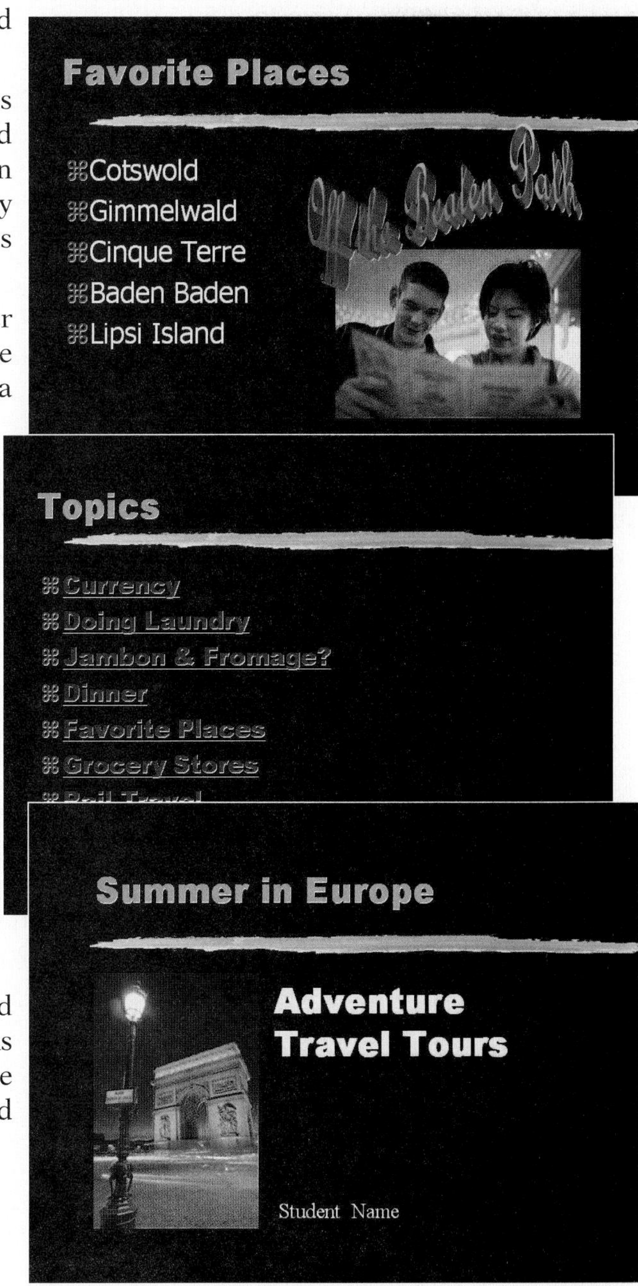

Fitness Web Page ★ ★ ★

4. The Lifestyle Fitness Club would like you to create several new pages for their Web site. The outline containing the text for the pages has already been created. You will create a presentation using the information in this outline. Several slides of the completed presentation are shown here.

   a. Create a new presentation using the Shimmer design template. Add slides to the presentation using the Word outline pp04_Fitness Outline.

   b. Delete the blank first slide. Apply the Title slide layout to the first slide. Add your name as a subtitle on the title slide.

   c. Change the slide layout of slide 2 to Title, Text, and Content. Insert the graphic pp04_Exercise.

   d. Change the layout of slide 4 to Title, Text, and Content. Insert the file pp04_Stretching in the placeholder.

   e. Add a sound clip of your choice to the presentation.

   f. Use the numbered bullet style to consecutively number the tips on slides 5 and 6.

   g. Insert a new slide at the end of the presentation. Use the Title Only layout. Title the slide **Why People Go to Fitness Clubs**.

   h. Insert a table with 3 columns and 9 rows. Enter the following information. Include appropriate column headings and formatting.

Tone my body	**41%**	**159**
Lose weight	**31%**	**119**
Meet people	**0%**	**1**
Reduce stress	**3%**	**12**
Bulk up	**11%**	**41**
Stay active	**13%**	**49**
Avoid feeling guilty	**2%**	**7**
Get out of house	**1%**	**2**

   i. Add home, back, and forward action buttons to the slide master. Appropriately size and position the buttons.

   j. Save the presentation as a Web page named Fitness Web Pages. Print the presentation with four slides per page.

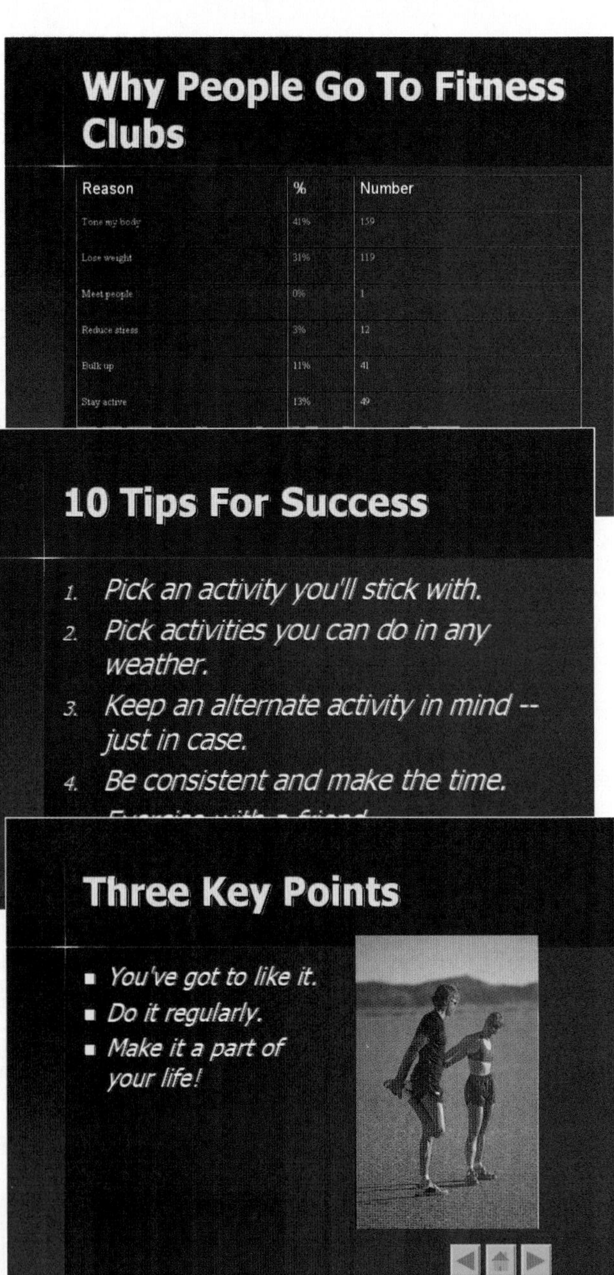

Sports Company Kiosk and Web Page ★★★

5. The Sports Company is expanding its advertising. They would like to have a kiosk presentation to send to their stores that features some special products in the stores. They would also like the presentation available on the Web. Several slides of the completed presentation are shown here.

   a. Create a presentation using the Orbit design template. Add slides to the presentation by inserting the Word document file pp04_Sports Company Outline.

   b. Delete the blank slide 1. Apply the Title slide layout to slide 1. Enter your name as a subtitle on the title slide. Insert the graphic pp04_Weight Lifter. Adjust the slide layout as needed.

   c. Make two custom slide shows, one for **Products** and one for **Services**. The Products custom show should display slides 4, 5, and 6. The Services custom show should display slides 7 and 8.

   d. Hyperlink the titles of the Products and Services slides to the appropriate custom show.

   e. Insert the file pp04_Tennis Racquet in slide 6.

   f. Replace the main title on slide 1 with an appropriately sized and shaped WordArt that contains the same text. Change the color to match the presentation design.

   g. Insert the graphic pp04_Mountain Bike on slide 4. Size and position the graphic. Adjust the layout as needed.

   h. Insert the sound file pp04_Onestop on slide 1. Set the sound to play when the presentation starts and to play for all slides.

   i. Add an animation of your choice to slide 8.

   j. Add home, forward, and back action buttons to the slide master. Color, size, and position the buttons appropriately.

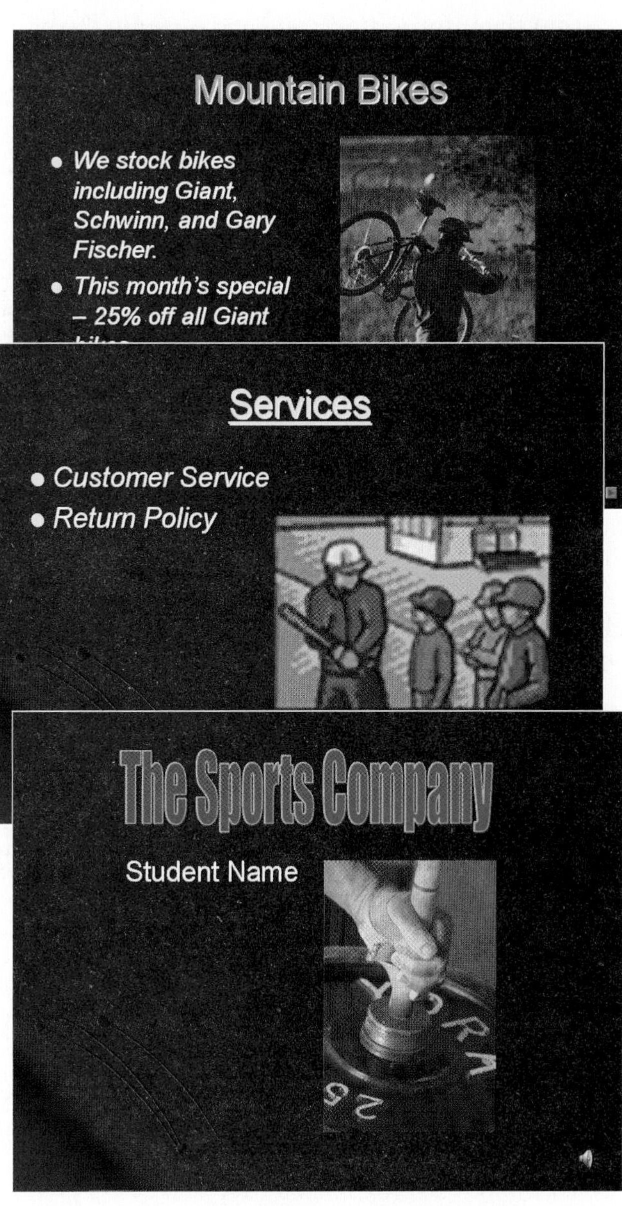

   k. Apply a random transition to all slides to advance automatically after 7 seconds. Set the slide show to run on a kiosk.

   l. Save the presentation as Sports Company Kiosk. Run the presentation to test the hyperlinks. Print the presentation with six slides per page.

   m. Remove the sound from the first slide. Remove the Products and Services hyperlinks. Add hyperlinks on the Products and Services slides for each bulleted item to the appropriate slide. Remove the transition settings and timings. Save the presentation as a Web presentation with the name Sports Company Web.

on your own

Pool Safety Kiosk ★

1. The response to your lifeguard safety presentation has been overwhelmingly positive. You decide that the information you have presented would make a good presentation to run on the kiosk in your public safety office. Modify the file Lifeguard Presentation for use on a kiosk. Add the name of your city in a WordArt design of your choice. Include appropriate animation and clip art, slide transitions, preset timing, and sound that runs continuously with the slide show. Set up the show to be browsed at a kiosk and to automatically play at full screen and loop continuously. Save the presentation as Pool Safety Kiosk and print the presentation with six slides per page.

Carpooling Kiosk ★

2. As cities surrounding Seattle get larger, rush hour traffic to the business district increases. You have been hired by the Washington Department of Transportation to create a presentation for their office lobby on the benefits of mass transit and carpooling. Use the information in the file pp04_Mass Transit to create a presentation that will run on a kiosk giving people information on how mass transit use and carpooling will benefit their city. Use the features you learned in PowerPoint, including sound and animation. Include your name in a footer on all slides. Save the presentation as Mass Transit and print the presentation with six slides per page.

Getaway Travel Club Web Page ★ ★

3. The Getaway Travel Club unanimously adopted your proposal to amend the itinerary for the Italy Trip this summer. They have asked you to post the information on the Web. Create a Web-based presentation. Open the presentation Favorites Travel (Lab 3, On Your Own 3) and create a custom show and an agenda slide with hyperlinks. Include action buttons, sound, animation, and WordArt. Include your name in the footer of all slides. Preview the presentation. Save the presentation as Travel Italy Web and print the presentation with six slides per page.

Storyland Fairytale Web Page ★ ★ ★

4. Your presentation on popular children's book titles was very popular with parents. Many have contacted the store owner, Susan, for more information. Susan has decided that the information you have compiled in your previous presentations would be an excellent Web page. Modify the Storyland Orientation file for use on the Web. Create a custom show and an agenda slide with hyperlinks. Include action buttons, sound, animation, and WordArt with the company name (Storyland). Save the file as Storyland Web. Print the presentation.

MusicFirst Web Presentation ★ ★ ★

5. MusicFirst, a large retail chain of stores that sells CDs, concert clothing, and jewelry would like you to create a presentation featuring a new artist monthly. This presentation will run on the company home page. Spotlight your favorite musician and his or her latest release. Create a presentation with the features you have learned in PowerPoint. Include music and custom slide shows within the presentation. Include your name and the date in a footer on the slides. Save your file as MusicFirst Web and print the presentation with six slides per page.

Working Together 2: Reviewing, Embedding, and Broadcasting a Presentation

Case Study

Animal Rescue Foundation

Now that the presentation to promote the Animal Rescue Foundation is nearly complete, you want to have several people review the presentation. To do this, you have sent copies of the presentation by e-mail to the agency director and several other administrators. You have asked them to add comments and make changes directly in the presentation and return it to you. When you receive the reviewed presentations back you will combine them with the original presentation and look at the comments and changes to determine which changes to make.

Once the kiosk presentation is finalized, you want to send a copy to the local shopping malls that provide a kiosk for use by local volunteer organizations. You decide to create a letter that contains the presentation embedded in it. You will then e-mail the letter to the shopping mall directors.

Finally, you want to see how you can distribute the presentation over the Web to audiences at different locations. To do this, you will look into broadcasting the presentation.

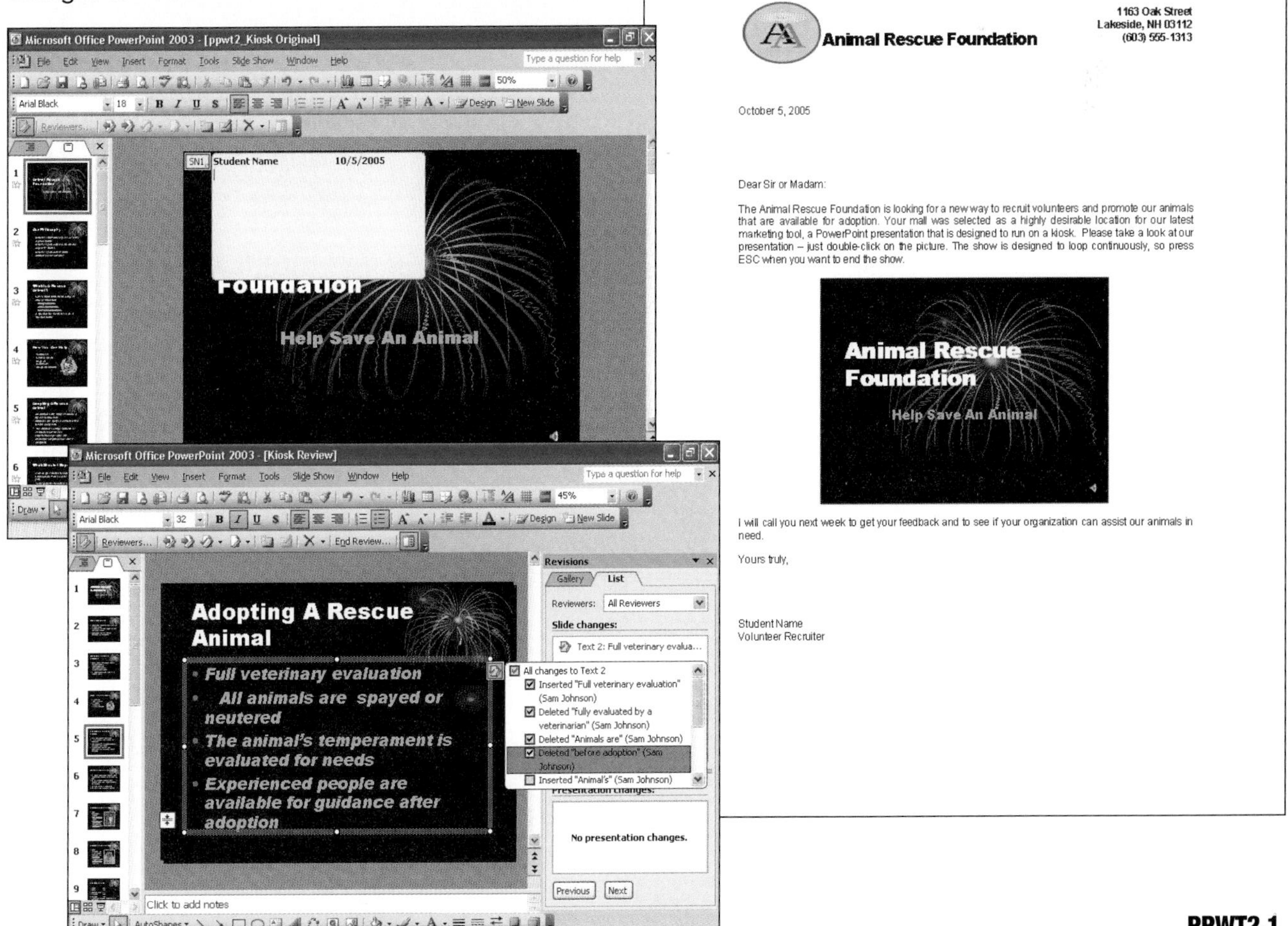

Animal Rescue Foundation

1163 Oak Street
Lakeside, NH 03112
(603) 555-1313

October 5, 2005

Dear Sir or Madam:

The Animal Rescue Foundation is looking for a new way to recruit volunteers and promote our animals that are available for adoption. Your mall was selected as a highly desirable location for our latest marketing tool, a PowerPoint presentation that is designed to run on a kiosk. Please take a look at our presentation – just double-click on the picture. The show is designed to loop continuously, so press ESC when you want to end the show.

Animal Rescue Foundation
Help Save An Animal

I will call you next week to get your feedback and to see if your organization can assist our animals in need.

Yours truly,

Student Name
Volunteer Recruiter

Reviewing a Presentation

Before sending the presentation to the shopping malls for use in the kiosks, you want to get feedback from several people in the organization first. You will do this by sending a copy of the presentation by e-mail to each person for review. The review process consists of several steps: prepare the presentation to send to reviewers, send the presentation, receive the reviewed presentations back, merge the reviewed presentations and respond to changes, and end the review.

Adding a Comment

Before you send the presentation for review, you want to add a comment to the reviewers. A **comment** is a remark that is displayed in a separate box and attached to a file.

1
- **Start Office PowerPoint 2003.**
- **Open the file** ppwt2_Kiosk Original.
- **Display slide 1 in Normal view.**
- **Choose Insert/Comment.**

Your screen should be similar to Figure 1

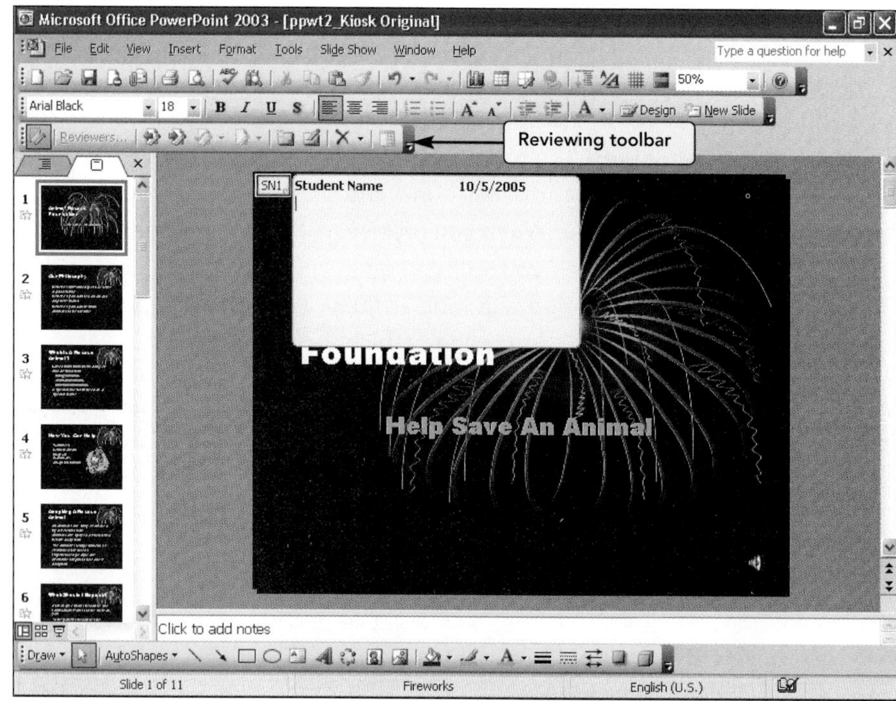

Figure 1

A comment box is displayed in which the text of the comment is entered. The name of the user inserting the comment appears on the first line followed by the system date. When you add a comment, the Reviewing toolbar automatically appears. You will use the Reviewing toolbar shortly, when you review the comments sent back to you by the reviewers.

2 • **Type the following comment text: Please add your comments and changes directly in the presentation and return it to me. Thank you for your help.**

Your screen should be similar to Figure 2

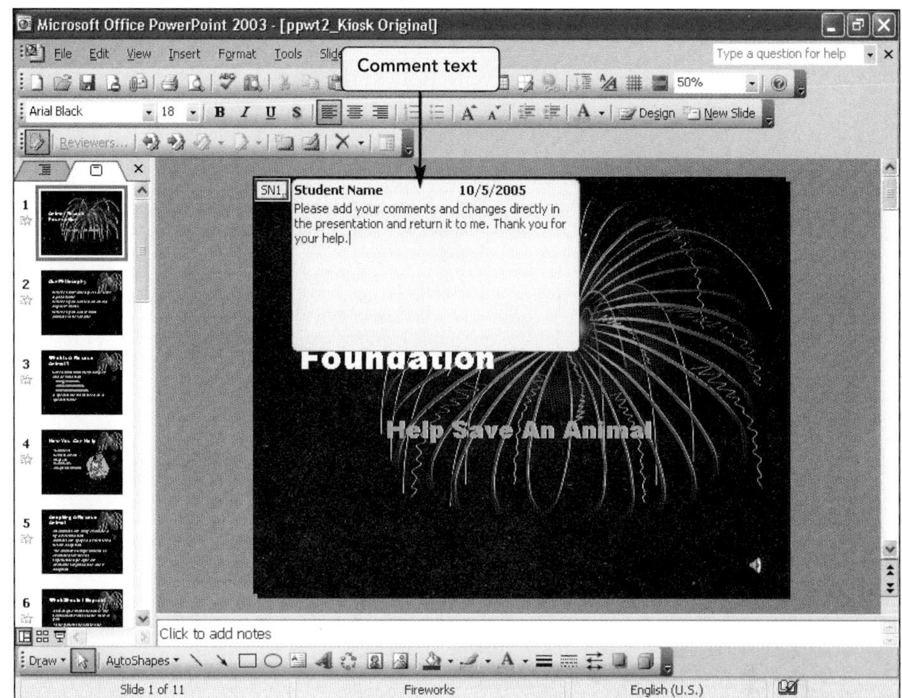

Figure 2

After entering comment text, clicking outside the comment closes it and displays an icon called a **comment marker** that indicates a comment has been added to the presentation. To see the comment text again, simply point to the marker.

3 • **Click outside the comment.**

• **Point to the comment marker.**

Your screen should be similar to Figure 3

Additional Information

If you need to edit the comment, click Edit Comment on the Reviewing toolbar or double-click on the comment marker.

Figure 3

The comment is displayed in a balloon that is sized to fit the contents.

4 • **Save the presentation as Kiosk Review to your solution file location.**

Sending the Presentation for Review

Now you will send the presentation to the director, Sam Johnson, and to the Fund Raising administrator, Mary Munson, via e-mail for them to review.

1

- **Choose File/Send to/Mail Recipient (for Review).**
- **In the To field, enter your e-mail address.**

Your screen should be similar to Figure 4

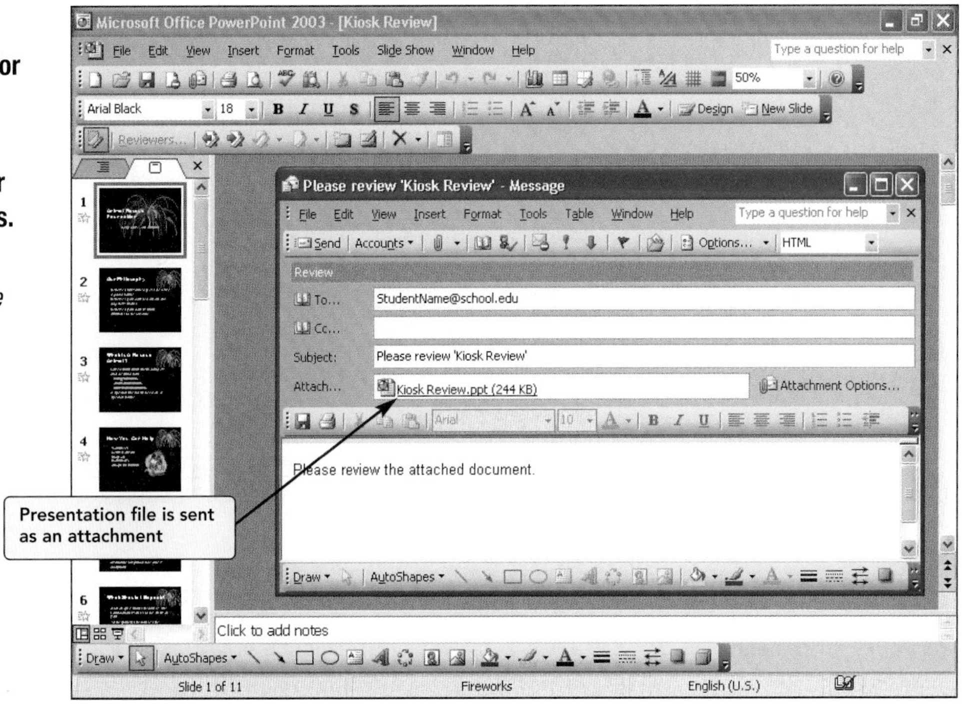

Presentation file is sent as an attachment

Figure 4

Because the command to send the presentation by e-mail was to send it for review, the subject and body of the message already include appropriate information. The presentation is included as an attachment to the e-mail message.

2 **In the body of the e-mail, type the following message below the default message: Please return your comments and changes to me by Friday. Thanks!**

- **Press ←Enter and type your name.**

Your screen should be similar to Figure 5

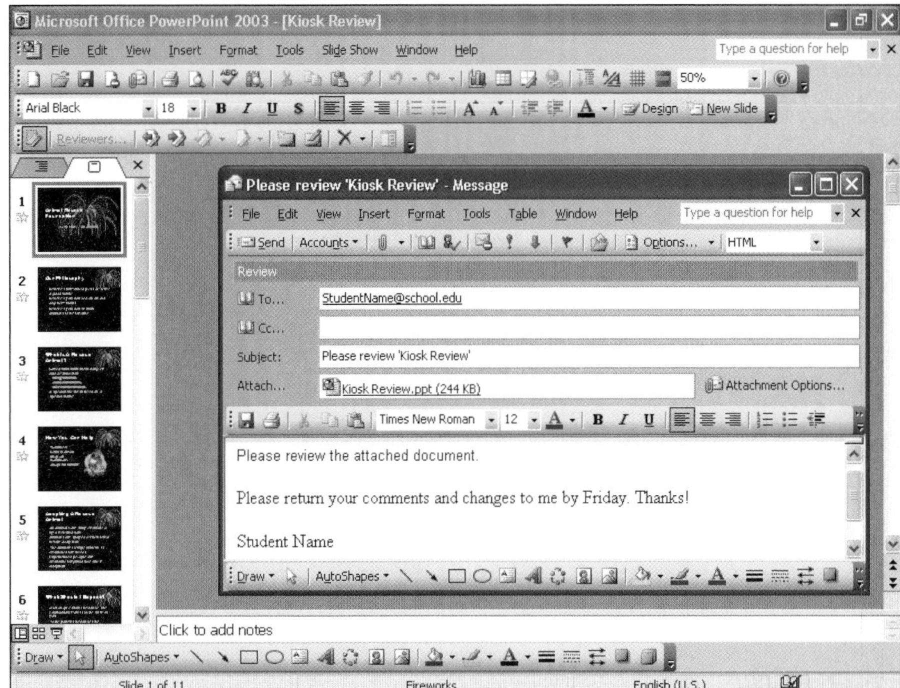

Figure 5

If you were connected to the Internet, you would send the message next. Instead, you will save the message as a text file.

3 **Choose File/Save As and save the message as a Word Document file type using the file name Kiosk Review E-mail to your solution file location.**

- **Close the e-mail window.**

Combining Reviewed Presentations

Additional Information

If all the reviewers are using Outlook, PowerPoint 2003 will prompt you to combine the reviewed presentations with the original when you double-click the attachment.

The next day while checking your e-mail for new messages, you see that both Sam and Mary have returned the presentation with their comments and changes. You have downloaded the attachments and saved them as files on your system. Now you want to review the suggested changes.

When you receive multiple reviewers' comments, the easiest way to review them is to merge the reviewed presentations with the original.

Choose Tools/Compare and Merge Presentations.

Change to your data file location and select ppwt2_Kiosk Review (1) **and** ppwt2_Kiosk Review (2)**.**

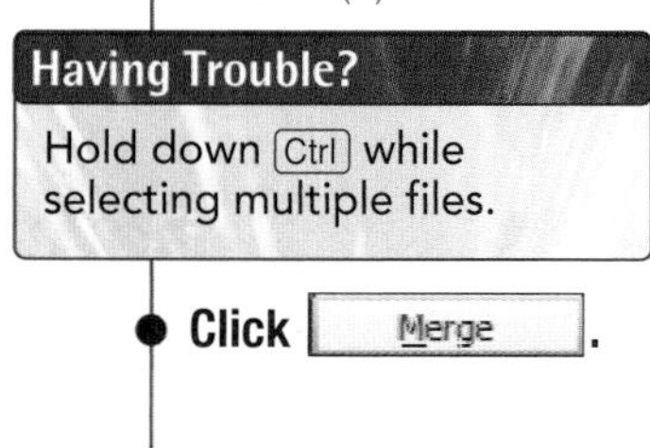

Having Trouble?

Hold down Ctrl while selecting multiple files.

Click Merge.

If necessary, dock the Reviewing toolbar below the Formatting toolbar.

Additional Information

When a presentation is sent for review, PowerPoint retains the name of the file but adds a number at the end in sequential order for each reviewer.

Your screen should be similar to Figure 6

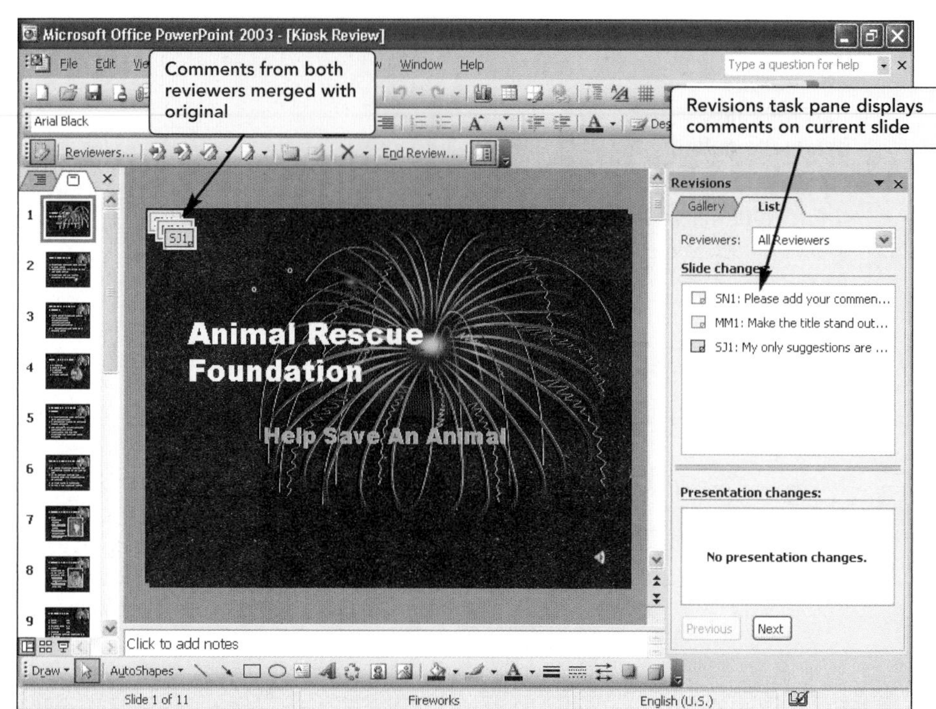

Figure 6

Having Trouble?

If the Revisions task pane is not displayed, click in the Reviewing toolbar.

The changes and comments from both reviewed presentations are now included in the original presentation that was sent for review. The first slide has three comment markers in the upper left corner with the reviewer's initials and the number of the comment. Each reviewer's comments appear in a different color.

The Revisions task pane also opens to assist you in reviewing the comments and changes. The Revisions pane displays the comments on the current slide.

Deleting a Comment

The comment you added when you sent the presentation for review is the first comment listed in the Revisions task pane. You want to delete this comment before you begin to review the comments from the reviewers.

1 Click the first comment in the Slide changes list of the Revisions task pane.

Your screen should be similar to Figure 7

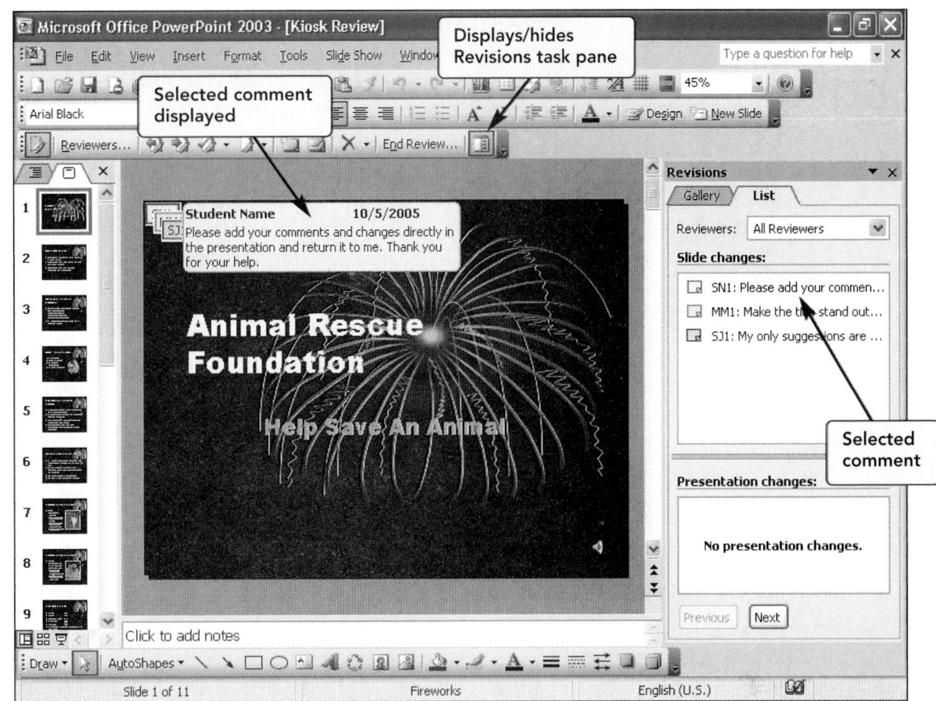

Figure 7

The comment box opens on the slide so you can delete the comment.

2 Click Delete Comment on the Reviewing toolbar.

Your screen should be similar to Figure 8

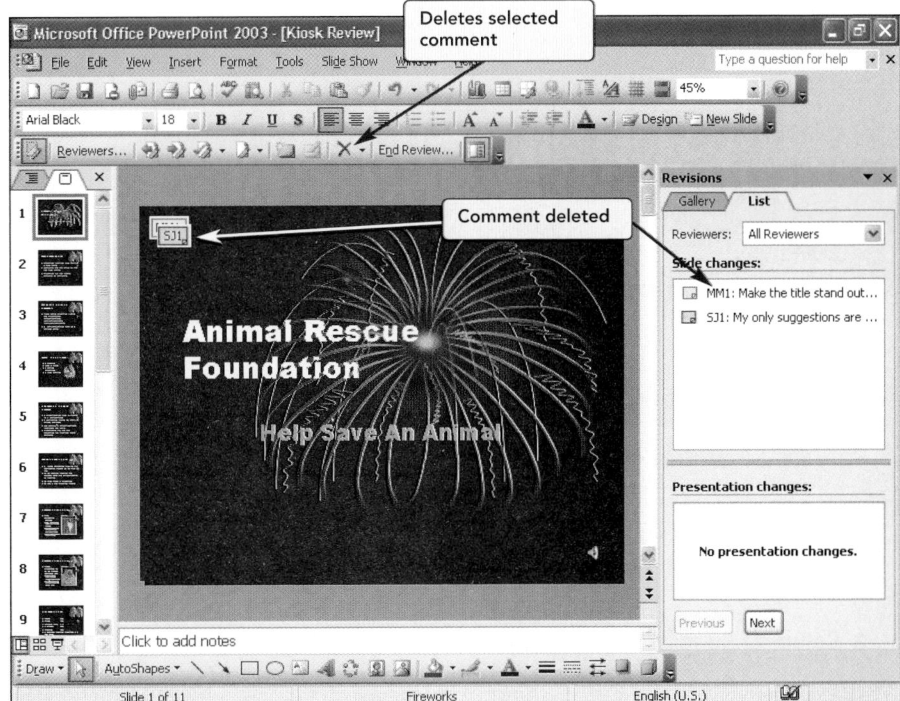

Figure 8

The comment is removed from the slide and the Revisions pane. You are now ready to start reviewing the comments and changes made by the reviewers.

Responding to Comments and Changes

You will use the Reviewing toolbar to navigate through the comments and changes made to the presentation by the reviewers.

1 **Click Next Item on the Reviewing toolbar.**

Your screen should be similar to Figure 9

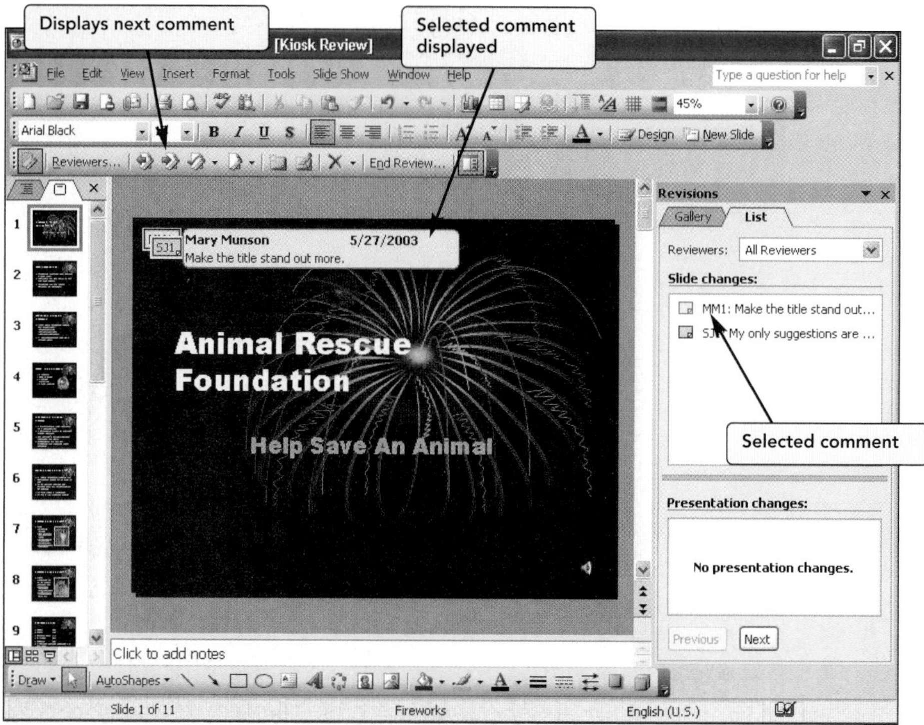

Figure 9

You think the suggestion in the first comment is a good idea. You decide to bold and make the title text larger.

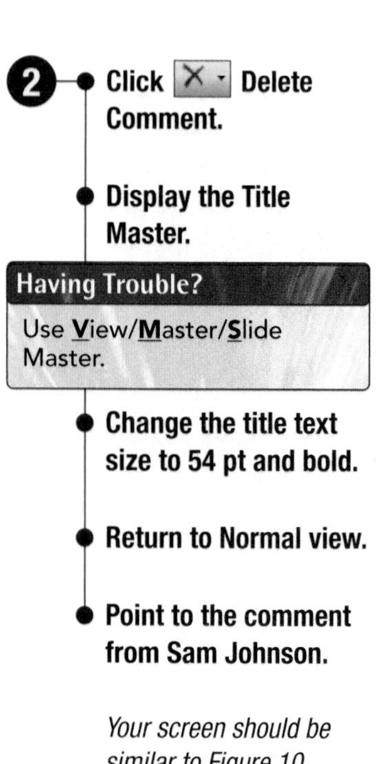

2 **Click Delete Comment.**

- **Display the Title Master.**

Having Trouble?

Use View/Master/Slide Master.

- **Change the title text size to 54 pt and bold.**
- **Return to Normal view.**
- **Point to the comment from Sam Johnson.**

Your screen should be similar to Figure 10

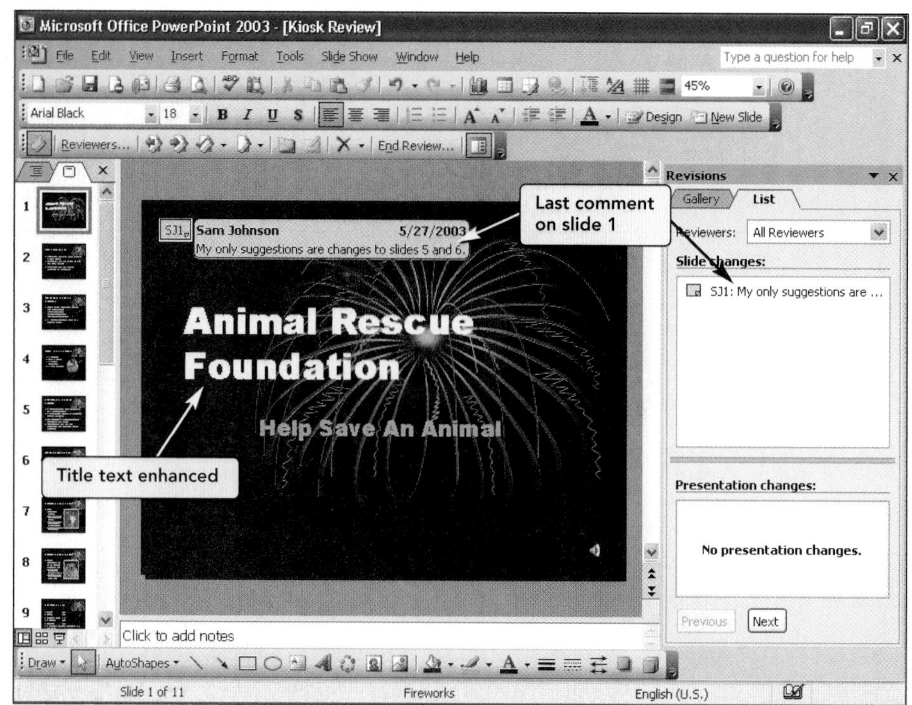

Figure 10

The title now stands out more. The last comment on this slide refers you to changes made to slide 5. You decide to go to slide 5 next and look at the changes.

3 **Click on slide 5 in the slide tab.**

Select the comment.

Your screen should be similar to Figure 11

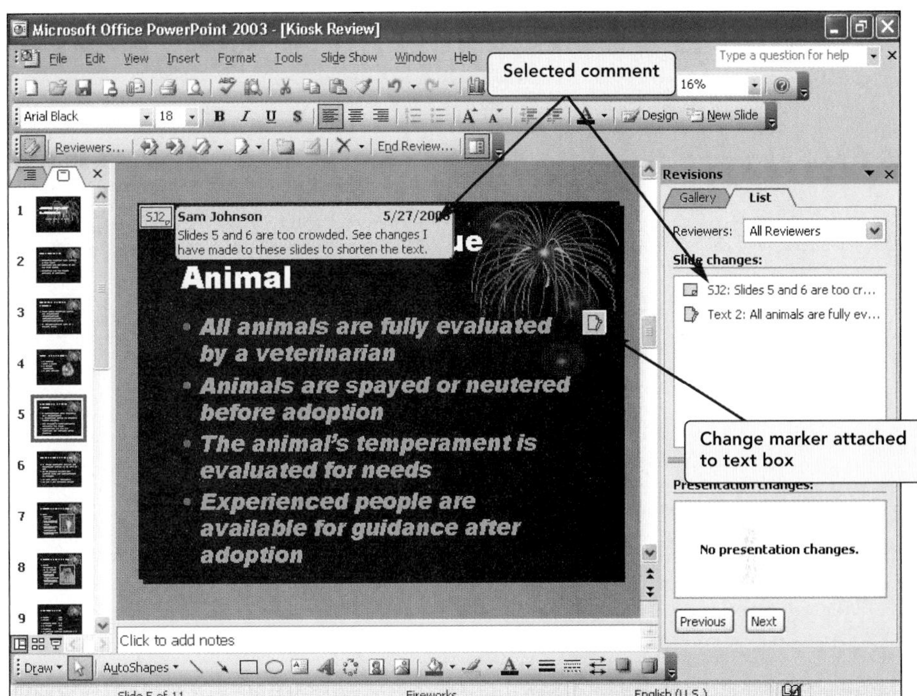

Figure 11

The comment on slide 5 notes that there is too much text on slides 5 and 6. The slide also displays a **change marker** attached to the text box indicating where a reviewer made changes to the presentation. You will delete the comment and look at the suggested changes.

4 Delete the comment.

Click [icon]**.**

Your screen should be similar to Figure 12

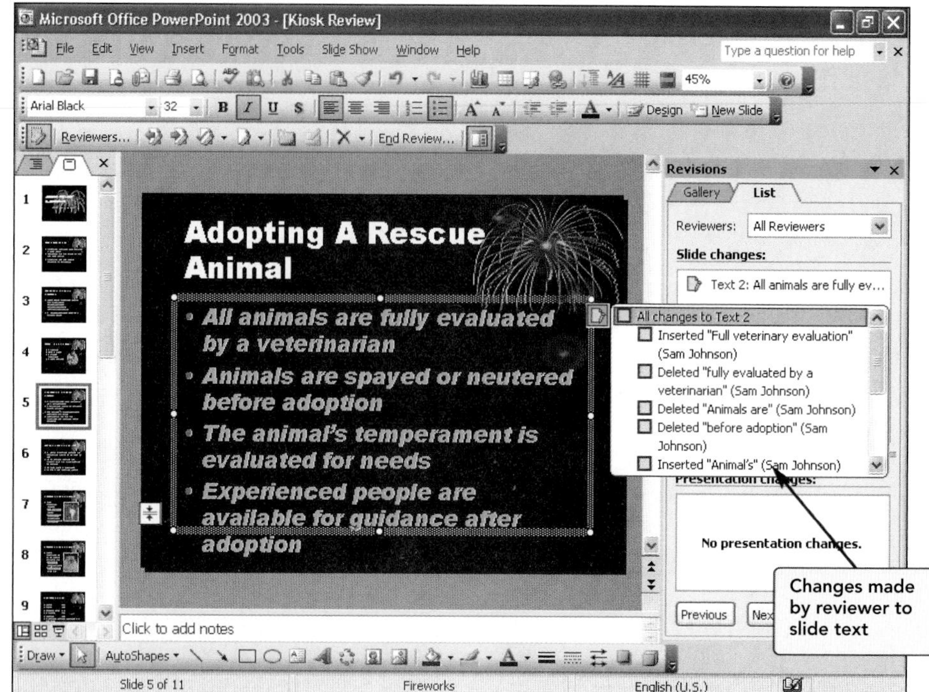

Figure 12

All the insertions and deletions that were made to the text are listed.

Applying Reviewer Changes

Notice that each item in the All Changes to Text 2 box is preceded with a check box. Selecting the item will display the change in the slide.

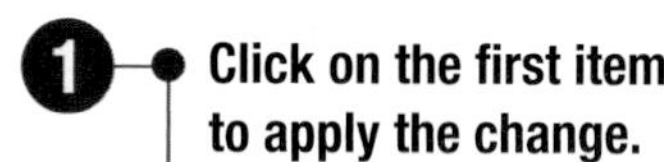

1 Click on the first item to apply the change.

> **Additional Information**
>
> The checkmark indicates that the change was added to the presentation.

Point to the second item.

Your screen should be similar to Figure 13

> **Additional Information**
>
> You can undo the change using [icon] Unapply on the Reviewing toolbar or by clicking on the item to clear the checkmark.

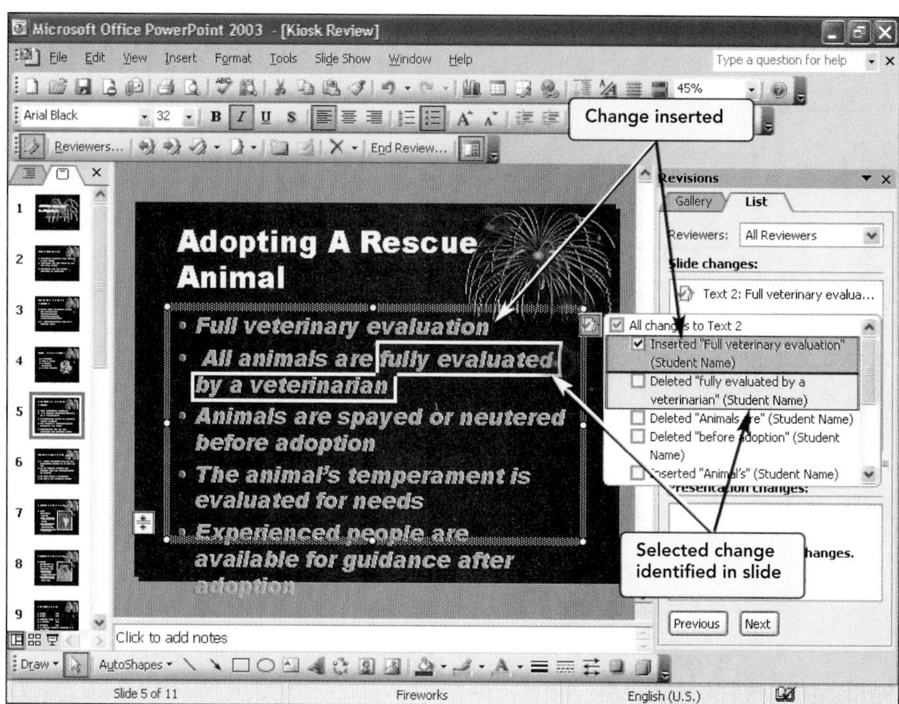

Figure 13

The first change is inserted, and the change you are pointing to is identified in the text box to show you the area that will be affected if you accept this change.

As you look at the next few changes, they all look good to you and you decide to incorporate them into the presentation.

2 **Click on the second, third, and fourth items.**

Your screen should be similar to Figure 14

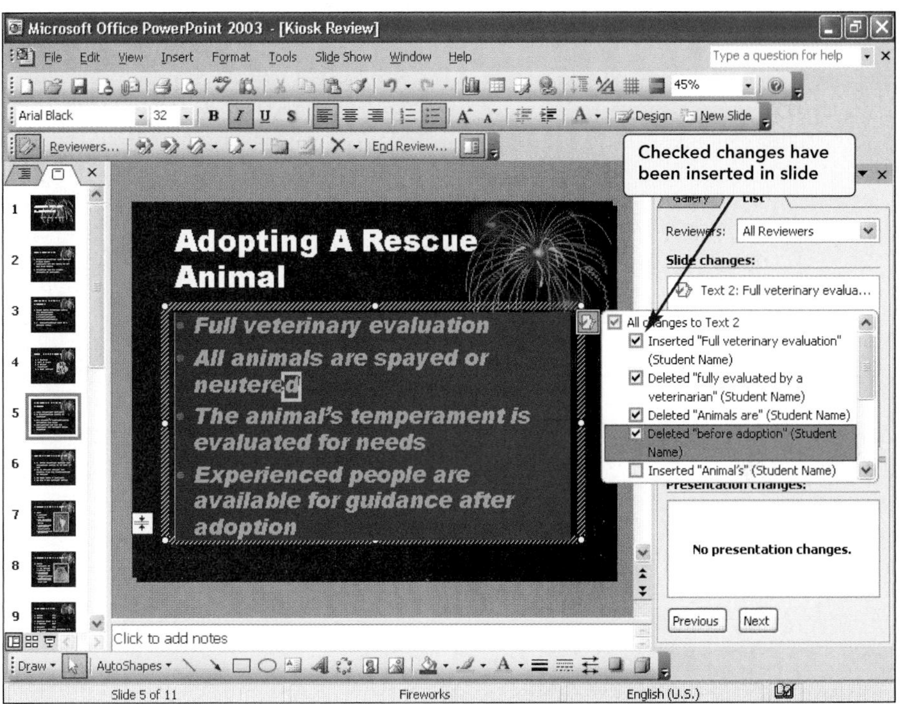

Figure 14

The three changes have been made in the slide. So far, you think all the changes look good and decide to just go ahead and apply all the changes to the slide.

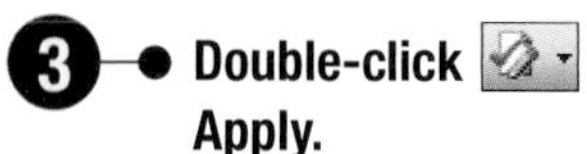

Double-click Apply.

Your screen should be similar to Figure 15

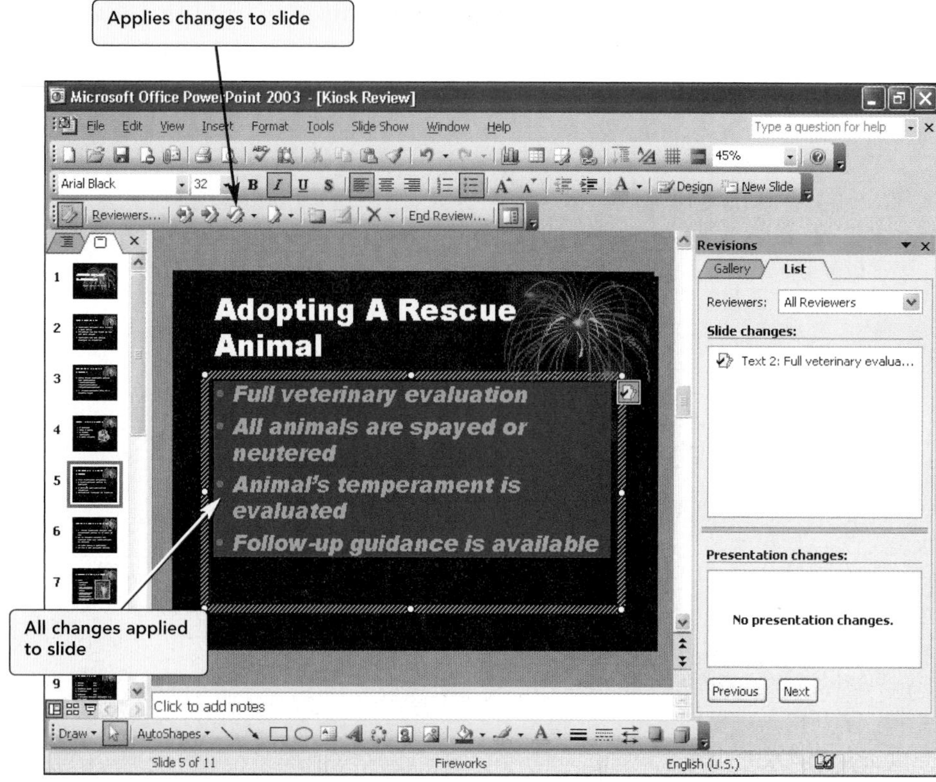

Figure 15

The changes look good and you just need to remove the change marker. Then you will look at the changes made to slide 6.

4

- **Click Delete to remove the change marker.**
- **Display slide 6.**
- **Click to display the changes.**

Your screen should be similar to Figure 16

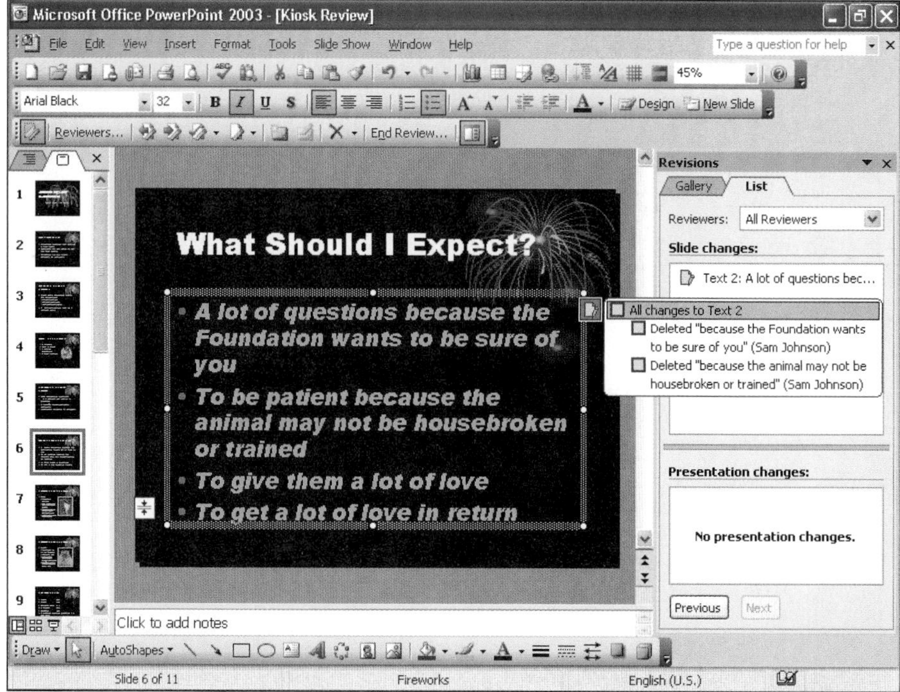

Figure 16

After reading the proposed changes, you again decide to accept them all. Then you will continue to look at and respond to any other comments as needed.

5

- **Click in the check box next to "All changes to Text 2" to insert all the changes.**
- **Delete the change marker.**
- **Click Next Item.**
- **Click Continue to look for more changes starting at the beginning of the presentation.**
- **Delete the comment on slide 1.**
- **Click Next Item.**

Additional Information

Notice the Slide Changes area of the Revisions pane indicates the location of the slide containing the next set of changes.

Your screen should be similar to Figure 17

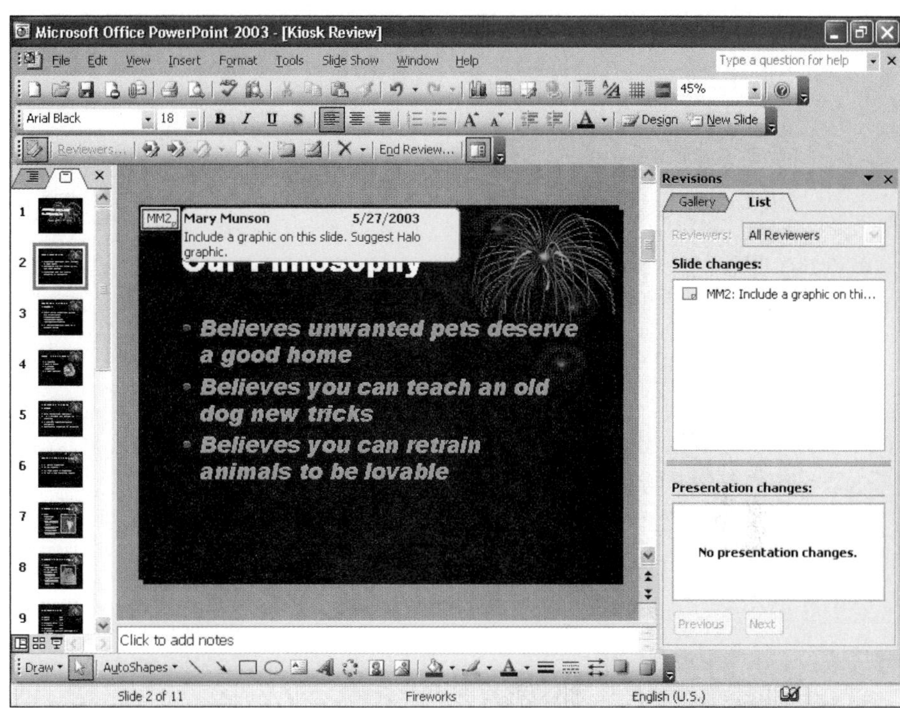

Figure 17

On this slide, Mary has suggested adding the Halo graphic to the slide. This graphic is one of the Animal Angels logo symbols that are frequently used in correspondence. Again, you like this idea.

6 Delete the comment.

- Insert the ppwt2_Halo graphic file from your data file location.
- Move the graphic to the lower right area of the slide as in Figure 18.
- Reduce the width of the text placeholder.
- Select the graphic.
- Increase the size of the graphic slightly.

Your screen should be similar to Figure 18

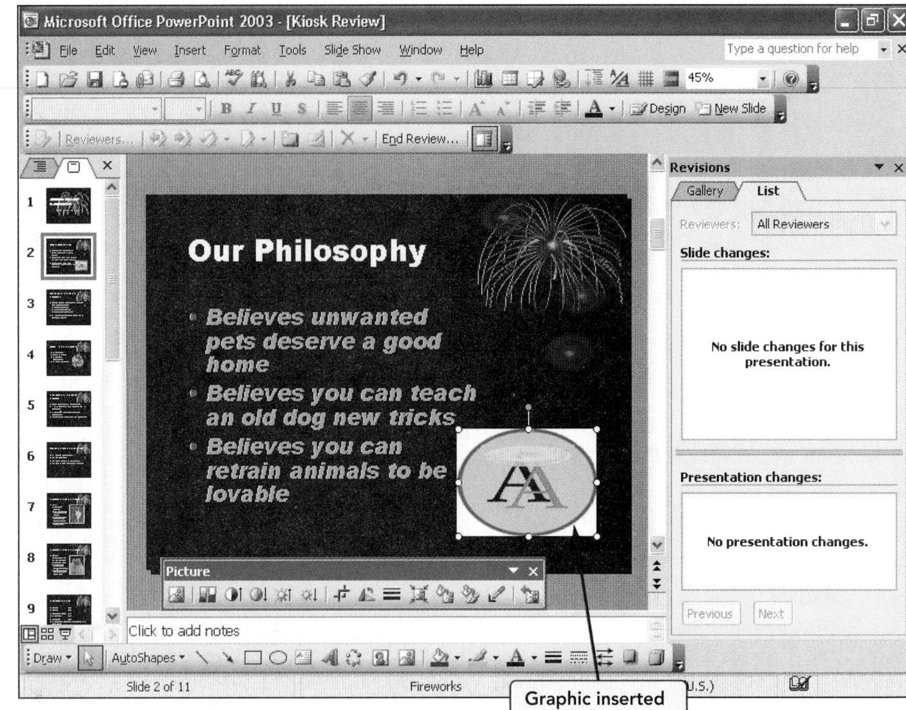

Figure 18

You think the graphic would look better without the white background. To quickly remove the background, you will make it transparent so that the slide background shows through instead.

7 In the Picture toolbar, click Set Transparent Color.

Having Trouble?

You may need to display and hide the Picture toolbar.

- Click on the white background of the graphic to make it transparent.

Additional Information

The mouse pointer appears as when this feature is active.

- Click outside the graphic to deselect it.

Your screen should be similar to Figure 19

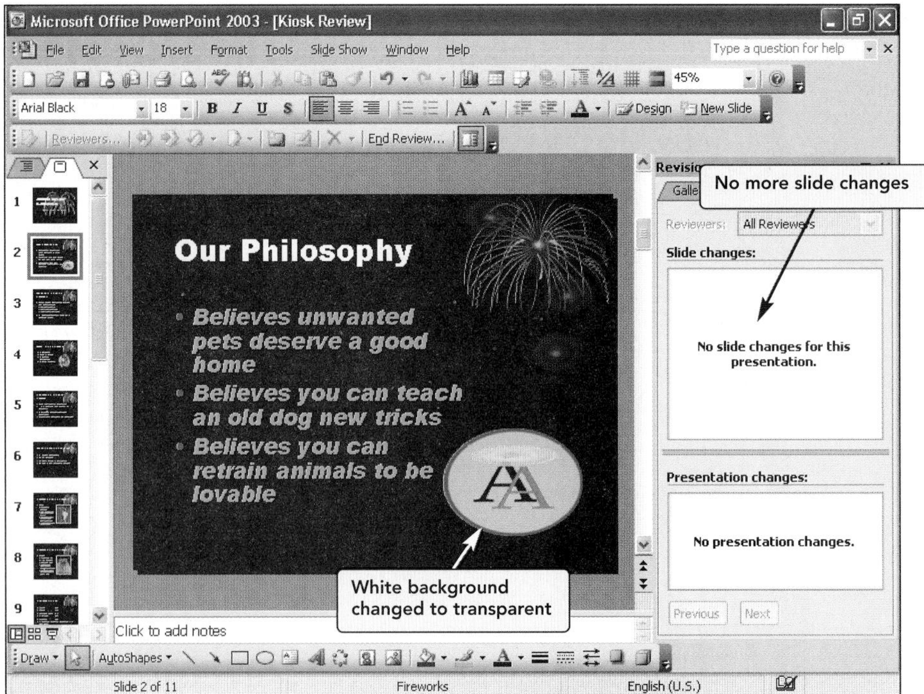

Figure 19

The graphic looks much better. Notice the Revisions pane indicates there are no more changes or comments in the presentation, and the buttons on the Reviewing toolbar are dimmed.

Ending the Review

Another Method

To manually end the review, click [icon] on the Reviewing toolbar.

PowerPoint automatically ends the review process if you have applied the reviewer changes you want, deleted all change markers, and saved the presentation. When the review process is over, you cannot combine any more reviewed presentations with your original presentation. Since you do not plan to get any more reviews, you decide to save the file.

1 Save the presentation as Kiosk Final to your solution file location.

Your screen should be similar to Figure 20

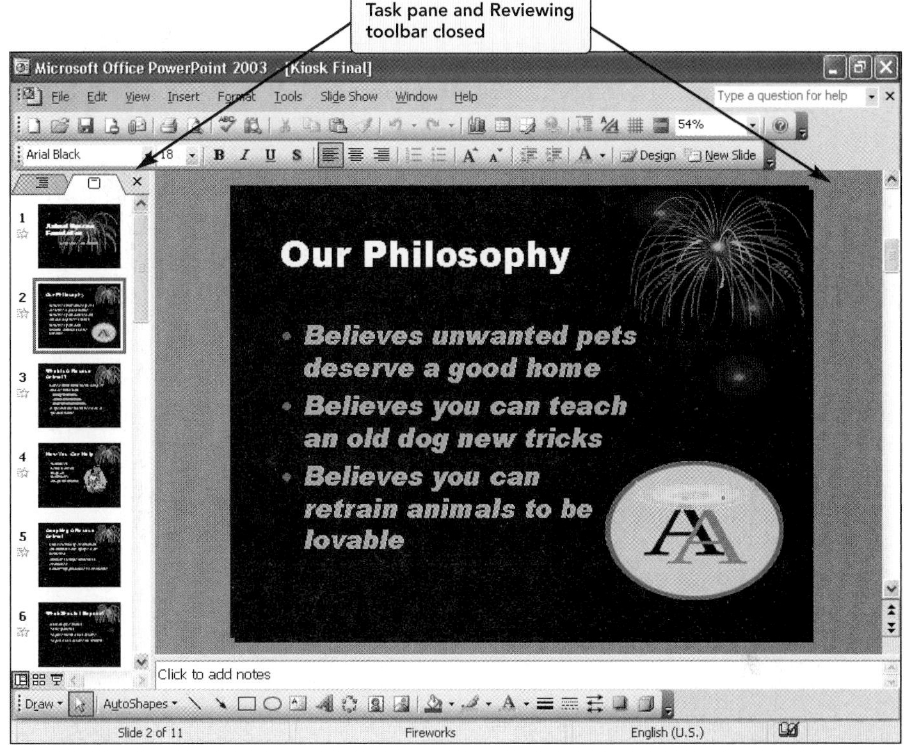

Figure 20

The review is ended, and the task pane and Reviewing toolbar are automatically closed.

Collaborating Online

As suggested by the agency director, you looked into other methods you can use to have the presentation reviewed by other animal shelters and members of the Animal Protection Association.

There are two ways that you can collaborate with many reviewers at once. The first way is to hold an online meeting using the Microsoft Windows NetMeeting feature. Each person you invite to the online meeting must also be running NetMeeting to receive your invitation. In an online meeting, you are in control of the collaboration. Each person in the meeting can add comments to the presentation in real time, if you give them access. When you turn on collaboration, each person in the online meeting can take turns editing the presentation. The person who is controlling the presentation is the only one whose mouse will operate, and that person's initials appear next to the mouse pointer.

The second way to collaborate is by using the Web Discussion feature, which needs to be set up by a system administrator. It enables you and other people to insert comments into the same document at the same time. This makes your job as document author much easier. You can see all the comments made by the reviewers, and they can too, which means if there is a question about a comment, the reviewers can discuss it among themselves.

Embedding a Presentation

The agency director is very pleased with the changes you made, and tells you to send out the presentation to the local malls. You have already created a letter to the mall directors and just need to insert the presentation file in the letter document file. Then you will send the letter as an e-mail attachment.

To insert the presentation in the letter, you will open the letter in Word and embed the PowerPoint presentation file in the document. An embedded object is inserted in a document and becomes part of that document, called the **destination document**. This means that you can modify it without affecting the **source document** where the original object resides.

1

- **Start Office Word 2003 and, if necessary, maximize the application window.**
- **Open the file** ppwt2_Mall Letter**.**

Your screen should be similar to Figure 21

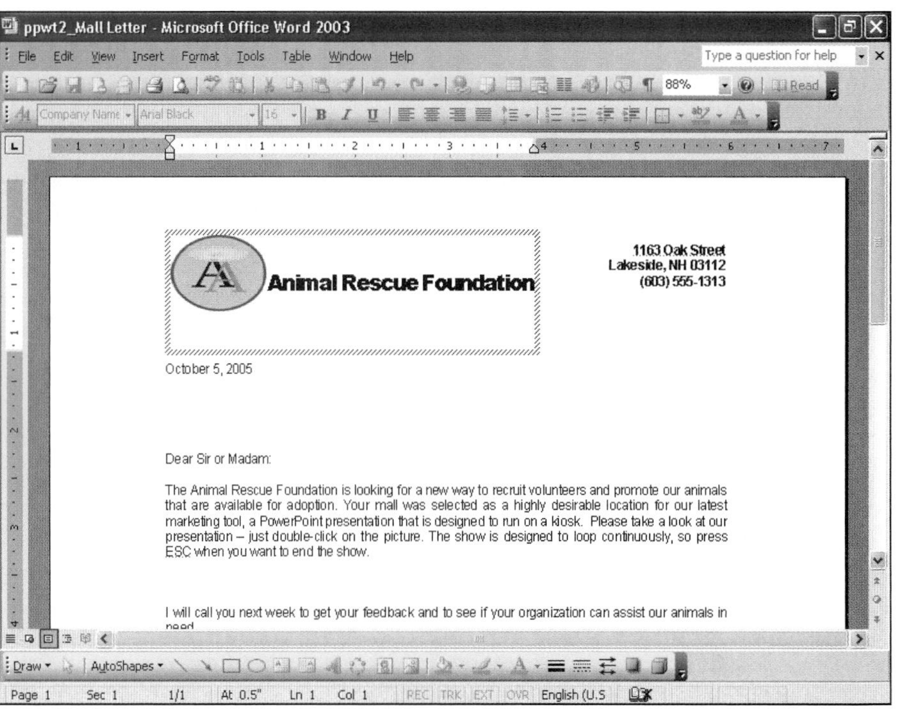

Figure 21

> **Additional Information**
> Always remove your personal information from the file's properties before distributing a presentation to avoid the distribution of this information to others.

Now you want to embed the presentation. When you embed a PowerPoint presentation, the first slide of the presentation is displayed in the document. You want the embedded presentation to appear below the first paragraph of the letter.

2

- **Move to the blank line below the first paragraph.**
- **Choose Insert/Object.**
- **Open the Create from File tab.**
- **Click Browse... .**
- **Change to your solution file location and select** Kiosk Final**.**
- **Click Insert .**
- **Click OK .**

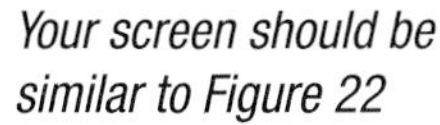

Your screen should be similar to Figure 22

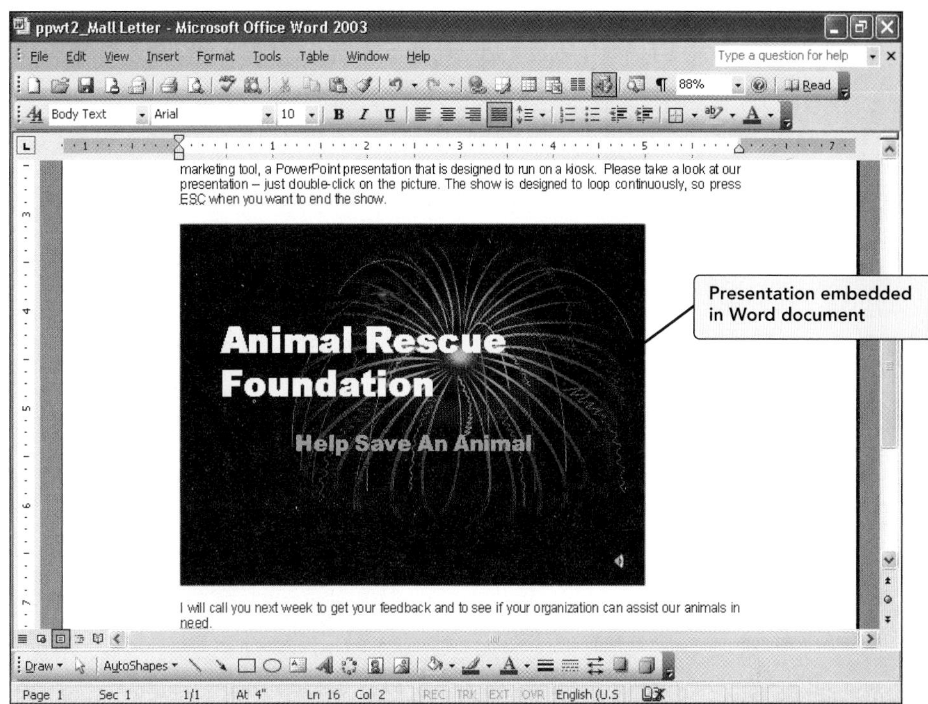

Figure 22

The opening slide of the presentation is inserted as an embedded object in the letter. Before you send the letter, you want to run the slide show to make sure that it looks good and runs correctly. The directions to run the presentation from within the Word document file are included in the first paragraph of the letter.

3

- **Double-click on the embedded object.**

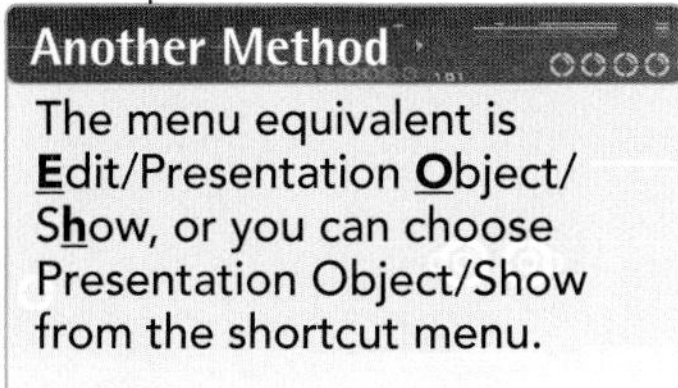

Another Method

The menu equivalent is Edit/Presentation Object/Show, or you can choose Presentation Object/Show from the shortcut menu.

- **View the entire presentation and press Esc to end the show when it begins over again.**

Editing an Embedded Object

As you viewed the presentation, you think that the last slide would look better if it included a graphic. You decide to add an animated graphic of a dog wagging its tail to the slide. Rather than editing the PowerPoint presentation file and then reinserting it into the letter, you will make the changes directly to the object that is embedded in the letter. The source program, the program used to create the embedded object, is used to edit data in an embedded object.

1 Choose Presentation Object/Edit from the object's shortcut menu.

Another Method

The menu equivalent is Edit/Presentation Object/Edit.

Your screen should be similar to Figure 23

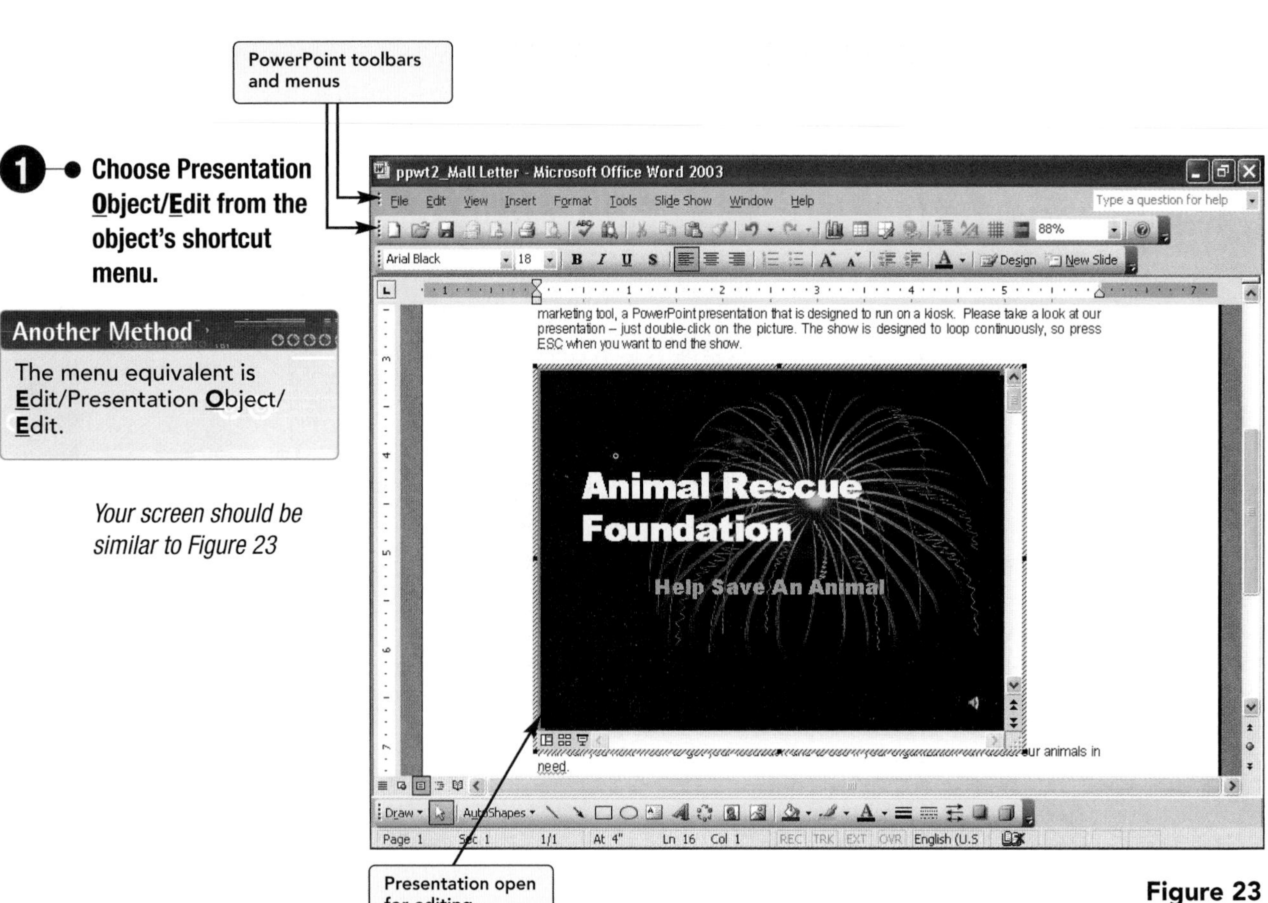

Figure 23

The presentation is open in an editing window, and the PowerPoint menus and toolbars replace some of the menus and toolbars in the Word application window. The first slide of the embedded object is displayed. Now you can use the PowerPoint commands to edit the object.

2

- **Use the editing window scroll bar to display the last slide.**
- **Insert the graphic** ppwt2_Dog Wagging **from your data file location.**
- **Position and size the graphic and text box as in Figure 24.**

Having Trouble?

Use the rotate handle to change the angle of the graphic.

- **Click Slide Show to run the slide show from the current slide.**
- **Press Esc to end the show after seeing the animated graphic.**

Your screen should be similar to Figure 24

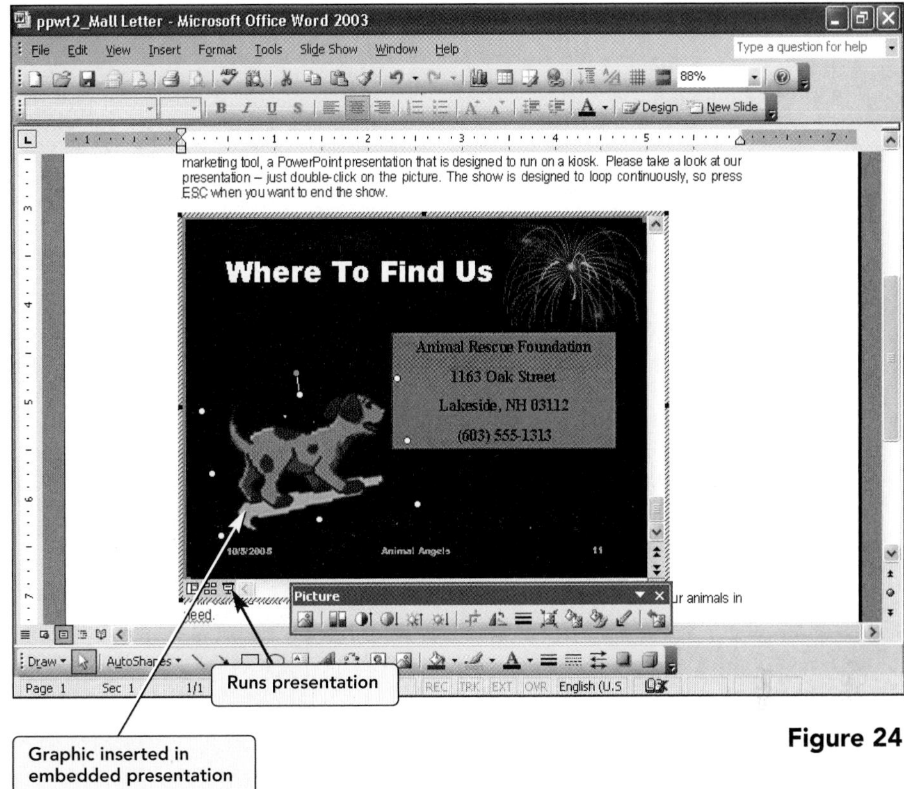

Figure 24

Now that the presentation is updated, you will close the source program.

3

- **Click outside the object to close the source application.**
- **Reduce the size of the embedded object and center it.**
- **Replace Student Name in the closing with your name.**
- **Save the letter as Kiosk Presentation Letter to your solution file location.**
- **Preview and print the letter.**
- **Exit Word.**

Your printed letter should be similar to that shown here.

1163 Oak Street
Lakeside, NH 03112
(603) 555-1313

October 5, 2005

Dear Sir or Madam:

The Animal Rescue Foundation is looking for a new way to recruit volunteers and promote our animals that are available for adoption. Your mall was selected as a highly desirable location for our latest marketing tool, a PowerPoint presentation that is designed to run on a kiosk. Please take a look at our presentation – just double-click on the picture. The show is designed to loop continuously, so press ESC when you want to end the show.

I will call you next week to get your feedback and to see if your organization can assist our animals in need.

Yours truly,

Student Name
Volunteer Recruiter

Next you will update the presentation in PowerPoint with the same change you made in the presentation in the Word document.

4

- **Display slide 11.**
- **Insert the ppwt2_Dog Wagging graphic in the slide.**
- **Position and size the graphic and text box as you did in the embedded presentation in the letter.**
- **Save the revised presentation.**

Additional Information

Most e-mail programs include the capability to create a distribution list that consists of the e-mail addresses of a group of people. The list is then assigned a name that is entered in the To box when you send the message. All addresses in the list receive the message.

Now that the letter is complete, you want to send the letter via e-mail to the list of local malls. This is only one way to distribute your presentation. You could also just send an e-mail with the presentation as an attachment or you could send a diskette in the mail containing the presentation along with a letter of introduction. By embedding the presentation in the letter, you create both an e-mail distribution method and also a printed letter that contains the first slide in your presentation as a graphic.

Broadcasting a Presentation

Note: To complete this section, the Broadcast feature must be installed on your system.

Additional Information

Use Slide/Show/Online Broadcast/Schedule a Live Broadcast to set up a live broadcast.

Another way to distribute a presentation is to broadcast a presentation over the Web. **Broadcasting** makes it possible to deliver a presentation to an audience at different locations. The viewers can view the presentation live or on demand. The presentation is saved in HTML format on a server that is accessible to the audience and is displayed in a Web browser. Your system administrator must set up a server location where you can store the files to be shared by all the viewers. Outlook can be set up to schedule and automatically start the presentation at a specified time. If you are using other e-mail applications, a hyperlink appears in the body of the e-mail and the audience double-clicks on the hyperlink to start the broadcast.

Recording a Broadcast

You decide to try out this feature to see if you want to use it in the future, by recording and saving a broadcast.

1. **Choose Slide Show/Online Broadcast/Record and Save a Broadcast.**

Your screen should be similar to Figure 25

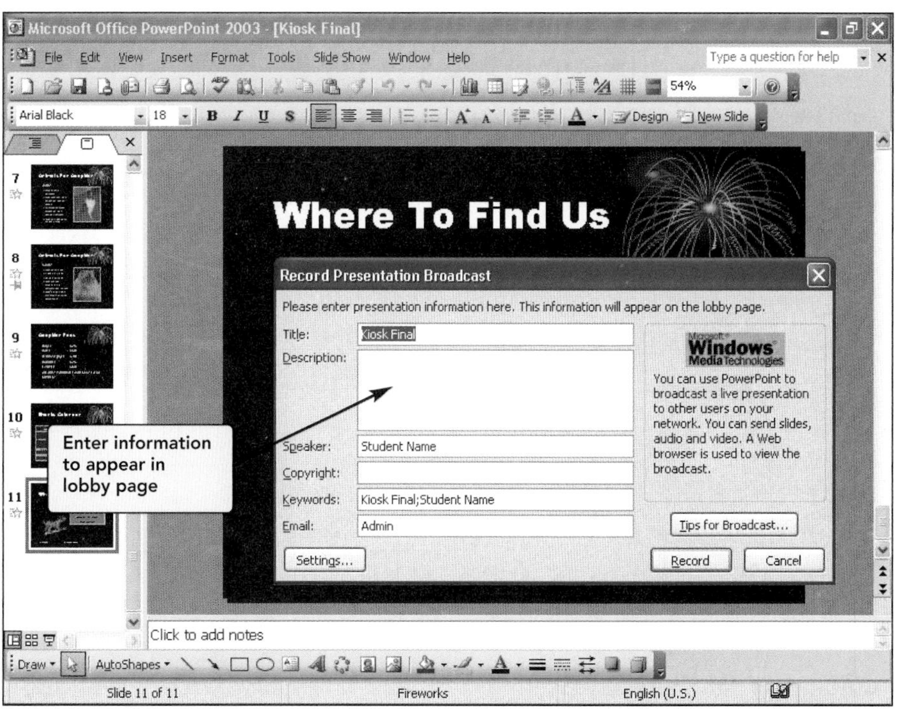

Figure 25

The first step is to enter information you want to appear on the lobby page. The **lobby page** is a page of information that is displayed in the viewer's browser before the broadcast starts. It includes information about the broadcast, including the title, subject, and host's name. It also displays a countdown to the starting time of the broadcast. The presentation file name is automatically displayed in the Title text box. You want to add a short description to appear on the lobby page when viewers receive the presentation.

2

- **In the Description text box type:** This presentation is designed to encourage people to help the Foundation by adopting an animal or volunteering.
- **Replace the name in the Speaker text box with** your name.
- **Click** Settings... .

Your screen should be similar to Figure 26

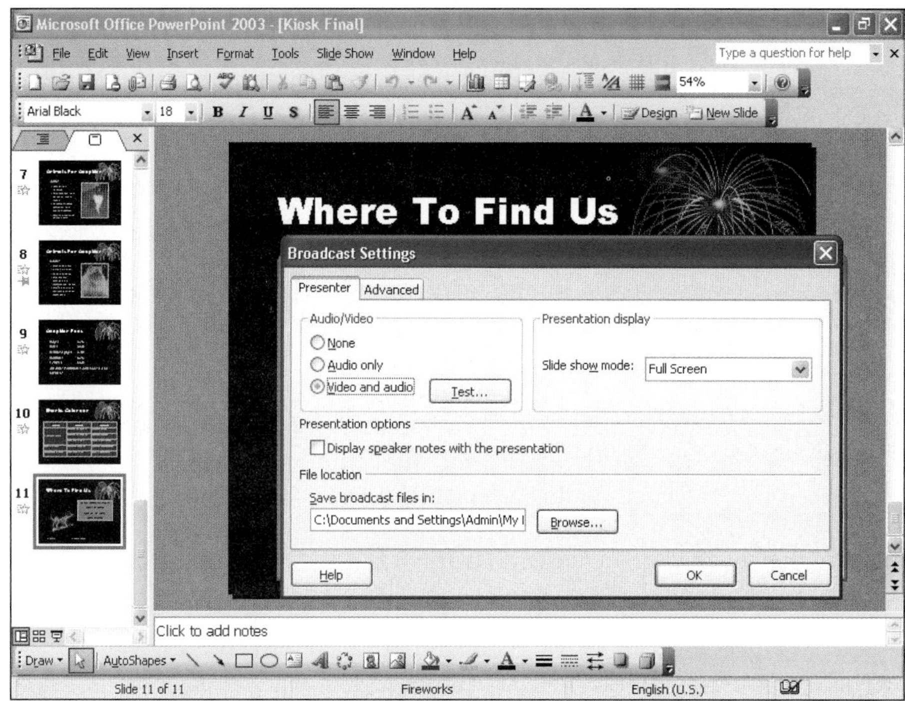

Figure 26

Next, in the Presenter tab, you define more features of the broadcast. You can send audio and video along with your presentation. Both of these types of files can slow down Web delivery, however, so you can turn them off if needed. You also need to specify the location where the broadcast files will be stored. If you are recording a broadcast, the location can be anywhere you want. However, when you actually schedule a broadcast, the location should be a server location that is accessible to the recipients. Once you have specified these items, you run the presentation to record it.

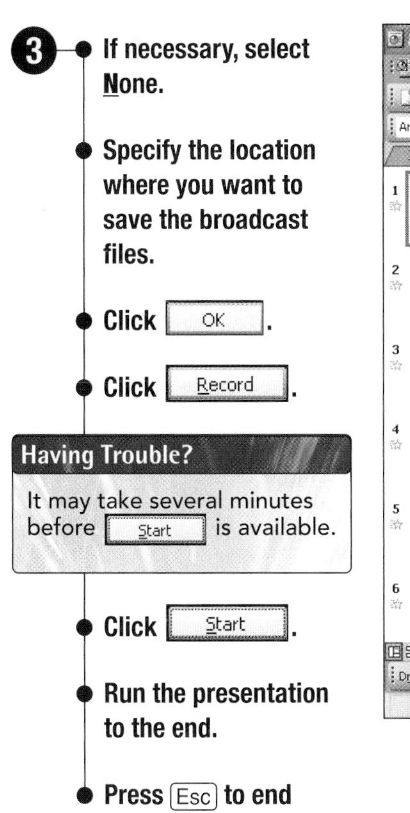

3

- **If necessary, select None.**
- **Specify the location where you want to save the broadcast files.**
- **Click OK.**
- **Click Record.**

Having Trouble?

It may take several minutes before Start is available.

- **Click Start.**
- **Run the presentation to the end.**
- **Press Esc to end recording.**

Your screen should be similar to Figure 27

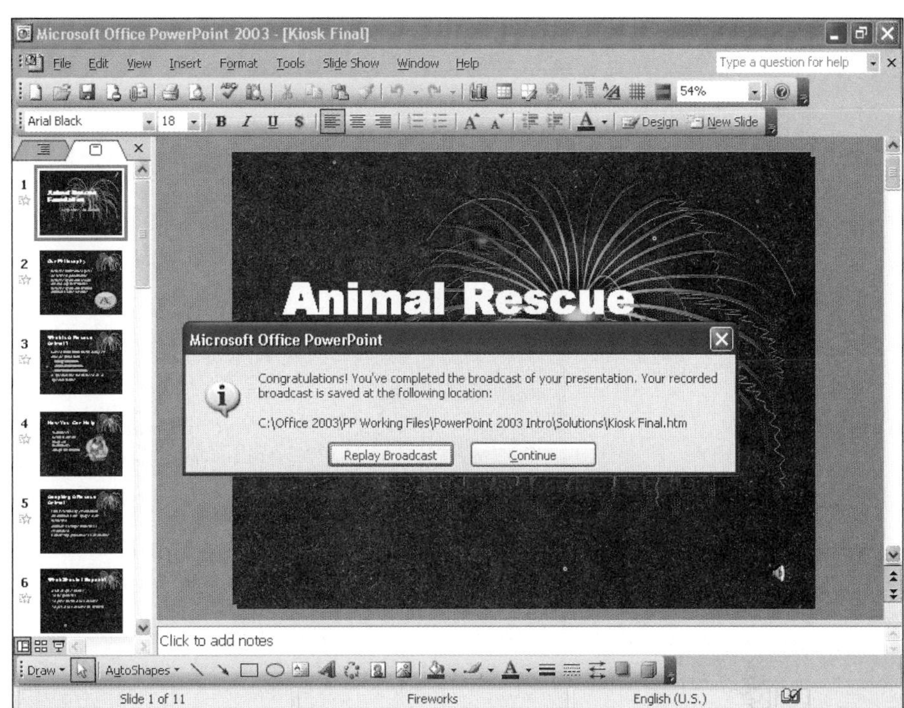

Figure 27

The slide show runs while it is being recorded. While it is running you could also record your narration to accompany the broadcast.

A congratulatory message appears indicating the slide show has successfully been recorded.

Playing the Broadcast

Next you will replay the broadcast to make sure it recorded correctly.

1 **Click** Replay Broadcast.

If necessary, maximize the browser window.

Your screen should be similar to Figure 28

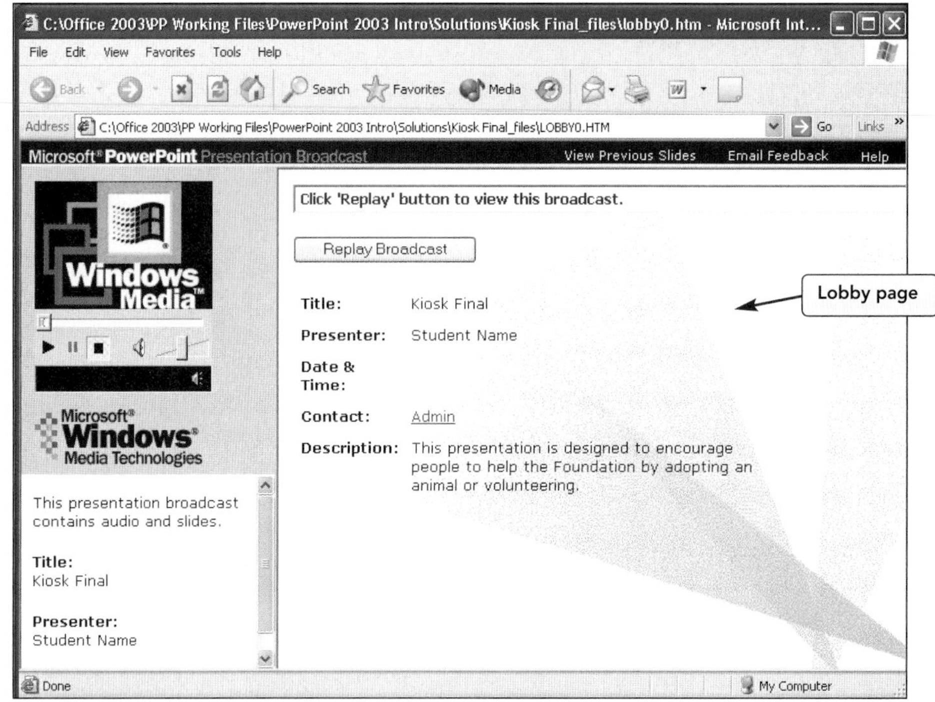

Figure 28

The lobby page with the information you entered is displayed in the browser window.

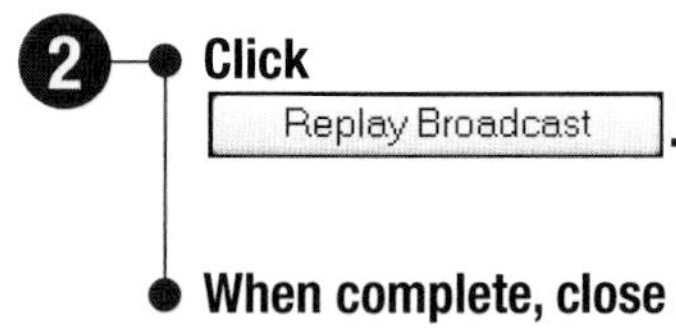

2 **Click** Replay Broadcast.

When complete, close the browser window.

Your screen should be similar to Figure 29

Figure 29

The PowerPoint window is displayed again.

Additional Information

Use File/Save as Web Page/Publish and specify the location of the Web server where the presentation will be stored.

The presentation is saved in HTML format. To make the recorded presentation available to others, a copy of it needs to be published to a Web server. Then, you need to provide the link to the lobby page to users so they can access the presentation whenever they want. All the audience would need to view the presentation is a browser.

When you schedule a live broadcast, the recipients of the invitation receive an e-mail message with the broadcast date and time. If they are using Outlook and accept the invitation, they will receive a reminder 15 minutes before the broadcast begins. The reminder contains a View This Netshow button, which they click to open the lobby page in their browser. The lobby page starts a countdown to the broadcast, and when the timer reaches zero, the presentation broadcast begins. Depending on the options the presenter selected, audience members might be able to chat with one another and send e-mail messages to the presenter.

3

- **Close the presentation.**
- **Exit PowerPoint.**

WORKING TOGETHER 2
Reviewing, Embedding, and Broadcasting a Presentation

key terms

broadcast PPWT2.21
change marker PPWT2.9
comment PPWT2.6
comment marker PPWT2.6
destination document PPWT2.16
lobby page PPWT2.24
source document PPWT2.16

microsoft office specialist skills

The Microsoft Office Specialist certification program is designed to measure your proficiency in performing basic tasks using the Office System applications. Certification demonstrates that you have the skills and provides a valuable industry credential for employment. After completing this lab, you have learned the following Microsoft Office PowerPoint 2003 Specialist skills:

Skill	Description	Page
Collaborating	Track, accept, and reject changes in a presentation	PPWT2.8
	Add, edit, and delete comments in a presentation	PPWT2.2
	Compare and merge presentations	PPWT2.6
Managing and Delivering Presentations	Prepare presentations for remote delivery	PPWT2.21

command summary

Command	Action
File/Save as Web Pa**g**e/**P**ublish	Saves presentation in HTML format to a Web server
File/Sen**d** to/Mail Re**c**ipient (for Review)	Sends presentation as an e-mail attachment and activates recipient's Reviewing toolbar
Insert/Co**m**ment	Inserts a comment into presentation
Tools/Com**p**are and Merge Presentations	Combines reviewed presentations with original
Sli**d**e Show/**O**nline Broadcast/**R**ecord and Save a Broadcast	Records a presentation for online broadcast
Sli**d**e Show/**O**nline Broadcast/**S**chedule a Live Broadcast	Sets up a live broadcast
Edit/Presentation **O**bject/**E**dit	Edits an embedded object
Insert/**O**bject/Create from **F**ile	Inserts contents of a file into document

step-by-step

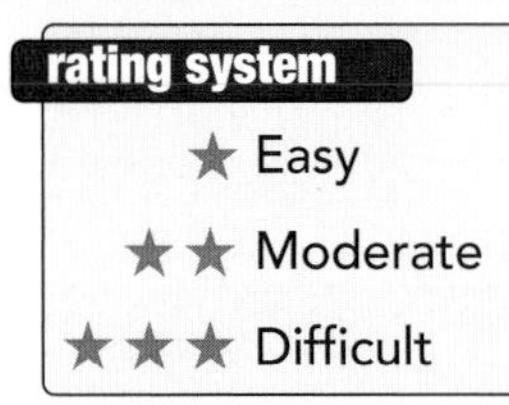

Distributing the Europe Presentation ★

1. Because the presentation you created on European travel (Step-by-Step Exercise 3, Lab 4) for adventure Travel had such a positive response, you have been asked to distribute it to other branches of the company. You will do this by embedding it in a Word document and sending it via e-mail. The completed letter is displayed here.

a. Start Word 2003 and open the ppwt2_Travel Letter file.

b. Insert the Europe PowerPoint file you saved below the second paragraph. Reduce the size of the object and center it.

c. Edit the embedded presentation by inserting a new slide before the last slide of the presentation listing the Travel agencies—**Flagstaff**, **Tucson**, and **Phoenix**—and the toll-free number of **1-800-555-5555**.

d. Replace the name in the introduction with your name.

e. Save the document as Europe Travel Memo.

f. E-mail the document to your instructor for review.

g. Print the letter.

h. Make the same changes to the Water Presentation PowerPoint file and save it as Europe Web Presentation2.

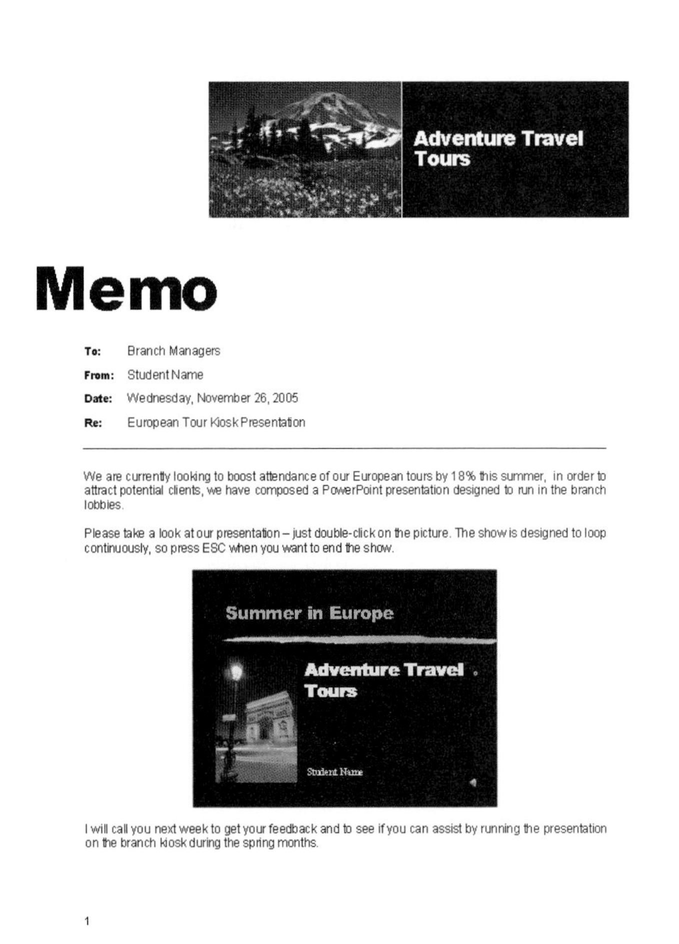

Adventure Travel Tours

Memo

To: Branch Managers
From: Student Name
Date: Wednesday, November 26, 2005
Re: European Tour Kiosk Presentation

We are currently looking to boost attendance of our European tours by 18% this summer, in order to attract potential clients, we have composed a PowerPoint presentation designed to run in the branch lobbies.

Please take a look at our presentation – just double-click on the picture. The show is designed to loop continuously, so press ESC when you want to end the show.

I will call you next week to get your feedback and to see if you can assist by running the presentation on the branch kiosk during the spring months.

1

Promoting the Fitness Web Page ★★

2. The Lifestyle Fitness Club presentation you created for the Web (Step-by-Step Exercise 4, Lab 4) has received positive feedback from the members. You would like to provide the Web pages to affiliated clubs in other states to use on their Web sites. You decide to do this by embedding it in a Word document and sending it via e-mail. The completed letter is displayed here.

   a. Start Word 2003 and create a letter to let the recipients know how to view the presentation.

   b. Embed the Fitness and Nutrition PowerPoint file in the letter. Reduce the size of the object and center it.

   c. Edit the embedded presentation to include comments about how the recipients can customize the presentation for their own use.

   d. Insert your name in the closing of the letter.

   e. Save the document as Fitness Presentation Letter. E-mail the document as an attachment to your instructor for review.

   f. Print the letter.

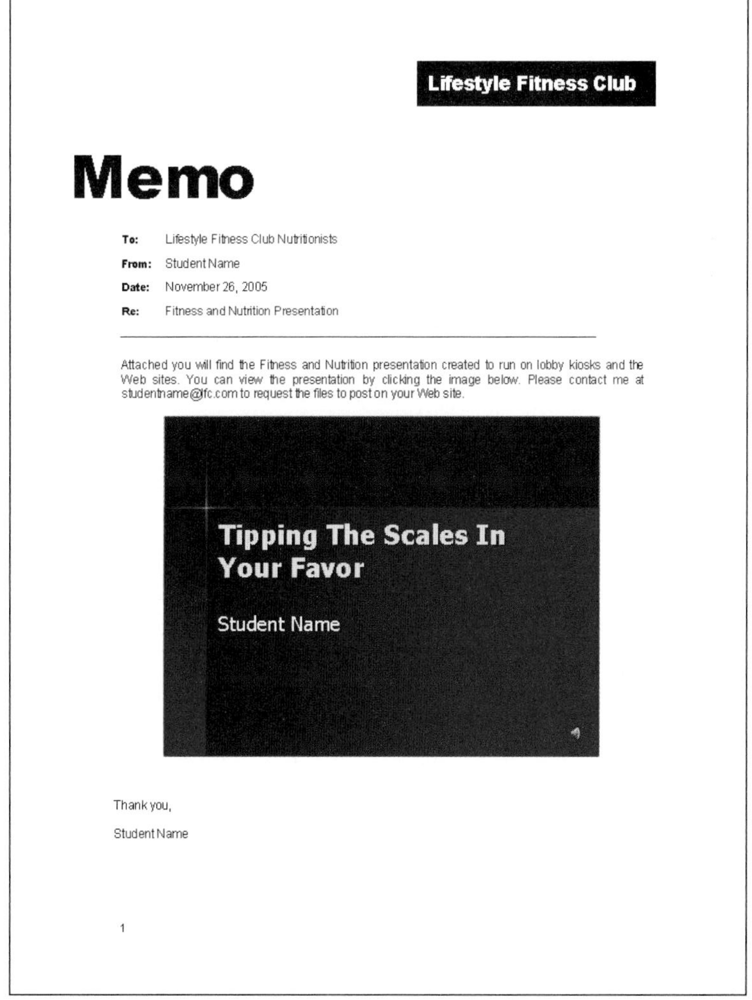

Lifestyle Fitness Club

Memo

To: Lifestyle Fitness Club Nutritionists
From: Student Name
Date: November 26, 2005
Re: Fitness and Nutrition Presentation

Attached you will find the Fitness and Nutrition presentation created to run on lobby kiosks and the Web sites. You can view the presentation by clicking the image below. Please contact me at studentname@lfc.com to request the files to post on your Web site.

Thank you,

Student Name

1

Distributing the Sports Company Web Page ★ ★ ★

3. The Sports Company's kiosk presentation has worked out well. The store manager would like you to send the presentation you created (Step-by-Step Exercise 5, Lab 4) to the store managers of the other stores in the state. The completed letter is shown here.

a. Start Word 2003 and create a letter that describes the presentation and how to access it.

b. Embed the Sports Company Kiosk presentation in the letter. Reduce the size of the embedded object and center it.

c. Edit the embedded presentation to include comments suggesting changes they might make to customize the presentation for their own use.

d. Insert your name in the closing of the letter.

e. Save the document as Sports Company Letter.

f. E-mail the document to your instructor for review.

g. Print the letter.

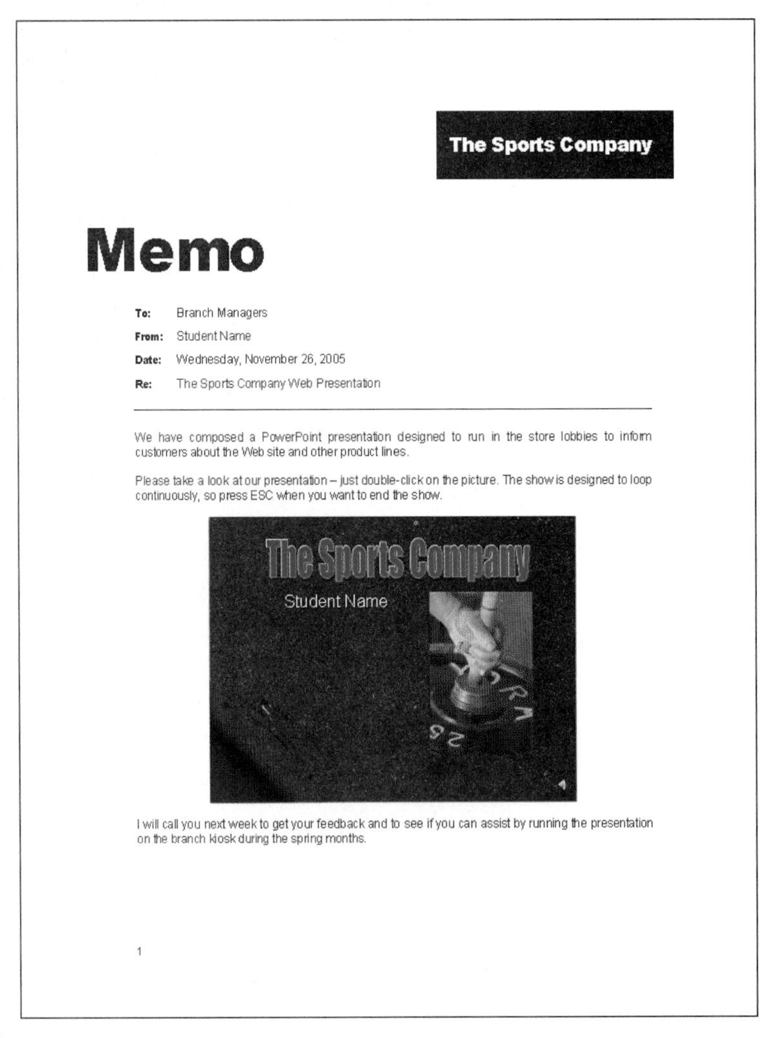

The Sports Company

Memo

To: Branch Managers
From: Student Name
Date: Wednesday, November 26, 2005
Re: The Sports Company Web Presentation

We have composed a PowerPoint presentation designed to run in the store lobbies to inform customers about the Web site and other product lines.

Please take a look at our presentation – just double-click on the picture. The show is designed to loop continuously, so press ESC when you want to end the show.

I will call you next week to get your feedback and to see if you can assist by running the presentation on the branch kiosk during the spring months.

1

Command Summary

Command	Shortcut Key	Button	Voice	Action
start/All Programs				Opens program menu
File/**N**ew	Ctrl + N			Creates new presentation
File/**O**pen	Ctrl + O		Open File open Open file	Opens existing presentation
File/**C**lose			Close presentation	Closes presentation
File/**S**ave	Ctrl + S		Save	Saves presentation
File/Save **A**s				Saves presentation using new file name and/or location
File/Package for CD				Saves presentation and all supporting files to a folder for use on a CD
File/Print Pre**v**iew	Ctrl + P		Print preview	Displays preview of slide
File/**P**rint				Prints presentation
File/Propert**i**es				Displays statistics and stores information about presentation
File/Sen**d** To/Microsoft Office **W**ord				Exports text of presentation to Word
File/Sen**d** To/M**a**il Recipient (as Attachment)				Sends presentation or selected slide as an e-mail attachment
File/E**x**it			File exit	Exits PowerPoint program
Edit/**U**ndo	Ctrl + Z		Undo	Reverses last action
Edit/Cu**t**	Ctrl + X		Cut	Cuts selection to Clipboard
Edit/**P**aste	Ctrl + V		Paste	Pastes item from Clipboard
Edit/Paste **S**pecial/<Object>				Inserts an item from Clipboard as an embedded object
Edit/Paste Special/Paste **L**ink				Inserts an item from Clipboard as a linked object
Edit/Select A**l**l	Ctrl + A			Selects all objects on a slide or all text in an object, or (in Outline pane) an entire outline

Command	Shortcut Key	Button	Voice	Action
Edit/**D**elete Slide				Deletes selected slide
Edit/**F**ind	Ctrl + F			Finds specified text
Edit/Replace	Ctrl + H			Replaces located text with specified replacement text
Edit/Lin**k**s				Changes settings associated with linked objects
Edit/Linked Worksheet **O**bject/**O**pen				Opens source application of linked object
Edit/**D**ocument **O**bject/**E**dit				Opens embedded object for editing by source program
View/Gr**i**d and Guides				Displays guidelines that help align objects
View/**N**ormal			Normal Normal view	Switches to Normal view
View/**Z**oom		45%		Changes size of onscreen display of slide
View/Sli**d**e Sorter			Slide sorter	Switches to Slide Sorter view
View/Slide Sho**w**			View show Begin slide show Start slide show Slide show view	Runs slide show
View/Notes **P**age				Displays notes pages
View/**M**aster/**S**lide Master	Shift + [Normal view button]			Displays slide master for current presentation
View/Tas**k** pane	Ctrl + F1		Task pane Show task pane View task pane Hide task pane	Hides or displays task pane
View/**T**oolbars				Displays or hides selected toolbars
View/**R**uler				Displays or hides ruler
View/**H**eader and Footer				Specifies information that appears as headers and footers on slides, notes, outlines, and handout pages

Command	Shortcut Key	Button	Voice	Action
Insert/New Slide	Ctrl + M	New Slide	New slide Insert new slide	Inserts new slide
Insert/Duplicate Slide				Inserts duplicate of selected slide
Insert/Chart				Adds a chart object to a slide
Insert/Picture/Clip Art				Opens Clip Organizer and inserts selected clip art
Insert/Picture/From File				Inserts a picture from file on disk
Insert/Picture/AutoShapes				Inserts selected AutoShape object
Insert/Text Box				Adds a text box
Format/Font/Font		Arial		Changes font type
Format/Font/Size		18		Changes font size
Format/Font/Font Style/Bold	Ctrl + B	B	on bold	Adds bold effect to selection
Format/Font/Font Style/Italic	Ctrl + I	I	italic	Adds italic effect to selection
Format/Font/Color		A		Adds color to selection
Format/Bullets and Numbering				Creates bulleted or numbered lists
Format/Background				Applies colors, patterns, or pictures to a slide background
Format/AutoShape				Changes characteristics of an AutoShape
Format/Alignment	Ctrl + L		Left justify	Aligns text in a cell or placeholder to left, center, right, or justified
	Ctrl + E		Centered	
	Ctrl + R		Right justify	
	Ctrl + J			
Format/Slide Design		Design		Changes appearance of slide by applying a different design template
Format/Replace Fonts				Finds specified font and replace it with another
Format/Slide Layout				Changes layout of an existing or new slide
Format/Picture/Recolor				Changes color of a picture

Command	Shortcut Key	Button	Voice	Action
F**o**rmat/**M**aster Layout				Selects the placeholder to be added
F**o**rmat/**T**able				Changes table border and fill color
Tools/**S**pelling				Spell-checks presentation
Tools/**C**ustomize/**O**ptions/				Shows Standard and Formatting toolbars in two rows
Tools/**O**ptions/Spelling and Style				Sets spelling and style options
Sli**d**e Show/Custo**m** Animation				Applies custom animation
Sli**d**e Show/Slide **T**ransition		Transition		Adds transition effects
Sli**d**e Show/**H**ide Slide				Hides selected slide
Slide Show Pointer Shortcut Menu				
Arrow	Ctrl + A			Changes pointer to arrow and turns off freehand annotation
Ballpoint Pen	Ctrl + P			Changes pointer to ballpoint pen and turns on freehand annotation
Felt Tip Pen				Changes pointer to felt tip pen and turns on freehand annotation
Highlighter				Changes pointer to a highlighter
Ink **C**olor				Shows color palette for annotation tool
E**r**aser				Erases selected annotations
Erase all Ink on Slide	E			Removes all annotations from slide
Slide Show Screen Shortcut Menu				
Go to Slide				Displays hidden slide
S**c**reen/**B**lack Screen	B			Blacks out screen
S**c**reen/**W**hite Screen	W			Whites out screen
Help/Microsoft Word **H**elp	F1			Opens Help window
Edit/Office Clip**b**oard				Opens Clipboard task pane
Sli**d**e Show/**S**et Up Show/**U**sing Timings				Sets up slide show to advance auto-math calls by preset timings
Sli**d**e Show/**R**ehearse Timings				Starts slide show and sets timings for slide

Command	Shortcut Key	Button	Voice	Action
Sli**d**e Show/**R**ecord Narration				Records narration while rehearsing the presentation
Draw /**G**roup				Groups objects together
Draw /**U**ngroup				Ungroups objects
Draw /Regro**u**p				Groups objects together again that were previously ungrouped
Draw /O**r**der/Send to Bac**k**				Sends object to bottom of stack
Draw /Grid and Guides/ Display grid on screen				Displays or hides grid lines
Draw /**A**lign or Distribute				Aligns or distributes objects
Chart				
F**o**rmat/S**e**lected Data Series	Ctrl + 1			Applies patterns, shapes, and other formats to selected data series
Data/Series in **C**olumns				Arranges chart based on columns in Datasheet window
Chart/Chart **O**ptions				Adds and modifies chart options such as titles, legends, and gridlines
Organization Chart				
Insert Shape /**S**ubordinate				Adds a box below selected box
Insert Shape /**C**oworker				Adds a box at same level as selected box
Insert Shape /**S**tandard				Applies Standard layout to selected boxes
				Applies selected design to boxes of organization chart
File/Save as Web Pa**g**e				Publishes presentation on Web
Insert/Slides from **F**iles				Inserts selected slides from another presentation
Insert/Slides from Out**l**ine				Creates slides from outline text
Insert/Mo**v**ies and Sounds/ Sou**n**d from File				Inserts sound or movie files into selected slide
Insert/Mo**v**ies and Sounds/ Play **C**D Audio Track				Plays a CD
Insert/Ta**b**le				Inserts a table consisting of the specified number of rows and columns

Command	Shortcut Key	Button	Voice	Action
Insert/Hyperl**i**nk				Creates a hyperlink
F**o**rmat/Aut**o**Shape/Size				Changes size and scale of selected AutoShape
F**o**rmat/**T**able				Formats borders and fill color of selected table
Sli**d**e Show/**S**et Up Show				Sets up presentation to run for specific situations
Sli**d**e Show/Custom Sho**w**s				Creates presentations within a presentation
Sli**d**e Show/Act**i**on Buttons				Adds navigation buttons to a slide
Sli**d**e Show/**A**ction Settings				Specifies action that is needed to activate hyperlinks
Sli**d**e Show/Custo**m** Animation				Adds motion and determines how sound is played
File/Save as Web Pa**g**e/**P**ublish				Saves presentation in HTML format to a Web server
File/Sen**d** to/Mail Re**c**ipient (for Review)				Sends presentation as an e-mail attachment and activates recipient's Reviewing toolbar
Insert/Co**m**ment				Inserts a comment into presentation
Tools/Com**p**are and Merge Presentations				Combines reviewed presentations with original
Sli**d**e Show/**O**nline Broadcast/**R**ecord and Save a Broadcast				Records a presentation for online broadcast
Sli**d**e Show/**O**nline Broadcast/**S**chedule a Live Broadcast				Sets up a live broadcast
Edit/Presentation **O**bject/**E**dit				Edits an embedded object
Insert/**O**bject/Create from **F**ile				Inserts contents of a file into document

Glossary of Key Terms

action button A special object that can be inserted into a presentation and assigned a hyperlink. Used in self-running presentations and presentations that work on a company network or Web site.

agenda slide A slide that lists the agenda items or main topics of a presentation from which viewers can select.

alignment Controls the position of text entries within a space.

animated GIF A type of graphic file that has motion.

animation Effect that adds action to text and graphics so they move around on the screen.

animation scheme A preset visual effect that can be added to slide text.

assistant box In an organization chart, a box representing administrative or managerial assistants to a manager.

attachment A file that is sent along with an e-mail message but is not part of the message.

attribute A features associated with an object that can be isolated and changed.

AutoContent Wizard A guided approach that helps you determine the content and organization of your presentation through a series of questions.

AutoCorrect Feature that makes certain types of corrections automatically as you enter text.

AutoShape A ready-made drawing shape supplied with PowerPoint.

branch In an organization chart, a box and all the boxes that report to it.

broadcast To deliver a presentation to an audience at different locations.

browser A program that connects you to remote computers and displays the Web pages you request.

build An effect that progressively displays bulleted items as the presentation proceeds.

category axis The bottom boundary of a chart, which is used to label the data being charted. Also called the X axis.

cell The intersection of a row and column in a table.

change marker An icon that indicates a reviewer made a change to a slide.

chart A visual representation of numeric data. Also called a graph.

character formatting Formatting features that affect the selected characters only.

clip art Professionally drawn images.

collect and paste The capability of the program to store multiple copied items in the Office Clipboard and then paste one or many of the items.

comment A remark that is displayed in a separate box and attached to a slide.

comment marker An icon that indicates a comment is attached to a slide.

co-worker box In an organization chart, a box having the same manager as another box. Co-workers from a group.

custom dictionary A dictionary you can create to hold words you commonly use but that are not included in the dictionary that is supplied with the program.

custom show A presentation that runs within a presentation.

data series Each group of related data that is plotted in a chart. Each data series has a unique color or pattern assigned to it so that you can identify the different series.

datasheet A table consisting of rows and columns that is used to enter the data that you want represented in a chart.

default Initial program settings.

demote To move a topic down one level in the outline hierarchy.

design template Professionally created slide design that can be applied to your presentation.

destination document The document where an embedded object is inserted.

destination file The document receiving the linked or embedded object.

docked toolbar A toolbar fixed to an edge of the window and displays a vertical bar called the move handle, on the left edge of the toolbar.

document window The area of the application window that displays the contents of the open document.

drawing object An object consisting of shapes such as lines and boxes that can be created using the Drawing toolbar.

Drawing toolbar A toolbar that is used to add objects such as lines, circles, and boxes.

embedded object An object that is inserted into another application and becomes part of the document. It can be edited from within the document using the source program.

floating object A graphic object that is inserted into the drawing layer and which can be positioned anywhere on the page.

font A set of characters with a specific design. Also called a typeface.

font size The height and width of a character, commonly measured in points.

footer Text or graphics that appear on the bottom of each slide.

format To enhance the appearance of a slide to make it more readable or attractive.

Format Painter A feature that applies the format associated with the current selection to new selections.

Formatting toolbar A toolbar that contains buttons used to modify text.

graphic A non-text element, such as a chart, drawing, picture, or scanned photograph, in a slide.

grid An invisible series of lines that form small squares on the slide and that are used to position objects.

group Two or more objects that are treated as a single object. In an organization chart, all the boxes reporting to the same manager, excluding assistant boxes.

guide A line, either vertical or horizontal, that you position on the slide. When an object is close to the guide, the center or corner (whichever is closer) snaps to the grid.

hierarchy A visual representation that shows ranking, such as reporting structures within a department in a business.

hyperlink A connection to locations in the current document, other documents, or Web pages. Clicking a hyperlink jumps to the specified location.

Hypertext Markup Language (HTML) The programming language used to write Web pages. It controls how information on the page, such as font colors and size, is displayed.

keyword A word or phrase that is descriptive of the type of graphic you want to locate.

landscape Orientation of the printed output across the length of the paper.

layout A predefined slide organization that is used to control the placement of elements on a slide.

legend A box containing a brief description that identifies the patterns or colors assigned to the data series in a chart.

level All the boxes in an organization chart at the same position in the hierarchy, regardless of the boxes each reports to.

linked object An object that is created in a source file and linked to a destination file. Edits made to the source file are automatically reflected in the destination file.

live link A link that automatically updates the linked object whenever changes are made to it in the source file.

lobby page In a broadcast, the page that displays information about the broadcast including the title, subject, and host's name.

main dictionary Dictionary that comes with the Office 2003 programs.

manager box In an organization chart, the top-level box of a group.

master A special slide on which the formatting of all slides in a presentation is defined.

menu bar Located below the title bar, this bar displays the application's program menu.

notes page Printed output that shows a miniature of the slide and provides an area for speaker notes.

object An item on a slide that can be selected and modified.

object alignment To position objects relative to each other by their left, right, top or bottom edges; or horizontally by their centers or vertically by their middles; or in relation to the entire slide.

organization chart A map of a group, which usually includes people, but can include any items that have a hierarchical relationship.

Outlining toolbar A toolbar that is used to modify the organization of the presentation text and slides.

pane In Normal view, the separate divisions of the window that allow you to work on all aspects of your presentation in one place.

paragraph formatting Formatting features that affect entire paragraphs.

picture An image such as a graphic illustration or a scanned photograph.

placeholder Box that is designed to contain objects such as the slide title, bulleted text, charts, tables, and pictures.

point A unit of type measurement. One point equals about 1/72 inch.

portrait Orientation of the printed output across the width of the paper.

promote To move a topic up one level in the outline hierarchy.

publish To save a presentation in HTML format to a Web server.

rotate handle The [rotate handle icon] on the selection rectangle of a selected object that allows you to rotate the object in any direction.

sans serif A font that does not have a flair at the base of each letter, such as Arial or Helvetica.

scroll bar Used with a mouse to bring additional lines of information into view in a window.

selection cursor A colored highlight bar that appears over the selected command.

selection rectangle Hashed border that surrounds a selected placeholder.

serif A font that has a flair at the base of each letter, such as Roman or Times New Roman.

server The computer that stores Web pages and sends them to a browser when requested.

Shortcut menu By right clicking on an item, this menu displays only the options pertaining to that item.

sizing handles Small boxes surrounding selected objects that are used to change the size of the object.

slide An individual page of the presentation.

slide show Used to practice or to present the presentation. It displays each slide in final form.

source document The document from which an embedded object was obtained.

source file The file from which a linked or embedded object is obtained.

source program The program used to create the linked or embedded object.

spelling checker Locates all misspelled words, duplicate words, and capitalization irregularities as you create and edit a presentation, and proposes possible corrections.

stacking order The order in which objects are inserted into layers in the slide.

Standard toolbar A toolbar that contains buttons that give quick access to the most frequently used program features.

status bar A bar displayed at the bottom of the document window that advises you of the status of different program conditions and features as you use the program.

subordinate box In an organization chart, a box reporting to a manager box.

summary slide A slide that contains the title of selected slides in the presentation.

table An arrangement of horizontal rows and vertical columns.

table reference The letter and number that identifies a table cell.

Task Pane Displayed on the right side of the document window, it provides quick access to features as you are using the application.

template A file that includes predefined settings that can be used as a pattern to create many common types of presentations.

text box A container for text or graphics.

thumbnail A miniature view of a slide.

titles Descriptive text used to explain the content of a chart.

transition An effect that controls how a slide moves off the screen and the next one appears.

typeface A set of characters with a specific design. Also called a font.

value axis The left boundary of a chart, consisting of a numbered scale whose numbers are determined by the data used in the chart. Also called the Y axis.

view A way of looking at the presentation.

WordArt Used to enhance slide text by changing the shape of text, adding 3-D effects, and changing the alignment of text on a line.

workspace The large area containing the slide where your presentations are displayed as you create and edit them.

X axis The bottom boundary of the chart, which is used to label the data being charted. Also called the category axis.

Y axis The left boundary of the chart, consisting of a numbered scale whose numbers are determined by the data used in the chart. Also called the value axis.

Reference 1

Data File List

Supplied/Used	Created/Saved As
Lab 1	
	Volunteer
pp01_Volunteer1	Volunteer1
pp01_Puppy (graphic)	
pp01_AnimalCare (graphic)	
Step-by-Step	
1. pp01_Triple Crown pp01_Jump (graphic) pp01_Stream (graphic)	Triple Crown Presentation
2. pp01_Resume (graphic) pp01_Success (graphic) pp01_Cover Letter (graphic)	Resume1
3. pp01_Relaxation	Massage Therapy
4. pp01_Logo pp01_Cuppa (graphic) pp01_Beans (graphic)	Coffee
5. pp01_Resume pp01_Biography (graphic) pp01_Meeting (graphic) pp01_Booth (graphic) pp01_Interview (graphic) pp01_Follow Up (graphic)	Job Fairs
On Your Own	
1. pp01_Internet Policy	Internet Policy
2. pp01_Memo	Phone Etiquette
3. pp01_Animals	Pet Activities
4.	Placement Services
5. pp01_Animal Careers	Careers with Animals
Lab 2	
pp02_Volunteer2	Volunteer2
pp02_QuestionMark (graphic)	
Step-by-Step	
1. pp02_ASU Presentation pp02_Arizona (graphic) pp02_Student Services (graphic) pp02_Library (graphic) pp02_Fine Arts (graphic)	ASU Presentation1
2. Massage Therapy (from Lab 1)	Massage Therapy2
3. Job Fairs (from Lab 1)	Job Fairs2

Supplied/Used	Created/Saved As
4. Triple Crown Presentation (from Lab 1) pp02_Read (graphic)	Triple Crown Presentation2
5. Coffee (from Lab 1) pp02_Globe (graphic)	Coffee Show
On Your Own	
1.	Interview Techniques
2. Careers with Animals (from Lab 1)	Animal Careers2
3.	Fad Diets
4. Internet Policy (from Lab 1)	Internet Policy2
5.	Travel Favorites
Working Together 1	
Volunteer2 (from Lab 2)	Volunteer2 Linked
ppwt1_OrientationMeetings (Word doc)	
ppwt1_RescueData (Excel chart)	Rescue Data Linked
Step-by-Step	
1. ppwt1_MassagePrices (Word doc) Massage Therapy2 (from Lab 2)	Massage Therapy3
2. ppwt1_Coffee Prices (Word doc) Coffee Show (from Lab 2)	Coffee Prices Linked (Word doc) Coffee Show Linked
3. Triple Crown Presentation2 (from Lab 2) ppwt1_Forest Use (Excel worksheet)	Triple Crown Presentation3 Forest Use Linked (Excel worksheet)
Lab 3	
pp03_Recruitment	Volunteer Orientation
pp03_Animal Angels3	Volunteer Presentation (e-mail)
pp03_Sunrise (graphic)	OrientationCD (folder)
pp03_Cat (graphic)	
pp03_Dog (graphic)	
Step-by-Step	
1. pp03_Employee Motivation pp03_Motivation (graphic) pp03_Success (graphic)	Employee Motivation2 Motivation Outline
2. pp03_Doggie Travel pp03_Auto	Doggie Travel Tips
3. pp03_Valley Soccer pp03_Futbol pp03_Varsity	Valley Soccer Presentation Soccer Outline
4. pp03_Exercise pp03_Fitness Trends pp03_LFC Logo	Fitness and Nutrition Fitness and Nutrition Outline
5. Job Fairs2 (From Lab 2) pp03_Hurry pp03_Jobs	Job Fairs3 Jobs (CD folder)
On Your Own	
1.	Family Reunion
2. pp03_Lifeguard	Lifeguard Presentation
3. Travel Favorites (from Lab 2)	Travel Favorites2
4.	Storyland Orientation
5.	Preventing Network Infection

Supplied/Used	Created/Saved As
Lab 4	
pp04_Promotional Outline	Animal Rescue Foundation
pp04_Animals for Adoption (Word document)	AnimalRescueCD (folder)
pp04_Foundation Introduction	Rescue Foundation Self Running
pp04_Jake (picture)	Rescue Foundation Web
pp04_Sadie (picture)	
pp04_Adoptions (graphic)	
pp04_Doggie (sound)	Self Running (template)
Step-by-Step	
1. pp04_Birds (graphic)	
pp04_Bird Outline	Betty's Birds
pp04_Dancing Parrot	Birds (template)
pp04_Parrot Talk (sound)	
2. pp04_Anthology Logo	
pp04_Anthology Outline	Anthology Cinema Web Presentation
pp04_Popcorn (graphic)	
pp04_Ticket (graphic)	
pp04_Film (sound)	
3. pp04_Europe	Europe Web Presentation
pp04_Champs Elysees (graphic)	
pp04_Dinner (graphic)	
pp04_Train (graphic)	
4. pp04_Fitness Outline	Fitness Web Pages
pp04_Exercise (graphic)	
pp04_Stretching (graphic)	
5. pp04_Sports Company Outline	Sports Company Kiosk
pp04_Weight Lifter (graphic)	Sports Company Web
pp04_Tennis Racquet (graphic)	
pp04_Mountain Bike (graphic)	
pp04_Onestop (sound)	
On Your Own	
1. Lifeguard presenation	Pool Safety Kiosk
2. pp04_Mass Transit	Mass Transit
3. Italy Favorites2	Travel Italy Web
4. Storyland Orientation	Storyland Web
5.	MusicFirst Web
Working Together 2	
ppwt2_Kiosk Original	Kiosk Review
	Kiosk Review E-mail
ppwt2_Kiosk Review (1)	Kiosk Final
ppwt2_ Kiosk Review (2)	
ppwt2_Halo (graphic)	
ppwt2_Mall Letter (Word document)	
ppwt2_Dog Wagging (graphic)	Kiosk Presentation Letter
Step-by-Step	
1. ppwt2_Travel Letter	Europe Web Presentation2
2. Fitness Web Pages (from Lab 4)	Fitness Presentation Letter
3. Sports Company Kiosk (from Lab 4)	Sports Company Letter

Reference 2

Microsoft Office Specialist Skills

Office PowerPoint 2003 Specialist Certification

Standardized Coding Number	Skill Sets and Skill Standards	Lab Exercises			
		Lab	Page	Step-By-Step	On Your Own
PPO3S-1	**Creating Content**				
PPO3S-1-1	Create new presentations from templates	1	PP1.7	3,4,5	1,2,3,4,5
		4	PP4.4	1,2,3,4,5	1,2,3,4,5
PPO3S-1-2	Insert and edit text-based content	1	PP1.16	1,2,3,4,5	1,2,3,4,5
		2	PP2.5	1,2,3,4,5	1,2,3,4,5
		3	PP3.5	1,2,3,4,5	1,2,3,4,5
		4	4.6	1,2,3,4,5	1,2,3,4,5
		WT1	PPWT1.2	1,2,3	
PPO3S-1-3	Insert tables, charts, and diagrams	2	PP2.9	4,5	3
		3	PP3.30,3.43	1,2,3,4,5	1,2,3,4,5
		4	PP4.12	1,2,3,4,5	1,2,3,4,5
PPO3S-1-4	Insert pictures, shapes and graphics	1	PP1.54	1,2,3,4,5	1,2,3,4,5
		2	PP2.23,2.24	1,2,3,4,5	1,2,3,4,5
		3	PP3.16,3.26	1,2,3,4,5	1,2,3,4,5
		4	PP4.20	1,2,3,4,5	1,2,3,4,5
PPO3S-1-5	Insert objects	WT1	PPWT1.11		
		4	PP4.26	1,2,3,4,5	1,2,3,4,5
PPO3S-2	**Formatting Content**				
PPO3S-2-1	Format text-based content	1	PP1.49	1,2,3,4,5	1,2,3,4,5
		2	PP2.13,2.15	1,2,3,4,5	1,2,3,4,5
		3	PP3.8	1,2,3,4,5	1,2,3,4,5
PPO3S-2-2	Format pictures, shapes, and graphics	1	PP1.61	1,2,3,4,5	1,2,3,4,5
		2	PP2.22,2.25	1,2,3,4,5	1,2,3,4,5
		3	PP3.19,3.23,3.28	1,2,3,4,5	1,2,3,4,5
PPO3S-2-3	Format slides	2	PP2.31,2.33,2.72	1,2,3,4,5	1,2,3,4,5
		3	PP3.10	1,2,3,4,5	1,2,3,4,5
PPO3S-2-4	Apply animation schemes	2	PP2.54	1,4,5	1,2,3,4
PPO3S-2-5	Apply slide transitions	2	PP2.51	2,3,5	1,2,4,5
		4	PP4.29	1,2,3,4,5	1,2,3,4,5
PPO3S-2-6	Customizing slide templates	4	PP4.50	1	
PPO3S-2-7	Work with masters	2	PP2.38	1,2,3,4,5	1,2,3,4,5
		3	PP3.13	1,2,3,4,5	1,2,3,4,5
PPO3S-3	**Collaborating**				
PP03S-3-1	Track, accept, and reject changes in a presentation	WT2	PPWT2.8	1,2,3	1,2,3
PP03S-3-2	Add, edit, and delete comments in a presentation	WT2	PPWT2.2	1,2,3	1,2,3
PP03S-3-3	Compare and merge presentations	WT2	PPWT2.6	1,2,3	1,2,3

Standardized Coding Number	Skill Sets and Skill Standards	Lab Exercises			
		Lab	Page	Step-By-Step	On Your Own
PPO3S-4	**Managing and Delivering Presentations**			**3,4,5**	**2,3,4,5**
PPO3S-4-1	Organize a presentation	1	PP1.12,1.40–1.45	1,2,3,4,5	1,2,3,4,5
		2	PP2.23,2.63	1,2,3,4,5	1,2,3,4,5
		WT1	PPWT1.2,WT1.9	1,2,3	
		3	PP3.5,3.24,3.44	1,2,3,4,5	1,2,3,4,5
		4	PP4.7	1,2,3,4,5	1,2,3,4,5
PPO3S-4-2	Set up slide shows for delivery	2	PP2.60		
		4	4.31,4.39	3,5	1
PPO3S-4-3	Rehearse timing	3	3.56	3,4,5	1,2,3,4,5
PPO3S-4-4	Deliver presentations	1	PP1.47	1,2,3,4,5	1,2,3,4,5
		2	PP2.56	1,2,3,4,5	1,2,3,4,5
PPO3S-4-5	Prepare presentations for remote delivery	3	3.57	5	3
		4	4.31	1,2,3,4,5	1,2,3,4,5
		WT2	WT2.21		
PPO3S-4-6	Save and publish presentations	1	PP1.31	1,2,3,4,5	1,2,3,4,5
		2	PP2.8	1,2,3,4,5	1,2,3,4,5
		4	4.45	1,2,3,4,5	1,2,3,4,5
PPO3S-4-7	Print slides, outlines, handouts, and speaker notes	1	PP1.62	1,2,3,4,5	1,2,3,4,5
		2	PP2.71	1,2,3,4,5	1,2,3,4,5
		WT1	PPWT1.14	1,2,3	
PPO3S-4-8	Export a presentation to another Microsoft office program	3	PP3.52	1,3,4	5

Index